SOCIAL RESPONSIBILITIES AND LIBRARIES

SOCIAL RESPONSIBILITIES AND LIBRARIES

A Library Journal/ School Library Journal Selection

Compiled and Edited by

Patricia Glass Schuman

R. R. BOWKER COMPANY
A Xerox Publishing Company
New York & London, 1976

Published by R. R. Bowker Co. (A Xerox Publishing Company)
1180 Avenue of the Americas, New York, N.Y. 10036
Copyright ©1976 by Xerox Corporation
Printed and bound in the United States of America

Library of Congress Cataloging in Publication Data
Main entry under title:
Social responsibilities and libraries.
Includes index.
1. Libraries and society—Addresses, essays,
lectures. I. Schuman, Patricia, 1943-
Z716.4.S6   021.4   76-27894   ISBN 0-8352-0952-0

Contents

v

Part III: SERVICE TO THE COMMUNITY

Part IV: SERVICE TO YOUTH

Part V: SERVICE TO STUDENTS AND FACULTY

Part VI: INVENTING THE FUTURE

Preface

How can libraries respond to social ferment? Should librarians be political activists or advocates for victims of social injustice? When must we take a stand on crucial issues? Can we respond to or even anticipate vast social changes?

These are but a sampling of what some call the "accursed" questions raised by the concept of social responsibility and libraries. *Library Journal* and *School Library Journal* have been in the forefront of publishing articles which not only debate whether or not these questions should be asked, but which offer answers—and more specific formulations of the questions. This collection of articles reprinted from *LJ* and *SLJ* has been compiled to present personal, professional, and institutional philosophy and programs which attempt to deal with the implementation of social responsibility; its purpose is not to present further debate over whether social responsibility is a valid subject for discussion.

Although American libraries, from their beginnings, have always had to deal with their role within the social structure, it was not until the late 1960s that an organized movement for social responsibility from within the profession began to highlight and attack the gap between the philosophy and implementation on a nationwide basis. The movement began on two fronts in 1968: the Congress for Change was organized by a group of library school students pressing for the relevancy of their education and future careers to crucial social issues; the Social Responsibilities Round Table was founded to move the American Library Association to deal with these issues. These two groups came together at the Atlantic City ALA convention in 1969 to present antiwar, intellectual freedom, and other socially topical resolutions to the profession. The ripples they caused are still being felt in the seventies. Spurred by the general social movement of the late sixties, and the excitement of Atlantic City, other groups like Librarians for Peace, Librarians for 321-8 (participatory democracy), the National Freedom Fund for Librarians, and the National Women's Liberation Front for Librarians were formed. Eventually, most members of these groups united under the umbrella of the Social Responsibilities Round Table (officially incorporated as a unit of ALA in 1969) and its issue-oriented task forces and local affiliate groups. Readers interested in historical details should consult the Annual and Midwinter Conference Reports of *LJ* and *SLJ*. Unfortunately, this same period was the beginning of budget bloodletting and retrenchment in libraries. The socially oriented programs of the sixties were losing their funding and few new ones were seeing the light of implementation.

How far have we come in the past eight years? What have we learned? These 51 articles have been selected for both timeliness and subject coverage from over 180 magazine issues representing over 600 articles in the hope that bringing them together will offer a perspective from which we can continue to build and refine our social responsibilities.

The book is comprised of six parts. *Advocacy and Action* presents a wide range of individual and group actions taken by librarians without institutional support, illustrating ways courageous and hard-working librarians have interpreted their professional roles. *Women and Minorities* delineates the problems of racism and sexism within the library profession and its institutions. Issues and Programs (successes and failures) in public libraries are dealt with in the section called *Service to the Community*. Academic, school, and children's and young adult services are examined in *Service to Youth* and *Service to Students and Faculty*. Social change, library education, relevant technical services, and technology are among the questions discussed in *Inventing the Future*. Bibliographic information for the articles along with biographical information on the contributing authors will be found at the back of the book under List of Contributors.

While the volume of material relating to social responsibility published in *LJ* and *SLJ* between 1968 and 1976 is immense (whole collections could be devoted to most of the chapter topics) this anthology pinpoints not only the questions, concerns, and programs of the profession, but the gaps—what is *not* being written. The need for better library service to prisoners, minorities, the aged, and the handicapped has been addressed frequently in the news and editorial pages of *LJ* and *SLJ* and sometimes in bibliographies. Unfortunately, editors can only publish what writers have the time, energy, and interest to write. Understandably, librarians working in exciting programs often do not have the time or inclination to write articles. It is hoped that this collection of articles will encourage librarians at every level to examine their own thinking, to formulate and refine programs relating to social responsibility, and to share this responsiveness with the profession.

PATRICIA GLASS SCHUMAN

I
Advocacy
and
Action

Librarian and/or Citizen?

Geoffrey Dunbar

Let us give the name of hypothesis to anything that may be proposed to our belief; and just as the electricians speak of live and dead wires, let us speak of any hypothesis as either live or dead. A live hypothesis is one which appeals as a real possibility to whom it is proposed. If I ask you to believe in the Mahdi, the notion makes no electric connection with your nature—it refuses to scintillate with any credibility at all. As an hypothesis it is completely dead. To an Arab, however (even if he be not one of the Mahdi's followers), the hypothesis is among the mind's possibilities: it is alive. This shows that deadness and liveness in an hypothesis are not intrinsic properties, but relations to the individual thinker.—William James, "The Will to Believe"

WITH another annual conference looming on the horizon, I for one hope that we've all had enough begging of the "involvement" question and that ALA members will again try to avail themselves of the opportunity to explore this complex issue on its merits, in a rational, sober, and reflective atmosphere. For, if the membership does not take pains to approach the issue in just this spirit, it is all too probable that a meaningful debate will once again be precluded by a failure of basic communication.

Unfortunately, the general direction of partisan commentary on this subject during the past two years offers little encouragement that such a fresh approach will be taken at Chicago; this direction, in fact, seems to have been set in the very beginning by certain remarks by David Berninghausen, director of the University of Minnesota Library School, past chair-man of the ALA Intellectual Freedom Committee, and spokesman for the School of ALA Non-Involvement.

No one present at the first membership meeting in Detroit two years ago can fail to recall the Director's well-distributed thesis that one's role as a "librarian" is (by virtue of nothing less than the very definition of the term, apparently) mutually exclusive of whatever role one chooses to fulfill as a "citizen." In his paper "Should ALA Take a Stand on an Issue of Public Interest," Berninghausen said:

. . . There are thousands of worthy causes, and each citizen chooses for himself some of these which, to him, are of special importance or urgency. For these few causes he makes a special effort. But, if this citizen is a librarian, he must distinguish between those causes, among the thousands, in which he has a direct inescapable interest *as a li-*

3

brarian, and those which may be equally, or even more urgent to society, but in which his direct interest is that of a *citizen. . . .* The new voices in ALA that urge members to perceive social problems as their problems are on firm ground when the appeal is to librarians *as citizens.* There are no grounds at all for their insistence that the critical social problems of the world are the problems of librarians *as librarians. . . .* It would be inappropriate, and probably illegal, for the ALA to take a position promoting the fluoridation of water systems, though most librarians would probably be ready and willing to take such positions as *citizens. . . .*

This facile librarian/citizen distinction clearly constituted the "big gun" in the Detroit professionalists' arsenal, and in terms of effective fire-power, it was a potent one indeed.

One wonders, in fact, if even Berninghausen himself was not rather startled at the feeble, low-level response to his argument. Looking back, it appears certain that the absence of a more effective, vigorous reply was due at least as much to rather indirect influences as to the intrinsic merits of the statement.

Although irrelevant to the central hypothesis, for example, much of the Detroit statement (particularly portions *not* quoted above) contributed to its success by means of diverting the counterattacking forces from what should have been their primary objective. Few of the "young Turks" at Detroit could ignore the almost sinister implications of such fillips as, "ALA members . . . should ask themselves why . . . (in many cases) they expect their libraries to pay their expenses to conference." But of even greater importance in the failure of the "involvement" advocates to put up a respectable resistance was the simple fact that few of them had even the foggiest notion of what the argument was really getting at; at the same time, Berninghausen's fellow professionalists at least *felt* (in terms of "gut reaction") that *they* understood and fully appreciated the cogency of what he was saying, whether in point of fact they did so, or not.

What little experience I've had in this area has convinced me that, in terms of improving communication upon such subjects with the so-called "younger generation," nothing could be more futile than to attempt to base one's argument upon the notion that one's choices of action are necessarily confined to a range determined by the kind of "role" one is playing at any given time. While many of us in the pre-activist generation of librarians are only too familiar with this line of reasoning (and duly grateful, too, for such a marvelously effective conscience assuaging device), there is abundant evidence that such a predisposition to schizophrenic, dysfunctional compartmentalization is *not* a distinctive characteristic of the emerging generation (facts that at least partially explain the widely divergent attitudes toward the Calley case, one would assume). If ALA can ever hope to get off dead center on the involvement issue, more groundwork in communication, in communicability to activist librarians must be done.

In short, as far as ALA's homegrown rebels are concerned, the principles of "professional," single-minded devotion to a librarianship defined most restrictively simply do not add up to a "live hypothesis."

To extend James' analogy further— those of us on the far side of Cobo Hall's generation gap were "Arabs" encamped in the very midst of seemingly ever-increasing hordes of hostile, howling nonbelievers. *We* understood those principles, in other words, whether we *believed* them or not (and most of us did); they, on the other hand, did not comprehend the very sense of the argument and thus were denied the opportunity of refuting it.

Obversely, of course, there is little evidence to indicate that ALA's elders have even begun to appreciate the premises upon which the Social Responsibilities Round Table members and their traveling companions have taken their stand —premises involving the nature of the individual (hence, also, the "librarian"), the nature of his relationship to society, and the nature of his responsibility to act upon that society.

Presented as it is with two fundamentally opposed hypotheses, ALA membership will have to make its choice, if it is to maintain any sort of rational collective stance regarding the issue of professional involvement in so-called nonprofessional concerns.

Personally, I believe that the familiar philosophy expounded by the Director of the University of Minnesota Library School represents a social outlook that has just about seen the end of its time. On the other hand, it appears obvious to me that the viewpoint that librarians not only can but *must* be involved in the resolution of fundamental social issues—*as librarians*—evident as it is on every quarter, and persistent as it is in the face of incredibly powerful opposition, represents the irrepressible next step in the evolutionary development of the librarian's store of social consciousness, whether any of us like it or not.

Considering the two philosophies in such a relationship certainly helps to explain a rather curious dichotomy between Berninghausen's Detroit statement and certain remarks of his to which students at the University of Minnesota Library School had been previously exposed. And as some of us sat in Cobo Hall listening to the Director, more than one must have recalled the brief statement entitled "Professionalism," which, for all I know, may still occupy its place as a "required" reading assignment in the loose-leaf binder of reserve readings for Minnesota's required basic course in library administration.

As it appeared in 1969, the two-page essay consisted of an elaboration of its opening sentence—"I often tell students in our professional library school that any professional person works 60 or more hours per week."

Although better than half of the piece is a synopsis of Marjorie K. McCorquodale's "What They'll Die for in Houston" (*Harper's Magazine*, October 1961, p. 179-82), the portion that is uniquely Berninghausen casts something of an eerie reflection upon his librarian/citizen pronunciamento in Detroit:

. . . What do I mean by saying that a professional works 60 hours a week or more? I mean that he is fortunate enough to have a bridge between his own world and the world of ideas. He is lucky enough to be alive all his waking hours. His "real world" and his "working world" are one and the same. He sees the connections between what he reads and what he does. There is simply no possibility that such a professional will seek a nine-to-five job.

A professional is one who has developed his attitude toward his work and his life. He may gripe at the unending procession of problems and projects to be done, but he wouldn't really want it any other way. He is a lucky man, and most of the time he knows it.

It is this attitude toward his life and work that marks the professional librarian. He is an intellectual, at home with ideas, acutely aware that ideas have consequences; that they are related to the real world. Because he knows this he cannot and does not regard his library as a safe, ivory tower. His library is the market place of ideas, and he is committed to an ideal of keeping books for people rather than from them.

For me, librarianship is so exciting, there is so much to do—so much worth doing— that I know there will never be time enough for me to tackle a tenth of what I can think up. Sixty hours a week is not nearly enough time.

Does this sound like the champion of role-playing who so boldly delineated the vast gulf between the individual as "citizen" and as "librarian" at Detroit? How can one reconcile the belief that the professional librarian's " 'real world' and 'working world' are one and the same" with "There are no grounds at all for their [the librarian-activists'] insistence that the critical social problems of the world are the problems of librarians *as librarians*"?

These inconsistent and contradictory statements on the part of the defenders of the *status quo* are ultimately more dangerous to the future of librarianship than even the most supposedly irrational outpourings from the activist quarter.

For, rather than having us focus our attention on visions of what, ideally, the world *might be* (as we are used to expecting from our young utopians), the elders demand of us that we place our belief and confidence in simultaneously conflicting descriptions of the world *as it is*, depending on the particular point they wish to make at the time. Pursued to its logical end, this direction can lead only to collective madness.

Despite their portentousness, however, such utterances may not be quite as disjointed and irreconcilable as they appear on the surface. For example, if the "Professionalism" statement is understood as having been originally enunciated during the identity-through-vocation syndrome that prevailed in this country in the late 40s, 50s, and early 60s (whereby an individual's essential worth was to be measured according to his vocational "contributions to society"—and especially so, with regard to so-called "professionals"), and the Detroit statement, on the other hand, as an attempt to stem the rising tide of identity-through-"social responsibility" backlash to that earlier preoccupation, there is a certain kind of fiendishly logical connection between the two preoccupations.

It is interesting, also, to speculate on the very real possibility that such attempts to justify one's existence by the extension of one's occupational role into one's "private life" contributed materially, themselves, to a quasi-merging of the two; who can be blamed if they did not foresee that, eventually, the so-called "private concerns" would begin to emerge *as dominant* over what had previously been a safely distinct and separate set of vocational concerns?

These views, of course, represent the speculation of just *one*—to paraphrase Berninghausen's term—"librarian/citizen." Until *all* of us undertake to think through the background, context, and implications of the "involvement question" *for ourselves*, it will remain with us, unremittingly, for an indefinite period of time.

Only time will tell if ALA membership is individually capable of coming to grips with the whys and wherefores of the variety of "faiths" underlying the arguments of the principal parties to the issue. Only time will tell, in others words, if the "profession" is capable of finding its own answers to such questions as: *If a professional librarian demonstrates his professionalism in the carryover of his "professional" concerns into his daily life, when (if ever) can the nonprofessional concerns of that daily life be justifiably allowed to influence the conduct of his professional life?*

Upon the answers to such questions depends the most important question of all: What does it mean to be a librarian?

Bearing Witness: Some Thoughts on Zoia Horn

Paul Cowan

Documenting Zoia Horn's Protest
Library Journal

AT THE American Library Association Conference in Dallas, 1971, Zoia Horn and Pat Rom offered the following resolution to the membership of ALA:

This year we two librarians hit the national press when we were subpoenaed by a federal grand jury as witnesses in a conspiracy case, then labelled the Harrisburg Six, now called the Harrisburg Eight, named after Harrisburg, Pennsylvania, locale of the grand jury hearings. What has happened to us is of extreme importance to our profession. We move: 1) that ALA Membership meeting at Dallas recognize the danger to intellectual freedom presented by the use of spying in libraries by governmental agencies; 2) that ALA go on record against the use of the grand jury procedure to intimidate anti-Vietnam War activists and people seeking justice for minority communities; 3) that ALA deplore and go on record against the use of the Conspiracy Act of 1968 as a weapon against the citizens of this country who are being indicted for such overt acts as meeting, telephoning, discussing alternative methods of bringing about change, and writing letters; 4) that the ALA Membership at Dallas assert the con-

fidentiality of the professional relationships of librarians to the people they serve, that these relationships be respected in the same manner as medical doctors to their patients, lawyers to their clients, priests to the people they serve; 5) that ALA assert that it is expected that no librarian would lend himself to a role as informant, whether by voluntarily revealing circulation records or identifying patrons and their reading habits.

The ALA Membership at Dallas passed the resolution and sent it along to the ALA Council where the preamble was changed to read as follows:

Whereas, ALA is concerned with the preservation of intellectual freedom and Whereas, the freedoms to think, to communicate, and discuss alternatives are essential elements of intellectual freedom, and Whereas, these freedoms have been threatened by actions of the federal government through the use of informers, electronic surveillance, grand juries, and indictments under the Conspiracy Act of 1968 as demonstrated in the case of the Harrisburg Eight, now, therefore be it resolved. . .

7

The Council inserted the original five points from the membership resolution following this new preamble, and then voted to pass the measure. To many, the passage of these two resolutions by the Members and their governing body put the Association squarely on the record against the use of the procedures, strategies, and laws cited to intimidate citizens. Zoia Horn refused to testify, despite a grant of immunity from prosecution by the Court, at the trial that stemmed from the findings of the same grand jury that indicted the Harrisburg Seven under the same act that the two ALA resolutions condemned. At the time of her refusal to testify, Ms. Horn made this statement to the Court:

> It is because I respect the function of this court to protect the rights of the individual, that I must refuse to testify.
>
> I cannot in my conscience lend myself to this black charade. I love and respect this country too much to see a farce made of the tenets upon which it stands.
>
> To me it stands on:
>
> *freedom of thought*, but government spying in homes, in libraries and universities

inhibits and destroys this freedom.

It stands on *freedom of association*—yet in this case gatherings of friends, picnics, parties have been given sinister implications, made suspect.

It stands on *freedom of speech*—yet general discussions have been interpreted by the government as advocacies of conspiracy.

The realities of overt killings in Vietnam have been obscured by the unrealities that I have encountered here.

Legally, I was advised to say that the court's decision denying my request for a wiretap hearing should be challenged and the improper procedure in issuing the grant of immunity should be legally questioned. I believe this.

Because of her refusal to testify, Zoia Horn was found guilty of contempt of Court and sentenced to jail for the duration of the trial of the Harrisburg Seven. She received the support of the Social Responsibilities Round Table (SRRT) of ALA and from the LeRoy Merritt Humanitarian Fund of the Freedom to Read Foundation in the form of grants totalling $1000.

ZOIA HORN is one of the gentlest people I've ever met. Though I don't have any first-hand knowledge of her work as a librarian, students at Bucknell, where she was employed for several years, say that she was dedicated and tireless. And she certainly is a very courageous human being.

Her decision to go to jail rather than testify at the trial of the Harrisburg Seven has to be understood in the context of that whole sordid affair. She would have been the most marginal of prosecution witnesses. (There was no such thing as a central witness, though the informer Boyd Douglas tried to play that role, since the government had no case.) She barely knew any of the defendants. At the most, her few minutes on the stand would have enabled the government to prove that Douglas had once used her house to entertain Father Joseph Wenderoth and Father Neil McLaughlin at a

meeting which the government called a luncheon. That's all.

The defendants wanted her to testify. Jane Hoover, Betsy Sandell, and librarian Patricia Rom—three other Bucknellians whom Douglas used in a similar way—all testified. But Zoia couldn't. She was so disgusted by the government's effort to weave a sinister conspiracy out of chatty, speculative letters and a few friendly social gatherings that she couldn't bring herself to cooperate with any portion of the ugly process.

Her refusal to testify was a spontaneous, outraged act of resistance by a quiet woman who had never before made a comparable political gesture. On another level, it was an example of a stern American sense of justice which, if it were multiplied by thousands of people, could serve as an effective buffer against any sort of government repression.

I first met Zoia in the spring of 1971, when I was investigating Boyd Douglas' activities at Bucknell for an article in the *Village Voice*. She was one of the last people to whom I spoke and, in her own sweet way, one of the firmest. Most of those I interviewed were still angry at Douglas, and very eager to share that emotion with me. But Zoia was wary of a reporter who might exploit those feelings for journalistic ends. We finally did have several long conversations and became warm friends; but when she talked about Douglas, she never failed to emphasize the fact that he was as much of a victim as the defendants, a piece of bait the FBI used to attract some radicals they wanted to trap.

That summer Zoia married Dean Galloway and moved from Lewisburg to Turlock, California. She was appointed Chief of Public Services at the Stanislaus County Free Public Library in Modesto. She wouldn't have come East for the trial if the government hadn't subpoenaed her to fly all the way to Lewisburg to testify that a single social gathering, which Fathers Wenderoth and Mc-Laughlin would have stipulated they'd attended, had actually occurred.

The nearer she got to the proceedings, the more they enraged her. In court, and in her statement to the press, Zoia called them a "black charade" and refused to participate. So Judge R. Dixon Herman declared her in contempt of court and sent her to jail for the duration of the trial.

One of Zoia's main complaints was that the government had sought to corrupt the academic community to win this case. In court, and in her statement to the press, she insisted that Douglas—and the Justice Department and FBI officials who used him—had perverted the function of libraries, speculative discussions, and friendships in order to obtain their evidence. That feeling, which was repeatedly borne out by Douglas' testimony, was at the heart of Zoia's decision to resist.

She had met Douglas while he was still a prisoner at Lewisburg Penitentiary (which was where he met Philip Berrigan), attending Bucknell on a study-release program. He had a part-time job in the library. (Each week he'd use one of the machines there to make copies of letters between Sister Elizabeth McAlister and Father Philip Berrigan, which he'd promptly send to the FBI.) Zoia had none of the rather dreamy, romanticized views of convicts which characterized the relations between Douglas and many people in the Catholic left and at Bucknell. She didn't particularly like him. But she did feel sorry for him.

But as testimony (including his own) at the trial records, Douglas was a hustler. He could convert any human feeling into currency. He'd had a starved, deprived childhood, had been a con man throughout most of his adolescence and young adulthood. He'd spent a total of ten years in jail; now, at 32, he was primarily interested in people and situations for their usefulness to him. That was probably why the FBI found him so easy to work with. He would make friends with Zoia, or with Bucknell undergraduates, or with anti-war faculty members. Then he'd arrange for them to meet Catholic radicals like Father Joseph Wenderoth or Father Neil McLaughlin or Sister Elizabeth McAlister, who came to Lewisburg to meet Father Berrigan. Then, he would tell FBI agents (who wanted to hear such information) about the "conspiratorial" conversations that were taking place between the clusters of people he'd just introduced. Each scrap of information, real or spurious, increased his worth to the Bureau. Of course, the FBI lacked the means, and the interest, to double-check his yarns.

He used books, many of which he borrowed from the Bucknell library, as bait to win people's trust or as a means of pushing people into illegal actions. That was part of what Zoia Horn meant when she charged that Douglas and his FBI handlers had perverted sacred freedoms of the library and of academia. For example, he had a brief, intense relationship with Jane Hoover, a Bucknell coed who had never before been political. He tried to radicalize her by loaning her books like Bobby Seale's *Seize the Time.* (He said scornfully on the stand that he'd never read the book himself.) He told her that he was a Vietnam veteran who was ardently opposed to the war; that he was in jail because he and some friends in California had been caught trying to blow up a napalm truck. (He'd never been to Vietnam, and he supported the war.) To buttress his story, he gave Jane Hoover a copy of Wilfred Gaylin's *In the Service of Their Country,* a book about draft resisters in the Lewisburg jail, and he told her that some of the passages in it were about him.

He wrote a letter to a Rochester resister named Susan Williams, whom he never met, which contained a slightly veiled appeal to join an illegal project in Washington, D.C. It also contained a description of himself as a "totally committed non-violent revolutionary, who believes in strategic sabotage." Where did those words come from? He'd copied them out of a book he found in the library, he testified on the witness stand. He didn't even remember the book's name.

In prosecuting attorney William Lynch's opening statement, he mentioned some ROTC manuals on explosives which Joseph Wenderoth had borrowed from Douglas and hinted that they would be one of the keys to the government's case about conspiracy. In testimony, it turned out that Douglas had asked the FBI to lend him such literature because he'd told the defendants that he was a demolitions expert, and he wanted to bone up on demolitions to keep from being exposed. So the FBI borrowed the manuals from Bucknell's ROTC library. Instead of reading them, Douglas urged Joseph Wenderoth to take them and copy them, which Wenderoth did in order to placate his strange new friend. As evidence of the route the manuals had travelled began to emerge, they melted out of the case.

Zoia Horn went to jail because she believed that Douglas and the FBI had sought to corrupt the academic community in general, not just the libraries. They certainly sought to twist one of Bucknell's most important experimental undergraduate programs, the Jan plan. In it, students are free to use the month of January to pursue independent studies programs; Douglas and his handlers sought to use the Jan plan as a cover for espionage.

Douglas had told Bucknell faculty members that he wanted to devise a Jan plan program which would allow him to travel around the country studying prison conditions. He was given permission to do that as soon as he received parole. In addition, the Bucknell faculty offered him a small grant and assigned two students to assist him with his research.

But Douglas and the FBI had their own uses for the Jan plan. During his travels Boyd would get in touch with as many movement groups as possible, focusing on the East Coast Conspiracy to Save Lives, a Catholic left group, and report on them to the Bureau. He would visit Philip Berrigan, who had recently been transferred from Lewisburg prison to Danbury prison. Would he tell the FBI that the bombing and kidnapping schemes, which had never been more than speculative fantasies, were still plots that the Catholic left planned to carry out? The FBI planned to pay him $1000 a month for six months to work as an informer. The plan only fell through when the Justice Department decided to blow Douglas' cover in December 1970 and bring the bombing-kidnapping case to court.

Zoia Horn was peripheral to all of these machinations. But by the time of the trial she knew how Douglas and the FBI had sought to use the facilities of academia as part of the trap they were laying. She found her own brave way to say "no" to that outrage.

I spent several hours with Zoia the night before she refused to testify. She was very nervous then. The prospect of jail unsettled her, as did the prospect of being so far away from Turlock and Dean Galloway. Since I thought that her presence on the witness stand would probably deepen the jury's sense of Boyd Douglas' shabby character, I thought that she'd spare herself and help the defendants if she testified. But it wasn't a question of personal comfort with her, or even one of immediate trial strategy. There was a deeper, purer moral impulse involved which I hadn't really sensed the first times we met, but which awed me when I saw it in Harrisburg. It was a simple, dear desire to preserve cherished values.

I saw her twice after she got out of jail at the end of the trial. She didn't seem very eager to discuss the experience. Evidently, much of it had been quite unpleasant, though she still seemed very cheerful and quite eager to talk about other subjects. I didn't want to push her to discuss the experience since I knew that she'd soon integrate whatever she'd learned into her character and share it with me the next time we met.

She'll be fine. In her middle age, she seems to be gaining strength year by year. And her earliest, deepest perception about the case—that Boyd Douglas was its true victim—proved to be a sound one in the end. My guess is that a year or two from now, when she's back in Turlock working as a librarian, she'll pick up her local paper and read a small article saying that Boyd Douglas, the informer in the Berrigan affair, was in trouble again. And at that moment she'll suffer for him, just as she suffered for the values he helped abuse. Perhaps, though, Zoia Horn will draw some comfort from the fact that she went to jail to protest Boyd Douglas' mistreatment, too.

A Boll Weevil
Six Feet Long

John M. Carter

ABOUT A MONTH before the Mississippi gubernatorial election of 1959, the Honorable Ross Barnett backed into the propeller of a private airplane and almost lost his honorable life. Sensing that this would probably be enough to win him the election, I left the state.

After four years of wandering in the wilds of Nevada and darkest Illinois, I returned in the early spring of 1964 with an awful mixture of emotion. Still frenzied was the panic that resulted from the Ole Miss debacle of 1962, which among other things, drove one representative to rise on the floor of the state legislature and demand nothing less than secession. Those who revelled in the death of John Kennedy had learned that Lyndon Johnson would be an even more zealous and effective advocate of Negro rights. State membership in the Ku Klux Klan had grown from a few hundred to a frightening ten thousand, and the more respectable white-collar Citizens Councils continued to expand. The State Sovereignty Commission, Mississippi's answer to the KGB, kept long lists of liberal traitors to the Southern Way of Life, representing a very real danger to any Mississippian who fought the "Closed Society." Indeed, James Silver, who that year coined and documented the phrase

in his book *Mississippi: The Closed Society,* was to resign his position at Ole Miss in 1965, and leave the state. Another turncoat, a newspaperman named Ira Harkey, who won the Pulitzer Prize for his editorial fight against the Barnett administration, had, in 1963, sold his Pascagoula newspaper and moved to Arkansas, having been boycotted by his major advertisers. Freedom Riders had come and gone, and in that spring of 1964, were being replaced by affluent young idealists who had at last recognized that the only way to equality was through suffrage. The Voter Education Project, sponsored by the first amalgamation of the five major civil rights organizations, was going into high gear, and white reactionaries were boiling a bitter brew. The smell of blood and burning crosses was in the air.

Not entirely unlike Mississippi being dragged bellowing into the Twentieth Century, I finally succumbed to the powerful urge to go home again. Two months later it was being said around the state that the three young troublemakers who had disappeared near Philadelphia, Mississippi, had actually gone "back to Cuba."

Since that time the nation has learned that violent racism is not peculiar to the South, that there are mad white men in the police forces of Northern cities as well as the sheriffs' offices of Southern counties. While race relations deteriorated in New York and California and New Jersey, they have improved in Mississippi. Perhaps, as one student recently remarked to me, they have deteriorated since November 1968. But as compared to the early 1960's they have improved. Juries have been hung and white Mississippians even convicted for shooting Negroes and bombing Jews, where a few years before such activities were looked upon by the genteel as questionable social behavior at worst, but certainly nothing for which to send a man to jail. Today it is difficult to find enough Klansmen to raise a decent cross. An enlightened populace has successfully demanded an end to the pompous hypocrisy of Mississippi's prohibition laws. And there are even signs that it may soon be completely legal to teach evolution.

But the old ways survive like stubborn microbes. As Mississippi's post-Reconstruction laws have been knocked down systematically by the Federal Courts, its majority of "right-thinking Americans" has stiffened, and reaction has become more devious. Many public library boards are still run, surprisingly in some of the larger cities, by aging retrogressives still dedicated to maintaining "separate but equal" facilities. Boards of education, run by brilliant Nineteenth Century minds but torn between the status quo and HEW guidelines, have devised rather ingenious plans for protecting their children from "foreign ideas."

The Board of Trustees of the Mississippi Institutions of Higher Learning, which controls the three universities as well as a bushel of smaller senior and junior colleges, adopted a policy in 1966 that read in part, "All speakers invited to the campus of any of the State Institutions of Higher Learning must first be investigated and approved by the head of the Institution involved, and when invited the names of such speakers must be filed with the Executive Secretary of the Board of Trustees." It is not difficult to anticipate what an imaginative board of trustees could do with such a policy. The only problem might arise from the fact that the Board would be informed only *after* the speaker was approved and invited. This problem proved to be the Board's undoing.

Two years before the Board unravelled over this problem, in the fall of 1966, a student group asked the President of Mississippi State University to approve a list of seventeen speakers for that academic year. He turned down five. (George Wallace; Aaron Henry, Mississippi NAACP president; Edward Kennedy; Bishop James Pike; Dr. Peter Bertocci.) When the students threatened a law suit the President reversed part of the decision on the grounds that the law suit would be more harmful to the University than the speaker, and allowed Negro leader Aaron Henry to speak. The speech was taped by the MSU Library. It might be speculated here that the Board of Trustees allowed the President to get away with this bit of vacillation because he was still in his honeymoon period as a new president.

The showdown over the Board's policy did not come until fall, 1968. In October, MSU President William L. Giles approved as campus speaker one Charles Evers, brother and successor to NAACP Field Secretary Medgar Evers, who was gunned down on his own front doorstep in 1962. The invitation to Charles Evers was issued, and President Giles, as the policy requires, reported this fact to the Board of Trustees. The effect was not unlike that of discovering that the Soviet Union had developed a boll weevil six feet long.

As this writer understands the events that followed, the Board of Trustees held a hasty meeting and ordered President Giles to "request" that the students withdraw the invitation to Evers. The students refused, so were told that

Evers would not be allowed to speak anyway. The students sued in Federal District Court. Charles Evers also entered the suit as an injured party. The faculty was silent.

Testimony was given in the court of Chief U. S. Northern District Judge William C. Keady on October 21, 1968. President Giles testified that he h⌐d originally approved Charles Evers as speaker because he did not consider it "out of order." Several students testified as to what they considered their right to hear speakers of their choice. President of the Board of Trustees M. M. Roberts, acting as attorney for the Board of Trustees, argued that his birthday was on the day of the proposed speech, and that if Evers was allowed to speak, he, Roberts, would not have a happy birthday. (Aaron Henry alledgedly sent Roberts a happy birthday telegram later.) Judge Keady refused to grant a temporary injunction allowing Evers to speak, but instead turned the entire matter over to a three-judge panel to rule on the constitutionality of the policy of the Board of Trustees which had come popularly to be called "The Speaker Ban." Keady did, however, state that the Board's action had been "arbitrary and irrational . . . a disservice to the state of Mississippi, and damaging to the independence of college administrators." He found that there had been a "varying if not curious application of the regulation."

On October 23, 1969, this writer was contacted by a group of students and invited to speak at a rally opposing the Speaker Ban. There had never been such a rally before, to my knowledge, in the state of Mississippi. Certainly not one involving members of a faculty. My first reaction, as the witticism goes, was to put on my pants and go home. But I had been openly critical of faculty apathy and cowardice, so could not in good conscience refuse to speak. On the steps of the Union at high noon the next day, I and one other member of the faculty spoke on the issue to a gathering of about a thousand students and faculty. We began a dialogue, often heated, that is still reverberating around this once placid campus. I said:

First of all I should like to disqualify myself as an expert on the events of the past few days. I have not talked with President Giles concerning the consequences of his decision to allow Charles Evers to speak on this campus. He would have no reason to discuss it with me. I do not *know* beyond doubt what mental processes caused the Board of Trustees to reverse the decision of President Giles, though having worked for the public library board of trustees in Jackson, I could make an educated guess.

But I did not come here to stand in judgment of the Board of Trustees. That has been done by a judge far more competent than I.

What I *am* concerned about is the awful silence of the faculty. I am concerned because I have heard no member of the faculty, or group, who is willing to speak out in favor of the students' right to know. And being thusly concerned, I could not very well turn down Sam Love's invitation to speak.

So I continue to ask myself, why is the faculty so *silent?* The Board of Trustees *knows* where the administration stands. The Board of Trustees knows where the *students* stand. But where stands the faculty? Why do they not rise to the opportunity to defend academic freedom for their students . . . and for themselves? (This is the case, you know. For when the Board of Trustees denies your hearing a speaker on campus, it also denies it to me.)

I should like to devote the few moments remaining to me to an attempt to at least partially answer these questions about our silent faculty.

The faculty at this university, based upon my observations for three years, may be divided roughly into three major groups. The first of these is the largest. How large is anyone's guess, perhaps 88 or 90 percent. This is that portion of the faculty that simply *doesn't care* about anything so ethereal and attenuated as academic freedom in Mississippi.

This group that doesn't care may be further divided into three sub-groups. The first of these we might call the Football for Lunch Bunch. They are occupied with little more than three squares per diem, and speculation as to the possibility of the football team's winning a game this year. It is the members of this group that I have heard say that "the administration sure is havin' a lot o' trouble with them students," not really able to understand that the problem the administration is having is not with them students, but with them trustees.

The second sub-group that doesn't care is perhaps more intelligent than the first. Indeed some of them are brilliant; and the university could not function without them. But they are so enmeshed in the narrow little world of their own academic disciplines, that they are not aware of the storm that rages about their heads. Some of them, even now, are not aware of the existence of a Negro leader named Charles Evers who has been ruled as unfit for human consumption.

The members of the last, and probably the largest, sub-group, may not belong at all with the group that doesn't care because they do care. They agree with the speaker ban policy of the Board of Trustees. They believe in the fundamental right of one group of men to decide what is fit for the ears of another group. One of these—a Ph.D mind you —told me on Monday of this week, "Perhaps Charles Evers doesn't have anything to say that the students need to hear."

The second major group cares, but is afraid to say so. There's really not much more we can say about them.

It is with the third group that lies the hope of full academic freedom at Mississippi State University. This is the group that cares, and says so. But its members are ineffective. There simply are not very many of them. When they speak they speak largely to one another, and agree with one another, which makes for a dandy argument. Perhaps if they spoke in unison—well, perhaps their few voices would make too little noise.

But we don't know, do we? They never speak in unison. They are too scattered, and often do not even know of the existence of one another. I know perhaps 20 . . . and I think they are all here today.

My plea is that they speak out—and let the administration and the Board of Trustees know where they stand. Perhaps in doing so this third group can give some courage to the second.

A few days after this rally an executive board meeting of the MSU chapter of the AAUP was held. After nearly a week of drafting and revising, the chapter issued a statement, abridged as follows:

We, the members of the Mississippi State University Chapter of the American Association of University Professors, aware of at least one occasion on which the Board of Trustees has refused to permit an individual to speak on a university campus, address ourselves herein to the speaker ban policy of the Board of Trustees of Institutions of Higher Learning. In view of the principles stated in the Joint Statement on Rights and Freedoms of Students adopted by the AAUP, we object both to the stated policy, and to the inconsistent manner in which the Board of Trustees has administered this policy and written or unwritten interpretations thereof.

The Joint Statement . . . reads, "Students should be allowed to invite and to hear any person of their own choosing. Those routine procedures required by an institution before a guest speaker is invited to appear on campus should be designed only to insure that there is orderly scheduling of facilities and adequate preparation for the event, and that the occasion is conducted in a manner appropriate to an academic community. The institutional control of campus facilities should not be used as a device of censorship. It should be made clear to the academic and larger community that sponsorship of guest speakers does not necessarily imply approval or endorsement of the views expressed, either by the sponsoring group or the institution."

This statement has been endorsed by many educational organizations, including the Association of American Colleges, the American Association of University Professors, and the American Association for Higher Education.

We believe that any policy designed to investigate and approve speakers has within it the possibilities of inconsistent application and censorship which are in violation of those principles of academic freedom for which the AAUP stands.

We therefore urge the Board of Trustees to rescind its speaker screening policy, and to consider the principles of the Joint Statement on Rights and Freedoms of Students in formulating a new policy.

The Board of Trustees responded by strengthening its policy and forbidding on-campus speeches by "any person who has been announced as a political candidate." (The invitation to Evers was originally issued by the Young Democrats. Evers presumably would have spoken in support of Hubert Humphrey.) The gauntlet had been dropped by the students, backed by the AAUP. The Board of Trustees had picked it up. It was now clear that the latter would not rescind its policy unless forced by the courts. Columnists, both liberal and conservative, had a field day. One Greg Adkins of *The Daily Mississippi* (University of Mississippi), in a column widely quoted in other state newspapers, likened professors and students who asserted their right to hear Evers to "anarchists, radicals, communists and subversives." He concluded, "if the liberals and their further Left [sic] friends . . . want to listen to anarchists, radicals and communists, then I would suggest they watch more T.V." This view probably was representative of the majority of Mississippians.

The three-judge federal panel, headed by former governor J. P. Coleman, now a U. S. Fifth Circuit Court of Appeals judge, convened to hear testimony on January 14, 1969. Other members of the panel were Judge William Keady of Greenville, who had previously issued an injunction to allow Evers to speak at Ole Miss, but refused to do so at MSU, and Judge Dan M. Russell of Bay St. Louis. Several prominent wit-

nesses had then returned to declare the Speaker Ban Policy "unconstitutional on its face." Said Judge Coleman, "These regulations can never again be enforced on any of these [state supported] campuses." The Trustees were given 60 days to write a more specific policy that was not "unconstitutionally vague."

During the second week of March, 1969, the 60 days expired, and the Board of Trustees for the Institutions of Higher Learning of the Great State of Mississippi, heretofore responsible only to God, but now like an errant schoolboy forced by his teacher to rewrite a sloppy term paper, submitted its new policy to the judgment of the courts. The new policy indeed eliminated any possibility of vagueness. It was so specific as to be potentially more crippling than ever. Banned were any speakers who *might* incite riots, destroy school property, disrupt college operations, or come from off-campus for a religious meeting. Banned also were announced candidates for public office and any speakers who, within the past 15 years, had advocated violence or caused violence to be used by others, "incited any group of more than three persons to enter a college or university building and destroy property," or been convicted of a felony or crime or moral turpitude. No one could speak whose *presence* might cause a riot. Further, only the president of the institution involved would be permitted to issue the invitation.

Not surprisingly, attorneys for the students who had challenged the original policy, now challenged the second. As of this writing the Court has not rendered its decision on the new policy. But when it does, no matter what the ruling, the case could very well go to the U. S. Supreme Court, setting a precedent on speaker regulations for the entire country. Both sides are prepared to go that far.

Other than the fact that the Board of Trustees is dying hard, there are several lessons from this episode that might be learned by librarians in general, and Southern and academic librarians in particular. My conclusion from my experience is that an element of academic freedom does at last exist in Mississippi. There is a crack in the door of the Closed Society, and it is opening more rapidly than most people realize. Several students, fewer faculty, and one lonely librarian publicly challenged the wisdom of their Board of Trustees—and got away with it. To my knowledge there has been not a single attempt at retribution. One student was threatened by an idle alumnus who said something like "we're going to get you Young Democrats." Another received a few silent phone calls. But that is all. I received no obscene telephone calls and no threatening letters. No crosses were burned in my yard. As of this writing I have not been lynched. As a matter of fact I have been offered a new contract by the hand I bit, the Board of Trustees, for the fiscal year beginning July 1969. Five years ago I would not have fared so well. In the climate of today's Mississippi, I did.

I have also learned that, despite their personal prejudices, most people deeply respect intellectual courage. To be sure a few faculty shunned me. Others wondered aloud before their classes what a librarian was doing making a speech on free speech. Why wasn't he over at the library stamping books? Or reading the unabridged dictionary? Or wiping his glasses? Or holding his index finger in front of pursed lips? But mainly I feel that I achieved a kind of respected infamy. One employee said to me exuberantly, "I'm proud that you're my boss!" Faculty members, while making cracks about not wanting to be seen with me, seemed actually to take a certain amount of pride in the association. Perhaps they will remember, and someday have occasion to defend the library profession with something like, "Who says librarians are sissies? Why I remember a librarian who. . . ."

But above all, I developed a mutual trust and respect with the students involved that I value most highly. They now talk to me and associate with me as if I were under 30. Several have even offered to keep me supplied with marijuana. And that, dear reader, in a state that can levy up to 20 years for so heinous a crime, is trust.

From Roswell to Richmond . . . to Your Town

Gordon McShean

THE TOWNS of Roswell, New Mexico and Richmond, California are a great distance apart, but it is remarkable how near they are to one another in terms of public attitudes toward censorship. And it would probably surprise you to find out how near your town is in its attitudes.

As the head librarian of Roswell, and a former resident of the Bay Area in Northern California (I had been a librarian at Stanford University for two years), my knowledge of the communities is reasonably intimate. There is nothing in either place to make one think that *this* town will embrace censorship and get rid of its librarian. They both have some history of intolerance, but what community does not? Both could be called medium-sized towns (Roswell has a population of 50,000 and is the second largest city in the State; Richmond, with a population of 75,000, is one of many similar towns making up the cosmopolitan sprawl of the East Bay); one is rural, the other urban; both are places where reasonably well educated, civic-minded people lived—perhaps like your town.

They didn't seem very close together when I arrived in Richmond in the summer of 1968, for I had traveled from New Mexico to California via Iowa and New York in a vain search for work following my experience with library censorship. I had resigned from Roswell subsequent to a controversy over a poetry reading which was opposed by a vocal, vicious minority and most of the city council (although it had been supported by the library board). I succumbed eventually to a continued campaign of vilification and spent a few months with a Job Corps program that never got off the ground. When I reached California I felt that only good things could happen. I met and befriended John Forsman while I was looking for work at his library in Richmond. I did not know then that the "trouble" he was experiencing over some magazines in his library was about to become another major censorship battle. We were soon to find out how near Roswell and Richmond really were. Since then, Farmingdale, Los Angeles, Martinsville, Memphis—a host of other towns—and even the whole State of Missouri—have seemed to be next door, for they have all experienced censorship attempts. When one adds to the toll the many communities which have been torn by controversies over sex-education-in-the-schools, the whole picture of censorship activity is awesome. We'll never know how many attacks have been made on libraries and schools which have resulted in a quick and quiet surrender by the administrator. I am prepared to believe that the number is considerable.

The censors, I am convinced, have little real interest in the offending materials when they first make charges against a library, a librarian or a library board. In Richmond, interest was first centered around the periodicals *Berkeley Barb* and *Avant Garde* but the real focus of the attack soon became the librarian and his presumed motives.

If you listen to the recording *What Shall They Read?* (released by Pacifica Archives in early 1969) which contains some of the testimony taken before the Richmond City Council, it will soon be clear to you that the attackers had very little knowledge of the materials they had chosen to attack—they were instead involved in what they considered a minor skirmish to rid the earth of one or two agents of a monstrous conspiracy which might somehow convince the poorer children in the community of the perspicacity of their own minds. "Law and order" to such people is mindless acceptance of the dictates of the elite (to which they obviously belonged); freedom is anathema to such people.

In my own case, in Roswell, the attack was even more blatant in its emphasis on motives, for the principal thrust was made against a program *title*, "Hippie Poetry" (it was one of a series of library readings). None of the critics had any knowledge of even the names of the poets who would be represented. It was enough that the librarian had extended the freedom of expression to poets who called themselves hippies—it was irrelevant that the librarian had previously presented other types of poetry.

The librarian *had* to be an agent of evil from abroad, the censors were convinced, for they credited him with such diverse immoral acts as having desecrated the memories of various individuals by weeding books from the library which had been given *in memorium,* and of moving the geneology collection to less accessible shelves without asking the permission of the Daughters of the American Revolution and the Daughters of the American Colonists. The ladies of the D.A.R. later marched into the library *en masse* and removed the books they had placed in the library (all on geneology)—without asking permission—mentioning to a staff member that they would not have their books in an "un-American" library.

Soon the rumors had grown to such an extent that the librarian was supposed to have taken the collection of local history and locked it away in a cupboard, refusing to permit anyone access; he had posted materials on the bulletin boards in the children's library which described the sex lives of priests; he had even been drinking on the job (believe me, it *was* a temptation). The Mayor finally went on record to make the suspicions of the censors quite explicit: mentioning the fact that the librarian had come from abroad, wore a beard and was a Buddhist (the man had attended the librarian's courtesy lecture on Eastern Religions at his own church to learn this much), he stated that one could therefore "know what kind of man he is." Are you still convinced of the censor's concern with *materials?*

Even in school censorship problems it is obvious that the concern is less for the repression of sex education materials than it is for the establishment of a general climate of repression based on the international communist conspiracy myth. A pamphlet on sex education in the schools which is put out nationally by the John Birch Society claims that there is a conspiracy to destroy "all civilized values." It goes on "It is no accident that Communists and others long associated with this conspiracy are among the staunchest advocates of the drive for continuous sex education." I find myself quite unable to visualize the cold and calculating communists chortling over the latest ploy in the conspiracy, dedicated this time to giving kids V.D. or whatever, like some medieval witch who was presumed to find joy in doing anything that offended God. Meanwhile I must presume that the forces of "American Morality" are busy in every state of the Union seeing that nothing is done to modify the "civilized values" of the sexual indoctrination each child presently receives in school or park restrooms.

The Martinsville, Virginia case (which is still being fought as I write this) leaves us little doubt that Ellis Hodgin was attacked not for what he had in his library, or even the manner in which he ran his library, but for his stand on the teaching of religion in the schools (*LJ*, September 1, p. 2853, 55). Since the attack began various charges relating to his conduct in the library have been made (as they are made, in some manner or another, in nearly every case involving an organized, serious attack on intellectual freedom as it relates to librarians).

I have talked to Ellis Hodgin and am amazed at the similarity of the attacks which have been made against him, John Forsman and myself. In every case the librarian is subjected to criticism of the fiscal management of his library (they went so far as to accuse me of attempting to destroy private enterprise with my coin-operated copier and my 10¢-discarded-book rack— these operations were distinctly leftist in their eyes). There is always a consistent pattern of insinuations in regard to the librarian's personal appearance, his life style and his religious beliefs as well.

The censor is a master at using the librarian's own weight to contribute to his downfall. The attacked librarian finds that such things as the length of his wife's skirts, the length of time he takes at professional meetings, and the prominence of the bags under his eyes

are all used as evidence for more serious charges. Despite the fact that many of these things seem to be discussed at gatherings of presumably responsible people (my wife's miniskirts were discussed by a ministerial conference in New Mexico!), the librarian is never able to quite pin down the origin of the rumors.

It is when the attacks reach your family that they start to become unbearable (I thought I had learned from television that only communists used that ploy). I know of two librarians who are presently in trouble because they broke down to such an extent— after their families had been subjected to numerous aggravation phone calls— that they swore at someone over the telephone. I know how they felt.

It is a strange thing that a measure of the ridiculous—even irrelevance and foolishness—seems to help the censors. They are obviously aware of this. The librarian and his materials are presumably at issue, and the curious logic of the principal opponents in a censorship conflict makes the librarian seem guilty even if the materials seem innocuous —after all, the community guardians wouldn't be making all that fuss over nothing, the logic runs. The librarian begins to feel the attack viscerally.

The same approach by the censors also has the effect of lulling supporters of the librarian to sleep. If the members of the support group know him as a good guy and conclude that the material being attacked is harmless—not *legally* indictable, and those of us who have been through it know that legality or illegality has little to do with an effective censorship campaign—they tend to feel that you are overreacting when you call for help. But it is my conviction that there is no way—short of suicide—to overreact when a serious censorship attack is launched against you. The evidence of the conduct of censors in other parts of the country is too strong. Do not expect the tactics of the moral defenders of the community to be moral.

The attitudes of your colleagues are worth some study as well. In most censorship cases a number of admirable documents have been produced, ranging from well-phrased statements of support and principle which may eventually enrich the literature of our profession, to personal accolades which the attacked librarian may have trouble living up to. Often these documents are the work of state library associations or other equally prestigious organizations. But in the end the librarian ends up feeling that he had more friends in the place he resigned from than elsewhere, librarians or anyone else.

One of these reasons for this is that "fighting the censorship nuts" is an adventurous theoretical exercise for library school students, bored acquisitions librarians and administrators, as long as it remains theory. With such exhibits as *the book, the community support* and *the legal question* to play around with it will remain a popular game. But the whole thing falls apart when you have to include *the victim,* especially if you find out (as I did) that the censored material is really not at issue. Then the fine public relations program fades to nothing in the face of the exciting dirt the censors think up, and the legal question is basically whether they can find official sanction for harassment. I have taken issue with officers of the American Library Association who have felt that *the law* and *justice* were an equation.

Abstract letters of support come to the attacked librarian from all over the country, and the unsuspecting person might be duped into believing that he had become very popular everywhere —if he did not occasionally meet some of the people who wrote. Because then he finds that many become embarrassed when faced with this unknown person: *the librarian who got himself in trouble while everyone else was managing to keep the lid on.* He will find that the letters were written only because it seemed like the right thing to do, in view of all the theories the writers had

been fed in library schools. He will find that too many of his colleagues will be willing to defend intellectual freedom as long as it is an abstract principle— but they resent it when that principle has to be invoked.

The attacked librarian can go back to the town where he struggled to maintain good library service, and he can count on the friendship of hundreds who knew him and knew what he was attempting to do—the censorship campaign only brought these people closer. He may be out of a job there, but at least he has friends.

But when he goes to other towns he will find that the only job available is in a quiet back room, and it's only available if he will take a cut in salary. University libraries are almost as bad as public libraries in this respect. The library profession unwittingly inflicts the punishment the censors demanded. It is time that we started to realize what we have been doing to ourselves and our colleagues.

The people who are taken in by the propaganda which casts doubt on the librarian and his motives fail to see that if intellectual freedom, civil liberties, and freedom of action for the individual are *truly* a first step in the achievement of the communist state as is so often charged then it is strange how few of the communist states now in existence offer these "privileges" (it is obvious that the forces on the left and the right consider them privileges). Our own profession is not free from this hysteria. I have recently read a letter written by a librarian very high in the councils of our profession which makes blanket charges about the furthering of the "International Communist Conspiracy" by those of us whose voices have been heard in defense of our Constitutional freedom. If these freedoms are really the basis for the spread of communism, then there must be something much freer about that movement than I had realized.

As one of the foreigners most likely to be suspect for having brought alien concepts to these shores, I can state that a great many of my convictions in regard to the need for freedom *everywhere in the world* have been gained from my studies of the traditions of the United States of America. The charge of "Un-American" is not valid.

We are indeed involved in a struggle for people's minds—and I know this is a claim generally made by the censors. I agree with the censors that there are people actively working to subvert our traditions and our way of life. I even agree that these people are often dupes of an alien ideology. But it is my firm conviction that the struggle for people's minds is in terms other than those we are used to hearing: the struggle is whether minds will be free or not. If we believe that the struggle is whether minds will be controlled by the left or the right, we have already forfeited our freedom. The people who are attempting to subvert our traditions, our way of life—the dupes of an alien ideology —these are the people who have no faith in our freedoms, whose narrow view of humanity forces them to conclude that most people need to be dictated to by an elite.

Advocates of authoritarianism on *both* sides want us to lose our freedoms. The cries of "communist" from the right are patently ridiculous in the context of the struggle for free expression. However, the arguments we are faced with in the "softening up" period before a censorship attempt is made are often more subtle. Sometimes the story is that we must suspect all information that is not the product of the "expertise" which has become so popular in our booming technocracy, and sometimes it is presented to us in terms of the need for conformity to ease social problems—but always the final message is that we must control expression and suppress initiative which does not serve an immediate practical end.

The arguments for authoritarianism, when stated in these terms, are easy for us to identify with. When we are so taken in, we become simple tools of the people who are in the vanguard of all efforts towards the establishment of a repressive society, all the censors, whose very methods belie their pious assertions of concern with defending "morality."

It is time the profession began to realize that the censorship situation today in American libraries amounts to an organized campaign to wear down those members of the profession who are capable of defending the citizen's right to know. It is time we stopped making our ritual gestures each time censorship happens. It is even too late for us to start weeping crocodile tears for the unfortunate librarians who are being attacked or who are soon to be attacked. It is time to realize that the librarian attacked will be hurt whether he technically "wins" or "loses"—look at me, I "won." We must recognize that we have allowed this situation to be created because of our failure to give more than support on paper for our principles, and by our failure to recognize the true nature of the attacks upon our colleagues. We need to act now to make the censors see that we believe in promoting freedom, not simply defending it! There is a difference.

The profession—the library schools, the committees, the associations and every individual librarian—must stop playing around with the supposed causes of censorship (usually an insignificant dirty book) and address itself to the *principle* of intellectual freedom. If it does this it is going to find itself very busy for a while, but it will be worth it in the long run. For instance, it needs to protest loudly, to "scream bloody murder" when it sees efforts being made to turn the National Commission on Obscenity and Pornography into a tool for the censorship conspiracy, as evidenced when Charles H. Keating Jr. of the Citizens for Decent Literature was appointed to the commission by President Nixon.

The profession must reevaluate its

own "experts"—venerable though they may be—who last summer at ALA thought that an "action" program meant a restatement of all the old principles, and who actually went on record to keep money from being used to further any action. If our experts are going to busy themselves with fancy words and "fight" only the peripheral misconduct charges which accompany all censorship attempts—while failing to address themselves to the principle and refusing to recognize the true nature of the attacks—then it is time we had new experts.

Beyond this, we need an action program that will set out to identify the items in the "attack blueprint" that is obviously being used by censors across the country so that we can anticipate attacks. Having done this, we need to approach our politicians and point out the nature of the conspiracy and the dangers it poses to our whole way of life. We must point out that our political representatives and our courts are being systematically and consciously used to undermine our free democracy through censorship. Let us hope that these representatives will neither like being used, nor sympathize with the ends which the censors espouse.

The person the librarian is most likely to have to deal with (at least until he reaches the courts or an open political deal when he may meet one of the conscious agents of authoritarianism who uses the censor merely to achieve his more comprehensive ends) is a *dangerous* person. His beliefs are based on the irrational. His is no dedicated political program to establish a state which would fit his philosophical tenets. His actions are taken in opposition to persons he believes are agents of evil, and these actions are almost invariably seriously anti-social in nature (even the minor malicious rumors have a dangerous potential, the ultimate death threats notwithstanding). These disturbed people do exist. Their dangerous potential is enhanced by the possibility of collusion with others similarly infected, and by the likelihood of support from organizations which need to justify their claims of civic "responsibility."

I have been questioned about the inclusiveness of my belief, and have been asked if I think that *all* censors are potentially dangerous. Much depends on the definition of "censor." The person who is *worried* about the effect of books or other materials on an impressionable person's mind may not be dangerous. I may yet be able to reach that person and set his mind at ease, at least in part.

There are sincere citizens who are confused about society's responsibility towards ensuring the freedom of each individual. Where there is doubt or simple confusion there is still hope that we can win one for freedom. But I have to agree with the controversial Dr. Szasz (*Science Digest,* December 1969, p. 7-14) that a person may come to a dangerously anti-social conclusion about the meaning of society or of one's own role in life without necessarily being a victim of mental disease; the vacillating censor may eventually go the way of the others (particularly in view of the amount of censorship propaganda which he may be exposed to which we have allowed to go unanswered). I have used the term "sick" to describe the censor. Yet even though I do believe that the censor's message may work to reinforce the attitudes of some other weak person and strengthen the tendency to use coercion and repression as social implements, we must tolerate even that message in order to ensure the free flow of ideas.

The attack which the censor mounts, when one looks at its most basic elements, is a sexual mind-exercise for those who get their kicks from imagining themselves as omnipotent, moral watchers in the various weird sexual and social dangers they dream up. They start by ascribing powers to an illustration, a taboo word, or a description of a taboo occurrence. This power is beyond reason, and they transfer this unreasonable power to any agent they can identify. The librarian—evil agent—makes obscure mystical markings on an order card which results in *Portnoy's Complaint* —evil object—appearing on the shelves. Placing the librarian in this role brings the evil force down to a size the censor feels capable of handling.

Don't underestimate the censor—I have already said that he is dangerous. If he was satisfied with those mere imaginings we might be safe, but he must always have a real victim, human or institutional, to give credence to the imaginings and ultimately to supply him with gratification, however perverted. In the absence of book burning (book burning is usually too reminiscent of Germany), the symbolic destruction of the librarian is the only gratification that will satisfy him.

Perhaps I have exaggerated a little. In the long run it is the concerted efforts of the various extremist organizations which are coordinating the censorship campaign on a nationwide and even an international level. They are fully conscious of the motives of some of the persons they enlist to gain their end. They have shouted "conspiracy"; it is time we openly conspired to halt their collusion. I am incensed that we have allowed these people to negate the efforts of some of our most forward-looking librarians. We have contributed to the ineffectiveness of these librarians in the future by refusing them responsible positions.

We have taken our freedoms for granted, paying them lip service. We have considered that a "professional" attitude amounted to showing a well-groomed staff in front of a neat and innocuous collection. But we have denied freedom in our library collections, in our professional programs, which are too often involved with techniques instead of the human beings we serve. We have denied it in our violent reaction to dissent, which is shown in our tolerance of and implied complicity in repressive official policies which ultimately manifest themselves in officially sanctioned violence and brutality.

My own experiences and those of my colleagues have shown that we— and the people we serve in our communities—are not free. I am calling for librarians to take a stand only on an issue we have always said we supported, an issue we have always taken for granted: intellectual freedom. If we can guarantee our communities access to knowledge, to expression—if we can make informed dialogue possible —we can ultimately guarantee them the freedom they are being denied.

When we see that our freedoms are so seriously under attack—when we see that we are losing—we must realize that our tactics have been ineffective. Our new organizations, the National Freedom Fund for Librarians, of which I am a director, and the Freedom to Read Foundation are to the good, but they are only *defenses,* together hardly a resistance movement.

What we need is an invasion force to confront the censors on their own grounds, a massive army of dedicated freedom fighters who will attack the censors and deny them every parcel of the community consciousness that they seek to control. We can confront them by exposing their tactics before they use them, by witchhunter-hunting in communities before the hunt gets started. We need only tell the truth about their backgrounds, their motives, and their tactics. The evidence is plentiful, and the threat is great and immediate.

How close is your town to Roswell, New Mexico? The attacks have brought us all, communities and libraries, closer together. Let's make the counterattacks complete the consolidation of our communities into a large, neighborly, free democracy.

Reconstitution
for Peace and Relevancy

Celeste MacLeod

MAY 1970. Berkeley, California. It is soon after the Cambodian invasion and the death of four students at Kent State University in Ohio.

In a small office on the third floor of the library school, a ringing telephone is answered by a student, Andy Hubbertz: "Campus Information Clearinghouse."

A student at the San Francisco Art Institute wants figures on government defense spending during the past five years. Andy records the request in the Daily Log, copies the information onto a card, and hands it to another student, Steve Sheldon, who goes out to look up the answer. The telephone rings again: students doing research in the Documents Department of the main library need translators of Vietnamese and French. Andy refers them to the Multi-Lingual Translation Center of the Comparative Literature Department, who had phoned the day before offering their services.

Two undergraduates come up to the Clearinghouse for help. They have joined "Project Silent Majority," a campus group that plans to visit cities across California and canvass against the war; they need information on Bishop, California. Sue Wrought, a 23-year-old student who heads the Recruiting and Training section of the Clearinghouse, takes the students down to the school's reference laboratory and helps them locate statistics in the *City and County Databook*.

Stanford University's Southeast Asian Study Group phones to ask for a copy of the bibliography that the library school's Community Committee has compiled; this 16-page document lists the holdings of public libraries throughout the Bay Area on the conflict in Southeast Asia and related U.S. foreign policy, annotated with library locations for each book or pamphlet. Requests for the bibliography have been so numerous that a "second edition" was mimeographed a few days after its completion. The Stanford group also wants copies of all documents received by the Clearinghouse that are pertinent to their field.

Annamarie Welteke, a 27-year-old library school student active in the Clearinghouse, visits the Geography Department of the University to get copies of their *Peace* newsletter. The geographers, one of many noninvolved groups on campus before Cambodia, express surprise that a library school even exists at Berkeley; but after talking with Annamarie they put the Clearinghouse on their mailing list and ask her to send them information on telephone

25

survey techniques, for use in one of their reconstitution activities.

In the cataloging laboratory on the first floor of the library school, a group of students are busy indexing and cataloging the documents that have been received by the Clearinghouse. Brian Galloway is working out descriptors to fit the special nature of the material. Louise Cavanaugh, a student with previous public relations experience, is one of the indexing subcommittee's most enthusiastic members. "What we're doing here fits in exactly with what we've just learned in our cataloging and information sciences classes," she says, looking up from a position paper written by a member of UC's Committee of Concerned Asian Scholars. "Our work here is so germane to librarianship."

At the desk of the Clearinghouse, Gloria Siegal answers a telephone call from the Italian Department, which wants the names and addresses of important Italian language newspapers in the United States and Italy so that their students who oppose the war can write letters to the editor in Italian. Gloria gives the request to another student, William Whitson. In a few days Bill will be writing "Proposals for a Redirected Curriculum" as a member of the Long Range Planning Committee, a faculty-student group who want the meaningful experiences of the Clearinghouse and other projects integrated into the regular program of the library school; but now Bill's thoughts are on Ayres' *Directory of Newspapers and Periodicals* as he heads for the main library.

Gloria, a married student with two children who manages to be on hand wherever there is work to be done, takes time out to talk about the students. "I think we're all happy to be united in one large effort against the war," she says. "Most of us have wanted to help stop the war for a long time, but we didn't know how."

Throughout the library school, students work at their assignments with an excitement unknown in regular classes;

the questions they answer, the material they catalog, the bibliographies they compile are not "make believe"; real people want this material and will use it for their own efforts to help bring about peace. "Relevant" is the word heard over and over again when one asks the students why these projects have special meaning for them. Some students find it hard to believe that they can work for peace, actively learn to be competent librarians, and yet receive credit towards their degree in librarianship at the same time. A month earlier no one would have believed this possible, but two weeks that included the invasion of Cambodia, the U.S. bombing raids over North Vietnam, and the death of four students in Ohio, followed by the death of six men in Georgia and two more students in Mississippi, caused a profound change on the campus of the University of California, a change that permeated even the traditional School of Librarianship.

For several years the Berkeley campus has been know as a center of anti-war activity, but this action involved only a segment of the 27,000 students at the prestigious university, whose graduates are sought-after in scores of fields and professions. While humanities and social sciences students were being gassed on the campus a year earlier during the People's Park incident, thousands of science students continued working diligently in their laboratories. Engineering students remained at their drafting boards, and most library school students kept their heads in encyclopedias and cataloging rules, while activist students protested the war, racism, and the depleted environment. Even though the bulk of the students were sympathetic to these causes, they felt they were too busy with their studies to become involved. But two days after the killings at Kent State, the anti-war movement shifted from the hands of the radical minority to the broad base of students from every department, as the majority of those on campus decided that everyone concerned about the future of this country must become involved.

The University Is Reconstituted

On Wednesday morning, May 6, more than 15,000 students attended a convocation in Berkeley's Greek Theatre, where they overwhelmingly approved the "Wolin Resolution,"[1] a proposal of the Ad Hoc Faculty-Student Peace Committee, which began: "This campus is on strike to reconstitute the University as a center for organizing against the war in Southeast Asia. We are curtailing normal activities for the remainder of the quarter. We pledge our time, energy, and commitment to stopping this war. We will open the campus to mobilize our resources—our knowledge and skills, our manpower and facilities." The resolution asked students and teachers in each class to discuss ways of reconstituting their courses.

A few hours later more than 80 students gathered in the cataloging laboratory and planned a meeting of the entire library school the next morning. They formed a telephone tree which contacted all of the 191 students and faculty whom they could reach that evening.

More than 90 students and faculty attended the meeting the next morning. It was held at a private home off-campus, because Governor Ronald Reagan had ordered all state colleges and universities closed from midnight Wednesday, until Monday. The group set up three committees within the library school: the University Committee, to act as liaison with all university departments and groups; the Community Committee, to bring news of campus anti-war activities to the general community working through public and school libraries, and to encourage libraries in the Bay Area to provide information about the war to their patrons; and the Professional Committee, to develop effective lines of communica-

tion with librarians and the professional library organizations, awakening them to the necessity of taking a firm stand against the war. All students were urged to join one of these committees and bring to it their suggestions for action.

The heads of the committees were called "Janitors" instead of "Chairmen" to avoid a hierarchical structure: they would have responsibility rather than power, doing the tedious work involved in organizing a group. All three committees scheduled meetings within a day or two.

The University Committee decided to set up an information center which would serve as a campus clearinghouse for material on Southeast Asia. The center would help prevent duplication of effort by various campus groups as well as enabling library school students to use their professional skills giving reference help to students from other departments engaged in anti-war projects. Marcia Bates, a doctoral candidate at the school and a former Peace Corps English teacher in Thailand, set the Clearinghouse into action with a few telephone calls, including one to Raynard Swank, Dean of the library school, who agreed to provide an office and a telephone, specifying only that the Clearinghouse remain a neutral information center, answering all requests. After making the arrangements, Marcia phoned the university's student government and announced that the library school would open a Campus Information Clearinghouse the next day.

The next morning the University Committee met hurriedly and outlined basic procedure. At noon the telephone in 310 South Hall began to ring. "It rang continuously at first," recalls Don O'Neal, the student on duty when the office opened. "I just kept writing down requests and passing them on to other students who were standing around. We had no reference books; the room was chaos. But gradually we've become quite organized."

When he is not manning the telephone, Don O'Neal works as Janitor of publicity and public relations for the Clearinghouse. One month earlier Don still tacitly supported the war; a brother serving in Vietnam had asked him not to get involved. After college, he studied art for a year at the University of Padua under the "Education Abroad" program, then took a job in the university library at Santa Barbara, California, cataloging books in Italian. When he entered library school, Don was nominated by the Dean and later selected for the Library of Congress Special Recruit Program for 1970-71. But he could not remain immune to what was happening in the world; two days before the invasion of Cambodia, Don wrote to his brother saying his conscience would no longer allow him to remain silent; he must oppose the war. He now works full-time at the Clearinghouse.

The same day the Clearinghouse opened, May 8, the faculty of the library school met and unanimously endorsed the Wolin Resolution. They issued a statement which said in part, "The faculty of the School share the views that the proposals of the Ad Hoc Committee do not in any way call for a strike against the University, but for an educational protest by the University, in concert with hundreds of colleges and universities across the United States, against what the majority of the university community sees as immoral as well as illegal actions. A University cannot take a position of moral neutrality."

With the faculty behind them, the students burgeoned into activity over the weekend of May 9-10, while the university was officially closed. The Clearinghouse remained opened, and the Community Committee began its bibliography on Southeast Asia, working with such perserverance that they completed the first edition in four days. The Professional Committee sent out letters to the 50 accredited library schools in the United States and Canada, explaining the school's project and asking for news of their own activities.[2] That Committee also went to a meeting of

the Northern California Section of the California Library Association, where they urged librarians to take a stand against the war through their professional organizations and to provide people with information about the war through their libraries. They handed out a flyer entitled "The Dead do not Read Books." Part of its message to librarians was, ". . . We must unite and say— No more war; the time has been long overdue for peace . . . If we are silent now as a profession, those of us entering the profession may well wonder if we have made the right choice."

When the university reopened on Monday, May 11, the library school achieved an all-time record when 170 students and faculty attended a meeting at a school where it is usually difficult to induce 25 students to come and elect a class president. The Janitors of the three Committees, who had met previously with a faculty advisor, presented their suggestions for reconstituting the school. They urged faculty members to discuss with students in each class ways of restructuring their courses to make them consistent with the campuswide educational protest, letting work on one of the three established committees count as course fulfillment, if possible. Students and faculty who wanted to continue their classes in the traditional manner should not be penalized, they stressed, but should not make demands that would impede those taking part in the reconstitution movement. A planning committee of students and faculty members should be formed immediately to consider longer-range plans for the continuation of the educational protest and the restructuring of the school.

A vote was taken on the suggestions: 148 voted in favor, 18 against, and 4 abstained. The University of California Library School was reconstituted.

Reconstitution at the Library School

The library school at Berkeley draws a heterogenous group of students, ranging from recent college graduates in their early twenties, often single and still supported by their parents, through middle-aged men and women with families who saved for years or borrowed money to return to school for a library degree. As in other schools, the students vary considerably in their political views and commitments; the degree of students' involvement in reconstitution has depended more on their political convictions than on their family situations—some of the most active workers on the Community Committee, for example, are women over 30 with three or four children at home, while a few of the youngest students in school have shown no interest in reconstitution.

About a third of the student body is actively involved in one of the three committees, and the majority of students have participated in reconstitution to some degree; but at both ends of the spectrum feelings run high. One active student is angry at the number of her classmates who seem more concerned about grades and coursework than about what is going on in Southeast Asia; she also feels that many students have become so excited about revising the library school curriculum to make it more relevant that they have lost sight of the original reason for reconstitution —opposition to the war. At the other end, one student was sufficiently upset by the changes in the school to write a vigorous letter of protest to Dean Swank, saying she felt socially ostracized by other students when she voiced her legitimate objections to the reconstitution of classes. She would like to see the war end but thinks the war is unrelated to her education as a librarian.

Under reconstitution the faculty has tried to let each student work out a program that satisfies his own needs and convictions. Carolyn Mohr, who teaches a course in government documents, continued lecturing because of student requests, but cancelled weekly quizzes and the final exam. She gave her students a number of options: complete the regular bibliographic projects, compile a special war-related bibliography from a list she suggested or of their own choosing, or instead work full-time on one of the committees. Mohr was amazed to find some of her students doing all of the options, as well as attending lectures. She had seen a new level of interest emerge among the students since the school was reconstituted.

"I couldn't believe the change that came over me after I started working in the Clearinghouse. I'd been bored with classes all year. Suddenly I had a definite purpose; I had the feeling I was helping someone besides myself."

"For the first time I got to know other students in the library school; we really began talking to one another. And I also started meeting people in other departments of the University."

"I think I've learned more about librarianship in the past two weeks than I had the whole year."

These comments by three students are typical of those heard again and again when students describe their recent experiences.

Patrick Wilson, Associate Professor of Librarianship at UC, noticed a profound change in the students working in the new program. "Students sense that being a librarian is worthwhile," Wilson says. "As librarians they are not changing an image; they are creating an image." He would like to see the meaningful features of the reconstitution program incorporated into the permanent framework of the library school.

Wilson served as faculty advisor on the Long Range Planning Committee. Bill Whitson, a student member of that committee, drafted some proposals for change in the school's curriculum based on the premises that library school students vary greatly in age, experience, competencies, and interests; he envisioned a less-structured program than is prevalent in most library schools, a program built around "core studies" that would enable each student, in consultation with a faculty advisor, to plan a program relevant to his own goals.

Social Responsibility
—A Progress Report

Patricia Schuman

"CELEBRATE National Library Week —Eat a book!" was one of the more pertinent comments recently voiced on Rowan and Martin's "Laugh-In." We can pat ourselves on our collective back —we rate mention in at least two TV commercials as well. Yet, how often does one see libraries or librarians mentioned in discussions of American life and culture? Most of us encounter frequently the question "What do you do, check out books?" and the comment "You don't look like a librarian." As sociologist William J. Goode pointed out several years ago, "lay opinion does not recognize any special talent for librarianship. Second, even if in fact librarians had such a body of knowledge, the public does not know it, but rather views the librarian as a gate keeper and custodian of the stockroom." Recognition of our professional attainments is sadly elusive.

There can be no doubt that both libraries and librarians are badly undersold. Can it be possible that the fault lies not with the "know-nothings" of the public, but within ourselves? If we are convinced that we are professionals who perform essential functions, we must face the fact that we have failed to convince anyone else. We're so far "out of it" where most of society is concerned that the question of the relevance of libraries is rarely raised anywhere but in our own professional journals. The limitations may be within our establishments, but they are mainly within ourselves. Change can and will occur only when we vigorously attempt to define our professional roles in relation to the issues which influence and mold our society. It is essential that we convince ourselves, as well as others, that libraries can perform and produce.

Our first step must be to examine the mythologies we have become geared to, as individuals and institutions. Marcuse poses a germane question when he asks how ". . . administered individuals who have made their mutilations into their own liberties and satisfaction, and thus reproduce them on a large scale [can] liberate themselves from themselves, as well as from their masters?" He does not believe that most of us can and advocates a "repressive tolerance" of our hopelessly warped ideas. If we are to escape this solution, one which has become most popular in some circles, we must search for viable alternatives.

While in the past we have been willing, even eager, to consider ourselves and our institutions instruments of service, it has been at a price. We provide service "for people," not "with people." A plethora of myths, rituals, rationalizations, and euphemisms have been developed to explain and postulate our services. (Is it possible that we still use the term "disadvantaged" officially?) Saul Alinsky scores the underlying fallacy: ". . . served people tend to be compromised people." Once we begin to do things *with* people, we share power, we lose some of our precious autonomy, but we may become just a bit more meaningful.

The sham and hypocrisy which pervade American society are intrinsic in our system. Most of us lack either the background or the experience to serve other than mirrors of our own egos. Our library schools have by definition excluded most minority groups from entering their doors. Traditional academic standards are the sole criteria, even in experimental projects such as High John. The training offered, once one is privileged with acceptance, is sorely insufficient. Few courses discuss and examine social issues; none aid us in the attainment of skills necessary to tackle them. The only real library eduaction I received was my experience as a trainee with the Brooklyn Public Library. Attending library school part time, I suffered through most of my courses, marking time until I could get back to work and learn.

More than a little of the blame for the gap between ideals and reality lies within the American Library Association itself. It articulates its platitudes well, although seldom very loudly. The Association went so far as to suspend several southern chapters and thus forced them to integrate. Yet, at the Philadelphia meeting of the organization committee of the Round Table on Social Responsibilities of Libraries, a black librarian present advised us that in at least one southern state librarians were refused time off to attend integrated meetings. Other professional associations have learned to exert eloquent pressures on society; ALA lags far behind. Certainly it has accomplished many significant goals, but far

greater gaps still exist. Few younger members of the profession, myself included, see little relevance in it, or ways we can participate within its confusing structure.

A study conducted by Mary Lee Bundy in 1965 underlines the fact that "ALA is in much the same position as the AAUP would be if its leadership structure were controlled by college presidents." Although the survey is dated, it seems doubtful that the structure has changed significantly. During the years 1960-65, it found that the average age of the Executive Board was 53.6; no one under 35 served on either body and over 60 percent were past 50; 52.3 percent were directors of libraries, 12 percent were library educators, and almost all of the others were in administration. "No practicing professionals served on either body." Age may not be an exclusive criteria, but surely these findings are indicative of the lack of opportunity for participation and for the injection of fresh perspectives.

The establishment of the Round Table on Social Responsibilities of Libraries is one of the more hopeful moves the Association has made. It can be a method through which we can improve our image, reexamine and change our services, and pressure ALA and the library profession to face up to the fact that for too long they have accepted the system in all of its reprehensible and irrational ramifications. My own personal approach has always been a kind of ad hoc activism. It may be possible to intellectualize the problems of the entire world, but I cannot grapple with them on an active basis. Perhaps I can do something about the things within my reach.

Many of the more "up tight" members of the library profession have automatically identified the germination of the Round Table as Radical, New Left, part of the Movement, the Underground, and other sundry labels popularized by the mass media. I may be expressing sentimental cliches when I say that I want desperately to live in a world that practices what it preaches; that I do not wish to see my husband or my brother sent to fight in an obscure part of the world for reasons so terrible most of America refuses to hear them, but can it be radical to insist that our institutions be accountable to those whom they profess to serve? Is it revolutionary to expect that the materials we provide be relevant? Is it audacious to ask that professionals be equipped with necessary skills? Is it extreme to demand concrete actions from those who mouth ideals? Perhaps Michael Harrington is right, "common sense has become radical."

Jean Paul Sartre has repeatedly expressed the belief that an individual's freedom is mostly negative and the Round Table seems to be saying no to things as they are. Not only do not most people "tell it like it is"; they do not "see it as it is." "You're young, idealistic, things don't work that way. You don't know how it used to be," is a favorite ploy of those who seek to convince us we live in the best of all possible worlds. "We were once idealistic too." Can it be that as I grow older I will shrink into myself, my frame of reference becoming smaller and smaller as I contract into my own minute portion of experience? No, I am not suggesting acid—or even pot—for expanding consciousness; just seeing, hearing, and feeling. It may be painful, but to feel pain is to exist; to be irrelevant is to die. If this be the alienation so many of us are accused of, so be it. It is alienation from the fact that things are not as they appear to be. Saying no is an affirmation that we can change.

I cannot offer any statement of purpose for a New Utopia. Erudite statements of idealogy will not change the facts. The rage which has engulfed a good portion of my generation, the trauma of confrontation between America as it is, rather than as it says, has left a sour taste in my mouth for idealogy per se. Those of us who still

have some hope for restructuring rather than razing must seek to learn inductively as we act. Rigidity has been exposed too often—we cannot allow ourselves to become hung up on words alone. The concepts of justice, decency, equality, and responsibility are not new or startling. The difference is to tackle them seriously, to demand their implementation. It is not that simple statements of ideals are without meaning, rather that they are abstractions. If society is to be changed, not merely assuaged, we must learn as we act.

Yes, the Round Table on Social Responsibilities presents a challenge, but challenge does not simply imply threat; it offers opportunity. It is unfortunate that to most Americans crusades against the status quo are suspicious. Those who seek change are apocalyptic, deluded. Our institutions are so pervasive that to suggest fault is to call for destruction. Yet, as society begins to crumble we cannot sit back and trust in the normal progress of man. Some of those who have sought change have been taught the fact that institutions react only when dramatically confronted. If we fail to commit ourselves, if we do not at least begin to discern the relevant necessities, we can expect repetition of these tactics. The choice, while it is still ours to make, must be made now.

When I joined the New York Round Table I made part of that choice. I have a full-time position which demands many extra hours of my time and I am on several faculty committees. I am pursuing further graduate work, belong to several other library associations and community groups, and have many interests outside the library world. Yet I felt I had to commit myself and whatever special talents I have as a librarian. I had talked and I had criticized, but it was time to act.

Action is not easy, as I discovered at our weekly meetings. When we met for the first time early in October, several of us had been to an earlier meeting at Drexel; many more had not. Public, college, school, and special librarians, as well as library school students, were represented. We were asked to concern ourselves with the problem of race. Unfortunately, most of us were white and at the very first venture our own prejudices limited us. It was a slow, painful process to conclude that we must tackle prejudice within the white community. The time was no longer ripe for the helpful white liberal in the black community. Even so, we were stymied. How could 20 concerned librarians attack the problem of race?

Someone suggested that each of us contribute $20 and place small collections of materials such as *Ebony,* paperback editions of Eldridge Cleaver's *Soul on Ice,* The National Advisory Commission Report and the like, in our local police precincts. After some discussion, we discovered that none of us possessed the sheer nerve it would require to walk up to the desk sergeant with a copy of *Freedomways* under his arm. We resolved to contact some outside agencies and offer our services to them. Most of the calls turned up very little aside from "If you have a packaged project we might help." But a suggestion made to one of our members by a representative of the Urban League did aid in the definition of our activism. "Since you are librarians, why not approach other librarians? Librarians are citizens of their communities, parents, voters, and professionals—there you have some common ground."

At this time, the school strike in New York City had begun to take on a decidedly racial tone. Hate literature, much of it fabricated out of whole cloth, flooded the streets. Advertisements, articles, and debates permeated the tense atmosphere. Here was our issue. During the next few months, we undertook several actions, sans funds or institutional backing.

Biweekly bibliographies were and are still being prepared on the issue of decentralization and community control of the New York City School System. Items listed are mainly limited to material not readily available through indexes, although particularly relevant materials are included even if available through indexes. Copies were distributed at a meeting of education librarians and to Columbia University School of Library Service students. Copies have been mailed to various libraries and other interested organizations. A small mailing list has been developed. Response has been uniformly enthusiastic. The materials listed in the bibliographies have been organized and are available through interlibrary loan from the New York City Community College Library. In addition, the Round Table cosponsored a discussion of decentralization and community control at the Columbia University School of Library Service; Geraldine Clark, assistant director, Bureau of Libraries, Board of Education, was the main speaker. Miss Clark expressed her personal views, not those of the Board, concerning the motivations which have led the black and Puerto Rican communities to insist upon the necessity of community control. Stating that many people "no longer have hope that their children's lives will be better than their own," she also suggested some creative possibilities for librarians under community control. The Round Table also circulated a petition in support of community control at the New York Library Association and among several libraries in the area. The petition, signed by 150 librarians, was sent to John Doar, President of the New York City Board of Education.

It is important to note that although we certainly were not a neutral group, there were many divergent opinions concerning the issue. Several of us, myself included, were convinced that the demands of the black community were just and that Albert Shanker of the United Federation of Teachers was clouding the issue in order to destroy the existing experimental school districts; others saw both sides as partially right, and still others were not convinced that the system of community control was the answer. The petition was written and circulated with the full knowledge of the Round Table membership, but not all signed it.

Some felt it an idle gesture, others of us felt it crucial to take a stand as librarians. Certainly we had gone to the trouble of collecting information; was it not part of our "social responsibility" to read it, to form, change, or reinforce our opinions and to vocalize them? It seems to have been this vocalization which has hit the hardest. Incredibly enough, because we had supported the black community, now being unjustly accused of wholesale anti-Semitism, we have been accused by some of anti-Semitism ourselves. (The fact that I, as well as many of the other signers of the petition, am Jewish is never even noticed.) Unfortunately, several of our members are in vulnerable positions within the institutions they serve. Although we did not have the funds to reproduce our kit of materials in quantity, it had been hoped that we might make it available in several of our libraries. We were refused in at least one instance because the institution itself had not propagated it. Some of the members were warned to make sure that their institutions were not identified with the Round Table in any way.

The pressures may be usual, but even more insidious pressures have begun to work on us. Suddenly we are VISIBLE. We are RADICAL. Several of us have been offered speaking engagements, and two of us have already written articles for major library publications. We are somehow being insidiously co-opted into the anti-establishment establishment. Several prominent librarians have told us frankly: "We intend to ride on your coat-tails." Great! We can all float our own professional balloons if we care to, but what about all the others out there who have heretofore been kept invisible. It is tempting to play a role in the spotlight rather than to operate as conscientious members of the library profession trying to improve the situation. One of the most important objectives the Round Table must have is to allow all those who care to participate. It was most interesting to observe that when the idea of a volunteer, rather than an elected, organizing committee was suggested at Midwinter, it was viewed with suspicion.

There are those who would like to see meaningful change within the library profession and its related institutions and those who suggest mere tokenism. The Round Table can take and demand meaningful action, or we can become sops to the consciences of those who wish to identify with us because it seems the liberal thing to do. It's easy enough to criticize and to mouth ideals, but to act is the challenge. We can attempt to persuade all those who feel they can contribute to do so, or we can slice up the pie among a few of us. Personally, I want to be part of the solution, not part of the problem.

Book Selection in Philadelphia

S. J. Leon

THE "Survey of the Handling of Certain Controversial Adult Materials by Philadelphia Area Libraries" was conceived in the fall of 1969 and executed in the spring and summer of 1970. The Social Responsibilities Round Table book list, therefore, inevitably reflects the social scene and literary politics of that time.

It was decided to study all major libraries in the area. In selecting academic libraries for study, we wanted to include a Catholic institution, a college whose administration was liberal, and an institution whose student body was predominantly black. In selecting public libraries for study, we weighed the general economic level and general social and political orientation of the community served and the size of the system. Here our aim was to contrast an urban system with a small town library and a library that serves a working-class clientele with one that serves more affluent readers.

In shaping our adult book list, it was obvious that the major areas of controversy in our culture today are psychosexual and sociopolitical. We wanted to include fiction of unquestioned merit as well as creative work of more questionable durability and finesse. Inevitably, we included imaginative writing that probes homosexual behavior, interracial sex, and political violence since these are

hot issues in today's social scene. Some of the nonfiction titles deal directly with sociopolitical unrest, and we tried to represent the radical right as well as the splintered left. We also included certain books written by practitioners whose work for different reasons is not accepted by their professions.

Among our periodicals is a local underground paper, *Thursday's Drummer*, and publications on the red and violet end of the social rainbow.

In constructing our questionnaire, we aimed to get as many statements of institutional book selection policies as we could. We also wanted a description of how restricted books are made available to patrons and what closed shelf procedures have been adopted by various institutions surveyed. Hopefully, we asked for specific descriptions of pitched censorship battles and, again hopefully, we tried for some indication of how censorship attacks have affected institutional book selection practices. Finally, we solicited administrative evaluation of anti-censorship apparatus existing within the profession and suggestions for making the apparatus more effective. We tried to ask questions which were specific but not so complicated as to discourage answers.

In order to elicit a better response we decided to omit the names of the 12 insti-

OWNERSHIP AND CIRCULATION OF CONTROVERSIAL PERIODICAL TITLES

Periodical Title	Four Public Libraries				Five University Libraries					Three College Libraries		
	PL 1	PL 2	PL 3	PL 4	UL 1	UL 2	UL 3	UL 4	UL 5	CL 1	CL 2	CL 3
American Opinion	X	O	O	X	X	X	X	O	O	O	X	O
Distant Drummer (Thursday's Drummer)	R	O	X	O	X	R	O	O	O	O	X	O
Evergreen Review	X	O	O	O	X	R	X	R	X	O	R	X
Human Events	X	O	O	O	X	X	X	X	O	O	X	O
Journal of Black Poetry	X	O	O	O	O	R	O	X	X	O	O	O
Liberator	X	O	X	O	X	X	O	O	X	O	X	X
Ramparts	X	X	X	X	X	R	X	X	X	O	X	X
Realist	O	O	O	O	O	X	O	O	O	O	O	O

tutional libraries involved. Rather than attempt direct interviews with library administrators, we decided to concentrate on a mailing piece. However, we also decided to supplement the mailing piece by sending members of the Intellectual Freedom Committee on independent surveys of institutional holdings and practices. Of the 12 institutions surveyed, 11 were scrutinized independently by committee members before the questionnaires were sent through the mail.

Four Public Libraries

The urban system surveyed reports a book budget of approximately $953,000 for the fiscal year 1970. In that year fully 61 percent of its book money came from local taxes; the remainder came from state and federal monies and private donations.

The library has adopted an official book selection policy. The director has final authority on all book selection matters, and that is delegated to him by the Board of Trustees. Standard book selection tools are used in building the collection, and staff reviews supplement commercial reviews in arriving at decisions.

The library maintains restricted collections of books and magazines. Restricted materials are shelved near the service desks but are closed to public access. They may be borrowed by persons 18 years of age or older. Restricted books are so listed in the public catalog, but no symbols are used in the catalog to show the location of any of these books.

The library reports that it has no formal program for the reevaluation of restricted or rejected titles. It adds, however, that "a responsible request for reconsideration of both rejected and restricted titles will be considered after a reasonable amount of time has elapsed following the initial decision."

During the past decade this library system has been hit by five significant censorship attacks. In 1961 the local District Attorney's office ordered all copies of Henry Miller's *Tropic of Cancer* withdrawn, but in 1964, after the Supreme

Court had ruled the novel was not obscene, all copies were returned to circulation and placed in restricted collections. Soon after publication, James Baldwin's *Another Country* was attacked by individual readers, but no copies of this novel were withdrawn or restricted. In 1963 Nikos Kazantzakis' *The Last Temptation of Christ* was attacked by individual citizens, but no copies were withdrawn or restricted.

In 1968 *Evergreen Review* was attacked by the local Constitutional Party, a local Chamber of Commerce group, and smaller community groups. As a result of this attack, two of the library's four subscriptions were cancelled and all copies are now placed on closed shelves. More recently the same groups attacked Jerry Rubin's *Do It*, demanding variously that it be removed from the library's collection or placed under restriction. The library, however, has not withdrawn or restricted any copies of this title.

The three smaller area public libraries studied vary in size and scope. The largest of the three serves a borough and adjacent county. Another serves a smaller residential community and is an autonomous unit in a county system. The third is a minisystem which serves a township and consists of six suburban libraries.

In 1970 the county system was given a book budget of $67,620 to serve 622,376 people. Its money comes almost entirely from local and state funds. In this system book selection is controlled by the director. Standard book selection tools are used, though staff reviews are not a factor in the selection process. In contrast to the large urban system surveyed, this library has no official restriction policy. However, books that are frequently stolen and mutilated are placed in a locked case, and there is evidence that this amounts to *de facto* restriction. The locked case is in the public service area and has glass doors so that restricted items are reviewed periodically in the same manner as all titles in the collection. The library further reports

that no serious censorship controversies have developed in recent years.

In 1970 the autonomous unit in the larger county system was given $28,830 in county funds to buy books for more than 141,204 people. Selection in this library is controlled by the director and a lay advisory committee. Standard book selection tools are used, and staff reviews are a factor in making decisions. This library also has no official restriction policy, but books that are habitually stolen or mutilated are placed in reserved stacks, and there is evidence that some controversial material is placed in the librarian's office. Reserved or restricted books are available to readers 14 years old or older who have adult cards. The library reports that when restricted material is stolen or worn out its repurchase is considered. It also reports that no serious censorship controversies have developed in recent years.

In 1970 the township system was given $66,600 in local and state funds to buy books for 68,000 persons. Selection in the six community libraries that comprise this system is controlled by the director. Standard book selection tools are used, but staff reviews do not figure seriously in the selection process. The library reports no official restriction policy, emphasizing that all books circulate freely. It indicates that lost, stolen, or worn out copies of controversial books are replaced. In recent years the township system reports that Gore Vidal's *Myra Breckenridge* was challenged by individual citizens but adds that this novel continues to circulate on open shelves.

Three College Libraries

The three college libraries surveyed vary in size and function. One serves a Quaker-affiliated liberal arts college in the Philadelphia area; another serves a coeducational satellite campus in the Philadelphia area; and the third serves a community college with a two-year program.

None of the three college libraries has written book selection policies, and none reports significant censorship incidents or attacks in recent years. In every case selection is controlled by the head of the library, and none of these administrators reports any special restriction policy.

The Quaker-affiliated liberal arts campus has a population of approximately 2000. In 1970 its library was given a book budget of $124,500, which came from the overall college budget and private donations. The book selection process involves the head librarian, staff members, and faculty. Standard reviewing media are used, and staff reviews play a role in selection. The library reports that "collections are built on pertinence and prospective usefulness without regard to controversy." It adds that books are restricted only because of their rarity and vulnerability to theft.

The satellite campus library serves a population of approximately 1600. In 1970 its book budget was $17,500, representing $1500 in state funds and $2500 in federal funds. Selection is a collaboration between the head of the library and faculty members. The standard book reviewing tools are used, but staff reviews do not figure in selection. This library reports that its selection is motivated by "courses taught, the ethnic composition of the student body, and the interests of the student body." It lists student requests as a significant factor in determining selection. This library reports that it restricts "only those materials placed on reserve for use in specific courses at faculty request or to discourage theft." It adds that repurchase of

lost, stolen, or worn copies of controversial materials is considered if the materials "are still of current interest or significance."

In 1969-1970 the community college library received a book budget of $75,000, exclusive of periodicals and films, to serve a population of approximately 7000 persons. Its money came from local, state, and federal funds. In this library selection is described as a collaboration between librarian, faculty, and students. The standard reviewing tools are used, but staff reviews are not used as checks on them. This library reports that "we do not purchase titles because they are controversial but rather we purchase to support the curricula primarily. If a controversial title is requested, we judge each request on its merit." Aside from regular reserved collections, the library reports that it restricts only "titles which tend to disappear from open stacks."

Five University Libraries

The five university libraries studied vary in size and function. All serve coeducational institutions. Two of the universities involved are large urban institutions. A third urban university has a heavy technological and business emphasis. The fourth is a suburban university with a predominately Catholic faculty and student body, and the fifth is biracial but predominately black.

None of the five university libraries involved has a written book selection policy, and none report significant censor-

NUMBER OF CONTROVERSIAL PERIODICAL TITLES OWNED

Periodical Title	Public Libraries			Academic Libraries		
	C	R	N	C	R	N
American Opinion	2	0	2	4	0	4
Distant Drummer						
(Thursday's Drummer)	2	0	2	3	0	5
Evergreen Review	0	1	3	3	3	2
Human Events	1	0	3	6	0	2
Journal of Black Poetry	1	0	3	2	1	5
Liberator	2	0	2	4	0	4
Ramparts	4	0	0	6	1	1
Realist	0	0	4	1	0	7

C=Number that circulate title R=Number that restrict title N=Number that do not own title

ship confrontations or controversies in recent years. Selection practices vary slightly, but in every instance selection seems to be controlled by the library administration. None of the university libraries report official restriction policies, restricting only for rarity or vulnerability to theft.

Perhaps because it was between administrations, one large university library responded to the Intellectual Freedom Committee's questionnaire in so fragmentary a fashion that information on budget and book selection practices is not available. This library indicates that it has no special restrictive practices; however, it does maintain special collections in its closed stacks, and one of the titles on the committee's controversial list does not circulate at all.

The second urban university library serves approximately 45,000 persons. In 1970 the book budget for the main undergraduate library was $700,000, of which approximately 50 percent came from state funds. Selection is accomplished by a bibliographical department of 13 persons; in addition, faculty and students participate in the process, but final authority rests with the director of libraries. The library reports that it has a blanket order for all current books in the English language, with some minor exceptions. Restricted collections are found in a rare book room and a restricted area in the stacks. Rare books can be used only in the room by any legitimate reader, and books in the restricted stacks can be used in the library. The library maintains a Contemporary Culture Center, which amounts to a special collection of periodicals, underground papers, and leaflets housed in a seminar room on the second floor. This arrangement is "because of the fragility of most of these publications." The library makes provision for replacing lost, stolen, or worn copies of controversial materials. Regarding censorship pressures, the director reports: "No sweat."

The third university library serves a "technological university with limited Humanities and Social Sciences collecting." Its population exceeds 11,000, and in 1970-1971 its book budget amounted to $80,000. Of this amount, 91 percent represented university appropriations; eight percent was federal funds; and one percent was gifts. Selection is accomplished by library staff members and faculty, and final authority rests with divisional librarians. Restricted collections amount to "archival and special collections and reserve books." This library circulates acquisitions lists in order to keep its clientele informed. Lost, stolen, or worn copies of controversial materials are replaced as funds permit.

The fourth university library serves a Catholic-related institution, with a population of approximately 8000 persons. In 1970 its book budget was $325,000, all of which came from church funds. Book selection in this library is handled by staff members and faculty, and final authority rests with the head of the Acquisitions Department. This library orders all university press books on a special approval plan. It also uses staff reviews to supplement the commercial reviewing media. The library reports that it has no special restrictive policies other than those customarily found in university libraries. Lost, stolen, or worn copies of controversial materials are replaced "if requested."

The Negro university library serves 1000 students, 125 faculty, and some 500 borrowers from adjacent local communities. In 1970 it received $50,000 for books from state and federal funds, private donations, and endowment. Selection is a collaboration between the head librarian, library staff, and faculty members. The standard reviewing media are used in selection, and staff reviews are a factor. The library reports that it restricts only rare books. Periodicals are kept in a locked stack, but there is an attendant on duty during library hours and access to them is freely given. Also a Special Negro Collection and an African Collection are shelved in a special room. The library reports that the repurchase of lost, stolen, or worn copies of controversial materials is periodically considered.

Public Libraries' Report

Reviewing the reports of the four public libraries surveyed, we find a few striking facts. The urban library system predictably holds the most controversial titles on the list—32 of 33—but it also restricts the most—nine. The other three libraries restrict relatively few of the controversial titles on the list, but the number of titles they hold is almost balanced by the number of titles they do not own. The county library system circulates 16 of the titles, restricts four, and does not own 13. The semi-autonomous unit of the larger county system, where selection is controlled by the director and a community advisory group, also circulates 16 of the controversial titles on the list, restricts two, and does not own 15. The township minisystem circulates 18 of the titles, restricts none, but does not own 15.

The urban library system reports five significant censorship confrontations during the past decade, but the other three public libraries maintain that there have been no significant confrontations with elements in their respective communities in the recent past.

When we examine the handling of specific titles by the four public libraries surveyed, a few patterns emerge. The books that are either significantly omitted and/or heavily restricted include William Burroughs' *Naked Lunch*, Jean Genet's *Our Lady of the Flowers*, Henry Miller's *Tropic of Cancer*, the Marquis De Sade's *Selected Writings*, Hubert Selby's *Last Exit to Brooklyn*, Le Roi Jones' *Dutchman and the Slave*, Timothy Leary's *The Psychedelic Experience*, Wilhelm Reich's *Selected Writings*, Arlo Tatum's *Conscientious Objector's Handbook*, and *The Kama Sutra* by Vatsyayana. Among the periodicals, the *Realist*, *Evergreen Review*, and *Human Events* are conspicuously either not owned or restricted.

Of the writers omitted or restricted in impressive quantities, Burrough, Genet,

and the Marquis De Sade deal explicitly with homosexual behavior on fictional, autobiographical, and other levels. Henry Miller and Hubert Selby deal more freely and less compulsively with sexual behavior. Wilhelm Reich is an orgonomist, therapist, and philosopher whose work in the sexual area has become more influential in our own day; *The Kama Sutra*, though a classic, deals explicitly with sexual techniques. Of the heavily restricted and/or thinly represented writers, Leary is a spokesman for the liberating effect of drugs, and Le Roi Jones, of course, focuses on the racial conflict in America and its implications.

But Jones alone, of all the writers on the racial conflict, is relatively ignored or rejected. Particularly well represented are Eldridge Cleaver's *Soul on Ice* and *The Autobiography of Malcolm X*. All four public libraries hold titles in multiple copies and circulate them freely. Also fairly well represented are Franz Fanon's *Black Skin, White Masks*, circulated freely by all four public libraries; James Baldwin's *Another Country*, held and circulated by three of the four public libraries; and Julius Lester's *Look Out, Whitey!*, also listed and circulated by three of four public libraries.

Norman Mailer's *Why Are We in Viet Nam?*, which mixes political and sexual iconoclasm, is freely circulated by all four public libraries surveyed and does not seem to fall into the pattern of sexual restriction suggested by the above noted holdings. On the other hand, Philip Roth's popular *Portnoy's Complaint*, which is circulated by three of the four public libraries, is restricted by the urban library system, which makes all 140 copies available only to readers 18 years of age or older upon proper identification.

Among the gingerly handled periodicals mentioned above, both the *Realist*, which is totally unrepresented in all four collections, and *Evergreen Review*, which only the urban public library makes available and that on a restricted basis, stand for political and sexual iconoclasm, while *Human Events*, represented in only

NUMBER OF CONTROVERSIAL BOOK TITLES OWNED

Author and Title	Public Libraries			Academic Libraries		
	C	R	N	C	R	N
Baldwin, J., *Another Country*	3	0	1	7	0	1
Burroughs, W., *Naked Lunch*	1	1	2	6	0	2
Donleavy, J. P., *Ginger Man* (Unexpurgated, Delacorte)	4	0	0	5	0	3
Genet, J., *Our Lady of the Flowers*	1	1	2	5	0	3
Lawrence, D. H., *Lady Chatterley's Lover*	3	1	0	7	0	1
Mailer, N., *Why Are We in Viet Nam?*	4	0	0	7	0	1
Miller, H., *Tropic of Cancer*	2	2	0	4	1	3
Roth, P., *Portnoy's Complaint*	3	1	0	7	0	1
Sade, D. A. F., *Selected Writings*	2	2	0	2	0	6
Selby, H., *Last Exit to Brooklyn*	0	1	3	4	0	4
Ginsberg, A., *Howl and Other Poems*	2	0	2	7	0	1
Jones, L., *Dutchman and The Slave*	1	0	3	7	0	1
Cleaver, E., *Soul on Ice*	4	0	0	8	0	0
Fanon, F., *Black Skin, White Masks*	4	0	0	8	0	0
Guevera, C., *Diary*	4	0	0	5	0	3
Guttmacher, A. F., *Planning Your Family*	3	1	0	4	4	0
Leary, T., *The Psychedelic Experience*	1	1	2	3	0	5
Lester, J., *Look Out, Whitey!*	3	0	1	6	0	2
Little, M., *The Autobiography of Malcolm X*	4	0	0	8	0	0
Masters, W. H., *Human Sexual Response*	3	1	0	8	0	0
Reich, W., *Selected Writings*	1	0	3	3	1	4
Tatum, A., ed., *Conscientious Objectors Handbook*	1	0	3	1	1	6
Vatsyayana, *The Kama Sutra*	1	1	2	3	1	4
Velikovsky, I., *Worlds in Collision*	4	0	0	6	0	2
Welch, R., *Blue Book of the John Birch Society*	2	1	0	1	1	6

C = No. that circulate   R = No. that restrict   N = No. that do not own

one of the four collections, deals with political and social currents from a particularistic conservative point of view.

Although all 12 of the libraries surveyed were invited to give reasons for purchase or rejection of specific titles, only two of the four public libraries responded to the invitation. Regarding this matter, the county library system replied: "No records are kept since all items purchased meet our library's book selection policy. Rejection of a title is on the basis of published reviews or examination of the book." The library noted that it has not purchased Le Roi Jones' *Dutchman and the Slave* because it is out of print; also, it has not purchased Tatum's *Conscientious Objector's Handbook* both because it is out of print and because it owns that author's *Guide to the Draft*. The library subscribes to *Ramparts* because it is indexed in *Reader's Guide to Periodical Literature*. Regarding restrictions, the library explains that it restricts *Lady Chatterley's Lover, Tropic of Cancer,* Guttmacher's *Planning Your Family,* and Welch's *Blue Book of the John Birch Society* because of repeated theft.

Of the four public libraries surveyed, only the township system, comprising six community libraries, attempted to comment on the literary or social value of specific titles. A closer examination of some of these comments is illuminating. One librarian replied: "Many books were not purchased by my predecessor, and I cannot give reasons for her." Since the titles so annotated included Burroughs' *Naked Lunch,* Miller's *Tropic of Cancer,* Ginsberg's *Howl,* Jones' *Dutchman,* Reich's *Selected Writings,* and *The Kama Sutra,* we can assume that this particular community library does not periodically reconsider rejected titles on the basis of shifts in critical attitude and general literary and social influence. Another community librarian had three of the 33 listed titles in her collection and justified their presence as follows: Baldwin's *Another Country:* "representative of our times"; Roth's *Portnoy's Complaint:* "popular demand"; Guttmacher's

Planning Your Family: "very much needed in this day of population explosion."

Still another township librarian wrote cryptically of *Naked Lunch*, Sade's *Selected Writings*, and *Look Out, Whitey!*: "Not needed." Her comment on Genet's *Our Lady of the Flowers*, generally regarded as that author's most powerful fiction, was: "Have other Genet." And her comment on Che Guevera's *Diary*: "Have other Guevera." However, this same librarian's comment on *Lady Chatterley's Lover*, which was well represented in her collection, was: "Classic." And she promised to pick up copies of Ginsberg's *Howl* and *The Kama Sutra.* Such positive reactions were rare among the commentators.

A colleague supported her rejection of *Why Are We in Viet Nam?* with the following comment: "Not even author's earlier reputation could redeem. Literary quality nil." Of Wilhelm Reich she wrote: "But Reich's thesis highly suspect. Unacceptable in standard medical circles. Therefore not acceptable for this library." However, she called the absence of *Our Lady of the Flowers* in her collection a "simple oversight" and said that *The Tropic of Cancer* was missing "through oversight, not design." A survey that can generate even a few instances of retrospective self-criticism has something to be said for it.

Comments by several of the community librarians in this township system would indicate that demand is the strongest single factor in shaping their periodical collections. As one librarian wrote regarding the eight periodicals: "Do not have any of these in our holdings. Up to the present, no demands or requests concerning these editions. *Ramparts* is the only one indexed in *Reader's Guide Index*, but have not found it to be in demand."

All four public libraries surveyed have book selection policy statements which they have forwarded, but the eight academic libraries do not. Since the four libraries do not comment on their statements, we can only assume that they have adopted them because they feel more susceptible to direct community pressures and feel more secure with guidelines.

A closer look at the four policy statements is useful. The urban library system's statement is the only one that explicitly provides for restriction. It reads in part: ". . . the Library is obligated to select works, often experimental, whose themes run counter to community mores, when these books have literary quality, represent a recognized development or trend in literature, or are of sociological importance. When suitable material is available, representative viewpoints of significant, though controversial, issues and questions are considered for the collection. Though anti-social in nature, certain publications of current or historic importance and examples of propaganda may be included for informational and educational purposes. The Library exercises judgment in restricting circulation of this material."

The restriction procedure is more explicitly explained elsewhere: "Two types of books are contained in these restricted collections. They are: 1) Books which are continually stolen or mutilated e.g., books on automotive mechanics, marriage manuals, etc. 2) Books likely to be regarded as pornographic by many patrons and which are predominantly unsuitable for persons under 18 years of age. Examples: *Memoirs of a Woman of Pleasure* (*Fanny Hill*) by John Cleland and *My Life And Loves* by Frank Harris.

"In the case of the first category it is up to the head of the agency to determine what titles should be restricted . . . Books in the second category are designated for restriction only by the Office of Work with Adults and Young Adults following administrative discussion. These titles are restricted in all agencies and circulated on 'pink pass' to patrons 18 years and over . . ."

The statement further provides that young adult books are to be restricted only if they are repeatedly stolen or mutilated and stipulates that restricted books are to be reviewed periodically by the Coordinator's Office. However, the fre-

OWNERSHIP AND CIRCULATION OF CONTROVERSIAL BOOK TITLES

Author and Title	Four Public Libraries				Five University Libraries					Three College Libraries		
	PL 1	PL 2	PL 3	PL 4	UL 1	UL 2	UL 3	UL 4	UL 5	CL 1	CL 2	CL 3
Baldwin, J., *Another Country*	X	X	O	X	X	X	X	X	X	O	X	X
Burroughs, W., *Naked Lunch*	R	X	O	O	X	X	X	X	O	O	X	X
Donleavy, J. P., *Ginger Man* (Unexpurgated, Delacorte, 1965)	X	X	X	X	X	X	X	X	X	O	O	X
Genet, J., *Our Lady of the Flowers*	R	R	X	O	X	O	O	O	X	O	X	O
Lawrence, D.H., *Lady Chatterley's Lover*	X	X	X	X	X	X	X	X	X	O	O	X
Mailer, N., *Why Are We in Viet Nam?*	R	R	X	X	R	X	X	X	X	X	O	O
Miller, H., *Tropic of Cancer*	R	R	X	X	X	X	X	X	X	X	O	X
Roth, P., *Portnoy's Complaint*	R	X	R	X	O	X	O	O	X	O	X	O
Sade, D.A.F., *Selected Writings*	R	O	O	O	X	O	O	O	X	O	X	O
Selby, H., *Last Exit to Brooklyn*	X	O	O	O	X	X	X	X	X	X	X	X
Ginsberg, A., *Howl and Other Poems*	X	X	O	X	X	X	X	X	X	X	X	X
Jones, L., *Dutchman and The Slave*	X	X	X	X	X	X	X	X	X	X	X	X
Cleaver, E., *Soul on Ice*	X	X	X	X	X	X	X	X	X	X	O	X
Fanon, F., *Black Skin, White Masks*	X	X	X	X	X*	X	X	O	X	X	X	X
Guevara, C., *Diary*	X	R	X	X	O	X	X	O	X	O	O	O
Guttmacher, A. F., *Planning Your Family*	X	R	X	X	X	X	X	O	O	X	X	X
Leary, T., *The Psychedelic Experience*	X	X	O	X	X	X	X	O	X	X	X	X
Lester, J., *Look Out, Whitey! Black Power's Gon' Get Your Mama!*	R	X	O	O	O	X	X	X	O	O	O	X
Little, M., *The Autobiography of Malcolm X*	X	X	O	X	O	X	X	X	X	X	X	O
Masters, W. H., *Human Sexual Response*	X	X	X	X	X	X	X	X	X	X	X	X
Reich, W., *Selected Writings*	X	O	R	O	X	X	O	X	O	X	O	X
Tatum, A., ed., *Conscientious Objector's Handbook*	X	O	O	O	O	X	O	R	X	O	O	R
Vatsyayana, *The Kama Sutra*	R	X	O	X	X	R	X	O	X	O	O	O
Velikovsky, I., *Worlds in Collision*	X	X	X	O	X	X	X	X	X	O	O	O
Welch, R., *Blue Book of the John Birch Society*	X	R	X	O	O	X	O	X	O	R	O	O

X = Library has   R = Library restricts   O = Library does not have   * = In Spanish quency of such review is not specified, and there is evidence that reviews of restricted materials are only sporadic at best.

The other three libraries do not mention restriction in their policy statements, but we have noted that they practice it. However, they do have something to say, and sometimes in considerable detail, about what they will not buy. The autonomous unit in a larger county system indicates that it will not buy materials inconsistent with current obscenity laws. "The library subscribes to the present laws dealing with obscenity and believes they should be vigorously enforced." The county library states: "Special efforts will be made to provide the best books on all sides of controversial issues, and those written in a sensational or inflammatory manner will not ordinarily be selected." The township library system's statement runs to considerable length, largely because it goes into forms and categories of materials, and it is heavily adjectival. It notes two areas in which exclusion may be necessary: "*first*, books which seem offensive to good taste or contrary to prevailing community moral and ethical standards, and *second*, books on public questions presenting one side of a question only, when written in a violent, sensational, inflammatory manner."

The township system's statement further provides: "The libraries may exclude from their collections a majority of the books representing views that are regarded by a consensus of responsible opinion—civic, scientific, religious, and educational—as unsound and have been so regarded over a period of years." Concerning fiction specifically, it notes: . . . it may be said that the libraries' policy is to acquire fiction, whether serious or amusing, realistic, or imaginative, which is well written and based on authentic human experience and to exclude weak, incompetent, or cheap sentimental writing, as well as the solely sensational, morbid, or erotic."

Three of the four statements explicitly mention censors and censorious pres-

sures as facts in a public library's existence. The autonomous unit in a larger county system observes that "there is no place for extra-legal efforts to coerce the taste of others, to confine adults to reading matter considered suitable for adolescents, or to inhibit the efforts of writers to achieve artistic expression. We will resist efforts of individuals or groups to deny access to materials on the part of other sections of the community whether in the name of political, moral, or religious beliefs. We believe it is against the public interest to force the reader to accept with any book the prejudgment of a label characterizing the book or author as subversive or dangerous."

The county system's statement reads more succinctly: "The librarian is responsible to the board for the selection and development of the collection and will not act as a censor for adult materials." The township system's statement reads diplomatically: "The libraries are opposed to the withdrawal, at the request of any individual or group, of books which have been chosen by the above principles. The librarian welcomes the opportunity to discuss the interpretation of these principles with representatives of such groups." It is the only one of the four libraries to provide that complaints about its acquisitions be filed in writing on standard forms provided by each of its six community branches.

As we have seen, one book selection policy statement cites two factors in restricting adult materials: frequency of theft and mutilation and the unsuitability of some adult materials for use by minors and adolescents. Obviously these factors frequently coalesce; it is precisely those adult materials that some deem unsuitable for minors and adolescents that are most frequently stolen or mutilated. This state of affairs enables some administrators to take or keep controversial materials off the shelves, citing theft and mutilation when they are actually more concerned with anticipating censorious pressures, real or imagined, in their communities. It is difficult sometimes to tell

TABLE ON USE OF REVIEWING MEDIA

Title	Public Libraries				Academic Libraries							
	1	2	3	4	1	2	3	4	5	6	7	8
Kirkus	X	O	X	X	X	—	X	X	O	O	X	O
Library Journal	X	X	X	X	X	—	X	X	X	X	X	O
ALA Booklist	X	X	X	X	X	—	X	X	O	X	O	O
Choice	X	X	X	X	X	—	X	X	X	X	X	X
New York Times Book Review	X	X	X	X	X	—	X	X	X	X	X	X
Saturday Review	X	X	X	X	X	—	X	X	X	X	X	X
New York Review of Books	X	X	X	X	X	—	X	X	X	X	X	X
New Republic	X	X	X	X	X	—	X	X	X	O	X	X
Commentary	X	X	X	X	X	—	X	X	X	O	X	X
Paris Review	X	X	X	X	O	—	X	X	O	O	X	O
Times Literary Supplement	X	X	X	X	X	—	X	X	X	X	X	X
Other	—	X	X	X	X	—	X	O	O	O	X	

X = Library uses   O = Library does not use   — = Information not forwarded

where safeguarding against theft and mutilation shades off into caution, fear, and self-censorship unless one knows intimately the library in question, its clientele, and the specific materials involved.

We have also seen that one of these policy statements gives detailed descriptions of materials that it will not purchase, but these details inevitably become adjectives which can be subjectively interpreted. Is *Naked Lunch* morbid? Is *Our Lady of the Flowers* erotic, and if yes, is it more erotic than *Lady Chatterley's Lover*? Is *Last Exit to Brooklyn* cheap and sensational? If one were to judge by holdings alone, at least one public library in this survey would seem to think that all of this is so.

College Libraries' Report

Closer scrutiny of the holdings of the three college libraries surveyed reveals a pattern of acceptance, rejection, and unawareness that sometimes coincides with and sometimes deviates from the public library pattern. To begin with, a few titles are well represented. All three academic libraries have Ginsberg's *Howl*, perhaps because of its influence on the Anglo-American poetic scene during the sixties, and two of three hold Le Roi Jones' *Dutchman and the Slave*, whereas only one public library has that title. There are also several titles which are held with the same frequency as public libraries, notably Burroughs' *Naked Lunch*, which

two of three college libraries have, and *Evergreen Review*, which one college library holds and restricts.

On the other hand, some of the holdings are almost inexplicably thin. *Lady Chatterley's Lover* is held by two of the three libraries, whereas all the public libraries hold it, some openly, one cautiously. Two of the three college libraries surveyed have Mailer's *Why Are We in Viet Nam?*, but Miller's *Tropic of Cancer*, which has grown in stature through the past two decades, is held by none of these libraries. The *Kama Sutra*, generally regarded as a classic of its kind, is also ignored, and Welch's *Blue Book* is held by one college library. Whereas two of the four public libraries surveyed have Leary's *The Psychedelic Experience*, only one college library has it. Likewise, Sade's *Selected Writings* is held by none of the three college libraries, though it can be argued that a complete work might have fared better than an anthology. Among the periodicals, *Ramparts* is held by two of three college libraries, whereas all four public libraries have it. And the *Realist* is completely ignored, even as it is by the public libraries surveyed.

The fiction and nonfiction that focuses on race seems fairly well represented in these college collections, and the fiction and nonfiction that explores human sexual behavior seems less well represented even as it was in the public library collections. There is virtually no restriction of access to materials reported—the *Evergreen Review* and Welch's *Blue Book* being two exceptions—but it is obvious that these college libraries show their negativism, not by restricting materials but by not buying them, whether through a process of deliberate rejection or blithe lack of awareness.

Since none of the college librarians surveyed gave specific reasons for acceptance or rejection of specific works, we do not know what book selection values were operative in these cases. However, a few of their comments are ironic.

The librarian who serves a Quaker-affiliated campus reports that "collections are built on pertinence and prospective usefulness without regard to controversy". This collection does not have *Tropic of Cancer*, Guevera's *Diary*, *The Psychedelic Experience*, or Wilhelm Reich's *Selected Writings*.

The librarian who serves a satellite campus located in the Philadelphia area reports: "Books not purchased were not actively rejected. None of these titles was requested by anyone—library staff, faculty, or students." And regarding the periodicals, she notes: "We have none of these ... We have had no requests to add them to our collection." We are asked to suppose an undergraduate institution which offers courses in modern literature where no student or faculty member asks the librarian for *Our Lady of the Flowers*, *Lady Chatterley's Lover*, *Tropic of Cancer*, *Portnoy's Complaint*, *The Psychedelic Experience*, *Dutchman and the Slave*, *Ramparts*, and *Evergreen Review.*

The librarian who serves a community college reports that his library has a book selection policy, "but not on paper." He adds: "... we purchase to support the curricula primarily. If a 'controversial' title is requested, we judge each request on its merit." His collection does not have *Our Lady of the Flowers*, *Tropic of Cancer*, *Look Out, Whitey!*, Welch's *Blue Book*, *Evergreen Review*, and the *Journal of Black Poetry* among other titles.

In all these cases, curriculum support and lack of requests are suggested as strong reasons for not including some controversial materials in collections. But in one or two instances one is sorely tempted to ask if the librarian's initiative and sensitivity both to modern letters and the current scene are not also legitimate factors in book selection.

University Libraries' Report

Closer scrutiny of the five university libraries surveyed shows that they hold more controversial titles than the college and in many cases the public libraries. They are apparently more alert to contemporary literary values and to social problems, though in some instances they are more restrictive, perhaps for security reasons.

RELATION OF OFFICIAL BOOK SELECTION POLICIES OF FOUR PUBLIC LIBRARIES TO THEIR ACTUAL HANDLING OF CONTROVERSIAL BOOKS

	PL 1	PL 2	PL 3	PL 4
Director Selects	X	X	O	X
Director and Community Group Selects	O	O	X	O
Official Restriction Policy	Yes	No	No	No
No. of Selection Tools Cited Used	All	10 of 11	All	All
Staff Reviews Used in Selection Process	Yes	No	Yes	No
No. of Titles on Controversial List Circulated	23	16	16	18
No. of Titles on Controversial List Restricted	9	4	2	0
No. of Titles on Controversial List Not Owned	1	13	15	15
No. of Censorship Controversies Reported	5	0	0	0
Librarian believes professional organizations should be more active in censorship controversies	Yes	Yes	Yes	Yes
Librarian believes profession needs a supportive agency in censorship controversies	Maybe	Yes	Yes	Yes

Four of five university libraries have *Naked Lunch*, which is the best group showing for that particular novel. Also four of the five university libraries have *Our Lady of the Flowers*, again a better group showing than the college and public libraries. All five university libraries have *Lady Chatterley's Lover*, and they all circulate it. All five university libraries have *Tropic of Cancer*, and though one library restricts it, the treatment of available copies is freer than it is among the public libraries. All five university libraries have *Portnoy's Complaint*, which shows more responsiveness to contemporary fiction than the college libraries evidence. Two of the five university libraries have Leary's *The Psychedelic Experience*, again a better showing than one finds among the college libraries. Four of the five university libraries hold *The Kama Sutra*, a better showing than the college or public libraries. All university libraries surveyed have Velikovsky's *Worlds in Collision* despite the scientific attacks leveled against his work.

Of the periodical titles, all five university libraries hold the *Evergreen Review* and, though two libraries restrict it, the group showing is better here than among the college or public libraries. Three of the university libraries have the *Journal of Black Poetry*, whereas only one college and one public library have it. All five university libraries carry *Ramparts*, whereas two of three college libraries carry it. And an urban university library is the only one among 12 surveyed to carry the *Realist*.

On the other hand, a few titles are not as well represented as they are in college and public library collections. Four of five university libraries have Ginsberg's *Howl*, whereas all three college libraries have that title. Three of five university libraries have Donleavy's *Ginger Man*, whereas two of three college libraries have that novel. Three of five university libraries have Guevera's *Diary*, and one of these copies is in Spanish, whereas two of three college libraries have that title. Only one university library has Welch's *Blue Book*, and only two have the *Se-*

lected Writings of the Marquis De Sade. Both titles emerge as public library items.

Though the university libraries hold more controversial titles on this list than the other libraries, they do not duplicate as heavily as the public libraries do, a practice which might reasonably be expected. The fiction and nonfiction which deals with racial problems is relatively well represented. Of the fiction and nonfiction that concerns itself primarily with sexual behavior, only the *Selected Writings* of the Marquis De Sade and Donleavy's *Ginger Man* are relatively weakly represented; on the political front only Guevera's *Diary* and Welch's *Blue Book* are comparatively overlooked or rejected.

Since none of the university librarians offered specific comments on specific titles on our list, we cannot evaluate more closely the selection and rejection processes involved. Whether the university libraries duplicate in sufficient quantities to meet their particular demands is a pertinent question, but we cannot answer it conclusively since that would require a familiarity with all five campuses and the internal operations of all five libraries beyond the scope and resources of this survey. There is some evidence that they do not duplicate some of these titles in sufficient quantities.

The library that serves a university with a strong technological and business emphasis reports divisional autonomy operating in book selection with this statement: "Our selections are left to the discretion of our librarians whose decisions are based upon funds available and priorities in their divisional collections."

The library that serves a Catholic-related university reports that there is no restriction in the handling of its materials, but this particular library does not have Donleavy's *Ginger Man*, Genet's *Our Lady of the Flowers*, De Sade's *Selected Writings*, Selby's *Last Exit to Brooklyn*, Ginsberg's *Howl*, Guevera's *Diary*, Leary's *The Psychedelic Experience*, Wilhelm Reich's *Selected Writings*, Welch's *Blue Book*, and the *Journal of Black Poetry* among other titles. In this library final selection authority rests with the Acquisitions Department head, and faculty recommendations are particularly important.

One urban university library has a blanket order for all current books in the English language, with some minor exceptions, which means that controversial materials in English arrive as a matter of course. The selection process is operative primarily with foreign language materials. In this library selection is handled by a bibliographical department of some 13 librarians supplemented by faculty and student recommendations. The library has an interesting Contemporary Culture Collection of more than 425 items. These titles are kept in a Contemporary Culture Center, which is open two hours every afternoon. Among the titles are *The Militant*, *New Left Notes*, and *Youth International Party News*, representing the radical left; the *Dan Smoot Report* and *Storm Trooper*, representing the radical right; *Thursday's Drummer*, *East Village Other*, *Los Angeles Free Press*, *Philadelphia Free Press*, and *Rat*, representing the underground papers; *Black Panther* and *Up From Under*, representing the Women's Liberation movement.

Conclusions

"The nightingale sings with its fingers," a line in Cocteau's film *Orpheus* reminds us. Moving from poetry and the literary history of the early 20th-Century to librarianship now, we are reminded that librarians sing with statistics and file with their fingers. However, sheer statistics have their crudities, and vital half truths are often hidden underneath, between, and around them. Figures don't lie: they merely make half statements much of the time, and much depends on how they are presented.

Given the ineradicable accomplishment of D. H. Lawrence, is it impressive that only one of the 12 libraries surveyed does not have *Lady Chatterley's Lover* and only one restricts it? Shall we say that 92 percent of the librar-

ies we surveyed have *Lady Chatterley*, or shall we say more accurately that one library does not have and one library restricts a significant novel by one of the major novelists of this century dead these past 40 years? Given the reputation of *Naked Lunch*, at least among many specialized critics, shall we say that only seven area libraries make freely available one of the significant avant-garde novels of our time? Shall we say that 75 percent of the libraries we surveyed have *Tropic of Cancer*, or would it be more exact to say that three libraries do not have and three libraries, including one university library, restrict a novel that is taught in American Literature classes in a steadily increasing number of academic institutions?

One of the limits of such a study as this is the absence of expansive statements to explain the responses. Are the four libraries that do not have the two plays by Le Roi Jones making evaluative judgments on the merits of these plays? Are they even aware of them? Are they reacting partially to the author's reputation as a militant in Newark's recent ghetto wars? Or are they reacting, perhaps, to his anti-Semitic diatribes disguised as poems? All these factors are separable, but only in the minds of knowledgeable collection builders.

As we moved from the sixties into the seventies, the following controversial areas dominated the thinking of our citizens and inevitably affected the judgments of librarians: 1) racial tensions, 2) radical politics and the war in Vietnam, 3) changing sexual mores, and 4) drugs. Reviewing overall holdings in these respective areas, we find first that certain titles which deal with racial problems, heavily publicized because of their substance and rhetorical force, are fairly well represented. All of the libraries surveyed have *Soul on Ice*, *Black Skin, White Masks*, and *The Autobiography of Malcolm X*, and some have them in quantity. When we move to the books that try to make literature of our racial problems, the showing is less impressive: one public library and one college library do not have Baldwin's *Another Country*, and three public libraries and one college library do not have the two plays by Jones. Among the periodicals, the showing is also less impressive: only four libraries carry the *Journal of Black Poetry*, and only half the libraries surveyed have the *Liberator*.

In the area that can be roughly designated as radical politics and Vietnam, the holdings are spottier, suggesting more caution and sharper differences of opinion. Of the 12 libraries, 11 have Ginsberg's *Howl* and Guevera's *Diary*, and one of these holds Guevera in Spanish only. Since Tatum's *Conscientious Objector's Handbook* is a title that is not widely known, the fact that only three libraries have it and one of the three restricts it may not seem particularly surprising, but only five libraries have the *Blue Book of the John Birch Society*, and only three of them circulate it freely—a

curious statistic that invites closer scrutiny.

Among the periodicals that belong in the area of radical politics, only *Ramparts*, which is held by 11 of 12 libraries, is well represented. *Evergreen Review*, which combines New Leftism with its own idiosyncratic version of sexual freedom, is held by seven libraries, four of whom restrict it for security reasons. Two conservative periodicals, *American Opinion* and *Human Events*, are held by six and seven of the libraries surveyed respectively, and the *Realist* is held by one university library only.

Turning to the fiction and nonfiction that probes our sexual mores, usually critically, the holdings reflect a clear-cut pattern of caution, restriction, and rejection mixed with unawareness. In this area the high publicized Masters and Johnson study is the only widely held title; all libraries have it, and 11 circulate copies freely. Of the creative works, *Portnoy's*

12 PHILADELPHIA LIBRARIES' OWNERSHIP OF 33 CONTROVERSIAL BOOK AND PERIODICAL TITLES

	Public Libraries				Academic Libraries							
Ownership of 25 Book Titles:	1	2	3	4	1	2	3	4	5	6	7	8
No. of titles owned, no restrictions	17	15	13	16	20	24	15	15	8	15	21	15
No. of titles restricted	8	4	2		1			1	1			1
No. of titles not owned		6	10	9	5		10	9	16	10	4	9
Ownership of 8 periodical titles:												
No. of titles owned, no restrictions	6	1	3	2	6	5	4	3		5	4	2
No. of titles restricted	1					3		1		1		
No. of titles not owned	1	7	5	6	2		4	4	8	2	4	6
No. of *combined titles* owned:												
(unrestricted)	23	16	16	18	26	29	19	18	8	20	25	17
Owned, with restriction	9	4	2			4		2	1	1		1
Totals, all ownership:	32	20	18	18	26	33	19	20	9	21	25	18

Only one public and one academic library have all book titles. No public library, and only one academic library (the same one) have all periodical titles. Only seven of the 25 book titles are owned by all four public libraries, unrestricted. An additional 12 book titles are owned, used with restrictions. Twelve book titles are lacking in at least one of each of the four libraries.

Only four of the 25 book titles are owned by all eight academic libraries; only four additional titles are owned, restricted. Twenty-one book titles are lacking in at least one of each of the eight academic libraries.

Only one of the eight periodical titles is in all four public libraries, unrestricted. Only one of the eight periodicals is not in any of the four public libraries, but another is in only one, and then restricted.

Total of 73 titles is owned by the four public libraries, making the average total 18.25, or 15.25 book titles. Total of 162 titles is owned by the eight academic libraries, making the average total 20.3, or 16.6 book titles.

Complaint, another highly publicized book, is held by 11 of 12 libraries holding the title in some quantity.

But the other titles fare feebly. *Naked Lunch* is freely circulated by six libraries who have single copies of the novel. The only library that holds it in quantity restricts it. Donleavy's *Ginger Man*, less influential and less iconoclastic, is freely circulated by nine libraries. But *Our Lady of the Flowers*, evocative autobiographical fiction by one of the most forceful novelists and playwrights since 1940, is freely circulated by six of 12 libraries studied, and the one library that holds it in quantity restricts it. *Lady Chatterley*, as already noted, is not held by one college library and restricted by one public library. *Tropic of Cancer*, freely circulated by six libraries and restricted by three, apparently still gives cause for professional anxiety almost 40 years after it was written. And Selby's *Last Exit to Brooklyn*, more dubious because of its one-dimensional realism but a representative novel nevertheless, is freely circulated by four libraries and restricted by one.

In the nonfictional area, the *Selected Writings* of the Marquis De Sade is freely circulated in small doses by four libraries and restricted by one. The handling of *Howl* has been noted. Wilhelm Reich is a catalytic influence on the sexual thinking and therapeutic techniques of the sixties and early seventies, but his *Selected Writings* are freely circulated by four libraries and restricted by one. And *The Kama Sutra* is freely circulated by four libraries and restricted by two. Among the periodicals, the handling of *Evergreen* and the *Realist*, which are anti-establishment in both sexual and political fronts, has been noted.

The one title that deals directly with the drug scene, Leary's *The Psychedelic Experience*, is freely circulated by four libraries and restricted by one. Only one university library makes it freely available in quantity.

We conclude from this mathematics that books that challenge conventional sexual mores meet with more caution,

anxiety, and defensiveness from our selecting and/or administrative librarians than books that challenge prevalent political values and practices. *Soul on Ice*, Guevera's *Diary*, and *The Autobiography of Malcolm X* will make their way more readily into our collections than *Tropic of Cancer* or *Our Lady of the Flowers*. Established novels, like *Lady Chatterley* and *Tropic*, which one might have hoped would be fully represented, are not, and creative works, like *Our Lady* and *Naked Lunch*, which are now tunneling their way into modern letters, are handled nervously or cavalierly. Also, recent censorship attacks have told us clearly that it is the bisexuality and the nudity in *Evergreen Review* much more than its New Leftism that sticks in the craws of our moralistic citizens and librarians.

We conclude further that the puritanical heritage we read about in our social and cultural histories still lives in Philadelphia area libraries.

One would find it difficult to assign an overall adjective to describe this state of affairs. Is the state of intellectual freedom in Philadelphia area libraries as reflected by the handling of these titles good, bad, or indifferent? The answer obviously depends on the values of the investigators making the judgment. One might reasonably have hoped that most, if not all, of these titles would be held by all 12 libraries surveyed, but such was far from the case. Only one public library and one university library had all of the book titles, and only one university library had all the periodicals. One would opt for a descriptive adjective like *indifferent* rather than *good* to describe the situation.

In extenuation of the mediocre showing these collective libraries make in the area of contemporary writing particularly, one might argue that each institution has its unique function and some, because of budget limitations alone, would give lower priority to such luxury items as *Our Lady* and *Naked Lunch*. One might argue further that the capacity of our student and adult masses to assimilate esoteric and arcane fiction is not as great as their supposed social and political sophistication, that they can more readily connect with a Cleaver, who is out on the street speaking colloquial Afro-English, than with a Genet, who weaves his sexual fantasies in dense symbolist prose. One suspects, however, that unawareness is a sizeable factor in the neglect of several of these absent or thinly held titles. The survey afforded occasional glimpses of indifference to certain authors and titles and suspicion regarding positive censorship stands that are far from reassuring to the members of this Committee and do not particularly augur well for the future. We can only conclude that librarians who care about contemporary letters, experimental approaches in art and social action, and the right of radical voices to be heard have cause for continued concern and ample reason for using their professional wits to try to improve this unimpressive situation.

Unawareness covers a wide stretch of territory, ranging from ignorance to indifference. The unawareness uncovered by this survey reflects, among other things, a professional overemphasis on administrative matters. Particularly does our professional literature prefer to dwell on bureaus rather than ideas, perhaps because furniture is more maneuverable and less explosive.

Even if differences in function and book buying potential are taken into consideration, some libraries are obviously more sensitive to controversial materials than others. We have seen that university libraries have a wider spread of titles but do not duplicate heavily. We have also seen that there are two modes of behavior in the public libraries surveyed: a few reject or ignore much controversial material, and one or two will add it, but often on a restricted circulation basis only. We see further that a few libraries with relatively large budgets tend to hold most, if not all, of these titles. The university library with a $700,000 budget has all 33 titles and circulates more of them than any other library surveyed—29. Two other university libraries, one with an un-

disclosed budget and a Negro university library with a $50,000 budget, circulate the next largest number of titles—25. The public library with a $953,000 budget has all but one of the 33 titles but circulates 23 and restricts nine. This same public library has multiple copies of all 23 titles that it owns, more multiple copies than any other library surveyed. But that is consistent with its function as a large distributing agency.

On the other end of the spectrum we find that the weakest showing is made by the area state college library with the smallest book budget—$17,500. This library holds nine of the 33 titles on our list, circulates eight, restricts one, and holds only one of these titles in multiple copies. On the other hand, the second and third weakest showings are made by libraries with relatively substantial book budgets. The community college library, with a book budget of $75,000, holds 18 titles on the list, circulates 17, restricts one, and holds only one title in multiple copies. And although it has the third largest budget reported in this survey—$325,000—the Catholic-related university library holds 19 of the 33 titles, circulates all of them, but holds none of them in multiple copies.

If we compare the community college library, which has a $75,000 annual book budget, with the Negro University library, which has a $50,000 annual book budget, we find that the library with the smaller budget holds more of the controversial titles on our list—25 against 18—circulates more of them—25 against 17—and holds more of them in multiple copies—seven against one.

We conclude that relatively favorable book budgets are no guarantee that the library's collection will include controversial materials in any significant quantities, that the values of the institution and the librarian inevitably come into play, and that some librarians with modest budgets and a sense of social and artistic adventure are building more contemporary and provocative collections than others, who have more money at their disposal but suspect or dislike the

I.F. SCORES OF 12 PHILADELPHIA LIBRARIES

I.F. Rating	UL $700,000 Bk. Budget	PL $953,000 Bk. Budget	UL Undisclosed Bk. Budget	UL $50,000 Bk. Budget	PL $66,600 Bk. Budget	UL $80,000 Bk. Budget
No. Controversial Titles Owned	33	32	26	25	18	20
Plus No. Controversial Titles Circulated	29	23	25	25	18	18
Plus No. Controversial Titles Circulated in Multiple Copies	18	23	9	7	9	5
Minus No. Controversial Titles Restricted	4	9	1	0	0	2
Equals Intellectual Freedom Rating	76	69	59	57	45	41

I.F. Rating	CL $124,500 Bk. Budget	PL $28,830 Bk. Budget	PL $67,620 Bk. Budget	PL $325,000 Bk. Budget	CL $75,000 Bk. Budget	CL $17,500 Bk. Budget
No. Controversial Titles Owned	21	18	20	19	18	9
Plus No. Controversial Titles Circulated	20	16	16	19	17	8
Plus No. Controversial Titles Circulated in Multiple Copies	1	8	7	0	1	1
Minus No. Controversial Titles Restricted	1	2	4	0	1	1
Equals Intellectual Freedom Rating	41	40	39	38	35	17

unorthodox or feel compelled to ignore it because of institutional policy.

At the close of our survey we asked the 12 librarians to evaluate existing anti-censorship apparatus in the profession and comment on the supportive role of existing professional organizations and agencies in censorship controversies. Nine librarians, a clear majority, thought that existing professional organizations should play a more active role in supporting libraries or librarians in censorship controversies. One Catholic university librarian did not. One college librarian hedged, answering: "I'd like to know more." And one university librarian did not reply.

All four public librarians spoke for stronger supportive organizational action in censorship confrontations, perhaps because public libraries are more vulnerable to direct attack by organized community elements, whereas college and university censorship problems are usually internal and frequently unpublicized. One supportive college librarian thought the recently established Freedom To Read Foundation proper. However, none of the eight who answered affirmatively were very specific or chose to elaborate on their views.

Eight of the 12 librarians surveyed thought that the profession needs an agency to give financial, legal, and moral support to a library or librarian with a censorship problem. One college librarian in this group thought that the Freedom To Read Foundation was the probable answer and could do the job. Also, one vacillating public librarian said that such an agency was needed only if existing agencies do not begin to do an effective job. However, one college librarian dissented from the majority view, stating: "Some librarians, I think, want a confrontation and create a situation which produces such." The inference here is that censorship confrontations are often devised by opportunistic librarians who are guilty of self-dramatization and self-aggrandizement, even though they sometimes risk their jobs. The Catholic university librarian again dissented, and one other university librarian did not reply.

Without overinterpreting these answers, we can say that most of the librarians surveyed seemed aware of the censorship problem, though some were tepid and none were particularly expansive. Dissenting voices among a few college and university librarians could mean that either they do not regard the issue as important or they regard themselves as removed from the censorship arena. Particularly does the militant dissent from the college librarian remind us that some professionals suspect or resent censorship fighters in their midst and continue to see intellectual freedom as a synthetic and manufactured issue as we move towards the Orwellian millenium.

Breaking into Jail

Sue Opipare Murdock, Peggy Porter, and Ida Reed

THIS IS A REPORT of one small event in the library world. It is important, we feel, not because of what was done, but why it happened. The library "zeitgeist" at the beginning of the '70s generated in us motivations and frustrations which we feel represent the emotions of many now in the profession who are trying in some fashion to meaningfully accommodate themselves to the call for change.

Simply attempting to define those charged words "Relevant" and "Socially Responsible" in terms of library programs has been a staggering process, which has stalemated meetings and developed armed camps of opinion in associations and institutions. Our "happening" was a way for us to demonstrate our understanding of these words' import.

The talk about such issues at Atlantic City in June 1969 developed in us a desire to find something which could be done now, something which would illustrate through action, not talk, the felt meanings of these battle cries. In such an atmosphere, a push to organize a local Social Responsibilities Round Table was launched in Pittsburgh in October 1969. Precisely at that moment, a coincidental opportunity arose which seemed designed to answer the

desire of some members of this group to, through action, refute the skepticism of those who mocked or rejected or simply yawned at the challenge of the SRRT invitation: "Give a damn!"

Warden William B. Robinson, head of the Allegheny County Jail in Pittsburgh, wished to organize a recreational library in the jail. However, funds were limited. The County Jail was in limbo, unable at that time to obtain adequate funding for programs from federal, state, or local sources, in part because the County Jail is considered a short-term facility. The average stay there is seventeen days, though some of the residents are there months and even years awaiting trial or appeals.

The jail, built in 1884, has been described as an outstanding specimen of 19th Century American architecture. The building is massive and seemingly indestructible. Adapting it to modern ideas for correctional facilities is a technically intricate process. It has a staff of 109, including the guards and matrons, nurses, and a baker. The resident population of the jail varies from 475 to 550. About six percent of the residents are women. Many of the residents are idle while inside, for there are internal jobs for only 25 percent of them.

Warden Robinson assumed his position February 15, 1967, after 14 years in the correctional field. His first steps were to initiate a jail newspaper, *Concern* (written and printed by the residents), to organize new recreational and entertainment programs, to upgrade the institutional food and menus, to begin education programs which enable interested residents to take the high school equivalency diploma exams while in jail, and to begin plans for the library. The warden was a determined man. He explored all avenues of approach to these projects which he felt were necessary in order to create a rehabilitative rather than a punitive atmosphere in the jail. Due to his own resourcefulness and contacts, Warden Robinson was able to obtain valuable donations of equipment and supplies from agencies in the community, and aid from volunteers like ourselves in developing these programs.

To establish a library, the Warden began by soliciting gift books from agencies and individuals in the city, and he accumulated over 7000 volumes which he stored in unused cells. He obtained $18,000 from the County to convert eight cells into a library. This conversion was a major construction feat as the old cell walls had been extremely thick structural supports. The result was a long narrow room with shelves for about 5000 books, and a small work area. While construction was underway, he approached the Allegheny County League of Women Voters, and they agreed to organize the books into a workable collection. The League in turn called the Carnegie Library of Pittsburgh, seeking the aid of a professional consultant, but unfortunately the library had no department or staff to answer this kind of community request.

At this point, we entered the picture. The League's call for help was casually discussed one day in the Carnegie Institute cafeteria, and that conversation sparked the chain of events which followed. Here, we felt, was a chance to do something positive, to use our professional skills in a worthwhile community project that needed doing now. We talked with the Carnegie administration, with associates we thought were interested in such a project, and with the League, and we agreed to serve as consultants in our free time. We decided to become a local SRRT task force, and in the sense of participatory democracy, as a committee, share the responsibility, distribute the labor, and bring a combined and therefore wider experience to the project. Eventually there were nine of us, ranging in age from early twenties to late forties, with library experience from one to 20 years, married and single, from public and university library systems in the city. The six who joined with us were: Dorothy Kweller, Mike Marino, Sheila Maxwell, Tina Meszaros, Carl Reed, and Kitty Smith.

We never presented ourselves as a task force, however, for the local SRRT effort fizzled. But we had committed ourselves and were determined to see the job done, and done as competently as possible.

Warden Robinson had certain prerequisites for the library. Once it was established, it was to be staffed by residents. The borrowers would not have direct access to the books, but would select from a list, or book catalog, kept on each range. No paperbacks were to be included, partly for security reasons. The Warden viewed the collection as recreational, and he, therefore, initially did not want texts. He also stipulated: no books of a sexually inflammatory nature and none "glorifying crime."

With these prerequisites in mind, we met at home in the evenings to decide how best to organize the books and utilize the independent work of the League volunteers. We quickly surveyed *Library Literature* for concrete help with little tangible results. We reviewed books on fundamental procedure and organization for small libraries. We strived for simplicity in our instructions and procedures, and soon became freshly aware just how much library technique and terminology taken for granted by us is totally unfamiliar to laymen.

In processing the books, the League volunteers were joined by volunteers from the women's section of the jail. The librarian-consultants weeded the accumulated books with the advice of the women residents. The League members and the women residents assisting us made simple catalog cards in duplicate, listing author's name, book title, date, and call numbers, which were simply accession numbers. The call numbers were written on the spine of the book and on the inside cover. The librarians added informal subject headings to the catalog cards. Because of the scattered conditions under which the work had to be done, no attempt was made to group duplicate titles together on the shelf, and though each book was given only one subject heading, attempts were made to give duplicate copies subject headings different from the first copy, in order to bring out as many aspects of the book as possible. *The Caine Mutiny,* for example, could be listed under Books into Movies, War Stories, Sea Stories, or Adventure, among other possibilities. One set of cards was filed by call number, for a shelf list, and the other set was filed by subject headings. From the subject cards, a book catalog was typed. A charging system was established to accommodate the special requirements of the jail, accounting for the books both by due date and individual borrower.

Work progressed slowly. Date "guess-timates" regarding completion of stages were forlornly passed, and work continued. Murphy's laws proved all too true in our case. "Nothing is as easy as it looks. Everything will take longer than you think it will. If something can go wrong, it will." When the project was finally completed, a member of our group presented each of us with a memento—a framed copy of Murphy's laws to caution us when ambitious projects arise in the future.

The project took us almost ten months, from October 1969 to July 1970. We sometimes worked in the evenings till 11 P.M. or later, sometimes on Saturdays or free week days. The League volunteers had ceased their activity in January 1970 when librarian-consultants began a review of the collection. The books were then housed in the library proper. Reviewing the collection and catalog cards, making necessary corrections, adding additional donations which materialized, and typing the pages for the book catalog continued till July, when the library finally opened.

The following announcement in *Concern,* written by one of the residents, preceded the opening.

Everyone of the tenants of the County Hotel shall be the recipients of a "windfall"; this shall be theirs by virtue of being occupants of said residence. The Hotel shall soon be accorded a somewhat ceremonious opening of a library.

This will be the first time in the history of the County Hotel that literature, lore, and the pursuit of wisdom and finally understanding will be made available to the occupants by the management.

The new Fountain of Knowledge is but another step toward providing occupants with ways and means of constructively filling the idle minutes, hours, days and oft times weeks and months . . .

We know that most of the tenants now residing within the premises pursue vocations and various types of hazardous occupations which keep opportunity to read at a minimum; to wit, dailies, and current magazines of special interest only. Soon the "lame excuse" that no time was available to quench the literary thirsts endured by many of the hotel's occupants will be just what it always has been, "a lame excuse."

During the months we labored on the project, we received dismal predictions from some of the jail staff regarding how badly the residents would treat the books, how the library would either be disused or destroyed, and how foolish we were to give so much of our own time to the effort. Similarly, we encountered the same response among some librarians, who were skeptical of both our motives and our results. We were considered "impetuous" by traditionalists and "do-gooders" by reformists. However, encouraging words, gifts of books, and money for new books came from other librarians, and from the Carnegie Library Staff Association as the project neared completion.

The first books were circulated July 11, 1970. After an initial flurry, the circulation figure for the summer and early fall leveled to about 900 books a month. As winter approached and outside activity became restricted, circulation began to increase. Vincent Davis is the resident who has supervised the library since its opening and is largely responsible for its smooth operation to date. These are his personal reflections about the library.

Every night before lock-up there was always a mad scramble to try and find something to read. During the day, there is only a limited number of jobs at which a person can utilize his time. It left a large part of the population with nothing to do, with time on their hands. . . .
. . . the weather has started to turn cold and we are lending about double the amount of books that were going out during the summer months. . . .
. . . they don't come in here asking for gangster books.
. . . they call for philosophy, psychology, Bacon and Emerson essays, black history —all history—general equivalency diploma test books. These guys are not asleep. They're trying to get it together. There are ones who said this would never work, but they (the residents) have shown it will by not destroying or mutilating any books.

What is the future of this library? At the close of 1970, it was functioning smoothly. Additional books in sports, history, and black studies were purchased by interested librarians and added, and the necessary supplement to the catalog compiled. One of the librarian-consultants has maintained a continuing interest in the library and still devotes personal time to it.

But a continued, sustained interest on the part of volunteers is not the answer to library service in this county institution. The current collection is but a beginning toward meeting the reading needs of the residents. While there are some universal request categories— black history and legal texts, for example—the range of the interests of 500 individuals can be readily imagined. Obviously, regular public library service would be better.

According to the news in professional journals, a number of libraries are establishing departments to serve institutions in their communities. A library department devoted specifically to the needs of local institutions and agencies could serve some now-unreached citizens, and the service provided should appeal to local government officials who are being asked to increase fiscal support for libraries. Staff could devote time to identifying groups needing service and to maintaining regular contact with them, beginning with such fundamental methods as bookmobile service and depository collections. An institution or agency already having an internal collection of books, or wishing to build one, should not be considered a "threat" or an indictment. Rather these small specialized collections could be looked upon as ancillary to the public system, to be encouraged as part of a community network of materials. In this regard, the staff could serve as consultants in the organization of these internal collections and recommend appropriate materials for the particular institution, while emphasizing the concept of the public library as a backup resource.

Our story halts at this point. The project was a unique experience for us as individuals. It was a beginning.

For others, it may illustrate that the time *is* ripe for such beginnings. Perhaps in your community a catalyst is needed to coalesce place, people, and events into a new, responsive library program. That catalyst can be you.

Prison Law Libraries and You

Celeste MacLeod

ME, YOU ASK? What have I got to do with prison law libraries? I don't work in one. I don't know anything about prisons, or law libraries either. Do they really let prisoners have law books, by the way? And what good does it do, if they aren't lawyers? Why, I thought most prisoners were practically illiterate.

A group of librarians in the San Francisco Bay Area might have reacted in the same way a year ago. None of us had ever worked in a prison library; none of us was a law librarian. But we were the kind of people I suspect many of you are—concerned with the mounting problems our country faces and newly awakened to the destructiveness of our prison system. We wondered if there was some way we could help prisoners *as librarians*, working through our profession.

We found that our group (and its official name is a mouthful), the Prison Task Force of the Bay Area Chapter of the Social Responsibilities Roundtable of the American Library Association, could contribute, both through education and action. We discovered that a specialty of prison law librarianship is needed in the profession. We found that the image of librarians needs upgrading (especially in the eyes of lawyers) and that to do this we need specialized train-

ing. We found that prison officials, in California at least, don't know what librarians and library systems can do, and they won't find out until we come to them under official auspices with information.

We sponsored a conference on prison legal libraries, and we filed an *amicus curia* brief, as librarians, in a suit concerning law libraries in prison. In order to understand why and how we acted, you need to know the situation of prisoners with legal problems.

Prisoners and the Law

Should prisoners have law libraries? Are they entitled to them, and could they make effective use of such materials? Prison officials have traditionally answered "no" to both questions, and until recent years most judges, attorneys, and librarians accepted their opinion as fact. The concept of rehabilitation flourished—belief that a stay in prison could turn a man into a useful citizen, if he accepted his guilt and looked to his jailers and their programs for help.

In those years a prisoner who protested either his sentence or his treatment in prison, and who tried to bring such grievances before a court, was seen as a malcontent with adjustment problems. He needed help—i.e., a period in solitary

58

confinement, his library privileges revoked, or some other theraputic measure that would lead him back to the path of rehabilitation. Jailhouse lawyers—prisoners who persisted in learning about the law and then helping uneducated inmates file legal petitions—were considered a menace, and stringent regulations were written to prevent these men from "practicing."

Long before prison reformers in the early seventies denounced the concept of rehabilitation as a hoax, prisoners saw it as a game played at their expense. Long before the Supreme Court ruled on November 8, 1971 that indigent prisoners have a right to adequate law libraries, prisoners looked to the courts for justice. Many persisted in the face of harsh punishment.

Prisoners have legal problems in three areas: 1) post-conviction relief (litigating their sentences), 2) civil problems, and 3) mistreatment or abridgement of constitutional rights in prison:

1) Most prisoners are poor and cannot afford a private attorney to defend them. Some were unfairly convicted, given unduly long sentences, or were innocent of the charges against them. In prison few volunteer attorneys are available, so often the prisoner's only road to the court is to file a *habeas corpus* petition himself.[1]

2) Civil problems include divorce, child custody, social security, veteran's claims, and others. Many of these problems are aggravated by incarceration.

3) Unfair treatment in prison can be the problem. For example, the prisoner may believe he was thrown into solitary confinement without just cause, that the food is inedible, that he is harassed by guards because he joined the Black Muslims, that he is not adequately protected against homosexual attack, or that he has a permanent ailment because he was refused proper medical treatment during an illness.

Most prisoners would not do their own legal work if they had the services of a competent licensed attorney, but the scattered public defender programs that extend to prisoners and the law student prison projects in this country reach only a fraction of inmates with legal problems. With a few exceptions the inmate who wants a court hearing must file his own petition or get help from a jailhouse lawyer.

Can prisoners who have not attended law school use law books to advantage? This question is answered by the many important cases they have won over the years, often in the area of prisoners' rights. You may have heard of *Gideon* v. *Wainwright*, the case that was initiated by a handwritten petition mailed to the United States Supreme Court by an uneducated Florida prisoner. It resulted in the landmark decision that indigent defendants in felony cases must be allowed court-appointed attorneys for their trials. (This 1963 decision did not extend the right of legal counsel to the convicted.)

Less known to the general public is *Johnson* v. *Avery*, the major decision for jailhouse lawyers. Willie Joe Johnson, a jailhouse lawyer in Tennessee, was put into solitary confinement in 1966 and his legal materials were confiscated, because he helped other prisoners draft their writs. He filed suit for relief. In 1969 the U.S. Supreme Court ruled that states could not outlaw the jailhouse lawyer, unless they provided "some reasonable alternative" (such as hiring a bevy of attorneys) to help indigent and uneducated prisoners draft their writs.

In 1966, after California set down a 12-title law book list for prison libraries and ordered all other law books to be destroyed, 90 prisoners from San Quentin and Folsom prisons joined together in a class action suit, *Gilmore* v. *Lynch*. After three years of procedural delays the Federal District Court, in May 1970, ruled in the prisoners' favor. Under the Fourteenth Amendment guarantee of equal protection for all citizens through access to the courts, the judges reasoned, indigent prisoners have a *right* to meaningful law libraries. The California Department of Corrections appealed this decision to the United States Supreme Court. On November 8, 1971, in *Young-*

er v. *Gilmore*, the High Court unanimously affirmed the decision of the California Court.[2] Thus it was not lawyers, legislators, corrections officials, or librarians who initiated needed changes in prison law libraries and in prisoners' rights—it was the inmates themselves, working through the courts.

The Library Profession in the Past

What *were* librarians doing during the prisoners' years of struggle? For the most part, they were silently upholding the viewpoint of the warden. The 1941 edition of *Objectives and Standards for Libraries in Adult Prisons and Reformatories* shows how prison librarians classified legal materials in the forties.[3]

"Books which emphasize the morbid, sex, and anti-social attitudes, ways of committing crime, disrespect for the law, religion and government, and such types as anatomical works, federal and state laws, as well as magazines of the confessional, sensational pictorial, and pulp type should be omitted."

What that paragraph says is that prisoners are like small children, so benevolent prison officials and librarians have a duty to protect them from materials that might confuse or corrupt their tender minds. People should be sent to prison for breaking the law, but they should not be allowed to know what that law says!

In the late 1960s, a number of people in our country began to take a close look at the prison system after nearly 30 years of neglect: what they saw made them call for changes. Some law librarians outside the prison began to take notice of prisoners' legal needs. Two excellent articles appeared in 1968 and 1970: "Reading Law in Prison" by Morris Cohen, Law Librarian of Harvard Law School, and "Law Library Service to Prisoners—The Responsibility of Non-prison Librarians," by O. James Werner, Law Librarian at the University of Oklahoma Law School.[4] Both found prison law libraries grossly inadequate. Cohen felt it was the responsibility of state correctional agencies to upgrade law libraries, while Werner urged outside law librarians to extend service to prisoners. Neither considered the possibility that prison librarians could play a role in law library service. (Both men are lawyers as well as librarians.)

Librarians Take Action

In the summer of 1971 librarians began to take affirmative action. The American Association of Law Librarians, at the request of the Conference of Concerned Law Librarians (a SRRT affiliate), set up a committee on Legal Services to Prisoners in June 1971 with Elizabeth Poe, Pennsylvania State Law Librarian, as Chairman. One section of the committee compiled a booklet showing what legal services are offered to prisoners by law libraries throughout the country, a state-by-state listing that prisoners, librarians, and others can use when ordering legal materials.[5] Another section has compiled a model list of law books for prison libraries.

In August 1971 the American Correctional Association established a Committee for the Provision of Legal Research Materials for Prisoners, with Marjorie LeDonne, a California librarian, as chairman. When the U.S. House of Representatives held hearings on prison reform in San Francisco in November 1971, LeDonne presented a list of recommendations for legal libraries on behalf of her committee.

Other wheels began to turn. Immediately after the *Younger* v. *Gilmore* decision, the West Publishing Company, a major law book firm, came out with a plan for law collections that would satisfy the court. Charles Kitzen, their manager of training and services, began visiting state departments of corrections across the country to sell the plan. Included in the price was a training program for inmates.

Both librarians and some corrections administrators became concerned that state systems would buy the West proposal as a convenient way to meet the court's directive, without first considering the reference aspects of library service, possible cooperative ventures among libraries, the use of modern equipment like photocopy machines or microforms, and the cost of keeping the initial purchase up to date. What was needed, everyone decided, was a seminar where experts in criminology and librarianship, as well as knowledgeable prisoners or former prisoners, could come together to discuss these alternatives.

Such a seminar was held in Washington, D.C. on May 22 and 23, 1972, under the joint sponsorship of the American Correctional Association and the Institute of Library Research of the University of California at Berkeley. Charles Bourne, the Institute Director, sent as his representative Marjorie LeDonne, who had recently been hired to conduct a survey of prison libraries in the United States. Other participants in the seminar—which was invitational—included librarians, corrections officials, attorneys, and the West Publishing Company representative, about 20 in all. A committee from that seminar is now working on recommendations that grew out of the talks. Their greatest agreement was on the possibilities for the use of microforms.

Bringing together people from many disciplines showed how each group views the same situation in its own terms. Everyone agreed that inmates can be trained as law clerks, but they disagreed about the role prison librarians should play in law libraries. The West Publishing Company felt that once it trained prisoners in the use of law books they could in turn train other inmates, so prison librarians would not need to know about the law books. Corrections officials saw the extension of legal reference services in their prisons as a way of upgrading positions for their employees—if corrections officers could be trained to do some legal reference work as part of their job, it might attract more highly qualified people to the corrections field. Attorneys thought law libraries could only play a minimal role in giving prisoners access to the courts, but that inmates were better able to administer them than librarians, while librarians felt that better trained librarians and a system of interlibrary cooperation for book and reference services were essential.

The opinion of prisoners was not heard because there were no inmates, past or present, at the conference. Two prisoners from the nearby Lorton Prison were scheduled to appear on the program, but for reasons that are not clear they never came.

Roney Nunes, a former prison and outspoken jailhouse lawyer (who was not at the seminar because he wasn't invited), feels strongly that inmate law clerks cannot do the job alone. Based on his experience in California prisons, he gives the following reasons: 1) If an inmate law clerk becomes too good and is effectively helping many prisoners, officials may transfer him to another institution (known as bus therapy) to get rid of him. 2) Some prisoners who become skilled law clerks may not want to share their expertise (all prisoners are not altruists). 3) Inmate law clerks may win their own appeals or be paroled at any time. Nunes believes that prisoners can make effective law library clerks, but they must be backed up by a professional prison librarian who can train successive clerks and give references services on a sustained basis.

The Berkeley SRRT Conference

A month before the Washington, D.C. seminar, there was a one-day conference on "Prison Legal Libraries—Idea into Reality" on the Berkeley campus of the University of California. It was jointly sponsored by the Bay Area SRRT and the Berkeley School of Librarianship.

After *Younger* v. *Gilmore* gave a strong mandate for prison libraries but left the details of what went into those libraries to the discretion of the Department of Corrections, SRRT members felt there was a need for an exchange of information about prison law libraries. We decided to hold a conference where librarians, lawyers, legislators, corrections officials, former prisoners, and students could come together for discussion. Having read the *Younger* v. *Gilmore* decision, we knew that the law libraries would only be as good as Corrections officials made them—and they were opposed to more than skeletal libraries.

In order to encourage student participation, we chose to hold the conference on a campus. Dean Patrick Wilson and the faculty of the library school at Berkeley were unanimous in joining us as cosponsors. The "we" of our Prison Task Force included librarians within a 30-mile radius of San Francisco: Joan Goddard, National Co-ordinator of the SRRT Task Force on Library Services to Prisons; Mary Stewart, who runs a bookmobile for prisoners as part of a job as an Alameda County Librarian; Carolyn Mohr and Fay Blake of the University of California library school faculty; Celeste West, who edited the *Synergy* magazine issue on prison libraries; Marjorie Le Donne; myself; several library school students; and other dedicated librarians.

On April 22, 1972 nearly 150 people (predominantly librarians and former prisoners) came together to hear talks and lively panel discussions on topics such as: What good are prison law libraries and the jailhouse lawyer? How can legal library services be extended to county and city jails? What role can legislation play in bringing law books to prisoners? The transcript of the conference has been published by the Berkeley School of Librarianship.[6]

The Librarian Image

During the conference organization and my own research, I was struck by the image that most lawyers I talked with had of librarians. With a few exceptions they viewed librarians as innocuous clerks whose sole function is to hand out books over the counter. When library school students at Berkeley offered to help set up a law collection for a nearby city jail system in conjunction with one of the courses, the staff attorney for the jails gave them a polite cold shoulder. He thought nothing was involved in a library except selecting the books and that only lawyers were qualified to do that. A participant at the Washington, D.C. conference noticed that lawyers discounted the role librarians could play in prison legal libraries, and the librarians would not argue back and defend their position in public even though in some cases they knew far more about the subject than the lawyers. Librarians have become so accustomed to being quiet and accommodating, she feels, that they are often afraid to speak out for what they believe in.

Not every lawyer has this narrow view of librarians. John Eshleman Wahl, the attorney for the prisoners in *Younger* v. *Gilmore*, was enthusiastic about the work librarians were doing. When SRRT decided to file an *amicus curiae* brief, evaluating the California Department of Corrections plan for legal libraries, Wahl welcomed our participation as a professional point of view that would be helpful to his clients, the prisoners. Two San Francisco attorneys, Fred Kurlander and Evander Smith, agreed to serve as our attorneys without fee, out of their own interest in helping prisoners.

The SRRT Brief[7]

Joan Goddard got on the phone to get national as well as local SRRT sponsorship for the brief, and we began formulating our arguments against the law library plan of the California Department of Corrections (CDC), which our lawyers then put into legalese. The final brief was in two parts:

1) *Service and training.* Our basic brief pointed out that the CDC plan made *no provision whatsoever* for reference services or for training prison librarians or inmates in even the most elementary knowledge of law books; also, that there is not a single librarian at the administrative level of the CDC. (In California,

prison libraries are under the administration of the Education Department.) We recommended placing the reference and service functions of prison law libraries under the administration of a group outside of Corrections, such as the State Law Library. It could hire a State Prison Law Library Consultant to visit prisons on a rotating basis to train staff and inmate law clerks. We also urged the use of photocopy machines, both in prisons libraries and at a state backup library, which would supply specialized books and reference services for prisoners.

2) *Need for lawyers.* Our supplemental brief emphasized that law library service alone cannot bring adequate legal help to prisoners. A combination of more lawyers in prisons and better use made of jailhouse lawyers, in conjunction with expanded law libraries, is essential.

The SRRT Brief was accepted by the Court when it held a hearing in San Francisco on July 14, 1972. The dozen librarians who attended the hearing were appalled to find that it was essentially a two-hour discussion between judges and lawyer on the merits of various law books on the CDC list. Reference services were not mentioned.

To date the decision has not yet been handed down. Our lawyers felt that the presence of so many librarians at the hearing, plus the arguments in our brief, would have a beneficial effect on the judges' decision. Some of our suggestions may also be used later by state senators writing future legislation for prison law libraries. The significance of the SRRT brief for librarians, I think, is that we made known to the courts both the views of librarians and the fact that we exist as a viable group.

Prison Library Training

If librarians are to play a significant role in prison law libraries, and if they are to speak out in favor of that role, they must have expertise in the field. Library schools, along with other related departments, need to set up training for: 1) *Specialists in prison law librarianship,* for those who will be law library consultants to large prison or jail systems, or who may direct a backup library; and 2) *those whose work includes some prison law librarianship,* general prison librarians whose collections will include a law section, law librarians whose libraries offer legal reference help to prisoners, and public librarians whose systems may extend their legal services to local jails and prisons.

The specialists will include those who will work full time in prison law librarianship and need a joint degree that draws on librarianship, law, and criminology, with possibly some courses in sociology and social welfare. They should be highly trained in legal bibliography rather than in the actual practice of law. Such a program might take two or three years after the B.A. If a few library schools set up a program with related departments, it should meet the need for specialists in this area.

Other librarians who will do some legal reference work for prisoners need special courses. Along with discussing book sources, a course on legal bibliography pertaining to the imprisoned could include information on procedure. For example, what are the various kinds of petitions a prisoner can file, and in what court do you file which form? At least part of such a course should be taught by a criminal lawyer or an experienced law librarian. (Note that none of this includes learning how to practice the law or give legal advice, the universal fear of prison librarians confronted with a law collection. It teaches the librarians to direct the prisoner to a book, form, or an agency—a reference function.)

Field work programs where law students work in prisons as part of their training are becoming increasingly popular. Why not set up the same type of field work for library school students studying law librarianship? Field work could be done both in the prisons and in outside law libraries that offer reference services to prisoners.

Role of Public Libraries

The *Younger* v. *Gilmore* decision has been applied mainly to state and federal prisons, but there is no reason why it cannot extend to county and city jails. A recent California decision, *Brenneman* v. *Madigan*, is a trend in that direction. In this case the court ruled that people in jail awaiting trial must have the same rights as those out on bail, or those already convicted.

City and county library systems are the logical institutions to provide legal books and services for the jails in their area. Many systems already serve other institutions such as hospitals and schools; extending services to jails is the next step. It is good economics for existing law libraries in cities to tie their services in with local jails, rather than attempting to set up whole new systems. In some instances the law library is in the same building as the jail.

When prisoners at the "Tombs" jail in New York City presented a list of grievances to the Mayor in 1970, one grievance was: "Because many of us feel that we cannot get a fair shake between the Legal Aid Society and the Courts, we find that we must prepare our own briefs and motions. This institution has law books in its library but does not allow the inmates to use the law books for reference data. In conclusion. . . WE DEMAND THE USE OF LAW BOOKS IN THE PRISON LIBRARY."[8]

Most Public Defender Offices and Legal Aid Societies simply do not have the staff and money to defend every prisoner the way a private attorney can, so material with which to do-it-yourself is essential in jails, along with more volunteer lawyers. Such help at this stage is crucial, for it can prevent innocent people from ever being sentenced to prison.

The San Francisco Public Library recently allotted $12,000 for a system of legal services in the city and county jails. Librarians Reed Coates and Linda Knutzen are now working out the details. Hopefully their experience will prove useful to other cities who may want to set up such programs in the future.

In 1972 Phyllis Dalton, president of the Association of Hospital and Institution Libraries (AHIL) and a long-time friend of prison libraries, appointed Barratt Wilkins, Institutions Librarian of the Missouri State Library, to head a new AHIL Special Committee on Library Services to Jails. Wilkins, whose committee is planning a pamphlet explaining how community librarians can set up such services, has asked Bay Area SRRT to write the section on Legal Materials.

Public Relations

How should librarians go about setting up library services in jails and prisons? I think it's a mistake to assume in advance that police officials will oppose your plan. In reading about general library programs that librarians set up in jails, I noticed that in several instances such programs were started at the request of the warden.[9] The major hesitation of sheriffs and wardens these days is likely to be one of security, i.e., fear that drugs and weapons will be smuggled in with the books, violence will ensue, and they will be held responsible. If you can allay their fears on this score, sheriffs may be more responsive to bringing in law books than will be lawyers and some law librarians you may have to convince.

The initial approach is important. I think there is a happy medium between our famed position of being "yes" men or women on the one hand, afraid to fight for innovative programs, and the other extreme of ultra-militants, who think that if the entire prison library isn't revamped by morning, to our specifications, forget it! The librarian who goes out to meet the sheriff or the warden needs an ability to communicate with people of many persuasions, as well as confidence and know-how.

Needed: More Women

The majority of prisoners in this

country are male; the majority of librarians are female. To give adequate services to inmates, we must have more women librarians working in the prisons. There is no valid reason why women cannot be librarians in men's prisons. California has the paradoxical situation where women are not allowed as librarians in men's prisons—too dangerous—but at Atascadero State Hospital, which treats the criminally insane (and doesn't come under CDC jurisdiction), they have had women librarians for years.

When I went to library school in the mid-sixties, the trend was to upgrade the profession by giving administrative positions to men. Hopefully the Women's Movement has stopped this sexist approach. We can upgrade the profession by being better trained and by actively pressing for responsible jobs and adequate recognition. The field of prison law librarianship should be open equally to men and women. We should use our professional organizations to make sure that when positions are open, qualified women are not passed over in the name of their "safety."

Prison Law Libraries

At our April 22 conference, I was surprised to hear two speakers say that law libraries are fine, of course, but they are the frosting on the cake. What is needed first is better living conditions, adequate medical facilities, and the like. I was surprised because, to me, adequate legal libraries in jails and prisons provide a major way in which the prisoners themselves can effect such changes.

Riots, as we have seen in recent years, rarely bring about needed changes. Once the prisoners are safely locked into their cells, officials can renege on promises made under stress, regardless of the merits of prisoners' demands. As we have also seen, in the past prisoners have not been able to depend much on the outside world for help. We have just been through "The Year of Prison Reform." The previous year ecology was *the* social

concern, and before that, Vietnam. Next year another important issue will probably capture the national conscience.

Small dedicated groups will continue to work for changes in prisons (many of them composed of former prisoners), but after the fanfare dies down, in the main the prisoners will again be left to make their own changes. Librarians can play a vital role as a profession, by making sure that prisoners have the legal tools they need in order to help themselves, and that they are not denied access to such tools by a bevy of restrictions.

Individual vs. System

When a group of lawyers in the San Francisco Bay Area set up an office to help prisoners who have legal problems, they soon broke off into two groups: the first wanted to work for major changes in the prison system by bringing class action suits that would benefit a number of prisoners. The other group felt their responsibility was to help the individual prisoner who had been unfairly convicted or badly treated in prison, even if his case was unique.

In the library field I think we have the same dichotomy. The librarian on the job in prison is responsible to his individual patron, the prisoner. If he becomes so involved in changing the system that he pays scant attention to prisoners, they will suffer—and he will probably be out of a job once prison officials get wind of his activities. Pressing for major changes is the job of organizations set up within the library profession. Such organizations could support the prison librarian (just as the ALA Intellectual Freedom Committee supports a librarian in trouble over a censorship issue). Since its members would not be employees of the prison system, they would be freer, both as library advisors to prison officials and, if necessary, as their adversary.

Prison Library Committees

The work now being done by the

American Association of Law Librarians, the ACA's Committee for the Provision of Legal Research Materials for Prisoners, and the AHIL Special Committee on Library Service to Jails are beginnings toward professional responsibility for law library services for prisoners. From this beginning we can expand to include more than prison and law librarians. National (and some state) prison library committees could be set up under our major organizations. One section, devoted to law libraries in prisons, could be subdivided to work in the following areas:

1) Training of prison law librarians in library schools: A committee that included faculty, prison administrators, prison librarians, law librarians, and other interested persons could set up suggested courses and perhaps seek funding for a pilot program at a willing library school.

2) Better librarians in prisons: Both a resource center for prison administrators in search of competent librarians with some legal training, and as pressure groups to protest sexual discrimination and other mistreatment of librarians in prisons.

3) Books and services for prison law libraries: The existing committees of the ACA and of law librarians seem suited to continue in this area.

4) City and county jails division: Working for legal services in this area, public librarians can play a major role. AHIL's leadership in this area can be expanded.

5) Watchdog of the prison library system: The group might function as a pressure group for needed legislation and as a Friend of the Court in cases that relate to law library services. The presence of an official library group watching over prison law libraries would have a beneficial effect on those libraries.

Not all librarians should or could become interested in prison legal libraries. A librarian with a social conscience, however, can go beyond his or her daily job to bring better library service to

people who need it. If our experience in the Bay Area Prison Task Force proves nothing else, it does show that an individual librarian, through his or her job, a professional organization, or a local group, can work for the provision of good library service to people who need it. And it can make a difference.

REFERENCES

1. *Habeas corpus*, literally "you have the body," a basic writ designed to enable the unlawfully incarcerated to obtain their freedom.

2. When *Gilmore* v. *Lynch* was reviewed by the U.S. Supreme Court, the case's name became *Younger* v. *Gilmore*, because Evelle Younger had succeeded Thomas Lynch as Attorney General. But it was *text of Gilmore* v. *Lynch* which the High Court affirmed unanimously.

3. Prepared by the Committee on Institutional Libraries of the American Prison Association.

4. Cohen, Morris. "Reading Law in Prison," *The Prison Journal* (Pennsylvania Prison Society), Spring-Summer 1968; O. James Werner, "Law Library Service to Prisoners—The Responsibility of Non-Prison Libraries," *Law Library Journal*, May 1970. See also Herman C. Spector, "A Librarian Looks at Writ Writing," *California Law Review*, April 1968, for a description of a San Quentin librarian's frustration when jailhouse lawyers monopolized the 32 seats in his library.

5. This list is scheduled for publication in *Law Library Journal*.

6. For a copy of the transcript, "Prison Legal Libraries: Idea into Reality," write to: Prison Law Library Conference, University of California, School of Librarianship, Berkeley, Calif. 94720. The book also includes a list of proposals for prison law library service made by Cy Silver, California State Law Librarian, for the Conference.

7. Copies of the SRRT Brief can be ordered for $1, postpaid from C. MacLeod, 2838 Woolsey St., Berkeley, Calif. 94705.

8. The text of "Grievances of the Tombs Inmates" appears in *Struggle for Justice: A Report on Crime and Punishment in America*, prepared by the American Friends Service Committee, New York (Hill & Wang, 1971).

9. For example, see the following articles, all of which appeared in *Library Journal*:

Brother Ignatius, "Had You Thought of County Jail Libraries?" February 15, 1946, p. 252; J. W. Kling, "Books Behind Bars," July 1967, p. 2488; and Opirare, Porter, and Reed, "Breaking Into Jail: Setting Up a Library in the County Jail," September 15, 1971, p. 2734.

Legal Citations to Cases Mentioned in the Article:

Gideon v. *Wainwright*: 372 U.S. 335, (1963).

Johnson v. *Avery*: 393 U.S. 483 (1969).

Gilmore v. *Lynch*: 319 F Supp. 105 (N.D. Cal. 1970).

Younger v. *Gilmore*: -US-, 30 Lawyer's Edit. 2nd 142, 92 SC -1971.

Brenneman v. *Madigan*: 343 F. Supp. 128 (1972).

II
Women
and
Minorities

A Healthy Anger

Helen Lowenthal

AS LIBRARIANS, we pride ourselves on our understanding of freedom—intellectual freedom, personal freedom, political freedom. We point with pride to *Portnoy's Complaint* and *Soul on Ice* on our shelves; with equal pride we point to publications of the Birch Society and the DAR. We are pleased that our liberalism gives readers a choice in the literature they read. We shudder at the thought of a library which expresses a single point of view, for certainly all freedom rests on the freedom of choice.

Women's liberation aspires to exactly that: the freedom of choice and equality of opportunity. As women, we are restricted in choosing careers, life styles, and behavior. We are channeled into the roles that we must play as women, and deviancy from these roles is considered abnormal behavior. Women who choose to step out of their traditional roles are branded "unfeminine" and must suffer the consequences of abnormal behavior. Men, too, suffer from being forced into restrictive roles, but the suffering of men is the suffering of the master who is chained to the slave: both are bound, but the conditions of their bondage are different.

Nowhere is woman's inequality and her lack of choice more plainly evident than in librarianship, the profession which claims such a profound understanding of freedom. Many a woman librarian is smug in the knowledge that her professional colleagues are predominantly women. Her smugness and contentedness have no foundation. Perhaps she ought to address a few questions to herself:

Why did she select librarianship as a career?

What were her options and how free was her choice?

Why are there so many women librarians?

Once she "chose" librarianship, how free was she to choose her position in the hierarchy of the field?

Once she reached her level of competency (woman's progress is usually halted before the Peter principle applies), was she rewarded on an equal basis with men in salary, recognition, and attitudes towards her?

When I was ready to graduate from college, my parents asked me what I was going to do. I replied that I did not know, but that I was *not* going to teach. Aghast, they asked, "Well then, what *are* you going to do?" So it goes with daughters. From the time we are born we are channeled into teaching, nursing, social work, and librarianship. For some reason, I was not expected to become a

71

doctor, lawyer, or college professor, as were all of the boys I grew up with.

Women are handicapped psychologically in that society's expectations for them are lower than they are for men. In those rare cases when a woman decides that she wants to enter the "male" professions, she is not patted on the back as are her male counterparts. We women confront raised eyebrows: "Won't you feel bad taking up a man's place in medical school?" and "Won't that interfere with marriage?" With no outside encouragement, we develop a "nigger mentality" and decide that we don't really want the prestigious positions anyway. We shuffle along, contented with serving others selflessly and stifling the urge to serve ourselves. I firmly believe that people cannot adequately satisfy others until they are satisfied with themselves. As women, we are the living denial of this statement.

So we choose librarianship, firm in the belief that we were meant to help others. If we are not helping our children and husbands, we are helping the public. If altruism is such an important quality in furthering social progress, why haven't more men entered the service professions? Why are these professions comprised predominantly of women?

Perhaps in librarianship it is because recruitment takes place on two different levels, one for each sex. Women are equal, but they are separate. This acts in the interest of women as well as it did of blacks before *Brown vs. the Board of Education.* In any hierarchy, by definition, there are fewer individuals at the top and more at the bottom. I maintain that women are recruited for the bottom and men for the top, and that this fact explains the disproportionate number of women in the field.

The appeal in recruiting women to librarianship is not only to our helping, serving-others, maternal "instincts" (instincts we are *taught* from the day we are born), but also to our "housewife" qualities. Those of us in public services

play mother to our patrons and those in technical services "keep house" within our institutions. Melvil Dewey admitted it: "The natural qualities most important in a library are accuracy, order (or what we call the housekeeping instinct)" and "executive ability . . ."[1]

Mr. Dewey mentioned executive ability as a librarian's quality. If we are looking for men in the hierarchy of librarianship, we would be advised to look to the top. Considering the percentage of men in librarianship, they overwhelmingly dominate the executive, administrative positions in the field. The higher we look, the more men we see. There are a number of studies which bear out this fact, and casual observation affirms their statistics.

In a 1968 thesis, Ben Bradley studied the characteristics of heads of the 50 largest academic and 50 largest public libraries, based on volume count. Of the public library heads, 86 percent were male, and *all* of the academic library heads were male.[2] Are we to believe that in the academic library field, two-thirds of which is female, there were no qualified women to fill any of those positions?

In *Esquire,* April 1964, an article entitled "Young Man, Be a Librarian" claims, "Most of the top jobs in the profession want male librarians to fill them as the running of library systems in most large urban areas of the nation is truly big business." Adrian Paradis tells us that "Men fill most of the top administrative posts . . ."[3] It's no secret. Men are the patricians and women the plebians in library science. With their Y-chromosomes, men inherit the top seats in the field; they are the aristocracy, the chosen few.

And we shuffle along and say, "But I really don't want to be an administrator. I truly enjoy doing the less prestigious work." This may again be a result of our nigger mentality or it may just be the absolute truth, but in either case we must realize that *we have not had a choice.* We frequently complain about the way things are being run, but we dare not aspire to taking over administrative positions. After all, everyone knows how level-headed and practical men are and how emotional and impractical women are. There are exceptions, of course, but we women know our place—at the bottom of the hierarchy.

Even if the library field placed fewer restrictions on women's ability to rise to the top, the restrictions imposed by society and our culture would have to be confronted.

Because of the lack of geographic mobility of the professional married woman, she cannot follow the opportunities in her field but must make the most of those that exist wherever she happens to be. Such a situation leads to exploitation . . . She will, for she must, accept conditions that her male counterpart would not . . . though this sort of exploitation often occurs with the knowledge and even with the approval of the woman, it impedes her professional advancement and hence increases the likelihood that she will find herself in a situation where she is superior—in ability, training, or seniority—to the requirements of her job and to the men classified as her equals or even as her immediate superiors.[4]

So we find women in their subjunctive role. Now, given "our place," how are we regarded and how are we treated by people within the profession and those outside it?

The librarian image is nothing new to any of us. The outside world stereotypes us as either effeminate males or old-maid, bookish females. In either case we are far from filling the ideal sexual roles that society and Madison Avenue dictate we should strive for. Women are supposed to be married; when little girls are asked what they want to be when they grow up, the answer is inevitably "a mother," and this presupposes marriage. Although we are allowed to be intelligent—or rather, "educated"—we should not be more intelligent than our

male counterparts. As any popular woman's magazine will tell us, the main reason we should pursue knowledge and broaden our horizons is so that we will be more interesting or helpful to men. Imagine a wife telling her husband to take a course so she'll find him more interesting!

Far worse than the treatment the outside world gives us is the total lack of recognition and respect from within the profession. When we enter the field, we are aware of the former, but the latter is hard to accept.

Anita Schiller's study of academic librarians' salaries indicated that in that group the median salary for men was $1500 more than that of women, and furthermore, as these librarians grow older, acquire more experience, and move further up the hierarchy, the gap widens.[5] These are examples of attitudes towards women expressed in dollars. There are other reflections of these attitudes.

My experiences in library school abound with instances of male chauvinism, a term that we in the women's liberation movement use when a person—of either sex—builds up the male ego at the expense of the female ego. (Strange, how the words "female ego" seem foreign on the tongue.)

At Simmons, where 84 percent of the students were female, only about one-third of the voting faculty was female, and neither of the two top administrators was female.

At an alumni function I attended, the entire head table was male, except for one woman, who was at least 50 years old. When the man at the microphone introduced her, he referred to her as the only "girl" at the table. His calling her a girl was vaguely reminiscent of a white person calling a 60-year-old black man "boy."

In library school courses where we used the case method, competent library administrators or promising young library students are consistently depicted as men, whereas the women are described as crotchety, conservative, and eccentric. And the worst part of these indignities is our unawareness that they exist. How subtle are the forces that elevate man's dignity above woman's and convince us that this is how things should be! What a brainwashing job has been done!

Who is to blame for the inequality and partiality towards men we see in our profession and in our culture? Men, women, the ruling powers in the profession (whoever they may be), the family unit which forces women to choose between a career and marriage are some possible scapegoats. But no amount of scapegoating will correct the situation. What are the positive steps we can take to correct such a deep-seated problem?

First, we must be aware of what is happening. How can we be free to choose a way of life if we are not aware of all possible choices? Up to now we have believed when we have been told that women must act in a certain way and men in another. We have not questioned; we have, nodding and smiling, accepted what we were told. We have clutched our femininity and masculinity as a child clutches its security blanket. What is femininity if not a set of attitudes and behavior, inculcated by sinister but effective brainwashing techniques, which give us security and limit our freedom to behave in other ways? How many of our feminine trappings are inherent in our biological makeup and how many are conditioned? We must challenge old assumptions at every step of the way and expand our consciousness enough to reject invalid assumptions about the traditional male and female roles.

Second, we must not be afraid of developing a healthy anger at situations and individuals which help perpetuate the inequalities in the sex roles. "Let it all hang out." We must not be afraid of

being mocked for daring to believe that we are entitled to more than we are getting. Mockery is the male-dominated society's strongest weapon. By refusing to take us seriously, our mockers totally negate our worth. There is nothing funny about the black man's getting a smaller piece of the pie than the white man; no less funny is this similar discrimination against women.

Finally, and most important, as women we must drastically change our attitudes about ourselves and cast off our nigger mentality. We must reassess our capabilities and try to win back what has been taken from us. We can no longer accept "You're a woman" as a reason for being shortchanged. Our choices in all areas of life have to be at least as free as those of our male counterparts. We must ally with other women rather than compete with them. Women across the country are uniting and discovering common problems and common angers. The most oppressive force we must face in liberating ourselves is not at home, nor at work, but in our minds.

REFERENCES
1. Dewey, Melvil. *Librarianship as a Profession for College-Bred Women.* Boston, Library Bureau, 1886.
2. Bradley, Ben W. *A Study of the Characteristics, Qualifications and Succession Patterns of Heads of Large U.S. Academic and Public Libraries.* Thesis, U. of Texas, M.L.S., 1968.
3. Paradis, Adrian A. *Librarians; Careers in Library Service.* Mckay, 1959.
4. Bailyn, Lotte. "Notes on the Role of Choice in the Psychology of Professional Women." *Daedalus,* Spring 1964, p. 700-10.
5. Schiller, Anita R. "Academic Librarians' Salaries," *College and Research Libraries,* March 1969, p. 101-11.

Women in Academic Libraries

Helen W. Tuttle

IS THERE discrimination against women in academic libraries? Yes, there *is* discrimination against women in academic libraries—in terms of equal pay for equal work and in terms of opportunities for advancement. After 30 years in academic libraries, I know by experience that there is discrimination. Everybody knows it, and I suspect we know it more strongly the longer we've worked in libraries. Anita Schiller's findings didn't surprise us. (Remember that her research was specifically in the academic library context.) In her article "The Disadvantaged Majority" (*American Libraries*, April 1970, p. 345-49) she verified the observations which we all had made: namely, that women in libraries make up a majority of the professional personnel (four out of every five being female); that women are paid less than men; that top positions in the large and influential institutions go increasingly to men; and that there appears to be a growing trend toward greater inequality between the sexes in the profession.

The financial inequality was confirmed by the salary survey of ALA members made late last year and reported in *American Libraries*, April, p. 409-17. Schiller found that in 1966-67, among professional personnel in aca-

demic libraries, the median salary for men was about $1500 higher than that for women. The ALA survey found among the same category of librarians in 1970-71 that the average salary for men was higher than that for women by $3,597.

No, Anita's thesis should not have surprised anyone. At ALA conferences, if you drift by the meeting of the Association of Research Libraries in the late afternoon when the door is open, you will see the group holding the top 75 or so research library jobs in the country relaxing with glasses in their hands. I understand that one or two females have the right to be there, but with the increasingly colorful male dress it's getting harder to spot any. In spite of an occasional female president, ACRL tends to lean toward male domination. Since the ALA reorganization in 1957, ACRL has had five different executive secretaries. All have been men. Its journal, *College and Research Libraries*, has never had a female editor. In fact, of the present nine editors and editorial board members who guide the destinies of that periodical, nine are males.

Actually, women in academic libraries tend to be a disadvantaged group. That is, on many campuses librarians are considered to be para-academics, people who work alongside the faculty but don't reach the faculty level. Some directors of academic libraries sincerely believe that librarians should not have academic status. I would be more comfortable with their sincerity if it were not true that in most such cases the director is the exception and has academic status himself. You notice that I said *himself.* I could reasonably have said *herself* 75 years ago. Not today.

Although the Schiller findings didn't surprise anyone, they are useful in several ways: they make it impossible to refute the existence of the problem; they provide factual proof of the extent of the problem; they will in the future furnish us with data for measuring progress in solving the problem; and most important, they push us ahead to the more useful consideration—how can the problem be solved?

In discussing the problem, I find it impossible to remain inside the library context. Discrimination against women in almost every field of endeavor except homemaking (you've got to admit that we have *that* field sewed up) cannot be usefully discussed in terms of academic libraries only. The situation in all libraries is simply a reflection of the total situation. All aspects of society have to be re-examined and readjusted if women are to become whole and happy individuals while following their intellectual bents. Like all disadvantaged groups, women are asking to be evaluated as individual human beings with unique abilities and limitations that should be used as creatively as possible. This is not an impossible goal. Throughout March and April, I served two days a week on the Mercer County Grand Jury. The group of 23 jurors, characterized by an earnest desire to arrive at just decisions, was not polarized along sexual lines. Indeed, I can't tell you offhand how many males and females were on it. What I can tell you is how the group lined up along a liberal-conservative axis. On the far right there were three persons; on the far left, two. The rest were in between at various intervals, not

always clearly defined. It was beautiful to work in such a context, where sex did not enter into consideration. Had there been only one or two female members of the jury, their contributions would have tended to be equated with the "feminine point of view." But with a fairly even mix, we were all just people.

How can women develop this unprejudiced climate for all of their activities outside the home? Recently, I asked someone about the authority of a new governing body added to the Princeton University Community. I was told in effect that it would define its own authority through its own actions, by the way it developed. It was a new idea to me, but I began to see that public bodies do indeed develop in that way.

Women must do the same thing. They can define their roles and assume authority as far as they believe in their own potential and ability. Is it reasonable to think that men will step aside and provide top administrative jobs for women in a fair proportion to the number of women in libraries? Time has shown that this is not the way it will happen. Our own attitude toward ourselves—isn't that the single most important factor in determining the attitude of others toward us?

I'm sure you will agree with me that women's position in our culture is not the result of one person or one biological condition or one group of people. The first general point I want to make, then, is that women are one of the chief architects of today's situation, that women must change their own attitudes and activities before they can change the attitudes of others.

I want to make a second point. Men are victims of this social error of discrimination against women, too, just as the white race is a victim of the discrimination against the black. When women are not permitted to be whole persons, men lose in all their relationships to them—as son, brother, husband, father, and friend. The breadwinner and final-authority stereotype imprisons the male, too. Too many women have been conditioned to grow up thinking of themselves primarily as a function, not an individual. When they realize that they can have the best of both the home world and the outside world, it will be a better world for everyone. I want to enlarge on that.

May I be personal for a moment? My husband has always been supportive of my career. He's back there encouraging and pushing me much of the time. He never complains about my 90 percent absorption in my profession. This is all part of his attitudes toward people and justice, which I consider to be ideal.

But one thing about him used to bother me. I realized that he would not want to be a woman. This implied that it was somehow "better" to be a man. This realization used to float to the top of my consciousness from time to time and annoy me. I'd cast it adrift, and it would move off for a while.

Finally, I picked it up and examined it and attacked it by asking myself if *I* would want to be a man. The answer was an emphatic *no.* I've always envied men their short hair and their flat, practical shoes. (When this paper was given at the SRRT luncheon during the New Jersey Library Association Spring Conference last May, Moderator Arthur Curley added a bit of information, pointing out that this particular female reaction is known as pedal envy.) But beyond that I couldn't possibly do many of the things men do.

Consider for a moment the My Lai incident and the trial of Lt. Calley related to it. The judge was male. The jury was male. The defendant was male. The witnesses were males. The attorneys were males.

The only role women played in that affair was that of victim. Think about it.

Many men look forward all year to their vacations. And what do some of them do? They spend them killing living things. Can you imagine looking forward all year to two weeks spent killing? I love to go to the woods and am excited when I can surprise small creatures going about their business. But *kill* them? Kill for *pleasure?* Incredible!

Can you imagine yourself hitting someone in a boxing match? Can you imagine yourself in Vietnam—or in any other war zone—bayoneting an enemy? Can you imagine yourself going to Vietnam, creating a child there, and leaving it to grow up under impossible conditions, which you had helped produce? Can you imagine yourself in My Lai shooting unarmed villagers? Can you imagine yourself sending someone else to do those things?

I can't. If you agree that you also could not, then *we*—women—are the people who should be involved in the decisions which lead to such activities so that we could keep them from happening.

In *Fortune,* February, p. 135, there is an appalling article by Tom Alexander entitled "There Are Sex Differences in the Mind, Too." But at the end the author says one encouraging thing, which is: "The importance of men's special traits may be on the decline. Aggression, preoccupation with technology, even competitive ambition itself seem to be counting for less and less as our society matures. Conversely, the especially feminine qualities of nurturance and concern for people may be assuming more importance in a society threatened with disintegration." Someday men will catch up with us, but only if we actively help them.

Getting down to the practical, action level, I want to suggest two areas in which I think efforts would have results which we want to see. Number one: Getting back to libraries, I would like to see women who are professional librarians take their careers as seriously as men, specifically their husbands, do.

Academic librarianship is a good profession in which to do this. Time and again, I have seen an unusually able female librarian ignore her own professional advancement to follow her husband on his quest for his advancement. I do not suggest that spouses should go their separate ways. I suggest that there should be an understanding from the beginning that the partnership called marriage will be a better relationship if both partners have meaningful careers which permit both to develop fully. Campuses are fine places for women to have independent careers while enjoying the advantages of family life. Two independent careers can be pursued on many campuses, and moves to new campuses can be restricted to those which would benefit both parents in the family without unduly restricting professional advancement for either.

Librarians are asked frequently to suggest candidates for top jobs in the library world. I always try to think of women to suggest. It's a little difficult because the supply of experienced, middle-management women is limited. I believe that the primary cause of this situation is that too many women choose to give their husbands' careers top priority. I believe that such self-sacrifice in the long run will recoil on the sacrificer, the sacrificee, and all the little sacrificants.

Area number two is a matter of semantics. Some words in common usage, not surprisingly, support the idea that men are superior to women and play the dominant role in human affairs. It would be useful if such words in the language could be replaced. What is needed is a group of impersonal pronouns and articles, words which mean human being without reference to a specific sex. With today's language, in order to refer to the generalized individual, we must say "he." Thus we're already at a disadvantage.

We can't say *it*—that's nonhuman. We can't say *she*—that's subhuman. We must say *he* to make the referral to a human being.

What about the word *mankind?* Shouldn't it be *humankind?*

The phrase *human being* could replace *man* as the generic term, but the two-word term is awkward. Ms., replacing Miss and Mrs., is a step in the direction we need. It's only half a step, unfortunately, since it is useful only in written communications. When we speak, we still must specify Mrs. or Miss. So let's get ALA to join forces with an appropriate group such as the Modern Language Association to add new words to the language which will permit us to include all human beings in our generalized statements without suggesting male domination.

To summarize, I'm suggesting two practical activities designed to move toward equality for women, one a group activity and one an individual activity. As a group, clean up language usage which suggests male superiority, and as individuals, each woman act like a responsible professional in developing her own career.

Lest I be accused of discriminating against men in libraries, I want to end by reassuring them. In academic libraries, we do *not* want to eliminate men from librarianship. We simply want to teach them to take minutes, to type, and to make coffee.

The Legal Status of Women

Kay Ann Cassell

I RECENTLY read the case study on married women in Kenneth Shaffer's article "Decision Making" (*LJ*, May 15, p. 1677-80), in which he stated that married women with families were unreliable employees. His statements surprised me since I had naively assumed that such attitudes were dying or at least were no longer being openly stated. But stereotypes of women employees die hard, and even the director of a library school hasn't gotten the message yet. Then where do women start to fight their case and change the picture of employment opportunities? I personally opt for the legal front as the first step.

Diane B. Schulder wrote in a recent article that "law is a reflection and a source of prejudice. It both enforces and suggests forms of bias." [1] The United States and many other countries have a tradition of sex-based legislation. These laws reflect societal attitudes towards women, and the extent to which they remain indicates present opinions on women's role in our society. Changes in the law do not bring about instantaneous changes in attitudes or behavior. But it seems likely that in the case of sex discrimination legal and attitudinal changes will proceed at about the same rate—each supporting and reinforcing the other.

With the 19th Amendment in 1920, women got the right to vote, but they are still trying to achieve equality under the law. Theoretically the U.S. Constitution grants equality to women. The 14th Amendment provides that no state shall "deprive any person of life, liberty or property without due process of law; nor deny to any person within its jurisdiction the equal protection of the laws." The federal government is similarly restricted from interfering with these individual rights under the "due process clause" of the Fifth Amendment.

But even with these amendments women have been largely unsuccessful in challenging the constitutionality of discriminatory laws. The President's Task Force on Women's Rights and Responsibilities noted in its report issued in April 1970:

It is ironic that the basic rights women seek through this amendment are guaranteed all citizens under the Constitution. The applicability of the Fifth and 14th Amendments in parallel cases involving racial bias has been repeatedly tested and sustained . . . The Supreme Court, however, has thus far not accorded the protection of those amendments to female citizens. It has upheld or refused to review laws and practices making discriminatory distinctions based on sex. [2]

In the 1908 U.S. Supreme Court case of *Muller vs. Oregon* which challenged the validity of an Oregon law limiting the hours of work for female factory employees to ten hours a day, the Court stated:

> The two sexes differ in structure of body, in the functions to be performed by each, in the amount of physical strength, the capacity for long-continued labor . . . the self-reliance which enables one to assert full rights, and in the capacity to maintain the struggle for subsistence. This difference justifies a difference in legislation . . . [3]

This trend has continued down to the present day. In 1961 a Florida law providing that a woman not be called for jury service unless she registers with the clerk of court her desire to serve was held not violative of the 14th Amendment.[4] In 1968, the Court upheld different treatment of men and women for purposes of computing social security benefits, stating that "the trend of authority makes it clear that the variation in amounts of retirement benefits based upon differences in the attributes of men and women is constitutionally valid."[5] The recent case of *Phillips vs. Martin Marietta Corporation* was the first test of Title VII of the Civil Rights Act. In this case a Florida court had ruled that an employer who hires women but refuses to consider mothers of preschool children, while hiring fathers of preschool children for the same job, does not violate the 1964 Civil Rights Act prohibition against sex discrimination in employment.[6] This ruling was reversed by the Supreme Court, who ruled that employers cannot refuse to hire women solely because they have young children unless fathers of such children are also denied jobs. However, the Supreme Court sent back to the lower court for a ruling on whether parenthood, if more relevant for women than for men, is a bona fide occupational qualification.[7] Thus the Phillips case is at best only a partial victory.

For 48 years women have been trying to get an Equal Rights Amendment passed by Congress. This amendment would in one swift act make unconstitutional a variety of state and federal laws which discriminate against women. The Amendment states: "Equality of rights under the law shall not be denied or abridged by the United States or any state on account of sex." It is badly needed because of the numerous sex-based laws that still exist and the lack of favorable Supreme Court decisions. Recent attempts to pass the Amendment have been halted by amendments to the bill, and its future remains uncertain.

One of the most crucial areas of discrimination is employment. It is the one that most concerns professional librarians since it is here that laws must be strengthened if we are to combat salary and promotional discrimination against women. Two acts passed within a year of each other jointly provided the initial steps in this area. The Equal Pay Act of 1963 provides for equal pay for equal work regardless of sex within a given establishment, but professional employees are not as yet covered by this act. It has been suggested that an amendment be added to this bill to include professional, executive, and administrative positions. This would be most useful to librarians in larger library systems.

Title VII of the 1964 Civil Rights Act covers private employers and labor organizations engaged in industries affecting interstate commerce as well as employment agencies. It declares that it "shall be an unlawful employment practice" for a covered employer, because of race, color, religion, sex, or national origin to:

> 1) fail or refuse to hire or to discharge any individual, or otherwise to discriminate against any individual with respect to his compensation, terms, conditions or privileges of employment . . . or
> 2) limit, segregate or classify his employees in any way which would deprive or tend to deprive any individual of employment opportunities or otherwise adversely affect his status as an employee . . . [8]

The law, however, exempts from coverage religious educational institutions and employees of an educational or a religious institution who further the educational or religious activities of such an institution; it also does not cover state and local government employees. Employers with less than 25 employees are also exempt. Furthermore, the law allows for exemptions where "religion, sex or national origin is a bona fide occupational qualification reasonably necessary to the normal operation of that particular business or enterprise."[9]

Title VII is weak because of the large number of exemptions it allows and because of its inadequate enforcement provisions. The Equal Employment Opportunity Commission (EEOC) is charged with investigating cases of discrimination brought to its attention and is directed to try to bring about voluntary compliance whenever possible. The EEOC has no enforcement powers but may refer a case of noncompliance to the Attorney General. The EEOC cannot investigate if the alleged unfair employment practices are potentially subject to redress under state or local law. Because of this situation Title VII places the main burden of enforcement on the individual complainant who must first bring a case of discrimination to the attention of the EEOC and then wait for the EEOC to investigate and try to gain voluntary compliance. If this procedure does not prove fruitful, the individual may have to bring a private lawsuit. In its 1970 report the President's Task Force on Women's Rights and Responsibilities recommended that the EEOC be given the power to enforce the law.[10] H. 1746 was introduced this year and would provide for such powers. Unfortunately the many exceptions to Title VII mean that many librarians are not covered under the present law.

Title VII has not rectified the many state protective laws which regulate employment for women. These protective laws vary from state to state and often regulate the number of hours a woman may work, the amount of weight she may lift, and the occupations in which she may be employed. Ten states have laws limiting the amount of weight a woman may lift while no state limits the number of hours a man may work. There are 38 states that limit the number of hours a woman may work while only three states limit the number of hours both men and women may work. There are 18 states that have laws concerning nightwork for women yet none that regulate nightwork for men.[11] Actually these laws work against both men and women. Men tend to be hired because they can be paid less and women lose out in the number of jobs available to them.

When these protective laws were passed, this legislation was badly needed. But today these laws hinder more than help women. Women cannot work at night when the pay is often higher, and they are restricted from some occupations. For instance, in some states they may work as waitresses but not as bartenders, who usually receive higher wages. Often women are not promoted because the new job will require overtime and the state law does not allow it. On the other hand, only 35 states have equal pay laws[12]; 37 states have mandatory fair employment practices laws; but only 21 prohibit discrimination based on sex.[13] Ironically a very important protection which is a guarantee of employment security while absent from a job for childbirth has not been provided for under the law in any state.

In August 1969 the EEOC issued guidelines indicating that "state laws restricting the employment of women are superseded by Title VII and, accordingly, do not justify the refusal to employ women. Two federal district courts which had occasion to consider the matter adopted the EEOC's approach."[14] Yet most states continue to enforce their protective laws.

Many librarians will also be assisted by Executive Order 11246 as amended by Executive Order 11375 which prohibits discrimination on the basis of sex by federal contractors and subcontractors and on federally assisted construction projects. The Women's Equity Action League (WEAL) has brought suits against a number of universities for discriminatory practices. Women in university libraries could pursue cases through WEAL. Libraries receiving LSCA funding can also be sued under this Executive Order.

Sex laws are often cited when someone discusses sex-based legal discrimination. A few examples will perhaps suggest the problems inherent in these laws. Abortion laws have been the focus of many recent attempts at legislative reform. But even with recent reforms only ten states allow abortions to protect both the physical and mental health of the woman and only 11 states allow abortions in rape cases. Most states still permit abortions only to save the life of the mother.[15]

In most states prostitution laws provide direct punishment only for the woman. There is, in fact, usually no direct punishment for the male who patronizes the prostitute. Although there are often in theory laws under which men may be punished, they are rarely used.

The statutory rape laws are designed to protect the woman, and they usually provide for prosecution when the minor in a rape case is female. However, only a few states have penalties for rape cases in which a male minor is engaged in sexual relations with an adult woman. The age of consent for the female varies greatly from state to state—from 14 to 21 years old. Some state laws even distinguish between cases in which the female was or was not chaste at the time of the act. In general, the state laws concerning sex vary greatly and are primarily based on societal attitudes as to the role of the female and male.

Married women bear the brunt of sex-based discrimination. It is ironic that the law indicates that a married woman by virtue of being married is less able to take care of herself than are single women, divorcees, and widows.

Discrimination for the married woman begins when she must give up her maiden name and assume her husband's name. Although most women probably wish to assume their husband's name, those who wish to retain their maiden name cannot legally do so. In fact, American judicial decisions have denied women's requests to retain their maiden name. This is not uniformly the pattern even throughout the Western world where Danish and French women may retain their maiden name both by custom and law.

In our increasingly mobile society the question of a married woman's domicile has become more important. "In effect, a domicile is the place where a person lives and has his true permanent home, to which, whenever he is absent, he has an intention of returning."[16] Many rights and privileges of citizenship depend on a person's domicile, such as the right to vote, to hold and run for public office, to receive welfare assistance, and to qualify for free tuition at state-operated educational institutions.[17] Men and unmarried women have a free choice of domicile, but married women do not. If a married woman chooses to live in a different state from that of her husband, many of her rights and privileges as a citizen may be lost to her. Only five states permit married women to have a separate domicile for all purposes although 42 permit her a separate domicile if she is living apart from her husband for cause.[18]

Although women are tried by juries for crimes in every state in the United States, until recently three states did not allow women to serve on juries. Even today only 28 states permit women to serve on the same terms as men.[19] In other states, such as Florida which I mentioned earlier, special rules apply only to women.

Starting in 1839 each state passed Married Women's Acts which granted women most of the following rights: to contract, to sue and be sued, to manage and control property brought with them to marriage, to engage in gainful employment without their husband's permission and to retain these earnings.[20] Yet pockets of discrimination still exist.

In ten states a married woman's contractual capacity is restricted, and in five states a wife cannot make a valid conveyance of real property unless she is joined by her husband. In other states women are limited in their right to serve in a position of trust and in their right to sue or be sued in their own name. In California and Nevada married women must follow a formal procedure of obtaining court approval to engage in independent business.

Control of property is another important area of discrimination. Four of the eight community property states permit the husband to have exclusive rights to manage and control community property even if money is contributed by the wife. In the 42 common law states, if a husband is the sole wage earner, he is free to manage, control, and dispose of the savings without consulting his wife. These laws fail to take into account the services performed by a wife who does not work outside the home.

To rectify this situation the 1963 President's Commission on the Status of Women recommended that each spouse should have joint rights in the earnings of the other and in their management and control.[21] The new Texas law is one of the first to rectify this situation; it states that "each spouse shall have sole management, control and disposition of that community property which he or she would have owned if a single person."[22]

Divorce and alimony laws discriminate against both men and women. Although the situation has greatly improved, various states still have discriminatory divorce laws. Twelve jurisdictions allow wives to divorce husbands upon showing that the latter has failed to fulfill obligations of family support, but few permit husbands a divorce for the same reason.[23] In Alabama a wife may divorce her husband if he is addicted to drugs, but the reverse situation is not grounds for divorce. Kentucky still has a law which allows a husband to divorce a wife for a single act of adultery, but the wife does not have the same right. Several states allow a husband to divorce his wife if she is pregnant at the time of their marriage, but they do not allow a wife to divorce her husband if he caused another woman to become pregnant prior to the marriage. (The man could be sued and forced to provide support for the illegitimate child.) An unwritten law in many states allows the husband to kill a man caught in the act of having sexual intercourse with the accuser's wife, but the wife does not have a similar right!

The alimony situation is bound up with the very complicated laws of support. Basically the law provides that the burden of financial support in a marriage shall fall on the man. This burden of support has been extended to alimony laws. Only 14 states permit alimony for husbands although seven states hold the wife liable for support if the grounds for divorce were mental illness.[24] Alimony has often been given because it was thought that the husband should continue to support his wife without considering the woman's ability to support herself. Many people now think that alimony should be based on need and should be given to either spouse.

Legal discrimination is endless, and every person faces some forms of this discrimination. Librarians as professionals are most affected by employment laws, yet other laws affect them daily in their public and private lives. I highly recommend Leo Kanowitz's *Women and the Law* for more information on this subject.

Women have been the largest number of workers in the library profession for many years. Yet even with their large number, men have often been in the positions of power and prestige. In recent years an increasing number of men have entered the profession. This influx of men has certainly improved the overall level of library salaries. But it was alarming to see the recent ALA salary survey which reaffirmed our previous information that the gap between men and women's salaries are widening. It revealed a $2,591 gap between men and women with M.L.S. degrees, a $4,157 gap between men and women with

Ph.D.'s, and a $4,944 gap between men and women administrators.[25]

Men have risen swiftly to administrative positions as capable women administrators have retired. Statistics show that men are about twice as likely as women to be chief librarians.[26] We know, for instance, that only four of the 74 largest college and university libraries have women directors[27] and that only three of the 26 cities with a population of 500,000 or more have women directors. Library schools as well as libraries discriminate against women. In 1969 only nine library schools were headed by a woman, and two of these were women's colleges. Only a third of the professorships at accredited library schools are held by women.

These patterns of discrimination will not be changed easily. Librarians will have to become activists, as have other professional groups, if they are to change their situation. They must use the laws presently on the books to work for them, and they must assist women's groups that are lobbying for new and stronger laws. Compiling bibliographies will no longer be enough! The fronts of attack are many. Library schools must be more responsive to women. Administration courses are for both sexes, as are Ph.D. programs. Boards of trustees must look for the best qualified librarian for their library director position. Women are equally good administrators. It doesn't take a man to play politics and deal with city officials. Librarians must rid themselves of sex stereotypes in judging the abilities of other librarians. They must not always judge a good administrator in male terms nor a good children's librarian in female terms.

Attitudes as well as laws must change if we are to build a more humane society which will allow each individual to express him or herself on their own terms. The time to act is now, and I hope librarians will respond to the challenge.

REFERENCES

1. Sculder, Diane B. "Does the Law Oppress Women?" in Sisterhood Is Powerful; An Anthology of Writings from the Women's Liberation Movement. Vintage: Random, 1970, p. 139.

2. A Matter of Simple Justice; the Report of the President's Task Force on Women's Rights and Responsibilities. G.P.O., 1970, p. 4.
3. 208 U.S. 412, at 422 (1908).
4. Hoyt vs. Florida, 368 U.S. 57 (1961).
5. Gruenwald vs. Gardner, 390 F. 2d591, at 592-93 (1968).
6. 411 F. 2d 1 (C.A. 5).
7. New York Times, January 26, 1971, p. 1.
8. 78 Stat. 253, 42 U.S.C. §2000e-2(a).
9. Ibid., §2000e-2(e).
10. A Matter of Simple Justice. p. 6.
11. Ross, Susan Deller. "Sex Discrimination and 'Protective' Labor Legislation" in The "Equal Rights" Amendment; Hearings before the Subcommittee on Constitutional Amendments of the Committee on the Judiciary United States Senate. G.P.O., 1970, p. 396-97.
12. Ibid.
13. U.S. Department of Labor. Wage and Labor Standards Administration. Women's Bureau. Laws on Sex Discrimination in Employment. G.P.O., 1970, p. 3.
14. Pressman, Sonia. "Legal Revolution in Women's Employment Rights," Florida Bar Journal, June 1970, p. 334.
15. Association for the Study of Abortion, Inc. Analysis of Abortion Laws in the United States. 1969, p. 5-6.
16. Kanowitz, Leo. Women and the Law; The Unfinished Revolution. Univ. of New Mexico Pr., 1969. p. 46.
17. Ibid., p. 47.
18. Ibid., p. 48.
19. Bayh, Birch. in The "Equal Rights" Amendment; Hearings . . . , p. 5.
20. Kanowitz, p. 40.
21. "Report of the Civil and Political Rights Committee to the President's Commission on the Status of Women" in The "Equal Rights" Amendment; Hearings . . . . p. 238.
22. "Report of the Task Force on Family Law and Policy to the Citizens' Advisory Council on the Status of Women" in The "Equal Rights" Amendment; Hearings . . . . p. 147.
23. Kanowitz, p. 96.
24. Bayh, Birch. in The "Equal Rights" Amendment; Hearings . . . p. 5.
25. American Libraries, April 1971, p. 410-16.
26. Schiller, Anita. "The Disadvantaged Majority: Women Employed in Libraries," American Libraries, April 1970, p. 345.
27. _____. "The Widening Sex Gap." Library Journal, March 15, 1969, p. 1098.

Toward a Feminist Profession

Kathleen Weibel

REDEFINITION of the role and position of women in society has again become a major social movement. Parallelling the first wave of feminism which culminated in the right to vote, the "women's movement" has made its way from the organization of a small number of middle-class women to a broad based movement of women working in homes, industry, and offices, gay women, single parents, and others. Their rejection of traditional social, sexual, and economic dependencies has already made an impact on individuals, both male and female, and on the institutions of society. The future of this movement ranges from potentially revolutionary to mildly reformist, with the ever-present danger that a male dominated power structure may become female controlled but equally oppressive. The direction of the women's movement will not evolve in a vacuum; a host of factors will help shape it, including the condition of the economy, racism, and scientific discoveries. With this in mind, then, what is the impact of the women's movement on librarianship?

One might expect it to be considerable. Librarianship as a profession is 84 percent female (unless otherwise noted all figures are taken from the U.S. Bureau of Labor Statistics' *Library Manpower*).[1] If statistics were available on all those employed by libraries, the percentage of females would most probably be higher. To varying degrees, issues of the women's movement such as child care, role definition, equal pay and opportunity have become concerns of the institutions which define libraries: schools, colleges and universities, business, government, etc., as well as concerns of the constituencies served by these libraries. Executive orders and legislation on equal pay and opportunity have also had a direct impact on a number of libraries, including the Library of Congress.

On the other hand, libraries have not been noted for their quick institutional response to social movements. Within the profession itself, organized activity on the part of women came a bit later than in other professional or academic groups, including those such as nursing also dominated in number by women. Organized participation in the overall women's movement has not yet developed as a vigorous concern of the profession. No library defined group, for example, is listed among the 75 diverse organizations (American Nurses Association, National Gay Task Force, Hadassah, etc.) contributing to the creation of the U.S. National Women's Agenda.[2]

While discussion of women in librarianship and action on the issues raised by women have increased greatly in the last five years, knowledge of the status of women librarians and their impact on library service is still limited to scattered data and research, and opinion pieces such as this. Anita Schiller has culled a description of female librarians from the literature which most librarians can corroborate from individual experience: women do not predominate, in top administrative positions, in large libraries, or in the "status" branches of the profession. The salaries of women are generally lower than those of men, and the average salaries of the profession are generally lower than those of similar male dominated professions.[3] The role of women in the initial development of the field is currently being explored by Garrison, among others. Schiller points out that the profession has not considered women an appropriate concern for a directed research effort since 1904.

It is the purpose of this article to explore the future impact of the women's movement on librarianship with the year 2000, the upward boundary. Anyone reading the projections of futurists written as recently as five years ago known the pitfalls of this type of forecast. (Since cliches about our rapidly changing society are all too true.) Our limited knowledge of the position of women in librarianship and the factors determining it, coupled with the fluctuation and conflict within the women's movement, and the potential for backlash against women's liberation, complicate the precariousness of such predictions. But, since problems, trends, and questions can be identified and discussion generated from futuristic musings, I'm willing to take on the role of seer.

The women's movement has effected libriarianship primarily in matters relating to employment. The affect on services and the nature of the profession is more subtle, if it yet exists. Certainly this effect is more difficult to observe and measure than the more visible discrimination suits, for example, although the impact of such actions are also difficult to determine. Assuming that the women's movement continues at least at its current strength, its impact could be felt by librarianship in three general modes: 1) as *a women's profession* in which females make up the majority of the work force; 2) as *a feminized profession* with the "negative" connotations of characteristics labeled female such as passivity, emotionalism, and intuitiveness, 3) and as *a feminist profession* operating on a feminist value system wherein traditional roles based on sex and power are no longer extant and life choices and ability determine functions. Of the three areas, the last is the most speculative, but the most far-reaching in its implications.

Librarianship as a woman's profession has received more attention in the literature and limited data gathering than the other two. The problems of a feminized profession have also been discussed directly and in the many considerations of the profession's *image*. Little research has been done in this area. Librarianship as a feminist profession has received the least consideration although the newly formed Woman Library Workers seems to be attempting to grapple with it, as a "growing sisterhood of non-submissive, life affirming women who are committed to action programs in democratically run libraries."[4]

A women's profession
Once fields become established as men's or women's professions they are very hard to change. —Anita Schiller[5]

Librarianship will continue to include enough women to remain a women's profession during the next 25 years. Whether the percentage of women will equal or continue to surpass the percentage of men depends on a number of factors. Although men have been attracted to librarianship in growing numbers in recent years, a proportionate increase in the number of women entering the field has caused the percentage of females to drop only a few points. The ratio of men to women in the under 45 age group is higher, however, than in the total profession. As of this writing, 44 percent of all employed librarians are age 45 and over. Almost half the women in the profession are in this age group and are likely to retire during the next 25 years. The ratio of male to female librarians replacing this 44 percent of the profession, and in the under 45 age group now practicing, will determine the sex characteristic of the profession in the year 2000.

What the influence of the contracting job market on the entrance of men and women into the profession will be, is difficult to say. Fields such as engineering and law, which had previously not been overly receptive to women, are now actively recruiting and may very well draw women away from the traditional women's fields. Consideration of desexualization of role may also make men feel freer to enter the women's professions.

At the same time that librarianship is placing a growing emphasis on the hard sciences as undergraduate preparation, fields traditionally dominated by men, business, industry, and academe, actively seek women with these qualifications to meet affirmative action quotas. Librarianship may not be able to compete for these women as a career option, meaning that entrants into the profession with scientific preparation are even more likely to be men.

The question of people with advanced academic qualifications in other professions, the humanities, and social sciences, moving into librarianship due to job shortages in their own fields will probably have an influence, but it is difficult to suggest a direction in terms of sex in these fields. Interest in part-time work and job sharing currently voiced by both men and women, but usually associated with women, will influence the availability of positions and qualified women to fill them. The effect of re-entrants into the profession, who will probably be women, and drop outs who may be either male or female, must also be considered. A safe projection, then, is that librarianship will continue to be a women's profession although the percentage of women will drop below the present 84 percent mark.

Librarianship as a whole may remain a women's profession in 2000, but men may very well predominate in certain types of libraries, particularly academic where they now account for 44 percent of the professionals. Special and public libraries will also reflect a change in the male:female ratio, with special libraries possibly swinging toward balanced employment of men and women. Even in school libraries, where women dominate in numbers greater than their percentage of the total profession, men may make considerable inroads. Projection by type of library must take into account growth possibilities in each type. Enrollments in elementary and high schools, for example, are expected to pick up during the 1980s and to drop in higher academic institutions during this period. Whether more men or women will move into the school library field where jobs should be more plentiful is an open question.

Staffing of the various library functions will also reflect the change in the numbers of men in the profession. In the case of administration, the push towards equal opportunity may counterbalance the projected increase in the number of males. Certainly it has already been an acknowledged factor in restructuring of procedures used to fill positions and in the actual filling of some jobs. It is safe to say that we will probably see more women administrators in the traditionally male dominated top positions in the larger, more prestigious libraries. Whether women will retain their rapidly diminishing predominance as administrators of the smaller institutions, particularly public libraries, is more questionable. These institutions are not as visible, the pressures in them less, and possibilities for reaction against the historical dominance of women greater.

At the same time that women have been pushing for admittance to higher positions, they have also sought the development of lateral career structures. Women who do not want to be administrators are actively seeking personal and financial recognition of their contribution to the profession. Revised career structures would also benefit those men who do not wish to take the administrative route which they are sometimes unwillingly nudged into. The plight of the excellent reference librarian, for example, forced into administration to advance his or her career has been a concern of the profession long before the women's movement. This additional impetus should speed the process. It may have a positive effect on services, as well as influence the balance of male:female administrators.

A gender breakdown of aspects of librarianship other than administration is not readily available (a telling fact in itself). Since the profession is 84 percent female and more males than females hold the bulk of administrative positions, one might conclude that the technical support and reader services are composed of women. There is a general impression that men may be more populous in the automation and information science areas of the field than in readers services. We just don't know. In public and school library youth services, an area most would agree is truly dominated by women, and where other factors, such as the long proposed merger of the two institutions' services and the growing acceptance of men working with children are known, questions can be raised. What will be the scope of opportunity for men and women in this service? Will men be more sought after than women? Otherwise, projection beyond a statement that change will occur because of the adjustments in the sexual makeup of the profession as a whole is not possible.

A feminized profession

I hope you won't repeat that quote from Justin Winsor again!—A Feminist Librarian Friend

"That quote" refers to Winsor's 1878 summary of the value of women in librarianship as cheap well educated labor with the additional service, softening, and housekeeping instincts needed in the profession[6] and characterizes much of the sentimental comment on women in library literature. Sentimentality is not the only response to women. An anti-feminine bias on the part of both men and women also exists and manifests itself in characterizations of niggling spinsters, uncommitted mothers, and the sheer number of women in the profession as a weakness. In fact much of the literature of women in librarianship treats feminine dominance as a problem: the problem of a feminized profession.

An acceptance and even affinity for bureaucratic and

hierarchical structures, humanitarian service rooted in the emotions, task rather than intellectual orientation, and compliance are the hallmarks of the feminized professions and are the subject of innumerable articles in the literature of librarianship. Whether one attributes these characteristics to the dominance of women alone, not at all, or in combination with other factors such as association with the educational, cultural, and nonprofit segments of society, these do seem to be the acknowledged generalizations about the profession and are voiced both within and outside of librarianship. Simpson and Simpson cataloged these and related tendencies and characteristics of feminized or semi-professions and concluded in the late sixties that "so long as our family system and the prevailing attitudes of men and women about feminine roles remain essentially as they are now, this basic situation seems unlikely to change."[7]

The women's movement, however, is challanging prevailing attitudes toward female and male roles. In addition, the literature concerning sex differentiation indicates socialized and not innate origins for the roles and characteristics identified by Simpson and Simpson and seen in library literature.[8]

Librarians concerned with the sexism of children's materials acknowledged the importance of socialization to the challenges of the women's movement. But what of the adults who inhabit Libraryland? Library literature offers no response. To project a defeminized profession it is necessary to move outside librarianship—toward those who are attempting to define feminist, not feminized, values and structures.

Women are seeking to define themselves through control of their bodies, equality in their relationships, and freedom of choice in their career. Participatory rather than hierarchical structures, the development of the individual as well as of the collective movement, and, responsibility rather than dependence are goals of the women's movement. Rather than replacing passive with aggressive behavior, new models such as assertiveness are being explored. As women pursue these and other changes it seems reasonable to expect that their work styles will reflect them.

Activity on the part of women librarians for their own liberation as women and as librarians has been growing. There is a proliferation of their literature, for example, *Women Library Workers* and *Emergency Librarian*, as well as an increase in the number of articles elsewhere. They are organizing new professional associations or groups within existing organizations such as the SRRT Women's Task Force. There is regional and local organizing of library women in Massachusetts, Chicago, California, New York and Connecticut. For those librarians active in or supportive of the women's movement, and this includes men as well as women, the characteristics of a feminized profession are in opposition to their commitments. These commitments require an assertive response to client information needs, practiced in an open flexible institution.

At the same time library literature indicates an increasing interest in nonhierarchical or collegial management styles, more autonomous practice of the profession, and flexible approaches to career ladders. If the increase in library science doctorates is any indication of an attempt to build a more knowledgeable base from which to design services, the profession is also moving away from its emotionalistic roots. Convergence of these with the similar interests of the library women's movement should strengthen librarianship so that the image can be overcome and the profession is no longer "feminized" in the pejorative sense.

The impact of women's challenge to traditional male and female roles in the next quarter century will also help shape the character and values of the men and women who choose to enter the profession. The direction and degree of their role redefinition will mirror the changing agenda and influence of the women's movement. Librarianship's own redirection will influence the values and characteristics of those who choose to enter the field. If the profession does not keep pace with the challenges of the women's movement and its own innovators, it may remain a feminized profession in the worst sense of the term, no matter whether males or females dominate in the year 2000.

A feminist profession
I hate not men but what it is men do in this culture, or how the system of sexism, power dominance and competition is the enemy—not people, but how men, still created that system and preserve it and reap concrete benefits from it.—Robin Morgan, *Monster*, p. 83.

Discussion of librarianship as a feminist profession is highly speculative. Consideration of the potentials of feminist values is essential to making the women's movement more than just a numbers game. The purpose of the women's movement is not more women administrators, male children's librarians, or clerk typists. These are manifestations of the central issue: the development of role-free human beings, they are not ends in themselves.

A feminism built on humanitarian values and advocacy of women's full participation in political, social, and economic spheres shares a call for the redistribution of power with other social movements. Feminism further calls for a transformation of our concepts of power: compassion and support rather than aggression and dominance. As a value system as well as a social movement, feminism demands a change in basic assumptions as well as an alteration in life style. While feminism is associated with the women's movement, belief in and actualization of its value system are not confined to women. Men may have a limited role in the women's movement, but they have a full role in the struggle for human freedom which is here labeled feminism. How they choose to develop that role is up to them as individuals and as a social grouping.

The potential for feminist librarianship lies in the men and women of the profession who hold feminist values. Their ability to implement the changes in the assumptions of the profession and to build new approaches is unknown. Brief examination of library employment and services through the focus of feminism is the only projection possible.

If librarianship accepted the feminist values of eliminating the dominant or single breadwinner per living unit and encouraged more people to work while balancing time for personal and community activities, the profession would be characterized by job sharing, serial, and part-time work arrangements. Individuals choosing these work styles would have the same benefits and career options as those who choose full-time work. Continuing education not confined to job related subjects will be available for all levels of employees with adequate counseling time and general encouragement provided. Acceptance of the potential for individual contribution should result in creative job design possibly crossing current professional/nonprofessional lines as well as participatory decision making. Equal pay for equal work is, of course, a given, as are just payment for ability and effort accompanied by adjustment based on need.

Implementation of feminist rooted library services would be based on a concept of equal services for all users: SDI for children as well as scientists. Free access to information will continue as a central tenet of librarianship in the year 2000. However, demystification of information and advocacy will be given equal billing. Rather than attempting to build institutional empires, libraries will act as catalysts in the larger communication environment. Service plans will be flexible and designed with user input and evaluation. Because feminist values imply a reworking of national priorities, more financial support will be available for institutions such as libraries, if they respond to needs in a feminist and humanist mode.

These employment and service scenarios drawn for feminist librarianship are but one possibility on a wide spectrum of potential. The year 2000 could just as readily see us only inches ahead of our present view of the profession or even behind it. Women and the women's movement are *not* meant to be portrayed as saviors of humankind nor of librarianship. A process of defining and working towards a realization of feminist values, however, is relevant and possible.

The spectre of a truncated women's movement, bereft of feminism, must also be raised. Freedom of choice for women, at the expense of the caring, warmth, and sensitivity to others so often associated with them, may be empty. In the thrust to redefine male and female roles, women must not become men; nor can men be permitted the continued dehumanization of their role.

For librarianship, triumph of the women's movement without feminist values may result in meaningless proliferation of networks, self-perpetuating institutions, service built on expediency, and a lowering of capacity to meet the user needs to a level below that of its worst days as a "feminized" profession.

REFERENCES

1. U.S. Department of Labor. Bureau of Labor Statistics. *Library Manpower: a Study of Demand and Supply*. Washington, D.C.: U.S. Government Printing Office, 1975.
2. Meyerson, Bess. "A Call to Action: The National Women's Agenda," *Redbook*, November 1975, p.71-75.

3. Schiller, Anita R. "Women in Librarianship." In: Voigt, Melvin, ed., *Advances in Librarianship*, v. 4. Academic Pr., 1974.
4. *Women Library Workers*. Special issue. September 1975, p.6.
5. Schiller, Anita R. "The Status of Women." In Sellen, Betty-Carol and Joan Marshall, eds., *Women in a Women's Profession: Strategies*. Proceedings of the Preconference on the Status of Women in Librarianship sponsored by the American Library Association, Social Responsibilities Round Table, Task Force on the Status of Women: Douglass College, Rutgers Univ., July 1974.
6. Conference of Librarians (1878). "Transactions and Proceedings of the Conference of Librarians held in London. October 1877." Trubner, London.
7. Simpson, Richard L. and Ida Harper Simpson. "Women and Bureaucracy in the Semi-Professions." In Etzioni, Amitai ed., *The Semi-Professions and Their Organization*. The Free Pr., 1969.
8. Maccoby, Eleanor E. and Carol N. Jacklin. *The Psychology of Sex Differences*. Stanford Univ. Pr., 1974.
9. Morgan, Robin. *Monster*. Random House, 1972.

Racism in the Library: A Model from the Public Schools

Mildred Dickeman

OÚR UNDERSTANDING of the functions of racism in the American school system is increasing. I believe that what we are learning about schools is applicable to libraries, and that it assists us to identify those points at which we can expect racism, and to comprehend the functions it serves; things which we must know if we are to eradicate racism in these institutions.

The basic characteristics of institutions are familiar, but need to be mentioned because they become important in understanding institutional racism. Institutions, in the sense in which I am discussing them here, are bureaucracies with a hierarchical structure. The ranking of individual positions within the bureaucracy results in a chain of command. Status is correlated with power and authority, and also with responsibility. Such bureaucracies all have a series of top administrative offices supervising a large rank-and-file. It is an important characteristic of such arrangements that the positions at the top, those with greatest responsibility, are granted greatest flexibility in carrying out the activities of the institution. It is the top administrator who is at liberty to bend and modify the rules and regulations. The further down the ladder one goes, the more constricting are the rules and regulations, the

less freedom of interpretation is allowed the worker in carrying out his job. The reason for this is simple: greater freedom is granted only to those who have been judged reliable and responsible in terms of the institution's goals and values. In terms of the institution, those at the bottom are less reliable than those at the top, and therefore allowed less opportunity for decision-making. But it is well to remember (and sometimes hard to remember when one is at the bottom) that all jobs within the institution require some judgment, some decision-making. No activity can be totally programmed. Emergencies occur; rules must be applied to specific situations. The important consequence of this is that all of the members of the institution, including the lowest of the rank-and-file, must be judged to have some degree of reliability, however slight. We will see the significance of this later.

Finally, one must mention that other group of individuals who interact with any institution: the clientele. Since all institutions serve some need of the society of which they are part, they interact with those whose needs they serve. As they do so, they define that clientele; not only do institutions tend to define the needs of the clientele for them, they also tend to define who is appropriately a member of that clientele. And since the clientele is outside the institution, and is not required to demonstrate reliability in carrying out the institution's tasks, the demands made on its members are minimal, and of a very different order than those made upon the staff. The consequence of this is an incipient kind of opposition between client and staff, which has important implications for our subject.

The institutional racism with which I am concerned here is a larger category than individual racism, because it refers to all those aspects of the structure and operations of an institution which result in discrimination. Whether or not the individuals within the system know that their acts have racist consequences is not relevant to this definition. We are concerned with the consequences of the operation of the system. Racism itself is also part of a larger system, and although I use that term here in recognition of its currency, I might more accurately employ another, like ethnocentrism, because as we all know, we are dealing with a kind of discrimination which is based not only on biological characteristics but on class and sex and religion and cultural or ethnic behaviors as well: a very complex cluster of characteristics, both innate and learned.

I would like to propose that libraries, like schools, are very special kinds of institutions, however, and that this explains the special quality of their racism. Most institutions in our society can be thought of as producing a product or carrying out a task: corporations produce material goods; the military carries out warfare, and so forth. But the product of schools and libraries is in essence *ideology*: our function is the preservation and the transmission of a body of knowledge, a tradition, and like all traditions, this Western European heritage is as much a matter of values and of mythology as it is of factual knowledge. It is the concern with values and with the preservation and inculcation of values which gives libraries and schools their peculiar character, in matters of recruitment and advancement,

in their functioning, in their relations to their clientele.

This complicates greatly our relations with the public. For the public knows very well that we are the central ideological institutions in this society; consequently the society as a whole has a stake in our activities. Our clientele thus becomes not only those individuals whom we directly serve, the readers and the students, but society at large. Hence, the public hysteria over pornography in libraries is paralleled by the public hysteria over sex education in schools, a concern not matched by public interest in corporations or the Pentagon.

Every ideology, every integrated body of social beliefs, accepted history and mythology is a support for a social system. It is a theoretical justification for a series of social and political arrangements, phrased in terms of a view of man and his history. The American ideology was many years in the forming, but one of its most significant aspects is its dedication to the notion of uniformity, or assimilation, the assumption that to be successful and acceptable members of this society, groups and individuals must conform to a rather specific set of characteristics, those that we popularly call "Middle Class" or "Midamerican" traits. Behind the myth of equal opportunity lies an unstated demand for conformity. But those traits are not merely cultural or learned. They are biological as well. From its beginning, American ideology has ranked individuals and ethnic groups on the basis of their conformance to an ideal set of characteristics which includes such biological traits as skin color. Thus the ideal American is not only Middle Class in values, language, religion, manners, and so forth, but white, indeed North European. The least North European in physical traits is the least "American" in this sense, and the least likely to achieve "Americanness." For behind the American myth of equal opportunity also lies the tacit assumption that those who are biologically distant from the ideal will be culturally distant, will be least capable of achieving conformity with the values and behaviors of Midamerica. Those individuals who have demonstrated a capacity to conform, in spite of being biologically "unamerican," are conceived of as "exceptions" to the racist rule, and are so treated and so labelled throughout American life.

The great era for the founding and expansion of public libraries in America was during the late 19th Century, overlapping that same period in which the public school system was established, and for the same reason. That period was a turning point in the history of this country and of its ideology. For the first time, this society was confronted with a large urban lower class, culturally and linguistically diverse, yet white enough to threaten the dominant Anglo-Saxon ruling class. That large mass of European immigrants had to be indoctrinated into the American value system, had to be taught their place in it, and to learn those behaviors and values and attitudes which were appropriate to "good Americans." Otherwise, their presence, their ethnic diversity, their social and political and religious differences would disrupt the very foundations of the society, and destroy the power of the existing elite. Thus the public school and the public library became the primary means for the indoctrination of the lower classes and the ethnically diverse into the dominant society. They existed, and still exist, to assimilate the restless masses into a belief system which will guarantee their acceptance of their place in society, and to recruit from out of those masses whatever individuals may be needed to replace and expand the upper classes. Those are the individuals who show most likelihood of conformity to Middle Class ideals, who show most promise of reliability and loyalty to that group and its institutions.

The consequence of this is a certain complexity to the recruitment and advancement procedures of schools and libraries. Because, if our ideology tells us which groups and individuals are worthy of inclusion in the dominant class, which groups are most likely to possess the necessary intelligence, responsibility, rationality and so forth, then the individuals who are to be entrusted with the transmission of this ideology to the masses and to the young must be selected with special care. These purveyors become models to society at large: representatives of the ideal. We should not be surprised to find that hiring procedures for schools and libraries have been, and are, unusually concerned with conformance to a variety of characteristics which may be irrelevant in other jobs. Standard English and appropriate dress, manners and lifestyle are indices of successful indoctrination into the dominant value system: they are guarantees of reliability of special importance for institutions with this function.

Racism in recruitment and advancement is often analysed as a product of job competition, of the perception by whites of a threat to their job security from minority groups. Certainly this is true, but while this observation may be central for understanding such racist institutions as building trades unions, it is inadequate for understanding the recruitment procedures of ideological institutions. Because the ideological requirements important for librarians and teachers are simply not important for construction workers. The latter are expected to accept the ideology; we are expected to demonstrate it and to transmit it. Consequently, librarians, like teachers, are hired on the basis of dress, dialect, body postures, hobbies, and family life. Of course those attributes have nothing to do with the skills of education or of librarianship. But they are absolutely crucial bona fides that teachers and librarians will serve as models, as screeners and enforcers of Middle Class values in the classroom and the library.

Hence, minority members may serve as school or library custodians without threat to the system, since custodians are not engaged in the ideological transmission process. In contrast, it is no surprise that, until a few years ago, blacks were not allowed to work at the circulation desk in the Library of Congress (*LJ*, January 1, 1972, p. 14), because "it was felt they shouldn't meet the public." I suspect that the entry of minority individuals into the lower ranks of both libraries and schools has not been so much the product of civil rights activism as it has been the consequence of the expansion of these institutions into large bureaucracies, with an extensive rank-and-file closely supervised by top personnel. As long as the school remained a one-room schoolhouse and the library a small-town institution, the individual running it had administrative, decision-making responsibilities as well as the drudgery of the daily tasks. It is probably the separation of those tasks, the specialization of the large bureaucracy, which has made possible the replacement of the well-mannered Middle-Class white spinster (how alike the job histories of these professions have been!) with the minority individual.

It has long been observed that the majority of teachers are recruited from the upper-lower and lower-middle classes, socioeconomically. There is good reason for this. These are the individuals who will be most loyal to the system: their security and acceptance is new and tenuous; they are on good behavior; they have, through entry into the institution, just made it into the Middle Class. They can be trusted not to rock the boat, to defend the Middle Class ethic with vigor and rigidity. Has not this been true of librarians, as well?

The implications of these observations on recruitment and advancement in ideological institutions are clear. If the educational model applies to libraries, then changes in recruitment policies, to be significant, will have to involve changes in the ideology itself. Only when these institutions admit the existence of a plurality of worthy individuals, groups, and cultures in this society, will they allow a plurality of diverse individuals to demonstrate that diversity to the public. Rather than attacking piecemeal all the specific requirements for job mobility in the system, from dialect to skin color to hair length, it might be more efficient to attack the ideology directly. What must be attacked is the implicit notion that individuals must be ranked on the basis of their group affiliations into a hierarchy of "Midamericanness." We must begin to destroy the myth that we have treated people as individuals in this society, and to recognize the ways in which we have denied validity, and indeed survival, to a variety of ethnic traditions and cultures. What must be killed, in short, is this society's "Uniform Code of Success." Until we admit equally to all ranks of librarianship and education not just members of the Middle Class, and not just those exceptions who have managed to achieve conformity, but people of clearly and openly diverse heritage and custom and values, we will go on fulfilling our functions as models and perpetuators of the racist ideal, as guards and policemen standing at the gates of entry to American acceptance and achievement.

Another aspect of the racism of the ideological institution lies in the roles and responsibilities of the rank-and-file. I have noted that, in bureaucracies, greater freedom of interpretation is accorded to the highest rank, but that there is always some freedom and responsibility granted to the lower ranks. This freedom, however small, is granted on the understanding that the employee will carry out loyally the ideological imperatives; that his or her interpretations will never question or contradict the ideology. The consequence of this is that employees of such institutions, who feel themselves to have little liberty, are in fact reinforcing and supporting the racism of the institution by their daily interpretations and applications of the rules.

By way of example, let me refer to Sanford Berman's provocative recent tract on the LC subject headings, *Prejudices and Antipathies* (Scarecrow, 1971), and to a review of it which appeared in *LJ* (February 15, 1972, p. 658-9). I believe that the reviewer raises a very important question in regard to Berman's analysis, but he does so in order to arrive at some rather disturbing conclusions. While the reviewer grants that "the LC headings cited incontestably reflect a pervasive bias and bigotry," the question he raises again and again is, "but *whose*?" "A good catalog," asserts the reviewer, "reflects faithfully the face of the literature represented by it, warts and all; and if that face is not pleasant to behold, it is not the mirror that is to blame." Likewise, "a list of subject headings is not a social treatise reflecting its author's philosophy or point of view. It is merely a list of the subjects with which the materials in the library's collections are concerned, and any imbalance in the character of these materials will naturally be reflected in the headings. The specification of Jewish, Negro, and Catholic criminals, and of no others, reflects only a hateful obsession with these groups by members of the community represented by that literature—and nothing else." Yet in reference to another heading, "Yellow peril," the reviewer concedes, "This heading is clearly a vestige of an earlier and darker age and, happily, now appears moribund. Its replacement by current terminology will only improve the usefulness of the catalog. . . ."

I can only understand these responses to mean one thing: that the "heading-manufacturers," whoever they may be, are and must be passive and unquestioning transmitters of the traditions of racism; that the acceptance of positions of responsibility within the library system must imply an uncritical acceptance of a role in which one's own judgment and values are sacrificed to the larger social responsibility of endless repetition of racist nonsense. And this must be so, even as in the case of yellow perils, where it is clear that society is undergoing change. Librarians and teachers may not participate in that change, much less lead or shape it. They may only reflect it, mirror it, transmit it. Is it not significant that the reviewer regards the "Yellow peril" heading as a matter of terminology, rather than meaning and value, as though replacement with some modern scientific epithet such as "Mongoloid threat" were the issue? By so doing he avoids recognition that the catalog of racism changes because it mirrors more than a literature.

In his concern to free the librarian from any responsibility, the reviewer has failed to see that the subject headings, while not an individual social treatise, are indeed a social treatise written by a whole society. This is precisely the significance of Berman's book. He has found here a detailed anatomy of the body of American racism.

Further on in his discussion, the reviewer takes a different stance. In dealing with the *see also* references, rather than the headings themselves, he takes no exception with Berman, and cites several examples of *sa* references which "should now be purged from a public catalog," or "should and can be easily remedied." Thus he maintains that while the librarian-cataloger has the right and responsibility to dismantle the muscle and nerve of the racist ideology, he has no right to destroy or remove the very bones of the structure which the *sa* references tie together. The reviewer has managed, at least to his satisfaction, to avoid the central issue which his original question implied: how *does* one avoid the transmission of and support for dangerous bigotry, while still carrying out one's responsibilities to provide a guide and access to an important body of literature, good and bad? Again, I do not see how this question can be adequately dealt with without attacking the more central question of one's loyalty to the ideology which the headings represent.

Finally, there remains the matter of clientele. Our racist ideology, like all ideologies, is composed of both sins of omission and sins of commission. While it includes within it mythological notions and falsified histories and traditions, it denies the existence of other traditions, other realities which are irrelevant to it, and which indeed might question its very validity. These omissions are of prime importance, for they tell the clientele that whatever is absent is not part of the Great Tradition, has no bearing on or relevance to his status as American. Libraries, like schools, are immensely selective. And I would suspect that, as is the case with schools, much friction with minority and youthful clientele is a consequence of this selectivity. What these disenfranchised groups are saying is that their traditions, histories, and mythologies are as importantly American as what is now contained in the archives and the textbooks.

Within the public school system, concern for the so-called "dropout" problem has reached obsessive proportions. Of course it is partly the practice of compulsory attendance which creates "dropouts" as an identifiable class of individuals. Libraries, less central control agencies for the young in our society, are spared this particular dilemma. Yet a superficial difference masks an essential sameness. Library systems are greatly concerned with the identification of the "nonuser" and the problems of service to a variety of traditionally non using communities. An understanding of the origins of the public school dropout will, I think, illuminate the nature of the nonuser as well.

The dropout is, simply, an individual who perceives, consciously or unconsciously, that the costs of assimilation into the Middle Class ideal are greater than he cares to pay and that the chances of success, even should he do so, are minimal. He is one who has understood the message of the institution, that as he stands, racially and culturally, he is an unacceptable human being, and that all of his behavior, values, and attitudes, and the heritage of his community, are likewise irrelevant and worthless. This message has been transmitted to him through every aspect of the racist institution which he has been forced to attend: the race, behavior, and ideals of his teachers; the nature of textbooks and curriculum, the bureaucratic structure from custodian to principal, and the rewards and punishments. All these inform him of his chances of success and of the sacrifices he must make to achieve it.

Likewise, libraries communicate the ideological message. From the moment he enters the library doors, the potential user is bombarded with communications, verbal and nonverbal, about the institution's ideals. The architecture, the pictures and posters on the walls, the signs (mostly negative) informing him of appropriate behavior, the people behind the desks (their race, manner, dialect, dress), the books, the catalog and the style in which library operations are carried out—all inform him that this is a temple of the Middle Class ideology. A fearsome place, the traditional library, for someone not already a member of that class. His own behaviors and traditions are absent, therefore unacceptable. No wonder that only those willing to abandon their traditional affiliations and willing to believe in the myth of individual opportunity will remain and return. Or that those who, as in school, are forced for external reasons to remain, will become restless and disruptive. Their disruption is a statement, however unconscious, of insistence on their validity as human beings, and of their refusal to accept the definitions of worth imposed upon them by Middle Class institutions.

Why, then, does the system resist their inclusion? Why all the difficulty about underground news media, popular music, militant minority literature? Because, as is now clear, to admit these into the ideological institutions is to admit their validity as part of the American heritage. And to do that is to say that America is not merely a mass of unassimilated individuals, all striving to conform to the Midamerican ideal, and ranked according to their success in doing so, but a *plurality* of *equally valid* traditions of survival and achievement; in short, a plurality of ways of being validly, fully American.

Choices

The choice of both libraries and schools, it seems to me, is either to continue to resist, to dilute and redefine and deny, to accept only as peripheral and secondary those other American traditions, or finally to call into question the very central assumptions of the American racist ideology and of the social order which it supports, to create on every level a commitment to plurality, and to begin to design a new and truer ideological basis for the transmission of all of American experience. The creation of a new ideology is but one part, but a significant part, of the larger job of creating a just American society.

Can Library Affirmative Action Succeed?

E. J. Josey

IN JANUARY 1974, the Bureau of Labor Statistics, U.S. Department of Labor, issued a preliminary draft of "Library Manpower—a Study of Requirements and Supply." The report indicated that there were 115,000 librarians working in libraries in 1970 and that school libraries employed nearly half of them. Of the total, 97,000 were female and only 18,000 male. The male librarians work mostly in academic and special libraries. The report estimated that 92 percent of all of the male librarians are white and 92 percent of the females are white. The nonwhites were not broken down by their ethnic groups— blacks, Chicanos, Native Americans, Spanish surnamed, and Asian Americans—but the small number of minorities in the profession is a dramatic indication that something must be done in the library profession to insure equal employment opportunity; and it goes without saying that each library in the country must have affirmative action programs. The American Library Association passed an Equal Employment Opportunity Policy Statement at the midwinter meeting in Chicago in January 1974. On the other hand, no mechanism has been established for libraries to file affirmative action plans with the Association. In truth, an affirmative action plan is at the very heart of the matter of a workable affirmative action program.

The Office for Library Personnel Resources of the American Library Association conducted a survey in May 1973 which is rather revealing. The Office sent questionnaires to libraries thoughout the United States in an effort to collect information about the ethnic composition of the professional labor force. Institutions were asked to identify in total number the ethnic breakdown of their staffs in five categories: American Indian, black, Oriental, Spanish surnamed, and others including Caucasians and all minorities not specified.

Although information was obtained for all levels of employment, only data for professional employees are presented here because of the national scope of the labor market. Within the classification, information was broken down into three categories based upon level of professional education; for example, some library education, a Master's degree in library science, or a Ph.D. in library science.

Let us take for an example one type of library, the public library. The public library employees in the sample with some library science education but not a Master's degree were: 0.2 percent American Indian, 4.5 percent black, 0.5 percent Oriental, 1.2 percent Spanish surnamed, and the remaining 93.6 percent either Caucasian or some other minority. Of the same group, 88.5 percent were women and 11.5 percent were men. And of course, the ALA survey provided data on the employment of minorities in other types of libraries.

The black caucus survey

While I have no quarrel with the ALA survey, in too many instances the respondent who answers an official Association survey represents the administration of an institution or the administration of a library or a library system and does not reflect the views of minorities who work in libraries and who are victims of discriminatory practices. Therefore, the Black Caucus of ALA in the spring of 1974 authorized a small survey to obtain information which would shed more light on a complex problem. Although this survey includes a small number of libraries, the information is valid, for in all except one large university library the data was sent to the Caucus. The respondents were told that the source would be strictly confidential. The confidentiality of the source was underscored in order that the respondents would feel completely free in presenting his or her views on the conditions of employment in the institution in which he or she is employed.

Twenty-four questionnaires were sent to 12 public library systems and 12 university library systems. Twenty-two of the questionnaires were returned, ten of which were from public library systems and 12 from university library systems. In short, information was received on black professionals employed in university and public library systems.

The public libraries

The public library systems which responded included the Atlanta Public Library, Brooklyn Public Library, Chicago Public Library, Durham (North Carolina) City-County Public Library, Cleveland Public Library, Milwaukee Public Library, the New York Public Library, Queens Borough Public Library, Rochester Public Library, and the San Francisco Public Library.

Atlanta reported a total number of 97 professional librarians in its system, and that of this number 32 were black. Brooklyn reported a total number of 280 of whom there were only 18 black librarians. The Chicago Public Library indicated approximately 300, and of this number there were 24 black librarians. Durham City-County Public Library reported a total of 15 librarians employed, of whom four were black. The Cleveland Public Library responded that there were a total of 201 librarians working full time and 20 librarians employed on a part-time basis. Of the total number of 221, only 17 librarians were black. The Milwaukee Public Library responded that it had 149 librarians in its system, and of this number seven were black. The New York Public Library respondent provided statistics from a 1972 published survey which indicated at that time NYPL employed a total number of 463 librarians, and of this number 41 were black librarians. The Queens Borough Public Library reported a total of 393 librarians, of whom 30 were black. The Rochester Public Library reported a total number of 98 librarians; of this number seven are black. Finally, San Francisco reported a total of 146 librarians with only five black librarians employed in the entire system. It is obvious but necessary to underscore the inequity which exists. The largest number of black librarians in terms of the library's constituent population seem to be employed in Atlanta, a Southern city, and even in Atlanta the 1970 census showed the population was 51.3 percent; therefore, in proportion to the black population there is much to be desired in Atlanta.

The third question asked for the total number of librarians in middle management positions: for example, branch librarians, supervising librarians, and those who were in coordinating positions. Atlanta reported 45 in middle management positions, and of this number there were 19 black librarians. Brooklyn reported 75, and of this number 12 were black. The Chicago Public Library reported a total number of 24 at this level with seven of these persons being black. Interestingly enough, Durham reported a total of five at the middle management level, and four of them were black. The Cleveland Public Library reported a total of 77 in middle management positions, and of this total number only 13 were black. Milwaukee reported 14 at this level, and only two were black. The New York Public Library reported a total of 150 in this category, and only 20 of these persons were black. The Queens Borough Public Library respondent indicated that there were approximately 75 middle management personnel, and only nine at this level were black. The Rochester Public Library respondent failed to give the total number at this level, but indicated there were only three blacks employed in middle management. The respondent from San Francisco reported there was only one black person employed at this level.

In terms of top management—that is to say those libraries that employed black directors, associate directors, personnel officers, or directors of branches—Atlanta and Durham each reported one in this category. Brooklyn, Chicago, Rochester, San Francisco, Cleveland, Milwaukee, and New York Public each reported no blacks in top management. Queens Borough Public at the time of the survey reported none, but since that time we are pleased to report that Milton Byam, a distinguished black librarian, is now the director. There were only three in top management in the 12 public library systems.

Upward mobility?

The next question was as follows: What do you think

of the outlook for upward mobility and/or promotion of blacks in your system?

Atlanta indicated "good." Brooklyn reported "fair," and that it would take pressure from organizations such as the ALA Black Caucus within the profession and pressure generally by militant blacks. The Chicago respondent replied "dismal." Durham reported that the outlook for upward mobility and/or promotion was good. Of course, the assistant director is black. Cleveland reported "prior to the appointment of two black trustees on the Cleveland Library Board by the local school Board, the outlook for upward mobility was dismal." The respondent also indicated that the former director of the Cleveland Public Library was interested in appointing blacks to administrative level positions. Milwaukee responded fair on the upward mobility question. The New York Public Library indicated that "there are five blacks and three Asians in the internship program, but I feel that there will be a limited increase in numbers of black librarians unless public libraries and library school faculty make a concerted effort to recruit and train black librarians." The Queens Borough response on upward mobility was negative not in terms of discrimination but that, "The senior librarian's eligibility list gets longer each month with few new positions open or available." The Rochester respondent felt that an affirmative action program did not exist at the Rochester Public Library. The San Francisco reply to the upward mobility question is interesting: "One librarian is a Librarian III, and she has been blocked from taking the examination for Adult Coordinator primarily because of racism." Continuing, the respondent declared that "one black librarian in a middle management position, who has a national reputation, has been blocked from becoming Assistant City Librarian because of racism."

The last question attempted to discover how other minorities were faring in the same systems. The question was stated as follows: "Are there general comments that you would like to add that might add light on how other minorities such as Chicanos, American Indians, Puerto Ricans, and Asian Americans are faring in your system?" From the responses the other minorities are not doing so well either. Atlanta reported that "among minorities, there is only one Puerto Rican." Brooklyn reported,

"Their condition is as dismal as blacks." Chicago reported, "I think what holds true for blacks is true for other minorities. It should be added that the Board of Trustees has one black person and recently added a Chicano to its membership." Durham indicated that "we work toward minority balance to the best of our ability." Cleveland provided an interesting commentary on libraries and politics. The respondent wrote: "Promotional opportunities for blacks and other minorities in this system depend upon the political climate." Milwaukee indicated that Chicanos are sought as paraprofessionals and professionals to serve a growing Latin community. There are *no* librarians of the other ethnic groups such as American Indians, Puerto Ricans, and Asians.

On the question of other minorities, the New York Public Library reported "that there is a small number of other minorities." On a hopeful note the writer stated, "A few more Spanish surnamed librarians will probably join NYPL as a result of the South Bronx Project. In future years NYPL may obtain minority librarians including blacks, Spanish, and Asians from among those staff members who are now studying for their undergraduate degrees with the assistance from a new scholarship program." Queens Borough felt that other minorities would fare well to the extent that federal funding remains available. Rochester reported that "there are no other minorities in our system." San Francisco reported "Minorities have been kept out of visible decision-making positions. Our struggles against institutional racism and for a meaningful affirmative action program have had no effect. All plans have been talked or delayed to death."

Academe

Turning to responses from academic librarians working in university libraries, questionnaires were received from Case-Western Reserve, University of Chicago, Cornell University, University of Illinois, Urbana, New York University, Northwestern University, Princeton University, Roosevelt University, Rutgers University, State University of New York at Buffalo, and the University of California, Los Angeles. At Case-Western Reserve there was a total of 63 librarians and of this

number, only two were black. Of ten librarians in middle
management positions at Case, one was black. The University of Chicago reported 82 librarians, and of this
number there was only one black librarian on the staff.
There were approximately 15 librarians who were at the
middle management level, and the one black librarian because he or she was the Assistant Head of the Cataloging
Department was considered middle management. The
University of Colorado had a total of 60 librarians and
only one black librarian in the system, and like the University of Chicago this person was a middle management
person. Columbia University reported a total of 136 librarians, and there were only two black professionals in
this number. Since Columbia University libraries are undergoing a reorganization as a result of a recent management study, Columbia was unable to report how many of
its librarians are considered middle management, but it is
my understanding that the two blacks have not reached
that state of grace. Cornell University has a total of 139
librarians and, like Case-Western Reserve and Colorado,
had only one black professional librarian. The University
of Illinois had a total of 180 librarians and only two black
librarians or 1.5 FTE black librarians. Illinois had 54 librarians at the middle management level none of whom
were black. New York University reported 80 librarians
in its system, and of this total, there were *no* blacks on
NYU libraries' staff. Northwestern University had a total of 80 librarians, and of this total, two were black.
There is a total of 22 in middle management positions,
and there were no blacks at this level. Princeton has a total of 79 professional librarians; of this total only two
were black. There are 30 librarians at management level
and only one was black. Roosevelt University is a small
university, with a total of 13 librarians on its staff, and of
this total, two were black; these two blacks were at the
middle management level. Rutgers has a total of 102 professional librarians, with a total of only six blacks. There
were 11 librarians in middle management, and there was
one black at this level. The State University of New York
at Buffalo had a total of 94 librarians, and like New York
University there were no black librarians in the system.
One encouraging sign at Buffalo is that a young black
scholar who is a personnel specialist and holds a Ph.D.
degree (but not a librarian) has been made an assistant to

the director of libraries for personnel, so the situation should soon change at SUNY at Buffalo. UCLA had 152 librarians. Of this total four were black. There were 28 librarians considered middle management, and two of the four black librarians were at this level.

With reference to top management, there were no blacks in this category at any of these 12 universities. Until very recently the prestigious Association of Research Libraries had a membership of 81 university libraries, all headed by white librarians. (Dr. Charles Churchwell was appointed director of libraries at Brown University in July 1974.) There are no blacks, Puerto Ricans, Chicanos, American Indians that are directors of these libraries, save Howard University by default, as it is a predominantly black university.

Like their public library colleagues, these black librarians were asked this question: "What do you think the outlook is for upward mobility and/or promotion of blacks in your system?"

The Case-Western Reserve respondent replied, "All top management jobs are now held by whites, and I suspect it will remain this way. So far, the two blacks in the system have not been offered a promotion." The University of Chicago response to this question is rather revealing: "Due to the local climate (union dispute) the administration might be inclined to move a black up (the one black librarian was recently promoted). However, the contradiction—no blacks hired at all." The University of Colorado respondent wrote, "Slender!" Columbia wrote, "For those in the system, better chance than new . . . Tight job area, people stay in jobs longer, therefore, less chance for upward mobility." The Cornell response went to the heart of the matter: "Upward mobility and/or promotion of blacks in this system depends on factors like the political and philosophical accommodation of black values and needs. The inclusion of such factors in the library's administrative, recruitment and allocation policies could enhance such upward movement."

The response from the University of Illinois was the following: "Considering the two positions involved, upward mobility is nil. Promotion in rank and/or tenure is presumably possible." The New York University has no blacks, and the respondent stated: "Since there seems to be little chance of expanding the present group of professionals, there seems little hope for a change."

Northwestern indicated: "It would depend upon the qualification of the person; the person would have equal chance for upward mobility." Princeton gave the general comment "Infinite" in regard to mobility. Roosevelt University's respondent was not as optimistic as the Northwestern correspondent: "I think the outlook for upward mobility beyond middle management is grim. The two librarians in the system were hired and promoted during the time when there was a shortage of librarians, and the system was less competitive than many systems in the area." Rutgers reported that those with appropriate credentials may be considered for promotion. There were no other minorities on the staff.

New York at Buffalo, although it had no black librarians, had a belief that "the chance would be better than average." UCLA believed "that upward mobility through the ranks (of assistant librarian, associate librarian, and librarian) is probably good; however, the situation appears bleak as far as top administrative positions are concerned."

Other minorities

How do academic libraries rate with the public libraries in the employment of minorities such as Chicanos, American Indians, Puerto Ricans, and Asian Americans? Case-Western Reserve stated that there were no other minorities on the staff and that "probably they would fare no better than blacks do here." The University of Chicago report indicated, "No Chicanos, American Indians, or Puerto Ricans. There are some Asians in a special area such as the Far Eastern Collection." The University of Colorado reported, "None in the system." Columbia's response centered on the budget regarding other minorities without answering the question. In essence the respondent once again indicated very little turnover on the Columbia staff and said that "positions that are opened are for usually highly specialized positions." Cornell had no other minorities. University of Illinois indicated that there were Chicanos, Puerto Ricans, and Asians but no American Indians. While New York University had no black librarians, it did have four Asian Americans and no other minorities on the staff. Northwestern had 1.5 FTE Asian Americans on its staff; Roosevelt reported three Asian Americans, and the writer said: "I predict that their outlook for upward mobility is no greater than, if not less than blacks." SUNY at Buffalo has no minorities except Asians. The UCLA respondent stated, "There are few minorities in the system. There are probably more Asians than Chicanos, American Indians, and Puerto Ricans. There is one Asian librarian in an upper echelon position."

There is no need to comment on the aforementioned sorry state of affairs with reference to the employment of blacks and other minorities in our nation's public and university libraries. Most of the blacks in the system believed the chances for promotion to be almost nil. To those of you who have read Charles J. Sugnet's penetrating article, "The University of Minnesota: the Uncertain Progress of Affirmative Action," in the May 1974 issue of *Change*, it may be quite evident that there are no real serious efforts in the nation to implement a real, meaningful policy of affirmative action. Writing about affirmative action at the University of Minnesota, Sugnet characterizes it as "a structure that exists largely on paper, having a hit-or-miss effectiveness at best ... The sense of urgency that inspired social change in the sixties has decidedly waned." Unfortunately, this is true not only at the University of Minnesota but throughout the country.

I applaud the American Library Association for having adopted an "Equal Employment Opportunity Statement" at its midwinter meeting last January, but as I stated earlier, unless the Association also adopts a strong implementation program, the EEO statement is only a worthless piece of paper.

Finally, talent search and recruitment programs have only begun to scratch the surface. There is a great reservoir of potential black and other minority librarians if employment officers will only try hard enough. The U.S. Bureau of Labor Statistics indicated that there were approximately 18,000 male librarians. Of this number six percent or 1,080 of them were black. Of the approximately 97,000 female librarians, seven percent or 6,790 were black. Of the total number of black librarians in this country, Dean Virginia L. Jones (in her essay in E. J. Josey's *The Black Librarian in America*) revealed that more than half of the black librarians in America were educated at the School of Library Service at Atlanta University.

Minority Americans are short-changed—cheated—when it comes to higher education generally. Not enough of them get in, not enough of them get up to top management following their higher education.

Higher education institutions and public libraries will not erase elitism or racism overnight, nor will they devise the most perfect and equitable ways of serving society in the twinkling of an eye; but they can change, and they have ample precedent for doing so. It is the fountainhead of my faith that, in spite of the small gains made by minorities in the library profession, I do have faith that change will come, if all institutions become committed to a real affirmative action program.

The Invisible Librarian

Edward Mapp

MY CAREER affiliation with libraries began over two decades ago on a brisk autumn afternoon. As I mounted the stairs leading to the public library's impressive entrance, I was excited at the prospect of capturing one of the part-time positions, sought after by high school students at that time. One hour later, I left the building, surprised, disappointed, and still unemployed. How could attendance at one of the city's honor schools coupled with a general familiarity with libraries have failed to satisfy my interviewer? Fewer qualifications than I possessed had been more than enough to win identical jobs for white acquaintances.

The matter came up again some time later, following a successful interview by a different interviewer and subsequent employment with the library. A co-worker said, "Of course, Mr. P didn't hire you then. He wouldn't hire you now for that matter. You just have to look at his staff to know that he only accepts whites." From prolonged personal observation in the immediately ensuing years, I came to learn that this gratuitous remark was unquestionably true.

I could hardly have foreseen then that other discriminatory incidents would track my life in the library profession. Time wove a tapestry of characters, kindred spirits, each one cut from the same fabric as Mr. P, in respect to white racist attitude. Unforgettable among these was the library supervisor who advised against librarianship as a profession. "No opportunities for your people," he said. "But what about Mr. J and Dr. C? They succeeded," I replied. He, clearly no recruiter of blacks, terminated the interview which I had naively initiated, with the wry comment, "They are two exceptional Negroes."

Library personnel had no monopoly on these curious behavioral patterns I was to be thoroughly taught by the vast and heterogeneous public. At one point in my career I manned a desk to which all readers using certain materials had to come. One white patron, anti-black to the point of psychosis, was compelled by his own bias to wait until my lunch hours or coffee breaks for the fulfillment of his library needs. Happy days were those in which I could arrange for another black person to relieve me. Such days meant no service at all for this intolerant "seeker of knowledge." Since black staff members were scarce, my sadism was not allowed to flourish frequently. In retrospect, I am convinced that this particular bigot inspired in me a permanent sense of punctuality. On my rare tardy mornings, he would rush to my desk moments after 9:00 A.M. in the desperate hope that some white "early bird" would assist him. Needless to say, I became a paragon of promptness in those days.

A telephone reference assignment became the setting of another strange encounter. A female caller with a pleasant voice was not content with a routine identification of an exiled Dominican Republic leader. "But is he white? Some of those people are colored, aren't they? I must know before I invite him to address our club," she queried. To this day I wonder what that "faceless Fury" actually looked like. The imminent advent of video-telephones will never be too soon for me.

Progressive achievement in a chosen profession cannot ameliorate the impact of racial injustice, as some might suppose. Nothing really changes, save possibly the conversion of overt bias to a more subtle operative level.

There is that look of astonishment mirrored in the eyes of so many white job applicants as they confront a black administrator for the first time. The glance may last only a split second or it may remain throughout the personal interview. Whatever the duration, the unspoken question is always there—how did you slip through the gate? Politely verbalized, the question is heard as: "Are you Dr. Mapp?"

Traditionally, administrators have assumed responsibility for the guidance, development, and evaluation of new staff members. One white probationary appointee came to me from a rigid and closely structured job situation, where he was accustomed to supervision. Although I established early a clearly democratic

professional relationship, he could not accept any criticism from a black man, probably at a subconscious level. "I don't have to kowtow to you," was his unwarranted rejoinder to constructive advice. At the opposite end of the spectrum was the response of a white employee during the initial period of her employment as my secretary. When required to correct dictation or typing errors or to file memoranda, she consistently remarked, "I don't mind." For what conceivable reason should she "mind" performing the duties routinely expected of a salaried secretary? The concepts implicit in these episodes are not exclusively white. Negroes, too, accept the racial images and psychic stereotypes imposed upon them by a white racist society. During a visit to a college, as a member of a regional accrediting team, I struck up a conversation with a young black employee. He asked me to step aside where we could chat freely, explaining that important visitors were roaming about the college. Although I was obviously a stranger on campus, this individual could not envision a black brother as one of the visiting dignitaries.

Fortuitously, on other evaluation visits I chose to observe certain classes at moments of unanticipated revelation. In one speech class, a student spoke extemporaneously on the familiar theme of "Why Don't They Lift Themselves Up By Their Bootstraps?," without any attempt by the instructor to correct him. A literature class was involved in a discussion of the characterization of nigger Jim in Mark Twain's *Huckleberry Finn.* Whether the observer or the observees were more anxious on both occasions is difficult to recall now.

Functioning as a regular reviewer of books on "the black experience" for a major library periodical, admittedly, does not make me an expert in this field. Yet, I was mystified when the editor of this same publication invited a white colleague, who reviewed books on other subjects, to specialize as a consultant on books about the Negro.

Whether an exclusive library fraternal group invites my membership or not is of little consequence. This probably encroaches upon the social sector, and the selection of friends should be a personal matter. However, I am affronted by the realization that my white peers and subordinates can avail themselves of more of the "creature comforts" than I, all other things being equal. Subject to ability to pay, they have equitable access to America's housing, restaurants, barbershops, private schools, medical care, and a host of other services. Professional achievement for me (or for any black man) is illusory to the extent that I am denied much that white men of comparable status take for granted. I rebel at having to live in an apartment building that "blockbusters" and fleeing whites have bequeathed to me. "Why don't I move to a place where faulty elevators, broken mailboxes, and antiquated boilers do not exist?" Most landlords and real estate agents, despite open housing laws, respond to the color of skin and not to academic degrees or professional appointments.

It is axiomatic that job mobility, especially at the highest echelon, depends to a large extent upon direct personal and professional contacts. At a meeting of library directors, the host thanked me for conveying some information to the group. "It's ideas such as this that we miss. We need you at our meetings." Then he announced news of a highly desirable professional opening, liberally singling out individuals, present and absent, as likely candidates for the post. My name was not mentioned, despite the earlier praise. I have been approached, recommended, and nominated for professional offices and re-

sponsible tasks by the same persons who have consistently forgotten me when a professional "plum" was in the offing. Black librarians are now sought after where "entry level" or token positions are vacant but when a major college or university library directorship becomes available, the experienced black librarian, with few exceptions, remains "the invisible man."

Each one of us has different perceptions based largely upon life's experiences. Undoubtedly, the preceding remarks will evoke mixed reactions. Some will diagnose advanced paranoia; others will recognize a justifiable hypersensitivity; still others (mostly blacks) will applaud "telling it like it is."

Sooner or later, one tends to weigh the good and the bad of every aspect of life. Librarianship has not been found wanting in the balance on my personal scale. The potential rewards of this profession for a black man are many and varied. I am not referring solely to monetary considerations, which are more appropriately left to the U.S. Department of Labor and to the ALA Office of Recruitment.

In the black chauvinistic sense, I can "do my thing" in many minor ways. These may include absence from duty on Black Solidarity Day, insisting that a library orientation film be racially integrated, honoring Malcolm X Day with posters, recommending recruitment of more minority personnel at every opportunity or appearing as a visible symbol to black high school students in attendance at a library career conference.

Personnel referral officers feel reasonably confident that "equal opportunity" prevails in a library administered by a black person. They do not hesitate to direct black applicants to me, a salutary situation which does not apply in many libraries across the country. With increasing frequency, administrators have bestowed upon me the welcome (when I can help) responsibility of finding black candidates for library vacancies. This awesome burden of procurement, ordinarily linked to the oldest profession, can be maddening. Prospective employers seem to emphasize the word "qualified" only when seeking black personnel. Then too, there appears to be no burning desire for significant integration of staffs. The "show Negro" is yet very much in demand.

The black librarian can make a distinct contribution to the development of collections reflecting something other than the traditional western civilization point of view. Imbalance and distortion are exceeded by overt racism more frequently than one might imagine. A standard college psychology review book defines "performance tests" as follows: "These are used to test people who can't take verbal tests (foreigners, infants, illiterates, negroes [sic], and feebleminded people)." I cannot deny having wanted to remove, surreptitiously, *Man and the Negro* and other loathsome titles from a distinguished research library in which I served. That I was able to resist the temptation is testimony to my contempt for censorship in any form. In a world with a majority of non-white peoples, the imbalance in many library collections is conspicuous, to say the least. With numerous librarians today making blanket purchases of every Negro reprint series to hit the market, I find satisfaction in attempting a degree of selectivity in the acquisition of materials on "the black experience."

My tenure as a teacher-librarian in a black neighborhood afforded an opportunity to infuse students with an interest in black celebrities. Book talks, exhibits, informal "bull sessions," and letter writing projects bore unexpected dividends. I remember Tom with his letter from Langston Hughes, and Henry with his autographed photo from Floyd Patterson. This tangible recognition inspired in both boys an aura of pride and a feeling of expectancy. They were motivated to read about other black men and women who had "made it." The habit of reading is not easily lost, once acquired. As Claude Brown wrote in *Manchild in the Promised Land:*

> She [a librarian] gave me a book on Jackie Robinson and on Sugar Ray Robinson. She gave me a book on Einstein and a book on Albert Schweitzer. I read all these books, and liked them. After a while, I started asking her for books, and I started reading more and more and liking it more and more.

More than ever before, black youths are searching for their own identities. Being a figure to whom they can relate comfortably in the library context is profoundly gratifying. Even in the seventies, young blacks will empathize with the sentiments expressed by Richard Wright more than 30 years ago:

> I knew of no Negroes who read the books I liked and I wondered if any Negroes ever thought of them. I knew that there were Negro doctors, lawyers, newspapermen, but I never saw any of them. When I read a Negro newspaper I never caught the faintest echo of my preoccupation in its pages. I felt trapped and occasionally, for a few days, I would stop reading. But a vague hunger would come over me for books, books that opened up new avenues of feelings and seeing, and again I would forge another note to the white librarian.

It has been customary for an academic librarian to be concerned with matters of curriculum, but the black incumbent has a unique role to play. When student demands for black studies courses were thrust upon the college administration, I became, among a predominant white faculty, a vociferous "minority of one" in support of the proposed curriculum. The critical comments of Bayard Rustin, Roy Wilkins, W. Arthur Lewis, and other Negroes notwithstanding, it is my firm feeling that ethnic studies have the power to enrich scholarship, research, and the entire realm of higher education. Furthermore, I believe that a black librarian has a social responsibility as well as a professional responsibility to his black patrons.

Southern Integration: Writing Off the Black Librarian

Patricia Schuman

"THEY THINK librarians can't affect students much, so we're the first one's they use to integrate white schools. They don't see that we're dealing with *minds*. They think all we do is check out books, so they're less scared of us than black classroom teachers," said a Mississippi black librarian when queried by *SLJ* on the effects of integration on the Southern black librarian.

Massive displacements, demotions, and disappearance of black teachers and principals in the South have been documented in recent months in separate reports by the Race Relations Information Center (RRIC), state NEA affiliates, the American Friends Service Committee, and several other civil rights groups. HEW statistics for 1968-1970 indicate that in Florida, Mississippi, Georgia, Louisiana, and Alabama alone over 1000 black educators have been dropped from school systems, while more than 4000 whites have been hired.

None of the surveys deal with the specific questions of librarians, so *SLJ* queried over 60 education officials, teachers, civil rights lawyers, educational organizations, and librarians in an attempt to delineate the specific effects, if any, integration has had on the Southern black librarian.

Statistics and hard facts are nonexistent. Most officials maintain that there are no problems under integration. Lawyers and education associations rarely make the distinction between librarians and other teachers; black librarians justifiably fear reprisals and few complain. Most of those who did provide some documentation on their own, or others', specific cases have requested that their names be witheld.

No shocking statistics were revealed from our telephone survey, or even very much hard evidence. What we did find were several recurrent discriminatory and racist patterns which seem to be prevalent among white school officials.

Shoved Around

Librarians seem to have been the teaching personnel least effected by displacement *per se*. In fact, they are usually the first teachers "integrated" into white schools. "We are continually moved around and shoved around," charges the black president of a Southern school library association. "We are sacrificed first."

This phenomena results for several reasons. According to black library educators and librarians we queried there is a shortage of certified librarians in the South. They report a definite "brain drain" of younger black librarians to the North. Many have to leave Southern states for graduate training and never return.

It's difficult to get black graduates to want to come," says Dudley Flood, North Carolina State Education Department's Division of Human Relations associate director. "We can offer few lucrative inducements and the kinds of things they hear about our school systems discourage them."

"Black librarians are shifted so frequently for integration ratio purposes that many have *asked* to return to the classroom. . . our ranks are being dissipated," charges a black library supervisor from Georgia.

The dominant "myth," according to a Southern library educator, is that librarians are "service" people who come into less formal contact with students than black classroom teachers, and who have much less influence over students and educational structure than principals—or even coaches (both of whom are rapidly disappearing in the South).

The library is considered so "safe" by some school officials, that black English and social studies teachers are placed in them. George Strickler of the Lawyer's Constitutional Defense Committee has several cases under litigation.

"Librarians may have been less effected by outright displacement because they are predominantly *female* and represent less of a threat than the black male," suggests Dudley Flood. A thesis on *The Status and Characteristics of Displaced Teachers in Arkansas 1954-1968* by Dr. Albert Baxter, professor of education, Arkansas A and M, confirms that black males are displaced at a much higher rate than females.

Not only are the black librarians transferred, but often the black clerks and library aids too. Joe Reed, chairman of the Alabama League for the Advancement of Education, says that predominantly black schools have sometimes been left without librarians, or staffed by less qualified or unsympathetic white librarians. His complaint was echoed by others in Arkansas, Mississippi, Georgia, Louisiana, South Carolina, and Florida.

Outergration?

One of the more insidious effects of integration in Southern school districts has been the closing of black schools entirely in some areas, making integration a one-way street for blacks, who must travel to white schools. American Friends Service monitors found that 163 school districts closed a total of 235 black schools in 1970 alone. AFS says that 51 percent of the schools closed were in good condition, 21 percent in fair condition. At least 43 of the schools had new additions or improvements built in the last five years. Black children in at least 45 of the districts are now attending schools in worse condition.

Dr. Horace E. Tate of the Georgia Association of Educators and Joe L. Reed of the Alabama group have started calling integration by another name— "outergration."

With the closing of black schools, though teachers and principals are displaced, the librarian is often "accepted" by the integrated school, though often with concommitant loss of pay and prestige.

Librarian Ollie Burns from Monroe, Louisiana, one of the few librarians willing to brave a public fight, complained to the Louisiana Education Association when the Booker T. Washington Elementary and Junior High School was closed and she was transferred to Shady Grove Elementary School and asked to teach remedial reading two hours a week in addition to her library duties. The school was smaller, with poor library facilities, and a lower grade level.

Mrs. Burns who holds a master's degree in library service, had requested transfer to the Lakeshore school where many of Booker T. Washington's former students were being sent, but the position was given to a white teacher who had just completed 18 hours of library science and received her certification.

A compromise was finally worked out, but it seems to have been a false one. She accepted a transfer to yet another school, Oachita Elementary and Junior High School, on the understanding that the school would soon be split and she would be librarian of the junior high. Though the white librarian who had been there for ten years was not officially "in charge," Mrs. Burns says that many white teachers still prefer to work through her.

Mrs. Burns has told the administration she is leaving in June, since the school board did not follow through on their promises by separating its grades. "They never expected me to stay."

"There is a prevailing pattern," she says. "Blacks are not supposed to have leadership. They're okay as figureheads and assistants, but not working shoulder to shoulder or above white people."

"Though many people will not speak up, I go on because I know where I am and the people with whom I work know that my qualifications and ability are superior to the person whom I work with: They're not going to do better unless they're made to do better."

Pairing of black and white schools has also taken its toll. The black high school head librarian remains at the black school—now the integrated junior high. Or, she is sent to the white school —now the integrated senior high—as *assistant* librarian. Sources in South Carolina, Georgia, Louisiana, and Alabama also report this trend in their states, "despite the fact that black librarians are often better prepared than white."

A black librarian from Georgia sees "the most desultory effect on black librarians as the combination of local schools and systems, particularly high schools."

Hiring blacks with federal funds, then abolishing positions when funds dry up, is another trend noted in the RRIC report. A Northern Louisiana black librarian, hired in a supervisory position for a Title I project after her school closed, had her job abolished after 18 months. She was transferred again to a non-supervisory position. Three months later the position was reestablished, and a white librarian hired. She did not pursue the case.

"When you have children . . . what would the notoriety mean to them?" she asked. "If I had gone through with this I would have had enemies, even within the profession, even of my own ethnic background. Rational or not, people don't want to question authority. The traditions are strong."

But Are They Qualified?

A frequent tale we heard was that of black librarians with master's degrees being placed as subordinates to white librarians with minimum certification. In Georgia, some experienced librarians with graduate training have been placed "in charge" of small a/v collections requiring little professional work and *no* contact with students. "The expertise and training of librarians is really being dissipated," says one Georgia library supervisor.

Dudley Flood says that there are many more qualified black librarians than white in North Carolina, particularly with respect to new media. Recent NDEA media workshops have been held at heavily black schools and few whites elected to participate. One of our South Carolina sources says that since her state has no graduate programs in library science, blacks, used to seeking education elsewhere, go out of state, while "white librarians get away with murder with just the few undergraduate courses required for certification. . . . Black women *have* to work, and they are used to enduring hardships to get an education."

But, qualifications notwithstanding, few black librarians are to be found in supervisory positions and promotions are scarce. Carrie Robinson, the Alabama State Education Department Library Consultant who charged that she had been denied a promotion as a result of racial discrimination, and received a favorable out-of-court settlement as a result of other Alabama State Education Department suits, is one of the rare black supervisors at the state level. (*SLJ*, February, p. 9; *LJ*, February 15, p. 677.)

J. K. Haynes, executive secretary of the Louisiana Education Association calls it "a conspiracy to phase out blackness. School boards dig up whatever whites they can get." He cited sheriffs, retired salesmen, and even a former bread man teaching in one Louisiana county.

Florida Blacks Caucus

Emily Copeland, chairman of the Department of Library Service at Florida A and M sent *SLJ* some notes on discussions among black librarians at meetings of the Florida Library Association and the Florida School Library Association. They complain that no blacks are employed at the state level, either as supervisors or consultants, while whites are hired without library service experience. In addition, state standards for school librarians were developed with little consultation with black librarians.

Generally, they feel that experienced and trained librarians have been "phased out" of positions and replaced by whites with less qualifications. One black librarian was asked by her principal to move to a lesser position because a recent white library school graduate would only accept the head position. (The principal later apologized, after the librarian complained to the school superintendent.)

In several counties, clerks in ESEA funded programs were elevated to supervisory positions upon their promise to seek graduate library education. Some did and some did not. In one county, though, there is a supervising librarian with two library school degrees and over

thirty years experience. She is working under a white librarian who has only library certification.

Florida black librarians also charged that blacks have almost totally been denied employment in county media offices. One librarian with two library degrees and advanced training in a/v is employed "way down on the totem pole."

Though in other states, new black graduates were said to be still in demand because of shortages, many Florida counties hire no black librarians. Though six new schools opened in Leon county, the librarians say, no blacks have been hired in three years.

At least 15 FAMU graduates applied for library positions during 1969 and 1970. None were hired, while whites with equal training received appointments. Of a total of 39 librarians in Leon County only eight are blacks. All 1970 graduates from FAMU applied for library positions but none were hired and the schools were staffed by white librarians.

There is one ALA accredited library school in Florida—Florida State University at Tallahasee—and black librarians charge it with discrimination. They claim that until 1969-70 not one black graduated from it and that blacks were kept out of library school because of a discriminatory requirement for graduate record scores not applied to whites.

Dean Harold Goldstein denied that no blacks had graduated, but admitted that there had been few, though he says efforts to recruit black students are now being made. Graduate record scores of 1000 or a 3.0 average is a requirement for *all* applicants, he says.

Merged or Submerged?

Robert Hooker, in the RRIC report noted that black teachers lost a strong voice and ally when state associations merged. Most librarians queried by *SLJ* said there were little means for communication between them within their states. Miss Copeland says that Florida black librarians feel that little effort is made to recruit black librarians in FLA —or ALA for that matter. "In fact, those that join or attend are discouraged subtly, at meetings and at work.

Though FLA has always worked hard to foster its image among black librarians outside the state, they complain that there is no effort to work within. "It's just show. . . ." Workshops, programs and institutes held at Florida State University, FLA and other library meetings, have invited outside black libarians without consulting or inviting Florida black librarians.

Also, there is little communication, planning, or mutual understanding about education and training of librarians among black and white institutions they charge. Inservice training programs are planned without them.

Florida black librarians feel that ALA has acted against their best interests through the years. "There was an active and dynamic association where black librarians could meet to discuss problems before FSLA (black) rescinded its application for ALA state chapter in favor of the white FLA group. "We expected and were promised full participation in the merged group," says Miss Copeland. "ALA has not followed through on its commitment to follow-up and implement these mergers." Less than 25 black librarians are now ALA members.

Black Materials

Southern black librarians seem to feel they have made some movement towards getting black studies materials into Southern school libraries, though Dr. Baxter reports that "the black man is still left out in Arkansas."

Most states at least have black history lists, and the Division of Educational Media of the North Carolina State Education Department has compiled a bibliography sources. Though Associate State Supervisor Doris Brown observes that more materials are being bought, Dudley Flood sees some room for improvement.

Title I and Title II funds had been used to build up black studies collections in black schools. But, when black students and teachers are transferred to predominantly white schools, they no longer have access to them. They have some difficulty buying them in white schools since few teachers are familiar with them and many white parents object to them. (In February, p. 15, *SLJ* reported on the removal of two textbooks from Rocky Mt. North Carolina schools. Flood reports that the local school board was recently overruled by the state textbook commission and the texts have now been reinstated. Though the official complaint was obscenity, Flood says it was actually objections to black writers like James Baldwin and the late Martin Luther King.)

A South Carolina librarian reports that the purchase of printed materials is improving, but media is still a grave problem "We have to comb the state to find films on social issues and about black culture."

There are a few reports of principals censoring orders, but the problem seems to be mainly one of education of white librarians. "When white librarians don't know what to buy, they often don't buy anything. And when they do . . . they buy it for black kids, though white students need them and read them avidly," notes an Alabama librarian.

A Professional Responsibility

The results of our telephone survey are not conclusive by any means, but it seems clear that the black librarian in Southern schools face some serious discriminatory practices. They are the first teachers used to integrate schools, the first transferred, often leaving children in predominantly black schools without a librarian—or without a sympathetic one. They are largely left out of the power structure, despite education and experience, and though the Black Caucus has made some inroads, too often we spoke to black librarians who do not participate in state and national library associations. Some attribute this to overt—or covert—racism, others to the expense of dues. It seems clear, in any case, that we have largely ignored them. If we don't act now, the prediction of one librarian is: "The black librarian in the South will soon disappear."

Recruiting Spanish-Speaking Library Students

Roberto Cabello-Argandoña

LIBRARY SERVICES to the Chicano community, by both public and academic libraries, have been plagued by shortcomings and lagged well behind the provision of library services to other publics. Inadequate library and information services are experienced by most members of the Spanish-speaking community.

Among the significant factors accounting for poor library services to this community are: deficient collections, inadequate staffing patterns, under-utilization of professional personnel, lack of significant bibliographic control efforts with a resulting lack of proper access to materials, and significantly low recruitment of Spanish-speaking students by U.S. library schools.

This article will focus on personnel training efforts and recruitment as factors contributing to the low level of effectiveness of library and information services to Spanish-speaking citizens. Hopefully, it will provide some basis for the launching of a sound recruitment program which would attract Chicano students to library schools.

While the difficulties encountered in the development of effective library services to the Spanish-speaking community are many, some librarians feel that the problem is mainly due to lack of serious efforts by the library schools of the U.S. to recruit minority applicants.

How many Spanish-speaking librarians?

A survey of minority graduate students done by the ALA Library Education Division and the Office of Recruitment in 1972 revealed a limited increase in minority representation in accredited library education programs. This survey reported an enrollment of 18 Spanish-speaking students as compared to 156 black students. The number of Spanish-speaking students reported in this survey represented a net positive increase of eight new enrollments as compared to 1969.[1] Despite the small size of minority student input, 18 schools reported "active minority recruitment programs."[2] Certainly this concept of "active minority recruitment programs" has never been defined.

The National Center for Educational Statistics of the U.S. Office of Education conducted a study of library manpower and the number of library science degrees awarded for the period between 1960-71. This statistical data was supplemented with additional surveys to determine the number of placements, applications, and staff limited to public libraries and to school media centers in 30 large cities and to 21 large academic libraries for the years 1969-1972.[3] The results of these studies indicated a total of 61,200 full-time and full-time equivalent professional librarians for 1960 and 97,420 for 1970. The number of library science degrees to be awarded between 1969-1970 were projected at 7,810 and at 8700 for 1970 and 1971 respectively.[4] The number of Spanish-speaking librarians graduated in 1972 reported earlier, is an insignificant number compared to the overall size of the human resources in the field of library science.

The size of the Spanish-speaking professional pool is relatively small compared to the size of Spanish-speaking population in the U.S. The urgent need to increase the size of the professional pool of Spanish-speaking librarians calls for active programs of recruitment and training of Chicano students. Rough estimates of the size of the professional pool as compared to the population provide a rough equivalent of one librarian per 40,000 Spanish-speaking people.[5] The ratio between professional librarians and population in the dominant society is of approximately one librarian per 2000 people. This seems to indicate that there is a serious shortage of Spanish-speaking personnel in this field. Furthermore, the Bureau of Labor Statistics of U.S. Department of Labor conducted a study to project the number of professional librarians for the period between 1970-1985.[6] This study projected that the total number of professional librarians will rise to 167,000 in 1985. This study also forecasts that 9000 new graduates are likely to enter the labor force as librarians every year. This figure is not at all unrealistic, since the study conducted by the National Center for Educational Statistics of the U.S. Office of Education mentioned earlier, had indicated 8700 library science graduates for the period of 1970-71. The problem here is to determine in general, what percentage of these yearly new graduates will be from minority background, and specifically from the Spanish-speaking community?

A nationwide library education survey conducted by ALA in 1973-74 indicates that the Spanish-speaking community has graduated 99 librarians between September 1, 1973 to August 31, 1974. This represents a minimal percentage (1.37) of the total number of 7,221 graduates for that period.[7] These figures indicate that 38 masters degrees in library science were awarded to Spanish surnamed students by nonaccredited programs and 61 degrees were awarded to the same group by accredited programs.

The statistical data in the ALA survey points out to two basic facts: first, one of every 100 library graduates is Spanish surnamed or seven of every 500 is Spanish surnamed. Second, the professional pool of Spanish-speaking librarians is increasing at a lower rate than the increase of the professional librarian pool increases in this country, the local pool of Spanish-speaking librarians is growing at a lower rate as compared to the professional librarian as a whole. Furthermore, the composition of the Spanish-speaking library graduates is made of only 62 percent of graduates of ALA accredited programs for the year 1973-74. Thirty eight percent of the Spanish-speaking graduates come from library programs unaccredited by ALA.

Too often it has been said that universities and other educational institutions ought to respond to the needs of the various population sectors which surround them. It is not surprising, then, that there have been increasing claims upon library schools located in areas heavily populated by Chicanos and other minorities to increase their minority enrollment and to adapt their curriculum to the specific needs of these groups.

The Los Angeles Urban Region and especially Los Angeles County are the most heavily populated areas of Spanish-speaking people in the U.S. Librarians and library schools in these areas must take an increasingly active role to extend effective library services and professional training to this increasingly important population group.

Conservative population projections for the Los Angeles County by 1985 made back in 1966 indicated that the combined non-white population would exceed the Anglo population by almost five percent or 51.44 percent to 48.56 percent. The Spanish surnamed population would account for the 25.04 percent of the population (2,356,452), the black population will account for 23.10 percent (2,174,300), and other non-white will account for the 3.29 percent of the county's total population (310,200). These projections, needless to say, have been progressively confirmed by later population reports stemming from U.S. Bureau of the Census, 1970.[8]

Pilot program

The issue raised by Spanish-speaking librarians, based upon the analysis of the manpower statistics, has political overtones. This issue can be formulated as follows: What are the policy alternatives available to insure a balanced Spanish-speaking representation in projected increases in professional library manpower for the next decade?

Some efforts have been developed to minimize the high costs of the underutilization of Spanish-speaking manpower. The Illinois State Library funded, with LSCA Title I monies, the Illinois Minority Manpower Pilot Project, initiated by minority community people in the Chicago area.[9] The scholarship recipients began their graduate library educational training in January 1973.

Other small efforts have been attempted to correct the existing underrepresentation of Spanish-speaking and other minorites in the library profession. The National Minority Referral Network established by the Office for Library Personnel Resources of ALA was a unit designed to assist graduate library school programs to identify qualified minority students interested in pursuing a library career.[10] Other minority recruitment programs have been reported in the School of Library Science at the University of Michigan,[11-12] and Columbia University.[13]

A good example of manpower training efforts based on mutual cooperation between the Spanish-speaking community and a library school was that of the Graduate Institute for Mexican American Library Science at California State University Fullerton. This institute made a significant effort at training Spanish-speaking professional librarians by other experienced community professionals; it was created as graduate program to train Chicano librarians and to improve librarianship and specialized library services for the Spanish-speaking people of the United States.

In 1968 three librarians, Elizabeth

Martínez Smith, José G. Taylor, and David Barrón, founded the Committee to Recruit Mexican American Librarians (CRMAL) in Los Angeles in an effort to establish a mean for developing library services to the community. In 1972, Patrick S. Sánchez working with CRMAL members proposed an institute to train 15 graduate students of Mexican descent as school library media specialists at California State University Fullerton. The project was funded by the Federal Government for the amount of $130,000; all 15 participants in the program obtained the Master of Science Degree in Library Science in July 1973. Since then, the Graduate Institute was funded in 1973-74 with an additional $130,000 and graduated another 15 librarians in July 1974. For the 1974-75 academic year the Graduate Institute recruited 20 students and expanded its training programs to include junior college librarianship and training in research. The Institute's funding for 1974-75 totaled $164,600 from three separate grants; the total funding for the past three years was $424,600.

To date, June 1975, the Graduate Institute has graduated 33 Chicano librarians and 17 completed their M.S. degree in July 1975. Chicano library science graduates will total 50 this year, representing one fourth of the estimated number of Chicano librarians since 1972. A total of 26 men and 26 women have been enrolled with the Institute at one time or another. Two persons dropped out of school before completing degree requirements.

Thirty graduates from the Institute were employed in libraries or library related work shortly after their graduation. Most have stayed in California, however, some were offered positions elsewhere (Michigan, Massachusetts, Texas). Present participants are on the job market since July 1975, some of whom returned to their home states of New Mexico and Colorado. Participants for the Institute were recruited from California, New Mexico, Colorado, Texas, and Arizona.

Many of the Institute courses were taught by Chicano librarians with first-hand experience on specific needs, methodology, research, administration, and media for Chicano communities. The Graduate Institute completed funding and demonstration as an Institute specifically geared towards Chicano librarianship at California State University Fullerton in August 1975. Specific aspects and course offerings in Chicano librarianship of this Institute that will be absorbed by the division of library science have not yet been determined.

To determine the impact of the Institute a basic survey of the participants was conducted by José Sandoval. The objective of this survey was to provide an insight to the makeup of the participants, their employment experience, publishing, and their evaluation of the training program of the Institute. The results of this survey indicated that the first group of students of the Institute was made up of 60 percent males and 40 percent females, while the second group was made of 66 percent males and 33 percent females. These figures clearly show that men outnumbered women by a two to one margin during the first two years of the Institute. This trend was reversed, however, by the third and final group where women outnumbered men two to one, 15 women and seven men. Overall figures of this survey have indicated that 52 students were enrolled in the program, 50 of whom graduated. In short, 96 percent of those enrolled successfully completed the program. The average age of the female participants was 29 and 31 for the males. The average age for all participants was 30. All the participants were born in Mexico or the Southwest with the majority being from California.

Partial records of the activities after graduation indicate that one participant is employed in Michigan and 29 are employed in California. Four participants obtained employment through the Institute. All of the graduates found employment within two months after graduation and most upon graduation. Seventeen graduates indicated that they have experienced employment discrimination. Twenty-three indicated that they had problems because of the nonaccreditation by ALA. Eighteen of the participants employed in positions such as media specialists, reference librarians, associate librarians community college librarians, and children's librarians have been promoted in their jobs. One of the participants has since enrolled in law school and four others are pursuing higher degrees.

The library training at the Institute was rated by 47 of the participants as good and by five as fair. Seven of the participants have either been published or have submitted manuscripts for publication.

Results of the recruiting lag

The underutilization of human resources and the insignificant recruitment efforts of Chicanos in library school have had a definite influence in the underdevelopment of the library services to Spanish-speaking people. This system does not have the capacity to reproduce itself, it is not self contained. Accredited and nonaccredited library schools, an integral part of the dominant system, should operate as an institutional mechanism available to our community to transfer and pass on the knowledge, do research in the area of Spanish-speaking librarianship and to increase the small number of scholars and researchers in this field . . . There is not, for instance, a single individual Spanish-speaking researcher currently working or interested in the development of adequate indexing systems for the Spanish-speaking population.

The work needed in this field exceeds the energies of any dedicated librarian. This task cannot be accomplished without proper institutional support on a long-term basis. Library schools historically have had an extremely low enrollment and a poor recruitment record of Spanish-speaking students. This fact ultimately is bound to affect the numbers of Spanish-speaking graduates from library schools and the size of the professional pool from where libraries draw the human resources needed to service the Spanish-speaking community. The Spanish-speaking community would, in principle, be the beneficiary of the library and information services and, at the same time, would provide the human resources for training in library schools. The schools would provide the necessary professional manpower resources necessary to manage and run the library systems providing services to the community. The insignificant efforts in recruting Spanish-speaking students, and the resulting low enrollment in library schools is bound to result in a low number of graduates every year. This leaves the libraries in a precarious condition and with no source from which to draw their manpower requirements. This in turn results in a gradual deterioration and decay of library services to the Spanish-speaking community.

There are a number of ways a university could interface with the Chicano community. Recruitment programs are one of the basic vehicles to insure an adequate representation of the Spanish-speaking community on campus. A program of recruitment ought to be the initial step for a more solid interchange between the community and the library school and the university as a whole. Furthermore, the library schools should have an active role in the development of undergraduate and graduate curricula in Chicano Studies, emphasizing graduate curricula. In line with the development of human resources and the development of curricula is the application of professional expertise and research to human resources in the classroom through faculty and curriculum development. Specially focusing on graduate studies where professional training pro-

vides the pool of professionals so desperately needed in Chicano Studies and
our community. Spanish-speaking leaders would be glad to cooperate in the efforts of providing a sound program-
matic vehicle for increasing the number
of Chicano students in library schools,
and the enhancement of curriculum and
faculty development in Chicano studies
librarianship.

REFERENCES

1. "Survey on Minority Graduate Students," *American Libraries*, October
   1972, p. 942.
2. "Minority L.S. Grads Still a Trickle,"
   LJ, February 15, 1970, p. 616.
3. S. R. Reed, "Library Manpower Statistics, 1969-72 and the Outlook for the Future," *Bowker Annual of Library and
   Book Trade Information, 1972*. Bowker,
   1972, p. 260–68.
4. S. R. Reed, *op. cit.* p. 262, Tables 1 & 2.
5. These estimates are based on an ap-
   proximated 200 Spanish-speaking professional librarians from accredited library schools and a total U.S. Spanish-
   speaking population of nearly
   8,000,000. This estimate is merely a
   rough indicator of the size of the professional pool of Spanish-speaking librarians. A more exact indicator was not possible due to difficulties in obtaining
   more accurate data.
6. "Federal Bureau Predicts 167,000 Librarians, 212 Support Staff, Job
   Squeeze for 1986, "*Wilson Library Bulletin*, March 1972, p. 529.
7. ALA, Office for Library Personnel Resources. *Survey of Graduates and Faculty of U.S. Library Education Programs Awarding Degrees and Certificates, 1973–74*. Tables 1 & 2. ALA,
   November, 1975, mimeo. Single copies
   of this survey are available from ALA/
   OLPR, 50 East Huron Street, Chicago,
   Illinois 60611, without charge.
8. Los Angeles County Commission on
   Human Relations. Los Angeles County—1985. A sociological review paper
   prepared by John A. Buggs, Executive
   Director, October 26, 1966.
9. "Minorities Manpower Pilot Project,"
   American Libraries, June 1973, p. 369.
10. Marilyn Salazar, "Referral Network to
    Assist Minority Applicants to Library
    Schools," *American Libraries*, Septem-
    ber 1973, p. 493–94.
11. "Minority Manpower for Michigan
    SLS," *Wilson Library Bulletin*, Decem-
    ber 1972, p. 327.
12 "Michigan U. Library School: Minority
    Students Drive Again," *LJ*, November
    15, 1972, p. 3951.
13. "Minority Recruitment," *American Li-
    braries*, May 1972, p. 447.

III

Service
to the
Community

Branch Power

Florence Field

THE CHICAGO Public Library is in the process of trying to find its bearings in the outside world after being shut away from it for many years. When I was hired two years ago last August, my task was to join in this process of discovering the ways and means by which the Chicago Public Library could again become a legitimate member of society. I was assigned to the Woodlawn Regional Branch, which is located in a low-income, black neighborhood on the Southside of Chicago.

With the advice and cooperation of various agencies, groups, and individuals in the community, we started programs which we hoped initially would accomplish two things: first, bring the library to the attention of community residents and agencies to whom we had become all but invisible; and second, change the image of the library to that of an agency more involved in the life of the community. Since we had no special funds or extra personnel, the kinds of programs we were able to develop were very much determined by the availability of resources. But it was an eye-opener to me to find out how much one can accomplish through the resource of interagency cooperation.

For example, our civil service examination training classes involved a teacher from the Board of Education; we have held three Job Fairs with representatives from 20 businesses, industries, and related agencies participating; we have an ongoing sex education program for teen-age girls staffed by a Woodlawn resident trained by the Lying-In Hospital of the University of Chicago; we have held an outdoor Afro-Arts Theater program with help from the Illinois Arts Council; we are starting a series on youth and the law for parents and youths by a lawyer from Legal Aid; and we have held a monthly series of panel discussion forums on such controversial issues as local control of schools, law and the black community, neo-colonialism in Africa, and the meaning of autonomous black studies programs, involving panelists from various agencies, community organizations, churches, and schools.

But as the months went on, I became convinced that the problem of converting a "traditional" library system into one more responsive to various community needs was more difficult and basic than I had realized. Adding on social workers and "social" programs to an already existing system simply were not sufficient for today's needs. The system, it seemed, was not ready for such a transformation. And I began to think about why the public library in Chicago, as well as elsewhere, had become so unresponsive and irrelevant to community needs.

Before going on, I should explain that my library experience has all been in Chicago, and, consequently, my examples will be from there. However, since large organizational systems all share common characteristics, I am sure my comments apply to other library systems as well.

An early, strong impression I got as an outsider was how little autonomy branch librarians actually have. In this respect, librarians and public school teachers find themselves in the same bag. They are both in organizations where rules and regulations are externally determined—by state and local legislation. Moreover, in such a setting, the rise of a highly bureaucratic system is all but inevitable. In such a system, as sociologist Robert Merton points out, "a high degree of reliability of behavior and an unusual degree of conformity with prescribed patterns of action must be attained."[1] Have we ever really thought about what this lack of autonomy means to the librarian and to the library? I think there are many consequences.

It is obvious that under such circumstances innovation is very difficult because, for one thing, rewards are more likely to be awarded to those who are "methodical, prudent, and disciplined,"[2] rather than to those who are innovative and experimental. For another, even a branch librarian who may have strong desires to make his library more relevant to the community finds himself bound by prescribed rules and procedures which have nothing to do with his situation. To paraphrase Wilensky and Lebeaux, two other sociologists, "between the dedicated librarian with the desire to help and the community with its need lies the bureaucratic ma-

chine, with its own 'needs.' And these 'needs' can result in an emphasis on technique and method, on organizational routines and records, rather than on people and service."[3] As a result, the demands of the system itself often overwhelm even the most committed librarian.

Further, a bureaucracy, especially when it is integrated with a professional culture, prides itself on being impartial and objective. For example, rules and regulations are made up and enforced "impartially"—the hidden assumption being that everyone and every community are alike, when in fact, they are not. Perhaps the most important, and therefore, the most critical, consequence of this view is the indiscriminate application of general goals to all the branches of a system—for example, the goal of book reading and the related one of high circulation figures.

Such a goal may do for some communities, but in those neighborhoods where reading is not widespread, it means, first, that if a nonreader should come to the library for information about black history, for example, he wouldn't be able to get it, whereas, if the library had an adequate film collection and personalized film viewers instead of shelves of unread books, the information would be available to him. But the book-oriented approach to the community by the library clearly means that services are available mainly to those who conform to rules of the game—i.e., by reading. There is no place for the nonreader. It is no wonder that the community is so often turned-off by such a one-sided approach.

And despite this emphasis on reading and circulation, the library also has rules, at least in Chicago, which make it impossible for a member of a family to get a library card if another member has a book delinquent. In an inner-city community like Woodlawn, this ruling leaves many children ineligible and unable to borrow books. Thus, despite the best intentions on the part of the librarian, such regulations, which are so blatantly unfair and inconsistent, make the library suspect in the eyes of our children, of their parents, of school teachers and administrators. In these and many others ways, the professional librarian finds he cannot use his skills or act out his responsibilities as he desires—he has, to a large extent, become a cog in the bureaucratic machine.

What can we do? Somehow and in some way, librarians must be given more autonomy—each branch must become much more of an autonomous unit than it is now. And what would follow then?

For one thing, I think we will find many more creative librarians within our system than now seems possible. I have read articles in your professional journals about the lack of imaginative librarians—but, given the freedom and the challenge, and, most important, given the proper support structures, in time I believe many people will respond positively, although of course there will be those who will not be able to cope with freedom. There seems to be quite a bit of attention given to curricula of library schools, but I imagine equally important might be the continuing education of librarians now in the system, once they are given the opportunity to reach out and become creative.

Branch autonomy will attract young, imaginative people into the profession, to stay and to develop and to help us make possible what now may seem impossible. These individuals, like the community residents of inner-city neighborhoods, are also turned-off by the meaningless red-tape of the system, by decisions in which they have no share.

Specifically, autonomy means, for example, that the librarians should be given a budget to use for programs that the staff, with the help of the community, decide are legitimate and necessary for the library and its programs. At Chicago, each branch gets a sum of money, but it is earmarked for certain items—books, audiovisual materials, display items—and whatever happens, in all 60 branches at the same time. But it may be that one branch needs more films or another more equipment. If so, the decision should be made at the branch level, not at the top, to be applied equally to all branches.

Of course, there can be no autonomy or freedom without responsibility (although mere conformity in a bureaucracy requires only obedience). Consequently, new ways will have to be devised to evaluate the librarian's performance. No longer will he be judged in terms of prompt paperwork or of common-sense administration (which, translated, means not rocking the boat) or of running a tight ship, but as much as possible in terms of programs that reflect the interests of the community.

Obviously, this is a much more difficult kind of evaluation; it implies an understanding of and a sensitivity to the changes taking place in our society. Moreover, it also means that the evaluation cannot be carried on by one senior librarian—the system must have on its payroll as consultants members of other disciplines—urban sociologists, educators, social workers—who will not only act as consultants to branch librarians but will share, along with the senior librarian, in the task of evaluating their performance.

It must be obvious to you by now that what I have been talking about is decentralization. Before going on, however, let me point out that decentralization does not necessarily mean community participation or control. Decentralization is an administrative concept, and in our context means local autonomy for the branch librarian. But a decentralized system needs new forms of internal control and coordination. In a bureaucracy, control and coordination are realized through directives from the top; in a decentralized system, control and coordination take place through communication. Thus, decision-making does not take place at the top. Instead, both vertically and horizontally, there is much more sharing, discussion, and communication.

The lack of mutual decision-making, both vertically and horizontally, is quite evident in Chicago, as I am sure it is elsewhere. For example, within each branch, staff meetings are held only a few times a year, mainly as an opportunity for the branch librarian to explain new directives or policy (such as a new pay scale) to the staff. I once asked one of our librarians if she were planning to call a staff meeting about coming programs, and her reply was she might—once they were decided on. Consequently, staff meetings are seen primarily as occasions for information delivery, rather than as occasions for free flow of ideas or for participation in decision-making.

Moreover, there are no staff meetings among the branch librarians themselves; in fact, contrary to popular belief, the branches exist much more as discrete, isolated units under a hierarchical bureaucratic system than they would under decentralization, where horizontal communication becomes the lifeline of the system. Questions and problems now go up the line separately, and the answers come down the line in the same way. This procedure is called, as many of you are aware, "going through channels."

As a result of the Lowell Martin survey, to give another example, the Chicago Public Library is undergoing some changes. There is now a committee on inner city libraries composed of two members of the Board of Directors and two top level librarians. Again, possibly, policy decisions will be made about inner city libraries without the advice or participation of anyone else in the library system. For example, we have a young librarian in charge of our recently initiated mini-libraries in various public housing projects throughout the city. She has, in a short time, gained tremendous knowledge and ex-

perience about inner city needs and about indigenous staffing of these libraries. She would be invaluable on such a committee, but her lack of seniority rules her out. Moreover, on matters as important as this, there is no reason the Chicago Public Library and its inner city committee should not hold public hearings, perhaps in each of the major inner city communities, to give residents and organizations an opportunity to voice their opinions. Since the Board of Directors in no way represent the voice of the poor and the excluded, public hearings seem only just for such a public agency. And, of course, I can think of no better way to get the community directly involved in the public library.

Consequently, what I am suggesting is a system in which branch librarians are freed from the limitations of bureaucratic control and are allowed to experiment and to find the best ways to apply professional skills to meet community needs. The librarian's identification, which at present is almost entirely with the library system, will in time begin to shift toward the community. He will begin to make demands on the system for personnel and other resources to implement the programs he feels are necessary. At present, branch librarians tend to work strictly within prescribed limits, within the realm of the now and the possible. But who is to say what the outer reaches of the possible really are?

Through action and commitment, librarians as well as teachers and social workers will find their professional identity and expand their professional skills. Decentralization surely has untold advantages for the community, but the other side of the coin is that it is also the only way for institutions to become responsive to the changes taking place in society today.

Librarians today are looking for new techniques of communication. I submit that we cannot begin to discuss problems of communication without taking into consideration the organizational setting of our library system. If we on our side are bound by limitations set up external to the situation (by city hall, by the state legislature, by the needs of the bureaucratic system itself), how can we enter into meaningful discourse with members of the community? These bureaucratic rules have no place in their lives; they serve no useful purpose for them; and often they hinder the kinds of services which are needed.

If we do not change, our libraries will become like the human appendix—a vestigial institution with no apparent function in society. But I am afraid the impetus for change will have to come from the community and particularly from the bottom ranks of the library profession. Decentralization means parceling out of decision-making powers—and no one who has power likes to give it up. Consequently, in the name of commitment to social needs and issues larger than the library itself, new librarians face a gargantuan task. Until the need for this undertaking is at least acknowledged, I can't quite see too much point in talking about innovation.

Let me end by saying it is really up to you, the librarians, to take upon yourselves the responsibilities of action you know will make the library work better, even though you may initially face official disapproval. We cannot have change without risks—I think one of the reasons we feel, despite the many new programs we have heard and read about, that things are more or less the same is because we are attempting to achieve innovation *without* change. If we really feel that there is a future for the public library, we must start acting now, no longer as dedicated bureaucrats but as dedicated professionals.

REFERENCES

1. Merton, Robert. "Bureaucratic Structure and Personality" in *Reader in Bureaucracy,* edited by Robert K. Merton, Ailsa P. Gray, Barbara Hockey, and Hanan C. Selvin, Free Press, 1952, p. 365.
2. *Ibid.*
3. Wilensky, Harold L. and Charles N. Lebeaux. *Industrial Society and Social Welfare,* Free Press, 1965 (paperback ed.), p. 243.

Libraries in the Marketplace: Information Emporium or People's University?

Fay Blake and Edith Perlmutter

SEVERAL RECENT DEVELOP-MENTS in the world of American libraries seem to foreshadow an ominous trend toward a new concept of library service. The concept is translated into a variety of proposals—the "information supermarket," "libraries for profit," "user fees," "user-based charges"—but what's really being proposed is an elimination of tax-supported library service.

Louis Vagianos in his article, "Libraries: Leviathanic Vagrants on a 'Titanic' Trip" (*LJ*, May 1, 1973, p. 1450), says libraries haven't increased their productivity in a century, so a "fair market price" or "real price" or user charge to the consumer of the information product is called for. "The information consumer," he says in attention-commanding italics, "has never really had to pay for his information and as a result has no conception of its cost, and therefore of its value to him as a product or service."[1]

Charles O'Halloran, Missouri state librarian, beats the same drum in a recent squib in *Show-Me Libraries* for September 1973. Libraries, he says, ought to take their chances in the "free market economy" just like franchise restaurants and Studebaker. Because of the "operation of the Law of the Marketplace which destroys the weak and the inept and the outmoded," he says, "some libraries

would certainly die" but "some would flourish and prosper."

O'Halloran fails to specify how exactly libraries would operate in this "free marketplace" he airily wants to consign us to (yes, the man has heard about Lockheed—he says so), but presumably free means not free so libraries would charge users for their services just like all the other enterprises in the free economy we operate in.

From still another source, the Information Industry Association, comes a proposal to set up an "Information Supermarket," a proposal for the funding of at least some library services through user fees for personalized preprocessed information packages prepared by specialized entrepreneurial libraries run for profit in the free market. In April 1973 the IIA Board Chairman, Eugene Garfield, testified before the National Commission on Libraries and Information Sciences that "user-based charges must inevitably prevail" and stressed that anything you get for nothing is worth nothing or, at any rate, valued at nothing.

At least one public library has already experimented with a user fee for some of its services. On April 1, 1970, the Minneapolis Public Library, in cooperation with the Greater Minneapolis Chamber of Commerce, inaugurated a special service to the business community of Minneapolis. For $18 per hour the library would provide abstracts, bibliographies, current awareness service, and searching within and outside of Minneapolis Public Library.

On the practical level, it is curious that, at this time when the "free market" is vanishing from what Galbraith calls the "new industrial state," suggestions for converting public agencies into for-profit businesses are increasing. Disenchantment with public sector performance has led to an irrational embrace of the market at a time when the market may itself be outmoded.

Now let's take a look at some of the rationale for this sudden flurry of proposals to turn economic history back to Adam Smith and to turn libraries loose in a "free market economy." Most of the reasoning seems to be based on muddy thinking and the uncritical swallowing of some undigested economic phrases. Vagianos, for example, says "The goal of society . . . has been . . . improvement in labor productivity . . . and the concomitant . . . (is) an improved standard of living for the individual . . ." Well, that sounds like an argument standing on its head. Even the greediest society would claim an improved standard of living as its goal and improvement of labor productivity as the concomitant, not the other way around. But be that as it may, Vagianos goes on to claim that the improvement of the library's labor productivity can be implemented through 1) the use of cost effectiveness to increase efficiency and, consequently, productivity and 2) the use of a "fair market price" user charge.

O'Halloran says, "In a free market economy, popular choices and preferences, competition, skilled versus inept management, imagination and boldness, or fear and hesitation can bring prosperity or ruin and it's brutal and jungle-like." The citizenry, O'Halloran claims, ought to decide freely what their money should be spent on, and if it decides that a huge defense budget is what we all need rather than continued funding for librar-

ies, then so be it. O'Halloran doesn't bother to mention that funds for libraries, even when chosen by the elected representatives of the citizenry, can be side-tracked by impoundment.

Zurkowski and Garfield both have personal association with the profit-making sectors of the information industry; they would naturally be expected to support more profit making. They don't confine themselves to such demands, however, Garfield says his association's existence in the free market will inevitably spur the development of new information technologies and an increased awareness of and expertise in the use of these new technologies.

Zurkowski on the other hand, speaks (*American Libraries*, May 1973, p. 258) of the IIA user charge suggestion "that in certain specialized areas where the available information services are very specialized and expensive, a for-profit library might well develop, thereby relieving some competition for the ever-diminishing public resources available for libraries.

So, the arguments for libraries as profit-making or, at least, fee-based information supermarkets are that they would: 1) increase the productivity of libraries; 2) increase the economic efficiency of libraries; 3) convince the user of the library's value; and 4) relieve competition for public resources. We maintain that none of these claims is true and that all these anachronistic proposals do the library user a serious disservice. We believe very strongly that today's library needs some drastic changes if it is to be an essential, functional social institution, but the changes need to be in the direction of more public support, not less.

Vagianos, O'Halloran, et al. have placed themselves in the position of the undergraduate who has taken the introductory course in Principles of Economics and proceeds to instruct the World Monetary Bank (not that the Bank couldn't benefit from some wise instruction). These gentlemen have confused the market mechanism in a private enterprise system with economic efficiency in public enterprise, in this case the provision of library services. Let us deal first with increased productivity in libraries. Vagianos claims that improved labor productivity has been an overwhelming success in the private sector but has not improved in the library since the Industrial Revolution. How he arrives at this conclusion or even how he defines productivity is left to the readers' imagination. We are defining increased productivity as either the increase of real output with a given real input or the decrease of real input for a given real output. The rate of growth of total productivity cannot be measured without the measurement of the rate of growth of the real product. How does Vagianos measure the rate of growth of real information product? The problems in measuring real input and real product in the private sector are immense (see, for example, "The Measurement of Productivity," *Survey of Current Business*, May, 1972). The problems of measuring productivity in service industries in the private sector are even greater. The problems of measuring real input and real product in a public service industry are still more formidable. Vagianos' airy assertion about the libraries' stagnant productivity flies in the face of the economists' admitted inability to agree on how to measure the productivity of public service industries. Let us search for the best techniques to achieve efficiency by all means, but productivity is only one aspect of efficiency.

Production is part of the question of supply in the economic equation. The other side of the equation—the demand side—, according to Vagianos, O'Halloran, and Garfield would be solved by charging the consumer of the information product "real prices," "fair market prices," or "a user charge." These are not synonymous, although the proposers do not distinguish among them. Ostensibly, a fair market price is determined by Adam Smith's famous "invisible hand" through the laws of supply and demand. Mr. Nixon's Phase 4 is ample evidence that the invisible hand is

palsied. One would think that a fair market price for instance, could rather easily be determined, but somehow meat prices do not seem to be in equilibrium through the laws of supply and demand. What makes these pundits believe that such an elusive product price as the library's could possibly be so equilibrated?

Public goods are, by definition, goods that are not financed through the private exchange or market economy. We assume, therefore, that Vagianos and the others substitute a "user charge" for public goods since there can be no "fair market price" for them. We deny that a user charge for the information product would increase economic efficiency. The price of a product in a private transaction takes into account only the private costs and benefits of the product. The price of an automobile, for instance, is based on the internal cost of the manufacturer and the utility of the car to the buyer. When the production and consumption of the automobile results in pollution, however, society is affected. The price has not, thus far, reflected the social costs to third parties or society, costs which are called "externalities" or "spillovers." In a competitive market the pricing mechanism would generally reflect a more or less efficient allocation of resources, but when the social cost has not been included, the pricing mechanism has been skewed and resources have *not* been efficiently allocated. The "spillover" may be either a cost or, as in the distribution of the information product, a benefit to society or third parties. The whole point of a public service industry like libraries or education is precisely the benefit spillover to society as a whole. No user charge could take into account this nonquantitative "spillover" or "externality." Therefore, a user charge would inevitably fail the test of efficiency.

Maybe the proponents of a user charge consider it an efficient technique because it seems to rid us of the problem of "free riders." You want our service? Pay for it! Here, too, they're off the track. The so-called free rider may very well be benefiting all of society. The individual who makes use of the library's product is not engaged in a private transaction which benefits and concerns only himself. He may be using his information to build a bridge, to show others how to build a better bridge faster, to write an opera; to use the computer to compose music, to cure a disease, or to invent a new prosthetic device. In other words, he may be increasing society's total productivity in ways not immediately visible from his library transaction alone. The private sector's overwhelming increase in productivity, which has so impressed Vagianos, may very well be partly the result of the free rider's utilization of the library's product. Our carrying of the free rider is, in effect, out investment in human capital.

But it is not efficiency alone that must be considered in the concept of a user charge. Vagianos and Garfield and O'Halloran say the user has no conception of the cost or value of the library's product because he hasn't had to pay for it. Have they access to some secret information which enables them to determine the value of a service to a user and to equate that value with the price? If two users each pay one dollar per unit of information service, one with an income of less than $4000 a year, the other with an income of more than $100,000 a year, do they assume that the value of the information product is the same for both? Vagianos says: "... as any economist knows, the best way of evaluating alternatives is by comparing cost benefits"— or, given the alternatives, will you spend your dollar on beans or books? But as any librarian knows, when you're trying to live on welfare, you haven't got alternatives—beans are more important than books. The library envisioned by these writers reminds us of Thoreau's comments in *Walden*: "I respect not his labors, his farm where everything has its price. . . . who would carry his God to market, if he could get anything for him . . . on whose farm nothing grows free, whose fields bear no crops, whose meadows no flowers, whose trees no fruits, but dollars; who loves not the beauty of his fruits, whose fruits are not

ripe for him till they are turned to dollars."

Even Adam Smith, the founder of laissez-faire economics, concedes in his *The Wealth of Nations* that ". . . the duty of the sovereign or commonwealth is that of erecting and maintaining those public institutions and those public works, which though they may be in the highest degree advantageous to a great society, are, however, of such a nature, that the profit could never repay the expense to any individual or small number of individuals, and which it therefore cannot be expected that any individual or small number of individuals should erect or maintain . . . . After the public institutions and public works necessary for the defense of the society, and for the administration of justice, . . . the other works and institutions of this kind are chiefly those for facilitating the commerce of the society, and those for promoting the instruction of the people.

That was in the 18th Century, yet in the last quarter of the 20th Century, our anachronistic library "economists" want to return to a real jungle where public works will become nonexistent and where the amenities public institutions have dispensed to all will become the possession of a tiny and moneyed minority.

The capstone argument for fee-based information supermarkets is that competition for public resources would be relieved. What makes these gentlemen think that removing an expenditure from a public budget would automatically create an alternative public use for the funds involved? The more likely outcome would be a decrease in taxes and the shift of resources to the private sector. The income increase due to reduced taxes would be spent on private goods, including information. And the resources formerly used to service public libraries, would now be employed in private information industries.

Competition for public resources would not be relieved, but on the contrary, increased by competition from the private sector which plow profits into advertising its wares. In a competition for the dollars of consumers and firms to buy private goods versus dollars for taxes which buy public goods for "others," the battle is rigged in favor of the private sector.

The thinkers who want to turn libraries into "efficient profit-makers" have succumbed uncritically to certain unwarranted assumptions. They have assumed without reason that the principles applicable to private enterprises can automatically be transferred to public enterprises. Beyond that, they have assumed that private enterprise in our society functions in a thoroughly free market, one that never existed fully free and is now an economist's chimera. The supermarket for information retrieval will resemble the telephone monopoly more than the competitive wheat market in economic textbooks or even the present-day grocery supermarkets. As in the telephone industry, duplications would be wasteful and technology would require large-scale operations for information retrieval. A third assumption is that private enterprise run with efficiency and a dash of imagination succeeds while "the weak go to the wall." A corollary of this assumption is, inevitably, that any private enterprise which survives must be efficiently run. We hate to be the ones to publicize the fact that some emperors are naked, but it is a fact.

There are private enterprises whose efficient management is not enough to overcome competitors with more sources of money, more political influence, more willingness or ability to cheat or connive or bribe.

The assumption that private enterprise produces what people need because of the exigencies of competition is also unwarranted. The supermarket which the library is to emulate is a prime example of the opposite. Milton Friedman, the eminent professor of economics at the University of Chicago and erstwhile advisor to President Nixon, supposes a fable in a recent *New York Times* article in which the retail provision of groceries has been organized like our elementary and secondary schools. "Would there be super-

markets and chain stores?" Friedman agonizes. "Would the shelves be loaded with new and improved convenience products? Would stores be using every device of human ingenuity to attract and retain customers?" Friedman fails to ask: Would stores be selling meats prepared with carcinogenic nitrites and nitrates? Would the shelves be stuffed with expensive and nutritionally useless foods? Would stores be adding to the cost of food a huge expenditure for vulgar, untruthful advertising? Would foods be offered in wasteful double or triple paper wrappings?

We already have an example of a few experiments in public services turned over to private enterprise. The U.S. Office of Economic Opportunity contracted with private educational firms in 1970 to teach school children in several grades. Payment was to be made on the basis of performance by the educational firms, and comparisons were to be drawn with the performance of children in regular classes. The result of the experiment seems to be one big mess. OEO says the experiment was a failure. There is apparently no evidence that the private firms performed the teaching function any better than regular school teachers despite the performance payment incentive. Could it be even that the powerful profit incentive doesn't guarantee efficient and effective public service delivery?

As a matter of fact, where we really care about results nobody seems to suggest putting the project into private hands. When is the last time anyone proposed that the Army ought to be farmed out to private enterprise? We could argue that such a step would make it more efficient: why leave the organization of the Army to dunderheaded public servants when it could be done by captains of industry for a profit? We could make the Army more productive: pay private companies by body count? Or number and size of wars they could arrange? And we could institute a user fee: anyone who wants a sophisticated protection packet including the latest in nuclear weapons can damn well pay for it; otherwise, how's he going to know the value of what he gets—and that'll get all those peaceniks off our necks, too. If they don't like the armed forces, they have the freedom of any citizen to opt out. You can try the analogy out on police forces or space exploration. Why not sell all public parks off, too, while we're at it?

This is not to maintain that we regard libraries as they are now run as models of productivity or efficiency or just plain utility. This is not to say that libraries and the library's product should not be improved. On the contrary. Today's library needs drastic improvement, but not via the thoroughly anachronistic proposals for the pricing of a public service in a society which has been growing more and more affluent, in which leisure is becoming more and more widespread, and in which more and more public services have become necessities rather than the luxuries they used to be. The "rigorous procedural standards," "the new techniques," "the budgetary and cost controls" offered as panaceas are only useful if the library's real productivity is increased. That means expanding and improving the quantity and quality of its products without increasing input, and that means substituting new services to new populations for traditional services to populations which can and do find them outside the library. This is not the place for a full exposition of these new services, but a few examples to consider are massive programs to serve the ghetto populations with information on employment and training or with programs designed to develop a sense of community and increased opportunities; or programs designed to provide prison and jail populations with extensive legal, vocational, and general information. We could provide extensive new leisure services for our population—not merely the traditional recreational books. How about mediating between filmmakers and their huge potential audience? How about helping users learn how to become filmmakers themselves? We could be providing information on controversial community issues as well as the rostrum and meeting halls for the discussion of community issues. We could be serving very young children and their parents and teachers before they enter the public school system not only with books but with toys or games or pets or whatever we can think of that expands the world of the next century's adults.

What's the social benefit of all these nontraditional services? Why *not* serve those who've already made it, more or less, and forget about the losers? Well, some of the reasons we'll just have to take on faith—and the words of people who've told us what libraries did for them. When Malcolm X told us the prison library turned his head and his life around, we believed him. We think it's worth a lot to society in human terms— and even in just plain economic terms— to turn someone away from a dead-end drug scene or a dead-end job or a dead-end holdup, and libraries can do something positive about this. *Free* and *public* libraries, that is, which accept their responsibility for serving everyone with the full range of information they need.

These services, especially those to populations the library has consistently failed to serve, will often have to be given instead of some of our extensive and expensive services to well-served populations, but the substitution could be economically efficient and could be increasing the library's real productivity. The library could become again the people's university we once were for the poor, the alien, the illiterate, and the disregarded as well as the source for information to a changing society.

Urban Information and Public Libraries: A Design for Service

Mary Lee Bundy

THE QUESTION of the role of public libraries in ghetto information dissemination cannot be addressed without first considering the more fundamental issue of the library's social commitments and particularly its stance with regard to the causes and solutions to poverty. An information system is neutral; it can be harnessed in support of many purposes. This is not to say that the information system in this country is neutral. The information deprivation which characterizes the situation for ghetto residents today is proof of a strong commitment to protect the status quo and a lack of genuine institutional commitment to change ghetto conditions. Information control and manipulation is one of the major means by which an oppressive status quo is perpetuated.

Denial of Human Rights

The major barrier to meaningful dialogue on the issue of the role of public libraries in urban centers is the same barrier which effectively separates libraries from their inner city communities—the profession's largely white and middle-class composition. This membership imposes blinders and reinforces engrained attitudes which allow the profession and its institutions to continue to be insensitive to the desperate plight of fellow Americans. The daily struggle merely to survive in the streets of the communities libraries purport to serve is not seen as requiring any serious response from this institution.

The inhumane liberalism in which the profession has indulged far too long allows the institution to maintain the importance of serving all comers equally and thus to treat as equally compelling a request from a suburban housewife wanting to plan flower decorations for a dinner party and the plight of a hungry child. The reality is that the deprived make next to no use of libraries and libraries do next to nothing to reach them.

When this basic hypocrisy is exposed, librarians fly to their own defense. They point out that they are not social workers or lawyers; they are not against helping the poor, but they cannot cross the boundaries of their professional territory. And so like the other professions, they allow people with needs to fall into the chasms which lie between the boundaries of the various professions because human problems do not define themselves neatly along these circumscribed lines and because the professions charged with a responsibility do not honor it in the case of America's poor.

Even more crucially, when poverty is

144

the issue, librarians like most middle-class Americans turn off their critical faculties so as to continue to avoid facing the reasons for poverty in the face of the most glaring evidence of it. The reality is that the social, political, and economic system in this country keeps large numbers of people dependent for survival on public institutions which deny them even minimum benefits and effectively keep them from getting out of this dependency. They are the victims of unscrupulous landlords and businesses which make exorbitant profits off them as consumers and discriminate against them as employees. They are left the easy prey of drug peddlers in a system which disenfranchises them so that they are always dependent on the benevolence of a larger system which has not been and is not disposed to alter the situation. The ultimate indignity is the educational system which demands of them that they seek to aspire to acceptance in this dominant system whose corrupt and twisted values have been historically and currently directed against them.

White Americans even more vigorously deny the racism imbedded in this system than the oppression. In a kind of fundamental perversion, the blame is transferred to the victims. The problem is cast in terms of crime, delinquency, and violence so as to countenance even the most extreme of measures in controlling the people thus unhumanly treated. It is because black people are seen as not quite human that they are considered suspect and ineligible for the same treatment and advantages enjoyed by members of the "superior" race.

The institutional accommodations being made to the "black problem" must be labeled for what they are—weak attempts of institutions to remove themselves from censure and to avoid having to make more major change. And so libraries, like other institutions, are currently involved in "hiring more blacks" and in setting up special—temporary—libraries in inner city neighborhoods, instead of giving the people who live there

at least library service comparable to that of branches in white neighborhoods.

Even the most service minded of librarians continue to treat of symptoms rather than causes. They will help a welfare mother get her check, but they are not actively engaged in working on local welfare rights programs or in bringing about badly needed legislative reforms in the welfare system. They will refer a drug user to a rehabilitation center, but they are not working with the groups seeking to stop the flow of drugs into the black community. They take books and films to prisoners, but they are not involved in trying to get information out about prison conditions.

Paternalism, do goodism, sympathy, and individual efforts accomplished within the constraints of the existing system are sorry substitutes for what people really want and deserve, their rights in this society. When practiced by librarians, they signify to ghetto people that here is one more institution unprepared to ally itself on the side of people in their struggle. For to stand idly by is to be supportive of the system of oppression.

Ghetto Information Needs

The reason why the failure of libraries to respond positively to the urban crisis is important is because the most critical commodity influencing change in the urban situation is information. The information needs of ghetto people grow out of and are made crucial by their human and social needs. They cannot be defined apart from a commitment to changing rather than perpetuating the conditions of ghetto existence.

Access or lack of access to strategic information can decide the success or failure of individual effort to solve problems and enhance life opportunities. It is important to the success of efforts to effect even minimal change and is essential in communities getting and keeping some control over the decisions affecting their welfare. It may be the last hope in stopping further repression from "coming down."

Survival necessity has dictated that ghetto people maintain a communication system which will come to their aid quickly in emergency situations. But this system is not a substitute for other vitally needed communication links. It is not sufficient to overcome the communication breakdowns which exist because public institutions are alien, unresponding, and hostile to them.

And information in and of itself cannot change reality. People can be made better informed of opportunities available to them and as a consequence some people gain advantages they would not otherwise have had. But this information transfer does not multiply the number of such opportunities. Investigation too frequently would show that proffered help through special minority programs is not actually available as advertised or has hidden barriers to "qualifying" for help. Special job training and other minority programs frequently give people expectations which do not materialize, thus adding to frustration and disappointment.

Informing a man of his rights does not ensure that he will receive them. Telling him where best to turn for legal help when he is arrested does not guarantee that the system will treat him justly if the very laws or the prosecution of them is unjust. Telling him he has a right to police protection does not force the police to provide it. Similarly, increasing his knowledge about how the system exploits and disadvantages him may only increase his feelings of powerlessness unless this knowledge is linked to knowledge about positive solutions.

Realization of the information potential in the urban situation lies therefore in putting information to work to help in the crucial task of organizing people to seek an end of their disadvantagement. For until ghetto residents unite to improve their power position, there is no real hope of any change in their situation. The established institutions simply cannot divest themselves of their vested interests and commitments so as to shift the terms of their operations. It is ridiculous to suppose that institutions of their own accord will turn their agencies over to communities whatever the gestures they may be making in this direction. The only hope lies in ghetto people organizing so as to achieve a power base from which to make themselves heard and responded to.

Under these terms giving people information which will permit them to cope may detract from the more basic goal of organizing people to achieve their freedom and rights. Indeed one of the strategies for keeping people disadvantaged is to make them vie for and grateful for small favors and fearful that if they protest on any issue, even these small benefits may be taken from them.

Linking individuals to the groups seeking to bring about more major change becomes then the more significant information task. Helping to form such groups where they do not exist even if only by letting people know that others share their problem and telling them how to get started in an effort to organize for collective action are informing tasks of important stature. Lending information support to community based organizations could make a very critical difference.

A range of community centered endeavors exist in the inner city and struggle to survive and be effective. Some render badly needed drug, crisis information, and other services. Others seek increased benefits from city institutions while others are organized around black and ethnic identification and unification. Many seek to lay the groundwork for long-term change even while rendering immediate services. All of them have critical information needs born out of the conditions of their existence, their purposes, and the fact that these goals put them in competition with, if not opposition to, established institutions.

The alternate programs which have stepped in to accomplish what establishment agencies are failing to do—street academies, free clinics, cultural programs, youth centered programs—

face a continual struggle for existence. They need to know where financial support can be found and aid in going about securing it. They need help in attracting users and members and in securing technical assistance for their ongoing programs.

Welfare rights and other rights movements have a particular information problem because the information they need to force reforms in city institutions is frequently in the hands of the very agency they are challenging and is, therefore, difficult if not impossible to obtain. Establishment agencies restrict information they make available about their own activities, engaging in what are actually public relations rather than public information programs. They also fail to collect vital information about their communities. An example is the lack of available information about the health situation in a community. The consequence is groups are forced to "prove" there are uncared for sick people in their community.

Decentralization of the school system and other efforts toward community control face this same problem. Reformers need first to collect information about the inequalities in the school system—how bad the situation is by educational standards—and then to disseminate it so as to educate people about what they have a right to expect. They need advice as to alternatives to the ineffective legal resorts open to them.

In a political system which effectively gives citizens no basic say, entire communities are left without information about developments crucial to their welfare such as urban renewal and expressway plans. The information people do get is presented from the point of view of the agency and political and private interests promoting it and is, therefore, one-sided in nature and does not give them what they need to weigh the pros and cons of the proposal. It certainly does not tell them about the private "deals" involved and leaves them usually much too late to fend off a fait accompli. Thus citizens are effectively denied par-

ticipation in the decisional processes which effect them crucially. Thus a central information task is the community-wide dissemination of information focused on current issues, problems, and developments. The need is for a medium of expression free of the biases and controls of the general media, prepared to focus on community issues.

Black people in this country have been and still are the victims of an educational and broader cultural system which has deprived them of knowing of their African heritage, from getting a proper perspective on the contributions black people have made, and the real story behind the treatment of black people in America. As a people, they have a major information problem and that is to disseminate black culture from a black rather than white dominant culture perspective. Black people also need an interpretation of issues and problems from the vantage point of their welfare so as to offset the current biased presentation they receive through the mass media and educational system.

The Information Situation

This overview of ghetto information requirements has suggested how access to information can be a powerful organizing tool in changing ghetto conditions. It also exposes the same neglect, domination, and racism in the information system as characterizes the social system of which it is a part and requires conscious recognition and effort to overcome.

A further inspection of ways the present system keeps critical information from being known reveals how oppression is practiced in information handling.

Neglect: One of the chief causes of information mal-distribution is the way the government caters to some interests while neglecting the needs of urban residents. An example of the comparative value placed on public information is the U.S. Government Printing Office. Compare this still sluggish and archaic system and its depository arms with the advanced information systems which support scientific research conducted for defense purposes. The government regularly collects and makes available much statistical data in support of industrial activities as for instance keeping accurate account of employment trends. It requires the creation of special commissions to explore urgent social problems such as in housing or conditions in penal institutions or the treatment of minors by the courts and correctional institutions.

Suppression: Public agencies consciously suppress certain types of information so as to avoid a close scrutiny of their activities. A range of mechanisms are employed by local and federal agencies including such simple devices as delay in publishing an agency's annual report of expenditures until long past the time that its use of public funds can be challenged. In these and other ways, public and private agencies avoid inspection and censure. The deliberateness of this effort is exposed when groups try to secure information which could be used to challenge agency behavior.

Despite laws and Supreme Court rulings, agencies still continue to make it difficult to get information necessary to ensure that the law is carried out if they are basically uncommitted to it. An example is the lack of information with regard to violations of equal opportunity. As a consequence of agencies' own neglect in complying with the law, special watchdog groups exist. They too allow the law to continue to be violated by the simple device of not learning about the violations.

Agencies resist exposure of information about conditions of abuse for the very obvious reason that with their limited budgets they cannot correct the situation. Nevertheless, the failure of agencies themselves to press for increased resources and their unwillingness to put such information into the hands of groups who will seek reforms must be seen as the protection of this society from knowing the consequences of its unwill-

ingness to provide for the sick, the poor, and other elements who cannot fend for themselves and are dependent on public gratuity.

Discrimination and Disadvantagement: In many ways information suppression is more readily routed than is the racism which permeates information dissemination. Racial discrimination affects the transfer of information in every sphere. An example is the way high school counselors make decisions about which students are "college material" and will be told about available scholarships. The black student is assessed and judged by his conformance in a system which discriminates against him; if he succeeds, he is the "exception." Thus, the myth of the inferiority of black people is reinforced and accommodating blacks are advanced.

The overt racism in the mass media controlled by white interests has already been cited. Not only are the prejudices of whites reinforced, but black people as parents and citizens daily confront media which presents what whites in a racist society want blacks to feel, think, be, and do.

Official planning agencies collect mountains of technical data in support of their activities. The statistical formulas used to analyze this data obscure the discriminatory and exploitative value assumptions which underly its collection. As a consequence of these biases, the picture these information sources present may be faulty and inaccurate and incomplete representations of the reality of the urban situation.

When directed toward support of a governmental program, they may present a very one-sided view; from official sources one learns the positive benefits of an urban renewal program. But if the planners did not figure into their equation the human losses involved by thus uprooting people from their homes, they will have no data on the nature, extent, and cost of these losses. Thus under the cover of "expertise" the same manipulation of information occurs so as to take advantage of ghetto people.

Exploitation: This is one type of use of information to exploit. Perhaps the more inhuman form of information exploitation, even worse than the collection of data by the government census to sell more products to ghetto people, is the investigations done by social scientists designed to analyze the poverty situation for "scientific" purposes. This clinical interest in learning how people struggle to survive and respond to abuse without any commitment to ending the degradation is a chilling example of the disregard for people who are poor and black.

Indoctrination: The present information system must also be characterized as engaged in indoctrination whereby the general public is kept from knowing the truth about ghetto conditions, lulled into thinking something is being done, and convinced that the poor are the problem. The media and the educational system propagandize points of view, programs, and cultural values as universal which deny other people's culture. The public library is among the institutions which misuses its public charge to promote one set of cultural values and one cultural heritage as if it were superior to others. Imbedded in this culture and, therefore, in its literary products which libraries carry and promote, are values at complete variance with a democratic society and respect for human worth.

Surveillance: As we hear more arguments for and are given more evidence of the invasion of privacy as a necessity in a disturbed society, white middle America is evidencing a new concern over this historic issue. Ghetto people have long been aware of overt and hidden controls whereby the police, welfare workers, credit bureaus, and other interests collect information about them in order to exploit and control them. The technological means now available to keep people under continuous surveillance makes it imperative that we as a nation speak to the issue of people's right to privacy. Hopefully our ethical stance may not exclude people because of the color of their skin.

Information access and its corollary, the invasion of privacy, is the largest single issue before the public today. We cannot talk in any real sense about increasing citizen participation in government without stressing the importance of access to information. Gaining minimal benefits from the system and stopping further encroachments on freedom requires diligent watchdogging and alerting activities. Putting institutions into the hands of communities necessitates the generation and dissemination of information which is not now freely available and where important road blocks to getting it exist and are frequently insurmountable.

The Public Library's Response

This analysis of the urban information problem suggests three strategic information functions for the public library: reducing barriers to access to already existing information; collecting much needed information which does not now exist; and effecting the widespread dissemination of crucial information not now being distributed so as to reach ghetto people and the groups which are working with them. Following are eight information services in support of these information objectives. Offered in combination they would go to form a comprehensive information service for the people of the inner city.

1. *Reference Service.* Reference service, the supplying of information upon request to inquirers and including the related service of referral, would form the broad base of the library's service program. Reference would come to be a highly personalized, specialized form of service with a strong client commitment and a problem-solving approach to helping the inquirer.

The nerve centers for this service would be the local neighborhood outlets, whether branches or smaller sub-units. To supplement these fixed units, more informal street-oriented service would be provided, modeled along the lines of the street academies and possibly functioning from them.

The central library would be the back-up support facility and could be a central place for study groups seeking extensive information collections relating to specialized problems. While this concept does not depart radically from contemporary library organization, nevertheless a complete transformation of the central branch would be necessary. Departments such as fine arts, social sciences, business and technology, and geneology would become instead departments of welfare, housing, health, education, labor, the system of justice, and politics and government.

The traditional stance of the library, that is to provide, without critical comment or advice giving, materials and information, would shift. For to leave the inquirer dependent on incomplete, inaccurate information sources or frequently none at all is in effect to refuse to help him.

The individual drug user does not come to the library to get a list of all the drug rehabilitation centers in the city. People wanting to get on welfare do not want the welfare system explained to them; they want to know how to get on welfare. The library's contribution is to give them short cuts if only to save them eight or nine trips to the welfare department. The man going on trial in a domestic case does not want to know the law; he wants to know how to ensure that his case comes before a judge who understands his culture. Someone considering taking advantage of a low-moderate income housing program wants some realistic advice on what he is actually getting himself into. People in a tenement trying to force a landlord to make improvements may need help in finding out who he is and how to force him to make changes, not the law which is on his side anyway.

As proposed earlier, libraries can and should serve an important referral function and that is to direct inquirers to the groups in the city who are working on his problem. This is not to suggest that librarians not deal with the user's problem as he had defined it. But they should not

pretend there is an answer to his question when there is not, or an immediate solution to a problem where none in fact exists. Instead of such pretense, in the reference situation the librarian can take it upon himself to inform the inquirer that there are groups working on problems such as his or which have the experience to give him further counsel. This is not to send him to the established agency which should help him but which is probably the reason for his problem to begin with.

2. *Information Consulting Service.* Basic reference would serve not only individuals, but would also be invaluable to community groups, saving them such crucial time by having information on hand or getting it for them if it is not readily available. The library would develop reservoirs of data which could be drawn on by many groups. Examples include data on the voting records of political figures, information regarding the public and private interests of city council members and agency board members in the city, and the property ownership in poorer residential sections of the city.

The library would also assist groups in their information gathering and informing activities through the device of having library staff act as consultants to help groups plan their "information program." The program's design would encompass the following elements: the organization of the group's internal files and a communication system among members of the group; planning of its public relations program and other activities involving the public dissemination of information; establishing the means whereby the group arranges to collect general or particular information about its community and on such relevant aspects as the passage of legislation affecting the group's interests.

The library consultant might work with a group continuously on a project at the stage that information gathering comprised a key part of its effort, as in collecting information about the community's health situation. Library consultants would be called in from time to time, but one of the consultant's tasks would be to train group members to carry out various information tasks. Thus, while not able to assign a full-time librarian to every group in the city, groups could get some of the services which special librarians and information experts provide for business and industry.

I am talking about people's groups. On the basis of relative need only, the library would give service priority to community-based organizations over "establishment" agencies which can better afford to provide themselves with information services. Consistent with its "people's" orientation, the library would require of establishment agencies proof of community representation in any project for which they sought library help. One natural partner for the library not mentioned is the urban-based colleges seeking to reach inner city residents through community development programs.

3. *Public Information Dissemination.* Yet merely having information available for those who might want it is a totally inadequate concept for an institution centrally concerned with community-wide service. Reaching ghetto residents with vital information is one of the most challenging of the services for the library to undertake. It necessitates getting into nonprint media use for elements which are not strongly oriented toward printed medium. *The focus for a public information dissemination program would be community issues presented during the time an issue is pending and while there is still time for communities to act.*

Central to realizing this role would be watchdog and monitoring activities whereby the library would follow the deliberations of such groups as the city council or a school board with regard to a pending development, gathering relevant supporting material and presenting it in forms understandable to and from the point of view of the community resident. In this task, a range of groups exist already working in watchdog capacities and the library may need merely to be the medium of expression.

A medium which specializes in getting the facts out can play an important alerting, informing, and interpretation role for a community. Its impact should be increased citizen awareness and hopefully participation; it could become a force for reform in itself. It can also serve as a vehicle for helping to link people with community action groups.

4. *Advocate Information Service.* The foregoing services are not advocate services. They are services the people and groups of any community are entitled to receive. Advocacy service is defined as beyond these expected services and would be those library initiated efforts to get information to where it is needed at a time it is critically needed in an effort which puts it directly and immediately in challenge of an established institution's manner of proceeding with clients. This would include the stationing of library staff in hospitals and police stations to inform people being brought in of their legal rights.

5. *Cultural Transmission.* Key to the concept of the library serving an important role in cultural transmission is the notion of the library as a center for information and materials representing all points of view and differing cultural orientations. By this I mean far more than having four copies of a book by Rap Brown, all of which are out when anyone wants them—even while the library maintains classics on the shelves which are not read by poor or advantaged.

I am proposing the translation of this ethic into a reality through the device of separate culture centers, each oriented around a separate ethnic or ideological identification, fully stocked with materials and staffed with people who share the orientation and membership and can "rap" with people as they come in.

6. *Library Sponsored Courses.* In its service quest, the library would also undertake a direct educational responsibility, stepping in to offer needed educational programs when they were not available through another aegis. Two broad types of educational programs particularly relevant to ghetto people are

programs related to their survival needs and specially tailored cultural education programs.

Thus the library would sponsor courses in such areas as drug education, consumer education, and employment. In keeping with its change stance, the library would not so much teach people how to shop wisely but rather how to get local businesses to stop exploiting the consumer through price increases on inferior merchandise and foodstuffs and to offer a better and wider variety of food and other goods. The library's informal street service would be the obvious locale for drug education, with the lines between education and information service merging. The Cultural Transmission centers are the logical groups to offer cultural education courses as part of their service. Conducted by skilled teachers who understand and are themselves a part of the ghetto culture, they would employ educational teaching styles and approaches better suited to the participants.

7. *Information Education.* Libraries have a particular responsibility for generating public understanding of the importance of information in solving problems and some knowledge about the present information system and how it can be improved. The library would, therefore, translate its notion of teaching "library skills" into a program for emphasizing the importance of information in any effort to change life conditions. One key group for this kind of awareness program would be teenagers. A target group for information skills training is community workers, for they have a particular need for the technical skills of locating, organizing, interpreting, and disseminating information.

8. *Defender of People's Information Rights.* To hope to promote a service program of this nature in any real sense, necessitates that the library take a strong position with regard to people's "right to know" and that it make an organized and sustained effort to win public acceptance and appreciation for a public agency to serve this social defense role.

Otherwise the library would be simply inviting the unfavorable political repercussions which involvement in the proposed activities would produce. The firmness of the library's own convictions will go a long way to convince power holders that they must yield on this issue. Objection from ideological and other interest groups when the library presents material in contradiction to their point of view can be reduced if the library works to establish why in the long run it works to everyone's advantage to open and keep open the information system.

Establishing the legitimacy of this role will require that the public library act it out. It would seek to get information to which groups have a legal right but have been refused. The library would act as an intervening procurement agent in asking for such information, thus allowing its client to remain anonymous in order to guard his interests and to protect him against reprisals.

As defender, the library would go into court if necessary to gain the release of information and may engage in promoting legislation to better protect people's rights to information. Public libraries would seek alliances also with local groups fighting the "information war" in the mass media but also groups which are directing their efforts against racism and discrimination in these media. It would also ally with groups fighting the invasion of people's privacy by governmental and industrial interests, taking a particular interest in protecting the rights of the poor.

Personnel

Physical resources, technology, and management skill would be important in the design and implementation of this program. But the most important resource is service personnel. This program requires a combination of a range of expertises which do not follow and should not follow the traditional status and educational lines of the field and which will require wholly new concepts of work roles and the background and education for them.

Individuals who can relate at street levels must of necessity come out of and be acceptable in that culture, probably the immediate group in which they would be working. Group acceptance is also critical in working with community groups for they are hardly likely to invite into their counsels people who do not communicate a sympathy with their philosophy and aims. Library consultants must also be sufficiently experienced in the kinds of activities in which the group engages so that they do not require extensive training before they can be utilized.

Another type of specialization lies along the lines of the proposed library departments. Each system, for instance, would have at least one housing consultant who understood the complexities of government housing programs. Other specializations would orient around the technology, in particular the nonconventional media. The Cultural Transmission centers must have staff who are authorities on the particular culture.

To create an institution which is active and purposeful and relevant and competent requires these new expertises coupled with very specialized information preparation. A range of information skills and abilities are involved as this proposed design reveals. In addition to reference skills (information problem solving), skills in information program planning, information investigative skills, media exploitation, and ability to design street and other information services are required. Most importantly, the urban information specialist requires a problem solving orientation which he will bring to every information activity in which he engages.

In filling these various role specializations, libraries must actively seek out and recruit people with commitment who have a point of view and act it out in their professional as well as personal life. Only thus can the noncaring stance of institutions be shifted and the indifference and inertia which the bureaucratic form of organization imposes be overcome.

One of the realities most difficult to convince white professionals of is that no matter how committed they are and how much they want to help, there are limits to their participation imposed by the fact that they are white. Some whites can certainly win acceptance in black communities and so lend their technical skills but because they cannot be black, think black or feel black, there will always remain barriers to their acceptance and full participation. Above all, their whiteness dictates that they never put themselves in a position of dictating to or deciding for black people.

Here, then, briefly described, are the elements of a central city information system which while catering to immediate ghetto survival needs would be working toward more major change. Assumption of these service responsibilities offers the public library an opportunity to assume vital and unfilled information roles for the people of the inner city in contrast to the social control and indoctrination roles it presently plays.

Realization

The one essential point of this article is that any public institution exists solely to meet the needs of its community and if that community is disenfranchised and victimized, that institution must ally itself on the side of people to end their oppression. Each inner city community has particular needs and problems which should form the basis for the design of service programs but the general situation for ghetto people is the same. The same causative factors are at work. The same price for racism and social neglect is being exacted from America's urban poor everywhere.

I have proposed nothing here that departs radically from public library philosophy; each of these services had precedence in library practice. These proposals are consistent with the concept of an open society. There is already an advocacy movement underway in the profession.

Yet I am fully aware that what would be involved in bringing about these changes is an internal and external fight for control of libraries. Appeal to conscience and reasoned argument are not sufficient to overcome the very strong forces which support the status quo of the field. Overnight libraries are not going to develop a genuine commitment to their neglected constituencies sufficient to rout the very strong forces actively opposed to change.

Easily wounded sensibilities will object to this frank encounter with this profession's racism and social immorality. No one, certainly not affluent white Americans, can take any other position unless they themselves are prepared to live and have their family live in the same misery as that of the impoverished ghetto dweller. As a nation and as a profession we cannot go on ignoring such realities as a ten-year-old child admitted today to a Harlem hospital on drugs. If instead of social alarm, the response is to rationalize inaction, or ineffective action, one more time the people of Chicago, Detroit, Baltimore, Washington, New York, and every other inner city in the United States will have been sold out. Ineffective resorts are easily seen through by ghetto people and readily exposed within the profession once one looks at what would be involved in making a genuine effort.

Internal Decentralization

The tight grip which central managements have on public library systems would have to yield to transfer of authority to the local branches. These branches would become the point of involvement of the community in library decision making. Far more is involved than the central headquarters looking the other way when branch librarians break the rules in order to give effective service. Indeed branch representatives might well form a central professional committee which would make over-all internal policy for the system and decide what the central branch does in the way of support services.

Coupled with this decentralization would have to come a shift in the rigid rule structure which now gives library staff only very limited freedom to carry out their responsibilities. Released from punishing routines and clock punching, they can visit in their communities, attend meetings, work with groups, and take the time with the individual library inquirer which his question or interest requires.

Opening the System

Even more importantly, as I have discussed, community people must be brought into the library system under conditions of an internal reorganization which recognizes community expertise in more than the present subservient roles to which we assign noncredentialized personnel. The twin evils of civil service and professional education would have to be attacked in the battle to bring more capable people from the ranks of the poor into professional membership. It is simply not true that capable and committed and exceptionally qualified people cannot be found from among the poor of the inner city.

The fact that the personnel system needs restructuring and opening is evidenced by the very fact that we have to talk about recruiting more blacks or more people from the community. The situation ought to be completely reversed, whereby community interests decide how many noncommunity members they wish to retain in their employ. Only thus can capability and responsiveness to community needs be ensured.

Community Control

An institution cannot have a commitment to the struggle of a people to gain control over their own affairs and at the same time itself maintain a colonial empire whether the claim to right to control is made in the name of professional expertise or submission to external power and controlling interests. I am saying that libraries must be put into the hands of the communities to whom they rightfully belong. Decentralization—the establishment of representative community boards at the neighborhood branch level—is one way, provided they are not co-opted through the selection process or manipulated once into being.

The professional task is to arouse understanding of what the library as an information service agency can do for people and to provide needed and wanted services. It is not to decide for people. We have a long way to go before ghetto people would trust us enough to allow us to perform strategic services for them. Effective services must involve the community in their design; they must be subject to their continuous assessment.

I am here calling for a new statement of philosophy for the American public library which recognizes and commits the institution to helping to end social inequality and injustice through improved information access and by reconstituting the institution's government, structure, and staffing so that it can become and remain genuinely socially responsive.

If these developments do not occur, if libraries continue to proffer weak, ineffectual, and basically insulting service, no matter what the excuses, there will be no other alternative than for inner city residents themselves to insist that money to be spent on service to inner city dwellers be put into the hands of people picked by them, hired by them, and reporting to them at the top system level and in every branch in the city.

One way or another people are going to get the information services they need and deserve. The irradication of poverty and the future of a people are far too important to be left dependent on any institution's willingness to transform itself.

A Model Library
for Community Action

Major Owens

THE FAILURE of libraries is a failure to become relevant—*relevant* to the communities and institutions libraries profess to serve; to urban upheaval and its potential for constructive change; to the desperate race against our cultural lag; to that continuing evolution of democracy that reaches out and embraces the movement for full civil rights to all.

Democracy is at a critical point and libraries and the library profession can and should be more involved than ever before. To continue to be passive and nonrelevant, to continue to flounder without a professional imagination and sense of mission, and to accept failure is to deprive the nation's urbanization and democratization process of a vital point of view, of a unique approach to the useful harnessing of knowledge, and of a time-honored method of education which is still the most efficient and most modern method of all.

What harm to our society, what unfilled potential, what dangerous vacuums are we creating by our failure to be relevant? Before getting down to specifics, let me pose a few general questions.

In our public schools, which touch the lives of more of the members of our society than any other institution, how has the library profession failed to be relevant? Our librarians who sit by and allow the school library to continue to be a place where children are sent for an hour of quiet and rest are guilty of professional cowardice and neglect. Should not the library profession mount a campaign to show that a curriculum that continues to make the library a sterile unit of the English textbook is bad and inefficient? Should not the library occupy a more central place in the curriculum in order for our children to be launched into the educational world with the right attitudes and techniques for developing the capacity for independent study which is so important in later life? Does the concept of the school library as a supporting facility mean that it has a passive role? Should it not attempt to actively project a more relevant place for itself in the total pedagogical approach? Should the school librarian be assigned a position and rank on the level of assistant principal in order for the independent study approach to be integrated at all grade levels and all subject areas?

The narrow concept of education as that which takes place only in a classroom with a teacher begins in the early school years and unfortunately, too often, never ends. These same students grow up and become the voters and the public officials that are usually unwilling to consider public appropriations for libraries as another form of expenditure for education. The failure of school libraries helps to set the stage for the problems of our public libraries.

In the competition for the municipal tax dollar, most of our big city public libraries are facing a desperate situation. Some are on the brink of outright shutdown as final defeat. Is this negative expression of contempt for the public library merely a matter of cultural lag and voter ignorance, or is it a punishment that we must endure because of the failure to be relevant? Is there no vested interest group that will speak out for the library? Is the failure of the public library to build its own constituency an indication of a failure to be relevant?

Education and job training is a primary concern of the poverty areas within our big cities. In New York City there is a strong thrust by the black and Puerto Rican communities for community control of the schools. Why is the public library never mentioned by the leadership of these communities? Does this inattention reflect hostility or confusion and ignorance of the library's potential for helping to achieve the kind of education they are demanding?

Blacks and Puerto Ricans are striving to secure a place in the mainstream. How can the public library be relevant to their needs? Are they not the constituency which, although a minority, exercises and will continue to exercise increasingly more and more influence on what happens to our cities, including the appropriations of funds?

Can adult education take place at a faster and more efficient rate if the public libraries play a central role, especially in those activities that are in the poor, ghetto areas?

Should the young and floundering community action programs be encouraged to reshape the public library to meet their rather extensive needs in this area of adult education, of information, and of basic research facilities? Should we develop new, or improve old, ways to integrate community activities with library activities? Should the staffing patterns for public libraries be revamped in order to guarantee that they are staffed by local community residents in poverty areas?

And, meanwhile, back at the library schools, what is being done to prepare professionals who can deal with these questions? For any professional, the professional school is the fortress; the soldiers go forward to battle and they return periodically for inspiration and a new sense of direction and purpose. Library schools are the dominant force in the shaping of the mission for the library profession, if it is to have a mission.

As librarians, we know how to create order and structure out of any amorphous mass of information. We know how to channel any body of knowledge into a system and describe it in shorthand terms. We are the masters of abstracting the essence from media. We know how to select, classify, and efficiently store what is relevant. We are the masters of the art of selecting information from books or from other forms of information and matching it with the needs of individuals or groups.

We are specialists in adult education through independent study with professional guidance. Our modern society in general, and our cities in particular, are very much in need of the contribution that libraries can make.

This abstract and theoretical description of our reason for being can be translated into some concrete and practical examples in one area—the public library and its relevance to the urban ghetto.

Model Ghetto Library

Let us project a model public library for any one of the 26 poverty areas into which New York City has been divided. In any one of these areas, if a library is to serve as a model library, the branch librarian must, at the outset, identify fully with the community and see the library as an instrument for the total community action effort. In one form or another, these community action efforts are taking place all over the country.

The community philosophy and the mission must be known and understood if the library is to be relevant. Although it is not always clearly articulated, the concept of the mother community is what guides the thinking of leadership in most of the poverty areas. We often use the term revolution too loosely, but if there is anything close to a revolution going to take place, it will take place slowly and in the various ghetto communities throughout the entire country.

What happens at our colleges may be more dramatic and more exciting and look more like a direct confrontation with the power structure, but it takes many bodies, masses of people, people who are hungry. It takes people who cry out for decent housing. It takes people who are determined to have opportunity for their children to really make a revolution.

If those revolutions are to happen, whether they be revolutions or merely the accelerated evolution of democracy, they will happen in the communities which see their community action and the total community effort as being the answer to their ills.

The concept of the mother community with resident controlled institutions which cradle and nurture the young and the insecure, the mother community which encourages the striving and the talented and provides a place to practice and an audience to listen—this is the goal. The community effort, the mother community with group action as the only effective defense against powerful pressure groups, and the community-supported collective knowhow and funds to purchase the ex-

pertise as the only meaningful weapon in the increasingly intense war for survival in our competitive society—this is the objective of community action.

Individual courage, stamina, and ability will always be important, and a few young supermen will continue to emerge even from the most depressed and neglected slums. But the goal today is not the salvation of a few—the natural cream that rises to the top—but the development of the great masses. Every strata must be given an opportunity to rise to the limits of their abilities. The poor you have with you always, but it is our duty, our sacred mission, to keep pushing the percentage who are poor down towards zero.

We cannot do it case by case, with individual and family counselling or even group work. The only answer is community action, total effort, the creation, the building, the reshaping, the influencing, and the controlling of all vital resources and institutions within an area. To create the mother community, the community expects a special contribution from the library. We might call it information power.

Knowledge of the right facts and at the right time is a form of power. For example, on the subject of annual appropriations and budgets, it is important for the communities to know when the hearings are to be held; what the appropriations are for all agencies; the names of the city councilmen and the other officials primarily responsible for the budget review. It is important to note the comparative statistics on the city expenditures and to have simple explanations of program budgeting. All of this the library can supply.

Comparative statistics which show the cost of a hand grenade vs. the cost of milk for school children or the cost of a super bomber vs. the cost of a low-income project are the kinds of things that the community will need as weapons to battle for a greater share of the funds needed to improve their lives. These bits of information become weapons in the community arsenal.

While the average librarian would be able to secure all of this material within a relatively few hours, most community action personnel or the residents themselves would have to search for days or weeks, or are completely unaware of the fact that they can get such information.

The average citizen will be shocked to learn of the amount of time and effort expended by the government and its agencies to control the flow of information to the public and keep certain information out of the public's hands. Agency budgets are often written in anticipation of the public's ignorance of the services and benefits available. For many years in New York City it was almost impossible to obtain a full copy of the Welfare Regulations which provided interpretations of the law and the formulas for the computation of recipients' allowances. When community action groups began to mimeograph large quantities of the "Black Book" as it was called, the information was translated into power—the power to obtain larger allowances by insisting that they follow their own laws.

Action Bibliographies

The model library for community action would mimeograph such materials, and circulate them on a weekly or monthly basis at intervals. It could even establish a new form called Action Bibliographies on any timely or pertinent subject. Some examples of such bibliographies would be federal grants possible under new legislation, job training programs, comparative hospital care and cost in various cities, the legal rights of tenants, selection and purchase of public school textbooks, etc.

Why is it that year after year parents in the ghetto communities complain about the inadequacies of textbooks and how badly they depict minority groups, and yet year after year the same textbooks are selected? Who is the corrupt person? Who is being paid to continue to do this?

Such bibliographies must be compiled with the community need and point of view reflected. To be relevant, the librarian must often isolate that which is most significant and by the arrangement of facts throw a magnifying glass on certain aspects of a problem. For example, on the issue of law, order, and crime, the action bibliography could provide investigation reports, books, news articles, etc. on organized crime, on corruption and graft among police and public officials, on statistics for petty crime arrest vs arrest and conviction of known underworld bosses and their henchmen. From day-to-day observation, ghetto residents know that at the root of rising crime statistics lies organized crime, particularly the untouchable narcotics rackets. The contents of an action bibliography would provide ways for those residents to articulate their case to the mass media and to responsible public officials.

What is needed is an aggressive and involved librarianship that cannot be separated from the total community thrust. The library collection and its services must be a natural extension of this philosophy of the mother community. The reference collection should contain reports, proposals, directories, minutes, and other records of the local community action agencies. The expertise of the professional librarian should be placed at the disposal of the in-service training units and other adult education and training projects within the community. The book collection should specialize in ethnic history and cultural materials of interest, particularly to Negroes and Puerto Ricans, as well as job training and adult education. With the community action program, new possibilities for the library as an adult education center are now open. We run the risk of being super-sophisticated. Too many of us have tried experiments—community coordinators, supermarket libraries, etc.— and they all failed a couple of years ago.

There is a new movement now. Apathy is ended in the ghetto community. Any effort that is now carefully planned in conjunction with community action programs will probably yield significant results.

One final point: The current and coming confrontations between college students and the power structure and the demands for open enrollment are already taxing the budgets of our states and cities. This is producing the kind of confrontation which might make it possible for libraries, if they are imaginative, to reinterject themselves into the situation and to show how libraries, books and adult education, as promoted through the library, is still the most efficient and most effective form of education.

Some Experiments Fail: The Public Information Center Project at the Enoch Pratt Free Library

Joseph C. Donohue

THE PAST 20 years have seen the rise of many specialized information centers. Like libraries, they collect and maintain documentary materials. Unlike libraries, they do so only as an adjunct to providing information. Freed from the concern with maintaining a collection, an information center is often able to provide intensive information services within its restricted subject area. Since there is a continuing need for an agency that maintains documentary materials and assists in their use, the information center cannot replace the library, but as an adjunct or supplement to the library the information center has been found very useful, especially in scientific and industrial applications. Efforts have been made in recent years to apply the information center concept to problems of daily life in society, such as those of health, welfare, education, employment, and the like.

One such effort was the Public Information Center (PIC) Project, sponsored by the Enoch Pratt Free Library and the University of Maryland School of Library and Information Service. Its purpose was to find out whether or not a public library could be a comprehensive information center. The project originated with a suggestion from Paul Wasserman, dean of the University of Maryland library school, to the library's director, Edwin Castagna, and its assistant director, Grace Slocum, that such a study might be conducted at the Pratt Library.

Federal funds in the amount of $25,000 had been

made available for improving services in Maryland's five metropolitan library systems. At the request of the Enoch Pratt Library, and with the support of Nettie Taylor, state director for library development, the directors of the respective systems elected to apply these funds to the PIC project. The library then contracted with the school for the half-time services of a faculty member, the author, as director of the project, and other persons as needed in the study and planning of the service.

The library's interest in sponsoring the effort may be seen as a recognition of the changing conditions of urban life, and of resulting changes in the support base of libraries. The book-using middle class has to a significant degree deserted the city, leaving the continued viability of the urban public library in question. Nevertheless, people continue to need information; indeed, many kinds of information vital to survival in the urban environment cannot be found in books; some important information is not in published form at all. It was therefore appropriate for the library to extend its scope, in order to become a clearinghouse for information regardless of the format in which such information is to be found. Where the information needed was of a factual kind, such as could be obtained from publications, the center could direct the inquirer to such literature, either directly or through the appropriate department of the library. If what was needed was substantive help, the center could direct the inquirer to the social agency, organization, government department, or individual able to provide that help. In thus acting as a broker between people with needs and people with the resources to answer the needs, an information center would, it was thought, learn much about which kinds of needs are satisfied and which are not— data that would be useful to planners, to officials, and to voluntary citizens' groups.

Planning

Over a period of several months, project people from both the library and the library school met frequently, identified and reviewed useful documentary materials, and interviewed people in the community who had special knowledge of existing social welfare problems and services. While there is no dearth of potentially related literature, there seemed at the time very little that related directly to problems of setting up a service of the type envisioned. The most valuable reading was a report by Kahn and others (1966), *Neighborhood Information Cen-*

ters, which explored the potential value of several types of services, including the British Citizens' Advice Bureaux. Given the lack at that time of empirical research regarding the kinds and extent of information types needed by citizens, it was necessary to construct such an array *a priori*. After a study of relevant literature, Samuel Markson, a graduate student at Case Western Reserve University, now public services system coordinator at the University of Massachusetts, developed the following outline of subject areas:

Government in general

Legislative bodies in a given jurisdiction: how elected, their powers, structure, and operation, Office holders: responsibilities, committee assignments, powers, pay, how appointed. Courts: how judges get their jobs, their responsibilities, powers, and jurisdiction of respective courts. Taxes: kinds, how they are set, how collected, how taxes are earmarked for spending, how disbursed. Constitutions, charters, laws: which are extant, their import, how interpreted, how they may be changed. Influence: means of influence open to individuals, to groups, how lobbyists work, where they are registered.

Agencies

Responsibilities (of respective agencies), their normal work and normal clienteles, powers permitted to them and those they are required to exercise, their methods of operation, supervision, and control. Procedures to follow in order to get an agency to act on a problem, procedures for complaints about an agency.

Police

Citizen rights and obligations in dealing with police, and conversely the rights and obligations of police. How to get a lawyer to help in dealing with police. Bond procedures. Kinds of problems appropriate/not appropriate for police to deal with. Relationship of police to other government agencies.

Housing

Landlord/tenant relations: leases and rights of those who sign them, limits of lease. Rights in the absence of a lease. Determining ownership of a building. Getting landlord to make repairs. Rent strikes. Public housing: who qualifies, how to apply, who runs it, and by what rules and procedures. Urban renewal: effect on citizen, redress against actions under renewal programs. Housing codes and laws: coverage, impact, who enforces, how to get action under them, operation of rent control, of Fair Housing Laws. Significance of condemnation, of receivership. Housing purchases: how to find an appropriate house to buy, and how to buy it, problems and dangers in purchase. Significance of condominium and cooperative ownership, their respective advantages and disadvantages. True cost of purchasing. Insurance needed. Taxes on houses. Rented housing: deciding on desirability of rental property, responsibilities of landlord and tenant maintenance. Types of heating; determining degree of congestion in a building or rental neighborhood.

Employment

Training: where to get training, what is available and at what cost. Apprenticeships: how to obtain, their conditions, requirements. Employment agencies: availability of public agencies, private agencies, profit/non-profit. What the agencies will/will not do, costs. Job hunting: education, skills, other requirements for particular jobs. Unions: purpose, who needs to belong, how to join, laws governing unions, regulations of unions. Unemployment, disability, and workmen's compensation: who qualifies, how to apply, types of benefits. Social Security: how it operates. Compensation benefits. Appeal. Redress in unfair treatment. Labor laws: what laws exist, who enforces, how to get action under them. Labor statistics: on city, state, national level. Numbers of people employed, by job, by industry. Jobs available, growth trends.

Education

Courses, programs available (all levels). Entrance requirements, costs, scholarships, loans, and other support. Tutors: where to find, at what cost. Schools: how supported, their organization, curricula, local, regional, state control, governance. School districts: how they are set. Accreditation, availability of special schools and courses, e.g., for handicapped, etc.

Welfare

What public/private aid agencies exist and whom do they serve? Kinds of problems they handle. Eligibility to receive help.

Health

Medical problems: how to find a good doctor, how to determine competence of doctor. Public programs: clinics, hospitals available, health education programs, pollution control programs and agencies. Private programs: what services are available, their cost, how financed, who run by. Health insurance: costs, coverage, limits and conditions of payment.

Business and consumer affairs

Credit purchasing: interest charges, finding true interest, laws governing credit buying, who enforces laws, repossession for non-payment. Differences in borrowing from bank vs. finance company. Collateral, cosigners. Prices: determining fair prices, comparison shopping. Workmanship and service: how to get redress. Reputation of stores or products: how to determine. Establishing your own business: laws governing new business, help available from public/private sources, financing, costs and profits.

Determining needs & resources

Given the limited time and resources of the project, and the determination of the library director to develop a useful service as soon as possible, it was necessary to severely restrict the study phase. In addition to a literature review, this phase consisted of interviews with a series of persons involved in official and voluntary agencies and citizens' groups. By far the most informative of these interviews were with the staff of the Health and Welfare Council. Its Information and Referral Service (I&RS) was already operating on a 40-hour-a-week basis, giving referrals and advice, mostly by telephone. It was found that the capabilities of the I&RS and those of the library were complementary, though they overlapped in important areas. Much of the work of I&RS is beyond the competence of the library, involving as it does, highly sensitive casework, sometimes of a medical or psychiatric nature. However, other aspects of its work are purely informational, involving the identification, collection, analysis, organization, and dissemination of information. Much of what the I&RS and the Council's member agencies do in this area is really library work, involving operating their own special libraries, devising indexes, keeping data files, and the like. The suggestion was made during discussions with Council representatives that the library should do more to assure the availability of the publications needed by the Council and its member agencies, thus relieving them of the need for their own special libraries.

This would require close liaison between the library and the social agencies to assure the permanent availability of important planning materials, however ephemeral their form. The I&RS also scans newspapers and other publications for information about changes in the availability of social services in the community, thus to a large extent duplicating files kept in the library. Plans were made to reduce such duplication while assuring the ready availability of needed materials. Also, it became clear that the library could do a great deal more to inform its clientele of the availability of social services in response to particular needs. Its central and branch libraries could offer many points of initial contact for persons who could be referred to appropriate agencies either through the I&RS or directly, as appropriate.

Technical resources

There was general agreement on the need for an efficient system for gathering, processing, and retrieving data on the availability of official and voluntary services. Studies were made to determine the feasibility of computer methods or other electronic or mechanical aids, but these were not available to the project or to the library at acceptable costs. Instead, plans were made to adopt the "extract-clue-word" system which had been developed by the Battelle Memorial Institute in Columbus, Ohio for use by its own information analysis centers, and which had been successfully adapted to the needs of the Columbus (Ohio) Regional Information

Service, an agency similar in some ways to the service envisioned by Pratt. The extract-clueword system is particularly well suited to the needs of a small, specialized information center lacking computer support, where the information is to be derived from many formats and where a high value is placed on exact, timely, and accurate data. It is remarkably simple and economical, and it provides a format that allows easy transfer of data to machine-readable form for automatic processing. Through well-chosen extracts the system also provides more substantive data than does the conventional catalog, thus greatly reducing the need for referring to the original documents.

The first input to the central file was the data from current files of I&RS, most important of which was the file used to update its *Directory of Community Resources*, a guide to social services in Maryland. The PIC Project took on the task of preparing the index for the next edition. A computer program was written to sort and list the indexes by type of service, by agency, and by geographical area served.

A British model

An unexpected but highly beneficial opportunity arose to study a model of citizens' information service that has operated since World War II, the Citizens Advice Bureaus (CAB). Carole Peppi, the project's administrative assistant, returned for a visit to her native England. With CAB cooperation, she was able to study the system intensively and actually to work in several of the local bureaus. Among the matters that she studied, the following were considered most important in the context of PIC planning:

STRUCTURE: Enabling legislation, funding, governance, legal authority, legal vulnerability.

ADMINISTRATION: Staffing, training, centralization/decentralization, communication patterns both internal to CAB and external; relation if any to public libraries.

SERVICES: Extent and nature of services, clientele; problems of special types of clients; experience under normal and stress conditions, follow-up methods.

TECHNICAL SUPPORT: Facilities, communication, and cooperation with other agencies; types of documentary resources; files (types, structure, maintenance, integration); special talent, "resource persons."

A report of Ms. Peppi's findings was published as part of the project's final report. The influence of CAB was important in our recommendations for expanded services at Enoch Pratt, but as Kahn and others have recognized, it was necessary for us to develop approaches particularly suited to the nature of our society. Especially problematic are issues such as 1) the effective scope of service, 2) the degree of centralization or centralized support of services, and 3) the appropriate contribution of volunteer workers.

Educational efforts

Meanwhile, planning continued at the library, with a number of managerial structures being devised and considered, and suggestions received from members of a professional seminar conducted by the school in connection with the PIC project. The seminar brought together library school students, experienced librarians, social workers, and city planners in an exchange of ideas that served to stimulate interest beyond those immediately concerned with the project. Also, during the course of the project, two one-day institutes on public information services were held, to acquaint members of the professional community with the range of problems and opportunities attendant upon the project.

Recommendations

The project team made many recommendations to the library for the creation and operation of an information center. These have been fully documented in the final report of the project, published in 1971. The most important of these are summarized here.

The project team recommended to the library that it set up a new department which would be a special information unit, under the full-time direction of a senior librarian, and located in the most prominent place possible in the central building. Its function would be to assist its users, both individuals and organizations, to find information and information sources in answer to particular needs, especially those of a health and welfare nature. It would become the point of entry for users who were unsure of how to use the library, and a court of last resort for those who had exhausted the library's resources.

The Information Center, it was recommended, should continue to identify urgent information needs of the city's populace, including those people who do not use the library. Conversely, it should seek to identify resources, both documentary and institutional, and to develop excellent day-to-day liaison with the agencies that could serve in this capacity. It was envisioned that in addition to providing extensive information-handling capability to support these agencies, the library could serve as a point of referral, with its branches being feeders to I&RS where appropriate. We recommended that since I&RS already operated a telephone service, the library's Information Center should, at least initially, emphasize in-person services, though it should answer phone queries as received. The Center would not build a document collection, but would extract materials and pass the publications themselves on to the library's appropriate departments. The Information Center would build a file to lead to information sources, wherever located.

With respect to organization, it was recommended that a) the Center be created as a department of the library, under the direct supervision of a senior librarian, the peer of other department heads, who would be responsible *only* for the Center; b) staff should be composed of both librarians and others such as experts in social work, to complement the bibliographic and technical skills that the library's regular personnel would provide; and c) that it include technicians whose principal duty would be to maintain the files and answer routine questions.

It was further suggested that librarians from other departments and from the branches who had an interest in PIC-type services should be recruited to work full-time for periods of from three months to a year in the Center to help spread understanding of the Center to the staff generally. It was emphasized that the Center should be staffed by people with good general education, ability to learn quickly and to adapt to the fast-changing requirements of an evolving service, a commitment to service, and a healthy respect for people. Training was recommended along the following lines: a) the city and state, their political and social organization, and the organization of social welfare service; b) the library, its structure and operation, goals, and services; c) the center itself, the reasons for its existence, special features of its service; d) information needs of the urban setting; e) interview techniques; and f) systems of information handling. The library would not attempt to be an ombudsman or advocate, except to assure the citizen free access to information.

In late July 1970, these and other recommendations were made in an interim report to the library administration, which, agreeing that such a service should be instituted, began the necessary internal planning and training. The project team did not participate in this internal planning or in selection of staff for the center. At the request of the assistant director, the project team did set up and conduct the training course it had planned and completed the development of the resource file that was to be used jointly by the library and the Health and Welfare Council. In addition, the team completed work on the index for the *Directory* to be published by the Council.

Implementation

The new service was given the desired prominent location in the central building. No direct telephone service was provided (it was the library's policy for *all* calls to enter through its Telephone Reference Service). The service area was identified by a sign that indicated only that this was an "Information" desk. At no time was the unit identified to the public by any distinctive title such as "Public Information Center."

A leaflet was prepared and distributed, indicating that the library now had established closer ties with Health and Welfare Council, and could therefore provide more information in that area of need, but no indication was given that such service was localized in a particular unit of the library.

It may seem strange that after so much planning and effort, no publicity was given to the new service. It should be understood that because of budgetary stringencies there was doubt whether the new information service could begin at all. The library administration decided to go ahead with plans, but to do so in such a way that the new unit could be re-absorbed into the pre-existing structure with a minimum of difficulty if necessary. With this in mind, no publicity was provided at the beginning of the service. It seemed to the author that the important thing was not what the service unit was called, or whether it would have any fanfare, but rather what it would do. It seemed that if the staff began to provide information and referral services to even a few people a day in an active way, the word would spread. Anyway, the lack of publicity was expected to be temporary, until the service could get onto its feet and establish itself within the library.

The staff was comprised of four college graduates from the Library Auxiliary Service, all of whom had shown high aptitude for library work and who had expressed special interest in the new concept of an expanded information service. They responded well to the special training provided, and brought much talent and a high degree of motivation to their new assignment. At a later time, a clerical assistant was added.

The service was not established as a department; rather it was placed directly under the Office of the Assistant Director, and reported to her administrative assistant, who supervised it as a responsibility added to others, such as general administration of the Central building. These circumstances precluded his spending the time needed to establish the desired liaison with city, state and regional government, and voluntary agencies.

In addition to serving as a general inquiry point, the new information service was given the task of making all photocopies required by the library staff and patrons, as well as providing general directions about the building and the neighborhood. Thus, with the exception of maintaining the specialized information file on community Health and Welfare agencies, and querying that file in response to the few queries that required it, the new service became outwardly in no way distinguished from the kind of general information desk that had long been found in most large libraries. A study made of questions addressed to this information desk in the first year of its existence showed that less than two percent were related to health or welfare problems. Nevertheless, the staff continued to maintain the currency of the community resource file, and for a time made weekly visits to the Health and Welfare Council, working side by side with its Information and Referral Service staff contacting social service agencies in order to keep data current. Subsequent reductions in the staff resulted in these visits being discontinued.

In 1974, the library's General Reference Department was renamed General Information Department, reflecting the growing commitment to information service, which had been earlier seen in the creation of the Telephone Reference Service. At the time of the restructuring of General Information Department, the remaining staff of the information service

(PIC) were incorporated into it. The service location that had been set up inside the front door was vacated, and a large desk was placed in the center of the hall to serve all types of information requests, including those for catalog assistance. The resource file was placed at that desk and it continues to be used upon occasion by personnel of the General Information Department in answering queries made by patrons in person or calling the Telephone Reference Service. Plans are under way now (February 1975) to perform a complete update of that file.

What went wrong?

The Public Information Center Project cost $25,000 for salaries of personnel from the University, travel expenses, training, equipment, and overhead. The library may well have contributed at least an equal amount in the salaries of its staff who were involved in planning, training, and implementation. Today there is no visible evidence that the project ever existed or that a service resulted from it, except for the card file. Many have asked, "What went wrong?"

More than four years have elapsed since the project ended, during which the author has not had official contact with the library, nor any opportunity to observe closely the subsequent history of the service initiated as a result of the project. The following comments must be considered with those limitations in mind.

PIC was an experiment. It is in the nature of experiments that some of them fail, and PIC was one that failed. It may be useful to try to understand why, because there are still people who believe in the concept, and some may be in a position to try a similar experiment.

The officials of Enoch Pratt undertook a pioneering effort, attempting to create a new service under less than ideal conditions. The failure of the service is in some measure a result of inadequacies in

the planning, for which the author is responsible.

It is not possible to say to what extent each of the following deficiencies was responsible for the failure. A postmortem may be of some value to others who, like the author, are convinced of the validity of the PIC concept. Therefore, some of the deficiencies in both the project and the resulting service are sketched out here.

1) *Confusion About Mode of Service:* During the planning, there was a long period of discussion about whether PIC should be a telephone service, a "walk-in" service, or both. We had some concern about duplicating the telephone access service of Health and Welfare's I&RS, while leaving other potential needs unmet. Further, since the library had gone to great lengths to consolidate all incoming calls in Telephone Reference Service, there was a reluctance on the part of the administration to cause further confusion by introducing a new telephone service. The resulting decision to begin operating almost exclusively in a walk-in mode represented at best a compromise solution, since it made it difficult to present a clear and forceful image of the new service to either the library's staff or to the public. In retrospect, our concern over jurisdictional problems seems to have been unnecessary and vitiating. Experience of the I&RS indicates that the demand for telephone service is very elastic. Promotional programs, such as television spot announcements for I&RS regularly produce such response that they must be carefully spaced to avoid creating a demand beyond the service capacity. In short, there appears to be no reason to avoid competition in delivery of telephone service. The experience of both the I&RS and the library indicate that few people are inclined to come to a downtown building with questions of the health and welfare type; the convenience and anonymity of the telephone service has greater appeal. People at Pratt did express the belief that if the information service were available at the neighborhood branch libraries it would be used.

2) *Restriction on PIC-type Development in Branches:* The library administration elected to concentrate efforts on setting up the Central information unit. Community leaders in one branch area expressed considerable interest in starting a small PIC-type service at that branch. The administration agreed to make space available, but not to permit any other dedication of library resources. No one can say for sure what would have been the result if the branch had been allowed to participate fully in such an effort, but failure to do so seems like an opportunity lost.

3) *Organizational Structure and Placement:* It now seems clear that it would have been better either to have created a PIC Department as recommended, or else to have placed the new service in an existing department. Operating as it did for several years as a special project reporting to the Assistant Director's Office, and under a part-time supervisor, it could not establish itself and its role satisfactorily. The most crippling blow to the implementation of the unit was the failure to appoint a full-time professional with adequate time and the clear mandate to represent the new service to the library staff, to the cooperating civic agencies and to the public. Though the unit's staff were talented and well motivated, as paraprofessionals they could not perform the necessary liaison function satisfactorily. They did not have sufficient authority, and they did not have the necessary credentials in a society and an occupation that are to an ever increasing degree impressed by credentials.

It should be understood that though the staff of Pratt in general were interested and sympathetic to PIC, the project was resented to some extent as a dilution of traditional library resources at a time of retrenchment.

In the early months of the PIC project, each step was documented in "Project Notes" that were provided to the library for wide internal distribution, in the hope that these would generate wide discussion and input of ideas from the staff. After some months, it became apparent that these notes were not being read by the staff and were demonstrably ineffective as a communication medium. They were therefore discontinued as a poor use of project time.

In another kind of attempt at internal communication, a number of meetings on PIC were held with the library's staff. Unfortunately, these were too large and too highly structured to encourage two-way communication. Perhaps small meetings would have brought out better discussion among staff members and more suggestions from them, which could have been incorporated in policy discussion and planning. A complex organization such as Pratt cannot possibly include everybody in all its activities, but it now seems clear that we did too little along these lines.

5) *Failure to Publicize:* The new service unit was opened without publicity, a decision of the library, to which I did not object strenuously, because I believed—and still do—that if the will to serve is present, and resources are allocated to serve, the use of such a service will quickly grow through personal referral. Given all the other impediments to PIC's development, I now believe the decision a mistake. Even if publicity had temporarily swamped the library's resources, it would have been preferable to a still birth. In the absence of demand and without demonstration of the value of the service, there was no effective motivation for the library to continue the operation of the unit, and to devote adequate resources to it. The investments that had been made in conceptualizing, studying, planning, and developing were written off as bad investments without testing or marketing the product.

By the definition of survival, PIC was a failure. Its planning and execution were inadequate and/or inappropriate to the Pratt Library at the time. That does not invalidate the concept of providing greater depth of information services through the medium of the public library system. The public library has a traditional responsibility to provide documentary materials. If libraries do not do this, they are failing as libraries. But the world is becoming inundated with documents. Only a few of them are relevant to a given problem or a given library user. There is great danger that a library's pre-occupation with collections and its relative neglect of information services may render those very collections progressively less relevant to the needs of its patrons. In short, the quality of even the collection itself is subject to continued improvement through use.

Today's citizen needs information of many kinds just to survive. To supply information related to survival, such as was envisioned in PIC, is to build the library's capability to supply other kinds of information and documentary materials, including those traditionally provided.

Some traditionalists are concerned that the library's role as champion of literate culture will be diluted or cheapened by making it also an information and referral agency for a public, some members of which are indifferent to literacy or to high culture. But culture, in a deeper sense, is not divisible into "high culture" and the other things that people do, including basic survival. It is a single fabric. The citizen who can approach the library with confidence in seeking survival information will be more receptive to the library's potential as an educator.

In the view of this writer, the provision of comprehensive information services remains a valid function for the public library. The public library, more than any other agency, is suited to the task. While many kinds of agencies distribute information, the public library is unique in our society, in combining the following features:

1) Its primary function is to provide information and informational materials. 2) It exists to serve the entire community.

3) Its subject scope is virtually unlimited. 4) Its operators are specialists in document and information handling as such. 5) It is in principle impartial, being dedicated to the interests of society as a whole, rather than of a particular element of society. 6) While generally supported by public funds, its customary form of governance provides some measure of freedom from direct or partisan political control.

There is significant precedent for information and referral service in public libraries. Librarians have long maintained informal files of "resource persons" to call upon when the library, with all its books, could not answer the questions. In some communities, especially in periods of mass immigration, economic depression, or wartime, public libraries have served as liaison between official and voluntary organizations and the citizens. But even though one can present such a rationale as this, and such clear precedents as to make one wonder if the PIC is even a new idea, the creation of the information service along the lines that we attempted at Enoch Pratt is still a somewhat radical departure from tradition—at least in emphasis. It cannot be done successfully without a sizeable commitment of resources. It is a mistake to begin it unless the commitment is strong enough that it is likely to be continued in lean times, when to do so would mean perhaps retrenchment elsewhere in the library's program.

Like all institutions, the public library seems certain to change greatly in the near future. How it changes, and what will be its place in the society of the future will depend in large measure upon how effective it is in providing comprehensive information and referral services.

Hindsight on High John

Richard Moses

IT MAY WELL BE that by now the whole subject of High John has been beaten to death. I keep getting indications to the contrary, however—the October *Library Trends* which footnoted but otherwise forgot it notwithstanding. Whether or not the idea *cum* issue seems dead, I'm not sure it should be allowed to be buried without a suitable encomium. Actually, I do not think it is dead any more than any vivid experience ever is.

In any case, there has not yet been, to my knowledge, a proper summing up, an answering of the questions still being asked: Was it a success? What was learned? Would you do it again? How?

Difficult to say just where the idea for a combined classroom and field experience in servicing unserved publics originated. I can remember throwing such a thought to one of Mary Lee Bundy's seminars several months before there was any hard talk. At the same time, I know Paul Wasserman had been thinking along similar lines even before he opened the School of Library and Information Services at the University of Maryland. In any case, there was a luncheon in about April of 1967 at which, over the din of a million students eating out of tin cans and plastic plates, the Dean began to cast a long line of prose my way, to which, not knowing him very well, I listened raptly. After five minutes or so, Mary Lee blasted in with: "What Paul is trying to say, Dick, is that we'd like you to come to the school to teach the course and help set up the field program." Thus it was begun.

The Office of Education came through on schedule with the funding; Gerry Hall was stolen out from under Enoch Pratt's nose; applications began to come in from potential students; and by the end of summer 1967 not only was the program in high gear, but we were being asked to come out and speak on such topics as "Educating for Service to the Disadvantaged." This is a phenomenon known around libraries as "instant expertise": we had not yet seen our first student, but were already "authorities" on educating them.

The beginnings of the project were beautifully detailed in Eric Moon's piece in the January 15, 1968 *LJ* and Evelyn Geller's summary in the September 1, 1968 *LJ* of the workshop held later that year. Geller rivals Moon for insight and perspicacity. Both editors saw and articulated situations and problems which were unmistakable but had not been recognized or enunciated by us nearsighted ones. It is obvious in rereading these excellent pieces that some very real—in some ways desperate—excitement was generated by High John, i.e., the "fervent" hope of Moon.

As usual, the hopes were perhaps too high, the disappointments already being prepared offstage. But feelings ran deep: this tiny project—a dozen students that first year and a fistful of dollars—seemed significant out of all proportion, an intriguing comment on the urge for change in our profession. On its infant shoulders (it was never to learn to walk or talk) rested the hopes for public libraries, library schools, the library research community, and a whole new direction for an ambling profession.

Was High John a success? Unqualifiedly, yes. Like a Fourth of July—perhaps I'd better say Dominion Day—skyrocket, it did just what it was supposed to do, at least during its first year. Its mechanisms worked according to plan. Light, heat, and loud noise were generated right on schedule and, as one doesn't forget that first fireworks display, so neither will that doughty dozen (and more) forget those first months. But most important, change was generated: in the students who manned the lines and were thus educated in the true sense; in the community where the promise of an indigenous Library Council gutsy and knowledgeable enough to fight for continuing or better library service came exactly true; in the library school where Jim Welbourne and others created a sort of spinoff from High John's mistakes and evocations; perhaps in the research establishment where, hopefully, it was realized that there is more to measuring effect than "decent behavioral science." Alas, the primary target of the skirmish, the public library itself, may have benefitted least of all, enmeshed as it is in its fears and apprehensions, its monolithic insecurity.

Like the skyrocket, High John has ended—can there be any question of that?—with a fizzle and a settling of debris. But while it flew . . .

What was learned? A solid confirmation of George Leonard's observation (in *Education and Ecstasy*) that true learning involves internal change, often a physiological change in which the neuron synapses in the brain are actually rearranged, at least a "head" change enabling new directions and actions. And that change (learning) almost always requires the sort of active participation by the student that forces him to exercise those synapses and discover, for example, that they don't work in a new situation. In other words, do it! No other way works. Is it any wonder that library school students drift out having memorized a few things, but having learned little? Is it any wonder they are ill prepared to meet library service face on? What have they *done* to prepare?

Some High John students have probably never gotten over the experience of carrying that library with its mixed nut patronage on their very own head and shoulders, and that is as much a negative fact as a positive one. Some flunked the experience miserably; academic work complete, they were ready to become librarians, to pursue their interest in "helping the poor." They were wrong; they were not ready and might never be. At least one student was so culturally shocked by noise, numbers, thievery, and the general chaos that she fled, not to return. Another found himself so turned around by conflicting emotions about race that considerable trauma ensued, resulting in some real maladjustment for a while.

Others—calling upon those mysterious energies and resources still to be isolated and analyzed—found their footing and grew remarkably. The first year experience, the "pure" High John (before the program broadened out, with changed, eased requirements, and increased academic emphasis but decreased field experience) was quite possibly the toughest sort of ordeal any graduate student is subjected to outside of a medical internship at Bellevue; but for the success of the program it was absolutely vital. It is too bad that no way was found to research and measure this value. The academic interests in High John apparently did not comprehend the vitality of this aspect and could not measure it, nor could the extent of its impact be assessed so close in time. This intimate, burdensome, vital participation was the first casualty: gradually the student was no longer required to be the staff; he could nip in and out and not feel the weight of responsibility that forced the first few to sink or swim, i.e., learn.

The second realization has to do with the very nature of library service itself. We make sounds about the public library being middle-class in its orientation; we don't know the half of it. We say the words, but down deep we really mean, "It's okay for the library to be middle-class because all people are really, after all, middle-class; they just vary in the degree of middle-classness." Or, "They may not be exactly middle-class now, but surely they want to be!" We mean that there are some folks who are perhaps "reluctant," who need encouragement, who are closet bourgeoisie, latent grey flannelers, who, if given the right opportunities, will come along nicely and Fit.

To make the point, let us change the phrase "middle-class" to "English speaking." What we're saying then is that all the world's people really speak English, some better than others, to be sure, but given a good example, the right books, etc. etc. . . . What we "discovered" at High John was that, figuratively speaking, a great many folks don't speak English at all—they speak Russian or Chinese or Urdu—and they don't even want to speak English. It isn't a matter of degree at all; it is another country. And we went in there not grotesquely middle-class, but certainly a lot more middle-class than any of us allowed ourselves to admit. (The grotesque ones quickly crumpled.)

For example, we started with a library, i.e., building, books, shelves, charging system, films. Now that's about as middle-class as you can get. Such an approach already assumes an enormous number of conditions. It assumes moti-vation, curiosity, knowledge of means of satisfying that curiosity. It assumes acquaintance with the wide variety of interpersonal relationships we practice every day, instead of the one or two or three that were present for most of our patrons. It assumes a knowledge of knowledge itself, if not necessarily of school, then at least some respect for accumulated knowledge. It assumes acceptance of the old, familiar delayed gratification pattern. It assumes a long process of rearing, of precept, example, care and concern, of walking and talking, of gentle teaching, of admiration for someone grown-up who is somebody—and on and on.

It does not assume the child next door to High John with 15 brothers and sisters, no father, no language with which to communicate with the other world, a mother with no time, a neighborhood where day-to-day survival is the lesson; a child to whom you are either his best friend or nothing at all, for whom school means less than absolutely nothing. (He not only doesn't understand what is happening there, he is learning the "right answer syndrome": that it is wisest not to think but to reproduce as nearly as possible what you think the teacher or the boss or "Mister Charlie" or the librarian wants to hear.) There is far too little gentling in his background; his mentors are the worst, his heroes the blurry shapes on the TV screen. He is a child, furthermore, who is always hungry, usually nose-running, ragged, dirty, and always deathly bored—certainly one of the worst, and probably the most debilitating, aspects of poverty. And we young academics had the temerity to open up a middle-class library and fill it with books!

Well, many of the HJ staff had already passed through the shock and were ready to do some thinking about it all. The almost interchangeable staff meetings/class sessions that first year were, as I recall, education at a fairly high level. (One always manages to learn important things when one's head is just above the water.)

We had to examine closely the question, "What's a library doing in a place like this?" and/or look very closely at that library, at the very roots of its approach to its avowed goals.

Consider a sort of ladder of development of the personality and mind, with the lowest rung being that point where the infant or child (or adult) first learns the dialectic of curiosity (question-answer-new question), learns to trust others and through them himself, a ladder which reaches upward through stages of learning and satisfying curiosity, through reading and communication, to the highest forms of intellectual pursuit and self-teaching. It is obvious that the public library—even in its preschool story hours—is zeroing in on a point already several rungs up the ladder, a point where the middle-class four-year-old is jumping around, full of vinegar and itching to try that next step, let alone the same kid when he is eight or 12 or 15 or 19. The middle-class child, even in the face of the curiosity-crushing educational system, given a halfway decent home environment, can manage to hold onto some interest in the world.

But what about the child who sleeps three to a bed, eats potato chips for breakfast and grape soda for lunch, gets his answers *a la* Ring Lardner's, " 'Shut up!' he explained," who may never in four years on earth have heard a complete declarative sentence, and who doesn't have any idea that the world is or can be any different? What is the library to him? What it is is a home. It is a place to go and be, and it has "mothers" and "fathers" in it. And that, for the moment, is just about all it needs to be and have; that's where it all starts. And the children are not all four—they are eight and 12 and 15 and 19.

The single most important component of the "library" is the "liberrian." And an M.L.S. as we know it "don't mean shit." What counts is how gently tough you are and how long you can stay that way (no middle-class cat can hold on forever). By tough, I don't mean rough; I mean strong enough so you can be best friends with a hundred guys and a hundred girls and some mothers and a few dads and so you can listen and listen and listen and nod and understand and, as Gerry Hall once said, "find out things I don't want to find out, but if I don't listen, I won't be able to do anything else with them." And Gerry was tough. After the slums around Baltimore's branch libraries, she took on High John, virtually ran the place, the only full-time employee in the library, and cried heartbrokenly when she said, "I just can't leave—but I have to get away."

Jane Matthieu, mentioned in Moon's article as the founder of Baltimore's Echo House, recalls that for the first six months her experiment in social work (she was hired by a landlord to try to help his tenants in some way—as ombudsman, organizer, sympathizer, listener) was but a vague shape in her head and an empty house on Franklin Street. We must be willing to accept the same possibility with library service. For six months or more it might be just talking, knocking on doors, and chatting on corners: just being there.

"Hi, I'm Natalie Atired. I'm a librarian, I live in that house down there."

"Send your kids over some afternoon, we'll play some games, read some stories and stuff."

"We got this building, and we can do anything we want with it—paid for by the library. Come on by this evening for some coffee and let's talk about it."

"You need a ride downtown? Hop in. I'm going that way."

"Why don't you let me stay with the kids tonight while you take in the PTA?"

"Fix it up like a house? Great."

"Some books in it? OK."

"Call me if you need anything."

If we can revise the idea of library service to include starting at the bottom rung with a solid lump of one-to-one people stuff and be content to wait a while before trying to tickle the middle rung fancies that lead to reading and other Library joys, good enough. Otherwise, we may have to forget it, put the money into a good rec center, run a bookmobile in there for them as needs it (and there are always them as does), and let somebody else do the essential introductory one-to-one bit.

If we were to start all over again with High John, it would be with that empty house and the empty station wagon, and it might work better. Even if we decided to adapt a middle-class library branch approach, I'm not sure setting one up from scratch would be best. Better to take over an existing branch in some large system—D.C. Public, Pratt, New York Public. I've always felt that one branch in every system should be staffed exclusively by new M.L.S. grads anyway—let 'em go for broke. Why not another one, or the same one, for experimental service to nonusers. Double sized staff and budget, the center of activity for the system.

We learned, too, the value of indigenous support, whether called a Friends group, a Board, or a Council: the articulate community spokesman (and I challenge you to discover a single community without such) can make or break an operation. It is not so much a matter of what usually amounts to a token participation in programming and policy decisions; it is more the initiation of a group of library laymen into the whys and hows of library operations so they can understand and sympathize and defend. Three things, then:

1) Learning for a service profession such as librarianship must involve honest on-the-job responsibility where the "buck stops here" (not just "training" or "assisting"), with the immediate opportunity to discuss and analyze mistakes, failures, and triumphs.

2) Library service as we know and love it is far more class oriented than we ever imagined, and as such automatically excludes great numbers of potential users. Much more than a library school "community survey" is needed in order to identify and interact with potential users. Vital tips available from Saul Alinsky on the business not of studying a community but of becoming a part of it, learning its language, its grape vines, its people.

3) Library service must grow up and out of its community whether it uses a million dollar building or the back end of a Volkswagen bus, even if it means starting with nothing but "me and thee." Community support or lack of it at all levels and stages of development can mean life or death for the library.

Sad to say, all this may be moot for the moment, at least in many deserving communities. A return to the University of Maryland some months later for a superb idea festival produced and directed by Annie Reed, who was then heading up the project, showed that old High John may have been about the last instance of white folks making it in the ghetto. The understandable but adolescent blacklash had set in, and we flour faces were told to stay in the suburbs and lay it on the folks out there—not a bad idea, incidentally.

In the meantime, we can cache up stores against the day when open access reigns for everybody and assistance is again a nice word.

A Library in Search of Itself

Larry Earl Bone

*"If libraries tend to be poor in [quality], the reason is
that they are trying to serve everyone. They should set one
or two major goals to serve one or two major sectors and
give everything they have — top staff, top money — to this
effort." — National Advisory Commission on Libraries*

THERE IS an important scene near the end of the current Broadway production of *Follies* when the four principal characters come face to face with their individual self deceptions and their collective naïveté. In each case there has been a refusal to move away from the illusions of youth, to accept the changes that time invariably brings to one's being, and to make the life choices necessary to establish clear identities for oneself. It has been called a play about good-bys. The end of the play does not make it clear whether the characters will move forward or simply continue in their pathetically stunted states.

Many viewers of this play have regarded the characters' plights as a general American predicament— although as a country we seem most recently to have been forced to remove our rose colored glasses, to accept our weaknesses along with our strengths, and

to make hard choices forced upon us by our changing society. Yet no small parallel exists between the larger society and the institutions which help constitute its framework.

It now seems apparent that these institutions will either make new adaptations or will wither away and die. One cannot be a part of the public library scene today without realizing that the survival of this institution is very much in question. Of all the types of libraries it seems most under fire from a variety of camps. While all libraries are confronted with the need for change, the public library seems particularly challenged to create fresh directions, to re-orient itself to the dimensions of a rapidly changing society, and to justify its relevance. Like the cities in which they reside, the urban public libraries, particularly, seem at present to be engaged in a fight for their lives.

The lack of fresh direction, the lassitude within public libraries parallels the malaise in American society as a whole; both are often incapable of facing a necessary reorientation. Noble as has been the public library utopianism of "all things to all people," such can no longer be allowed to veil our present need for choice-making reorientation.

It seems not too much to hope that an educational institution of the public library's significance could serve as a model for the society in which it stands. That those in the profession engaged in public library work have not been able to clarify the library's purpose in American society, to provide the leadership necessary to guide their constituencies in a selection of priorities is in a sense a failure. It should not mean defeat.

Of late there has been a rising chorus of voices calling for self-renewal. Loudest among these is that of John Gardner. "That human institutions require periodic redesign (if only because of their tendency to decay) is not a minor fact about them. How curious it is, then, that in all of history no people has seriously attempted to take into account the aging of institutions and to provide for their continuous renewal. Why shouldn't we be the first to do so?"[1] One of the more articulate spokesmen for the library profession, Lowell Martin, has extended the challenge to libraries when he says: "A library, like other organizations of workers, must have goals to achieve and principles for guidance. Without this animating force, an agency becomes bureaucratic, following established patterns without enthusiasm and without concern for the public served."[2]

No such animating force was lacking in the public library's genesis. Compare the clear direction that the public library had in its beginnings. In a refreshingly direct document, a committee of the Board of Trustees of the Boston Public Library suggested that the public library's purpose was to supplement the city's system of education. "For it has been rightly judged," the report stated, "that under political, social, and religious institutions like ours—it is of paramount importance that the means of general information should be so diffused that the largest possible number of persons should be induced to read, and understand questions going down to the very foundations of social order, which we as a people are constantly required to decide, and do decide, either ignorantly or wisely."[3]

The present official standards for public libraries—the *Minimum Standards for Public Library Systems*—seems to be all-inclusive in its statement of purpose for the public libraries. No suggestion seems to be made of the need for establishment of priorities.

What has happened to make the purpose no longer clear and the mission less precise is something for library historians of the future to divine. The explanation, as suggested before, is perhaps intricately woven into the whole fabric of American society, but the result is unquestionably the malaise in which the public library presently finds itself.

It does not seem unduly optimistic to suggest that the "animating force" which Lowell Martin considers so necessary can again be achieved in our public libraries. The following is an account of the movement of one public library in this direction. It is the process itself, rather than the story of one particular library, which may be of interest.

Early last fall the administrative council of the Memphis Public Library and Information Center agreed that the library's purpose and function were not clear, that overall objectives had become extremely vague to all concerned—both staff and trustees. The council could foresee that Memphis, like other large cities, would be facing a financial crisis in just a few years. It was not possible to make decisions about the library's future programs or even to adopt a meaningful materials selection policy unless such objectives were clarified.

Clearly, decisions on priorities would have to be made. What was or should be the library's role in the community? Was it responsive to the real needs of the community? Was its identity clear to its constituency? Was it playing and could it play a part in the lives of all segments of the population? These and other questions concerned the director and his advisors. To wait for the American Library Association or others in the profession to provide the leadership to determine, among the various opportunities for service, the public library's major responsibilities seemed to mean a loss of time that could ill afford to be lost. It seemed warranted, therefore, to proceed with some kind of self-examination. To this end the director, C. Lamar Wallis, appointed his Assistant Director for Public Services as chairman of an Objectives Committee. The committee, he said, should take enough time "... to reflect on proposed objectives of the Memphis Public Library for the 1970's." An eight-member committee, four men and four women, was appointed in addition to the chairman. Two were senior staff members; one was a black staff member; five were young staff members who had attained department head status in the last two years.

It was a particularly appropriate time for such a re-evaluation of this library's purpose. A decade of unparalleled expansion was coming to a close; 12 new branch libraries of a 17-branch system had been erected, and the new main library was scheduled for completion in the summer of 1971. The decision to reorganize completely the main library along subject department lines offered more fertile ground for new concepts of service. In short, the library had grown from a medium sized system to one capable of serving more than 770,000 people with more sophisticated and complex needs. Finally, whatever changes might come from a re-examination of objectives had been facilitated by the recent retirement of 12 senior staff members, including five department heads. Replacing them was a considerably younger corps of enthusiastic and dedicated professionals with strong social awareness.

The director communicated to the entire staff the news of the creation of the committee and its purpose, inviting suggestions for the entire staff for recommended goals and priorities. Assisting in this invitation, the editor of the staff bulletin, *Undercurrent*, directed the editorial staff over the next several issues in a canvass of library patrons and staff to determine what they thought the objectives and purposes of the library should be.

Meanwhile, in a memorandum to his committee, the chairman prepared the committee for the difficulty of its mission: "There will be many opportunities for our services in the 1970's. Our difficult task is to recommend to the director and the Board of Directors those areas which we see as priorities. The decisions we make, if accepted, may determine this library's future existence." To this end he directed a number of questions to the committee: 1) What are the present strengths and weaknesses of the Memphis and Shelby County Public Libraries? 2) Among the traditional functions that the public library may serve, which ones, if any, are the Memphis and Shelby County Public Libraries serving? 3) Are there important groups not being served by the library? 4) Are there important services which the library is not giving? 5) Does the Main Library have a role distinct from the branch libraries? 6) Is the library providing all forms of materials adequately? 7) What can this library do more effectively than any other agency?

Such questions, while proposed for discussion in the opening meeting, were to recur in subsequent meetings and were not to find their answers until much later. Still, they provided a platform from which the discussions could be launched. The chairman appointed a secretary to record the minutes of all of the meetings, which were to be distributed after each meeting to each committee member, the director, and the editor of the staff bulletin. One committee member recorded the sessions on cassette tapes, making the deliberations further available to any other interested staff members. Notice was given to the staff at large that throughout its sessions the committee would be receptive continually to their suggestions.

In the beginning session the chairman briefly traced the historical development of the American public library. Members of the committee were expected to have read from a brief select reading list. One committee member also prepared a profile of the community, both statistical and narrative—a profile that would point to some of the major changes in the community in the past ten years.

For purposes of organization, the chairman outlined for discussion in the next several months some major areas of services. There were Culture and Recreation, Continuing Adult Education, and Reference and Information. The groups to be considered for service were General Adults, Students, Children, Economically Disadvantaged, Businessmen, and the Senior Citizen and the Shut-in. Each member was assigned to one of these areas, usually to work with another member in preparing a case for or against the service. While the director had instructed the committee "to take its time and deliberate carefully," the chairman felt it wise to set a date for completion of the assignment. Six months with twice monthly meetings of two to three hours each seemed an adequate amount of time to reach conclusions.

From the beginning it was obvious that the committee's task would not be easy. While it would be most inaccurate to say that each member began his work on the committee with a clearly developed philosophy of service, almost all of the members had strong convictions in some areas. Each member brought his own set of values and at the same time his respective limitations of vision, and while some of these limitations remained intact, in terms of group dynamics the articulation of these values and limitations helped set free some of the blocks to growth and change.

That age old tension among public librarians—the quality and demand conflict in service to the public—was soon to surface. Some members echoed Mary Lee Bundy's statement about the public libraries of Maryland and saw the Memphis Public Library as "the same agency passing out the same old wares at the same old stand as twenty years earlier." [4] Others disagreed. It was not hard under close examination, however, to recognize that social change coupled with the changing nature of communication had, like it or not, rendered certain aspects of traditional public library service obsolete.

The group did not take long in gravitating towards its central concern—that the library could generally play a more important role in the community as an agency of continuing, informal education and as an important center for community information. For many years the library had developed an image as a recreational home reading agency catering principally to the demands of a small, vocal group who wished its reading provided inexpensively. Like many other public libraries throughout the country, the library had directed its attentions to satisfying those temporary, seemingly insatiable demands for the popular which resulted in a collection that had little potential for contributing to an informed populace. The arguments of some committee members in favor of a continuation of this role were based, it was discovered, largely on fears that a lessening of this service as a result of changed objectives would damage the library's support in the community. This fear seemed to provide some committee members with the most difficulty and produced the greatest disagreement when it was discussed.

A great deal of discussion, moreover, was generated by those members who held to the traditional viewpoint that one must give the public what it wants. When the searchlight was turned on that "public," it was apparent that it was not easy to speak of one public in this urban community of 774,000 people. As one writer, cited by a committee member, had expressed it: "We must avoid using the word *public* as though it were one entity. We would be much safer if we talked about publics. . . . A program may have a large audience and still be a minority audience."[5] Finally, the majority of the committee seemed forced to conclude that in the face of competition from television and other mass media, the library could not compete as recreation and "escapist" entertainment. Some of this service, the group concluded, might continue to be provided, but it should not be given top priority.

One of the most important reasons for the committee's recommendation that the information function be a major objective for the library in the 1970s was that such a need existed, in fact, at all levels, and that this was an area in which the library could play an important, distinct role. It was difficult for the committee to draw a clear line between the library as information provider and as an instrument of continuing education. The

OBJECTIVES FOR THE MEMPHIS LIBRARY

Library Functions to be Served

The Information Function:

Reference and information service in the Memphis Public Library and Information Center should be the primary objective in the 1970's.

The reference and information function should cover all types of service, all age groups and all financial and educational groups.

In accordance with this objective, the development of the Main Library as a major resource center should be a priority in the 1970's in compliance with the recommendations of the Hamill survey.

Service to business and industry is an important aspect of this objective and should reflect the needs and resources of the total community. Every effort should be made to coordinate the role of the business and industrial services with the information efforts of other community agencies.

The branch library network of Memphis Public Library and Information Center is a relatively strong unit of the system. With the development of strong central resources they will provide reliable outlets for the reference and information function.

The Education Function:

The Memphis Public Library and Information Center feels that the original objective of public libraries—continuing adult education—is as valid now as it was in the nineteenth century. It also feels that it is very difficult to separate the information and education functions. The library will attempt to define its educational role in terms of continuing *informal* education rather than as an agency of formal education, duplicating the services of institutions better equipped to serve the formal function.

The Cultural and Recreational Functions:

Culture, as defined by the Memphis Public Library and Information Center, is the "enlightenment and refinement of taste acquired by intellectual and aesthetic training." The library considers its role in this respect as important, but secondary to the information and education function, since other agencies in the community share in this endeavor.

Recreation, defined as light and escapist entertainment, will be low among the priorities. While the library will continue to offer some recreational service, it feels that because of competition from other sectors it should not try to compete heavily in this arena, thereby weakening the educational and informational potential.

two roles seemed integrally connected. The committee recommended, therefore, that continuing adult education on an informal basis be a major objective, but that the library not attempt to duplicate services to formal education which other institutions might better provide.

Furthermore, the committee felt that if the information and education role were to be backed up with resources in depth, it was development of the main library collection which deserved priority in the 1970s. While the branch collections were strong, only the business and technical department had depth. This collection strength of the business and technical library, which functions separately as a division of the main library, was one of the factors which led to the additional decision by the committee that provision of information to the general business community should be

AND INFORMATION CENTER FOR THE 1970's

Groups of the Public to be Served

Service to Adults:

As implied in the information and education function, adults will be one of the primary groups to be served.

Service to Young Adults:

No basic distinction will be made by the library in the service to young adults (10th grade through the fourth collegiate year) since the growing sophistication in education as reflected in library use would indicate such distinctions to be artificial. Some efforts will be made, however, to increase programming to attract the young adult.

Service to Children:

Children's services should continue as a significant function of the system, but increasing national and local emphasis on school libraries should limit *expansion* of public library services in the 1970's.

Service to the Disadvantaged:

One of the major objectives for the 1970's will be service to the disadvantaged, but the library feels an obligation to continue good library service also to the large middle class group who have been the greatest users of the libraries up to this point.

The library system should make every effort to obtain state and federal assistance for service to the disadvantaged and should devote local funds to this service so long as service to the long established users is not seriously impaired. Experimental service in ghetto areas other than through traditional branches should be tried, and where needs in such areas are specifically shown, branches should be erected as part of the capital improvement program.

Service to Other Disadvantaged Groups:

Other disadvantaged groups such as shut-in's, the penal inmate, and the senior citizen should be given service as part of the library program insofar as personnel and finances permit.
These objectives will be reviewed at the end of each calendar year and revised wherever appropriate.

Adopted December 15, 1971
Board of Directors
Memphis Public Library and
Information Center

an important objective. Realization by the business community of the public library's value, it seemed, would assist the library in its efforts to obtain support.

The committee concluded more regretfully that the library's cultural role had to be secondary to the information and education functions. While all members felt that the library could be an important influence in the raising of taste and encouragement of creativity, they saw other institutions in the community sharing in this endeavor.

When it came to groups to be served, the committee was clear in its priorities. "Service to the disadvantaged," it observed, "should be a major objective for the Memphis Public Library and Information Center in the 70's. With an economically deprived population estimated at 200,000 persons (by federal government guidelines), it seemed obvious that greater efforts needed to be made than in the past to reach this large segment with meaningful library service. Members of the committee, moreover, felt that the information role was just as valid for the disadvantaged as for the businessman, the general adult library user, or the student.

Some committee members felt strongly that provision of service should not depend on state or federal funds. The board of directors, in the formal objectives statement later, seemed, however, to suggest that federal and state funds should be an integral part of this program's support.

A further question was raised as to the type of outreach service to be provided for the disadvantaged. Some felt that the traditional branch service with new and attractive buildings would be the more effective way to serve this group. One of the closest decisions came when the committee voted five to four in favor of exploring types of service other than branch libraries and the use of types of material other than print. Here was the clearest example of how strongly librarians are sometimes bound by tradition. It was not easy for some of the committee members to give up a concept

of library service in terms of buildings and/or to accept the possibility of other outlets for service.

The committee's top priority rating for continuing education suggested a priority for service to adults. Because of declining juvenile circulation and the improvement of school libraries, it was felt that before expanding the service to children, the library should follow closely national developments in this area. This conclusion caused concern to some committee members, as it later did the board, although basically the committee was suggesting a wait-and-see attitude.

Members of the Objectives Committee soon learned that service on the committee was a responsible activity—neither comfortable nor easy—which could not be experienced passively and which required active participation on their part. Those with strong egos had to adjust to having their carefully prepared cases riddled by the other members' criticisms. Sometimes feelings ran high. As in any group situation, every member seemed to have to give in at some time or other. Yet several members commented before the deliberations had ceased how significant a learning experience the participation had been for them, and how for the first time their own ideas about the library had been crystallized. One sensed that some of the members emerged from the discussions with a philosophy of library service where little had existed before, or if existent, had lacked clear focus.

The committee, after their own deliberations, concluded that if some of the decisions were accepted it could be most difficult for some staff members to adjust to an informational/education emphasis, as opposed to a recreational one. The rebuilding of the library's program to suit different clienteles would test some staff members' ability to change in order to meet changed needs of the community.

It is not easy to convey the excitement of many of the discussions or the intellectual stimulation of the interchange of ideas. Moreover, it was interesting throughout to see general staff interest in the committee's deliberations. Before the final recommendations had even been made public to the staff, certain staff got word of one tentative decision of the committee—that service to shut-ins should be "part of the library program insofar as personnel and finances permit." The committee was criticized for such partial commitment by an editorial in the staff newspaper.

After the last meeting when the final recommendations were summarized for the director and board, a staff association meeting was held at which the Objectives Committee chairman discussed the recommendations before a large part of the staff. The director, meanwhile, had accepted the committee recommendations and had submitted them to his board of directors.

The board deliberated over the committee's recommendations at several of its meetings. At one of these meetings the chairman of the Objectives Committee was invited to answer questions concerning the recommendations. The board could see the need for the library's playing a strong information role in the community, and as a consequence, voted to rename the library the Memphis Public Library *and Information Center.* Two points troubled the board the most: the recommendation that service to children not be *expanded,* and the lack of precision, in their eyes, in the statement concerning service to the disadvantaged. After considerable discussion, the board accepted the statement concerning service to children, but insisted on changes in the wording related to service to the disadvantaged. The trustees were particularly anxious to assure that existing services would not be allowed to deteriorate because of the library's effort to serve this other pressing need. The committee's wording, they believed, could be interpreted to mean that the library's total effort would be in this direction.

Now that they are approved, will these objectives be easily translated into action? One may observe that no original concepts or new values were unearthed, but one can again cite John Gardner's encouragement in this respect when he says, "We have in this nation a well-tested framework of values. Our problem is not to find better values, but rather to be faithful to those we profess—and to make those values live in our institutions, which we have yet to do." [6]

Furthermore, the significant accomplishment seems to have been clarification of purpose and the suggestion of a clearer identity for the public library in this community. The future challenge will be in enlisting the commitment of those engaged in this institution's work. As Lowell Martin was to say to Chicago: "This statement of goals and principles is offered as a rallying point. The Chicago Public Library can be significant in its city. Chicago desperately needs a library that will bring the record of facts and knowledge and wisdom and expression into the lives of people. The wellspring of such an agency is not buildings or even money, but clear purpose and complete commitment." [7]

The advice need not be confined to Chicago. Like those characters in *Follies,* we in Memphis have seen where we have been. What matters now is where we will go.

REFERENCES

1. Gardner, John. "Toward a Self-Renewing Society," *Time,* April 11, 1969, p. 30.
2. Martin, Lowell. *Library Response to Urban Change.* American Library Assn., 1969, p. 23.
3. Report of the Trustees of the Public Library of the City of Boston. City Document No. 37, July 1852, p. 6.
4. Bundy, Mary Lee. "Factors Influencing Public Library Use." *Wilson Library Bulletin,* December 1967, p. 382.
5. Dale, Edgar. *Can You Give the Public What It Wants?* World Book Encyclopedia and Cowles, 1964, p. 3.
6. Gardner, John. *op. cit.,* p. 30.
7. Martin, Lowell. *op. cit.,* p. 23.

A Tip from Detroit

John Berry

THEY HEARD about the branch librarian who followed
up a question about treatment for alcoholism by driving
the shaky patron to a Salvation Army treatment center . . . and the librarian who moved into an inner-city
neighborhood from a middle-class suburb to function
more effectively . . . or the librarian whose perseverence
on the telephone to an urban renewal agency got it to fill
and cover dangerous holes in a vacant lot in response to
complaints from a block association. Then there were
those Latino construction workers who had been cheated
out of a month's pay, or the woman who was in deep domestic conflict over her decision to have an abortion.

They also heard how the providing of information
and referral service had transformed a major library system and had rebuilt deteriorating relations between another and its city hall. They heard how in Houston the development of Neighborhood Information Centers had
uncovered gaps in library service, how the federal funds
from the NIC Project had proved the validity of the program to the mayor, how the library's budget has since increased by 50 percent, how the library's telephone reference service has grown from 30,000 calls in April 1973 to
78,000 in April 1975 because of the famous "Watergate
Commercial" publicizing the library's information and
referral services . . . Said Houston Library Director David Henington, "The NIC program has turned our Public
Library around, we're finally doing something right!!!"

The occasion for all of these stories was the Conference on Information and Referral Service in Public Libraries held in the bowels of the Detroit Public Library on May 7, 8, and 9, 1975. The Conference was sponsored by the NIC (Neighborhood Information Centers Project) Consortium comprised of the public libraries of Atlanta, Houston, Detroit, Queens Borough (New York City), and Cleveland. The Project has been funded since 1972 by the Office of Library Research and Demonstration of the Department of Health, Education, and Welfare. After three difficult years of planning, operating programs, collecting documentation, and dealing with major changes in the leadership of the libraries and the project, "We have moved past the experimental stage to incorporation of 'I&R' into the structure of bona fide library work." So said project chairman, David Henington, director of the Houston Public Library.

It was an invitational conference, and the roster of those present read like a mini *Who's Who* among library leaders. Directors or their delegates were on hand from public libraries in Brooklyn, New York, Philadelphia, Cleveland, Wayne County, Baltimore, St. Louis, Tulsa, Lexington, Chicago, Denver, Los Angeles, San Francisco, Memphis, Dallas, and Chicago, along with deans or surrogates from such library schools as those at Columbia, Michigan, Wayne State, Illinois, Drexel, Simmons, Atlanta, Western Michigan, Toledo, Kentucky, and North Carolina Central. Supportively watching this first public presentation of the success of the NIC Project was HEW's Henry Drennan, the fed who has seen NIC through all of its ups and downs, and who has provided a certain stability through the tough period of leadership change and early inability to find directions.

NIC beginnings

The beginnings of the project date from the development of a funding proposal at the Cleveland Public Library, through the efforts of Dorothy Turick and then director of the library, Walter Curley. Curley was made project director when the proposal was funded, a post later assigned to Houston's David Henington. NIC seems to have had one of its most important successes in Houston, and it has revitalized a "tired" public library. It

is, however, in Detroit, under the committed direction of
Clara Jones, and with the implementing leadership of her
associate director, Bob Croneberger, that the concept of
Neighborhood Information Centers really got its first
complete practical application. Detroit, on its own funds,
began the development of its TIP Program ("The Information Place") in 1971. After four years of difficult staff
orientation, file building, organizational change, and the
most comprehensive and searching program of community study we have observed, Detroit decided to "go public" with its TIP program at the conference. Among the
NIC participants, the Detroit TIP program, a model of
I&R services for urban libraries everywhere, has made
the most progress. It is now solidly operational, and there
has been little professional ballyhoo or publicity. The library wisely waited until it could show results and a functioning, effective program.

The philosophy of I&R

Detroit's statement of philosophy for the TIP service is a fine definition for other libraries: "1) information
and referral service is simply a broadening and deepening
of the library's traditional function; 2) as in every aspect
of service, the public librarian serves as ombudsman or
expediter, not as advocate; 3) the necessity of follow-up is
emphasized as a strength unique to the TIP service and to
make sure that the patron has actually received the help
he or she needs . . ."

It was the question of whether I&R services should
be an integral part of library service, or operate as separate service that engendered much debate as NIC developed. For instance, one of the causes of the failure of the
Public Information Center Project at the Enoch Pratt
Free Library in Baltimore (Joseph Donohue, "Some Experiments Fail," *LJ*, June 15, p. 1185-90) was the library's unwillingness to give it a separate identity, or
even a telephone number. On the other hand, Bob Croneberger, one of the architect's of Detroit's TIP service,
told *LJ* that he felt that integration of traditional reference service with the TIP concept was not only possible
but desirable. Lamar Wallis, director of the Memphis
Public Library and Information Center, reported that the
problem was solved in Memphis by making I&R service

the top priority for the whole library. Here again Detroit provides the best model so far. The commitment of the library administration under the leadership of Clara Jones has given TIP the internal importance that its survival demands, and has clearly shown that in Detroit I&R is very much a part of total library service. Recent increases in other kinds of library use in Detroit are attributed to TIP's success. A similar story has been forthcoming from the other successful model, the Houston Public Library. If the commitment of Chairman Dave Henington is any indication, in Houston administrative commitment has been translated into a daily working role for the library administration from the top down.

Community needs

In Houston, where other agencies were involved in some provision of information and referral, to overcome their jealousy the library spearheaded a movement to form a Council of community social agencies. It worked. The library's role in I&R was eventually accepted. In Memphis, on the other hand, when the Shelby County Court system decided to fund I&R service in the county, the Memphis Library and Information Center was forced to compete in a bidding situation to provide the service. The library's proposal won in competition with others, particularly from a proposal brought in by the United Way. In Detroit the TIP program is now widely accepted by other community agencies and is apparently perceived as an important aid to their activities, rather than as a rival. Part of the reason for Detroit's acceptance of TIP may be the careful way in which the library has avoided presenting itself as an advocate, while meticulously following up on all inquiries and referrals. Marcia Allen, head of the TIP Department in Detroit's Chaney Branch, put it this way: "The Library is not designed, by definition or purpose, for direct social action . . . Our genius, if you will, is in locating, indexing, arranging, and making accessible information about the community and its resources, in a free atmosphere, so that such information can be applied to problems." But even with this basic point of view, the librarians in Detroit often find the line between the "ombudsman" concept and the followup required with other agencies, and the idea of "advocacy" very hard to draw. Lamar Wallis of Memphis, where a new I&R service is just being developed, wasn't that worried: "We'll just have to do it when it's necessary." Henington said that the problem hadn't occurred to him at first, but there had been scrapes with other agencies. Houston finally decided that a "degree of advocacy" was necessary or the service wouldn't work. Sam Lacey of Queens Borough reported that that library had run head on into New York City politics. One of the city's most powerful councilmen, Matthew Troy of Queeens, complained: "This kind of service belongs in a Democratic club!" Most of those present seemed to be satisfied with Marcia Allen's distinction between "social change advocacy and individual ombudsman action."

Starting the service

The original NIC proposal planned to set up two branches in each city as models for further I&R development. In Detroit the concept had roots as far back as World War II when the library ran a War Information Center, but as Marcia Allen pointed out, the needs of today's urban dweller are different, oriented "toward basic human services that deal with the problems of living and 'coping.' " Detroit initially opened two branches, publicized the event, and discovered that demand outstripped the initial ability to provide the service. Faced with the response, the Library decided to install TIP in all 30 Detroit branches. From the beginning funding came from the library's regular budget. Federal funds were added in 1972 and were used to beef up the TIP Clearinghouse staff and accelerate the extension of the service to all branches. According to Allen: "Federal monies have not had a direct influence on the long-range economic commitment of the administration." The Clearinghouse began the long task of developing the resource file for TIP. This required systematic gathering of information about services and capabilities in a host of areas: aging, children and family, education, health and mental health, legal, business and consumers, recreation, housing, finance, and taxation. Data was acquired from grass roots clubs and associations, government agencies, volunteer groups, professional associations, and just about every group organized to deal with people's problems. Full information, including some evaluation of an agency's ability to deliver service, was collected, and is continuously updated. Subject headings were carefully selected, mostly from standard library lists and indexes, but with great care taken to avoid the jargon of the various professions engaged in social service. Supported by all of Detroit's holdings, the file is also supplemented by pamphlet, clipping, and document collections at the TIP Clearinghouse.

Reaching out

To publicize the service, and at the same time develop information on community needs, a two-pronged effort was launched. Librarians from Detroit's branches were sent to speak on an unbelievable variety of community and neighborhood groups ranging from block clubs or boy scout troops, to penal facilities and nursing homes. Branch librarians were given maps of their service area, and from these they developed a system of community walks in which every business in the neighborhood would be called upon, informed about the service, and tapped for information regarding local information and service needs. Ultimately each branch had its own TIP service, but even now most inquiries are eventually referred to TIP Central at the Main Library. TIP Central expects to exceed 100,000 inquiries this year. Telephone connections allow an inquiry to be made from a branch with TIP Central and the agency being queried to be on the line, too.

Staff training

In all the NIC libraries there was considerable resistance from the library staff to the idea of providing I&R services. The commitment of the Detroit administration, coupled with a tough-minded implementation in the early stages tended to harden resistance in some cases, but ultimately got the message across to the Detroit staff that I&R service is the library's number one priority. Workshop series, that begin with Detroit's philosophy, and a general orientation to the I&R concept are then developed into actual training in the skills required to do I&R work. Frequent formal and informal staff meetings continue the process in Detroit. Finally, one of the best ways the library has found to build confidence and enthusiasm for the TIP program, as well as to overcome the resistance of staff to participating in it, has been the requirement that branch and central staff frequently meet with community groups ȧnd take those community walks. In publicizing the service to others, Detroit's staff often sold themselves on it.

In Queens, according to Sam Lacey, there was staff resistance, too, and he attributed most of it to older members. There are 15 Queens branch librarians still opposed to the idea. In Cleveland, where the program still falters in an experimental mode, Robert Vokes attributes part of the problem to a decision to begin with staff from outside the library. This has been changed. Staff attitudes in Atlanta were equally resistant, and the program there is still very much in an experimental mode.

In both Detroit and Houston, where the most successful I&R programs exist, outside agencies (Detroit's City Planning Department for demographic data, its Wayne State University School of Social Work for counseling and guidance, and Houston's Community Welfare and Planning Agency) were brought in to help with the staff orientation and training. In Detroit a social work graduate from Wayne State, Carolyn Luck, eventually joined the library staff.

Status of the NIC project

From the Detroit sessions one could develop the following assessment of the development of NIC models in the five cities. In Cleveland changes in the leadership of the library, and some mistakes at the outset, have prevented full development of the NIC concept. In Queens, the project foundered with the death of Director Harold Tucker and political problems. It is only coming "back to life" now. Atlanta appears to be suffering from leadership crisis with its NIC program. But in Detroit and in Houston the program has already developed beyond the initial plans and expectations. It has brought about significant revitalization of both library systems. In Houston, Director Henington attributes a 50 percent budget increase, 142 new positions, and a much improved level of credibility with city hall to NIC. Detroit reports a similar set of successes. More important, the NIC project has provided two exceptional models for other libraries throughout the U.S., and those models are already being copied.

In addition to providing a model for other libraries, Detroit has begun to export talent as well. Former Deputy Director Bob Croneberger and Community Social Work Consultant Carolyn Luck, the team that got the TIP program off the ground, have just been appointed Assistant Director for Public Services and Head of Community Information and Referral Services respectively at the Memphis and Shelby County Public Library and Information Center. This kind of leadership, which has already characterized Lamar Wallis' efforts to bring change in Memphis, should go a long way toward insuring the success of the new I&R program there. Croneberger and Luck will be authors of a series of articles on information and referral services in public libraries beginning in *LJ* in October.

I&R services are a fact in dozens of public libraries serving cities of varied sizes and types, from the ghettos of Detroit to the affluent exurbs of Greenwich, Connecticut.

To succeed, we have learned from Detroit, Houston, and Memphis that the first requirement is total commitment by the library administration. Without leadership and commitment the service just doesn't get off the ground. We have learned that it ought to be part of total library service, not broken out as in Baltimore or Cleveland. Detroit showed that it is better to involve and train existing library staff than to superimpose specialists on the library organization. We have also learned from the bad luck at Enoch Pratt and the successes in Houston and Detroit that it is probably better, if possible, to put I&R components in every branch, rather than in one central place.

NIC disappointments

When the question of community involvement came up at the conference, there was little to report. Most of the libraries had avoided citizen advisory groups and citizen committees, despite the fact that the original grants required a level of citizen involvement. The NIC program has failed in this regard, unless you feel as Detroit's Clara

Jones does, that it is better to go to the people with an existing program fully operational, and involve them at that point than at the beginning stages.

The other disappointment at the conference was the session devoted to education for I&R service. Miles Martin of the University of Toledo effectively described that library school's ambitious plan for educating staff for I&R service. The program includes a one-third commitment to training in information handling, a third on people and politics, and a third devoted to internships with community agencies. Most of the participants, while curious about the Toledo program, expressed fear that it would train I&R specialists only and thus limit the career development of the librarians trained. Dick Darling of the Columbia University School of Library Service described, briefly, the special Urban Information Specialist program there. It seemed better integrated with traditional librarianship, thus producing a graduate better founded in both urban information service and other kinds of librarianship.

Unanswered questions

Detroit's TIP program and the NIC project have not solved all the problems connected with I&R service in public libraries. There is no concensus yet on whether or not the files developed should be shared with other groups or individuals. The question of when and to what degree users of the service should be involved in its governance and operation is very much an open one. (It was, for example, disappointing to hear Lacey describe developments in Queens, with no references at all to the fine Langston Hughes Branch in which community control is a fact.) Libraries are still struggling with the question of integrating I&R with existing reference departments or not, and most are still struggling with the hard economic fact that to support the service you may have to take funds from something else. Issues related to the political sensitivity of persistent follow-up with city agencies, or the provision of information that may cause problems for other agencies and constituencies (in the area of housing, for instance) were not dealt with in any direct way.

The I&R future

Information and referral service is obviously now a part of public librarianship in America. It is no longer an experiment. The NIC project is proof that federal aid can provide support for meaningful programs that ultimately not only strengthen public libraries, but provide urgently needed human services. NIC proves that federal support can even change the direction of institutions, provide new vitality in "tired" ones, and even show one direction libraries must turn if they are to survive these depression years. Detroit's success, despite the fact that the library exists in possibly the most depressed economic situation in the U.S., is a clear indication that change in the direction of real human need can bring new life. Clara Jones has shown American librarianship that firm commitment to change, deep belief in the power of information, and leadership in the face of crisis can succeed, and in that success the Detroit Public Library has given all of us a tip on what the future holds in store.

Defining Information & Referral Service

Robert Croneberger, Jr. and Carolyn Luck

INFORMATION and referral service has become an increasingly familiar topic in library literature. We have read reports of disastrous failures, outstanding successes, and everything in between. In our experience with the TIP Service in Detroit, in workshops around the country, and presently in establishing the LINC (*L*ibrary *IN*formation *C*enter) Service in Memphis, we have learned a great deal about the state of information and referral in libraries. There is a danger that it has become the new "toy" for librarians and library schools, and we are concerned that different people mean different things when they talk about information and referral, attempt to teach it, or to do it. In light of the confusion and controversy over information and referral in libraries, we would like to present our definitions, opinions, and ideas, and to share what we have learned. Among topics to be covered in this series are: what information and referral is and is not; the need for a systems approach in planning so that the service is integrated and not isolated; the need for training and the kind of training needed; the necessity for community analysis; staff and community resistance and how to deal with it; and models for cooperation with other agencies.

Approaches to I & R

Information and referral in libraries has, in the past five years, passed from possibility into practice, but there

194

has been a lag in what has been written about it. Most of what is available are arguments for or against it or tentative speculations about what would happen if libraries did it. There is a disturbing approach in teaching, writing, and talking about information and referral which we call the "What information and referral means to me" approach. This approach permits people to give testimonials covering a wide range of services from the distribution of pamphlets about service agencies to publishing service directories to acting as "advocates" (a term of even more diverse interpretation than I & R). Similar essays and oral renditions on "What America (or Beauty or Truth) means to me," and other such inspirational topics are okay as long as they remain in the realm of the abstract where they can be governed appropriately by personal taste and subjective reality. However information and referral is not an abstraction, and subjective definitions are neither appropriate nor productive. This approach frequently includes rhapsodic accounts of "how we done it good (whatever it was we done)." What is needed is honest and tough-minded evaluation of successes and failures. This cannot possibly be done without clear definitions of what it is we are trying to do, and how we will know we did it good.

"Tell us the secret"

Another disturbing approach is the "tell us the secret" approach of many people interested in doing information and referral who have assumed that there is a secret which can be packaged and paid for and applied for successful information and referral. We believe that we have found some factors which apply in varying degrees to most library systems. We do not believe, however, that there is a formula or a single model for how to do it. This is because the inherent differences in any library system must be recognized to develop the best possible information and referral service for that particular system in that particular community.

Not a library invention

One of the major reasons common goals, methods, and terminology must be established in the library field is that they have already been established in the field of information and referral, which exists outside the traditional sphere of libraries. We detect a tendency to forget, or fail to recognize in the first place, that libraries did not invent information and referral. It has been developed and practiced for at least 30 years by various types of service agencies. Recognizing this, the assumption that libraries must now step in and "take over" information and referral because it has been badly bungled by social agencies is erroneous and unfair. It has, rather, been a stepchild of human services which nobody wanted to own but which could not be gotten rid of. Since I & R is not a direct social service (i.e., social casework or the provision of resources), but is vitally important in providing access and coordination of direct services, the problems have always been: where to locate it (as an independent agency or as part of an existing one) and how to support it. Consequently, information and referral service has frequently been the object of territorial struggles for inadequate funds. It has frequently been the service component which gets tacked onto an agency by necessity or by governmental mandate. It is the first to be cut back when funds become scarce and the last to get additional funds because direct services are always more important and more clearly the function of social agencies. Under these constraints, many social agencies, many local United Ways, and many other volunteer groups have struggled to provide good information and referral service with inadequate support. There is a high level of awareness among helping professionals of the need for information and referral and of what it is as opposed to social work. If libraries are going to share in meeting the need for information and referral, they must speak a common language with the others in the field.

Defining I & R

The definition of information and referral which we use is consistent with the national standards of both United Way[1] and AIRS.[2] We acknowledge that a small but increasing number of libraries are aware of this common definition and are using it. The definition: Information and referral is the active process of linking a person with a need or problem with a service which will meet the need or solve the problem. The link between the person and the service is made up of information. It is because the success or failure of the information link depends on communication involving specific individuals in specific problem situations, that we emphasize that information and referral is a process and not a product. The distribution of pamphlets describing social services, the addition of a director of community services to the reference collection, or the addition of a desk labeled "Information" where help with the card catalog or yellow pages is available are all fine services, but are not information and referral.

The linking process

The person in need of information and referral service may need help in articulating what his problem is (or what he thinks or feels it is) and what he wants to do about it. It is just as important to use active listening with the person who articulates well to be sure you understand each other. This kind of communication is essential in the first step of the information and referral process which is identifying the problem(s). This means getting enough information from the patron to be able to proceed in locating information/services which will be helpful. Skilled communication continues to be important in the next stage: searching for appropriate resources. Accurate information is useless if it is not presented clearly and in a form that is useful to the person who needs it. Only the patron can judge the usefulness of information or say whether he understands. The information and referral worker must actively seek feedback from the patron throughout the process in order to be effective. It is important to provide options (more than one agency or approach to the problem) whenever possible so that the patron can make his own informed choice. The process is complete when the link is made to the appropriate service or resource to handle the problem(s). Depending upon the patron and the situation, different degrees of active helpfulness may be required to complete the link. For example, it may be necessary to phone an agency to make an appointment for a patron who is not able or comfortable in doing that for himself or to arrange transportation to an agency if the patron's lack of transportation prevents him from getting service. When the process leads to referral to an agency, and there is reasonable certainty that the link has been made, the remaining step in the process is follow-up, which is made to the patron to find out whether he got what he needed and whether he needs further assistance.

It is clear from this definition and this description of "the process of linking . . ." that information and referral is not a product (directory, card file, computer print out). Rather, the product of information and referral is the effective communication of information to help people solve problems and to get services they need, creating the link between problem and solution, need and resource. The data base which is essential to the provision of I & R is a reference tool to be used along with others, but it is the use and not the existence of the tool that counts.

I & R is not social work

Another definition which we think is useful in helping people to understand that information and referral is not social work (because, after all, it is "helping people with problems" which may be of a serious nature) is a definition of social casework. The text book definition is: "a psychosocial treatment method."[3] The goal of social casework is change in the individual, but since it treats the individual in society (psychosocial) it may involve making changes in the environment, i.e. helping a person to find another living situation than one which is destructive, or the direct provision of resources, i.e. adequate food and clothing to permit a child to attend school and to function with alertness because of improved nutrition. Casework is based on a diagnosis of the immediate and underlying, long-term problems of the client and the development of an appropriate plan for treatment: helping the client to solve his problems and to make changes which he desires to make. Casework depends upon the development of a relationship between the client and the worker, which may be short-term or long-term in which the worker may act as a role-model or a resocializing influence, as a teacher, or an advocate.

It should be clear that social casework is much different and can be clearly separated from information and referral. The only relationship information and referral has to treatment is to link people

who want/need it to local agencies which offer treatment. The problem identification in the information and referral process might be called diagnostic, but it is preliminary and aimed at finding an agency which can meet the need as presented. For example, when a person who calls for information and referral says "I need counseling" the information and referral worker needs to know very broadly what kind of counseling (to be sure the person doesn't mean credit counseling or legal advice) and whether the person needs immediate help before beginning to search for appropriate agencies. The information and referral worker has no need to know details of the specific problem, why the person decided to seek counseling, or what related, deeper problems may exist, but the caseworker/counsellor to whom the referral is made will need to know these things in order to be helpful. This distinction between information and referral and social work applies whether I & R is done in a library or a welfare office or a crisis intervention center. The information and referral worker who dabbles in counseling or probes for unnecessary details (details which are not relevant to referral to an agency) is taking risks for the client, himself, and the agency which employs him.

Advocacy

In addition to the confusion over what I & R is (and is not), there is a related confusion over *advocacy* which we think has recently degenerated into semantics. Advocacy has become a dirty word with frightening connotations of politics, struggle, and sacrifice, and many people in libraries choose to avoid it at all costs, devising other, more acceptable terms to apply to what they think might be misconstrued as advocacy. Others choose to apply the term to a variety of phenomena precisely because it is a dirty word, guaranteed to evoke some response from everyone. We prefer to look at the phenomena related to information and referral and to define what is an appropriate role for the library as an information and referral agency.

In general, people need information and referral service because they cannot get information or find services for themselves for a wide variety of reasons. The task of the information and referral worker, then, is to help people get information and services which they are unable to get on their own. In some cases it may be necessary for the information and referral worker to intervene more directly between the patron and the agency than it is in others in order to accomplish that task. The appropriate role when such intervention is called for is that of an interpreter. Some patrons quite literally need an interpreter to deal with agencies, because of language difficulties or because they do not communicate well on the telephone. People may call for information and referral service because they have been given the runaround by another agency (or think that they have). If it appears that they should receive the service they want, a call to the other agency is in order to interpret the patron's situation to the agency and the agency's response to the patron. If there has in fact been a runaround, the involvement of a neutral third party is frequently enough to attach a priority to the case in question. If there is a valid explanation for the delay or lack of service, it is more likely to be given to the third party than to the patron and is more likely to be accepted by the patron in this way. In no case is it appropriate for an information and referral worker to approach a situation involving dissatisfaction with another agency as an antagonist or Public Defender. If satisfaction cannot be obtained for the patron on the direct service level, and the patron chooses to pursue the issue further, the information and referral worker should contact the appropriate agency supervisor, again acting as a neutral third party and interpreter. If the matter is still not resolved and the patron wants to continue, the I & R worker should check into whatever complaint mechanism may be available or contact the next highest level

of authority. At each stage in this process of intervention/interpretation, the *patron* and not the I & R worker must make the decision to go ahead. If the patron is a welfare client who must go back and deal with the same caseworker next month, he may not want to enter a formal complaint or even go to the supervisor. It is the patron's choice because he has to deal with the consequences. No one needs help that hurts.

We think that advocacy is as good a term as any we have heard for this type of interpretation/intervention. We think that intervening on the patron's behalf in this way is vital to effective information and referral service. It has been well received by other agencies in our experience and has not created problems for the library. Our definition of advocacy, then, is: helping a person to get information or services which he cannot get for himself. Then by definition, information and referral is advocacy which may require varying levels of interpretation and intervention. We think this kind of advocacy is needed, appreciated, and safe.

Helping agencies improve

It is not appropriate for a library as an information and referral provider to rate service agencies or to eliminate them from their files or directories if they do not perform satisfactorily. Libraries have no expertise for evaluating the professional services of other agencies. Libraries cannot recommend a "good nursing home" although they can refer to an agency which does inspect, rate, and recommend them or provide information (books, pamphlets, interpretation) about how to select a good nursing home. Nor can they tell people not to use certain agencies because they are "bad." Informal knowledge of agencies' shortcomings is an important part of information and referral work, and it is certainly legitimate to tell a patron that Agency X has a six-month waiting list, but there is no legitimate means for a library to say to the general public or press, "Agency X is no good." Mechanisms can be developed to communicate with people who can take action to improve services. This may mean the library administration communicating with the administration of the agency about a problem which has been documented by library staff, i.e. "Of 200 referrals made to Agency X last month, only 29 were handled to the patron's satisfaction," to see if it can be resolved. It could be that the library is making incorrect referrals or that the agency is simply overburdened and can use the library documentation in asking for more funds or that the administration has been unaware of direct service problems. It is also possible for the library to provide such information to city-wide or county-wide planning and/or governing agencies which could work to improve the overall delivery of services. Such avenues for communication and change can be developed positively without the library becoming a tribunal.

The definition of information and referral given in this article is not original, nor do we think there is any room for originality in redefining an existing field. There is plenty of room for originality in developing working models for the provision of information and referral services in libraries. We have shown that information and referral is not social work, and we believe that it is clearly library work as a public information function. We do not mean that information and referral is the exclusive province of libraries or even should be, but we emphasize that it is *library* work and not some experiment tacked onto the "traditional" library. Our next article will explore the need for a systems approach, the organizational change involved in incorporating information and referral into libraries and the folly of attempting to do information and referral as an isolated experiment apart from the internal organization of the library.

REFERENCES

1. Alliance of Information and Referral Services. *National Standards for Information and Referral Services*. Phoenix: The Alliance, 1974, 11p.
2. United Way of America. *National Standards for Information and Referral Services*. Alexandria, Va.: United Way, 1973, 16p.
3. Hollis, Florence. *Casework: A Psychosocial Therapy*. Random, 1965, p. 9.

I & R=Reference

Carolyn Luck and Robert Croneberger, Jr.

IN THE FIRST ARTICLE in this series, we discussed what information and referral is and is not, the distinguishing factors between information and referral and social work, the concept of advocacy as it relates to information and referral, and the importance of recognizing that information and referral is library work and not some "special service" attached to an existing institution. This article will deal with the reasons why so many "services to the disadvantaged" and other innovative projects end up being *disadvantaged services*. The public is the obvious and most important loser when this happens, but the public library loses a part of its future as a service institution each time it fails in another effort to serve the unserved. We think the major factor in the creation of disadvantaged services (to the "disadvantaged") is the "special service" status which isolates them from the library system, denying them support, authority, resources beyond special funding, and prevents them from providing first-rate library service. This is the same factor which too often allows the "regular" library to abdicate its responsibilities to the disadvantaged.

The introduction of information and referral service into a public library system is a change in that system. In order to manage change and not be victimized

by it, it is necessary to view the system as a whole and analyze how this new component moves the system toward the achievement of its goal and objectives. How can it fit in and work as an effective part of the system? If the new component is in conflict with the goals and objectives or (as is much more likely) the goals and objectives have not been formulated clearly enough for judgment of conflict or compatibility, the goals and objectives must be changed (or articulated and examined) or a rational decision must be made against introducing a change which will be counterproductive. If, for example, a library is defined through its goals and objectives as a place where books are kept and no decision is made to change its conscious role, the introduction of information and referral is clearly counterproductive. Efforts to do information and referral, or any other service which is antithetical to the stated or implicit goals, is likely to create internal disaster through staff conflict or end quietly in frustration and disappointment for the proponents of the change.

Change without conflict

The issue is really a choice of strategies for change. Obviously, it is possible and sometimes useful to make a deliberate choice to go against what is traditional in order to create change through conflict. In extreme cases (of organizational paralysis), this may be the best choice available. However, this strategy has a high mortality rate both in terms of the projects which are its vehicles and the people who take the personal and professional risks. A more subtle consequence of this strategy is the gradual institutionalization of resident troublemakers and in-house adversaries which has taken place in a number of library systems since the sixties, and by which people interested in change have created their own tokenism. If an in-house adversary is tireless, self-sacrificing, extremely dedicated to serving people through libraries, and extremely knowledgeable in dealing with conflict for positive gains, he may have impact on the system which will result in more effective services. If he is lacking in any of the above attributes (which means if he is human), that impact will be diminished. If, however, the person who adopts a conflict strategy is someone who thinks librarians are no good and libraries have nothing good to offer (except his new service, if they would only let him do it), he should not be in a library system. His destructive contributions will far outweigh any positive benefits as his long-range strategy is probably to wipe out libraries for the good of society.

I & R equals reference

We think that a cooperative approach which recognizes the strengths and weaknesses of a system and aims at improving that system in terms of the services it provides by making the whole library accountable for serving its publics is more likely to be more effective than a conflict strategy launched by a "special" department, project, staff, or individual. We believe that the major goal of public libraries should be to provide useful and needed information to the citizens who support it, and we have found compatible goals and objectives here at the Memphis and Shelby County Public Library and

Information Center. Information and referral is one type of service which can meet that major goal if coordinated with other library services (traditional and innovative).

The need for coordination of information and referral services and reference services is clear when the nature of "I & R" questions is examined. A high proportion of the requests received by most nonlibrary information and referral centers are information requests, for example: "What is the telephone number of 'X' agency?" Is there a local chapter of 'X' organization?" "How can I get in touch with them?" Many of these questions are regularly answered through the reference services of libraries not actively involved in anything called information and referral. There is a fuzzy line between "I & R" questions and reference questions, and only the most arbitrary distinctions could separate the "Information" in information and referral from reference. In other words, the content or source should not be the criteria for classifying an "I & R" question. The outcome is the operative distinction: information-giving, or referral to an agency for service. The first category cannot be clearly distinguished from reference questions, at least not by content. A question on venereal disease might be related to finding out where to get tested or treated, but it might also be an inquiry to the medical or social issues of VD which would be handled through reference tools other than the information and referral file or directory. They cannot be distinguished by source. The appropriate referral may be found through use of any number of reference tools including those in subject departments and the telephone. They cannot be distinguished by patron. It is absurd to classify reference questions asked by "the disadvantaged" as "I & R" questions. The only clear distinction is between reference and referral, and that distinction can only be made by the outcome—by the service rendered, whether it is the giving of information only or referral to an agency for service. Obviously, referral services cannot be offered separately from information services because frequently the combination of both is required.

The "funny files"

Given that many "I & R" questions turn out to be reference questions (or reference and referral) the effective use of the entire information system which is the public library is essential to good information and referral service. For example, at Memphis and Shelby County Public Library and Information Center, the Literature Department maintains a file of translators and also an interdenominational file of local ministers (since the department includes religion). These are valuable reference tools in the provision of information and referral services but should not be taken over by some special information and referral staff or incorporated into an information and referral file. The practical impossibility of creating an all-inclusive file is easily seen by taking an inventory of the "funny files" which exist in subject departments. Criteria for inclusion, consistency of format, the need for highly specialized information in a file designed to serve the *general* public, and the physical problems of reproducing and housing a large file in all branches would be some of the problems created. However, the mere fact that specialized files of important information exist in reference departments does not make them accessible.

There are four factors which make such files accessible and thereby part of the information system: 1) Cooperation among departments and branches to serve the public is essential. A patron is a patron and information is information. No service system can operate well on the assumption that "my patron is more important than your patron" or that "my information is mine." 2) There must be sufficient access by telephone within the library system. It is farcical to masquerade as an information system if you have too few telephone lines for efficient internal communication, not to mention lines to provide adequate public access. 3)

There must be knowledge throughout the system of where to check for various types of information. In developing the subject index to the information and referral file at the Memphis and Shelby County Public Library and Information Center, we are listing main library reference departments when appropriate as one means of letting branch library people know where to look. 4) Such files and current information in subject areas must be viewed as important enough to be kept up-to-date and in sufficient depth. A decision to leave subject files intact and make use of them as part of a total information system is a decision to enhance subject specialties as something beneficial to that system, enabling the system to provide more benefits to the public. It is a decision against taking information away from the specialists, who have the readiest opportunities to gather it and who can probably make the best use of it, because it may be in a different format, be current, or come from people rather than from print. This is not unlike a decision made recently in this library to transfer spoken-word recordings from the Music Department to appropriate subject departments or a decision to intershelve cassette tapes with books.

The other major reason for building information and referral services into the total library system is to maximize the benefits of decentralization. The decentralized branch-main library structure of urban public libraries facilitates both the collection and dissemination of community information. It is the only existing structure which holds the potential of creating neighborhood information centers. Doing information and referral systemwide and making it regular library work can multiply the support and resources applied to its success.

It should be clear from what we have said about building information and referral services into the system and doing the service systemwide that we do not see information and referral as a service to the "disadvantaged." Rather we see it as a service to the citizens of the city and/or county which supports the library. All citizens have needs for information which are currently not being met by existing sources. Because funding and community interests are frequently tied to the idea of service to the disadvantaged, it is not a term or a concept which libraries can get rid of entirely. More importantly, because of the unmet needs of segments of the population, it is important to develop ways to serve them and ways to evaluate the services provided. However, we think it makes more sense to make every service outlet in the system responsible for meeting the needs of its community in the most appropriate and effective ways. Some people react to the idea of integrating services to the disadvantaged into the regular library with suspicion that it may be a sinister cop-out or subtly disguised racism. Our view is the reverse: that the creation of *disadvantaged services* for people who need first-rate services allows library systems to cop-out on their responsibilities, in effect discriminating in the provision of public services.

A systems approach to establishing information and referral services has far-reaching effects on the library. Priorities need to be clearly defined, and budget allocations must be aligned accordingly. It is useless to say, "information and referral is top priority," unless the necessary changes are made to translate that statement into workable reality. If more staff is needed, if clerical procedures need to be reviewed and streamlined in order to make staff time available for information and referral, if more telephones, extended hours, publicity, etc. are needed, hard decisions must be made and clearly communicated in order to make the updated priorities real. Crisis management (reacting to whatever happens in the way that seems best at the moment) will not work. Planned organizational change is the rational alternative, although it is by no means mistake-proof or problem-free.

Authority

Hiring an "outreach librarian" (who is usually young, enthusiastic and fresh out of library school) to be in charge of a new, *priority* service with no clear authority to do so is a contradiction. It will most likely lead to staff resistance to that new "radical" and to frustration of the isolated project librarian who is unable to do his job because of lack of guidelines, authority, and expertise. An expert in information and referral or an enthusiastic idealist committed to change cannot fairly be expected to be an expert at planning, organizational change, or staff relations.

There are some very practical administrative problems involved in setting up information and referral services which can only be dealt with by proper systemwide authority. For example, the telephone changes we have referred to (additional lines, instruments, three-way devices) are important and must be planned for. These seemingly small changes involve allocation of funds, assessment of needs (which can only be done by visits to branches and consultations with the branch librarians), and working with the telephone company to be sure that they do what you want (do they have to dig trenches in cement floors in order to install required equipment?). Perhaps you discover a branch which doesn't have an information desk. Perhaps the branches in the low-income areas of the city or county are only open part-time and are staffed by one or two people. Perhaps there is another innovative service going on in the library (i.e., Adult Basic Education or Cable TV) which should be coordinated in some ways with information and referral. None of these practical problems can be handled effectively without proper authority. They are all important to the provision of information and referral services.

Full service to all

In summary, it is essential that we not create isolated and poorly administered "disadvantaged services" which are disguised as service to the disadvantaged. It is equally essential not to isolate information and referral services either in terms of the back-up resources of the library system or by limiting public access to them. We end up ripping off the "disadvantaged," and the dedicated, enthusiastic staff who expect to accomplish so much. Without a coordinated system-wide service directed toward all citizens, we are turning our backs on the very people we claim we wish to reach. Full service to all citizens must be the goal.

Our next article will deal with outreach methods aimed at achieving this goal, and how "outreach" service has been misplaced in public library service.

Help!
A Crisis Services Project

Richard Parsons

WHEN I was approached by representatives of the Baltimore County Board of Education to 'cooperate' in the production of yet another pamphlet on drug abuse, I came to three conclusions. The first was that everyone and his cousin had something out on drugs—lists of symptoms, lists of books and films about drugs, and so on. The second conclusion was that the traditional brochure format which appealed to librarians and other adults had to be scrapped. The third conclusion was just as important; if the Baltimore County Public Library (as it turned out) was to do all the work, prepare the manuscript for printing, and come up with the financing, then, we had to have a free hand as to design and content.

The people at the Board of Education agreed. Instead of another award-winning glossy job listing the current crop of pro and con material about drugs, we would issue in tabloid newspaper form a *Directory* of crisis intervention services in nine areas of concern to young people. These areas were: Alcohol; Draft Problems; Drugs; Family Hassles; Legal Problems; Pregnancy; Runaways; and T.B. and V.D. We set out to identify four levels of intervention service available to Baltimore County residents. These were: hot line, or referral; counselling; professional legal; and professional medical.

We aimed to provide avenues of help for fundamental problems, and not to offer just a band-aid or an aspirin tablet for a symptom. Availability to Baltimore County residents was our only criteria. Whether the service was outside of Baltimore County or, in Baltimore City was not important.

With the consent of the liaison man from the Board of Education, I appointed myself chairman of a committee, initially composed of the two of us, now joined by a delegate from the Mental Health Association of Metropolitan Baltimore. She had come to ask the Baltimore County Public Library to create just such a directory as we were setting out to produce.

Without the support of the Bureau of Mental Health of the County Health Department the project might have failed. This cooperation was essential. After talking for about two hours with an exceptionally conservative, foreign born psychiatrist, I was given the liaison of two key doctors on his staff. The roadblock in the discussion with this psychiatrist was his inability to understand why we were getting out the directory in the first place—there were all sorts of directories out already. "See," he said, "I have a whole drawer full of them." "Who else is using them, besides you?" I asked.

"Who else needs to use them?" answered the doctor. "They're for doctors and professionals." "What about the kids," I asked, "who are in trouble and are afraid or too embarrassed to seek help?" I was looking for some slight sign of service orientation in this public health officer. "You mean," he said, after a long pause, in a heavy Bela Lugosi accent, "you mean you propose to put this in the hands of young people?" Shock reduced him to momentary speechlessness.

The round was ultimately won—(mainly to get rid of me, I think), and shortly thereafter I augmented the committee by adding: The Chief of the Drug Abuse Division, and the Chief of the Comprehensive Alcoholism Division from the Health Department; the woman from the Mental Health Association; a delegate from the County Department of Social Services; a young seminarian who was head of Crisis Intervention Network, a loose affiliation of all the youth group hot lines and drop-in centers in the metropolitan area; a major from the County Police Department; and representatives from Legal Aid, Inc., and ACLU.

Everyone was put to work. Though the police had deep misgivings about something which resembled an underground newspaper—an anathema to them—we calmed their fears. The seminarian assured them that this was the only format which the kids would accept, and I promised that *this* tabloid would have no porno words or intimate personal ads!

We identified all the available sources of help in the metro area. A guide in this part of the project was an outdated directory prepared by the Health and Welfare Council of Central Maryland. We included many services, and sought types of information not available in this or any other directory.

We broke down our list of available services by types—pregnancy oriented, draft oriented, drug oriented, alcoholism oriented,—and gave appropriate agencies to contact over to the component parts of the committee. With a questionnaire we had devised, the professionals were to canvass the *heads* of certain identified services in their area of specialty by phone. Ambiguities in the resulting questionnaires could be resolved by a quick conversation between me and the agency head, *after* the ice had once been broken by my phalanx of professionals. The doctors were indispensable in getting the emergency clinics in hospitals, and Maryland State and Veterans Administration medical services on board.

We mailed the questionnaires with a covering letter on library letterhead to most of the identified services and a self-addressed stamped envelope for the return of material.

The questionnaire covered the following points: name, address and phone number of the agency/institution/service; name of person(s) in charge; hours of service; nature of services rendered (within the scope of the nine problem areas); charges, if any, for services—fee schedule requested; limitations in service to minors; geographic limitations to service.

When the questionnaires were returned I decided to alter the traditional directory format. Assuming that a youthful clientele was interested in the agency's location (and phone number), the nature of the services offered and the hours, we listed all that ahead of the name of the person in charge. We typed a manuscript following this format, and sent each agency a photo copy of its entry for corrections. (The covering letter noted that unless corrections were received by a certain date, the entry would be printed as was). We wanted to be absolutely certain that what was printed was both seen and approved by the agencies in advance, so that neither they nor the public could raise a legal storm in the sensitive areas of pregnancy counselling, draft counselling, runaways, etc. We printed a disclaimer that listing a service did not constitute either an endorsement of the agency or the service. We merely took note of the existence of the service.

While all this was going on, ACLU and Legal Aid, Inc. had been busy. At the suggestion of both the police and the youth group hot lines, we created a dictionary of those felonies and misdemeanors most frequently caused by youngsters. Legal Aid was asked to write in the definitions and the existing penalties for the 18-year-old and older, under Maryland law. The dictionary, which has fascinated both parents and teenagers, ran the gamut from Accessory, Assault, Auto Theft, Disturbing the Peace, Drugs, Drunk Driving through Harboring (as of runaways), Hitchhiking, Larceny, Runaways, Shop Lifting, to Sodomy, Unlawful Assembly, Vagrancy, and Weapons (possession and use of), with much in between.

ACLU did a 20 point section derived in large part from an existing pamphlet of theirs, on the rights and duties of teenagers. This covered basic human rights under the law in matters of search and questioning, as well as the code of civilized behavior expected of youngsters in their dealings with the police (don't shout at them, or use obscenities, or try to run them down with your car, etc.)

The Maryland State Department of Juvenile Services and the County Police collaborated on a section describing the processes a minor (under 18-years-old) followed under Maryland law if he "came to the attention of the police."

We had determined that a run of 250,000 copies of the tabloid, which came to 16 pages, would cost about $7300, with an approximate unit cost of 2¢ each. We raised the money outside of the Baltimore County Public Library budget through visits to State and County department heads, and talks to service clubs in Baltimore County. The table below shows how *HELP!* was funded:

Maryland State Dept. of Education Division of Library Development & Services LSCA Title I	$4,500
Maryland State Drug Abuse Administration	500
Baltimore County Board of Education	500
Greater Towson Council on Drug Abuse (through Sheppard & Enoch Pratt Hospital)	1,000
Kiwanis Club of Towson	500
Towson Business Association	250
Total	$7,250

In developing the market in advance of the printing (which was done by a community newspaper), I took the manuscript and visited the superintendent of Catholic Education, the headmasters of 17 private schools, the police and fire chiefs, the metro area heads of both the Boy Scouts and Girl Scouts, and several other potential "big" clients. We later sent a sample copy, with a covering letter offering unlimited quantities, to all the clergy in the County, and the presidents of all identifiable organizations in the County (about 700 such organizations). We got good spot announcements promoting *HELP!* on both TV and radio. The bulk distribution in thousands of copies went like this:

Distributed as an inserted supplement in seven County community newspapers. Had we had an additional $5000, we could have distributed an additional 108,000 copies in five more local papers. We were charged stuffing and inserting charges in all instances.	70,000
Baltimore County Board of Education (for controlled distribution in one or two high school grades)	38,000
The Archdiocese of Baltimore (for general distribution in Metropolitan Area Catholic high schools)	16,000
Scout Council of Central Maryland	5,300
Maryland State Drug Abuse Administration (for distribution through youth-group hot line drop-in counselling centers)	10,000
Maryland State Department of Juvenile Services	7,000
Baltimore County Health Department (for intended distribution and display at a heavily attended open air fair)	2,500

Baltimore County Dept. of Recreation & Parks	1,000
Two Real Estate Companies	1,500
Baltimore County Police Department	10,000
Baltimore County Fire Department	1,000
Welcome Wagons of Maryland	1,000
Enoch Pratt Free Library	5,400
17 Private Schools in Baltimore City and County	8,500
Inserted as a supplement in the seven student newspapers in the two- and four-year-colleges in Baltimore County (no charges involved)	25,000
Boy Scout Council	10,000

These quantities were ordered before printing. The library delivered them to the clients. Later, when an individual or a church or school ordered copies, the client was referred to the nearest branch of the Baltimore County Public Library, to which we would send the bundle marked with his name. All distributions were free.

The response was staggering! Nine months later *HELP!* is virtually out of stock. We get letters daily from schools, libraries, health agencies, and federal departments all over the country requesting samples. Right now I am trying to raise the funds for the second edition.

Busy or distressed people *often require prepackaged service* to answer serious informational needs. They do not want, and I submit don't need, the traditional library brochure. This would just tell them which books or pamphlets to ask for (if in) which *might* give them the answers they need desperately—NOW! Though we mentioned no book, film, or pamphlet, this was an in-depth library information service in which we strove to achieve the greatest possible accuracy. As gremlins got into the type setting and transposed some phone numbers, I sent out two sets of corrections to all listed agencies, noting the corrections and also additional agencies offering services which had been drawn to my attention after *HELP!* was printed.

Along these same lines, with the Baltimore County Public Library in a catalyst role, we produced (with the help of the police department's bank of IBM cards) a *Street Guide*, which we sell; an illustrated guide to the County's historic buildings (from an unused manuscript found in another County department), which we also sell; a three-page brochure giving the name, address, and phone number of the appropriate County agency official to contact to have neighborhood nuisances and code violations abated. These run from abandoned cars and roaming dogs to broken street lights, mini-bikes, and junk yard conditions.

Utilizing many of the people I met and worked with during the eight-month preparation of *HELP!*, I was able to join with five other people from different parts of the community in preparing an immensely successful workshop this past November.

The object of this all day affair was to examine Baltimore County from a total community viewpoint, what it had going for it and what its problems were. This was a call to inject human values into planning, to provide community input into the governmental planning process. In the words of a corporation president who participated, we should strive to abandon our traditional adversary postures and find ways of working things out together for a better community for us all.

We had participating 170 organization and business people whose hands are on the levers of policy making within their corporation or organization. The group included corporation executives, management people from the utility companies, public, private and parochial school administrators, merchants, developers, home builders, real estate companies, representatives from the American Institute of Architects and the American Institute of Landscape Architects, groups concerned with the aging, retarded children, and kindergarten age children; and recreation council officers.

A really fantastic process has been begun, one so big that the original six of us (the Coordinator of Curriculum Development representing the Board of Education, an architect, the Executive Vice

President of the Central Baltimore County Chamber of Commerce, the Executive Vice President of a national corporation, the President of the League of Women Voters, and me.) cannot really come to grips with the potential. Spin-offs are already occurring: by deliberately seating the Mountain Club of Maryland representative at lunch with the Regional Supervisor of the Maryland State Department of Juvenile Services, talks have begun whereby potential runaway or predelinquent kids will be taken on hikes and other excursions sponsored by the Mountain Club. This, hopefully, will help defuse a youngster's hostility, create a new adult authority figure against which he has no hangups, and perhaps provide a new perspective from which to cope with his own legal family. Besides which, it will be a healthy use of energy. Other unlikely spin-offs are taking place every other day. The library has joined the Chamber of Commerce, to which I am now a delegate. I have reasonable hopes of having the second edition of *HELP!*, through the Chamber, funded by corporations and businesses which are being vandalized and shoplifted by drug addicts. The Chamber of Commerce wants the library to join with it in publishing an annual market guide to Baltimore County. The library is going to take over, manage, and purchase materials for a special collection in the Baltimore County Department of Planning and Zoning. The library will probably do a survey of slide, tape, film, and map collections in county government departments. At this point nobody knows who has what—if anything, and much duplication exists. During the workshop, for example, I used 300 slides pulled from six

county and state agency collections, two nonpublic organizations, and three private collections. In the case of the public collections I examined (I looked at thousands of slides), there was gross duplication of material. Some of the best slides illustrating a basic point germane to a subject area (soil erosion for example, or historic buildings) were *not* in the collections of the departments where one might expect them. A superb presentation in slide form on automobile accidents had been put together by the State Police; the County Police didn't know of its existence until I told them.

The League of Women Voters, forced to vacate its present offices, is talking meaningfully with the Chamber of Commerce at the Chamber's invitation about moving in with it and sharing space, office equipment and rental costs. This is an incredible alliance with a sprawling power base which should alert politicians that a more responsive community is being structured. And, for the first time, radical kids from the hot lines and corporation officers sat down at the same table together, on a friendly, first-name basis, and really began to find out some things about each other.

The Baltimore County Public Library is at the very center of all this, printing materials as needed, arranging meetings, offering suggestions of unlikely combinations of organizations, providing equipment and library materials as required, and my time and services. Which is where the metropolitan public library has to be—in the midst of, and actively participating in, the ferment—if it is to survive as a meaningful service institution worthy of tax support.

Ohio's BOOKS/JOBS Program

Joseph F. Shubert and C. Edwin Dowlin

IN 1967 with 115,650 men and women registered as unemployed, Ohio's state government had programs to create new jobs and provide vocational training. As librarians we may have viewed our role as essential in supplying information for both programs. But even to other professionals we were invisible.

"We never thought of the library," said Mrs. Lois Rush, the Human Resources Planning Coordinator for Ohio's Office of Opportunity, in discussing her office's work to help the unemployed. "BOOKS/JOBS has brought the librarian out of his ivory tower in the eyes of the community. And placing books in neighborhood centers has made the library a part of everyday life for those we are trying to assist."

Three years after the launching of Ohio's $371,000 BOOKS/JOBS program unemployment is still a stark reality for a great number of Ohioans. Nor has the knowledge that the percentage of unemployed Ohioans is slightly less than the national percentage decreased the efforts of state government agencies. Thus, although BOOKS/JOBS has not yet reached all its goals, it has proved that the public library can be a valuable ally of these other agencies.

The concept of BOOKS/JOBS began with a conversation. In the spring of 1967, Ohio's state librarian commented to Ralph Gabele, chief of the counseling section of the Ohio Bureau of Employment Services, that the informational resources of Ohio's public libraries were being ignored by most of those unemployed and underemployed who already had the educational background to use these services. Even the staffs of community social agencies often failed to recognize the value of organized information as a social tool. Mr. Gabele agreed. He pointed out, however, that the job materials in the libraries he had visited were almost all out of date.

Within weeks the outline for the BOOKS/JOBS project was developed under the joint sponsorship of the State Library of Ohio and the Ohio Bureau of Employment Services. The State Library Board allocated federal Library Services and Construction Act funds for a statewide project and appointed an 11-member steering committee. Six members were librarians and five represented the Bureau of Employment Services, the Ohio

Office of Opportunity, and other community affairs agencies. BOOKS/JOBS was, as far as we know, the first library outreach program for the unemployed to be conducted statewide.

What was the purpose of BOOKS/JOBS? Our intention was certainly not to encourage librarians to become social workers. Instead the objectives of the program were to help Ohio's libraries reach and serve, both those needing information and skills in order to obtain and hold jobs and also the staffs of government and social agencies which work with the unemployed and underemployed.

The steering committee translated those general objectives into three specific aims:

1. To provide libraries with more information and greater understanding of the needs of the unemployed.

2. To develop effective communication between libraries and agencies that deal directly with job-seekers.

3. To assist in providing materials.

For the first time in Ohio an LSCA project was directed at one specific group of people who had special informational needs. And, although 70 percent of the funds were eventually spent for materials, the program's primary aim was not to put books on shelves but to encourage librarians to reach out to serve new readers. BOOKS/JOBS was created to help any unemployed or underemployed person who could use library materials. The only unemployed persons we did not attempt to reach through the program were those who could not read.

By the end of 1967 the steering committee had developed a three-part plan. Investigation had proved that library materials for job seekers were indeed obsolete, as Mr. Gabele had suggested. Two parts of the program, therefore, provided for massive purchasing of books, pamphlets and filmstrips. The third part financed experimental pilot projects conducted by local libraries. Because most BOOKS/JOBS staffing was to come out of local library budgets we hoped the new services would become integral parts of library programs, rather than a temporary overlay which would end when the federal funds had been spent.

In supplying materials, BOOKS/JOBS first offered a core collection of 16 books and pamphlets to every public library agency, including branches, bookmobiles and deposit stations. Fern Long and Mary Adele Springman of the Cleveland Public Library prepared both this basic list and also a lengthy supplementary list. These lists were based largely upon their experience with the Cleveland Reading Centers project which helped new readers use library materials and services (*LJ,* September 15, 1967, p. 3004-7). The core collection included practical guides like *How You Can Get the Job You Want* by Glenn L. Gardiner, Arco's *General Test Practice for 92 U.S. Jobs* and the U.S. Department of Labor's *Occupational Outlook Handbook*. To order all the books, a library needed only to return one card to the State Library.

After receiving the core collection a library was eligible to request funds for supplementary materials, including films and filmstrips. Funds were allocated to counties in proportion to the number of unemployed persons who had registered with the Bureau of Employment Services (BES). The grants of $1.27 for each unemployed person ranged from $63.50 in rural Vinton County to $27,051 in populous, industrial Cuyahoga County. Although BOOKS/JOBS offered a list of suggested titles, local libraries chose their own materials and were not limited to those on the list. Libraries were encouraged to buy materials in such areas as techniques of seeking employment, basic education, self-improvement, skill building, and human relations. Supplementary grants were made only after local committees of librarians, representatives of the Bureau of Employment Services, and others involved in helping the unemployed had assessed the information needs of the unemployed and had prepared a plan for the use of the materials. There were no restrictions on where the books and films were to be housed or how they could be used. Local BOOKS/JOBS committees were also encouraged to develop plans for experimental pilot programs for which grant funds were available.

This pattern of cooperation between libraries and other agencies was the theme for the one-day statewide conference which in January 1968, launched the program. Ninety invitations were accepted by librarians, BES staff and representatives of other community agencies. Almost none of the librarians had met the head of his local BES office before attending the conference.

In her keynote speech Evelyn Levy, the Enoch Pratt Free Library's representative on Baltimore's Community Action program, told the audience: "Today acquiring a job can mean a fight. Libraries and librarians have an important role to play in this fight."

By the end of the day, participants had heard reports on unemployment and on what agencies were doing about it. The BOOKS/JOBS project was described and plans were made for six regional meetings in February. During the regional meeting, which followed the pattern of the statewide conference, librarians and agency representatives from the same area met to plan local activities. Although personnel men from business and industry were invited to the meetings, few came.

"Some of the librarians were skeptical at these first meetings," Ralph Gabele commented later. "All of us in public service tend to forget to reach out to those who don't come to us. But there is a close correlation between education and employment. And once you start on an educational quest you can't avoid the library."

At the statewide conference and the regional meetings a pamphlet on BOOKS/JOBS was distributed. The folder was also sent to libraries and other community agencies throughout the state as were two later pamphlets, one directed to the job counselor and one to the job seeker. Regular reports in the State Library's newsletter also kept those working on BOOKS/JOBS informed about programs in other communities.

After the regional meetings, the program moved rapidly. By the April 1 deadline, 22 committees had submitted proposals for pilot projects. Later that month the State Library distributed the first books and pamphlets in the core collections.

If this was the blueprint for BOOKS/JOBS, what kind of structures did local committees actually build? Although the steering committee had hoped every library would order the core collection, 50 of the state's 257 public libraries failed to do so. Requests for 695 sets of these basic books and pamphlets, however, came from libraries in every county in the state. And even some of the librarians who did not order the core collection were later drawn into the program when librarians from nearby communities began to plan BOOKS/JOBS activities.

To order the supplementary materials a library had to be both committed to the goals of the program and willing to allocate staff time for it. A total of 159 libraries in 57 communities seized the opportunity and worked with the BES office and other agencies to assess local needs and prepared plans for the use of materials. These libraries were aware of the need to serve the unemployed and also were flexible enough to rearrange priorities to allow staff time for a new project.

In 31 rural, semi-rural and suburban counties, however, libraries did not participate. Unemployment may have seemed less important, or may have been less visible than in urban centers, but 18,250 men and women were then registered as unemployed in these counties. The $23,177 allocated for the purchase of supplementary materials in these areas was transferred to the pilot projects.

Wood County, near Toledo, was among the counties in which librarians found the core books and pamphlets useful but did not prepare a plan for the use of supplementary materials. "This county has less than two percent unemployed," explained Marian Parker, librarian of the Wood County District Public Library, "and most of them are probably migrants for whom you'd need a specialist. We have all we can do to run our libraries on a day-to-day basis to take on a new project which would not bring worthwhile returns."

In the town of Delaware the initial idea for a three-county committee came not from a librarian but from a Community Action Center staff member who read a newspaper article about BOOKS/JOBS. His enthusiastic offer to help form a committee was accepted by local librarians.

The 317 organizations represented on the 57 BOOKS/JOBS committees reads like a *Who's Who* of community action. Among them are such agencies as: NAACP, Allen County Extension Agency, Miami Valley Institute of Technology, AFL-CIO Labor Council, Urban League, Inner City Family Life Ministry and the Lima Joint Vocational High School.

The steering committee urged libraries to use the supplementary grants for books, pamphlets and films relating to the local employment needs as identified by local committees. Few libraries, however, selected materials which were not on the BOOKS/JOBS list. Dennis Day, who worked on BOOKS/JOBS at the Dayton and Montgomery County Public Library, believes that the initial seeking out of materials should stay at the state level but wishes librarians would be more experimental in selection. "It is a lot of work to dig up special materials," he commented, "but at Dayton we identified some of the non-traditional ones, such as those Du Pont developed for the functionally illiterate, and they were valuable to us."

BOOKS/JOBS placed much of this material in centers which serve the unemployed—taking the library to the people. For example, in the Marion BES office books and pamphlets are used regularly by job-seekers, perhaps because the receptionist not only points out the display but also helps them choose books. At the request of this office, the Marion Public Library continued to supply materials after BOOKS/JOBS sponsorship ended.

Probably the major change in library service resulting from the supplying of the supplementary list material was that many librarians now were working with agencies from which they had formerly been isolated. In communities which developed imaginative programs these patterns of joint action are continuing.

New communications links between libraries and agencies working with the unemployed and underemployed were also a major part of the eight experimental pilot projects. Activities ranged from jobmobiles to rotating book collections, from placing mini-libraries in community centers to lending films for industrial training courses. In many projects pamphlets were given away with no more than a stamped name to indicate the source.

Pilot projects in Portsmouth, Mansfield and Columbus placed collections of books, pamphlets, and films in job counseling and adult education centers. G. D. Reeg, manager of the Portsmouth BES office, said job counselors continue to use the BOOKS/JOBS materials extensively and the film strips and records have become popular additions to the orientation of job-seekers.

As one of two BOOKS/JOBS audiovisual projects, the Cuyahoga County committee created a materials center at the Cleveland Public Library. To promote the use of the films, which were a major part of the center's collection, the committee presented a day-long Job Film Fair for librarians, job counselors, social workers, businessmen and others from the manpower field. The Cuyahoga County pilot project included the production of a 17-minute film, *A Whole New World*. Developed by the Cleveland Public Library, the film tells the story of a man whose early library experiences turned him against books but who is reintroduced to the library during a job training program. Reaction to the film has varied. Some librarians have been disturbed by the "image" of the librarians in the film. Many job counselors and others who have viewed the film say it has given them a new concept of libraries and usually mention specific ways in which it can be used with individuals and groups with whom they are working.

The BOOKS/JOBS committee in the Akron area, which developed the second audiovisual project, worked closely with personnel staff from local industrial firms. Almost 45,000 persons who were enrolled in employer or agency training programs attended film and filmstrip programs on such subjects as: getting and holding a job; health, grooming and courtesy; consumer education; and the economic and political factors leading to unemployment. The Akron project appeared to be the only one which captured the interest and support of businessmen.

"BOOKS/JOBS is the greatest thing that has happened to us in a long time," commented John Rebenack, director of the Akron Public Library. "It got us involved in new areas of the community and showed us how complex the problem of unemployment is. The real secret of the success of BOOKS/JOBS was in the way the program was sold by the State Library and the Bureau of Employment Services through both channels."

In Cincinnati the Ohio Library Association's Junior Members Round Table, which was until then a primarily social group, initiated a pilot project in which mini-library collections were set up in six inner city neighborhood centers. The Junior Members, both as a library assignment and on their own time, helped train the six library aides who were hired to work in their local communities. At the request of these aides the collections were expanded beyond materials on job skills and job-finding to include books on black history and culture. In addition to supplying materials, two of the aides conducted film programs and one arranged an exhibit which was a popular feature of a two-day workshop held at the center.

Mrs. Margaret Sanger, Head of the Readers' Bureau of the Public Library of Cincinnati and Hamilton Country, said: "The program has not only brought a valuable resource to the neighborhood centers but it has also had an impact on the lives of the six aides. One has returned to high school and another became so active in neighborhood affairs through BOOKS/JOBS that she was hired by the Model Cities program."

Cincinnati's project also financed the placement of three library collections in community centers, including one which serves former Appalachia residents. "This collection," said a library staff member, "has been moved from its second floor broom closet location to a comfortably furnished first floor storefront room. The director plans to add a study room and we hope it will eventually expand into a full-scale branch library."

Last year when BOOKS/JOBS support ended, the Cincinnati Public Library provided local funds to continue operation of four of the mini-libraries and all three community center collections. In one of the centers a man in his early 20's recently asked for a book on hot rods. When the staff member discovered that he needed help in filling out an application for a library card, she showed him a paperback primer for adults who are learning to read. He borrowed the book with the comment: "I want to learn but I don't want anyone bugging me." Not ready for an adult education course in which the teacher might "bug" him, the independent young man willingly accepted this offer of help through his community center library.

Laurel Krieg, librarian of the Martins Ferry Public Library, says that the Belmont County pilot project which financed the purchase of reference materials for four libraries had as its main benefit a "cooperative spirit" which grew among the librarians. "This was the first time our four libraries had worked together," she said, "and it was a revelation to me how successful it was." These libraries are now working on other cooperative projects, a significant step in the development of the library systems which are a major part of Ohio's new library development plan. And as preparations for these systems develop throughout the state, it is evident that the BOOKS/JOBS experience has helped shape ideas for improving services through system development. Charles E. Blakeslee, a public library trustee and Meigs County Agricultural Extension Agent credits BOOKS/JOBS with opening

the door for a variety of cooperative programs which the Ohio Valley Area Libraries are now developing.

Although lack of staff to develop BOOKS/JOBS projects handicapped the work of many committees, the Stark County project included funds for a full-time coordinator, Philip Koons, who has his headquarters in Canton's Office for Economic Opportunity. Asked to evaluate the project, Mr. Koons gave this low key answer: "We've had some success." The local BES manager, however, calls the program "innovative, creative and dedicated to people." "Mr. Koons has been the greatest single factor in promoting a successful project," he wrote in a report to his supervisor. "The feeling of our staff is 'Three Cheers for BOOKS/JOBS.' This is one of the best programs in which we have been involved."

"We've placed books and pamphlets in abundance in neighborhood centers," says Mr. Koons, "and the materials have been used by the disadvantaged. The primary result of the program is that the library has become known to people in the disadvantaged areas." The project lends films for programs, issues a newsletter and has been trying, although unsuccessfully so far, to serve the migrant worker.

How successful in general has BOOKS/JOBS been? And why did it succeed or fail? Although individual projects within communities have ranged from solid success to complete failure, the program has accomplished its three aims. Some Ohio librarians do have more information and a greater understanding of the needs of the unemployed. Effective communication has been developed between many libraries and agencies dealing with job-seekers. And large quantities of current materials have been acquired.

Perhaps even more important than these results has been the demonstration by BOOKS/JOBS that the library's information services can be useful to the staffs and clients of social service agencies. The project has also shown that when the State Library plays a leadership role in developing programs with other state agencies, the pattern of cooperation is extended to the local community.

BOOKS/JOBS succeeded when initiative, imagination and commitment by the staffs of local libraries was coupled with equal skill and hard work by the staffs of the cooperating agencies. In the communities in which libraries and other agencies forged a strong cooperative link, activities are continuing. For most libraries these were new outreach programs. In some cities, such as Cleveland which was serving the Spanish-speaking population through the Reading Centers project, BOOKS/JOBS offered resources to enrich on-going programs, and led to new services in Project *Libros*.

In the major libraries, however, there probably has not been widespread change in branch services although the branch library is the nearest "community library" for most job-seekers. Specialists at headquarters worked closely with other communitywide agencies and in many cases there was little involvement by the staffs of the branch libraries. Some branch libraries even within these large systems did become deeply involved.

A more lasting effect on library service might have taken place if more money had been spent on personnel. A. J. Goldwyn, associate dean of Case Western Reserve Library School, suggests in an informal evaluation of the project which he calls an "experiment in aggressive librarianship," that instead of 70 percent for materials and 30 percent for staff, the percentages might have been reversed.

Certainly increased staffing at the state level was a major need. The project had a full-time coordinator only for the first few months; any project of this magnitude needs a full-time professional coordinator with supporting clerical staff. Limited staff at the State Library also forced us to curtail the educational component which should be in every program of this type. The most serious omission was the projected series of workshops on services and materials which were to have been conducted after the granting of funds. These workshops would have helped fill the requests by librarians for help in understanding the problems of unemployment, guidance in program planning and assistance in the promotion of projects.

Reports from participating libraries name lack of space and staff as the major problems of BOOKS/JOBS. Lunch hours and trips to and from work were the only times some librarians could spend in making contacts and delivering materials to agencies. In many communities it was difficult to locate places to display and distribute materials. In addition, limitations of time caused hardships at both the state and local levels. We rushed to develop the guidelines, produce materials and arrange the statewide conference, but still local communities were allowed only three weeks to form committees and prepare proposals. Given more time some communities which did not participate would have submitted proposals. We also saw the need for a strong statewide publicity program to interpret the goals of the program. Even without this, press coverage of local projects totaled more than 6000 column inches.

Any evaluation of a decentralized program in which participants are self-selected is difficult. Narrative reports from all libraries which received BOOKS/JOBS funds for supplementary materials or for pilot projects have helped us assess this program.

Even more important, perhaps, than these evaluations of a diversity of activities has been what we all have learned about the design and operation of a statewide undertaking. BOOKS/JOBS demonstrates the importance of broad involvement in planning and designing a project. Its successes show the importance of allowing participants to identify the need for services themselves. (The distinction between needing services and wanting them is one which librarians are wise to remember.) Finally, the project shows that offering resources to local libraries can both strengthen their capabilities and also encourage them to reach out to new publics.

The changing nature of urban, rural and suburban areas has meant a shift in leadership, often to groups for whom the public library is viewed as irrelevant. Through BOOKS/JOBS some Ohio libraries have reached out in creative, experimental programs to a variety of new publics. It may be that the benefits will be as great to the libraries as to those we are serving.

BOOKS/JOBS: WHAT IT COST

Statewide and Regional Conferences		
Committee Expenses	2,165.32	
Conference Catering	1,660.81	
		3,826.13
Printing, Supplies, Travel		
Part-time staff	252.00	
Supplies	344.14	
Travel	296.95	
Communications	2,225.28	
Equipment Rental	242.12	
Printing	2,876.13	
Other	27.00	
Miscellaneous	385.01	
		6,648.63
Books, Pamphlets, Filmstrips, Films		
Core Collections	94,887.95	
Supplementary List	144,001.29	
		238,889.24
Six Pilot Projects	122,238.00	
		122,238.00
TOTAL FY 1967 FUNDS		$371,602.00
Two Additional Pilot Projects		
(FY 1968 Funds)		34,610.00

This report includes only expenses which were financed by LSCA funds during fiscal 1967 and 1968. Except for some pilot project positions no staff salary costs were reimbursed, either at the state or local level. After 1968 some pilot projects became a part of local library programs, while additional LSCA grants continue to support projects which have grown out of BOOKS/JOBS.

PILOT PROJECTS

Belmont County—$8,000 (Bellaire, Barnesville, St. Clairsville, and Martins Ferry Public Libraries)

Established a job information network and specialized collections for job training programs and individuals.

Cuyahoga County—$41,860 (Cleveland Public Library)

Established a center for audiovisual materials to be used by all libraries of Cuyahoga County and other agencies; produced "A Whole New World," 17-minute sound film, Edward Feil Productions, 1514 Prospect Avenue, Cleveland 44115.

Hamilton County—$19,576 (Cincinnati Public Library)

OLA Junior Members trained local library aides to use collections which were placed in Neighborhood Centers and assist readers.

Franklin County—$32,940 (Columbus Public Library)

Operated a Jobmobile in cooperation with BES; provided neighborhood collections of books and materials and expanded its film collection.

Richland County—$13,862 (Mansfield Public Library)

Established an employment information library in the Opportunities Industrialization Center Office which provides training programs for hard core unemployed.

Summit County—$6,000 (Akron Public Library)

Developed its audiovisual collection and services, particularly those for community agencies working in the jobs and vocational information field, including business firms developing job training programs.

Scioto County—$11,000 (Portsmouth Public Library)

Established collections of printed and audiovisual materials in Opportunity and Adult Education centers; worked with job training programs.

Stark County—$23,610 (Canton, Alliance and Massillon Public Libraries)

Established "Job Information Centers" in neighborhood centers for informal use by individuals and as support of tutoring programs; program coordinated by librarian attached to the County OEO office with assistance of sponsoring libraries.

Libraries and Hunger

Agnes M. Griffen

EMPTY STOMACHS NOT ENOUGH PROOF FOR U.S.
OFFICIALS...SPECIAL SESSION ON HUNGER URGED.
SOLONS TO GET PETITION...RISE IN EMOTIONAL
INSTABILITY LINKED TO SEATTLE'S DEPRESSED
ECONOMIC CLIMATE...

THESE have been typical headlines on front pages of newspapers in the state of Washington since the effects of the decline in the aerospace industry and the collateral effect on secondary and service industries hit the area early in 1970. Current unemployment rates in the four-county Seattle-Tacoma-Everett area are officially acknowledged at 16 percent (seasonally adjusted), but reliable sources indicate an actual rate exceeding 20 percent. For many, unemployment compensation benefits have run out, and there are no jobs in sight. In the meantime, layoffs continue.

A fairly reliable indicator of the seriousness of the situation is the increase in the number of free school lunches provided to children of families with limited income in the King County area, which jumped from 222,299 in 1969-70 to over two million in the 1970-71 school year.

An even more dramatic development has been the growth of a huge grass roots-generated, church-sponsored free food program. "Neighbors in Need" has involved over 300 churches in the Seattle area, working out of 35 "food banks" to distribute donated food to an estimated 170,000 people in six months.

It becomes obvious that in addition to worsening the plight of those already trapped in the poverty cycle, the present downturn in the state's economy has brought new members into the world of the hungry. These "new poor" are the urban and suburban families formerly considered well off, who had secure middle-class jobs, above-average incomes, two cars, a boat or camper, a heavily mortgaged house in a "nice part of town," and who have suddenly discovered that they have little or no money to make all payments due on these externals of respectability. Those who swallow their pride and apply for unemployment benefits, and later for public assistance, soon find that the below-subsistence level income provided cannot possibly cover both payments and daily living costs. As anyone knows who has had to live on beans the week before payday because of poor management of the personal budget, food is the most flexible item in the budget and the first to be cut. The result can be widespread malnutrition and in many cases, actual physical hunger.

Many of these "new hungry" are among the half million people who live in the 1,984 square mile area served by the King County Library System. In response to these evidences of critical human need, during the past year the King County Library Board and staff have been exploring ways in which to do their part in alleviating the problems of unemployment, hunger and malnutrition, and related social and health problems among the people they serve. Since the problems are enormous and interrelated, no one problem can be addressed in isolation from others, nor can one person or agency work alone. It has been evident from the beginning that the library could be of greatest value in meeting human needs by providing information on services provided by other agencies; and in the face of the most critical, immediate, and urgent need— for food and help in making the food dollar stretch—cooperation with those governmental and private agencies and groups responsible for this area was imperative.

Much has been written about library "outreach" programs and efforts to publicize and develop programs for unserved groups by working in cooperation with other agencies that serve the same population groups. There has been less said about how libraries can be of assistance in informing potential recipients of services offered by these other agencies. Although librarians talk about the "information function" of the library, when applied to providing information about public services, this is usually limited to information hidden away in a pamphlet file under an obscure subject heading— the traditional reference department approach that is actually useful only to

those people sophisticated enough to know where to ask.

Community agencies have the same need as libraries do for comprehensive outreach programs to inform the public of their programs, yet it rarely occurs to them that the public library might be of real help in reaching people who may need their services. Witness the proliferation of "information and referral systems" operating totally outside of library networks. Librarians often hesitate to become involved in promoting public services by participating in public education campaigns, even to cooperating with government agencies offering tax-supported services! This is especially true about public services that may be controversial. Librarians' professional timidity toward such programs reflects average middle-class American attitudes.

One of the most controversial programs supported by people's taxes has been the Food Stamp program, operated by the U.S. Department of Agriculture and administered by state welfare agencies to combat hunger and malnutrition among low-income families.

Under this program, families trade the amount of money they normally spend for food for coupons that are worth more. The U.S. Government pays the difference between the amount each family pays and the total value of the coupons. The coupons are then used to buy food in retail stores.

Criticism has been justifiably leveled at this program because it is a totally inadequate approach to solving the problem of hunger in America. The controversial nature of the program can be explained more simply by reference to the common attitude that it is not the government's responsibility to guarantee every citizen a nutritionally adequate diet.

In the book *Let Them Eat Promises*,' one of the best introductions to the "politics of hunger," journalist Nick Kotz points out a strange inconsistency of attitudes towards federal aid. Affluent Americans, who can understand crop subsidy payments, oil depletion allow-ances, ship building subsidies, or government-guaranteed home loans and loans to big industry, are quick to insist that if a man will not or cannot work, then "neither let him eat."

While it may be true that most Amer-icans are humane enough to admit that if a person is truly hungry, he should be fed, the real problem is that most citi-zens will simply deny that there is such a thing as actual hunger in this country, and certainly not in their own commu-nity! Perhaps in this society we have come so far from a basic experience such as hunger that we are not able to believe in it until we experience it per-sonally. This is unlikely to happen to most employed individuals who may be in a position to do something to al-leviate the situation—until it is too late. Awareness must be heightened by some external factors that will serve to shock one into action.

It was in the midst of Christmas prep-arations for my family that a friend gave me some copies of letters written earlier in the month to various elected officials by the chairman of a "Washington State Committee to Follow Up on the White House Conference on Food, Nutrition and Health." Although I had been aware of the souring of the local eco-nomic scene, and of the numbers of skilled workers being laid off by Boeing, it had not really affected me personally. These letters hit me with a jolt.

The request being made to the Gover-nor and to Senators Jackson and Mag-nuson of Washington state was to "use any means at your disposal to influence Secretary Hardin and/or President Nixon to declare a major economic dis-aster in Washington State," thereby making it possible for residents in the state to qualify for distribution of dona-ble foods and free food coupons under the Disaster Relief Act of 1969 (Public Law 91-79). The partial list of commit-tee members attached to the letters was impressive. It included representatives of all the major organizations concerned with nutrition, health, and child care,

from Head Start to the Washington State Cooperation Extension, the PTA, the state medical association, and many others. This was hardly a wild-eyed bunch of radicals, but the Establishment itself speaking these unpleasant truths. In the face of such evidence, how could one *not* act?

During a lengthy phone conversation with Ann LeVasseur, chairman of the Committee and Nutrition Consultant in the Maternal and Child Health Section of the State Department of Social and Health Services, Division of Health, we discussed some possible ways in which librarians could work to alleviate the distress caused by hunger and malnutri-tion. I then drafted a letter to the State Librarian, Maryan Reynolds, outlining some courses of action, with the sugges-tion that library cooperation with the Department of Public Assistance, the state agency responsible for administer-ing the Food Stamp program, be coordi-nated on a statewide basis by the State Library.

Response by the director of the King County Library System, Herbert F. Mutschler, and by Maryan Reynolds, was heartening. Both agreed that the library had a definite role to play in in-forming the public of the Food Stamp program. But beyond this traditional role, they also endorsed the idea that meeting rooms in library facilities should be made available where needed as temporary outlets for the Food Stamp certification program. This was not a new idea. One of the smaller branches in the King County Library System had been quietly cooperating in this manner for over six months with the endorsement and support of the Library Board and director.

By the first week of January, Miss Reynolds had sent out an urgent letter to 13 major libraries in the state, in-forming them of the need. Prior to this, she had checked with the supervisor of Consumer Food Programs in the Divi-sion of Public Assistance to ascertain which areas in the state might have the most critical need for additional outlets and for cooperative efforts in informing the public about the program. Along with her letter she sent a copy of the first report of an ad hoc committee of King County Library staff to which the director had given the go-ahead on taking the lead in exploring possible ways of coopperation between local representatives of Public Assistance and the librarians of the system.

The KCLS Committee on Food, Nutrition and Health Information first met with two representatives of the Department of Public Assistance on the last day of the year. Discussion focused on the need for factual information and for the elimination of the great amount of misinformation about the Food Stamp program, such as the idea that Food Stamps were free handouts for hippies and that it was easy to cheat the system. Even among the members of the committee there had been some uneasiness and negative feelings about the program.

The two men from Public Assistance quietly outlined details about the wide range of eligible persons, many of whom were unaware of their eligibility. Included are senior citizens, students, households with extraordinary expenses, families of servicemen, private pensioners, beneficiaries of unemployment compensation, the underemployed, large families, and welfare recipients. Any limited household consisting of persons who cook and eat their meals under a common roof and are within the established monthly income and ready cash limits may be eligible.

The description of the experience of proving one's eligibility for the program was convincing. The committee members could almost smell the crowded waiting room and feel the personal embarrassment of having to bring birth certificates, unemployment compensation books, or alimony letters. The librarians began to realize that certain of their own library users, such as the elderly pensioners who dress so carefully to visit the library, may be hiding the fact that out of $65 total monthly income, $15 might be budgeted for food. Tea and toast is hardly an adequate diet to maintain one in good health during the time of life when one is most vulnerable to illness and can least afford its costs.

The result of this first meeting was a systemwide campaign of Food Stamp and other consumer information. The plan was to be developed in close cooperation with other public and voluntary agencies. It was designed to go beyond the usual library practice of distributing pamphlets and government documents destined for a short half-life in a vertical file, yet remain within the information-gathering and distributing role of the public library.

The Committee felt that the common negative attitude towards "welfare"-related programs such as Food Stamps was based on a belief in the American "work ethic" in combination with misunderstanding or ignorance of the basic facts. Since this attitude was probably keeping many potentially eligible users such as the newly poor, the elderly, and the underemployed from applying for a certificate of eligibility, an active information program about Food Stamps, originating from such a bastion of respectability as the public library, might help to eliminate some resistance to the program on the part of those who really needed Food Stamps. Since the 40-plus outlets of the library system were serving many citizens falling within this category, it was seen as a logical responsibility of the librarians to inform their patrons of a program which would provide immediate assistance to individuals, as well as benefit society in the future.

As many social and health service workers have pointed out, in the long run the taxpayers will pay more for bad health, malnutrition, and chronic and severe conditions occurring during a period of economic depression than they may pay for preventive measures. Researchers have established a definite link between inadequate feeding and mental retardation. It has also verified the self-perpetuating effects of malnutrition upon individuals who grow up, become parents, and again produce infants who will be subjected to poverty, probably again including malnutrition.[3]

After discussion of possible library involvement with the food banks, the Committee agreed that, in order to avoid confusing the issue, these two programs should not be stressed at the same time. One objective of the information campaign was to inform the public that Food Stamps were not "charity." To date, if librarians have worked with Neighbors in Need, it has been as private citizens.

Four major elements of the Committee's strategy were designed to provide the facts about Food Stamps and to make it easier for people to utilize the program:
a) publishing an information brochure and poster on the Food Stamp program; b) informing the Department of Public Assistance of the availability of branch library multi-purpose rooms for the Food Stamp certification program; c) distributing books and materials, including handouts of free government publications; d) planning and presentation of consumer education programs in branch libraries.

The Brochure and Poster

A brochure was drafted and issued first in booklet form, with a second revision as a one-sheet flyer. The heading was carefully worded but to the point: WOULD FOOD STAMPS HELP SOMEONE YOU KNOW? IS SOMEONE YOU KNOW UNEMPLOYED?   UNDEREMPLOYED? HUNGRY? With the help of the Public Assistance staff, Lynn Lancaster, chairman of the Committee, wrote an introduction and compiled information not previously brought together in any one government publication on the Food Stamp program. Included were facts on who might be eligible, what to bring to the interview to prove one's eligibility, an example of a typical cost of the stamps (which is dependent upon

monthly income and the number in the household), and lists of both certification offices and sales outlets in the King County area.

This flyer was printed by KCLS and distributed by the thousands through all branch libraries and other outlets, as well as through cooperating agencies. It was later reproduced by the Seattle Public Library with information on certification and sales offices for the city area, and distributed through its branches.

A poster publicizing the fact that local King County libraries had information on Food Stamps as well as books and other materials on nutrition and "stretching the dollar" was designed and printed by the system in a 10" x 14" format. This was used in displays and for posting in stores and other locations in the community.

Public Assistance Liaison

The King County Library offered the use of meeting rooms in its libraries in key locations to Public Assistance staff as emergency Food Stamp certification outlets. This was to provide additional certification offices, especially to serve the more sparsely populated areas of the county. It was agreed that availability of these facilities could be a positive contribution. Many people newly eligible for Food Stamps had never been in such straits before and would understandably be reluctant to enter "welfare" offices. They would not feel this stigma in going to a public library.

In addition to continuing the once-a-week use of the Maple Valley Library multi-purpose room for this program, use of the meeting room in the new Federal Way Library (about 25 miles South of Seattle) was negotiated on the same basis for an interim period. It was used once a week as a certification office for a period of about six months, until a permanent office was established a few blocks away. Although a separate outside entrance was used by most people applying for certification, the librarians,

Meredith Wallace and Isobel Willson, did make an effort to lure people into the library itself. A sign reading BE SURE TO VISIT YOUR NEW LIBRARY—NO LIBRARY CARD NEEDED, was placed in the room, and books and magazines from the regular collection were provided for the waiting applicants.

Although efforts were made to extend this program into other strategically located libraries in the county, Public Assistance was able to find other locations for the program so no additional libraries were involved in this part of the campaign.

Ironically, the KCLS offer of library facilities seemed difficult for the Public Assistance officials to absorb. It took a number of persistent phone calls and follow-up efforts by librarians before any action was taken. (When one tries to synchronize the gears of *two* bureaucracies, the wheels move more slowly than ever!) The shock (and pleasant surprise) expressed by other government officials, including the director of the regional office of the Department of Agriculture, when they learned what one library was trying to do, verifies the assertion that libraries are rarely considered as part of existing information networks.

It should be stressed here that in cooperating with this program, library staff were not directly involved in the certifying process but only in making library facilities available. Because of publicity in local papers about the library involvement in the Food Stamp program, many librarians functioned and continue to act as referral agents, relaying information on location and hours of Food Stamp program offices.

Librarians of the two branches cooperating with the certification program reported no negative reaction from either staff or public to having a "welfare" program in library facilities, as the Committee had anticipated. Instead, the public response was one of gratitude. The Food Stamp brochure could not be kept in print to meet the demand in all the branches. As Claire McGrew, Burien Librarian, reported, "You didn't realize how many people were concerned until you got the information out."

In contrast with the above, the problems encountered by the Department of Public Assistance in establishing Food Stamp sales outlets have been overwhelming. Insufficient transaction charges for banks selling the stamps, as well as the need for liability insurance, bonding requirements, and vulnerability to theft and holdups are typical of the reasons given by agencies pulling out of the program during the past few months.

A solution to the problem may be found soon. Post offices in the area are expected to begin selling Food Stamps within the next few weeks, according to a recent press release from the office of Governor Dan Evans. While libraries have neither the staff nor the security requirements to act as sales agents, the post offices would seem to be the logical federal agency to do this. It is distressing that it has taken so long to get cooperation between two federal agencies for this program, especially in an area of such critical need.

Distribution of Material

Materials distributed to the branch libraries and other outlets as giveaways included several thousand U.S. Department of Agriculture pamphlets and Washington State Public Assistance brochures on the Food Stamp program. These were provided free by the agencies.

"Money-saving Ways with Food," a brief annotated list of books and other materials in the system collection, was prepared by another committee member, Muriel Hain. This list included titles on growing, purchasing, and preparing foods inexpensively, as well as a list of subject headings for materials in the pamphlet file. A problem encountered in compilation of this list, which the committee hoped would be endorsed and distributed by professional nutritionists and home economists with whom we had been working, was the inclusion of books appealing to counter-culture "organic freaks." Because Adele Davis' books were listed, endorsement of the "nutrition establishment" was withheld. When I attempted to revise the list and remove them, on the basis of the specialists' indictment of the content as being nutritionally inaccurate, it was with an acute feeling of discomfort. When does the attempt to provide accurate information, especially about a subject that can have such long range effects, become censorship? No wonder the consumer becomes confused.

During preparation of this booklist, a check was made of library holdings in these subject areas and additional titles or volumes were added to meet the anticipated demand for information on home budgeting, nutritious and low-cost cooking, and other subjects.

Committee spokesmen urged community librarians to use the lists, posters, and handouts in displays featuring consumer education and the Food Stamp program. Press coverage of the campaign was excellent, as many local newspapers carried an article written by KCLS Public Relations officer, Cari Carter.

Consumer Education Programming

During the following months, consumer education programs were held in several libraries in the system. The most extensive programs were scheduled from late March through June in the multi-purpose room of the Burien Library. This active and community-oriented library serves a highly dispersed population in an unincorporated suburban area just south of Seattle; a large proportion of the people are former Boeing employees.

Loralyn Young, responsible for adult programming at Burien, and also a member of the KCLS Committee on Food, Nutrition, and Health Information which planned the campaign, worked successfully with the King County Cooperative Extension Service

to present three programs on "stretching the home dollar." The first program, concentrating on "how to stretch your food dollar," was the most popular, attracting about 100 people on a weekday morning. Additional programs on clothing and home furnishing were not well attended, which may verify the findings of caseworkers that the food budget is a greater problem to the homemaker on a limited income than other items. As one has said, "It takes experience to live poor."

Other similar programs were held in libraries in Federal Way, Bellevue, Newport Way, and Bothell.

Following the first series at Burien, a seven-session training course for leaders in consumer education was presented by the Washington Committee on Consumer Interests. (This statewide action group, affiliated with the Consumer Federation of America, works on legislation and education in consumer concerns, and has been especially active in the Burien-Highline area.) Average attendance at these sessions was 50, with 38 receiving certificates as trainers or speakers who would be available to work with other community groups.

Videotapes which were made of these sessions are currently being edited and will be made available through the Highline Community College Library. There are plans to transfer two of the programs to 16mm film for distribution through the Washington State Library and public libraries in the state.

As a direct result of these programs, channels of communication have been opened between librarians and the State Attorney General's Consumer Protection Division; additional cooperative efforts are being planned.

Looking Ahead

As of September 11, Washington Congressman Brock Adams had introduced legislation in the House to amend the Disaster Relief Act which, if passed, would provide food and extended unemployment benefits in cities designated as "economic disaster areas." Earlier, government officials in the state had been told by the Federal Government that there was no such thing as an "economic disaster." Perhaps the Great Freeze indicates a change of heart.

In the meantime, libraries in the area, along with other agencies, were scrambling for allocations to hire some of the unemployed under the Emergency Employment Act. During the summer other programs have also been tapped, such as the Employment Supplement Program and the Neighborhood Youth Corps. But these programs cannot begin to put everyone to work.

At the King County Library System we feel that what we have done thus far is hardly enough. People cannot eat promises, neither can they eat information. During the coming winter the picture is grim. Our branch libraries are receiving heavier use, and circulation continues to increase, a further indicator that people are looking for information on survival. We are asking what more we can do. Here are some possibilities:

a) Should libraries be designated as collection points for donated food for the Neighbors in Need program?

b) What more can we do about Food Stamps beyond updating the information sheet and giving it even wider distribution?

c) What additional programs, especially on nutrition and the food budget, should we promote in our branch libraries?

d) Should we open our multi-purpose rooms to organizations promoting short-term group therapy for "surplused" people who are suffering from the shock of being useless to a system they have supported all their lives, and are increasingly anxious, fearful, suicidal, with all the consequent effects on the stability of family life?

What more can we do as a public service to a community in need?

REFERENCES

1. Puget Sound Governmental Conference, *Situation Report of Recent Developments in the Region Relating to Food, Health and General Welfare Problems.* Memorandum to HEW Policy Advisory Committee, July 21, 1971.

2. Kotz, Nick. *Let Them Eat Promises.* Doubleday Anchor, 1971.

3. "Nutrition Survey Prompts NARC Position Paper; NARC Board of Directors Approves Statement to Spur Public Awareness," *Mental Retardation News,* December 1970.

IV
Service
to Youth

Bureaucracy or Commitment?

Geraldine Clark

SCHOOL LIBRARIANS are well imbued with the concept of service. Our standard texts tells us that the main task of the school library is to promote the school's educational program. The multitudinous questionnaires which pass our desk invariably ask how well the librarian believes he is meeting the needs and interests of his students and faculty. And the implications are always that the needs and interests deserving first priority are those closest to the school curriculum. The school librarian often justifies his program by citing his excellent relationships with his faculty—his *teaching* faculty—and pointing to his collection, in which he gathers the offerings of the institution. He is so proud that he is a faculty member and takes part in their meetings.

Yet he is rarely involved in the shaping of educational policy or the provision of educational leadership. In the main, he neither seeks, nor do his colleagues seem to expect him to play a major role in directing the educational policy of his institution. Major Owens has asked whether the school librarian shouldn't be an assistant principal. I would answer yes. But he will never be until he envisions a different role for himself within the school, until he sees as his responsibility the provision of

the understanding of learning—self-directed learning; the provision of the resources and techniques which will help not only those so ably suited for our present educational system (if there are such) but also those who are the powerless in our society. Before the school librarian can move into what should be his proper role, he will have to resolve the conflict that sometimes arises between his position as supporter of the status quo in the educational institution—his feeling that he is there to execute a policy which he has little role in determining—and his commitment to the needs of his students as these *students* see them. The educational policies of many of our institutions are being challenged by students as irrelevant and in some cases harmful.

The library is a part of its parent institution, and is set up in most of our schools to provide white middle-class and upper-class young people with the knowledge and skills they need to secure the continued control of our society, and to preserve our culture and its values as standards against which all the world's peoples are judged. With Victorian missionary zeal, innumerable plans are now being devised to accommodate the black, the Spanish-speaking, the poor—in other words, the

229

powerless in our society—within this middle-class stance and to fit them for a proper role: a role determined, of course, by the "haves."

Yet a large, and certainly a vocal, portion of the library's main clientele, its student body, has become increasingly disaffected from the educational program and, as a matter of fact, with most of our institutionalized culture. Many of the "haves" resent the preeminence the accumulation of wealth takes over the conservation of human values. Some actually believe that even if peace cannot be made as profitable as war (and thus as viable a state to their elders as what we have now), nevertheless, peace should be sought.

To the powerless, the school system is remarkable for its record of failure in their behalf. It is increasingly clear that their situation is neither an accident of history nor a natural phase of their upward mobility. Rather it reflects their place in an institutional system which well serves those who control the system, and which allots to them a perpetual peasant status.

The instant communications of our global village are making our young people the best educated—and I use that word advisedly, as opposed to "schooled"—generation, and the most socially responsible and aware, that we have ever worked with. Whether they will eventually opt to continue our society in its basic form, or to reform it, or to destroy it, they are eager to have at their disposal the representative thinking of all major points of view on the social issues that face us: race, drugs, war, sex, poverty. They wish it in the forms most congenial and familiar to them from birth in an electronic age.

The powerless want to learn the meaning of power and the way to get hold of some of it. For them the library should be the source of information that helps them learn about power.

And yet too many of our librarians demur as they talk about the "immature mind." They attempt to shift their responsibilities for providing their clientele that which it desperately needs to other people in the school system. Thus they forfeit their right to lead.

Not too long ago, I was at a meeting of school librarians at which we were discussing the provision of material, including that which may advocate violence for the correction of social wrongs; or suggest to those who would at all cost avoid involvement in the Vietnam war how it can be done; or provide an unconventional position on drugs. I was disturbed by the indecisiveness of most of our librarians.

We are, in fact, part and parcel of the establishment and balk at that which goes against it.

We who decry violence so vigorously nevertheless, I am sure, include in our collections our Declaration of Independence, the history of our country's involvement in the Spanish-American War and numerous others right up to Vietnam. Violence in the cause, the causes accepted by the majority, is fine; but violence for change by the minority must be avoided at all costs.

I am not passing judgment on what is the effective action for the powerless to take, or for those who belong to our majority but wish to change our society. I am saying that *we should have a commitment to present to these young people the thinking and the alternatives* so that they, in fact, may come to their own standards and their own judgments. And that we will never have a position of influence within our school communities until we see ourselves in that role and take the initiative.

We are the eternal pedagogue thinking that wisdom resides in the teacher and is passed down to the student, rather than seeing ourselves as a more experienced mind reacting with other minds, seeking from all available resources solutions to our problems.

At the meeting I've mentioned, we had suggestions for avoiding the problem which ran this way: "There are particular teachers who requested some material, so we'll buy it; but these teachers wish to know which students are reading it, so we'll keep records on students' reading." The invasion of privacy, the student's right to pursue his own interests, to make his own mistakes and not be bound for the rest of his life like that, did not upset some others as much as it appalled me.

The notion that a student's reading should be limited by a parent's social consciousness or intellectual curiosity is to me equally appalling. Somewhere along the line, we have got to say that, as professionals concerned with—and more, knowledgeable about—child and adolescent development and needs, we must take the responsibility for providing materials and programs which speak to these youngsters today.

Like Harry Truman, somewhere we've got to say "The buck stops here."

Now I am aware that the librarians cannot single-handedly change society, and I am not suggesting that there are specific techniques we all need to follow. But I am suggesting that we can find allies if we seek them and if we are clear in our own minds about what we are looking for, if our commitment is truly to our students as we find them and as they see themselves. Nor do I mean asking the student how he enjoys the library. His expectations are limited by what it is already doing.

What I am concerned about are some institutional procedures of finding out *what* agitates, *what* concerns, and applying that information to effective library service. This is *our* job—not the parents', teachers', or the students'. We are also concerned with providing materials in the forms that students best react to. I so frequently am told, oh yes, we will get some audiovisual materials for the slow learners, for those who don't use print effectively. It is time for us to wake up and look at our most academically talented and realize that we are in the communications business and need to find out about all aspects of it. Let us go back and look at our collections. Are we suffering from the Buckram syndrome? Where is the Jefferson Airplane in our collection?

Bob Dylan? Do we really know what our students can use and care about, and in what form?

In this discovery, I would hope that we'd begin to employ some of the sophisticated research procedures and machinery now available to us. The library schools may have let us down in the areas of information science and retrieval, but the pressure will have to come from us. The techniques will be provided, whether in library schools or in other institutions, if we feel that we need them. The research needs to be done, but we must first be committed.

We must above all have a commitment to self-directed education. Too often what we are speaking about is an easy way of programming a student. We limit ourselves to learning all about what the teacher says a student can do, then put him in the right slot and let him work along. We are not concerned enough about giving him the skills that enable him to pursue his own interests at his own rate and in his own ways.

If we, in fact, are willing to stand up for what we think is possible—and this is in a way a plea for *personal* involvement in our role as the school librarian —we will find that the techniques and knowledge and the courses will come, and that the allies can be found. We will find that if we are willing to be accountable and responsible to all in our communities, including those who are powerless—the parents of the black and Spanish-speaking and the poor—if we are willing to work with them even when they have the leadership role, then we can make some changes in our libraries. We will not become the least relevant of what is becoming a very irrelevant institution, our school system.

Many of us are afraid that if we try to make these changes, we won't be around long enough to carry them out. Will the administration back us up? I think I've alluded to some allies who can be of service in our behalf.

Let me close with the words of two spirituals. (You know this is all in vogue now. Black is most marketable, extremely profitable—not to blacks, but still extremely profitable.) I would remind you of one song that goes:

*You've got to stand your test in
   judgment.
You've got to stand it by yourself.
There is no one that can stand it for
   you.*

You've got to stand it for yourself.

And as an encore we might say:

*There's no hiding place down here.
There's no hiding place down here.
I went to the rock to hide my face.
The rock cried out, "no hiding place.
There's no hiding place down here."*

Bureaucracy
and the School Library

Lillian L. Shapiro

Bureaucracy defends the status quo long past the time when the quo has lost its status.

Laurence J. Peter
The Peter Prescription
(Morrow, 1969)

OF LATE there has been much excitement in the educational world about "accountability," especially the financial kind. The big thing is PPBS (Program Planning and Budgeting Systems), made famous by McNamara when he applied it to Department of Defense spending.[1] Intent on being as businesslike as the Department of Defense is, school librarians are urged to plan budgets more efficiently, as the Pentagon does. It is then disheartening to read that the budget of the Pentagon (PPBS or just BS?) has not come out quite right. An item in the *New York Times* says that the "Department of Defense has conceded that the Navy broke the law governing Congressional appropriations of funds on three separate occasions ... Defense Secretary Melvin R. Laird. ... said that the reports from the Navy reveal no evidence that the violations were willful. They were caused by mismanagement, poor judgment, inadequate or nonobservance of procedures and controls, and personnel turbulence associated with the Southeast Asia con-

flict."[2] Oh, well—nobody's perfect. The geometric theorem carefully learned in high school says that things equal to the same thing are equal to each other. To what same thing are school libraries and the Department of Defense equal? "Bureaucracy."

Most of us have a reaction as immediate as the patellar reflex to the term, but as sociology students and other readers of Max Weber know, bureaucracy had its beginning as a means of insuring *efficiency* in royal households of the early Middle Ages. Over long periods of change it finally developed into what we now see as a phenomenon of big business, government, and other large structures, including libraries. The word itself has acquired a pejorative meaning, since the common denominator of all of these organizations is red tape (as contrasted with red corpuscles which have to do with living entities).

An attempt to explain how this state of affairs has come to be is the message of C. Northcote Parkinson's law, "Work expands so as to fill the time available for its completion."[3] Any period of employment spent in the main offices of a board of education will reveal the motive forces generating this law. There are two reasons for the proliferation of papers and people to push them:

233

—"An official wants to multiply sub-ordinates, not rivals,

—Officials make work for each other."[4] Of course, they also create problems for us.

Officials, driven by a need to strengthen their position within the pecking order, bombard each other with memos and minutes. The result for the school librarian, among others in the system, is the request to fill out reports which often appear to have no discernible purpose.

People vs. Machines

If science can translate dogs and pigeons into people, it surely is no great feat for a bureaucracy to translate librarians and teachers into machines. A recent bit of legerdemain permitted the principals of a large city system to purchase computer-time which would do schedules, student grades, etc. The catch-22 was that the school had to pay for the computer out of its own budget—they were allowed to swap personnel to equal $25,000 worth of computer service. To help the principal make his decision, the average salaries of staff from assistant principal to school aide were listed. You could trade one teacher plus one secretary and make it; in fact, all kinds of combinations were possible. In one school, not unexpectedly, the principal traded a librarian and a secretary to buy the computer's services. (I trust he got the kind of service he deserves. My own experience with billing from telephone companies, department stores, and other users of computer services indicates that people did it better. There might be an occasional error, rectifiable as soon as one human told another about it. The computer makes an error in the grand style and getting it corrected takes almost an act of Congress, certainly a letter to the Better Business Bureau.)

Donald Arnstine, in an excellent essay ("Freedom and Bureaucracy in the Schools," *1971 Yearbook* of the Association for Supervision and Curriculum Development), develops the theory that

bureaucracy, in its pursuit of efficiency and education—as envisioned in our professed democratic ideals—are antithetical. Dr. Arnstine writes that, "Despite the practical inefficiency of schools, efficiency has been the overriding aim of school administrators ever since the growth of efficiency as the dominant consideration in business and industry. It may be recalled, for example, that accelerating bright students through the school grades got its impetus not from any considerations of the child's benefit, but from the belief that a child who spent less time in school was cheaper to educate."[5] His thesis is that where a question of freedom is at issue, it comes into conflict with notions of preciseness. But citizenship—a prized goal for education—cannot be defined as one set of behaviors. "The point of this discussion is not to suggest that aims in education can be dispensed with altogether; it is rather to emphasize as strongly as possible that aims in education are necessarily general, idiosyncratic, and alterable."[6]

In other words, the flexibility to which we point as a keystone of the kind of learning which can happen in a media center is, presumably, just what the bureaucracy does not underwrite, philosophically or in budgetary terms. Under the heading of efficiency, however, we find social studies teachers assigned to medical-room coverage and attendance procedures. Would it not be more efficient, and more economical, to have the teachers in the classroom, or better yet in the library with their students, and hire nurses for the sick-room and clerical staff to check on attendance?

Communication

Bigness is a fundamental element to be reckoned with in a bureaucracy, and it compounds the problem of too little and too late dialogue between administrator and those on the practicing end of the two-way street (in our case, the librarian). "Dialogue" may be a too-euphemistic word for what passes for communication between the actors in the educational performance. Since the decisions are made, not by those active in the direct service to students and faculty, but by the head bureaucrats, we find that programs are planned, steps are approved—nay, mandated—by those who are rarely, if ever, involved on a visceral level with what goes on in a school library, media center, classroom, et al. It is commendable that in some school systems the principal assumes the responsibility of teaching a class each term. I would applaud—even stamp my feet—if that class were not usually an "honors" class. A so-called ungraded class would test the imagination of, and be a challenge to (are these not the words always directed to teachers and librarians?), the chief school officer, who could then serve as a model for the beginning teacher. It was assumed, in the past, that the principal was a master teacher, not just another bureaucrat.

Laurence Peter describes "Peter Palaver:" as "words to mystify rather than clarify." It is well known to all of us that each profession has its jargon. Education, including instructional technology, is no exception. Lawyers and doctors, for example, toss out Latin phrases and indecipherable prescriptions which leave their clientele so overcome with awe and fear that no questions are asked. In education, of which school libraries are an integral part, there are no perceptible reasons for this special language except to impress each other.

The language is readily recognizable to anyone who has taken "ed" courses. In one school some 15 years ago, I knew a group of talented teachers with an irreverent sense of humor who produced a parody of the official daily bulletin. It was so close to the language that daily assaulted us that several of the newly appointed teachers were almost panicked by a directive which seemed to say that all the papers in the wastepaper baskets were to be alphabetized that day in order to tighten up on efficiency. This is not the time nor place for me to present arguments for "that old-time religion" but the regard for language which was taught

us way back in my youth did develop in us an ear for cadence, an appreciation for the infinite variety possible, and a respect for meaning and intelligibility. Is it possible that there might be some correlation between the exponential growth of bureaucracies and our increasing lack of regard for communication, written and oral, as a fine art?

I doubt that anyone who cared about clarity of language could have prepared the directives for purchasing school library books. An opening statement in one such says that it is "designed to facilitate and expedite their receipt by the school library." There then follows an outline of some seven items, each with three to seven subheads. The Internal Revenue Service directions are easier to follow. As for the outline, I note with regret the passing of the Harvard outline, now replaced with the use of numerals only so that one has an item designated as 2.2.2 or 6.1.1. (Could it be that bureaucrats do not know their Roman numerals from their Arabic?) Also of interest is the use of quasi-military or machine terms. Identifying code numbers are called "program" or "function". One notice reads "due to conditions peculiar to the *procurement* of library books. . ." (italics mine). A librarian would surely have written "acquisition." Just as surely the head office did not consult librarians as to what procedures would be best for them.

After you have waded through pages of instructions, special code-numbers, how to order for purchases under $100, over $100, change-order directions, one communication then requires eight copies of the lists of books. The number is not surprising since the school librarian is at the bottom of a ladder of communication which goes something like this—superintendent, associate superintendent, assistant superintendent, director, assistant director, principal, librarian. One must add that each superintendent and director usually has an administrative assistant through whom information must also trickle. Today, additional authority might come from the local school board.

Each of these could be sending the school librarian some instructions. Anthony Downs explains it: "The proliferation of a bureau's subformal channels and messages will be greater: (a) the greater the degree of interdependence among activities within it; (b) the higher the degree of uncertainty inherent in its functions; (c) the greater the time pressure upon its operations."

School librarians, at the bottom of the chain of command, have the greatest pressure put upon them since the time permitted for preparation of book orders is generally shorter than it should be because the notices, or approved lists, or other required materials fail to arrive on time. From Downs again we learn, "The most common bureau response to communications overloads is slowing down the speed of handling messages without changing the communications network structures or transmission rules." (If I use the word "books" it is not because I am unaware that libraries are media centers. It is only that in the city I know best—New York—there is no established procedure for school libraries to order nonprint materials.)

If you wonder what happens in any specific office to the copy of the form, the possibilities are listed on a printed routing slip which I saw recently. Choices of what you may do with the paper you have received include the following: "For action, for approval, for signature, prepare draft, for comments, may we confer?, your attention, as discussed, as requested, note and file, note and return, for information." No vote allowed for throwing it all out. Faced with such an array of possibilities, one might conceivably be hypnotized for hours.

School librarians, certified as teachers, have been exposed to the education jargon virus and now must guard against the added temptation to use the media jargon. One feels that if a list of some 20 words were declared out, there would be great holes in the fabric of media communication. A few of my current nonfavorites include "input, relevant, potential, interface, viable, meaningful,

concept, and maximize." In communicating with bureaucrats I have to use this language and then wanted to go home and wash my pen out with soap. It is not that these words are useless; they all started out with good meaning. It is only that they are used so tiresomely often and in such incongruous contexts. We who are supposedly specialists in the field of communication should set a better example. If these terms are used with the expected result of obtaining an automatic reaction in the reader or listener, then we are disciples of the behavioral learning philosophy exemplified by Pavlov and his dogs and Skinner and his pigeons. *We* deal with *people*. We have read ad infinitum, if not ad nauseam, that all children are different and that difference must be reflected in the kinds of opportunities offered them for learning, at their own pace, in their own lifestyle. How does one write behavioral objectives for that? I do not know of any research about individual differences among pigeons although, thanks to Richard Bach, we do know one seagull who is different.

Channels

We know the verse that ends with "the Cabots speak to the Lodges and the Lodges speak only to God." This is rather the way communication within the educational bureaucracy works. At an architectural conference concerned with the construction of a new high school building, an assistant director would not be allowed to speak in the presence of a director even though the assistant might have had 20 years of experience in that area of library service. Some stunning errors often resulted and, in the way of bureaucratic behavior, they were likely to be repeated in the very next school built, since there *seemed* to be no way of not using the same blueprint. Using a committee of school librarians actively engaged in their profession over a long period of time *never* seemed to occur to the planners on high as a way to get some suggestions for good planning.

Clearly, going through channels is the

way of bureaucracy; the trouble is that those channels are so arteriosclerotic that important information is not able to get through.

Whose Fault?

We come now to the possible core of the conundrum. Whose fault is this condition which causes such varying effects as despair, anger, incredulity, corruption, cynicism, and—finally, and most destructive—apathy? Shakespeare would have it that, "The fault, dear Brutus, is not in our stars but in ourselves, that we are underlings." As one of the studies undertaken by the Social Science Research Council in 1946 (concluded in 1949), at the request of the American Library Association, Dr. Alice I. Bryan did a revealing investigation into who entered the profession of public librarianship. It did not indicate that it was a profession that appealed to fighters; in fact, submissiveness was a more recognizable trait. (For a while, dating from the ALA Conference in Atlantic City, it looked like a new ball game. I think that shot of adrenalin has just about worn off by now.)

Such a survey into school librarianship is long overdue and might be useful as needed data to chart where the school librarian school media specialist issue is headed. Submissiveness is not a trait likely to further the aims of American education as they are stated to be, but then it is not unusual for us to profess to certain ideals in theory and find them too dangerous in reality. If the ideal of an informed citizenry was the great hope of our 18th Century leaders—educated men themselves—then those librarians who have tried to further the cause of independent thinking should have been honored rather than to have come a cropper. Whatever we have said or written in the endless educational guidelines about wanting our young people to think for themselves, to be independent in their pursuit of knowledge, the rise of underground school newspapers some years back proved that schools, as bureaucratic

agencies, did not really want students thinking critically and freely, in an unorthodox way. A study of issues of the *Newsletter on Intellectual Freedom* (ALA, Office of Intellectual Freedom) shows how much conformity is still expected of students across the country. Controversy is dangerous and, therefore, if it's controversial, throw it out— whether it's Darwinian theory or that old whipping boy, *Catcher in the Rye* (Bantam, 1970).

A study similar to Bryan's might tell us whether the bureaucratic climate appeals to teachers and school librarians, who feel comfortable in the hierarchical arrangement where you do as you are told, and do it conscientiously, for the rewards promised—money, security, and fringe benefits. The other side of this question has to do with whether the system, like a Procrustean bed, turns all who enter it, many with high hopes and great ideals, into the same product, not only through rewards but, in many cases, through fear. As Arnstine puts it, "The strict and often zealous adherence to rules is so commonly seen in teachers as to have become stereotypical. While such people may be attracted to a career in teaching, it is also the case that educational bureaucracies help to create and strengthen such traits of personality."

The bureaucratic Procrustes is even crueler than his forerunner. Not only are people stretched or shortened to perpetuate a predetermined model but today they may also have their hearts removed. It will never be known, since the New York City Board of Education will never tell—nor cared to find out—how many good people have been lost to the system because they did not pass examinations, or departed within a short time because of intolerable conditions. Furthermore, it is depressing to note that even among those who came through the rites of passage (written test, oral test, interview test, conference test, etc., etc., etc.) and stayed out their full course of years, the heart beat more and more mechanically, waiting only for its release from bondage.

Even more depressing is it to read in

The New American Society, "It would appear that survival in bureaucracy depends upon suspending conventional moral codes and developing a multiplicity of moralities, each specific to specific significant others. Bureaucracy destroys all older forms of conscience."[10] One should indeed weep for Adonais.

The very atmosphere of schools has encouraged a childishness among "adults" that prevents their achieving full status as partners in a process. (Paternalism has been the hallmark of employment in schools, and it has been that root "Pater" rather than "mater" since, even when the majority of elementary school teachers and librarians have been women, the Head has usually been Big Daddy—(not Big Momma.) In Rollo May's recent book on power and innocence he cautions, "There is another kind of innocence, already hinted at in Melville's novella, *Billy Budd, Foretopman.* Billy's type of innocence is that which does not lead to spirituality but rather consists of blinders—Pseudoinnocence, in other words. Capitalizing on naïveté, it consists of a childhood that is never outgrown, a kind of fixation on the past. It is childishness rather than childlikeness."[11]

Such nonadult behavior permits a climate of fear and repressiveness to exist in the school system. For example, in a bulletin to teachers from the principal's office, some years back, many items were listed for attention. They included a warning to female teachers about sitting on desks and this statement about unlisted materials, "The principal, or school officer appointed by him, must approve each unlisted item before it is used in the classroom. I am appointing department chairmen (ed. note—this did not include head librarians) as my representatives for this purpose and a teacher wishing to use such material must submit it to his chairman. The chairman must scrutinize the material most carefully and present to me any questions concerning it." Note the picture of the child (read "teacher") referring to Daddy (read "chairman") who must be approved by the father of them all (the principal).

In this same atmosphere of keeping teachers, librarians, and other subordinates in their place and fixed in the relationship of fearful child to authoritarian parent, a superintendent may instill, or wish to, such awe in a subordinate as to make a meeting between them tantamount to the privilege of conferring royal audience on a commoner. In one large city system, a while ago, the president of that city's school library association sought a conference with the superintendent who was charged with the responsibility of school library matters to discuss serious problems concerning library staffing and budget, both of which were minimal. The correspondence from the association was a model of deference, respect, and patience, and was finally rewarded with a scheduled meeting. The superintendent had allotted something less than an hour, came late for the time he had set, and sat turned away from the librarian so that she might not gaze fully upon his countenance ("Euclid alone has looked on Beauty bare"). He brought the meeting to a dramatic close with the statement that he would "think these matters over, since I do not wish to be prematurely stupid." The word order and vocabulary are exactly quoted, indeed indelibly remembered. It is no surprise to tell you that the sorry list of library problems was not alleviated, in fact, may still exist. Librarians' woes had—and have— a low priority in the educational bureaucracy.

This incident is only one illustration of what is at best an indifference to, at worst a contempt for, those who service the bureaucratic machine. In a *New York Times* editorial [12] commenting on the projected dismissal of thousands of civil service workers from federal agencies, the low status of the worker within the system is in the adjective "faceless." In the school libraries of large school systems, as in other hierarchies, that facelessness is often descriptive of all staff members other than the head librarian. Bureaucratic leaders expect the soundless (no questions, no cries of outrage) operation of the wheels, based on an accepted pattern of command and obeisance. It is obvious from the *Times* item that good behavior is no guarantee that the worker will be cherished for his loyalty. Librarians are traded in for clerical staff in the main office, computer time, or even untrained volunteers. There is, in the final analysis, no enduring satisfaction in one's work, material gains notwithstanding, when dignity and integrity are lost. If workers have never had it so good in terms of paid vacations, sick benefits, pensions, and annual raises, why all the evidence now surfacing about the anomie among workers—an alienation and malaise so acute that the work hours lost through absence are astronomical, and in some plants, actual sabotage has been evident?

Robert Townsend has not written a sociological treatise but he *has* been an organization man. He describes two opinions available for choice in determining how we shall live:

"Solution One is the cop-out: you can decide that what is must be inevitable; grab your share of the cash and fringes; and comfort yourself with the distractions you call leisure.

"Solution Two is nonviolent guerilla warfare: start dismantling our organizations where we're serving them, leaving only the parts where they're serving us. It will take millions of such subversives to make much difference." [13]

Power

We have heard often enough that power corrupts. Rollo May tells us that *powerlessness* also leads to corruption—and to violence. The latter as a course of action for school librarians is out of character, and I must confess that it is not in my lifestyle to leap to the barricades. Something *is* needed at this time of most serious challenge to the place of the school librarian in the educational scheme. (This threat has no relationship to the bookie/lookie schism which re-

quires a whole other investigation and report.)

The answer may be an ombudsman. But who will speak for the school librarian with a voice commanding attention? In 1960 there was a dream in New York City. It had to do with a strong, and needed, union which would carry enough authority so that bureaucrats and teachers could talk as equals. In many ways, some of the dream has been realized—for teachers. The material gains, of course, have affected school librarians. But the dream begins to have some nightmarish quality as the illness of bureaucracy infects the union itself. Since numbers equal strength, school librarians rank low in the esteem of an organization in which they are vastly outnumbered by teachers, and even by secretaries, counselors, and paraprofessionals. In a recent issue of the union newspaper almost every group of school personnel is mentioned, except librarians, as receiving attention in the presentation by the union to the central board for funding. Programs named were: Early Childhood Education, More Effective Schools, Junior High Schools, Vocational High Schools, Teacher Internship Program, Paraprofessionals, John Dewey Program, Guidance Counselors and Attendance Teachers, School Secretaries, Bilingual Teachers, Bureau of Child Guidance, Handicapped. Nowhere in that entire article is there any mention of the school library, its need for a better ratio of number of librarians to registration of the school, the lack of clerical assistance, the necessity for more flexible purchase of materials in all formats. It is possible that they had librarians in mind in the sentence, "In addition, guidance, psychological attendance, and other essential school services have been slashed, Levine said." [14] Another instance of union indifference was reported in *SLJ* in the case of librarian Arch Caliguri, who has been seeking exemption from an administrative assignment, namely proctoring during examination periods. "Court action or an appeal to the New York State Education Department is under consideration by Caliguri and Pankin, who have been pursuing their case with their own funds and others' contributions. When *SLJ* asked Caliguri why the UFT had not offered their own legal services, he replied: 'It's a teachers union. Unless it's a contract issue that affects other teachers also, they don't seem particularly interested. In fact,' he points out 'representatives to the library media committee are appointed by the UFT itself, *not* elected by the librarians, so there is some question as to accountability'."[15]

Leadership is needed to turn about the present relegating of school libraries to the position of low man on the totem pole, though, with our dizzying fall from national grace, some analogy to the maypole might be more apt. School library leadership will not spring full-grown like Minerva from Jupiter's head. It requires the total and concentrated effort of all of those involved in the profession. We have, understandably, looked to organizations to provide the leadership, but at this moment school librarians are underrepresented in teachers' organizations and have often been given short shrift in library organizations which cover the whole library profession. That is not entirely due to benign neglect. The total membership in organizations represents a small fraction of those employed in school libraries, and the number of active members in an organization, compared to those who just pay their dues and sit back, is even smaller. Admittedly, it is not unusual in organizations that the same people are called upon for service time and again. They may be the only ones who accept an assignment; a determined *member* can get himself involved actively. There is a serious need to investigate why teachers do not feel impelled to support librarians in their struggle for intellectual freedom, sufficient budget, status, and other school library problems. For a short time it appeared that the Connecticut Education Association and the Ridgefield Teachers Association (*SLJ*, March, p. 65; *LJ*, March 15, p. 961) would walk out of their jobs because of an issue of censorship, rather

than salary. The beau geste seems to have evaporated. It almost appears that teachers ally themselves with administrators in their indifference to school libraries. This does not mean all teachers but it does indicate grave insufficiencies in the professional preparation of teachers—who go on to become administrators and most important, superintendents.

Daniel Bell projects a future in which, "The relation of the individual to bureaucratic structures will be subject to even greater strain. The increasing centralization of government creates a need for new social forms that will allow the citizenry greater participation in making decisions. The growth of a large, educated professional and technical class, with its desire for greater autonomy in work, will force institutions to reorganize the older bureaucratic patterns of hierarchy and detailed specialization."[16] I find it difficult to share his optimism, first because it was born in the rather quiet seclusion of the company of scholars rather than in the troubled arena of education today, and second because the growth of an educated professional and technical class has been accompanied by the growth of institutions that have tended to evaluate security rather than freedom as an ultimate good.

We all have to consider this fundamental question: Can a bureaucracy exist without the covert consent of its constituent parts? We say that people get the kind of government they deserve. But the years of unrest on our campuses and the growing dissatisfactions reported among blue-collar workers, white-collar middle-management, and professionals seem to indicate that we are not getting what we want. The difference between "deserve" and "want" may lead us, eventually, to choose "better" over "more."

REFERENCES

1. Meyers, Judith & Raymond Barber. "McNamara, Media, and You," *School Library Journal*, March 1971, p. 1079-1081.

2. *New York Times*, January 8, 1973, p. 1+.

3. Parkinson, Northcote. *Parkinson's Law: and Other Studies in Administration.* Houghton, 1957.

4. *Ibid*, p. 4.

5. Arnstine, Donald. "Freedom and Bureaucracy in the Schools," in Association for Supervision and Curriculum Development, 1971 Yearbook, *Freedom, Bureaucracy and Schooling*, ed. by Vernon F. Haubrich. ASCD/NEA, 1971, p. 24.

6. *Ibid*, p. 15.

7. Downs, Anthony. *Inside Bureaucracy.* Little, 1967.

8. *Ibid*, p. 270.

9. Arnstine, p. 19.

10. Bensman, Joseph & Arthur J. Vidich. *The New American Society: The Revolution of the Middle Class.* Quadrangle Bks., 1971.

11. May, Rollo. *Power and Innocence: A Search for the Source of Violence.* Norton, 1972.

12. *New York Times*, February 4, 1973, Sec. 4, p. 14.

13. Townsend, Robert. *Up the Organization.* Knopf, 1970.

14. *New York Teacher*, January 28, 1973, p. 3.

15. *School Library Journal*, November 1972, p. 10.

16. Bell, Daniel. "The Year 2000—The Trajectory of an Idea" in *Toward the Year 2000: Work in Progress.* Beacon, 1967.

What Price Professionalism?

Renee Feinberg

"In the library you can take a deep breath and walk out and face everything."—Student at Performing Arts High School

WHEN I WROTE up my resumé the summer before last, after my first year as a school librarian, I was so impressed I couldn't reread it to check for grammatical errors. I left that to the friend who typed it for me. She assured me it read correctly. What I wrote had impressed me so much I couldn't read it. I had written this impressive resumé because I was out of a job.

September, 1969. High School of Performing Arts, New York City. In the school system, new staff appointees arrive the Wednesday before the Friday (when old staff return) before the Monday. The library when shown to me was barricaded—large teacher desks, three of them, in a classroom-size library. I smiled at those who found the library for me. and who pointed with pride and said that those adorable travel posters from Greece and Spain had to stay, and split.

The next day I wore my jeans and my special six-pocket Mexican work shirt, carrying my screwdriver, hammer and pliers, my scissors, penknife, two reels of masking tape, dust rags, paper flowers, posters. crazy contact paper and, ripping off the tallest ladder in the school, ten foot, took down the travel posters, put up ones of movie stars; borrowed a dolly to move out the desks. . . .

FURNITURE CAN'T BE MOVED OFF THE FLOOR!

Hello, I'm the new librarian. Do you need a desk? A file ·cabinet? A chalk board?

THE CHALK BOARD WAS BOUGHT OUT OF LIBRARY FUNDS FOR THE LIBRARY. DON'T MOVE IT.

DO YOU REALIZE THERE'S A WAITING LIST FOR TEACHERS WHO WANT FILE CABINETS? THE PREVIOUS LIBRARIAN DEMANDED THEM FOR MAGAZINES.

On Friday, my friend Lillian Shapiro introduced me to a date stamp, pointed out that books were double stacked on each shelf, kissed me and left.

Monday. The opening of school. I dumped back issues in boxes for students, put some large art books on the tables, and turned on the radio. The first order of the new term was to OK uncleared library accounts so students could get their new program cards. Wow! How-do-you-do authority! I got to meet a few delinquent library users. We agreed to talk someday about their debts, library fines, and overdues.

Some of last year's student aides dropped in to sign up for service credit and wondered how they were to take care of circulation and control without each of them having a desk. One student explained that a great many overdue notices had to be sent since books were only checked out overnight. The other aide shelved and received books because the students weren't allowed to go to the shelves. In her spare time she helped collect the fine money.

I explained why I had removed the desks and put books on the tables, and asked if they didn't think that, in a school with only 600 students, we might dispense with formalities, fines, and overdues, just letting students keep the books until they had finished them. They didn't think so.

I turned up the radio, walked to the fire escape, and watched a frisbee game in the courtyard below. It's an old school, city elementary, baroque type, five floors' worth. (Sophomores direct new freshmen to the swimming pool on the fifth floor.)

And so I dusted each morning, seized some bulletin boards around the school, walked through the halls with my pass jangling keys . . . *"Hey, the librarian wears earrings"* . . . sat in the teachers room . . . *"Yes, I did go to Scarsdale High"* . . . spent lots of time writing post cards to "Inc.," museums, college admission offices

. . . sent out some innocent questionnaires to students about their preferred paperback titles, to teachers about their favorite magazine titles, and wondered what the hell I was doing sitting in an empty library.

Where's the little lady with glasses with the little file you'd put your 10¢ into?

That Belmondo or Bogart?

Look at these movie stars from the olden days.

The Board of Education began its rain of directives, circulars, memoranda and supplements and new instructions. Seems I had to spend about $250 on a book order, ON LIST. Some more money was to be spent OFF LIST. That's a dollar per pupil or about $600. The New York City list came in. Wow! Those titles. . . . The 1000-page list and its supplements are an unending series of titles, titles, titles. I was unfamiliar with the books, books. There weren't any reference tools in the library, but Bowker was up the block. During the day I familiarized myself with the collection, asked the staff and students about needs and preferences, spent my afternoons in the Bowker library, and soon gave up. Time is the great leveler of good intentions. Money, too, sets limits. Once I really realized how few books I could buy with the allotment, I took out the latest supplement and plowed through those few sections whose subject content I knew well, and had students from the drama, dance, and music departments advise me in other areas.

I think most of my time was spent copying the order from inside the book to the front and juggling numbers of copies to make sure I fell within the allotment. It is always essential to work backwards, from the given money and time to the preferred books and methods. So much for hindsight. At the time, however, as a new librarian handling new procedures, I had to deal with patronizing, noninformative answers, with deceit and indifference, and with an attitude of don't bother headquarters—even though the decentralized school program had brought specialized high school libraries directly under "headquarters." But no matter. I prefer to work things out myself, and the message I was getting was to do that.

LAST YEAR'S BOOK ORDER IS IN THE OFFICE.

I don't think all of last year's money was spent.

SHE WASN'T A LICENSED LIBRARIAN.

Well, where's the money? Can I spend it now?

I DON'T KNOW.

Who Knows?

WHO KNOWS?

Can you prepare a list of books for dance history? Historical fiction?

Where's Shakespeare?

Hey, man, no Panther paper?

Where's WNEW on this radio?

You oughta get "Psychology Today," "New York," "Ramparts," "Scanlon," Zapp." We'll make a list. Got any money?

You've created a human environment here, but————WHERE'S YOUR PASS?

THOSE STUDENTS ARE CUTTING, FOR YOUR INFORMATION. THEY WERE NOT EX-
CUSED TO GO TO THE LIBRARY.

In time I heard about the school's furniture fund and invited an architect friend down. She planned to pull two stacks out from against the wall and turn them perpendicular to the wall, creating aisles and freeing an area so I could put in two new stacks. I informed the principal in a covering letter, enclosing a scale drawing of the planned change and requesting him to order two new book stacks. He forwarded my request to maintenance.

The students began to come, god-blessem, and with them, the excitement of young people capable of articulating their needs and interests, as yet unwilling to demand service. In time . . .

I'm writing a term paper on Women's Lib. You've gotta have something. You wear Women's Lib shoes.

Renee, is it Canada or jail if I don't register?

Hey, where are the sign-out cards for these paperbacks? Take it?

I walked out of class.

No fines?

He's got a $10 habit.

Can I take out five?

But I returned it. I put it on the mess on your desk.

I love them—their entrances and exits from the fire escape, the messages they left me on the sign-out cards, their patience as I learned the library, learned what they needed and when. They taught me well.

Tell Scott he left his shoes under the magazine rack.

Why can't we eat here today?

Can we stay till four?

Listen, I've no time, but I need to borrow that encyclopedia.

How do I add a bibliography to my term paper.

Renee, you got "Portnoy"? "The God-father"? "Dr. Hip"?

I've gotta tear this out.

Where's your tracing paper?

Can I use your typewriter?

That record player stinks.

Renee, the WHOOPIE LADIES are out, give me a pass back to class.

Can I use the library for my acting class? They need an environment that's alive to come alive. Let me try it on your lunch hour.

By now, in response to student requests, I began to draft counsel in the library. Hearing conversations about the draft in the library made me realize how little information was available.

As the students began to organize to pressure for changes in the school, the library became a focal point for planning and comforting. The place had become the kids' place with radio, flowers, I. F. Stone, posters, a place for a good time, a haven from class.

Renee, you've got to stay this afternoon. We need a place to meet.

They stayed, and they stayed late, though they came from the five boroughs and often worked in the evenings. They spoke of school, of intimidation, of arbitrary rule, of harrassment and embarrassment. They

shed tears, and they consoled each other, and they reached out and organized.

They sat down one morning in midwinter, a small group, by the sink in the basement lunchroom. Nobody knew. They held sings about the war, black people, students, me and you. Others dropped by to talk to them, stayed a while, and returned to class.

GET BACK TO CLASS OR YOU'LL BE SUSPENDED.

The students remained. As the threats escalated, others milled around. By noon, as word had got around, the school sat down with those four students in the basement, protesting the world they had inherited and the school that intimidated them. They spoke to each other, a small community who had recognized each other but hadn't had time to say hello. Parents rushed down to protect those who were threatened with immediate suspension. Even the principal descended from 135th Street to this annex to meet with the students whose school he regulated and whose faces he had never seen.

The students of Performing Arts remained that afternoon a¬d spoke to each other. And everyone listened, and no one interrupted his friend. The teaching staff was extraneous to the educational process conducted that afternoon, and we felt it.

The students agreed on representatives who would present the principal with their grievances about school and the quality of their education. They agreed to try to reach out to those they had turned off among their number, to speak to teachers and administrators. They decided to talk to their parents.

The principal refused at first to meet with them in an open meeting, with the student body in attendance. They waited until he agreed. Though the principal explained tirelessly why things could not happen their way, the students explained why it was necessary to have draft, abortion and drug counseling, to have a governing board involving the entire school community, the right to access to all the school facilities, to print a newspaper freely, to have redress to arbitrary and inconsistent rulings, to correct the racial imbalance of a predominantly white NYC high school, and to update the curriculum. The principal agreed to continue talking. The students submitted their proposals and their blueprints and went back to class.

April 1970. The Cambodia invasion. Vietnam became the Indo-Chinese War, and the students sat down again in the basement to talk. They organized peace actions and after-school street theater, planned for a city-wide high school communications network, and asked that the principal adopt the crisis curriculum they had presented to help them "get together" the crises in their world. And they went back to classes.

Kent State. The students demanded action and refused to return to class. Derogatory comments were entered on their permanent records, jeopardizing scholarships that many had applied for and carrying untold weight into the future.

Jackson State. The students walked out of school. They threw up picket lines. I marched with them for three days and clung to the building for protection as the construction workers—the same guys who for three years had shared the luncheonette counters on the block with us—pelted us with asphalt chips and beer cans. I joined them at Strike Central in the New School for Social Research.

Renee, why are you going back into school?

I had remembered a conversation we had had earlier, pointing out that the student movement was on its own and could do its own thing, but that for me there was a conflict of interest at the outset: that my job was not going to be put on the line for just any issue, no. My job was not going to be put on the line regardless of the issue. I'd wanted to indulge in the fantasy of guerilla professionalism, working within the system. When I returned to the library, I had blown that myth. I had felt the need to protect my job and argue with striking students to protect their scholarships and college acceptances.

They responded.

You have to know when to make certain all-out radical decisions, because then you limit yourself, you have a record, you get busted. You're perfectly justified in saying you're not going to put your job on the line. For us, in terms of high school education, it was kind of an all-out thing to do. The fact that we were striking and getting mass things in the basement at that moment meant so much more to us than taking a stinking Regents. We could have gone overboard and really messed ourselves up. But here we are, helping each other for the Regents. We did what we had to do.

In time these young people who had shared the same school building for four years shared their interests, their convictions, their money, their sweaters, their homes; they spoke with other high school students about their actions. Having petitioned hopelessly, they asked their administration to allow them to return to school with some token promise of change, in honor of their own commitment and as an honorarium to those young people of Nam and Mylai, of Kent and Jackson State. At an open meeting of the Board of Education, they again petitioned to be allowed to return to school with some pledges by the administration that meaningful changes would be made in the curriculum so that they could come to understand the world they had inherited. It was not enough now to "go back to classes."

Some Board members even listened to the students that night. After all, when middle-class, articulate young people come before them to speak of their concerns and propose changes and ask for help and guidance, surely we are all for peace in the world and relevance in education.

June, 1970. Business as usual. The students had trickled back to school. Five of us had been let go—of the seven teachers who had supported the students, all five who were non-tenured—and for good bureaucratic reasons. One of the parents talked about teachers as professionals: why not bring a malpractice suit against the principal? Those who had been fired had been respected professionals who had coincidentally established rapport with the children and stuck by them. (The principal told parents who confronted him: Had it been up to him, he would have kept the teachers.)

Regents were coming. The library magazines bristled, new and untouched. We no longer played the radio. The masking tape had dried and the signs fell down, the "Let's Be Friends" poster dangling by one corner. The library got dusty, the center light blew. Quiet cigarettes on the fire escape . . . the unshelved books rested. . . .

Renee, I'm taking Fanon. Where's Grotowski?

I'm not graduating.

I got 100 on my history Regents and my class grade was lowered, but I still have my scholarship to Swarthmore.

Where's "Rat"?

Have you got a job for next year?

Hey, I'll see you around.

Tell Scott to come get his shirt.

Finished with the Gemini poster?

TURN IN YOUR LIST OF STUDENTS WHO HAVE NOT SETTLED THEIR ACCOUNTS.

There is no list.

STUDENTS WHO CAN'T STAND THIS SCHOOL SURE SPEND A LOT OF TIME HERE WHEN WE'RE TRYING TO ENTER GRADES.

This is their library. There's room for you to work.

Hey, library lady, where you working next year?

Renee, we're doing street theater tonight in El Barrio. Supper's at my house. Coming?

Two Years After
. . . Reflections from YAP

Regina Minudri and Reed Coats

YAP is a link between the older people and the young. Using a library for this was a beautiful idea. As for the (YAP) library itself I do use it much more than the main (library) because the employees don't act as if they are superior to anyone, and above all, I can go to just sit and talk to people about things on my mind and *know* they are being listened to.

THE ABOVE STATEMENT is a direct quote from a young man who had used Young Adult Project facilities regularly. For him, it wasn't madness; it was what he expected library reality to be. For many young adults the centers that we ran for about 18 months were more than teen centers and more than libraries, they were a bit of both, with a soupçon of talk, a good deal of listening, and a whole lot of communication.

The Federal Young Adult Library Services Project began on April 1, 1968 (we always thought April Fool's Day was a rather auspicious time). It was planned as a cooperative effort between two independent library systems in Santa Clara County, California. The heads of the five cooperating libraries: Mountain View, San Jose, Santa Clara City, Sunnyvale, and Santa Clara County, formed the governing and administrative board for the

project. The funds were granted through LSCA Title II.

The approach of the project was to be experimental, nontraditional, and outside the library walls. Centers seemed to fill this bill of particulars. They did attract nonlibrary users, nonreaders, minority youths, and dropouts. But, they also attracted the wrath of part of the local communities because the very young adults the project was charged to reach looked different, behaved differently, and really cared little about what adults thought of them or their life style.

As a result, the history of the project, like anything dealing with young people, was somewhat stormy. We were attacked on several fronts by parents, teachers, and school administrators who either did not understand what we were attempting to do or who disagreed with our methods. Since we were not entirely without community or library support, we generally managed to maintain the programs, even though at times we felt somewhat paranoid about strange or unknown adult visitors.

Project activities fell into five phases.

1. *Satellite locations:* Unmanned drugstore-style spinner book racks placed in youth opportunity cen-

ters, teen centers, parks, juvenile halls, etc.

2. *YAP Centers:* Staffed locations providing paperbacks, films, records, posters, and programs in a relaxed, nonauthoritarian atmosphere conducive to talk, discussion, and communication. Honor check out of books.

3. *YAPmobile:* A brightly painted, renovated school bus which traveled to high schools, parks, recreation centers, and circulated books in much the same manner as a YAP center.

4. *In-Library Work:* An experimental program wherein a YAP staffer was assigned to each of the member libraries on a rotating basis. YAP staffer brought paperbacks, records, posters, and ideas with him and worked with local staff to upgrade Young Adult sections and collections.

5. *In-Service Training:* Coordinator conducted semimonthly sessions in each of the member libraries, working with librarians and library assistants in basic Young Adult work such as selection, reviewing, book talks, programming, techniques and psychology.

Where Do We Go From Here?

A comment we heard frequently from colleagues when discussing YAP was the seeming inability of public libraries to provide special or extended services to Young Adults because of lack of money, staff, room, and time. Interest in Young Adults and recognition that something needed to be done was rarely denied. Mostly, we were asked what parts of this project and philosophy could be implemented within the library as it is presently structured.

Applications for the public library can be divided into six major categories:

1. *Staff*—Professional, paraprofessional, and clerical. Attitudes, philosophy, training.

2. *Materials*—Paperbacks, magazines, records, films, games, posters.

3. *Design*—Atmosphere, color, informality, flexibility.

4. *Community Awareness*—Young Adult needs, adult reactions, resource people, local groups, and clubs.

5. *Programming*—Young Adult direction and cooperation, special projects, speakers, activities.

6. *Outreach*—Its ramifications for the library as a whole.

For the purposes of this article, we will concentrate on three of the areas mentioned above. Staffing, design, and outreach have a great impact on the Young Adult library user, or prospective user. In meeting and talking with many Young Adults in the course of the project we found that they feel strongly about the kind of staff they meet and the treatment they encounter as well as the appearance of the collections and areas they are expected to use. Outreach, of course, permeated all of the levels of service.

It is all well and good to go out into the community, do some image bending and present the library and its services in a favorable light, but what are we pushing our intended clients into? Is the library ready for today's Young Adult? Can the staff cope with his life style and habits? Do they understand him? Is the area stiff and brown and formal, or is it something he can meet and grok on? If not, why not?

Staff

We hear much about the image we have as librarians, but what about the mental picture we have of kids? Our vision of young adults is of vast importance because it colors, in many ways, our reactions to them; it often causes prejudgments, inaccurate appraisals, and downright fear. We frequently see kids as scruffy, noisy, bothersome, lively, impatient, often rude, and perhaps just a bit of a bother. One of the first things we need to inculcate in staff serving young adults is the realization that they are people, not all perfect, but people.

These views are mere facades, protective coloration, and akin to the stereotyped image of librarians and libraries held by many young adults and other library patrons. We are seen as establishment, aloof, busy, older, someone who puts them down, someone it's fun to bug, an authoritarian figure. Of course, we all know we aren't like that, don't we?

In reply to "Why do you use YAP and not the public library?" we got answers like this:

"Cause no one at the library ever wants to help us."

"The librarian is always on a coffee break."

"She looks mean, and throws my friends out, she even threw me out and I hadn't done anything, even."

Now, believe us, we're not of the opinion that all teenagers have halos and wings. We know too many who would be far more comfortable with red capes and cloven hooves, but mayhap some of these criticisms have a certain validity. We ought to listen, and while listening, hear; and after hearing, act.

Staff attitudes toward Young Adult patrons, at all levels, molds and determines teenage response, as seen above. Openness, friendliness, availability, humanness, respect, and very real interest in the young person as an individual undoubtedly wins friends and influences . . . It only takes a few muscles to smile, use them. We're far from perfect ourselves, and the ability to see humor in our own mistakes makes us more human. Clerical and paraprofessional staff are very bit as vital to the effectiveness of YA programs as the professional librarian because much good floor work and rapport can be undone by desk personnel if they do not understand young adults. We cannot overemphasize this and regret that in many areas these are the last persons to receive training in dealing with the public, but are often first to be criticized for problems.

Training programs for all levels of staff should include role-playing, self-awareness, identification, and psychology. These programs can be formal or informal, rigid or free flowing. Whatever they are and however they evolve it is essential that they present as true and accurate a picture of the young adult and his relation to the library as possible.

Role-playing, when done in a positive manner, gives many insights and some perspective. Simple scripts can be used, with the Young Adult librarian taking traditional roles and other staff acting as the teenager facing the inevitable hassles of libraryland. These sessions are frequently hilarious and usually people can't help but seeing the reflections in the mirror. Some libraries have access to videotape, which provide visual replays, a valuable asset. Self-awareness follows closely upon role-playing, as it helps to put us into contact with our own attitudes and the reasons for some of them.

Identification of the genre Young Adult is easy, primarily because they are of a specific age group. Training sessions go farther, they isolate and note trends, changing patterns, variances in mood, and causes of problems. Sometimes problems can be alleviated by small procedural changes and suggestions, for these adaptations will come easily from staff who have been responsive to earlier parts of the program.

Psychology of young adults needs background material and reading to supplement general knowledge. Ginott's *Between Parent and Teenager* (Avon, 1970), Friedenberg's *The Vanishing Adolescent* (Dell, 1968), Fader's *Hooked on Books* (Putnam, 1968), Goodman's *Growing Up Absurd* (Random, 1960), Gardner's *Excellence* (Harper, 1961), Edward's *Fair Garden and the Swarm of Beasts* (Hawthorn, 1969), and Carlsen's *Books and the Teen Age Reader* (Harper, 1967), all present viewpoints worth exploring. Other books dealing with adolescent psychology should be used and all need to be adapted for use within any particular localized framework and milieu.

In essence, we are advocating strong

training programs which will help library employees understand their young adult public. Programs which will suggest and encourage staff to change or adapt themselves, to relax, to make young adults feel welcome, to temper discipline with good nature, to help tell the difference between teenage exuberance and willful disturbance. Such programs require open minds, demand that we strip off our cultural filters, see ourselves as others see us, and respond to that individual we call Young Adult.

Outreach

For every teenage person with parents, teachers, librarians, or counselors who care about what he reads and how he is developing through his troublesome, frenetic age, there are four, five, or maybe more for whom reading, books, and the library experience mean nothing. These people haven't been reached, they haven't been touched, no one has found them yet. Who is this kid who hasn't been reached? Where is he? Why isn't he reached, why don't books turn him on, why doesn't he see reading as a valuable asset, a pleasurable experience and a mind-expander par excellence?

Who is he? He is black, white, Chicano, Indian, Oriental, he's everybody. (And for the benefit of Women's Lib, he is just as often she.) He lives everywhere—in small towns, in the barrios and ghettos of large cities, on reservations, and in upper and middle class suburbia. Somehow our friend, and he must be our friend because he is our future, has been through elementary school, and, hopefully, has learned a few things. But there are lots of things he hasn't learned yet, experiences he hasn't had, sights he hasn't seen, and people he hasn't met. Some of them can be found in books, others in films, others in music, or elsewhere. But our friend doesn't really use books, he often doesn't even realize that he might like them, and that's where library outreach enters the service picture.

In recent years many governmental agencies have embarked on programs designed to get to the people. Libraries are no exception. For the most part, these are usually special projects that have had many different approaches but which have had one basic goal in common: reach out to those who don't use the library and/or those who don't read, show them what the public library has for them, demonstrate its value and versatility, and try to get them hooked. In other words, be a pusher. The means for attaining these goals vary from area to area and group to group, but projects generally agree on the necessity of going outside the confines of the library, working with the community and its agencies, and developing contacts previously ignored and often unserved. As they proceed, one of the first things that outreach programs realize is that traditional methods, old-fashioned ideas and time-worn cliches just don't work with individuals who haven't been brought up within the usual structured library framework.

Individuals—that is an operative word in this context. As institutions grow and numbers increase, as budgets expand and machines enter the field, it is all too easy to lose sight of the very reason for libraries. All the information, books, films, records, magazines, etc., are superfluous if people don't use them. The slogan "Libraries to the People" is more than just a handy catch phrase among librarians. It needs to be a way of life. Books, films, etc., may be our commodities, but people are our business. Libraries serve individuals, human beings who need attention, want response, recognition of special needs, and specific materials which are relevant for today and tomorrow. Outreach programs try to do this. They try to cut some of the red tape surrounding the library as an institution which often can frighten and scare away potential users. They try to humanize the institution, make it listen, make it act, make it real. Librarians working on outreach programs are militants. They fight for and with their libraries and identify with the people they serve.

Involvement—another operative word.

People acting together for a common cause, whether its libraries, reading, or whatever. Action programs attempt to involve themselves in the heart of the community, bringing the library into focus as a community resource instead of a dry, dusty building full of a lot of musty tomes guarded by a lady with a pencil stuck through the bun of hair at the nape of her neck. Involvement changes images, it produces ideas, it asks questions, and it requires answers as well as action.

What then does library outreach mean when applied specifically to programs for Young Adults or Teenagers? It means going out and finding the young person, treating him like a responsible human being, dealing with him honestly, fairly, respectfully, objectively, and with spontaneity. One of the wonders of the the teenager is that he is never dull, he is always in a state of constant flux. Responsiveness is vital to this kind of relationship and quick action is almost imperative.

Outreach in this case means recognizing the taste of teenagers and not attempting to fit them into a mold which does not suit them. Take music, for example. Most, if not all, young adults listen to music, be it rock, folk, blues, or soul. It is an universal means of communication with them and one of the best methods available to libraries for quickly implementing their services to youth. For many years libraries looked down their noses at so-called popular music. It wasn't up to library standards, it was too ephemeral, it would be worn out, the tapes or records would be stolen. If the same standards were applied to general selection of books we would have much smaller collections. But libraries often established extensive collections of recordings of classical music, jazz, and dramatic readings. These very collections were usually instituted in response to user requests, yet the same type of requests from teenagers were ignored. It's no wonder that many young adults stay away.

Outreach for teenagers also means a lessening and dropping of the barriers, both formal and traditional, that have kept them away or caused them to be ejected. One of these is the rule of silence and the study hall atmosphere of public libraries. Outreach programs say "No Silence," talking encouraged, and communication wanted. Young people are most responsive to this type of attitude and, for the most part, do not take undue advantage of the situation. With music in the background, or foreground, and with easy, relaxed, informal surroundings, the teenager can be himself instead of an automaton. The attitude of outreach programs focuses more on communication with the individual than the institution. It encourages youth to comment and staff to listen, to respond, to help.

A variety of materials have been mentioned so far; recordings, films, books, magazines. All these, plus other things like games, imaginative displays, posters, use of bright colors and attractive furnishings, not necessarily new, generally contribute to the setting mentioned above. Materials have to be selected with the particular community and type of youth served in mind. Materials should reflect, as much as possible, the feelings of the young adults as well as those items which will be of potential interest. This means that those working with youth need to know them, to be aware of the changing currents of interests and needs. It means reading, listening, watching.

Design and Color

As necessary as it is to have the needed staffing, materials, and information available, it is of equal importance to attract the public to the library through design and color. Young adults, especially the nonbook-oriented, are in large part not often self-motivated toward library use, and every effort on our part needs to be made to attract their presence and attention. Only then can we begin to discuss and select appropriate items for them and show them that libraries really are more than book storehouses.

Splashes of color and areas of fluid design not only appeal to the young. Why is it that adults visiting the bright, multi-hued YA area in the San Jose Public Library have been heard to remark, "Gee, I wish there was a place like this in the library for adults to go." Perhaps we need to think of highlighted areas throughout our buildings that not only focus on best sellers or books for Negro History Week or objects d'art but also on music, banners, mobiles, table games, local handicraft exhibits, amid the comfortable chairs and pillows, ashtrays, and posters. We would at the same time realize the need to balance these areas by retaining the more traditional quiet study and reference locations.

We do not see this as a gimmicky come-on to snare people into looking at *real* library material. Public libraries, and to a lesser degree, school libraries, have an obligation and responsibility to *all* of their potential public. Eye-blinking colors, striking designs (freely borrowed from advertising and store display), and creative use of sounds are an integral part of the world outside the closed Carnegie (and Edward Durrell Stone) walls. If we see our primary function as *Communication*, and we should, for this is what we are all about, then we need to think in terms of relating to people through sounds—conversations, records, tapes and speakers; through tactile experiences—statuary that can be touched, games, especially wooden puzzles, feelable objects of leather, rock, metal, fur cloth, and wood; through olfactory experiences—flower, incense, fresh air; through visual experiences—film screenings, book jackets, pictures, and use of color and design. But, you point out, we have abdicated our responsibility as librarians and have become keepers of a conglomerate museum/rec center/hippie pad. All we are saying is that by understanding the broad definition of communication we can come to explore all facets of how people in dialog learn, mature, expand, and develop as whole human beings. We cannot, of course, be all things to all people, but we can show our

real flesh and muscle and say that the storehouse of information knows that learning happens on many levels.

We are not unaware that lists of reasons, "why we can't do those things in our library" have grown to astounding lengths. Sometimes our profession seems to take pride in excuse-giving. To rather badly paraphrase *Hair*, we ain't got no space, no money, no talent, no time, no guts, no staff, no control, no inclination, no ideas; ad nauseam, even if true.

The addition of pleasing colors and pleasant design is not dependent on an inordinate amount of time, talent, or money. Once you decide to take a step in this direction, the fun of creative finagling takes over. Posters—hero, ecology, psychedelic, protest, musical, peaceful—and mobiles—op, pop, and funky homemade—are actually very inexpensive and a few at a time will fit easily into most petty cash expenditures. Letter patterns can be easily obtained from art supply stores and with proper wording and placement, a new image can be achieved with these alone. For example, we have used 18-inch red and purple letters which read FEEL FREE and NO SILENCE going sideways up architectural pillars. Also, don't overlook the talents and donations of an interested public. Many of our more clever signs and announcements were happily constructed by kids, male and female, glad to have their art on display. We also obtained macrame hangings and collages in the same manner.

The use and flexibility of space is naturally dependent on the structural design of the building. But it is a rare place that cannot release a corner, slightly partitioned, where you could add a throw rug, a pillow or two, and a moderately volumed AM-FM transistor. This will attract the young of all ages, so that they may enjoy one another, the games, the visuals, the sounds; and yes, Virginia, it does work, even books get read.

To do any of these things we need to examine our philosophy of library service. (Why are we here? What is our purpose? Who do we serve? What do they want?) From time immemorial libraries have been book collectors, selectors, and keepers, allowing the public the great privilege of borrowing from us, providing that they are good and true and bonafide residents with clean hands. If libraries are viable institutions (and this is debatable in this age of accelerated information, mass distribution of paperbacks, and nonlinear people) libraries need to meet their publics where they are, not where we wish them to be.

The King County Youth Service Center: A Case Study in Library Cooperation

Eleanor F. Klepeis

HANDS ON HIPS, the youngster disdainfully replied to Librarian Susan Madden's invitation to see if there were something she might like to read. "I've seen libraries before. You got *nothing* I want to read." "This library is different. What do you want to read?" "You got *Pimp*? (Holloway, 1967)" "It's right over there on the shelf." "No jive! You not kidding? Where?"

This was the culmination of over four years' work by five Seattle-King County agencies to give library service to the King County Juvenile Court's Youth Service Center. The Youth Service Center provides detention or shelter care to youngsters from several political jurisdictions. None of the following agencies, Seattle Public Library; King County Intermediate School District #110; King County Library System; Seattle School District #1, or the Juvenile Court itself, felt that they had either responsibility or funds for the needed school/public library service.

In 1968, the King County Library Board of Trustees gave approval to Institutional Libraries Coordinator Agnes M. Griffen's proposal that King County Library take the initiative in calling together the principal agencies concerned to try to bring library service to in-

carcerated children with time on their hands and little to read.

All five agencies concerned responded favorably to the King County Library offer to coordinate library efforts. An advisory committee for library service to the Youth Service Center, with a representative from each of the five agencies, became concerned with emergency and long-term planning for library service.

The Youth Service Center, built in 1952, had become so overcrowded that the living units were frequently at 100 percent over capacity for the entire year. The number of children admitted for detention had risen from 1,852 in 1960 to 2,493 in 1968, and the average daily population in the same period of time, from 113 to 160 children. Overcrowded facilities and lack of money prevented the Committee from placing more than a minimal paperback collection, furnished by the special Education Department of the Seattle Public Schools, in the halls and living units of the Center.

The Committee, however, became familiar with the Youth Center functions, facilities, and the nature of its school. All children detained ten days or more were eligible to attend school, regardless of their school district.

The average monthly enrollment in

255

1967 was 70 children, with 1000 children enrolled during the school year. The teachers felt an acute need for supplementary material, coupled with a shortage of basic general and science reference books as well as a lack of contemporary poetry. They were making a concerted effort to use materials familiar to each student, but with 23 school districts represented, books were a real problem.

Both school and Youth Service Center representatives stressed the need for public facilities for after school hours, evenings, and Saturdays.

In November 1968, the people of King County, deeply concerned about their troubled children and realizing that juvenile delinquency was rapidly becoming a major criminal issue, voted a $6.1 million bond issue to modernize and expand the Youth Service Center.

Already functioning as an interested group, the five agencies became the official Advisory Committee to facilitate a dual school/residents' library in the newly approved Center and to make recommendations for a staff library to serve the varied professional, child care, and operational personnel. Legal staff had their own library.

The Committee, drawing on its previous findings, was able to forward by March 1969 its first recommendations to the architect on furnishings and utilization of the library.

The Committee identified three major uses for the residents' library: 1) to supplement the school curriculum by providing a variety of motivational materials and activities for teachers and students to use; 2) to provide study space and supplementary materials for a few extension school students who had been released from detention and were continuing their studies with Youth Service Center staff because they were expelled from or had dropped out of the regular school program in their home communities; 3) to provide materials and activities for recreational purposes after school hours for the children in the school program and those in detention who were not in school. The architect was instructed to design a residents' library space that would convey a relaxed, comfortable atmosphere, i.e. as much like a living room as possible.

The Committee recommended that a staff library supporting the work of professional and nonprofessional staff members, be provided, preferably adjacent to the residents' library. This location recommendation was not met; space was allocated in a former judicial chamber.

As the Advisory Committee continued to work, changes in the Youth Service Center itself affecting the library, were brought to the group's attention by John Liljegren, assistant administrator for Child Care Services for the Youth Service Center. Liljegren had been appointed library liaison between the Committee and the Youth Service Center. By the end of 1970, careful screening had reduced the number of actual admissions. Most children under the age of 13 were being placed in receiving homes rather than in detention, resulting in a marked decrease in shelter care.

Four and one-half percent of the population in 1971 was aged 13 or older. The population narrowed to almost exclusively a teenage and preteenage group of delinquent and rebellious youth. Beds formerly occupied by younger nondelinquent children were available to rebellious youngsters. Despite this, the junior boys unit in 1970 remained 100 percent over capacity for the entire year and continued operating at over capacity in 1971.

Young people's disaffection with society becomes readily apparent in looking at the children brought to the Youth Service Center by the police or their parents. Delinquents can no longer be dismissed as poor, of a minority race, and from the ghetto. Forty-four percent of the boys and girls came from families with parents married and living together; 76 percent were white; 28 percent of those with known family incomes were in the $10,800 or over annual bracket; 46 percent had fathers as their source of support. Unemployment, divorce, personality conflicts, ill health, alcoholism, and parental immaturity are frequently found in the family circle of the child.

In 1970, the largest number of delinquency referrals was for burglary/ unlawful entry, followed by auto theft, trailed by shop lifting and drug charges. In 1971, burglary/unlawful entry continued the cause of the largest number of delinquency referrals. Liquor use/ possession, auto theft, and shoplifting followed in that order.

About 600 youths were enrolled in the school program over the course of the school year, with an average of 60 students at any one time. Academically, children in the school program were often behind, but not excessively; students represented a broad range of ability. The drug culture seemed to have brought in a more intelligent child, who needed extra challenge in a school program.

When the architects' preliminary drawings indicated that the new addition to the Youth Service Center would provide 1600 square feet of library space, the Committee was ready to provide for furnishings, equipment, school and public library collections. Specifications for furnishing and equipment were given to the Juvenile Court administrator.

The largest mistake in all of the planning was failure to assign responsibility to one person to monitor library design and equipment specifications. Once the approval had been given for the space, a single committee member working with the architect could have prevented such errors as the librarian's office being too large and the workroom too small; lack of built-in shelving; windows occupying wall space needed for shelves and a roll top metal shutter over a counter set into the wall dividing the librarian's office from the entrance corridor. Bid specifications on shelving were not exactly what library standards call for; periodical shelving specifications furnished by the Committee omitted color choice and, consequently, were not ordered; paperback racks and bulletin boards did not

arrive on time. One person, closely cooperating with overworked Juvenile Court officials, could have prevented some of these errors.

On the advice of the Staff Department of Education, the Committee decided that ESEA Title II Special Needs Project Grant, with Intermediate School District #110 agreeing to administer the grant, was the most efficient method to establish the school collection. Members were appointed to draft the letter of intent and the proposal itself, with Children's Librarian, Kathleen Sullivan and Young Adult Librarian Jan Knape of King County Library System, being appointed to see that the proposal was written and submitted by the deadline of December 15, 1970. The proposal included the basic assumption that a librarian would be available to staff the library.

To solidify the Title II proposal requirements, the King County Juvenile Court Board of Managers and King County Library District Board of Trustees entered into a formal agreement. In it, the Juvenile Court agreed to provide facilities, furnishings, equipment, and maintenance of the library; one half the salary costs of a full-time professional librarian; and clerical assistance in support of an ongoing library program. King County Library agreed to provide administrative supervision of the total Youth Service Center library program; to hire a full-time professional librarian and to contribute one half the salary costs of this librarian; to provide the services of additional professional librarians as needed in children's and young adult services and in services for staff employed at the Youth Service Center; to provide access to its collection, through requests and loans, for materials not available in the Youth Service Center to both children and staff; and to provide additional materials to meet the public library needs of children in detention; and to meet the special library needs of staff.

Sister Beatrice Marie Farrell of Immaculate High School, Seattle, accepted an invitation to join the Advisory Committee and gave her experience and advice regarding the content of the Title II proposal. The proposal followed *Objectives and Standards for Libraries in Correctional Institutions*, prepared by the Committee on Institutional Libraries of the American Corrections Association, 1962; *Minimum Standards for Public Library Systems*, 1966, prepared by the American Library Association, 1967; and the State of Washington *Standards for Integrating School Library and Media Services: Program for the Learning Resources Center*, prepared by the Office of the Superintendent of Public Institutions, 1968. It requested a balanced collection, at a cost of $45,000. The letter of intent was accepted by the Washington State Superintendent of Public Instruction, and the proposal was returned with the request that the goals, needs, and evaluations be rewritten. Sister Beatrice Marie, Jan Knape, and Kathleen Sullivan rewrote the proposal in Title II language, and resubmitted it. The proposal was accepted and funded with $8000.

Authorization to purchase materials was received only six weeks before the deadline for final expenditure of funds. Although teachers had prepared selection lists and orders had been placed by Marilyn Wilkinson, Educational Media consultant for Intermediate School District #110, her office was in the throes of processing four other grants; verification of materials fell principally upon Jan Knape, who, being a public library specialist, felt handicapped by her lack of familiarity with school materials. Ninety-six periodical subscriptions were ordered; half of the money was spent for audiovisual materials, and the balance was used for basic reference materials.

Processing of Title II materials posed a real problem. Title II regulations allow $1 per item, which is sufficient for ordering, property stamping, pocketing, and perhaps covering a hardback with a plastic jacket; it does not begin to cover the cost of processing some of the highly sophisticated audiovisual materials. Until Title II administrators are convinced

that technical processing of an item is an integral part of its efficient usage, librarians will find themselves in the same situation as those responsible for the Youth Service Center—using valuable time to do what could be done more efficiently by the processing department of a library service center if only funds were available to pay for the service.

As soon as the Title II orders were submitted, King County Library System made available to the Youth Service Center Library a special grant of $2000 to be encumbered within four months for recreational reading. This was spent by Jan Knape for a variety of paperbacks and magazines especially geared to the Youth Service Center residents. Special care was taken to cover a wide range of materials, based upon the assumption that public library selection would provide what youth actually would read, rather than what they were supposed to be reading. Choice of paperbacks was based on Daniel Fader's selection lists in "Hooked on Books." Large paperback purchases were made of black, Indian, inner city, drug culture, counter culture, civil rights, pop music, riddles and jokes, and science fiction literature. Personal grooming, music, motorcycle and car magazines, comic books, and about 250 "fun" magazines selected from jobber's shelves were included.

As the proposed library emerged, Agnes Griffen, who shepherded the Advisory Committee from its inception in 1968 through July 1971, prepared drafts of a memorandum of accord to delineate responsibilities between the five concerned agencies, with the purpose of ensuring staffing, materials, and continuation of library service.

Recognizing their joint responsibilities to provide a continuing program of library services, the agencies agreed to the following divisions of responsibilities:

Intermediate School District #110:

1. Be responsible for funding for materials related to the curriculum of the school, and for administering

such funds, through purchase, processing, and distribution of all materials for the Youth Service Center Learning Resources Library.

2. Work to negotiate an agreement between King County School Districts that will provide a financial basis for continuing school library program at the Youth Service Center.

3. Make available the service of the School Media Consultant and the District's Learning Materials Production Center.

Seattle School District #1:

1. Continue its support of the school program in the Youth Service Center.

2. Provide one full-time certified teacher with library experience to guide and assist students in the Youth Service Center library during school hours.

3. Make available on a per capita basis for Seattle residents any monies allocated for school library resources for the purchase of materials for the Youth Service Center library.

4. Make available on a consultant basis the services of the District School Library Supervisor.

King County Library System:

1. Provide administrative supervision of the total Youth Service Center Learning Resources Library program, by hiring a full-time professional librarian, sharing salary costs with the Juvenile Court, and by assigning this librarian to be responsible for overall scheduling of staff and programming for the library, working in close cooperation with the Learning Resources library teacher.

2. Provide the services of additional professional librarians as needed, particularly in the areas of children's and young adult's services,

and in services for staff employed at the Youth Service Center.

3. Provide access to its collection, through requests and loans, for materials not available in the Youth Service Center, to both children and staff.

4. Provide additional materials to meet the public library needs of children in detention, and to meet the special library needs of staff, with appropriate budgeting, to be allocated from Rural Library District funds.

Seattle Public Library:

1. Through its existing contract with the King County Library System, will provide access to additional materials on request.

2. Make available for additional consultation and programming the services of children's and young adult's specialists.

King County Juvenile Court Youth Service Center:

1. Provide suitable library facilities, furnishings and equipment for the library and staff, as well as heat, light, and janitor service and maintenance and replacement of furnishings and equipment as needed.

2. Contribute to the salary costs of a full-time librarian, to be hired by King County Library System.

All five agencies agreed to enter into separate and contractual relationships for the provision of materials or services with any other parties to the Memorandum of Accord as the need might arise.

King County Library entered into two separate agreements: the first being with the Juvenile Court to hire and provide administrative supervision for the Youth Service Center librarian, supplying half of the salary costs; the second being with Intermediate School District #110, in which King County Library agreed to process the Title II materials with King

County Library contributing to the differences between allowable Federal grant and actual costs.

As soon as the agreement regarding the hiring of the librarian was signed, King County Library prepared and circulated a job description and began interviewing applicants. Those who had been most intimately concerned with the planning of the library were in complete agreement that although professional competence was primary, the determining factors in choosing the librarian would be ability to relate to the current teenage population naturally and without reaction to the inevitable testing that they would give; ability to work within the structure of a detention facility; and ability to cooperate with the needs of the school and yet maintain the free choice atmosphere of a public library.

Susan Brooks Madden was selected by a joint decision of both King County Library and the Youth Service Center personnel with whom she would be working. Her training and orientation to the King County Library System and its several institutional libraries extended over approximately six weeks. Then followed an introductory period with the staff of the Youth Service Center and the several agencies involved with the new library. The Youth Service Center contractor was behind schedule; the furnishings and supply ordering and delivery were behind schedule, and Susan immediately became involved with the details of pushing through the opening of the library. Unordered shelving, which had understandably a far higher proportion for periodicals and paperbacks than ordinarily found, had to be selected and ordered. Previously bought collection lists were checked, desiderata lists prepared and order information checked for the second Title II grant proposal, which had been prepared and submitted in late December by Jan Knape.

The second Title II proposal was designed to strengthen weak areas of the collection for which there had been insufficient money in the first grant and was allocated $7000, including processing costs. Selection focused on science, social sciences, arts and crafts, ethnic studies, phonograph records (soul music is by far the major preference of these youngsters), posters, and included heavy purchases in remedial language arts. These areas are those in which there is greatest demand and heaviest usage by both teachers and residents. The Title II grant also served to renew the 96 periodical subscriptions.

Work started in March 1968, was carried out by determined and dedicated personnel, culminating in the dedication of the Youth Service Center Library on Sunday, June 11, 1972. The comments of adults present at the dedication ranged from, "I've always wanted to read this book," to the remark of Ms. Lura Currier, head of the Pacific Northwest Bibliographic Center, "This is the first book collection that I've seen in my long years as a librarian that is completely suited to the needs of the people who are going to use it. You don't have everything you need, but what you have is just right."

Resident reaction is equally illuminating. Youngsters regularly comment, "God, what books!" or "I've never seen a library like this before." A 16-year-old, holding the *Underground Dictionary*, gave the ultimate compliment, "Far out. Far out. Even the reference books are Far Out."

The school library teacher reports an angry youngster storming at her, "I hate to read. I hate to read. I hate to read!" When confronted with the fact that she had read two books and been in the school program only five days, the youngster retorted, "But that's different. You let me read what I want to read."

In addition to books that they want to read, jigsaw puzzles have proved popular to residents, who make a game of timing themselves on the smaller puzzles. Pocket puzzles, of the two bent nails joined together type, are useful with hyperactive youngsters and give a child something to do when he first enters the library. As expected, paperbacks are preferred far above hardbound. Fiction *about* drugs, gangs, blacks, and anything that has become a movie is always in heavy demand. Poetry is the most popular area of creative work, enjoyed by both girls and boys. When bulletin boards arrived for each individual room, posters were lent as library materials and are much in demand.

Pimp, with its unromantic view of street life, has become the favorite book. One girl, in and out of the Center for the last five years, told Susan Madden that *Pimp* had made her decide to never join a "Stable" and to curb her own prostitution activities.

After the library had been opened, it became apparent that some of the materials were overprocessed. Dewey Classification was not necessary, nor were pockets for date due slips. New material is now property stamped, and given a subject heading. Fiction goes with the subject. Fiction of general interest is color coded for location, to make request filling and reshelving faster.

Residents like to work in the library, and can be used for stamping, typing, filing, color coding, shelving, and art work.

Any programming beyond regular open hours, such as rock groups, story hours, or films are cleared to ensure nonconflict with volunteer planned programs or court needs. Anyone coming from the outside has a briefing on contraband materials (cigarettes are not allowed) and the necessity for keeping Youth Service Center keys on one's person at all times.

The discipline supervision is furnished by unit staff, who accompany their unit members to the library, and by teachers, leaving Ms. Madden free to work as a librarian.

Teachers are most responsive to the presence of a professional librarian. They rely heavily on Susan Madden not only for materials, but to give reference service to their students, and are generous with their thanks to her.

Not every child in a detention center will respond to library service. But for many of these children, a pleasant, casual atmosphere; a selection of high interest, easy reading materials and, most importantly, a friendly, unshockable librarian are the pathway to the hitherto unknown experience of reading for sheer pleasure.

Crisis Information Services to Youth: A Lesson for Libraries?

Carolyn Forsman

YOUNG ADULT SERVICES in public libraries are being threatened with extinction. The elimination of separate departments and of their specially trained librarians in Chicago, Montgomery County, Maryland, and other library systems may signal the beginning of a national trend. The New York State plan to give the school library sole responsibility for services to youth is another step in this direction.

At the same time a new phenomenon, the Crisis Intervention Center, which provides counseling as well as information and referral services to troubled youth, has emerged within the last four years in hundreds of urban, rural, and suburban areas: Anchorage, Atlanta, Denver, Des Moines, Long Island, and Long Beach. Your community probably has one or soon will. Crisis Centers explain themselves by such evoking names as Hotline, Switchboard, Free Clinic, Rapline, Help Line, No Heat Line, Y.E.L.L., Rescue, H.I.P. (Help Is Possible), Somebody Cares, We Care, Inc., Listening Post, Night Line, Drug Aid, Y.E.S. (Youth Emergency Service), Community Youth Line, Your Information Unlimited. Crisis Centers are there to serve the needs of youth ten to 25, not only as students, but as whole persons.

The history and development of young adult services has yet to be written,[1] but young adult librarians have always taken pride in their ability to change with the times, to be sensitive to their clientele's needs and to be innovative in services and programs. Perhaps we can learn from the Crisis Intervention Center new ways to serve the young adult in his complete range of information needs.

Crisis centers in philosophy, organization, services, training methods, publicity, and insight into youth's problems contrast sharply with the whole concept of library service to young adults. They suggest possible new roles and directions for libraries and librarians.

The Crisis Center developed as an alternative to traditional community mental health and medical services. And because information and referral are an integral part of its concept, Hotlines, Switchboards, and Free Clinics can also be looked at as an alternative to traditional library service to young adults.

As with any new phenomenon, the definition of terms used to describe it are often not clear, concise, nor consistent with each other. However, agreement seems to be growing that the term "Crisis Intervention" includes three fairly distinct types of crisis services: Hotlines, Switchboards, and Free Clinics.

A Hotline is an emergency anonymous telephone service for young people in crisis providing a listening ear, with referral to agencies and professional back-up when necessary.

A Switchboard is primarily a telephone information and referral service as well as a message center. Unlike a Hotline, it may also have a walk-in or drop-in facility for visitors.

A Free Clinic is basically a walk-in center that provides direct medical services. It also has facilities for individual or group counseling in both medical and nonmedical problems, such as birth control and the draft.

An example might better explain the relationships and differences between these facilities in a community. A teenager thinks she is pregnant. If she calls the Switchboard she will be referred to the local Free Clinic for a pregnancy test. At the clinic, in addition to the free test, if she chooses, she will be counseled on birth control methods as well as possible solutions to her immediate situation. She might also be counseled on her relationship with the father. If she calls the Hotline instead of Switchboard, a nonjudgemental anonymous voice will direct a few questions to determine if she might indeed be pregnant, and also refer her to the Free Clinic for a test. The listener will not advise her to have an abortion, nor to marry the suspected father, nor otherwise tell her what to do. He will instead, in a series of questions and replies, let the caller discover the options for herself. The Hotline will more likely be used for this type of problem since Hotlines emphasize and specialize in interpersonal and individual psychological needs. Switchboards tend to satisfy more concrete needs, such as food, housing, transportation, and information on political and leisure activities. If a call to the Hotline requests a place to crash for the night and the caller is over 18, he more than likely will be referred to Switchboard. If he is a minor who's run away, the listener will encourage the youth to question his action in terms of himself and his family.

Hotlines, Free Clinics, and Switchboards do not advocate or encourage illegal behavior, including the harboring of runaways without the parent's permission, or the use of drugs.

In certain crises, the person is not in any state to be referred to another agency, no matter how logical it may seem. Persons experiencing a "bad trip" on drugs or contemplating suicide or who are in other life threatening situations, and who call in a state of panic, are handled by whichever of the three services he or she happens to call.

Switchboards

Switchboards and Free Clinics arose out of the counter-culture of white alienated youth: The first Switchboard began in the summer of 1967 in San Francisco to serve the Haight-Ashbury community as a message and referral service. It's prototype was the old "Central" switchboard in American communities which not only connected telephones, but was also a source of solutions to human problems. Its initial use was primarily as a crisis and problem center (what the Hotline now serves), but it soon expanded into a "community resource center." The Switchboard, with the help of its community, created a "human resource file," a list of people willing to teach and to share their skills and knowledge with others. The philosophy is to help people control their own lives by providing them information to make their own decisions. Other files developed to further this goal show the extent of Switchboard services: Jobs, Housing, Transportation, Buy and Sell, Music, Theater, Education, Messages.

A Switchboard is usually reached by telephone (San Francisco had 150,000 calls in their first two-and-a-half years). Its number will be found in a local alternative newspaper listing of frequent phone numbers. Some have a walk-in service, where visitors can read bulletin boards for notices on survival, politics, the youth culture pleasures, or leave and pick up messages. The message service is also used by parents of runaways as a possible point of contact.

✓ In all cases dealing with youth, his or her privacy and confidentiality are respected. Switchboard workers are volunteers from the community who try to make decisions in a democratic manner. When there is a coordinator, he or she has no more rights than the volunteers. Often the staff lives together as a collective. Switchboards are funded by donations from the community, including local ministries.

The manuals of the Berkeley and San Francisco Switchboards detail the philosophy, services, and policies of two of the oldest and most stable information services to the youth community.

Free Clinics

The first Free Clinic opened in Los Angeles in November 1967 as a drug treatment center for the free community. The philosophy of the Free Clinic movement is to treat the whole person; and so, it was natural that it would extend its services to include counseling on birth control, abortions, diet and nutrition, and drugs, as well as such nonmedical areas as the draft and law. Counseling is performed by community volunteers, professional and nonprofessional.

A client who enters the clinic is assigned a "facilitator" or "advocate" who is responsible for seeing that his or her needs are met by doctor and/or counselor. The facilitator is there to determine the person's needs, to put him at ease, to refer him to the right services(s) and to post-treatment follow-up.

Free Clinics are supported by donations, foundations, and federal dollars. The latter are sought reluctantly because of the restrictions often attached. Like Switchboards, decision-making is communal or by a board of directors composed of volunteers, the few full-time staff on subsistence salaries, and members from the community.

Free Clinics are loosely organized into a National Free Clinic Council, which facilitates communication via national meetings and a journal.

Hotlines

The use of community volunteers, the nonbureaucratic organization, the sensitivity to community needs and the ability to adapt and expand services in response to these needs, are significant features of Hotlines, as well as of Switchboards and Free Clinics.

While the Free Clinics originated in response to the drug problem, Hotlines evolved from suicide prevention centers and the community mental health movement. In 1958 the Los Angeles Suicide Prevention Center opened its telephones and doors to answer the *"Cry for Help,"* described by E. S. Schneidman, its founder, in the book by the same name. Experience and research indicated that most of the persons responding were not contemplating suicide but were nevertheless in a "crisis" situation, i.e. a point of extreme stress in which a decision must be made, but the person feels immobilized and unable to cope and is liable to behave in a self-destructive manner.

Adolescence is a "crisis of status discontinuity," socially, psychologically, and physiologically,[2] and in April 1968 the Los Angeles Children's Hospital began its Hotline for Youth. Hotline, the "port of call for angry, frightened, and frustrated young people."[3] Hotline, a personal, anonymous, emergency telephone service for young people in crisis.

Interdisciplinary Approach

Crisis intervention is a human problem and is therefore the responsibility of no particular profession or discipline. Though it arose out of the medical community, it soon aroused the interest and cooperation of professionals from the fields of psychology, psychiatry, therapy, health education, social work, pastoral counseling, nursing, and even law, anthropology, biostatistics and logic, but not librarianship. Its multidisciplinary approach is paralleled by the multi-service functions of Switchboards, Free Clinics, and Hotlines.

Confidentiality

Implicit in the provision of crisis intervention services is an atmosphere of Trust, as one hotline is aptly called. To engender this, a potential source of financial support will be refused if it threatens the center's credibility. There can also be no trust without confidentiality.

The relationship between caller and listener on the Hotline, between patient and counselor at the Free Clinic, and between person and staff at the Switchboard is confidential, whether adult or minor. Respect for the confidential nature of the client-Crisis Center relationship when the client is a minor is a unique feature of Crisis Centers. "We are responsible to the youths who come in, not to their parents." Hotlines, in particular, can guarantee confidentiality to both the caller and the listener by means of the anonymity of the telephone. In fact, the location of a hotline is often kept a secret to protect both parties. Should a parent inquire as to whether and why his or her child has used the Hotline, the listener can honestly reply that he doesn't know and can explain the Hotline's purpose.

Can public and school librarians honestly make the same claim with respect to their circulation records? How often are they guilty of telephoning a parent even prior to a teenager's or child's use of materials on, say, sex or drugs?

Alternatives

Hotlines do not advocate drugs, but neither do they preach their evils. Free Clinics are not pro-abortion, but neither will they moralize to an unwed parent. Switchboards do not encourage runaways, but neither do they turn them in. A nonjudgmental approach toward the client characterizes the variety of crises services to youth. They do not judge the person, nor do they recommend one solution, but for each of the range of alternative solutions, crisis centers do try to evaluate and recommend the best resource, whether it be a person, agency, book, or pamphlet.

For example, an unwed pregnant teenager, during a telephone encounter might discover that abortion or adoption are among her alternatives. The listener would not judge her predicament, nor ask her how she could have been so cruel to her parents, etc. If the caller should consider adoption, she would be given a list of recommended adoption agencies and homes for unwed mothers. In contrast, if the same young woman had asked a librarian, she might very well have received a short sermon or even an unintentional casual remark about the *badness* of her condition. Then the librarian might have handed her an outdated health and welfare directory for her to evaluate by herself!

Or if a young man were contemplating shooting heroin or smoking marijuana and let the librarian know this, it would not be surprising if he were told about the evils of drugs in general. But the librarian would not feel responsible for misinformation in any book or pamphlet the person might find by himself and would probably not feel confident to recommend one title over another. A Hotline or Free Clinic worker would discuss with him the possible consequences of drug use and would be prepared to recommend a particular book that had been evaluated to contain accurate information in a nonsensational way.

Hotlines do not advise, but they do more than listen. The aim of a crisis line is to provide constructive alternatives to a problem, to help the caller examine it from all angles, making use of his own resources to the fullest extent possible. If it is necessary, to go beyond this, the volunteer listener will "patch-in" to the telephone line, from his file of human resources in fields relevant to youth, a lawyer, doctor, psychiatrist, or minister, who has volunteered to be on call as a professional back-up. Alternatives might also be sought from the community resources file for the caller to contact later himself. Crisis centers hope to alleviate the immediate crisis, but also, just as important, to prepare the caller to deal with future crises, to become a better problem-solver. The repeat caller to a Hotline is a problem and is not encouraged.

Contrast this to the dependency relationship implicit in library services, e.g. "hooked on books," "book bait;" not only is one encouraged to frequent the library, but once inside, he is expected to have to "ask the librarian" to utilize its resources to the fullest. The reader's adviser hopes that a satisfied reader will return to him for additional advice.

Volunteers

Hotlines are operated primarily by volunteer youth. In the mental health services community, aides were used initially because of the shortage of professional manpower. Experience proved them to be more than an inexpensive second-best substitute. Their knowledge of the community and similarity to the clientele were qualities that the professional could not substitute with skill, and they became recognized members of the mental health team. It was only natural that youth would have a similar role in helping troubled peers who did not use and were not reached by traditional facilities.

Though the structure and organization of Hotlines is more varied than that of Switchboards and Free Clinics, even the most traditional, those organized by mental health and religious associations, have a youth advisory board and utilize teenagers and college students as volunteers.

Other Hotlines are sometimes part of a City Youth Agency, a University Counseling Center, or are nonprofit corporations. Support comes from their parent organization, if there is one, as well as from civic groups, personal donations, benefits, and foundations and federal grants. In any case, their budget is miniscule compared to that of health or information services in their community.

Problems

An analysis of the problems that are brought to these centers is possible because of the detailed records kept of each contact, whether by telephone or in person. A data log sheet will include age, sex, marital status, and first name; the degree of crisis, the attitude and approach the listener took; whether the problem was resolved by referral, professional back-up, or went unresolved; and where the caller heard about the service.

Though no systematic analysis exists at this time comparing one center to another, a general picture does emerge from inspection of the records of several crisis centers. Most calls involve interpersonal relationships: mainly boy/girl, peer, or family conflicts. Problems arising from an internal mental state, especially loneliness and depression are the second largest category. Suicidal calls are listed separately and are relatively few in number, though they are the most serious and have the greatest impact on volunteers. Medical problems, including drug information, drug overdose, tripping, pregnancy, venereal disease, and other sex problems rank third. Only about ten percent of the calls are drug related. Questions about the legal status, rights, and obligations of youth, including the draft, runaways, parental support, and marriage make up the next significant block. School-oriented problems occur less frequently, but enough to be a category. Only a small percentage of problems involve employment or housing.

Crisis Centers do not give advice, including medical or legal advice. Volunteers are not engaged in the practice of medicine or law without a license, but they are nonetheless able to serve youth in many sensitive areas with legal and medical implication, especially runaway, sex, and drug information. The possibility of legal suits has been raised both by Kahn [4] and Leviton [5] on hypothetical and empirical grounds and dismissed by both. It's these very sensitive areas that public and school libraries have feared to tread.

Crank calls, including put-ons and obscene calls, are generally treated seriously. The rationale is that the caller has a problem but is afraid to reveal it, perhaps even to himself.

Compare this attitude to the library's response to "troublemaker," which not infrequently is to ban him from the building.

In every Hotline, female callers predominate over males, between two to one to as much as five to one. But boys, when they call, have more specific problems than girls, who comprise almost all of the "lonely" calls.

The average caller is about 16, though older at college crisis centers. In one county, 16 percent of the callers were 12 or under. If this is not an unusual number of preteen callers, what implications are there for the present boundary in libraries between children and young adult services at 13 or 14 years, or the programs and materials in the children's room? Should the territorial boundaries in both libraries and library associations be re-drawn to include 11- and 12-year-olds in Young Adult services? Should junior novels be written, reviewed, and selected with the ten to 14 rather than the 12-to-16-year-old in mind?

Many Hotlines receive over 2000 calls a month. In the Washington, D.C. area alone, over 50 Hotlines, Switchboards, and Free Clinics were identified as providing a configuration of listening, counseling, and information or referral services to young adults. This is not an unusually large number for a metropolitan area. The combination of many centers, each with a potential large volume, indicates the possible, if not actual, impact of these services upon other information and referral services.

Referral Files

A referral system of community agencies and professionals is an essential element of any crisis center: Hotline, Switchboard, or Free Clinic. The degree the problem can be matched to referrals is one measure of the effectiveness of the center. Before an agency is used, as much information as possible is collected about it, including the identification of a particular contact person, so that a client is told who to see and not just where to go. Sometimes, an agency is checked out by means of a fake call.

Crisis Centers rely on users to improve their files. Volunteers are guided to ask the person for feedback on how helpful the referral was. If the center is unable to provide the information needed, he might be asked to call back and make the files more complete should he discover other sources. This mutual learning process also takes place between the center and the agencies themselves. The crisis center influences and educates professionals and agencies in more effective ways of handling the problems of young people, while the professionals and agencies provide training and expertise. Both user and agency feedback to the Center provide a mechanism for the continual up-dating of the files' "vital" information. The data sheets also encourage the search for and development of new referral resources.

Advocacy

Crisis centers not only intervene in individual immediate crises, the "band aid" function, but work to prevent future crises in a community. With the data collected on user problems and the follow-up and feedback provided on referrals, they function as a social indicator of the needs and gaps in community service. Perhaps the hours or regulations of an agency inhibit or prohibit its use by potential clientele, or there may be no agency at all that is concerned, or maybe a local ordinance on minors' rights needs changing. With data in hand and a constituency of community groups and professionals behind them, the crisis center is a powerful persuader to appropriate bodies to alter services or regulations. Alfred Kahn [6] names this "Program and Policy Advocacy" in describing the range of services a neighborhood information center could provide.

The library could assume the function of group advocacy. Even if it is not an advocate for individuals, it could use its accumulation of "unanswered questions" to be used by appropriate groups or organizations to substantiate and justify changes in services.

Access

Since crises can occur at any time and by their nature require rapid intervention, Hotlines and other crisis centers try to be open 24 hours, seven days a week. When this is not feasible, it is the daytime hours during the week that are closed, those nine-to-five Monday-to-Friday hours when public and especially school libraries are open, since emotional emergencies tend to occur most often at night. Crisis centers seem to have no problem recruiting staff for these hours, yet libraries base their limited hours as much on the unwillingness of paid employees to work at other times as on budgetary constraints.

It is not enough to be open, a service must be made known to its target audience by any media necessary: calling cards distributed at schools, stickers in phone booths and on cars, public service announcements on TV and local radio rock stations, stories in the local paper, listing in the alternative press, posters in neighborhood stores. These are the imaginative ways crisis centers try to reach troubled youth, while parents are informed by a Center's Speakers' Bureau, PTA's, and periodic written reports to the communities. Ironically, the one point of access that has been a stumbling block is the telephone directory and operator. Some directories require an address in order to be listed, and those Hotlines that demand anonymity have been refused a listing. In addition, there is yet no agreement by the phone company as how to list these Centers in the Yellow Pages, regardless of their name.

Training

The philosophy, services, and techniques of crisis intervention are initially conveyed to volunteers through a short training period, of not more than a dozen sessions, which utilizes role-playing, sensitivity groups, outside experts, and real crisis situations. It is necessary to understand oneself before one can help others and make oneself sensitive to the real but unstated and hidden needs of people seeking help, and so the volunteer is placed in situations which reveal his own biases and hang-ups. Authorities on subjects likely to be problems provide the information to answer these needs. Instruction in the content, organization, and update of the referral files is additional input into the volunteer's subject knowledge. The data sheets are a check that his training is consistent with the user population and its problems. Telephone techniques in particular are explained, demonstrated, and practiced through role-playing and actual supervised calls.

The initial training period, during which some volunteers are asked to drop out or do so by choice, is followed by weekly or monthly meetings to discuss problems, unanswered needs, and internal policies. Though written material plays a minor role initially, most crisis centers develop a training manual for future reference. The manuals describe the goals and services and emphasize the importance of follow-through, feedback, and up-date, so that services and resources will reflect community needs.

Is your library manual an adequate reflection of your library's stated priorities? Or does it contain more "don'ts" than "do's"? Would you be uneasy if your public read it?

Resources

Several crisis centers have indicated the desire to establish a resource library in their facilities (for reference by both staff and clientele) made up of handbooks, pamphlets, periodicals, and directories. One newsletter, the *Confederation*, mailed a questionnaire to crisis centers asking for recommended materials for such a basic collection. Materials so identified would be likely candidates for inclusion in a library's collection. Perhaps the library could provide them on indefinite loan to its local crisis center.

An informal network connects the over 750 crisis centers in the U. S. and Canada. The total number is increasing rapidly, despite the high death rate for new centers. *The Exchange* has established its responsibility for the production of the *National Directory of Hotlines, Switchboards, and Related Services.* At the International Hotline Conference, regional divisions were organized. The network also consists of smaller metropolitan area councils, such as in Long Island or Baltimore, and national research centers, all of which publish newsletters or journals and hold conferences and workshops. But there is great resistance to any strong network with regulatory powers. A proposal for national standards and accreditation was defeated in 1971, but the minimum criteria suggested: 24-hour-access, continuous training, justification of need for a service, formal evaluation to include feedback, are an accurate reflection of their importance to the crisis center philosophy.

Summary

In summary, a crisis intervention center is an easily accessible storefront or telephone community facility, counseling, advocacy, information, and referral service feeding into a larger human services network, using paraprofessionals from the community, who are peers of the clientele, with professional back-up when needed, and providing stopgap crisis services until more comprehensive and preventative services can be found.

When phrased this way, the crisis services image is parallel to storefront library "outreach" programs. Librarians are searching for new and innovative ways to reach the nonuser. Can we learn anything about changes in services, hours, personnel and training, and public relations from a similarly nontraditional service? In addition, several public libraries have gone into the information and referral business themselves,[7] so it is not entirely academic to ask if and how libraries, both school and public, should become a part of this network and cooperate with crisis centers as equals. Third, if we can accept as fact that we will never serve everyone directly and personally, can we perhaps serve our public indirectly by providing information and back-up services to the staff of our local hotline, switchboard, and free clinic, i.e. consciously serving community groups. Fourth, how can we apply the information crisis centers are collecting about the needs of troubled youth in our communities to even traditional library services, e.g. in areas such as book selection or programs.

"Every community needs a police department, a public school system, a mental health clinic, a welfare agency, a fire department, . . . and a suicide and crisis intervention service . . ."[8] Is the library ready to assume its place among these community helping systems?

REFERENCES

1. Braverman, Miriam. Ph.D thesis in progress at Columbia University School of Library Service.
2. Sebald, Hans. *Adolescence; A Sociological Analysis.* Appleton-Century Crofts, 1960, p. 24.
3. Bell, Joseph. "Take Your Troubles to the Hotline." Seventeen, August 1970.
4. Kahn, Alfred J. *Neighborhood*

Information Centers. Columbia University School of Social Work, 1966. Reprinted by University Book Service, Brooklyn, N.Y., 1971.
5. Leviton, Dan & Stanley Parey. *Proposal for a University of Maryland Crisis Intervention Center,* 1970. 8p. mimeo.

6. Kahn. *op cit.*
7. Donahue, Joseph. *Public Information Center: Final Report.* Enoch Pratt Free Library, February 1971.
8. McGee, Richard K. "Toward a New Image for Suicide and Crisis Services." *Crisis Intervention.* vol. 2, no. 3, 1970, p. 63.

DIRECTORIES OF CRISIS CENTERS—NATIONAL

National Directory of Hotlines, Switchboards, and Related Services. Ken Beitler. The Exchange, 311 Cedar Ave. South, Minneapolis, Minn. 55404. January 1, 1972. 50p. $2
The most complete directory at this time. Arranged geographically, including Canada.

Win with Love! A Comprehensive Directory of the Liberated Church, Including Peace Organizations, Youth Switchboards, National Resource Groups, Immigrant Aid Centers in Canada. Part I, October 1970, no. 4, 63p; Part II, June 1971, no. 5, 63p, Berkeley Free Church, Free Church Publications, POB 9177, Berkeley, Calif. 94709. $1.50
Geographically arranged.

Radical Therapist Rap Center Directory. Radical Therapist, Hillsdale, N.Y. 12529. June 1971 Supplement, p. 1-7. 50¢
Does not include hotlines and switchboards and so complements Beitler. Geographically arranged. Indicates type of services provided.

Switchboards and Hotlines. Appendix One in Ambrosino, Lillian. *Runaways.* Beacon Pr., 1971, p. 109-116.
An example of incomplete directories appended to books which are not updated.

Directory of Suicide Prevention Facilities. Bulletin of Suicidology. March 1969, p. 47-58.

DIRECTORIES OF CRISIS CENTERS—LOCAL

If your region does not produce its own directory, your library or librarians' association can offer to create and update it.
Survey of drug abuse programs for the Washington Metropolitan Area, Information Document. January, 1971. Metropolitan Washington Council of Governments, 1225 Connecticut Ave., N.W., Washington, D.C. 20036. 55p. mimeo. Free.
Arranged A-Z within the regions of Washington, Maryland, and Virginia. Services not exclusively drug-oriented, e.g. Hotlines are included. For each program affiliation, goals, hours, clientele, facilities, and funding are indicated as well as contact person.

New Jersey Drug Help Centers and Hotlines; a Preliminary Working Directory. Jana Varlejs, comp. Montclair Public Library, 1971. 5p. Dist. by the N.J. Librarians for Social Responsibilities, Princeton Public Library, N.J. 08540.
Librarian originated directory.

DIRECTORIES OF COMMUNITY RESOURCES

Every crisis center (and library!) needs an accurate, up-to-date guide to community resources. Many centers have created these in the form of files. The following are a sample of published directories that show their variety in depth and origin. If your community does not have such a guide, create one.

Direct Action. Philadelphia Librarians SRRT. October 1970. 2p.
A simple alphabetical list of community organizations with telephone numbers.

Free for You. Help Center. Univ. of Maryland, College Park, Md. 20742. Fall, 1971. 8p. mimeo. Free.
From Abortion to Zoo. Aimed at the local college student.

The Golden Goose. No. 1, 1972. Sue Critchfield, Bay Area Social Responsibility of Librarians Round Table, Community Resources Committee, 72 Ord St., San Francisco, Calif. 94114. Bi-monthly.
"The newsletter that intends" to list resources, to find lists of such resources.

Health Counseling and Crisis Intervention Referral Resources (for the Washington Metropolitan area). Prepared by Dr. Catherine M. Miller, Dept. of Health Education; Univ. of Maryland, College Park, Md. 20742; n.d. 1970? 8p. mimeo.
From Abortion to Venereal Disease, for each service, address, hours, fee, services, and personal contact are included.

People's Yellow Pages. Vocation for Social Change, 351 Broadway, Cambridge, Mass. 02139. 93p. 75¢
A meaty directory, arranged by subject with many "see" references to the appropriate term used. A model community resource guide for the alternative culture of Boston.

"Phones," *Quicksilver Times*, listed in every issue. Many of the local alternative presses have similar listings, e.g. "Frequently Called Numbers," *Los Angeles Free Press*.
These are the barest of guides, giving telephone numbers only.

A Questionnaire to Gather Information for the Interagency Information Referral Resource Committee. Sponsored and supported by the Prince George's County (Maryland) Health Planning Advisory Council and the Health and Welfare Council. July 1971. 10p.
An excellent model for preparing a directory.

Social Action Organizations of New Jersey. N.J. Librarians for Social Responsibility, Princeton Public Library, N.J. 08540. May 1971. 12p.

PERIODICALS

American Journal of Orthopsychiatry American Orthopsychiatric Assn., N.Y. Five times yearly, $16

Bulletin of Suicidology. National Clearinghouse for Mental Health Information, NIMH, Chevy Chase, Md. 20015. Spring 1970 special issue commemorating the tenth anniversary of the Los Angeles Suicide Prevention Center. Might be discontinued.

Confederation Newsletter. Main Line, Cornell Univ., Sheldon Court, Ithaca, N.Y. 14858.
College oriented.

Connection: Newsletter for New England. Project Place, 37 Rutland St., Boston, Mass. 02118.

Crisis Intervention. Suicide Prevention and Crisis Service, 560 Main St., Buffalo, N.Y. 14202. Vol. 1, No. 1, 1969. Index to 1969 and 1970 in Vol. 3, No. 1.
Includes annual bibliographies, 1968-.

The Exchange. 311 Cedar Ave. South, Minneapolis, Minn. 55404. Monthly. $6
"A national newsletter for hotlines, switchboards, and other youth-oriented projects." Ken Beitler, ed.

Free Clinic Journal. National Free Clinic Council, 701 Irving St., San Francisco, Calif. 94122. Annual. $5

Northeast Hotline Bulletin. Hotline, 1355 Northern Blvd., Manhasset, N.Y. 11030.

Radical Therapist. Hillsdale, N.Y. 12529.

SCHNEIDMAN, Edwin, ed. *Life-Threatening Behavior.* Avail. from Behavior Publications, 2852 Bdway., N.Y. 10025. Quarterly: $10 (indiv.); $20 (institutions).
Official journal of the Assn. of Suicidology.

The Vita. $1
Newsletter of the International Assn. for Suicide Prevention.

Vocations for Social Change. Canyon, Calif. 94516. Bi-monthly. $10
Source of information about new services, directories, alternative institutions.

ORGANIZATIONS—NATIONAL

American Assn. of Suicidology.

Center for Studies of Suicide Prevention, NIMH, Chevy Chase, Md. 20015.
A joint sponsor of the *Bulletin of Suicidology.*

Center for the Study of Crisis Intervention. Univ. of Florida, Gainesville, Fla. 32601.

Los Angeles Suicide Prevention Center. 2521 W. Pico, Los Angeles, Calif. 90026. Has produced studies on adolescent crises. "Student-packet" of article $3.

National Clearinghouse for Drug Abuse Information, NIMH, Chevy Chase, Md. 20015.
Among its many publications are its *Report Series* and its *Selected Reference Series.*

National Clearinghouse for Mental Health Information, NIMH, Chevy Chase, Md. 20015.
Publishes the *Bulletin of Suicidology.*

National Free Clinic Council. 701 Irving St., San Francisco, Calif. 94122.

Technical Information Section, NIMH. Will provide computer research on crisis intervention.

The International Assn. for Suicide Prevention. Newsletter *The Vida* and conferences.

BIBLIOGRAPHIES

Bibliography on Suicide and Suicide Prevention. Prepared by the Los Angeles Suicide Prevention Center. National Clearinghouse for Mental Health Information, NIMH, Chevy Chase, Md. 20015.
3300 items, covering 1897-1967.

Crisis Intervention. Annual bibliographies on crisis intervention.

Drug Dependence and Abuse, a Selected Bibliography. National Clearinghouse for Drug Abuse Information. March 1971. 50p. GPO. 60¢
Arranged by subjects, e.g. socio-cultural aspects, law and public policy, information resources. An annotated edition is planned.

Student Suicide, a Bibliography. 3p. mimeo. Available from NIMH.

TRAINING MANUALS PRODUCED BY CRISIS CENTERS

The following is not a comprehensive list of such manuals. Virtually every hotline, switchboard, and counseling center has an in-house manual. All that are listed below have been inspected by the compiler. Librarians would do well to compare them to their own policy and training manuals.

Advocate Guide. People's Free Medical Clinic, 3028 Greenmount Ave., Baltimore, Md. 21218. July 1970. 8p. mimeo.

Berkeley Switchboard Operators Manual. Free Church Publications, BPOB 9177, Berkeley, Calif. 94709. April 1970. 24p. $1

Community Relations. Tom Paine Society, 31 W. King St., York, Pa. n.d. 4p. mimeo.
A practical guide for other centers as well.

Drugs: Information for Crisis Treatment, a Manual. Matthew Lample, Drug Help Inc., POB 366, Ann Arbor, Mich. 48107. 1971. 25p. 75¢

Drug Abuse: Acute Treatment Manual. California Medical Assn. 1970. 8p. mimeo.
Includes suggested resource directory form.

A Drug Manual. Richmond Crisis Intervention Center. November 1970. 48p. mimeo. Available from Hotline Coordinator, c/o Adolescent Clinic, Box 151, Medical College of Virginia, Richmond, Va. 23219.
Includes a 14-page dictionary of slang drug terms and drug profiles for every drug including usual dose, duration of effect, effects sought, physiological effects, possible ill effects, withdrawal symptoms, etc.

Guidelines for the Establishment of a Hotline Service. Developed by attendees at Conference on Emergency Telephone Service, Children's Hospital, Los Angeles, Calif. February 24 and May 26, 1969. 21p. mimeo.

A Letter to All Telephone Volunteers. Drug Aid Program, Catonsville, Md. 1971. 6p. mimeo.
Their training and policy manual.

Manual. Franklin County Hotline, POB 307, Greenfield, Mass. 01301. n.d. 12p. mimeo.

MOYER, Beth. *A Descriptive Analysis of a Personal Emergency Telephone Service Used in Crisis Intervention for Youth in Richmond, Va.* Thesis. Write Ad. Clinic.

Richmond Hotline Training Manual. September 1971. 12p. mimeo. Hotline Coordinator, c/o Adolescent Clinic, Box 151, Medical College of Virginia, Richmond, Va. 23219.

San Francisco Switchboard Operating Procedures. Haight Ashbury Switchboard, 1826 Fell St., San Francisco, Calif. 94117. September 1970. 13p. mimeo. Free.

Training Manual for Telephone Evaluation and Emergency Management of Suicidal Persons. Suicide Prevention Center, Inc., Los Angeles, Calif. n.d. 27p. mimeo.
One of the first crisis centers in the U. S.

CRISIS CENTERS

The following are articles or documents directed toward the public that describe the purpose, services, and history of local centers in the Washington area. Similar documents are available from crisis centers themselves in your community and in articles in your local alternative press.

"Connection." *Harry*, March 29-April 8, 1971. p. 8. Describes and compares six Baltimore area hotlines.

"A County Mental Health Association's Hotline." *School Health Review*, September 1970, p. 27-30.
Describes the Montgomery County, Maryland, hotline. The entire issue is on Crisis Intervention.

Hotline, Could an Anonymous Listener Help? Information Sheet. Northern Virginia Hotline Inc., Arlington, Va. 22205. flier. n.d.

MCCARTHY, Barry & Bermna, A.L. "Student Operated Crisis Center." *Personnel and Guidance J.*, March 1971, p. 523-8.
Describes the American Univ. hotline.

"Switchboard—Our Community Headphones Offers . . ." *Quicksilver Times*, June 2-16, 1971, p. 5.

Statement of Purpose. Washington Free Clinic, Washington, D.C. n.d. 9p. mimeo.
Includes history and services.

For articles on other hotlines and crisis centers, see Readers' Guide and Education Index under "Telephone in Counseling" and "Suicide-Prevention"; Psychological Abstracts under "Crisis Intervention"; Alternate Press Index under "Movement Centers"; and from your local crisis center. Documents not found through these indexes include:

CLARKE, Nancy B. "Help." *Youth Magazine*, 1505 Race St., Rm. 1203, Philadelphia, Pa. 19102, October 25, 1970, p. 1-10.

JAFFE, Dennis. *Number Nine: Responses to Youth Problems at a Crisis Center; an Investigation of a Social Experiment.* State Street Center, 266 State St., New Haven, Conn. 06511. August 1971. 106p. mimeo. $10

An extensive description of a crisis center operation, based on survey data. Divided into nine sections that include background in community mental health, telephone and storefront counseling, staff, a survey of community attitudes, a bibliography, and a directory of Connecticut crisis centers.

"Help!" 25 min. color. $265. Avail from: Concept Films, 312-1155 15th St., N.W., Washington, D.C.
Describes the Philadelphia Volunteer Youth Crisis Center.

CRISIS CENTERS—THE PHENOMENON

AGEL, Jerome, ed. *Radical Therapist Anthology.* Ballantine, 1971. $1.25

AGUILERA, Donna. *Crisis Intervention, Theory and Methodology.* C. V. Mosby, 1970.

BELL, Joseph N. "Take Your Troubles to the Hotlines." *Seventeen*, August 1970, p. 242-3. Reprinted in pamphlet form by Social and Rehabilitation Service, Youth Development and Delinquency Prevention Administration, HEW, Washington, D.C.

FARBEROW, Norman L. & Schneidman, Edwin S., eds. *The Cry for Help.* McGraw, 1965.

GARELL, D. C. "Hotline Telephone Service for Young People in Crisis." *Children*, September 1969, p. 177-80.

JAFFE, Dennis. *Number Nine.* See above.

LEVITON, Dan & Stanley Pavey. *Proposal for a University of Maryland Crisis Intervention Center.* n.d. 18p. mimeo.

RUITENBEEK, H., ed. *Radical Therapy.* Bantam, 1972.

POTTER, Gus. *Hotline Story.* Paper presented at Hofstra Univ. Symposium, September 9-10, 1971. 17p. mimeo. Operation Hotline, Town of North Hemstead, 220 Plandome Rd., Manhasset, N.Y. 11030.
An excellent summary of hotlines: history, philosophy, services, finances, staffing, callers.

PARAD, Howard H., ed. *Crisis Intervention: Selected Readings.* Family Service Association of America, 1969.

V

Service
to Students
and Faculty

A Screaming Success
As Study Halls

Billy R. Wilkinson

AN UNDERGRADUATE library is defined as a separate library building on a university campus designed especially for undergraduates and which has as its purpose a full range of services for these university students; it may attempt to serve all undergraduates, but it is particularly concerned with the students in the College of Arts and Sciences, the General College, or whatever this part of the university is called.

To set the stage for the past 20 years when the Lamont Library at Harvard and many other undergraduate libraries sprang up on American campuses, two antecedents of undergraduate libraries are of interest.

Frederick Wagman, director of the University of Michigan Library, has traced the development of undergraduate libraries back to 1608 in England when Thomas James was head of Bodley's Library at Oxford.[1] James proposed the establishment of an undergraduate library to help the younger students, but Sir Thomas Bodley would have no part of it and dismissed the proposal in a letter to James. Bodley wrote:

Your deuise for a librarie for the yonguer sort, will have many great exceptions . . . there must be a keepre ordeined for that place. And where you mention the yonger

sort, I knowe what books should be bought for them, but the elder as well (as) the yonguer, may have often occasion to looke upon them. . . . In effect, to my understanding there is muche to be saide against it. . . .[2]

There was so "much to be said against it" that for the next 299 years, no American university actually tried, on any significant scale, a separate undergraduate library for its students. Then, at the beginning of this century, Columbia University created the Columbia College Study.

James H. Canfield, Librarian of Columbia University, wrote in his 1907 Report to the President that:

the establishment of the College Study—undoubtedly the best lighted, best ventilated, and most commodious reading room on the campus—is an excellent illustration of our desire to help undergraduates to help themselves, our constant effort to develop in the student self-reliance in the selection and use of books. It also enabled us to test the theory which is not new, but which thus far has never been put into actual practice. That is, that a collection of not to exceed 6000 volumes, carefully selected and kept fresh and up-to-date in every sense of the word, is sufficient to meet all the ordinary demands of the undergraduates of the average college. This has been given just a half year's trial, and the result is entirely satisfactory.[3]

After reading of the virtues of Columbia College Study, the present day undergraduate libraries do not seem so pioneering. To borrow a phrase from the musical *Guys and Dolls,* the Columbia College Library is "the oldest, established, permanent, floating" undergraduate library on the campus of an American university.

These two excursions into the past were to illustrate that separate undergraduate libraries are not a new concept in university library service. However, the real period of accelerated development of the undergraduate library began only 20 years ago in 1949 with the opening of the Lamont Library at Harvard. The early planning, the actual design, the functions, and an evaluation after the first years of the Lamont Library are all well documented in the literature. In fact, the Lamont Library is probably one of the most documented events in the history of American libraries. Keyes Metcalf and the other librarians associated with Lamont, perhaps sensing the importance of what they were doing, took time to record it.[4]

The following summary of the total Harvard situation is necessary to give an understanding of the Lamont Library.

Metcalf became librarian at Harvard in 1937. By that time, the Widener Library, which had been opened in 1915, was regarded as "cold, impersonal, and even unfriendly," to quote one observer. It was also full. Metcalf's first decision was whether or not to plan on the construction of a new central library for the university. He has written that "the conservative thing to do"[5] would have been to build a new central library. But the cost was prohibitive—an estimated $10 million. No suitable site in a central location was another objection. A third and equally important deterrent was that a building of the size needed would be so large as to be unwieldy from the

standpoint of service. The idea of a new central library was given up, and plans for expansion were developed along the following lines.

A study of Harvard's library disclosed that more space was needed for books, staff, and readers. Two other problems required attention. There were no adequate quarters in Widener for valuable collections of rare books and manuscripts, and no way had been found for providing proper facilities and services for undergraduates in a building where the pressure for service for researchers was so great; where undergraduates must use a catalog containing millions of cards; and where, it was thought, they could not be given direct access to the main book collection.[6]

With these needs and disadvantages in mind, plans were developed for four new units to house parts of the Harvard Library. The first would store less-used books; the second would satisfactorily house and service the rare books and manuscripts; the third would provide underground stacks in Harvard Yard, connected to Widener by tunnel; and the fourth would give undergraduates separate library facilities. The Houghton Library for rare books and manuscripts became a reality in 1942. The New England Deposit Library was also opened in 1942 for the storage of less-used books.

Thus, it is clear that the Lamont Library was not an isolated event, but part of a four-pronged solution to the problems facing Harvard.

Lamont was planned on three suppositions: 1) that undergraduates will make more and better use of a library designed expressly for them; 2) that this was the best way to relieve the pressure in the Widener building and make unnecessary a new central library building; and 3) that if that pressure were relieved, the Widener Library building would become a more satisfactory research center than it had been in the past.[7]

In planning the Lamont Library, the

Harvard staff and architects wanted it to be:

> conveniently located and inviting of access . . . on one of the main undergraduate traffic routes, and there should be no flights of stairs to climb to the entrance or monumental vestibules or foyers to traverse before coming to the books. Once within the Library, the student should find the entire book collection as accessible as possible.[8]

It is generally acknowledged that Lamont met these requirements.

Thus in the late 1940s, Mother Harvard had started something—in fact, she greatly influenced several ideas which are still very much with us in the world of university libraries. Separate undergraduate libraries, separate buildings for rare books and manuscripts, storage libraries, and underground libraries all got this early boost from Harvard. Indiana with its Lilly Library, Yale with the Beinecke Library, and Kansas with the Spencer Library are other very famous examples of separate rare book libraries. Several libraries are now going underground—the best illustration is the new Undergraduate Library at the University of Illinois. A sacred experimental corn plot on the campus could not be shaded by any new building. Therefore, the Undergraduate Library was built under the quad. There are also many examples of storage libraries, such as the ones at the University of Michigan and Princeton.

But the idea of a separate undergraduate library got the biggest boost of all by the building of the Lamont Library at Harvard. Almost overnight Lamont became a beautiful legend. It was idealized. Many of us made pilgrimages to the shrine. Even though university librarians were keenly interested in this separate approach to library service for undergraduates, no university built a separate undergraduate library during the next nine years. The University of Minnestoa did open its Freshman-Soph-

omore Library in 1952 in a classroom building. Then in 1958, Lamont's eldest son was born. The University of Michigan opened its Undergraduate Library, and during the past ten years new and separate libraries have been erected at South Carolina, Texas, North Carolina at Chapel Hill, Stanford, Ohio State, Penn State, Tennessee, and Illinois. New buildings are being planned or are under construction at Wisconsin, California at Berkeley, Oklahoma, Washington, Maryland, Massachusetts, and British Columbia.

There has been another approach to the separate undergraduate library. A new research library is built and then the old main library is renovated into an undergraduate library. Cornell, in 1962, was the first university to do this. UCLA and Michigan State have also taken this route, and currently Duke, Hawaii, and Emory are remodeling their original library buildings. Nebraska has remodeled part of a university building for its undergraduate library. If anyone has been counting, this all adds up to 24 separate undergraduate libraries, and several have probably been missed. There are also many undergraduate libraries which occupy extensive quarters in the central university library. Indiana University, which had a separate undergraduate library, has recently built a new university library which features undergraduate services in one section of a three-part building.

For additional details on this library phenomenon of the 1960s, refer to the writings of Irene Braden,[9] Warren Kuhn,[10] Elizabeth Mills,[11] Robert Muller,[12] and Jerrold Orne.[13]

So much for the historical background. There is a current rage for undergraduate libraries. Many millions of dollars have been spent on them. The buildings are there or they are rising. The book collections are there or they are being assembled.

The big questions are: What do we have? Are undergraduate students getting decent service in these libraries?

In an attempt to answer these questions, I have divided what happens in undergraduate libraries into seven functions or services. These are:

1. The undergraduate library as a study hall—students coming to the library with their own books and using them exclusively.

2. As a social center—students meeting and talking with other students. One librarian has called it "face time"—you get your face seen and see other faces. The library is a perfect place for this.

3. As the reserve book dispenser—books segregated onto special shelves at the request of professors.

4. As a browsing collection—the main collection with open-access for all students—there is just no such thing as a closed stack in any undergraduate library which I have seen.

5. As listening facility—audio rooms or listening rooms—the equipment plus records and tapes of music and spoken arts.

6. As visual materials center—films, filmstrips, pictures, paintings, prints, etc.

7. As a center for reference services —the assistance given students by librarians—what happens at the reference desk or in an encounter between student and librarian.

How do undergraduate libraries rate? Have they been a success or failure in these seven areas? You are warned that the following comments are generalizations and that naturally there are exceptions.

All undergraduate libraries have been a screaming success as study halls. The Undergraduate Library of the University of Michigan may be the smash hit of all time; the attendance in that library during 1968-69 was 1,899,000. This is 8000 to 10,000 students per day. The New York Public Library at 42nd Street does not have as many users each day. Studies have shown at Michigan and elsewhere that from 40 percent to 65 percent of those in the library are studying their own materials. Thus, the major function is a study hall.

Undergraduate libraries are also highly successful as social centers. Perhaps here is where the phrase "a screaming success" should have been used. If this is doubted, just go to one of them around nine o'clock on any night (except Saturday, that is). Some librarians resisted this function, but they were fighting human nature and lost. Luckily, carpeting and other acoustical treatments have helped tremendously in keeping the study hall from being taken over by the social center.

So far, undergraduate libraries chalk up two complete successes which have one great advantage: the students are there. They do not have to be pulled in off the campus. They are there.

But what else happens?

The Reserve desk is probably the busiest service point in the entire building. In 1968-69 Michigan had 50,000 volumes and 10,000 periodical articles on closed reserve with a total circulation of 276,000. There are many librarians, however, who question whether a booming reserve book business equals good teaching in a university. Studies at Cornell and elsewhere have shown that 40 percent or more of the volumes on reserve are dead wood and are not used. A healthy sign has been detected at several undergraduate libraries because the number of volumes requested for reserve by faculty has been whittled down by strong librarians. But then it is appalling to read that one university is planning shelving space for 65,000 reserve volumes in its undergraduate library now under construction. In case one wishes to cite the thousands of students as an excuse for so many reserve books, another example of the abuse of reserve services may be given where there is *no* excuse: a college library has 8000 volumes on closed reserve and another 10,000 volumes on open shelf reserve. It has *only* 1,114 students and is in a new $3 million library with completely open stacks.

Is this success or failure? If the number of volumes on reserve is gradually being decreased each year, it may be more of a success than if the librarians are still gently receiving long, out-of-date lists from lazy, unconcerned faculty, and laboriously processing the volumes to hide them away so that no one uses them. That submissive attitude perpetuates stagnant service.

Do the undergraduates use the freely accessible main collections which have been selected for them? The answer is yes, and it seems to be getting better each year. Cornell with over 85,000 volumes in its Uris Library has experienced an increase in use with each passing year. Michigan with 155,000 volumes had a home circulation of 245,000 in 1968-69. Many thousands more are used in the building. Perhaps one of the most worrisome aspects of undergraduate libraries has been the selection of this basic collection for undergraduate use. The Lamont catalog was published and served as a basis for some of the selection. Then, the Michigan shelf-list was made available, and now *Books for College Libraries,* developed in California, is used. There is not enough space to go into this aspect. Suffice it to say that the selection processes have been very detailed and elaborate with the involvment of both faculty and librarians. A great deal of time and energy has been spent on selecting individual titles for the collections. They are good, small collections. But we must realize that they will never come close to satisfying all the needs of undergraduates. The collections may now contain titles that students and faculty never use.

Almost every undergraduate library has some equipment for listening to records and tapes. The extent of this audio service varies greatly. Music and spoken arts recordings make up the collection at Michigan; only spoken arts recordings are in the Cornell Listening Rooms. At Stanford the language laboratory, consisting of four classrooms and an audio-control center, occupies about one-fourth of the ground floor, but the laboratory is not administered by the library. Have these audio facilities been a success or failure? At Cornell, the number of listeners increased each

of the first four years of operation, but has drastically declined each of the last three years. My evaluation is that the library had a moderate success at the beginning, but is now going downhill toward failure. The reasons for this deteriorating situation at Cornell are a lack of communication with appropriate faculty members by librarians concerning the record collection and also a lack of communication with students. Since the abandonment of the freshman orientation lectures several years ago, most Cornell students do not even know of the existence of the collection.

Going from the audio to the visual is painfully easy. University libraries barely know that films exist. They have done little or absolutely nothing with films. A complete failure is the mark for most undergraduate libraries.

Reference service is the final aspect of undergraduate libraries to be considered. I am currently working on a dissertation at the Columbia School of Library Service entitled: "Reference Services for Undergraduate Students: Four Case Studies." The cases are two undergraduate libraries on university campuses (those at Cornell and Michigan) and two liberal arts college libraries (Swarthmore in Pennsylvania and Earlham in Richmond, Indiana). My wife and I have completed a 10-week trip in which we visited each of these libraries on two separate occasions. I interviewed at length some 50 reference librarians and administrators; we also briefly interviewed many undergraduates at Michigan and Cornell who were in the main research library using the union catalog of campus holdings. We then monitored all questions asked by undergraduates at the reference desks of both the undergraduate library and the main university library at Cornell and Michigan and at the one reference desk at Swarthmore and Earlham for two different one-week periods during the 1969 autumn semester. Documents concerning reference services for undergraduates were also consulted. The following is only a brief report of the study.

The difficulties facing reference librarians in undergraduate libraries can be illustrated by relating the responses to one of the questions asked of librarians in the interviews. When asked if they, as undergraduates, had requested assistance from reference librarians, most of them admitted they had never, or rarely, ventured to ask for help. If those of us who go on to a career in librarianship did not approach librarians, what of those millions of students who have never given library school a thought?

The remainder of this paper will concentrate on the reference services of the University of Michigan and Cornell University. The reference services in both of these undergraduate libraries are in a state of decline. The total number of questions asked at the reference desks in the Michigan Undergraduate Library has decreased by 22 percent when the first full year of operation—1958-59—is compared with 1968-69. More alarming is a 55 percent decrease in the category of substantial reference questions (as opposed to the brief information and directional questions) from a high of 31,844 in 1963-64 to only 14,110 in 1968-69. During these 11 years, the home loans, in contrast, have jumped by 117 percent, and total book use has increased by 91 percent. The undergraduates enrolled in the College of Literature, Science, and the Arts (the primary group of students served by the Undergraduate library) have increased by 70 percent.

Cornell's Uris Library, which serves fewer students than Michigan's Undergraduate Library, has experienced a similar trend. The number of substantial reference questions rose each of the first years, and then, during three of the four most recent years, has decreased. The year 1968-69 was 17.7 percent below the best year of 1964-65.

I link these decreases in demand for reference services with the failure of the professional staff to pursue aggressively an active service program. Last summer before my field observation, I hypothe-sized that communications between the staff in undergraduate libraries and the faculty concerning reference services for their students have been minimal when contrasted with communications between liberal arts college librarians and faculty concerning available reference services for their students.

I also hypothesized that no effective means of stimulating use of reference services have been attempted by reference librarians in undergraduate libraries. There has been only a reliance on brief and general orientation lectures or tours at the beginning of the students' freshman year with no bibliographical lectures or discussions by librarians integrated with courses at the exact time students have need of such assistance. My findings, I am sad to say, confirmed both hypotheses.

But what are the students who do come to the reference desk in undergraduate libraries asking? During the two periods of monitoring questions at the Michigan Undergraduate Library, brief information and directional questions accounted for 48 percent and 53 percent of the totals with the more substantial reference questions (which required the use of library resources and more time on the part of the librarian) amounting to 52 percent and 47 percent. At the Uris Library, information questions were 32 percent and 40 percent while reference questions were 66 percent and 59 percent.

Bibliographical assistance with the library's own catalog and holdings constituted the bulk of the reference questions. There was very little assistance with the holdings of other campus libraries. In only one instance in 1,191 reference questions was there assistance with noncampus holdings. Although the official philosophies of reference services for undergraduates portray the librarian as teacher, little personal instruction is given in the use of the library or any of its resources. Retrieval of factual, nonbibliographical information took place more often than instruction. Librarians rarely counseled students in a reader's advisory capacity.

What was happening at the same time at the reference desks in the main library? At Michigan during the October week, the Undergraduate Library reference librarians were serving almost seven times the number of undergraduates as were served by the reference staff in the General Library. Undergraduates comprised 21 percent of the persons asking questions at the General Library's reference desk. During the November monitoring, the Undergraduate Library staff served over five times as many undergraduates as did the General Library staff. During this second period, undergraduates asked 23 percent of the questions in the General Library.

Cornell presented a contrasting situation. During both periods, the reference librarians in the main library served almost as many undergraduates as did the reference staff in the Uris Library. Undergraduates also formed a slightly higher proportion of the total users of the Olin Library Reference Department —23 percent the first week and 34 percent the second week.

What kind of responses are students getting to their questions? They are receiving very brief assistance—from a few seconds for some information questions to a few minutes for reference questions. Of the 961 reference questions asked at the Michigan Undergraduate Library, only in 19 instances did the librarians spend more than five minutes with the students. At the Uris Library, the librarian assisted the student for over five minutes in only eight of 230 reference questions.

Leaving the case studies briefly, more subjective impressions will be given of the calibre of reference service that students receive in many libraries, not just in the limited number of case studies. Librarians, in too many instances, make no attempt to understand what the students are trying to ask. The student asks a hesitant question which is not what he really wants to know. The librarian, however, answers the question and makes no attempt to get at what was actually wanted. At some reference desks, one has a feeling of watching a traffic cop pointing to possible locations of information. There is little exchange, little dialogue, little interplay. The most important first step in giving good reference service is poorly performed. At other reference desks, the librarians must have been chained at birth to their chairs—they are still in the fetal position with heads down and almost hidden from the view of any potential questioner. Only a few reference librarians ever approach students who are clearly perplexed, uncertain, and in need of assistance. Some reference departments give no telephone service. Others have official policies that questions will not be answered over the phone for students. I am *not* describing 1920; I am talking about 1970.

In summary, I believe that reference librarians are reaching few students and that those who are reached sometimes receive poor and indifferent service.

The job of undergraduate libraries has been only half done in the first 20 years. Good study space and small collections have been provided. Most of the time, energy, and money has been spent in these areas. The same effort, or even greater effort, must be put into reference and other services—and the advertising of these services. One of the places to start in this unfinished task is with the faculty. Faculty members are a key to successful and meaningful use of an academic library. Unless the faculty know and respect how much a librarian can assist students, the great potential of undergraduate libraries will never be realized. But first, last, and always, librarians must get intimately involved with students. We can no longer sit comfortably at our reference desks waiting for something to happen. I used to think that this was a hopelessly romantic dream, but I now know that this mix of students, faculty, and librarians can be attained. It exists at the Lilly Library of Earlham College. Evan Far-ber, James Kennedy, and the other Earlham librarians give superb reference service and have an excellent library instruction program. They know and work intimately with the students and faculty.

The times cry out for every undergraduate library to become as good as the Earlham College Library. Instructional methods are gradually shifting from textbooks, reserve books, and lectures to independent study, seminars, and reading courses. Today's students resent the monolithic and impersonal character of universities. As Fay Blake reported on a paper given by C. R. Haywood at a conference on the Library-College movement:

> Paternalistic, impersonal, undemocratic academic libraries are hung up on their own efficiency and develop acquisitions and reference departments which are neither student-oriented or student-determined. . . . To the undergraduate it must often appear that mechanization has become the library's raison d'être, and that the ultimate goal of the academic library is to narrow human contacts to the last possible minimum. When the institution as a whole adopts such an impersonal bureaucratic stance, the student demonstrates. When the library follows suit, he is more likely simply to avoid it—so far, at least.[14]

My experience on university campuses strongly confirms this. As we interviewed students using the union catalogs, several of them wanted to talk to us. They were not so much interested in talking about the library as they were in discussing the university. What they said can be summed up in one sentence: "The university doesn't give a damn about its undergraduates."

American universities in the 1970s must either get out of undergraduate education or they must do a much better job than was done in the 1960s. If universities want to flourish as centers of undergraduate education, let us start with undergraduate libraries fulfilling their promise.

REFERENCES

1. Frederick H. Wagman, "The Case for the Separate Undergraduate Library," *College and Research Libraries*, March 1956, p. 150.
2. Sir Thomas Bodley. *Letters of Sir Thomas Bodley to Thomas James*. ed. by G. W. Wheeler. Oxford, 1926, p. 18.
3. Columbia University, Library. *Report of the Librarian*, 1906-07.
4. Keyes D. Metcalf, "The Lamont Library, Part II, Function," *Harvard Library Bulletin*, Winter 1949, p. 12-30. Morrison C. Haviland, "The Reference Function of the Lamont Library," *Harvard Library Bulletin*, Spring 1949, p. 297-99. Philip J. McNiff, "The Charging System of the Lamont Library," *Harvard Library Bulletin*, Spring 1949, p. 438-40. Philip J. McNiff & Edwin E. Williams, "Lamont Library: the First Year," *Harvard Library Bulletin*, Spring 1950, p. 203-12. Richard O. Pautzsch, "The Classification Scheme for the Lamont Library," *Harvard Library Bulletin*, Winter 1950, p. 126-27. Henry R. Shepley, "The Lamont Library, Part I, Design," *Harvard Library Bulletin*, Winter 1949, p. 5-11. Edwin E. Williams, "The Selection of Books for Lamont," *Harvard Library Bulletin*, Autumn 1949, p. 386-94.
5. Keyes D. Metcalf, "Harvard Faces Its Library Problems," *Harvard Library Bulletin*, Spring 1949, p. 185.
6. *Ibid.*, p. 185-86.
7. *Ibid.*, p. 187.
8. Shepley, p. 5.
9. Irene A. Braden. *The Undergraduate Library*. ACRL Monographs No. 31, ALA, 1970.
10. Warren B. Kuhn, "Undergraduate Libraries in a University," *Library Trends*, October 1969, p. 188-209.
11. Elizabeth Mills, "The Separate Undergraduate Library," *College and Research Libraries*, March 1968, p. 144-56.
12. Robert H. Muller, "The Undergraduate Library Trend at Large Universities," in *Advances in Librarianship*, ed. by Melvin J. Voigt. Academic, 1970, p. 113-32.
13. Jerrold Orne, "The Undergraduate Library," *Library Journal*, June 15, 1970, p. 2230-33.
14. Fay Blake, "The Library-College Movement Dying of Old Age at Thirty: A Personal View," *Wilson Library Bulletin*, January 1970, p. 558-59.

Ivory Tower Ghettoes

Bill Hinchliff

EVERY ONE OF US is involved to some extent in converting the world into one vast "Auschwitz." Like Eichman, we execute antihuman orders from above. Being aware of fiendish phenomena, observing but not protesting, is comparable to the attitudes which prevailed while the Nazis were gassing and incinerating millions of Jews. Sane scientists—there are many —give us less than a 50-50 chance of surviving to the year 2000 unless we alter our death-dealing course.

Our nation has become a war-lubricated techno-corporate state. Universities, financial institutions, and labor unions have joined the military-industrial "cosa nostra." Deluges of death-dealing dollars have radically altered our national economy. War industry has plenty of money with which to "influence public policy." The same suicidal syndrome has seized other "major powers" and is spreading to all industrialized nations. It means war after war after war. It means one, two, three, four, five, six lobbyists per politician. It means socially irresponsible associations outworking us on Capitol Hill.

In each of the world's "great cities" and each of the world's major universities the problems are compounding. Smoldering discontent has given way to blind rage. Peaceful leaders have been displaced by ruthless ones.

As media distributors we must try to understand our media-polluted, war-prone, pseudo-civilization. We must try to understand the tyranny of television which haunts our children; makes actors and politicians interchangeable; prevents us from thinking about the real world. Truth needed for survival is buried under piles of . . . ugh!

The human race will go down the drain unless librarians and other responsible knowledge distributors help citizens to cut the media fog and focus knowledge on crucial problems in ways that will lead to effective remedies. The Social Responsibilities movement and the new Congress for Change represent American librarians' perhaps last opportunity to use their knowledge and leadership talents for human survival.

As Buell Gallagher put it: "A society that does not correct its own ills cannot expect peace." Can we expect our hungry, rottenly-housed, poorly clothed, intermittently employed, education-deprived, police-abused brothers, and our war-forced sons to be "socially responsible"? If you had to endure those conditions, would you be socially responsible? Yet they are often far more socially responsible than we comfortable librarians.

Our democracy is an unfinished experiment. It is late. The clock moves faster. Are we too timid, too obsessed with trivia? Shouldn't we join our impatient black brothers and our restless students to wake the people up? Including our fellow librarians?

Our most notable failure is in the realm of human relations: recruiting and developing librarians able to serve all students, including black students, effectively. We attend to *things* better than we attend to *people*. Many of us minimize human contacts and some of us avoid them altogether. Some of us concentrate on serving faculty, graduate students, and undergraduate elite students. How many of us would care to canvass our respective student populations for their criticisms and suggestions, and then discuss the results with student leaders, and follow through with corrective action?

Conventional library philosophy, like so much of our conventional wisdom, has lost its power. ALA standards for college and university libraries are obsolete. The Standards Committee does not meet often enough. It needs new members, fresh ideas.

The time has come to publicize the best, most innovative university and college libraries as the Knapp Project publicized the best school libraries; to facilitate much heavier use of the most important, most socially relevant media; to involve faculty and students who are not reached by conventional practices.

What might a team of economists say about college libraries? That costs are rising, efficiency falling, staff and users' time being wasted, backlogs higher, productivity lower, cost controls lacking, quality controls nonexistent, busy-work abundant, mechanization stalled, obsolete activities maintained? That most college libraries are weak, bogged down, underutilized?

What might a team of psychologists and sociologists say about attitudes toward college libraries? That faculty and students feel their resources are inaccessible; librarians unknowable; that librarians' efforts to gain understanding are feeble; that some teachers view the library staff as rivals, exposers of teachers' limitations, potential diverters of students' interest? Would the psychologists and the sociologists agree that bored, frustrated librarians create their own emotional ghettoes?

Might they not suggest that psychologists and sociologists be added to college library staffs, that they study faculty attitudes toward media and toward independent study; discover how some teachers motivate their students to read a great deal; help involve faculty and students in reorganizing the library for greater effectiveness?

Large-scale behavioral research would probably not only confirm the findings of Shores, Jordan, Knapp, Gaver, Monroe, Wasserman, and Bundy on the failures of conventional libraries, but might result in a recommendation for a million-dollar filmed "master course" in media utilization. Such a filmed course, while not a panacea, could multiply public understanding and use of libraries.

The quality of the college library depends not only on able, socially responsible staff members, but also upon the leadership, social commitment, and media sophistication of the faculty, the top-level college administration, and its governing board.

Is the college's "governing establishment" sensitive to human needs and willing to commit the college to the pursuit of a less destructive, more just, society? To focus the college's available knowledge and skill upon the removal of obstacles to the advancement of the people of the community? Do the college's policy-makers and leaders read and discuss the most authoritative sources on war and peace; racism; urban problems; the student rebellion; the social effects of the mass media? Do they favor a less regimented curriculum and more independent study? Do they recognize the fundamental importance of media utilization?

Is the purpose of education to stimulate independent thinking or is it to condition young people to submit, to obey, and to kowtow? If the latter is the case, college libraries should be abolished. Required textbooks will suffice. To the extent that students do not realize the liberating power of their libraries, college librarians have failed.

So let's attend closely to the young men and women for whom the college library exists. Unlike their forefathers, they refuse to submit to boredom, intimidation, indoctrination, and exploitation. Increasingly they refuse to be ignored, mistreated, or subjected to unreasonable, capricious, discriminatory military and educational compulsion. They are bitter toward bureaucracies that retard progress and degrade people. They want less emphasis on hardware, more emphasis on human beings.

A measure of the effectiveness of a college library is the quality and quantity of two-way communication between librarians and students. Do the librarians know how students feel about their college library? Are students' impressions, opinions, and suggestions for library improvement actively solicited, respected, acted on? Do most students feel that their library is irresistible or do they feel it is *unattractive*?

The movement toward student published course and teacher evaluation is spreading. Perhaps student evaluation of college libraries and librarians will come next. Some successful college libraries, anticipating this development, have placed suggestion boxes at heavy traffic points and have promptly posted "action taken" answers and explanations. Many progressive college libraries have student-faculty library committees which consider library problems, recommend solutions, and participate in planning better policies, services, and resources.

What responses could your college library administrators offer to a dele-gation of faculty members and students asking such questions as these: What major improvements in service has the library made recently? What service improvements are scheduled? What are you doing to increase faculty and student media sophistication and use?

Do you have accurate records of complaints? Books and other media requested but not supplied? Reference queries not answered? Waiting time for books to be retrieved from closed stacks? Photocopying service? Faculty members who do *not* use the library? Students who do *not* use the library? Cataloged titles lost, strayed, or stolen? Average time elapsed from selection of a new title to its availability on the shelf and in the catalog? Based on this information, what actions are taken?

College library collections: What proportion of them will never be used? How many college libraries have aggressive acquisition programs on racism; militarism; urban rot; sex; drugs; crime; political, bureaucratic, and police corruption; mental illness; capital punishment; and world government? How many have respectable holdings on Africa, Asia, and Latin America? When will college libraries begin to supply new books as fast as bookstores do, and receive the same discount?

Are most college libraries hopelessly behind with respect to the flood of non-print media: phonograph records, tapes, films, slides? How many college libraries are acquiring some of the interesting experimental motion pictures which are being produced by college students?

When will cataloging arrearages become a nightmare of the past? What would the hypothetical team of consulting psychologists say about the depressing effects of card catalogs upon those who must use them? Might they recommend that our new book catalogs become motivational as well as informational devices? That they use illustrations, photographs, cartoons, excerpts, and quotations, with color, style, and flair? Publishers' catalogs: Bantam. Grove, Doubleday, New American Library, Ballantine, Simon & Schuster, and of course, the New York Graphic Society catalogs are irresistible. We should learn from them.

How about our bibliographies? Do we confine them to "safe" subjects? What results do they produce? Would they be more effective if they dealt with major issues and were printed in the college newspaper? What if an urban college library cooperated with the public library, the leading newspapers, and the leading TV broadcasters in promoting selective, annotated bibliographies of paperbound books and other low-cost media on socially crucial subjects? A community resident would simply telephone the college library and receive by return mail a media-packet containing all of the items in the bibliography; he would thereby become an extension student.

Media utilization and educational effectiveness could be rapidly increased by providing "free" packets of course-required media to students at registration. At an estimated cost of less than $100 per student per year this measure would increase students' achievement, reduce their frustration, and raise morale very substantially. It would reduce strains on the library and on the bookstore. The cost of the proposed media packets would subsequently be repaid by the students themselves through taxation.

Prevailing book and media display practices fail somehow to uplift the human spirit. What if new multi-media shelving were designed which would attractively exhibit all types of media on a subject of major social importance? What if this multi-media display contained a special section for FREE materials: catalogs, lists, bibliographies, syllabi, reprints, reviews, guides, pictures, and pamphlets? Another special section for SALE materials: paperbacks, maps, posters, discs, kits, replicas, slides, and diagrams? Another section for the usual LOAN items? Another section for NONCIRCULATING REFERENCE works? These collections on subjects of greatest interest could be arranged in attractive bays with lounge chairs and "wet" carrels at hand. Although they would take up more space, much heavier media utilization would follow. Media-circulated-per-square-foot is a more relevant ratio than media-stored-per-square-foot.

A special exhibit version of the new model shelving loaded with media on a currently pressing social problem could be placed at the college's heaviest traffic point. An attractive "new image" librarian could be stationed there to explain it to students who have not yet been "hooked on the library." The new model media counselor would also engage in recruitment. She, or he, would probably talk with more unsuspecting potential librarians than would be possible in any other context. The library manpower crisis is no myth. Thousands of librarians are approaching, or have already passed retirement age, but they continue to fill key positions for which younger, more aggressive librarians are better qualified. Thousands are equipped neither by training nor by inclination to reach out with new, more effective media services to the poorly served black children and youth of the inner cities.

Recruitment: the most conspicuous disaster of contemporary library leadership! Who plans and directs recruitment for your library? Does he visit library schools and college placement offices, including that of your own college? What are his demonstrated recruitment skills? How effective are his interviews? Are group interviews conducted? Do students and subprofessionals participate? Are detailed records of interviews kept?

Does your library have a recruitment brochure or information kit? What is in it? Do you have position descriptions? Are they true? Do they describe the actual work? Do they sound as if Great Aunt "Bureaucratia" had written them?

Your job offers: are they being accepted? Are your starting salaries and fringe benefits competitive? Do you pay, or share, costs of candidates' visits? Are such visits carefully planned? In your library are beginning librarians given challenging, diversified, growth-conducive work? Who appraises the recruitment program?

Does anyone analyze your library's staff turnover, especially the reasons why you may be losing your best younger librarians? What libraries are attracting them? Why? Has your library a well-budgeted staff development program and a well-understood promotional ladder by which an aide may become a technician, a technician an intern; an intern a librarian, media counselor or specialist, and on up to an administrator? Do black librarians have equal opportunities for promotion to administrative posts?

The nation needs at least 100,000 new librarians to meet minimum standards which are already obsolete, particularly with respect to inner-city media services. Of these at least 15,000 should be black, including at least 8000 males. The members of the American Library Association should hammer out an enlightened national library manpower policy and action program including definite specifications for recruitment of blacks, especially males. Black librarians communicate, inspire, and motivate young black people more effectively than presently available whites.

There is no surer way for librarians to help end racism in this country than to recruit large numbers of talented, warm-hearted, socially responsible young black men and women to become children's, school, college, public, special librarians, and library administrators. Prejudice takes root in the very young. It must be stopped there. Our libraries need thousands of black librarians, a few of whom, in addition to their "regular duties," may do for libraries what the Holts, Hentoffs, and Herndons, the Kozols, Kaufmans, and

Kohls have done for ghetto schools. I don't mean that those authors were black, but that they exposed horrible conditions.

Black males are needed for many powerful reasons, chief of which is their ability to encourage and to convince ghetto children, particularly boys and youth, that education, libraries, books, and media are respectable and necessary to survival and progress.

The members of the American Library Association should raise five million dollars for a ten-year program to recruit 1500 black graduates per year for preprofessional internships or for immediate entrance to accredited library schools. The job must be done even if it costs ten million dollars. This is like a mere trace of moisture in the bucket when compared with the social costs which result from the failure of city people to educate their heirs. It is less than *one millionth* of our total national warfare expenditures which are at a rate of *over a trillion dollars per decade.* Over $5000 of military spending for every man, woman, and child in the United States of America!

The cause of the relative failure of college libraries is not too few *ideas* for programs, but too few librarians willing to support them; too few librarians willing to agree on priorities; too few librarians with the leadership, guts, energy, and persistence to bring about desperately needed changes. Successful innovation requires vast cooperation, tremendous thought, unremitting effort.

Let's shoulder our share of responsibility for constructive concerted action on society's major problems. Ivory towers, like lilywhite suburbs, are ghettoes too.

Working at Federal City College has convinced me that whites will gain as much—personally, I believe more—from the complete emancipation of blacks as blacks will gain. Understanding, mutual respect, pride, and affection will replace ignorance, prejudice, fear, rage, and violence. Instead of sitting busily out of it, we will have been in there digging it.

Ordeal at San Francisco State College

Barbara Anderson

ABOUT THIS TIME last year I read my horoscope for 1969 and it said, "This is the year to improve your life and to experiment in new areas . . . you will be making money by bizarre means. . . . " Come January, I found myself being pressed into such work-related library tasks as: a) hunting through book stacks for "suspicious looking objects" (especially those that might be ticking), b) sniffing out the sources of "stink bomb smell" and disposing of said objects, c) crossing picket lines daily with shouts of "scab," "fink," and other less delicate epithets ringing in my ears.

How did it all begin? I think our story was sufficiently publicized to forego all but the basic details in order to refresh your memories. On November 5, 1968, a group of students from the Black Student Union presented our then President Robert Smith with a list of ten "nonnegotiable" demands. Among other things, the demands ordered the college to establish at once a Black Studies Department with 20 full-time faculty members. They insisted that the new department be controlled by its faculty and staff, free from interference by college administrators or the statewide Board of Trustees. They also demanded that the college

accept all black students who should apply for admission in the fall of 1969 without regard to the academic qualifications of the applicants or the numbers that might apply.

The students were aiming at a crash program for the immediate and massive upgrading of the education of blacks in order to break the cycle of poverty in which they are trapped. They felt, perhaps rightly, that only through such drastic efforts could enough black teachers and community workers be trained to return to their communities with a new sense of black identity and goals of more relevant education in order to change the situation in which they lived. They claimed self-determination over their lives. They recognized that it was through education that they could rise out of the ghettos in which they were born, and they saw that the education they were receiving in the ghetto schools did not prepare them for admission to college. They also pointed out, correctly that the percentage of black students admitted to San Francisco State College had been gradually diminishing over the years, from ten percent in 1958 to less than four percent in 1968.

President Smith was unable, either administratively or legally, to agree to

290

all of the students' demands; he offered to discuss them with the students. They refused, insisting on a yes-or-no answer to all ten demands. The next day, November 6, the black students launched their strike against the college. Soon after, the Third World Liberation Front, a loose confederation of Chicanos, Latinos, Philippine-Americans, Chinese-Americans, and Japanese-Americans joined in the strike with a parallel five demands asking for acceptance of all nonwhite students who apply for the fall semester of 1969 and that 50 full-time faculty positions be appropriated to the School of Ethnic Studies, 20 of which would be for the Black Studies program. A week later 65 faculty members joined the students on the picket lines.

In the following weeks, the college was the scene of violence unmatched in the history of American higher education. At first, tactics took the form of daily rallies after which the strikers would break into groups and go through the buildings where classes were in session, yelling in the halls and pounding on the doors, or, in many cases, entering classes, dismissing class, sometimes knocking students out of their chairs, and physically confronting the professor. Two reading rooms in the library were disturbed in this way; students were shoved out of their seats as they studied. Small fires were set in restrooms, pictures were taken from the walls, a few windows were broken. Campus security at this time was only in the form of plainclothesmen throughout the campus. Strikers attacked two campus security officers, who carry no billy clubs and no guns.

Eventually, as the administration and the Trustees showed no response (indeed, two of the demands would require an act of the State Legislature to meet), the 15 demands were no longer the major issue on campus. The medium of the power struggle and the strike itself became the message; the protest became an end in itself. The campus became occupied by police on a con-

tinuous basis over several months and it was only the daily presence of 200 to 600 policemen which kept the college open from the start of the strike on November 6 to the end of the fall semester.

In January, the American Federation of Teachers local at San Francisco State also went on strike, partly for their own demands and partly in support of the student strike. By the end of the semester there had been 731 arrests on campus, more than 80 students had been reported injured as they were arrested, and others were hurt and not arrested. Thirty-two policemen were injured on campus. Damage to the campus buildings exceeded $16,000; there were scores of small fires and a major one in a vice-president's office. Eight bombs were planted on campus, and two fire-bombs were hurled at and into the home of an assistant to the president . . . and so on; you have read the stories.

In the Middle

During all this, I was probably the prime example of "fence sitter" on our staff. It was people such as myself who made up what the press liked to label "the silent majority." We were not really apathetic: indecisive is the better term. We were not blind or oblivious to the problems; rather, we were torn among the issues flying around us. We were the people who found most of the famous 15 demands reasonable, and just a few of them unreasonable. We were people who recognized the plight of our minorities and were well aware of the history of racial injustice in this country and of the need for massive and drastic measures to be taken to improve their lot. We were people who also understood the miseries of dealing with an impersonal bureaucratic structure which is bound by duly passed legal rules and regulations which take time in the democratic process to change. In short, we were people who understood what is meant by the thing the students like to call "The System" or "The Establishment" and were somewhat in sympathy with their frustrations.

On the other hand we also recognized that blind emotional reaction to long standing injustices was not the answer either. Basic realities of life such as legal authority, definitely outlined programs, budgetary allocations, and procedures for implementation also had to be part of the picture; if they were not, a signature approving 15 demands would be a meaningless gesture.

Those of us who chose to remain at work became part of "The Establishment." The significant realization of the strike was that it affected everyone, at all levels of the institution from the top administrators down to the custodians and gardeners. Everyone was involved; everyone was faced with day-to-day decisions about matters that were often so complex that he was thrust into agonizing reappraisals of his total value systems. Various factions on the various issues arose: Pro-student strike vs. Anti-student strike, Pro-all 15 demands vs. Pro-part of the 15 demands, Pro-AFT strike vs. Anti-AFT strike, Pro-police on campus vs. Anti-police on campus, Faculty control vs. Administration control, even Pro-violence vs. Anti-violence. Attitudes toward these issues did not necessarily follow a regular pattern. People were selective. For example, they may have been for the student strike, but against the AFT strike. They may have been against the student strike, but also against having police on campus. There was no regular "party line."

We were faced with seemingly endless petitions for one cause or another; whether one signed or didn't sign placed him in one category or another, and in the supercharged emotional atmosphere of the time, signing or not signing petitions either insured the friendship or incurred the enmity of the petition bearer, who was often a long-standing friend. Indeed, this was the most frustrating tactic of the strike. The entire confrontation plan was to polarize the sides in order to "radicalize the liberals." Thus when faced with a viewpoint on the 15 demands, one either had to be for *all* 15 demands and if not, was thereby considered to be against *all* 15 demands. There was no possibility of being for perhaps 11 or 12 of the demands; if you were not for all of them, you were against all of them.

It is a very effective confrontation tactic for it simplifies the conflict into "good guys" vs. "bad guys" and regardless of complexities, compels the split into opposing factions. At this point the common expression to be heard was "I agree with the principles, but not the methods." This became a well-worn cliché by the end of the strike.

As there was no possibility for a middle-of-the-road position in the view of the strikers, if you were not out on strike in the picket lines, you were thus considered to be a "Racist Fascist." And thus, we all became part of the problem. Those of us who chose to remain on the job arrived at work through a barrage of unprintable invectives (formerly unprintable, that is); we stayed at work amid the adverse conditions of bomb threats, stink bombs, cherry bombs, and the like. We also suffered through all the usual conscience pangs of the liberal.

Library One-Upmanship

How did all of this turmoil affect the library and what were the problems we faced and the responses that we made? The library did anticipate some of the problems and pressures. Months in advance (i.e. as much as six months to a year before any of the demonstrations) we were taking note of the movements toward Black Studies and Ethnic Studies. As responsive librarians, we naturally set about ordering the important books and periodicals in these fields. Bibliographic sources for materials on the various ethnic studies areas were searched out, ordered and a bibliography of these was prepared early in the summer of 1968.

When dealing with the initial planners of the Black Studies and Mexican-American Studies departments, again long before the strike began, we suggested that they select a library department with which to affiliate, thereby having a librarian who would be designated as responsible for dealing with their particular library problems. Nathan Hare chose to affiliate the Black Studies Department with the Social Science Library; Juan Martinez selected the Education Library for the Mexican-Americans. What the Social Science Librarian and the Education Librarian did was to keep constantly "tuned-in" to anything and everything involving these subject areas. They suggested purchases, prepared special bibliographies, did special searches, answered correspondence, helped student assistants working for those departments, and, in general, became the clearinghouse and designated liaison for the library. This has been quite successful because there are clear lines of administrative responsibility. The activities of the library for these areas proceeded throughout the strike. Despite the picketing, shouting, and bloodshed, we continued building our book collections, sometimes even with the assistance of those nominally on strike. When the strike was over and the Black Studies Department and the School of Ethnic Studies actually began functioning, the library had the needed materials for them.

Whenever interested students or faculty members came into the library to inquire about library holdings in the various ethnic areas, they were asked to "Give us a list of what you feel you need; it would be helpful if you would check the card catalog to see if we have the books first." They usually went away all fired up to prepare their lists. What they most often found was that the library already had nearly everything they wanted. Few lists were actually submitted. We then offered the aforementioned bibliography of sources as a guide so they would have some means to make further selections of materials about which they did not know. A few submitted lists of various local ethnic periodicals; we placed subscriptions for about 20 of these.

It is my feeling that the above procedures were one reason for the fact that we have not yet had pressures brought upon us to set up a separate Black Studies or Ethnic Studies room in the library. We have been playing a game of library one-upmanship and so far we have won.

Damage and Morale

As for the issue of what happened to our library during the strike, this discussion has two facets: 1) What damage or what pressures from outside were brought to bear on the library? and 2) What effect did the campus turmoil have on the internal morale of the library staff? These were not entirely separate issues, as nothing was during the strike, but both have to be considered in order to have a total picture of the problems faced on a campus in crisis.

The library became the choice vantage point for demonstration watching. Our library faces the central quadrangle of the campus. There are three floors of unobstructed viewing windows overlooking the area where most of the demonstrations were held. Depending on the particular day's activities, great crowds would congregate at the windows on all three floors to watch the happenings from the safety of the building, and many of the television shots were taken from library windows. On this side of the building, the noise of the loudspeakers and the shouting and yelling was often so disturbing that little work could go on; however, on the other side of the building which faced the street, work proceeded as usual except when a student assistant would burst in with stories of the events taking place outside. Watching from the vantage point of the library was an experience not to be forgotten. On the day of the massive demonstration which drew in local civic leaders, there were thousands marching around and around the central square on campus all shouting "On Strike, Shut it Down." Regardless of where you stood on the issues, it was a most impressive display of strength, one that all who looked on could not help but observe with some awe.

As for action against the library, as the strike wore on, the library, like every other building on campus, became regarded as part of "The Establishment." Efforts to close down the campus were felt in the library in terms of gradual forays of harassment. At no time did we feel that the strikers were anti-library so much as just anti-Establishment. The strike demanded the closing of the entire campus until the 15 demands were met; thus any building remaining open became an enemy camp. The actions felt by the library were similar to those being felt all over the campus:

We had bomb threats. Our library has had a history of bomb threats over the past several years, so this wasn't a new problem, except that the threats became more frequent as the strike wore on. Our procedure soon became to "avoid undue alarm," to call the campus security officers, and to set out in search of suspicious looking objects in the book stacks, waste baskets, restrooms, etc. This became a rather blasé operation at first; that is, until the first actual bomb was found on campus outside a faculty member's office. We then began to have second thoughts every time we received such a call. One of the rather memorable comments at the time came from a member of the Presidio Bomb Squad; he described his procedure upon finding a suspicious looking object: "When it starts to swell, run like hell."

There was a book-in. It came midway in the strike and was aimed at making the library shut down. The students didn't bother with checking out the books, but merely wandered around our open stacks pulling off the books and placing them on the floors, or on the tables, or on other shelves, or even on different floors of the building. It involved literally thousands and thousands of books misplaced all over the library. The problem was compounded by our centralized shelving situation and open stacks. Most of the student shelvers had gone out on strike in sympathy with the 15 demands. As you might expect, after four months of almost no shelvers, combined with massive harassment, we had books stacked all over the floors and all over the tables. It was impossible to track down a particular title. After the press reports on the situation, we had numerous calls from people who volunteered to come and help us. These were frustrated and concerned citizens and neighbors who had been reading of our strife for months and were desperate to find some way in which they could do something to help. They were housewives, faculty wives, high school students, women's clubs, and even an army colonel. One weekend, we had as many as 50 volunteer workers. We even had a wonderful little lady from the neighborhood who claimed, "I have supported revolutionary causes all my life, but when they touch books, that's the end!" On the weekend that these people came to volunteer their help, they faced harassment from the regular library student shelvers who supported the strike. To enter the library, they had to pass through the usual revolutionary verbal abuse to which we librarians had become accustomed. As the afternoon wore on, the students decided to move their harassment inside. They circulated around the book stacks shouting "Scabs! Scabs!" at the volunteer workers. One faculty wife, a big buxom woman, had come equipped with a police whistle. At the arrival of the students she began blasting away.

It became rather like a slapstick comedy scene.

We had stink bombs. For those of you who have not yet been treated with such things, these so-called "bombs" are really small laboratory bottles filled with a clear liquid which has an extremely vile odor and can be nauseous. The technique was to bring the bottles in brown paper bags, walk to a stack area, open the bottles, dribble some of the liquid on the floors and then walk off leaving the open bottle, lid, etc. on the book shelves or on the floor. Our main problem was to get rid of these in order to stop the smell. Sometimes the little lids of liquid were very cleverly hidden behind the books and it meant running around sniffing like bloodhounds for the strongest scent in order to detect the cause, for if we didn't find it, the smell would continue to grow stronger. The Chemistry Department analyzed the liquids and pronounced them "non-toxic," but nevertheless, the smell was so vile that for all practical purposes library work in the chosen areas came to a halt. We opened windows and sent out for aerosol spray. Some even lit little blocks of incense; others splashed cologne round. After a while the incense and aerosol spray was equally as foul. I might add, that scrub as we might, the liquid did not wash off the floors with soap and water; it lingered on for months afterwards. In some areas, we can still smell it. The Chemistry Department never found an effective neutralizer. They did suggest that we air out the books that had been splashed in order to protect the pages.

We had cherry bombs. Cherry bombs are like big fire crackers. (They are the things that make the loudest bangs during Chinese New Year and Fourth of July celebrations.) The technique was to slide a cigarette over the wick, to light the cigarette and lay it on the book shelves in the stacks and walk off. When the cigarette burned down to the wick, the blast was not serious enough to damage the books, but it frightened anyone who happened to be in the area. One of our student assistants found one of these objects that had burned out before going off. The librarian took it to a policeman who was stationed in the library. He told her that all it would take is a small spark to have it go off and had it gone off in her hand as she brought it to him, she could have lost a hand.

The card catalog came in for various sorts of abuse. The abuse was done surreptitiously and we are not even sure we know of all the attempts made against it to this day. One day glue was found in a few card trays, another day, handfuls of catalog cards were found in the sink in a women's restroom. The Hayakawa entries had been removed one day. Some cards were found in a women's restroom in the Administration building wrapped in paper with the message "On Strike, Shut it Down." Library response was first to station a worker in the card catalog area to watch over the situation; later we rearranged the card catalog to allow better surveillance of the area. We have also had the author-title catalog microfilmed since the strike.

Other harassments included such things as small fires in the restroom wastebaskets, clogged toilets, broken windows, slashed tires in the library parking lot, and paint sprayed on restroom walls with the message, "On Strike, Shut it Down."

Carrying On

Throughout the period of harassment, we still managed to continue doing things that come naturally to librarians: we kept a bibliography of the articles about the strike, a giant scrapbook of the newsclippings was prepared, and collections of leaflets and broadsides that had been handed out on campus by the various striking and anti-striking organizations were sorted out and arranged by name of organization (AFT, BSU, SDS, etc.) and date. This collection numbered over 800 items and has been microfilmed. Written copies of the addresses given by our faculty members on the strike were solicited, posters done by the Art Department were secured, and the college Audio-Visual Department collected copies of the KQED video-tape of the convocation and the student-produced video-tapes.

Facing the Issues

In regards to the issue of library staff morale, as the harassment tactics escalated, police were assigned to each floor of the library and often several more were on duty on the first floor on particularly bad days. Pro and anti-cop factions among the library staff arose and discussions raged on about whether police were really necessary on campus. As time wore on, we became so obsessed with the strike that few of us could discuss anything else; we talked and debated and went through all sorts of internal agonies; some friendships were broken. It was apparent that the police were necessary for the protection of property, but some felt that rather than having police, we should shut down. Others felt (myself included) that if the library closed down, the entire campus could well have followed, for sheer employee jealousy would take over—the "why are they off and not us?" type of thing. Petty as it sounds in a crisis situation, it does happen.

The question of the real value or virtue in closing down the entire campus was also a matter of lively discussion for the battle cry and seeming objective of the whole strike was: "On Strike, Shut It Down." Opinions were as varied as confused. Questions regarding matters of ethics and values were in the forefront: How can we go on with our work as usual when chaos is going on all around us? Do we not have an obligation to some ethical and moral standards? Do we not have an obligation to show the students that we are not part of The Establishment so they

will not damage the library? Should we not, as a staff, take a stand on the issues? When then about the dissenters? Do they not have rights too? What is our obligation to the students who want to use the library even though there are riots outside? Are we somehow morally different because we are a storehouse of information? Do we not have an obligation to make materials available to people with all viewpoints just as we feel that we have an obligation to house within our libraries materials of all viewpoints? These questions led to the consideration of such thoughts as: Are conditions in our society at this stage so bad that remaining neutral is being part of the problem? Are conditions such that these excesses are warranted? In short, it all comes down to one question: does the end justify the means? At this point you might ask, was the battle really against the S.F. State administration since the administration clearly did not have the legal authority to grant the 15 demands even if it had wanted to? Or, was it really against the Trustees? Or the Governor? Ultimately, it was concerned with the whole "System" itself. If closing down S.F. State was the means, what kind of end was expected? Would the closing of the college really have accomplished the aims of the 15 demands—that is, more and better education for nonwhites? Or, was a different "end" really implied?

As we went through some pretty harrowing days, internal conflicts arose in the library over staff safety and welfare and over whether the building should close down for the safety of the employees. The types of questions that arose are: If someone is afraid, should they be permitted to go home? If you let that person go, then what about everyone else? What do you do about the person who is easily excited? Or the one who is hypertense? People have different fear levels; what may make one person terribly frightened, may not bother another person at all. Should then, the library be closed down every time one person is afraid? On the other hand, should that person be made to sit at work if he is really in fear? Furthermore, what happens when threats become so common as to be as frequent as every day? And on another level: What does one do about rumors? Rumors fly around constantly in crisis situations. We had rumors which frightened staff members. Someone would overhear a remark that students "were going to attack the library on Friday." The rumor would spread and before long there was a petition and a delegation of staff members to close the library for "our safety." There was some feeling that many of these people were not really frightened themselves, but were merely using the issue of staff safety and welfare to pressure the library into closing in support of the strike.

Our main problem was that we had no policy governing riot situations. We had no guidelines with which to work other than an official statement regarding the closing of buildings during emergencies which placed the responsibility in the hands of the college librarian "when the danger is imminent." Just when is imminent danger really imminent? Does it apply only to your building? What if a bomb is detonated in the neighboring building? What if there is a fire reported in a building across the campus quad? What if windows are being shattered in a building half-way across the campus (i.e. a good block away)? These things happen, and they did happen to us.

These are the issues which divide a library staff. In some departments of our library, communication completely broke down as staff chose opposing sides to the issues; in others, they babbled for hours over the issues but at least kept some semblance of rationality. We coped with the situations as best we could; we tried to maintain an understanding of the issues and of the emotions that drove people to join in the confrontation. We sought to maintain an openness and an awareness; a stance of "keeping cool" and "hanging loose." There are no real answers or rules for governing the library in a crisis situation as circumstances always vary. We can only strive to be responsive to problems as they arise and try to remove the basic causes of dissatisfaction, but, in doing this, we must also keep realistic goals in mind as we act for these causes.

College Libraries for Students

Robert P. Haro

WHY SHOULD academic librarians take a keen interest and become more involved in campus problems? Mainly, because we are members of the academic community and have an obligation to students, our colleagues, and society to participate as partners in the educational process, rather than continue to play passive roles. Also, a more active campus role by librarians, quite apart from being an educational responsibility and a vehicle to increased status, will be required if disruptive confrontations between students and academic libraries are to be avoided.

How can academic librarians make their libraries more receptive and responsive to student needs? Fortunately, this task is not impossible. There are three areas in which academic educators and librarians should consider and make necessary changes that should allow more meaningful student participation in the operation, planning, and implementation of library programs and services: 1) students on library advisory committees; 2) library support of experimental college programs and their libraries; and 3) student control of browsing collections. It should be obvious to the reader that the above three areas are interrelated and, also, that they are not the only available avenues

for achieving more meaningful and harmonious student-library relations.

What is the purpose of a college or university library? Mainly, it is established to provide necessary library materials and services to support the teaching and research programs of the institution, with leisure and recreation aspects of secondary importance. Theoretically, the students—undergraduate or graduate—should be the principal beneficiaries. In practice, however, most academic libraries, and especially the larger university ones, are more responsive to faculty and research staff needs than those of the students. In fact, library administrators are so removed from the students that on many of our campuses they are unknown. That the head librarian and his upper echelon library staff should be nonentities, as far as students are concerned, must seriously undermine our cherished belief that the library is "the heart of the campus!" Unfortunately, librarians themselves are mainly to blame for their failure to relate with the students. How can this situation be alleviated and what more can the library do for the students?

At most academic institutions, there is a committee of faculty members that serves as an advisory body to the library. On some campuses, such committees are very influential, often going beyond an advisory capacity to decide on policy for the purchase of library materials and the types of services offered. What about a student voice in how the library is run, what materials are ordered, and what kind of services are offered? Here I propose that academic educators and librarians consider the appointment of graduate and undergraduate students to serve on faculty library advisory committees. Students, after all, deserve as much of a say in library matters as do faculty. Furthermore, students appointed to these advisory committees should share the same responsibilities and duties as faculty members. Otherwise these appointments will be meaningless, and will be rejected by the students as just "tokenism" or a "cop-out." What can students do on such committees?

When new library facilities and services are contemplated, discussed, planned, or under construction, students are seldom provided with a voice in the planning process. At best, they might be allowed to name a new structure or facility once completed. What makes academic librarians, who have too little contact with students, feel they sufficiently understand student needs to dispense with their direct opinions and rely on second hand information from the faculty or other indirect methods in planning and implementing library facilities and services? After all, faculty, through library advisory committees and other means, have an opportunity to express themselves directly concerning these proposed facilities and services. Why not allow students to express *their* desires directly, and on a regular basis, to the library? Meaningful student participation on library advisory committees would do much to identify librarians to students and bring students into a closer association with the library.

As for library materials, they are ordered by faculty and librarians to support established and proposed teaching and research programs. The students are treated more as childlike patients than concerned individuals. The professor and librarian seem to say, "We are ordering some library medicine for you. Take this reading medicine as prescribed and you will be all right." No wonder students ignore the resulting collection and turn to other information sources and centers.

In the beginning of the current wave of student activism action against the library was passive and nondisruptive. The possibility of disruption, if not outright violence, has been amply demonstrated since. Events such as the "library book-in" at San Francisco State College, although it was not undertaken as a protest against the library *per se,* should dramatize for us, as librarians, the potential results if students should take serious issue with library policies or practices. A form of passive resistance to library policies could easily take the form of student libraries, established and run by students.

Across the United States, college students have begun to create their own libraries within experimental colleges. What are experimental colleges? These colleges were established by students to provide them with an opportunity to initiate new courses and experiment with new methods of education. The much publicized course on the Berkeley campus of the University of California involving Eldridge Cleaver was part of this innovation in college education. To satisfy the information needs of these programs, students have taken it upon themselves to create libraries quite apart from the main library systems on their respective campuses. Why have they seen fit to ignore our established academic libraries and create their own? The answer, I believe, is based upon various prejudices and "hang-ups" under which librarians labor; principally, that they are "book bound" and "up-tight" about controversial issues and materials. These two conditions demand further explanation and closer analysis.

Too many librarians are still living in the world of the bound monograph as the major learning and information tool to be possessed by libraries. The book also serves librarians as a highly sophisticated art form. There is really nothing wrong with considering the book as a work of art. However, when this view begins to overshadow and prejudice a librarian's decision-making concerning the format of information which he will select, catalog, store, and retrieve, then he is not adequately serving the student. Our academic libraries reflect this prejudice in various forms. We tend to evaluate an academic library in terms of the number of its bound monographs and serials. We prefer to accession bound monographs and avoid the procedural problems associated with ephemeral and often fugitive nonbook sources of information despite its content.

Students, on the other hand, when they want information on the Third World Liberation Front, or Students for a Democratic Society, or whatever student group, will not find it in a bound format, nor in conventional periodicals. In other words, books about many of the topics which interest students are not available in most college libraries, mainly because of the format in which they appear.

Then too, librarians, bless their souls, are not always the liberals they profess to be. Extramarital sex, contraceptives, drug use, militant racial groups, and underground literature are usually too controversial for most academic libraries to handle, at least openly. Academic libraries, of course, do have erotica collections, rare book rooms, restricted circulation collections, and vertical files in which descriptive literature concerning all or some of these topics may be found. However, the paucity of available, pertinent materials and the restrictions imposed upon their use all but drive students away from these resources.

Students want to know about highly controversial topics and to be able to read about them on short notice, not within certain hours, not after waiting for days until they are secured from another library. They genuinely feel this information is necessary in their learning. When the rules governing this material grow too restrictive, or the material is unavailable, they turn their backs on our academic libraries. Therefore, they have created experimental college libraries to actively solicit these items and make them available with few or no restrictions. Many of these libraries purposely employ nonlibrarians to run them. They have open stacks, and are open on a 24-hour basis. Some of them, in fact, serve as distribution points for highly controversial materials, such as those dealing with draft resistance methods.

The message for academic librarians in the development of experimental college libraries is that something is wrong with our present libraries and services. But the development of experimental college libraries need not be an ominous spectre for academic librarianship. Rather, it can serve as an excellent vehicle for attracting college students to libraries and also allowing greater student-librarian involvement. Librarians should not attempt to duplicate the collections of existing experimental college libraries, hinder their efforts, nor ignore them. Rather, we as librarians should become actively involved with these experimental college libraries in an advisory capacity. Participation should be *strictly* advisory and in the role of a concerned observer only. This involvement should allow librarians many opportunities to communicate with the students. Through such a dialogue, we can more clearly discern student information needs, what library services they want, and how we can best serve them.

Too often browsing collections, if they exist at all, are merely light reading for librarians, faculty, staff, and students. They are often administered with little or no awareness of student interests. At best they are a casual place for students to unwind. For every situation where one finds *Playboy*, the latest records of the Beatles, Miles Davis, or Herb Alpert, there are ten where the librarian favors *Harper's* and *Punch* or Beethoven and Bach, or the materials he thinks students *should* be interested in. It is another instance of the librarian deciding what is good for students without consulting them in a more than casual manner.

I suggest that the library subsidize, on a matching fund basis with the students (perhaps the student government), a browsing collection that would be administered by and for the students. The collections should, ideally, be located outside the main library, in or near a student center. The main library could provide technical advice and assistance necessary to insure smooth operation of the collection. After all, don't most research libraries do as much for certain strong departmental libraries outside their administrative control, especially when the service is supported by influential faculty? If students want to read Marcuse, Reies Tijerina, and *Playboy* or listen to the Beatles, they should have the opportunity. Of course, librarians,

faculty, and staff could have equal right to use the collection and recommend material for it.

The areas I have discussed above—students on library advisory committees, the development of experimental college libraries, and student control of browsing collections—are not ends in themselves, nor are they a panacea for avoiding student-library related problems on our campuses. These suggestions, I hope, will serve more to prod us, as librarians, into questioning some of our traditional beliefs, the sacred cows concerning student-library involvement.

Students are very aware of themselves on our campuses and are demanding more of a voice in their education, especially what they are taught and how it is taught. That same questioning process may soon bring into focus the role and significance of academic libraries in their educational process. The day is past when academic librarians were uninvolved in campus problems, worked from eight or nine to five, and seldom encountered or cared to encounter the students. Students used to ignore college and university libraries as issues for confrontation. If the trouble hasn't already started, get with it before they start picketing doors, breaking windows, knocking books off shelves, and scattering the contents of card catalogs to the wind.

The Useful Academic Librarian

Fay M. Blake

WE ACADEMIC LIBRARIANS are rather a useless lot. We're not unique in our uselessness, though. Lots of other people are useless, too. Tom Wicker, speaking at a New Democratic Coalition meeting a few months ago, said:

> I think that one of the things that's really bothering the American people today is that too many of us, in effect, in whatever field of work we're in, are setting bogus type.
>
> I mean, we're making our living not doing anything that matters. You drive down the streets of Los Angeles or Phoenix or any of the new automobile cities and look at the business establishments on either side, look at them with the single criterion of how many are absolutely essential to the sustenance of life in Phoenix or Los Angeles. And they're damn few. And there are people in there who are manufacturing soft ice cream and running bowling alleys, whose livelihood is not necessary to the maintenance of the community. Now some of these things are marginal. Sometimes you can say, well, I'm advantageous to the community even if I'm not necessary to the community. But there are a hell of a lot of people who exist there, and they make relatively good livings in a material sense only because they are able to con people into thinking they need whatever it is that they're selling.
>
> I hesitate to say what the problems of young people and black people are because

I obviously don't know, in either case. But it seems to me that one of the major problems for younger people in the country today is that they don't have anything useful to do. When I grew up, not too many years ago, in the South, I had lots of useful things to do. If I didn't bring in the wood and coal at night, my family didn't keep warm. That was a useful thing to do. My children don't have anything useful to do.

And as they go into life and beyond the schools and are trying to spend their lives as citizens, people want to have something useful to do; they don't want to sell soft ice cream. The man who is convicted like a criminal to setting bogus type for the rest of his life—they may be paying him three dollars an hour, but his life is as empty as a basket with all the eggs taken out of it.

Living in England, I got some interesting insights into just who is useful and essential to the community. While I was there, Edward Heath, the Prime Minister, kept zipping in and out of the country. He went to Washington to hold hands with his pal Nixon; he went to Singapore to get hell from the Commonwealth heads for selling arms to South Africa; he went to the Mediterranean or wherever to show off his yachting skills. But as far as I could see, my life wasn't significantly affected by his comings and goings. But when the dustmen went out on strike and stayed out for six weeks, that was a different story. (Incidentally, here in the States we call dustmen garbage collectors, which probably shows the genteel effect of having and losing an empire.) Anyway, when the dustmen went out and the garbage started collecting in the streets and when everybody was getting a skittish stomach from the polluted water, we all got a dramatic lesson in who's useful to the community.

Now let's try to imagine what would happen if every academic librarian in the city or the country went out on strike —or was suddenly struck down with leprosy—who would know or care? The population as a whole? Not likely. They don't know we exist. The faculty? In a pig's eye. They regard us as nuisances anyway. The university administration? Don't you believe it. The only time they think of the library is just before an accreditation team swoops down, and you can always divert them to a new cyclotron. The students? Well, maybe a few who use the library, but only if the libraries closed down—and our clerical staffs could probably run them quite well without us. Academic librarians have certainly been saying: "Well, we're advantageous to the community even if we're not necessary to it," but on the whole that's not true. We've also been setting bogus type.

We say some of the things we're doing in the academic library are advantageous to the community. Speaking from left to right, we have those academic librarians who: 1) are going to start the coming revolution in the library, or put into the hands of the revolutionaries the information they need to bring the revolution about. Hogwash! If you want to be a revolutionary, go and be a revolutionary, but don't kid yourself or anyone else that revolutions start in libraries. Karl Marx didn't start socialism in a British Museum reading room. He had to go out and do a few things like organize a Socialist International. Revolutions have been begun and carried through by millions of people who never saw the inside of a library. What we've

got here is the typical arrogance of the half-baked intellectual who thinks all knowledge comes out of books. People, all people, know an awful lot of important things they never learned from books.

So you're not going to change all of society, but you're the librarian who: 2) is going to revolutionize the university. The library is the heart of the university, isn't it? And we're going to give it a transplant. Forget it. The university doesn't have a heart. The university, as a matter of fact, doesn't exist. Like a corporation, it's a legal fiction. What does exist is a group of people who function together in many different ways. If there are changes to be made in the university—and Heaven knows they're long overdue—they will come about and have meaning only through the effect of individual human beings on each other and not through some mystique about "the heart of the university."

All right, so you're not a revolutionary, but you're going to do what we've always done in the academic library only you're going to do it better. You're the librarian who: 3) is going to put the right book into the hands of someone who wants it—our classic example of the usefulness of the academic librarian. Well, that's all right, but what's so great or useful about it? Of our whole population, only the tiniest percentage wants a book. Even out of the academic population, only the tiniest percentage wants a book. You know as well as anyone in the university that it's quite possible to be a better than average student or a better than average teacher without setting foot inside the library. So at best it's a very small community we're advantageous to.

So maybe you'll be the librarian who: 4) is going to expand the community we can be advantageous to. You'll get out among those students, especially the new types from the ghettos who are "culturally disadvantaged," and let them in on some of our arcane secrets, teach them how to use the library. Very laudable, but you're heading for trouble.

We all carry with us one of the burdens of the American tradition, which really says: "If you're poor or ignorant, it's your own damn fault. Why didn't you work hard like me and make yourself a bundle or get yourself a doctorate or become a nice, useful academic librarian?" There are a few faint signs of change. We say now: "If you're really starving and we've got stockpiles of food rotting away, we'll give you some; but you really don't deserve our 'charity.' If you're really clamoring for knowledge (not wisdom—we're not giving any of that away), we'll teach you how to use the library—which we made difficult to use in the first place—but we won't let you have a hand in how we run it, what we put into it, how we arrange it, or what hours we keep it open." You just don't become a librarian without absorbing some of the underlying concepts of the society, and one of those concepts is that some people are better than others.

Well, then, you're not going to change anything. You're the librarian who: 5) is a conservative in the old sense of that word. You'll use the library to conserve the heritage of Western culture. You'll serve the small, select body of scholars for whom the university really exists, and you'll beat off the long-haired, ignorant rabble with their kooky demands for black studies and women's lib and nonsense like that. I'm afraid that stance is a pretty useless one. Even if not much has really changed, changes are coming about. They always do. And one of the changes that seems here to stay is a new definition of education. It's becoming evident, not just here but everywhere in the world, that everyone has the right to and the need for knowing—and knowing those things that will make his life longer, better, and easier. So the small, select group of scholars is inevitably expanding, and the small, select areas that used to be defined as scholarship are expanding, too.

So whether you're revolutionary or conservative or somewhere in between, you don't seem to be doing much good. We all seem to be setting bogus type.

We're a pretty useless lot. But I think we can become a bit more useful, and I think we should try. The reason I think we should try is that it's the only way I know to give sense and meaning to living our lives in the midst of absurdity. I have no illusions that the academic librarian can ever be absolutely essential to mankind, not even as essential as garbage collectors, but I think we can and should be advantageous to the community, much more advantageous than we are now.

✔ First of all, we have lots to learn. We have to learn how to become scholars—not pedants, but scholars in areas of real social concern. We need to learn how people learn, what they want to learn about, how the whole man is put together and how he functions. We need to learn other languages and other cultures, and we need to learn that all of man's cultures are equally inventive and equally important. We need to learn how a scholar looks for his materials and how he arrives at his conclusions. And we need to learn how to discriminate between useful scholarship and arid scholasticism.

We have to learn how to become politicians. We need to discover where real power lies in our universities, in our profession, and in our communities; and we need to learn how to use or how to subvert that power in order to give more people a crack at tasting knowledge. And we need to learn how to discriminate between the deadly game of politics played to give a few power over the many and the use of organization to protect everyone's right to decide what's good for him.

Most of all, perhaps, we have to learn how to become human beings. We have to come away from the desks we barricade ourselves behind and mix it up with students and faculty. We have to see them not only as library users but as people. We have to resist becoming numbers or dossiers in an Army or FBI or university file. We have to become convinced that everyone can help us organize good and useful libraries—if we listen to what they have to tell us. We have to recognize that the most important thing about a library is not how it's organized but why it exists and that it exists to put people in touch with each other. The only reason we collect books in a library is that a book is one way—only *one* way—in which people can talk to each other, and we have to look for ways, many ways, in which we can help people communicate with each other.

We have lots to learn, but lots to teach as well. I think we can teach, and I don't mean just show them how to use the library. I think we can teach both in the classroom and in the library. Some of us are and more of us will be in the classrooms, teaching in various subject areas. More of us should be in the classrooms teaching how to find materials in the particular interests of the students—not "how to use the library," but what the library has or can get for a study of African influences on West Indian literature or the role of FRELIMO in the guerrilla war in Portuguese West Africa, or what have you. We must turn the library itself into classrooms.

Conspire with the students to organize library-based programs and classes in subjects that are not part of the orthodox curriculum. Find out from them what they want to explore; use the riches of the library to back up forums and discussion groups and seminars which you and the students organize together; use your own knowledge to help lead some of the discussions, and convince or coerce or bludgeon faculty members to join in, too. Let it be known that you're ready to turn out annotated bibliographies or current publication information for students and faculty on their particular fields of study. That kind of teaching requires at least two things from us: 1) that we know something. Really know something. If you're bluffing, it'll soon be evident; 2) that we insist that both the library and the university administration let us do what we know how to do.

There is still another way in which we can teach in addition to what we do in classrooms and in the library. We need to communicate simply and clearly the results of our own scholarship. As a frequent offender myself, I can say in good conscience that most of what we communicate in our library journals is drivel, and badly written drivel at that. But we *can* explore areas of social need, and we *can* learn to write it down so it makes sense not only to ourselves but to the layman. Arnold Toynbee has written:

. . . in our time the enormous increase in the amount of things there are to know has conspired with the comparably great increase in the exactingness, in every profession, of the demands on the practitioners' time and strength to drive a wedge between the general cultivated public and the specialists in the increasing number of smaller and smaller patches into which the broadening field of knowledge has now been broken up. We are in danger of relapsing into the pre-Renaissance condition of Western Christendom in which the "clerks" possessed an esoteric knowledge which was beyond the laity's reach—a state of affairs in which some clerks abused the privilege of their benefit of clergy by keeping their knowledge to themselves . . .

If the divorce between specialists and the public were to go to further extremes, the achievement of the Renaissance might be undone; the Republic of Letters might dissolve, and culture might come to be in danger of dying from a plethora of uncommunicated and therefore unutilized knowledge.

I think Toynbee's emphasis is a bit wrong. I don't think the Renaissance ever created the Republic of Letters he thinks exists, and I don't think Western Christendom is the repository of all that's wise and good. But I think academic librarianship, along with the other professions, has wrapped itself in a protective cloak of jargon which is divorcing us from both the understanding and the needs of the community we claim to be advantageous to.

Finally, we can teach the new kind of student beginning to enter our universities and beginning to demand that they serve his needs—very different needs from the traditional student's. But we can teach him only as we recognize our own shortcomings. And I don't mean that we'll recognize or change them by reading a book. The academic librarian needs an alliance with blacks and browns, with the poor and with the outsiders. We need to make sure that minorities form an active and significant part of our own ranks at all levels in the academic library. As colleagues they can help to give us some insight and understanding of the minority community. We need to insist that our library schools make special and extraordinary efforts to recruit from the minorities and from the ghettos. We need to establish close ties with the minority group students in our universities, to put them on our library policy committees, to let them tell us what they need in our libraries. We need to insist that the ghetto is actively represented in all university decisions.

The reason I'm stressing our need for communication with and guidance from the minorities is that our long years of neglect have led to a wide chasm between us. The few black librarians who ever made it into our university libraries did so only at the cost of becoming white —at least in outlook—so that whatever we may know about the people in the university, we know almost nothing about what blacks, Mexicans, Puerto Ricans, and Indians need from us; and we won't be advantageous to that part of our university community until we find the ways to listen to it.

What I've been talking about requires a lot of hard, slogging work. To do it will require giving up some of the traditions we clutch pretty tightly—most important, our habit of talking to each other instead of listening to what users and potential users of the academic library want. If we really want to be useful, we shall have to learn to suspect every activity of ours in which librarians speak only to other librarians—which probably means that a nice old lady like me shouldn't be writing today.

A Wind Is Rising

Bernard E. Richardson

IN JANUARY 1969, the first students enrolled in Navajo Community College, the first and only institution of higher education on a reservation. After a history of almost 40 years of fruitless discussion, the Navajo Tribe finally abandoned hope of the federal government meeting the ever-increasing necessity for education of the Navajo and established a community college with Robert Roessel as president, Ned Hatathli as vice-president, and an all Navajo Board of Regents.

My first contact with the college was in October 1968, when I was asked to serve as a consultant. By March, the administration recognized the immediate importance of a library in the development of the college, and the need for an experienced, professional librarian. Approximately 200 applications were received in response to an ad in *LJ*. About 175 of these applicants meant well, but had little comprehension of the task or of their own limited qualifications. During a conference in which the remaining 25 sound applications were evaluated, the position was offered to me. I accepted and have been on the job since June 24, 1969.

Navajoland is a vast, semi-arid expanse of beautiful but desolate mountains and plateaus in the Four Corners Region where Colorado, Utah, New Mexico, and Arizona share a common boundary point. The Navajo Reservation today is a mere fragment of the land which once belonged to the Tribe; nevertheless, it still encompasses almost 25,000 square miles (16,000,000 contiguous acres).

"Today, there are approximately 120,500 Navajo Indians comprising the largest Indian tribe in the United States."[1] Figures vary but all are high, and it is generally accepted as a fair estimate by most who are familiar with the Navajo birthrate that 60 percent of all Navajos are 18 years of age or younger. "When birthrates were recorded among a carefully observed segment of the Navajos . . . , a six-year average (1955-60) was found to be 49.1"[2] (per 1000 population). Infant mortality among "Navajos in the period of 1955-59 had an even higher rate—58.5"[3] (higher than the national average for all Indians). "In 1944 the figure was 135.3 deaths per thousand live births, three times that for all races in the United States (41.4) in 1945."[4] Coupled to birth and infant mortality rates is this statistic: "In 1959 the average age at death for Indians was 41.8 years in the twenty-four federal

307

reservation states, compared with 62.3 for all races."[5]

"Most Navajos live in hogans—mud and log huts, often windowless and with earth floors—long distances from their neighbors."[6]

To alienate readers with depressing statistics is witless; nevertheless, it is important that a frame of reference be established for a non-Indian to comprehend the need for this estimable Navajo Community College project. Any librarian can readily document as fact that Indians have the highest rate of unemployment, the least and poorest education, the most difficulty in assimilating, the longest unbroken record of treaties broken by the U.S. government, almost 200 years of harassment and neglect by state and local governments, and a sordid history of exploitation by the white man which extends back to Columbus. Is it any wonder they also share the highest suicide rate in this country?

One difference between Navajos and most other Indian tribes is their resistance to almost all policies advocated at one time or another by Washington. Navajos not only resisted the policy of allotment (assigning ownership to individual Indians so it could be more easily stolen), but also used tribal funds to buy or lease more land even when they were literally starving. Navajos were permitted to resist since most white men assumed Navajoland was uninhabitable, unprofitable, and not worth stealing. The present importance of oil and mineral deposits may alter attitudes and increase pressures for elimination by allotment of land or by assigning responsibility from the comparatively benign federal government to rapacious states which are very susceptible to local political pressures.

Before letting that happen, Navajos are attempting to educate themselves to a competency which will enable them to deal with the dominant white majority. An important component of this preparation involves Navajo Com-

munity College—truly a community college established by a unique community. No Navajo is excluded; anyone is eligible for admission.

Since its start, Navajo Community College has shared the plant of a new Bureau of Indian Affairs Boarding High School at Many Farms, Arizona. In spite of the cooperative high school staff and its librarian, the college suffers from space problems in all areas. Eight trailers house members of the staff in excess of those quartered in the BIA homes. Two expanded trailers provide offices for the college administration and the faculty. College student affairs offices share quarters in the high school administration wing.

The Navajo Community College Library is located in half of the BIA High School Library shelving-and-study-space but has no workroom quarters. Space will remain a prime problem until the college is able to construct its campus on the 1200 acres on Lake Tsaile in the Lukachukai Mountains—acreage reserved by the tribe as a permanent Navajo Community College site. In the meantime, library collections and services are being developed to meet the needs of an evolving community college program.

To be critical of the BIA schools is too easy. A charitable stance is to recognize that the general failure of 100 years of BIA programs reflects the attitudes and goals of the dominant white culture and to acknowledge those rare individual BIA employees whose kindness, awareness, and dedication have permitted individual Navajo students to benefit from being turned into pseudo-white men. The difficulty is that most products of BIA schools do not go on to college. Of those few who do, the vast majority become early dropouts. The few who finish college and graduate schools seldom return to the reservation; so, inasmuch as it succeeds at all, the BIA program achieves its goal of eliminating the Indian problem by assimilating individuals into the larger culture.

Navajo Community College exists to educate its people while retaining their unique heritage and enabling them to function in a hostile culture which is attempting, in a fumbling way, to absorb them.

A great obstacle to the education of the Navajo has been the accumulated experience of a century of BIA schools. Until recently, all BIA schools were boarding schools. Because of the Navajos' warranted reluctance to send their children to be de-Navajoed, non-English-speaking children as young as six years of age were actually kidnapped by BIA officials—snatched from family, freedom, and childhood, and removed to prison-like compounds, some of them hundreds of miles from Navajoland. The use of their native Navajo language brought punishment. Who could learn anything at six years of age in such a setting with all classes conducted in a foreign language? Runaways were frequent. Animosity was widespread. Those who survived this trauma learned English and graduated from high school, but seldom returned to the reservation to help their fellows make the transition more easily.

Then came World War II. Navajos, along with all Indians, are inexplicably super-patriots and demonstrate it by their military service. Their most famous World War II service was the Navajo Code talkers who simply relayed messages in their native tongue which is such a difficult language that the enemy was never able to decipher it; however, code-talkers made up only a small percentage of the Navajos who served in the armed forces in World War II. These thousands of young Navajo men returned to the Reservation, but no longer the same. Even in war, they had been exposed to the creature comforts of the outside world.

Since the late 1940's, few Navajo children have to be kidnapped for school. On the contrary, parents de-livered them in such numbers that the gross inadequacy of the school facilities became a national scandal. The federal government embarked on frantic building programs. The inherent cruelty of boarding schools was recognized, and they were replaced by day schools and fleets of school buses. However, all classes continued to be conducted in a foreign language—English. Not until the late 1960's was there a single Navajo school with classes conducted in Navajo, English taught as a second language, and a local school board to make decisions. Even today, only Rough Rock Demonstration School retains the distinction of having a local, Navajo school board.

In addition to a changed attitude toward school attendance, the influence of the automobile has been significant. In one sense, Navajos are more American than any other Americans. Navajos are pragmatic. When exposed to alien cultures, they examine new ideas and select only those they want. They learned pottery-making from other tribes, adopted the horse for transportation and sheep for food and wool for weaving from the Spanish, silversmithing from the Mexicans.

From other Americans they have selected the pick-up truck. With it, travel to school, to town, and to ceremonials is no longer a major undertaking. The pick-up permits work off the reservation or miles from home and a return to home daily. The pick-up is the key to employment and economic improvement. It allows the Navajo the best of two worlds: to visit the confusing white world of speed and tight schedules and yet to return to the splendid isolation of the vast reservation to restore his noncompetitive soul by participating in the old chants and songs and dances of his religion and his culture.

Where does Navajo Community College fit into this compromise with the future? It is focal in an evolving way. Classes are already popular in auto repair and welding. Someone has to service those pick-ups. "Navajo boys often show a near genius in tinkering with cars which their white brothers would throw on the junk heap. No license is required on the reservation, and a speed of ten miles an hour was at least better than horse and wagon."[7]

The first semester found the largest enrollments in typing and business courses since someone must operate the craft shops, restaurants, and motels to serve the increasing hordes of tourists. Approximately 80 students are taking the standard academic classroom transfer courses this term; obviously, some Navajos must go on to the professions. These are examples of ordinary courses to be expected in a junior college, but how many other community colleges offer courses in Resources and Development of the Reservation?

Most important, every student is required to select six credits of work in Navajo Studies from a wide range of offerings in silversmithing, pottery-making, basket-making, weaving, the Navajo language, or Navajo history and culture encompassing art, music, dance, religion, and family and clan relationships. The first grouping is designed to equip tomorrow's Navajo to exist equally in the economic life of America; the second is to instill pride in his heritage, his people, and his Navajo self.

Who are Navajo Community College students? June graduates from high schools and illiterate non-English-speaking adults without a day of formal education. A variation of team teaching is used; e.g., auto-repair students learn English appropriate to the service-station, garage, and cash register from an instructor who conducts classes in the shop.

Where does the library fit into the picture and how will it develop? It cannot be patterned after any existing junior or community college library, since there is no model to follow. Nav-

ajo Community College Library will, of course, have a proper number of appropriate volumes to meet North Central Accrediting Association Standards. We will not attempt to create an isolated, peculiar, and whimsical monument to anyone. The staff consisted of the librarian and one Navajo clerk until September 15, when a second Navajo clerk was added.

The Library of Congress classification system is used not for any inherent present advantage but with an eye to the distant future. Only the usual disadvantage exists: a slow trickle of returns for cards ordered. Since July, we have placed 3000 classified, cataloged, and processed titles on the shelves for use and have a backlog of 6000 titles with cards ordered but not received.

About a hundred periodicals are now received, many of them Indian publications. No backfile exists yet. Desperately needed are backfiles of the expensive scholarly and technical periodicals.

The large and important pamphlet file is divided into two separate sections: one, a general information file with access only by alphabetic entry of folders; and the other, an Indian materials file which is fully cataloged by author, title, and subject.

Phonograph records—Indian chants, songs, music, and oral history—are being added to the holdings. A tape recorder and tapes are on order to initiate an ongoing Navajo oral history collection.

Gifts pour in from individuals and organizations. Some are valuable additions; many are not. A retired couple in New Jersey send regular gifts of wisely selected Indian materials. The usual boxes contain ancient trash which should have been hauled to the local dump instead of having to be burned at Many Farms. Quality is more important that quantity, pertinence more significant then prevalence. After all these years, Navajos deserve the best available.

Two significant gifts have been received. The students and faculties at Sacramento College, American River Junior College, and Sierra College in California had a drive and in August delivered to us nine and a half tons of books. This was not junk. The bulk of it consisted of multiple copies of textbooks; however, a copy of some of these was added to the library collection along with the truly appropriate books. Some of these titles are being used as textbooks. Many are placed on a table for the taking and the library distributes hundreds of titles weekly. It is seldom that there is not a cluster of students browsing and selecting from the gift table. There have been few books in windowless mud and log hogans.

The other noteworthy gift makes the real difference. The tribe appropriated an adequate minimal budget for operation and book purchase. The library did not request more because the entire college operates with precarious financing.

The bulk of our collection development this year will come from the interest and generosity of Mrs. Lucy Moses of New York. Mrs. Moses gave $50,-000 for the building of a collection of Indian materials and the Donner Foundation matched it. What do we buy? There are three immediate needs: any title an instructor needs for use, reference and bibliography, and Indian materials—anything by or about Navajos, much on Southwestern tribes, and a general interest in all American Indians.

Material abounds: "Indians, far out of proportion to their numbers, have enjoyed the attention of people who write books and of those who read them. The New York Public Library requires 23 drawers in its card catalog for its holdings on American Indians, while 16 drawers suffice for the Jews and 7 for Negroes, and certainly neither of these latter groups has been overlooked by writers. The Library of Congress devotes 18 drawers to Indians, 17 to Jews, and 7 to Negroes."[8]

I am beginning to agree with the old joker who said that the average Navajo family consisted of a mother, father, brother, sister, and two anthropologists. I think that both anthropologists published regularly.

To build a collection of Indian materials is not only possible but intriguing. Of particular help in acquisitions has been T. N. Luther, Kansas City dealer in Indian materials, who has donated time, money, and expertise.

The library will evolve. The standard foundations now exist. How it will evolve depends entirely upon the Navajo. Navajos dreamed the college into existence and keep it going; and the library will try to reflect Navajo needs.

One of these needs is for community service. Navajoland, the size of West Virginia, is without a vestige of public library service if you except the recent Window Rock and Shiprock volunteer community library efforts. Groups in Tuba City and Chinle have contacted NCC for help in establishing some kind of public library service. This is difficult but possible; both are small but definite population centers. What about the isolated hogans and the little sheepherders who leave school weeks before the term is over and are still appearing in late October to register for the fall term at Many Farms BIA high school, a term which began the last week in August? Some revolutionary scheme can provide them with reading from April 20 until October 15. Instead of acquiring and keeping books, could a public library service obtain and give them away? Is there an agency to fund a program to provide every little Navajo sheepherder with three or four selected titles for summer reading while he (or she) watches the flocks which are the backbone of the meager Navajo economic existence? There must be, somewhere.

For some months I have thought about and worked on an encompassing, interrelated proposal to accomplish the following: 1) at least three books for summer reading to the little herders; 2) serve isolated hogans by four-wheel-drive pick-up-mobile libraries which could traverse the paths and roadless expanses of rough terrain; 3) establish a formal program at NCC to train Navajos as library-aides not only to man the potential community reading room-service centers at Chinle, Kayenta, Shiprock, Ganado, and Tuba City but also to fill the clerical vacancies in libraries in the entire Southwest; and finally, 4) conduct a ten-week library-college summer session which would bring Navajo graduate students back to NCC as instructors in a program designed to equip June high school graduates to avoid being dropouts during the middle of their freshman semester. These are only parts of a complicated scheme to provide a bare minimum of community library service where none exists. True, even these bits make it sound grandiose: however, when a problem is monumental, it is doubtful that thinking wee thoughts about wee pieces of it could bring surcease.

My first memo to the President expanded my contention that "my eventual successor as College Librarian should be a Navajo or at least an Indian." I believe that a successor should be found as soon as possible because in spite of all my good intentions and my efforts to learn the Navajo attitudes toward life, I will always be non-Indian. However, the thought of inevitable departure saddens me.

The Navajo will not only endure, he will multiply and overcome. It is a cathartic experience to be even a small part of this particular time in Navajoland.

Níyal haaghááh (A wind is rising)!

REFERENCES

1. Vital Statistics Section, Bureau of Indian Affairs.
2. Brophy, William A. & others. *The Indian: America's Unfinished Business.* Univ. of Oklahoma Pr., 1966, p. 162.
3. *Ibid.,* p. 163.
4. *Ibid.,* p. 163.
5. *Ibid.,* p. 163.
6. Harman, O'Donnell & Henninger Associates, Inc. *Program Design Study for the Navajo Tribe.* Navajo Tribe, Window Rock, Arizona, March 1969, p. 1.
7. Underhill, Ruth B. M. *The Navajos.* Univ. of Oklahoma Pr., 1967, p. 245.
8. Berry, Brewton. *The Education of American Indians.* HEW, December 1968, p. 1.

VI
Inventing the Future

The Changes Ahead

Lowell A. Martin

THE WORLD won't stand still long enough for me to see what it is really like now, let alone say with certainty what libraries will be like in the year 2000. But it may be that we can get a little perspective on ourselves today by trying to look ahead at least a few years. What is coming, what will libraries be called on to do, and how ready are librarians for the changes they must face?

When you pick up your pencil to set down various scintillating predictions, a few sobering thoughts occur. Let me remind you of a current example of misplaced prediction. In most discussions of the future the starting point is population. So and so many people by 1980, so very many more by the year 2000. As to the world as a whole, it seems that we will run out of standing room. But hardly has the print on the predictions for the U.S. dried before the birth rate takes a significant drop. Have you noticed the recent scurrying about by the population experts, who a few years ago were pronouncing predictions with great confidence, adjusting now to this elementary fact of the number of new youngsters born in the country today? Who can predict how rapidly or how slowly birth con-

trol will spread over the face of the earth? Would-be prophets should take a lesson from the triumph of the pill over the statistician.

A more defensible approach is to try to see ahead to alternatives. I would like to set a few of these alternatives before you, and then you can predict for yourself just where the library will come out and what the new perspectives will be.

Technological Change

I am not going to regale you with a long list of glittering gadgets that are just around the corner. One of the most penetrating and at times terrifying documents on coming technological change that I have seen is the 1964 report of the RAND Corporation, issued under the deceptive title of *Report on a Long-Range Forecasting Study*.

Supersonic travel and space exploration we know about. I will not speculate on the exact form of the library that will be established on the moon in 1975. But think of the implications of widespread weather control, or even more of genetic control. I do not believe the gene for reading has yet been identified, but it will be,

315

and then the American Library Association can lobby for its inclusion in the approved serum.

The technologies that come closest to home for the library are those of computerization and of communication distribution. A library is a place for storing knowledge under a system that facilitates identification and retrieval as needed, which is also a definition of a computer. The printed page is a means for transmitting content from a source that knows to a recipient who wants to know, and this is also the function of the new communication devices.

How will the two relate, the library and the computer, the printed page and the electronic image? I don't know, but the basic alternative is clear enough. Either they will be coordinated or they will go their separate ways. Either the library will prove flexible and will utilize the new technology where it does the job better, or the library will remain primarily book-oriented, steady in its tradition, while the computer for information storage and retrieval, and electronic devices for distant and convenient communication will develop separately.

Both we will have, whether in one structure or more. It is clear that our society approaches an information overload, and that new means will emerge to handle it.

I do not believe that the library will promptly disappear if a separate computerized information system develops. What is a library for? Have I exhausted the possibilities when I say that it is for information? By no means. It is also—indeed it is fundamentally—for background or interpretation or insight or expression or whatever term you choose. Will we prefer to read a biography of Jefferson in facsimile? Will Toynbee be better if programmed? Do you look forward to poetry on a computer printout? These are corny questions, but not irrelevant, because despite all the talk of new communication the most remarkable fact is the continued prevalence and the durability of the printed page. We are all familiar with the predictions of the demise of the book by Marshall McLuhan, which predictions I note are set down neatly in very traditional linear print.

But it does seem to me that the library will be diminished unless it absorbs and exploits the new technology. We often go to extremes in reacting to the computer. Let me try to be just a little more specific on its prospects for libraries.

Distinguish if you will between the computer for bibliographic control, for documentation reproduction and distribution, and for information retrieval. The alternative on the first, so far as libraries are concerned, has I believe about been chosen. Within the next decade many libraries will be utilizing the new technology to rebuild their bibliographic systems for identifying and locating resources. A national record of publications on machine-readable tape is undoubtedly coming. This will be used not so much by individual libraries as by regional cataloging centers, with products from the same record ranging from book catalogs for individual libraries to bibliographies for individual readers.

We may well find it practical to do the bibliographic job more intensively; for example, I suspect that under this new system we will be cataloging individual chapters of books as well as the whole volume as a unit. But note that this does not imply some brave, new, and basically different library world, but rather an extension, automation, and centralization (f what has been occurring all along: the making of an organized record of holdings, known as the catalog. The computer in this development will not perform some remarkable new function, and certainly will not make the tough decisions of intellectual identification and classification, but will simply be the computer as the librarian's little helper and more flexible record keeper.

By the second step of documentation control I mean not bibliographic identification of a publication, but mechanical access to the publication itself, from which photo-images and copies will be made for use at a distance—distance meaning anything from a faculty office a block away on the campus to another library at the other end of the country. This is not in never-never land but with us now; it is not only possible but probable that a reader will go this morning into a member agency of the library system of New York state, request an article in a journal located several hundred miles away in the State Library in Albany, and have a copy back by facsimile before he can pick up *The Carpetbaggers* and locate one of those juicy passages. I am confident that libraries will increasingly utilize the new technology for what I will once again call a traditional function, getting the required document off the shelves or out of the file and spread out in front of the reader.

The picture changes when we go to the third and most complex step of computer applications, that of information storage and retrieval on any significant scale. Here I doubt whether the leadership and fresh new applications will come from libraries, but I would be the happiest person in the world if events prove me wrong. You recognize that I am referring now to communication between a record of knowledge and a searcher for knowledge without going through the intermediate step of print or near-print duplication—instant publishing or individual custom-made publishing, if you will. This requires first an information orientation as distinct from the librarian's usual book orientation. It calls for imaginative new classification systems which libraries have not thus far shown much inclination to

explore. It requires huge original capital investment, which is more likely to come either from large government installations, NASA for example, or from large commercial enterprises, the recently-organized combines of machine and publishing firms, for example. Finally, this development will call for area-wide concepts of resources and of users, rather than an institutional approach tied to a single municipality, or a distinct school system, or one university campus. I am not very sanguine that these new information networks will build up around libraries, with librarians taking the lead, particularly when I note how slow we are in achieving any genuine regional cooperation even in our traditional functions.

Information banks I suspect will first be built by special interest groups —scientific associations, for example —and then by private commercial interests. In time they will be consolidated into regional and national networks, very possibly under governmental or quasi-governmental authority, for soon or late we will challenge the holding of sources of information in private hands. Whatever the structure, in time—and very possibly in not too much time—everything from the price of eggs in the supermarket this morning to the latest analysis of the composition of the surface of the moon, will come directly into the private home, the office, the laboratory, and the classroom by electronic image rather than by means of a library reference book.

In this whole area of technological development, one must resist being seduced by sirens. Do you know what was one of the earliest and most persistent predictions about the communications revolution? The facsimile newspaper received by television or telephone. But somehow this has not reached my neighborhood. The newspaper still comes as old-fashioned print on old-fashioned paper. The newsboy still delivers it in the morning—usually a little late, but with unerring accuracy in tossing it precisely into the firethorn bush.

Permit me one more crack at the computer, with which I trust we will maintain a healthy scrap in the years ahead. I take as representative a little scene I witnessed recently in a printing plant. A tape was feeding rapidly into a computer, which was activating a high-speed photo-typesetting machine, justifying right-hand margins and hyphenating words, and laying out columns on pages, all at a great rate. There was a steady, impressive hum as the machine carried on. Suddenly the computer came to a word it could not hyphenate. Everything stopped. A bell sounded. A high school girl went over to the computer, and with a pencil indicated how the word should be divided, after which the half-million-dollar computer resumed its steady and mysterious pace. There you have it: a mechanical marvel so long as a human being has told it what to do—a helpless pile of junk the moment it gets one step beyond that point, waiting on the assistance of a high school girl.

New Forms of Materials

Quite separate from future mechanical marvels, new forms of material are already with us, starting with the paperback book and extending to the newest photo-records from moon probes. We don't have to try to peer into the future to get an indication of how libraries will react to nonbook sources; we can look around and see what is happening today.

The alternatives are clear: either the library as of today, book-centered plus appendages in nonbook form, or the library as a resource center, with a new materials mix, the multimedia collection, determined by purposes and clientele. Libraries of course have film departments and record collections and microfilm sections. But in most cases the user finds these at the periphery of the library organization, serving as adjuncts to what is thought of as the regular collection. The book is the center—other forms are thought of as supplementary.

Even when the book remains the same in outward form, but changes in kind of content, it is slow to appear in the library collection. I am thinking of programmed books, one of the hot items in publishing. The programmed text is a subject book with an extra education element built in; one would think they would have a special appeal for libraries. Yet you can look long through most libraries without getting any inkling that this interesting new form of educational publishing has occurred.

One does not have to use even as contemporary a form as programmed materials to make the point. Current reading studies indicate that while the amount and range of book reading has not increased much on the part of the general adult public since World War II, magazine reading has increased significantly. Libraries have magazines, primarily as a reference adjunct to the book collection. Librarians do not often think of them as a resource in their own right; they do not inquire as to what magazines regular patrons would find valuable separate from their extension and updating of information in books, nor do they capitalize on magazines as a means for reaching the disadvantaged, although studies show wide reading of such material by the undereducated. The book is the touchstone; other forms are acquired only if they relate to this center. It is therefore not surprising that studies of the public image of the library consistently show that it is thought of as a book institution but not as a source of information in other forms. If the librarian thinks of his institution as primarily or essentially a collection of books, naturally the community resident, the student, the businessman, the specialist, and the undereducated think of it in the same way.

Will the library of the future continue to be predominantly a book-oriented institution, with a smattering of nonbook forms, or will it encompass the full range of present and forthcoming materials in a new multi-form resource center? I don't know the answer, although I can venture a guess. The book still plays a central role in educational communication, and will continue to do so in these next years. The book is what librarians know best and what they are organized for. The library will probably be book-dominated for some time. However, as we go along, new forms will force their way not only into the fringes of the traditional library world but also into the central resources. For example, there is no question but what most libraries must turn more and more in these next years to utilization in some coordinated plan of resources at a distance, in other libraries, in order to meet demands of an increasingly specialized public. Our standard method for accomplishing this is interlibrary loan—another book-oriented concept, and one that is dependent on the mails, a method of communication more suited to leisurely correspondence than to the pace of present-day activity. Interlibrary loans in the future will seldom involve the originals, but will be in the form of photographic or electronic copies.

New forms will spread and libraries will utilize them more and more. In time a new resources mix may well emerge, and it will not necessarily be centered on the bookstack. But how widely and how rapidly this will occur will depend as much as anything else on whether the librarian's concept of his role evolves more toward functional use of resources, the point of contact between material and people, or whether it stays primarily with the subject concept of resources, the building of a reservoir.

Social Changes

So much for technology, the future shape and form and distribution of materials, the library hardware of these next years. What of the social and human changes in prospect? Here we usually get the litany of population, urbanization, and suburbanization. These are very real factors having to do with where people are and will be. We know of the population trend to urban centers and then of the movement of people outward in the urban complex, and following them the wave of slums. But sometimes we seem to assume that the wave will conveniently stop where it is now. We speak of the "inner city" as though we were dealing with a limited infection, when the truth is that city dilapidation is a cancer that is spreading throughout the organism. Urban rehabilitation—and by extension urban library rehabilitation—is obviously a priority social item of these next years.

But I suspect that if we project this all too familiar urban decline to the year 2000 we may be underestimating man's power of self renewal. Certain of our older cities—Philadelphia, Baltimore, and Atlanta for example—show evidence of regrowth at the center, not only for commercial but for residential purposes. Several miles of Manhattan's East Side, which is as inner city as you can get, already constitutes the highest rental residential area in the world. Don't write off the central city library as an anachronism in the center of physical, cultural, and educational desert. Its patronage has held up surprisingly well in the face of the suburban trend, and within the time period we are discussing it may find itself in the very center of a revived urban landscape. A city library that is planning its central facilities and its future branch program on the basis of past trends would do well to look afresh at the ground rules, consulting with the most visionary urban sociologist that can be found before buying a single piece of land.

But I am less interested in where people will live, whether in the man-made excitement of Safdie's new Habitat or in the sylvan glens of Reston and Columbia. The more vital question is what the values of these people of the future will be, what the texture of their lives, what the range and depth of their culture.

If we should by any chance be on the verge of a renaissance, when man will really develop as an individual and as a citizen, as well as a worker, then there is little in present experience to guide us in the future. We don't have a populace thirsting for knowledge today and filled with civic responsibility, and we don't know what it would mean for libraries if we did. Assuming any such project, we might do better to go back and read about ancient Athens, rather than consulting the latest statistics issued by the state library agency.

What really has been our central goal and highest value as a people thus far in the century? All fancy phrases aside, what have we been after? At the risk of being labeled an economic determinist, I see the central goal that has prevailed and dominated as increased productivity. For the individual this has meant a higher standard of living. For business it has meant increased profits. From the standpoint of society, the best and most charitable phrase I can think of is greater productivity.

The application is not to business and worker alone. This has been the motivating force of the school—to produce economically self-sufficient and productive individuals. This has also been the main impact of the university—to prepare graduates for more complex jobs and to conduct research which contributes, directly or eventually, to greater productivity. When we refer to the knowledge explosion we mean primarily utilitarian knowledge.

We wanted greater productivity and that is what we have achieved. The result is the affluent society. If you want to put it cynically, first we wanted enough to eat, then enough to be comfortable, and now enough to impress the neighbors. Small wonder that some young people, who already have a Mustang automobile and who spent their junior year in Paris, do not find this a satisfying statement of their life goals.

What other underlying goals might pervade these next several decades? No doubt pleasure, physical and psychological, will be pursued assiduously. Man has worked; now he is learning to play, and given his ingenuity in whatever he puts his mind to, his forms of play will no doubt be wondrous to behold.

Other than the producer and the hedonist, there are the humanist and the civic man. I use humanism in the classical sense, the cultivated life of the mind and of the senses. We have no accepted word for this goal, the closest being culture, which usually carries overtones of superficiality, in the same way that the term intellectual carries overtones of ineffectuality. We all know of the spreading interest in art, music, the theater. I refer not only to museum art but to the play of design and color in advertising, clothes, household furnishings, even kitchen appliances. It is multimedia art that accounts in good part for the success of Expo '67. Is this a temporary cultural kick, or a significant popular movement? In my own view it is more than a temporary fad, and constitutes part of contemporary man's search for meaning.

I can conceive of popular humanism, cultivated sensitivity, as a prevalent motive of these next years. Culture can be an appealing package, combining pleasure and mental exercise and a touch of creativity. The arts in the broadest sense may become the respectable person's LSD.

However, it stretches my credulity to believe that public responsibility, active civic concern on a wide scale, will come to the fore. We have not shown this quality in the face of the civic crisis of our time, that of relations between the races and genuine opportunity for all. This and other problems we see not as our personal concern but as the responsibility of an abstraction we call government, and we have a slightly indignant feeling that government is really not doing as much as it should about the matter. Whether businessman or professional, we are likely to work in the city and depend upon it directly or indirectly for our livelihood, but come five P.M. we escape, even at the cost of a long and expensive commuting trip, leaving the city with what we conveniently consider "their" problem.

If and as the cultivated individual and the civic individual appear, the library will indeed come into its own, or at least will have a golden opportunity to move into that central role in the school, in the community, and in the society as a whole that is claimed in the literature.

One increasing aspect of our society can be predicted with assurance. We are becoming more specialized, producing more highly trained individuals, with growing dependence upon a professional and technical class. Almost surely, well before the year 2000 college attendance will become as customary as high school attendance today. An even greater increase of these next years can be expected in the graduate divisions of universities. We are moving rapidly into a period when our greatest resource will be human intellectual power rather than machinery or technology. The business that does not proceed to build up its human resources, creative as well as operational, does not make a good long-term investment on the stock market today.

We are becoming a society of specialists, not just in our universities and laboratories, but increasingly throughout the fabric of national life. A specialized society, but where are the specialized libraries? Here and there we find a municipal library with some capacity to serve specialists; university collections at intervals, again with some specialized capacity, but distinctly uneasy as to how far they can serve beyond the campus; specialized government collections that have seldom been made widely available. We have been engaged in a paradoxical experiment for some time, to see if we can sustain quality education without adequate libraries. Soon we may try to sustain a specialized society without access to specialized libraries of real depth and scope. Without libraries equal to the task we will not be able to maintain specialization at a full level any more than we have been able to maintain education at a quality level.

It is said that we are entering a period of vast educational development. The other day President Johnson, between speeches on Vietnam, referred to the present "years of education," and just recently he called for an international year of education. I know about the increased number of students and I have seen the figures for new school and college buildings. What I don't know about is the quality of all this education. When I see statistics that relate to quality rather than quantity—salaries of teachers and librarians, for example, or average class size, or ratio of library staff to enrollment— the picture looks much less rosy. In a recent study of public libraries in California, the number of professional librarians per thousand population was found to have decreased by 20 percent between 1950 and 1965.

What of the years ahead? Will we stop talking and really act on quality education? If we do, the implications for libraries will be profound, for we know that students use libraries, whatever question there may be about other categories of readers. Project, for example, the implications of the educational goal of developing the individual capacity of each young person in school, after a long period when the underlying aim has been to bring all up to a level needed by the economy. If this new goal of developing individual capacity were really to prevail, the school of the future would no longer be organized into groups learning a lesson, like a platoon in an army marching up the hill and down again. Picture rather a beehive of human energy, of activity of individuals, each marching to his own drummer. Within this center of youthful growth, think not only of the gifted child spurting ahead but equally of the disadvantaged child catching up. This activity in the school of the future will lead increasingly to the library, for the library is more a place of the individual than it is a place of the platoon.

I think it more than possible that this country will really devote itself to education in these next decades. We have not discovered any substitute for individual capacity as the essential means to achieve whatever goals we adopt, nor have we invented any way other than education for developing individual capacity. Despite the premature pronouncements, we may really be entering a period of quality in education—preschool, elementary, secondary, collegiate, graduate and professional, and continuing education through life.

If this is in prospect, the next question is whether libraries will reach out to the new opportunities, whether within schools or in educational development in the widest sense in the community. We have many potential sources of strength—the continuing educational value of the book, the considerable measure of intellectual freedom that has been preserved by the institution, the general public acceptance which it enjoys. When you think about the wide range of human educational interest, only libraries really have the matching range of faculty and subjects and curricula.

But I am not sure that all this is enough. You can have a powerful resource that is not used to capacity unless it relates itself to people. Librarians have been more resource-minded than people-minded. A book is more likely to be acquired because it fills a topical gap in the collection than because it fills a discernible need of readers. We have not probed as to the resource requirements of portions of the population who do not customarily turn to libraries, whether the very undereducated or the very highly educated.

In the past the librarian's question has been: how can I get the learner to the library? The future question will take another form: how can resources be projected to the learner? There is an important difference between these two. Librarians have pictured library use as people turning from what they are doing to come to the resource center we have built. In a time of new communication media, we should more picture how resources can be carried to people where they are, to be used as an integral part of ongoing activity, in the classroom, the home, the marketplace, the government office. Let me suggest that the building of strong central resources, on which we have made some progress, is only a first step. The next is to project the resources into the lives of people, by means of pipelines into the fabric of life. This is alien to the librarian's concept of a reservoir to which the eager learner will come to dip up his pail of knowledge. Either we will learn to project our resources, or commercial and academic and governmental agencies will, and the library will come more to be a standby or reserve. These next years call for an outreach on the part of all libraries, which in the earlier years of the century have been more concerned with inreach and the building of collections.

I remember the educational thrust among librarians in the 1920's. This is what attracted me to the profession. For a quarter of a century I have watched this educational motivation weaken, while librarians try to stay afloat by providing subject collections and handling information inquiries. Could it be that one of the drives that kept the public library going has faded just at the stage where it is most needed? Is this an institution for a minority at a time when culture finally seeps out through the majority? I mean this as an open question, not as a disguised criticism.

Conclusion

This has been a most fragmentary review of the changes, technical and social, which will redefine the library job. But in summary I have touched on enough changing perspectives to keep us all out of mischief for these next years:

from a people seeking productivity alone to a people also seeking value and fulfillment;

from an educational system concerned with numbers to one seeking to develop quality;

from a society of workers to a society of specialists;

from a readership limited to the elite to a readership extended to the underprivileged;

from the first step of building strong collections to the further step of

outreach of resources through the whole society;

from the traditional book to communication in new and ingenious forms;

from routines that sap our time and energy to machines that free us;

from your own separate library to a unit within an area-wide resource;

most important, from an assumption that what we do is automatically socially significant to a professional recommitment to library purposes.

Will librarians climb to a new perspective? Some clearly display a spirit of search and experiment. Others stand on what they have, defensive if challenged, scornful of the new. I leave you to judge which group predominates. Perhaps the prevailing attitude is one of watchful waiting and cautious trial. Certainly in a period of substantial change in education and communication, there has been relatively little change in libraries.

We are agreed that library perspectives are changing. But what do we mean? A little adjustment here, a new program appended there? I believe that much more is at issue and in prospect.

It could go either way. The school, the college, the laboratory, the community, indeed the basic social organization—all stimulated and nurtured from the nerve center of the library. Or the library as the respected matron of a bygone age, a little out of the mainstream, somewhere at the fringe of the action. I honestly believe that the institution has more than a gambler's chance of moving toward the center.

I know a way that librarians can hedge their bet, assuming they want to go for broke in the knowledge game. This can be accomplished by sponsorship and utilization of fairly basic research into how people use and misuse reading and information. Following research should come controlled experiment, to determine how the library can increase its impact. The winner will not be the group with the biggest computer; the prize will go to the one who understands people and communication.

I am sure that the year 2000, like 1900 and 1800, will include, on the one side, old and new means for communicating knowledge, and on the other, old and new people seeking to develop their capacities. Where the library will stand in this depends, it seems to me, not on hardware nor on organization but on what has counted all along—how much the librarian understands and commits himself to the aims and motives of his users, present and potential.

The key is not the library as an establishment but the librarian as an individual. May the Good Lord bless him with hope and with skepticism, with principle and with flexibility, with knowledge and with feeling, and above all with a sense of adventure.

Community, Library, and Revolution

Leonard H. Freiser

TRUE REVOLUTION begins when you see what is in front of your nose; its archetype is "The Emperor's New Clothes." Today, we are in the tail end of one revolution and in the beginning of another. The rise of capitalism and industrial states made possible by movable type and supported by the Reformation brought with them public schooling. The schools resembled the factories and clerking establishments they were set up to feed. Raw material entered this assembly line at regular intervals and was graded and processed in uniform steps to emerge as factory hands or workers in the supporting trades and professions. In the midst of this mechanical organization was a safety valve: the public library. In the public schools we were prepared for Henry Ford; in the public library we discovered Walt Whitman. The library must now be more than a safety valve. Our job is to catch up with this fact.

Some see today's revolution in terms of the shift from rigid mechanical technique to fluid electronic systems; in terms of new concepts of space and time; in terms of the loss of innocence. To me, the key to our time is the rediscovery of the human scale. Large government agencies, data processing, library reports are all phantoms without human reality. Our libraries are filled with a highly imaginative literature describing programs and gadgets which either do not exist or don't work. Here our catalogers have let us down; the literature of innovation belongs in 817-American Satire and Humor. Innovation is not revolution. Innovators devise new lids for cans, they don't get rid of the garbage.

With the rediscovery of the person we seek a style of life which has meaning beyond materialism. We are looking for honesty in ideas and education as well as training, esthetics not packaging, neighborhoods not shopping plazas or junk jungles. We are seeking a style of life which leads to healthy communities and which accommodates people. If we set out to create a style of service to help us in our search we would reinvent the library style. The public community library is the only institution available to every person in our society which is not out to sell, convince, deter or train. The library style serves the person, the community—not the institution. Our job is to catch up with this fact.

Our country needs us to such a degree that the expansion of library services which is now necessary may well be considered as revolutionary. Expan-

325

sion includes the provision of personnel and facilities for educational programs generated in the community; helping children and adults with reading and other learning problems; bringing in specialists in various aspects of community life so that accurate information and consultation can be locally available; providing people with the information they need concerning specific issues within the community.

My central thesis is that expanded community library services are as vital as are school systems and should be budgeted on equivalent levels. Our job is to insure all persons the freedom and the means to benefit from the one institution which they can use—the one institution which does not use them.

Immediately we face two groups of problems: one in the stubborn present, the other in the possible future. First is the resistance of librarians to accept active educational and social responsibilities. Modesty or timidity are not solely responsible for this. Rather, it is a credit to the intelligence of librarians that they are suspicious of anything which can be interpreted as being grandiose. But their intelligence is keeping them from their intuition and their sense of the moment. The 1970's is the time of the community library. Now is the time to say, "Yes, Commissioner Allen, the community libraries of the United States accept your challenge of The Right To Read. By the end of the 70's no person reaching maturity will be without competent individual reading services."

In an editorial "A Nation of Illiterates?" on September 30, 1969 the *New York Times* states, "The youth who leaves school without being able to read—and read well enough to cope with the demands of modern life and employment—enters society crippled. Worse, his deficiency is likely to impel him to become a drop-out, a frustrated embittered and easy victim of delinquency, drift and crime. At present, an estimated one-third of the nation's

schoolchildren are embarked on such a dismal course, and in the nation's big cities, the hopeless army is probably closer to half of the total enrollment. It is to this intolerable situation that James E. Allen Jr., the United States Commissioner of Education, addressed himself in opening a nationwide war against reading retardation. His target is to make sure that by 1980 no youngster will leave school unable to read. Few priorities ought to command more unquestioned support. Dr. Allen is justified in asking for a public determination as compelling as President Kennedy's earlier goal of landing a man on the moon."

We are uniquely suited for this big job and we don't know it. One group thought we were "It" back in the 1950's —the students. We told them to get out. We lost that moment, let's not lose this one.

In the *New York Times* story, "Illiteracy Considered Nation's No. 1 Education Problem," October 11, 1969, William K. Stevens states, "In addition to the 24 million illiterates, an estimated eight million to 12 million children now in school (exact figures are not available) have such serious reading problems that they are headed toward functional illiteracy as adults. 'Illiteracy is really a much greater functional handicap than is the loss of limbs,' says Dr. Grant Venn, Assistant United States Commissioner for Vocational and Adult Education . . . How will his program of wiping out illiteracy be pursued? 'No one knows yet,' said an aide to Dr. Allen . . . Although reading is probably one of the most investigated areas in education, relatively little is known about the exact process of eye, ear and brain by which individuals learn to read . . . It is now widely held that no one method works for all children and that a combination of methods—primarily phonics and whole-word recognition—is usually required, the mix and timing varying from child to child. During the last five years, concern has concentrated on the intellectual conditioning that a child brings to the moment when formal reading instruction is to begin. It is here, many believe, that the root causes of functional illiteracy are to be found. Dr. Conrad of the Office of Education's bureau of research believes this strongly. He would like to see the establishment of a system of 'early education centers,' where pre-school children essentially would play at speaking games; where adults speaking fluent, grammatical English would read to them and talk with them; where spoken communication would become enjoyable and increasingly sophisticated."

Reading grows on literature, individual attention, and a civilized manner. Learning thrives in an atmosphere of searching and discovery. This is the library we are talking about, nothing less. We are not committed to raise anyone to a particular set of pedagogical, occupational, patriotic or consumer specifications. The library's job is to maintain and transmit learning and information. I object to the limited interpretation some librarians have of the job we can, and must, do. Reading is the heart of the library, yet we have stood by while children leave our schools as illiterates and millions have not found out that they can enjoy a book. Information is part of the power of the library, yet we still stand by, waiting for people to come to us, when we know that out there are millions whose struggle for better lives and communities requires accurate and understandable information.

We are the powerhouse. Education and information are part of the hot core of community regeneration. It's our kitchen and now is the time to face up to the heat.

Some of my friends suggest that we can't go out and say these things; we need proof, feasibility studies. In our work there is only one feasible way to run a feasibility study and that is to get on with the job—go out and do what has to be done and make it work. I'd rather have taken part in important failures than sit around waiting for pallid studies to dribble in.

My antagonism to the entire engineering approach to social and educational situations is that it is philistine and depersonalizing. It is not uncommon, for instance, for library directors to devote themselves to studies and meetings (and meetings, and meetings) concerning information systems and networks and at the same time permit sorry reference service to the public.

Continuing in the stubborn present there are some librarians who say, "This is not our job. We are not teachers, welfare workers, town planners or what have you." In saying that we are not any of these, my friends are sitting on crucial information and miss the point completely. We in this country no longer want to be the unasked, unconsulted recipients of other people's programs. We do not want to be taught at, we wish to learn. We do not want to be taken care of, we want to be part of the planning. People want locally accessible facilities, personnel, and services which they can use to generate programs which are satisfying and important to them. The community public library, expanded and with budgets equivalent to school systems, is uniquely suited to meet these needs. Our job is to catch up with this fact.

The serious problems will hit us as soon as we reach our goals. The danger is that once we have the power to meet our responsibilities, this power will corrupt us. One answer is that we are a country of checks and balances— of alternates. Children and adults must have alternate ways to poetry and information. The schools have a bigger monopoly than the "Little Red Book" of Chairman Mao and this way is not good enough. We require alternate ways—equivalent ways. And if our way brings power it is inevitable that this power will be challenged. This is a very familiar dialectic except that in our intelligence, in our reasonableness we are unable to accept power. Like libraries without censorship problems because they have no controversial titles; like countries without white-black fights because they only have one color; we have no problems with power.

Equal to the debasement of power is the debasement of our objectives under the heady influence of bigness. We can see this operating today when we mimic industrial engineers and educators. The bookkeepers, the gadgeteers, and the jargon throwers are rampant in our field. They are interlopers in the country of Mark Twain and John Milton and Thomas Mann. It is not that we can't use competent technicians but we find them directing libraries. It's time to chase them out of our marketplace and into some quiet temple.

Another problem we face is our confusion about information. Information service involves a process which includes an actuality on one hand and learning on the other. The print in between what happens and what you learn about what happens sometimes helps and sometimes doesn't. The computer is not going to be much use to us if our reference desks continue to hand out misinformation in correct bibliographic form and continue to serve only those who think they can get information from us—which, in itself, may indicate that we have yet to serve the more sensible members of the public. For one thing, no one wants information per se; what is wanted is the knowledge which results from information. We are involved in the learning process as well as in the nature of information. Perhaps we should take this one more step: often, what is wanted is not knowledge but a change which knowledge may help bring about. At this point we become fully engaged in both educational and social action.

These, then, are some of our problems: our resistance to taking a more active part in educational and social programs; the presence of pedantic,

philistine and depersonalizing influences in our field; our inability to see the similarities between the public temper and the library style; the debasement of power; the debasement of objectives; and confusions concerning information.

To these problems I should add one more: once we have a few communities with successful programs we may then be tempted to impose these solutions on others. Therefore, you will understand why the following description is general rather than specific. Libraries and their programs will vary from place to place and they will be autonomous. They will contract with information and technical services networks; the growth of networks and improved technology supports the autonomous and expanded programs of community libraries. The library will derive part of its power from having comprehensive access to information and, especially, from its ability to get this information out into the community to individuals and to groups where it is needed. The library staff will be drawn from a variety of professions and trades such as reading specialists, film producers, politicians or political scientists, writers, musicians, teachers, etc.—either full-time or as consultants. The library will not be a building but a program which utilizes the qualities of a variety of structures: buildings—permanent, inflatable, geodesic; vehicles—express delivery to patrons, movable office for the librarian to enable her or him to get into the community, bookmobiles, film and TV trucks; and parts of existing buildings —police stations, courts, movie theaters. There will be facilities and personnel for literacy and literature programs for nursery and pre-school through adult. Many libraries will produce newspapers, books, magazines, plays, films, oral histories—both as educational programs directed by professionals in these fields and for the intrinsic value of the products. The program will support individuals who have no university affiliation and who wish to engage in independent research with grants and study facilities. The library is the center of community planning and activities. The library is the community ombudsman.

These and other programs will be spelled out in as many ways as there are communities. Some will have studios, some will have shops, others may publish, but all must continue the integrity of scholarship, of esthetics and of free and effective access which make them worthy of these responsibilities.

The cost of this program, especially when seen parallel to school system costs, may well be the factor which could get it launched. The argument that money is hard to get today does not apply to the changed conditions which now place the community library in a pre-eminent position in our society. My argument is not that public libraries need larger budgets, but that needed expanded operation puts the library in a different level of budgeting. I am not suggesting that a city library's budget go from $8 million to $12 million, but that the city library must develop an expanded program which reaches a budget level of $200 million. This figure brings our case into focus. If we can do the things I know we can do then we have to set the price consistent with the scope of the job. How would you react to someone who offered to build a house for you for $327? The question is not that money is short but that the expanded community library program is an essential and primary social and education necessity. Our job is to catch up with this fact. Now, we have to change the battleground from increments on $8 million to a leap to $200 million. We may have to face a variety of reactions but the important thing is to reach the right battleground. Let them cut our budgets—but cut them from $200 million.

We are faulted not by what we do but by what we do not do. I have spoken to many laymen, trustees, who condemn librarians for keeping libraries down. We have among us those who are unafraid to challenge national and domestic policies, bigotry, and repression of intellectual and academic freedom. The one thing which we do fear is the place waiting for us on center stage.

Civil Liberties, Libraries, and Computers

Joyce Crooks

The civil liberties issues involved in the keeping of public records certainly arose prior to the use of computers, but automated information systems have, beyond any question, aggravated those issues involved in all areas of application and have made the need for legal protection crucial, if we are not to see a synergistic development of national dossiers in our time.

Librarians have not been significantly concerned with the questions involved in debates on the Right to Privacy and access to public records in the past, and they seem reluctant even now to realize that these issues will be of increasing concern in the future. All of us must become much more cognizant of the civil liberties implications of computers in general, and of the specific character of library computers for record keeping, especially borrower's records and personnel files. In addition to the question of violation of privacy, networking and large-scale information retrieval applications have other ominous implications and must be discussed widely and knowledgeably if we are not to find ourselves with a national library information network which will be a dybbuk for generations to come.

Borrower's rights

The question of the rights of library users has arisen increasingly since the McCarthy era, usually in the form of a request to view the records of a particular borrower, or to see the names of all the persons who read a certain kind of book. Typically, such requests come from people representing considerable authority in a community, such as law enforcement personnel or members of city government, or from parents with what seems to be a legitimate request to see what their children read. Librarians who wish to refuse such a request often find themselves on very shaky ground; and while some who successfully resisted

330

have been reported in the library press, it is unfortunately likely that many quick capitulations were never reported. I know of several such incidents from the San Francisco Bay Area, although they have been less frequent in the last couple of years, owing to the increased political sophistication of librarians, and to the official policy statement of the American Library Association, however nebulous a help it may be in a showdown.

Until the recent Texas case no librarian has ever had any legal justification for such refusal. Before the Privacy Act of 1974, it has not been that simple to "establish" a right of privacy based on the Constitution alone, although the American Civil Liberties Union has expressed great interest in taking such a case. One of the especially thought-provoking and somewhat amusing precedents in the Texas case is that establishing the right of a man to read pornography in his own home.[2] If you can read pornography without undue interference of the state, you can read library books without undue interference of neighbors! In any case, it seems fairly certain that this will serve as a precedent to help protect libraries and librarians from casual violations of borrowers' records.

There still remains the problem of protecting the integrity of the files against law enforcement bodies with subpoenas in hand. The Privacy Act[3] is intended to protect individuals from the abuses of federal government files and is particularly applicable to automated retrieval systems and data banks. A data bank is very carefully defined as a combination of retrieval systems designed to gather otherwise scattered material in one place for more effective use regarding one subject.[4] It is intended to insure that citizens will know that information has been collected on them, and for what purpose; that the accuracy and timeliness of such information may be challenged; and that the file cannot be shared with other departments for other than its original purpose without the individual's consent. Exempt from the Act are all law en-

forcement agencies, or agencies claiming to be collecting intelligence data for law or national security purposes. In these circumstances, the citizen or library patron would have no protection. If a law enforcement office, FBI agent, IRS agent, or whatever, persuades a judge to issue a subpoena, however ill-advised, the librarian must obey it.

The buddy system

Although there has been some discussion about the integrity of borrowers' files, another form of widespread abuse—that of records of employees, public and private—has generated very little concern. This absence of concern is the result of two major factors: 1) The "buddy system" of casual information-sharing on individuals, between offices, colleagues, jurisdictions, to and from police, credit bureaus, etc., is so common that it rarely elicits any comments at all, although the effect of the exchange sometimes amounts to a "black list" based on hearsay, or inaccurate or biased information (Westin and Baker note that these exchanges are often in direct violation of laws or official policies); 2) an individual, particularly an applicant, is unable to challenge such information when he cannot usually even prove that such an exchange has taken place.[5]

One of the most sensitive areas in this regard is the arrest record. It has long been common practice for all civil service and governmental recruiting applications to include the question, "Have you ever been arrested?" It is also very common with large private employers. To answer "yes" often meant one would not be hired. There are 7.5 million arrests a year, of which one quarter result in convictions. Sixty percent of white urban males are likely to be arrested during their lifetime, compared with 90 percent of black urban males. Civil service jurisdictions did query applicants on arrest, according to one study, and 75 percent of the employment agencies studied in the New York area "would not accept an applicant with an arrest record ... *without* conviction.''[6] The innocent and the guilty suffer alike!

Since the mass arrests of large numbers of middle-class activists and bystanders in the 1960's, questions of police and FBI information exchange have received greater notoriety, insofar as such records are often incomplete and/or inaccurate. The information on dismissal of charges, or a not guilty verdict, is often omitted from the FBI or police records, since these verdicts are not of primary interest to these agencies. Consequently, many have been denied jobs almost automatically without any cause, and certainly without due process or recourse.[7]

Civil rights legislation now requires that only conviction questions be allowed on job applications, and that a job cannot be refused on the ground of conviction unless it can be shown that the offense directly relates to the prospective position.[8] But the casual sharing of police information with employers, and credit bureaus, remains a basic and major problem of due process and privacy for most library employees.[9]

An especially heavy stigma surrounds ex-drug users and those who have a history of mental health problems.[10] Activism in college can cause trouble, too, so much so that many colleges have stopped keeping files on club memberships,[11] so that FBI agents and other investigators simply cannot obtain such data, even with a subpoena. Many students have stopped joining clubs at all, for fear that participating in fully legal dissent activity in college could haunt them in later life.[12]

The Privacy Act no doubt has foreshadowed many attempts on the part of state and local governments to enact regulations and laws which will protect personnel files from casual intrusion. Solano County, California, has drawn up such a personnel rule.[13] This document includes some procedures that are notable in their regard for due process and fairness. Among these are: 1) Before information from the master personnel file is given to any law enforcement agency, the employee shall be notified so that he may obtain counsel if necessary. 2) Without a demonstrable "need to know," only public information can be revealed, for instance the fact that the employee works there, his salary range, length of service, etc. 3) The permission of the employee is not sufficient reason to reveal contents of a file. This last point brings up the question of the "informed consent" of the employee.[14] That is, is the employee necessarily the best judge of what s/he should or should not reveal? Credit bureaus, in particular, often operate in flagrant disregard for the rights of privacy, and often of the law; and the person applying for a loan, credit to buy a house, or whatever, is often reluctant to refuse information if it might jeopardize these services.[15] Present practice, that is, the routine invasion of privacy in which we are all used to living our lives, makes the refusal of information under conditions such as these seem like an act of heroism.

Libraries have not been in the forefront in computerization of files, or in the development of data bases for multiple functions, nor are they uppermost in the mind of the public with regard to needed controls. But because of the increasing reliance on information for decision-making in all areas of American life, libraries, too, will find careful planning of systems design and objectives mandatory, if they are not to find themselves embroiled in lawsuits and besieged by angry taxpayers. Those who have not had problems of protecting confidential information in the past will most certainly have them in the future.

The obvious question here is: why do computers make that much difference? There are a number of reasons: 1) A switch to computers means there is a tendency to collect more information on individuals than when that information had to be handled manually. 2) Protection of the system is more difficult as more points of access must be controlled, if the information collected appears more valuable than before (for example, increased inquiries into loyalty of personnel, or reading records) this can become a protection problem that could prove costly to solve. 3) The tendency to share information or a computer system within a jurisdiction or a network means many more persons have access to your files who do not share your priorities or loyalties, as in "time sharing" situations with other governmental offices. This can also be an enormous problem where libraries share a computer in a network, where there are state systems planning to add circulation programs to existing bibliographic ones, it is potentially a major civil liberties problem, and careful attention must be paid to what information is to be collected, and how it is to be protected, if individual rights are not to be violated.

As long ago as 1965, I heard a very forward-looking librarian say, while contemplating the possibility of a giant computer serving all of the libraries of the San Francisco Bay Area, "Just think, if someone had overdue books from Richmond, we could stop them from taking out books in San Jose." Which brings us to the final difference between manual files and computers: the astronomical difference in surveillance capacity.

Circulation control is surveillance

Since so many large and hitherto bibliographic or acquisition systems are considering this move to add circulation files and presumably borrowers' files, it is time to talk about the real nature of circulation records, in whatever form.[16] (Both Stanford's BALLOTS and OCLC are discussing plans to add circulation to their systems.) Circulation systems, put simply, are social surveillance systems. Any information retrieval system meets this criterion if: it "in general enhances the ability of organizations . . . to achieve their ends. In other words, 1) whenever a bureaucratic agency seeks to make and enforce discriminating decisions concerning a mass clientele, and 2) whenever these decisions must accord with details of clients' past circumstances of behavior, and 3) whenever they entail points of potential conflict between system and clientele, it is advantageous to the system

to develop the maximum possible surveillance capacity." And further regarding the potentiality of library systems, ". . . centralization of filed data allows any system to bring the full weight of clients' records to bear in any decision-making concerning them, and prevents clients from evading the effects of their records through flight. It should likewise be clear that the extension of points of contact between system and clientele, by maximizing the incorporation of pertinent data and the ability to act aggressively towards clients when necessary, helps the task of surveillance."[17]

Note here that this does assume on-line capability—the ability to query the computer as to past performance of any patron within a few seconds. Technology is making the combination and sharing of files more possible than ever before. Although there certainly are manual files of data bank nature, the public has a justifiable fear of any mechanism that allows for increased surveillance.[18] Black people seem to be more aware, both of the necessity for giving up privacy to obtain public services, and of the violation of privacy in questionnaires for all purposes, and of political surveillance, as both Neier and Ervin point out in the works cited elsewhere. This might be one of the primary reasons public libraries have found it almost impossible to increase their clientele significantly in minority communities. The spread of computerized circulation networks, with their much more active surveillance nature, could mean fewer persons will be willing to trade additional invasion of privacy for library services.

General sensitivity to potential misuse of computerized information is of course increasing among all classes, which is what generated the study leading up to the Privacy Act.[19] The study was undertaken in response to widespread public apprehension about data banks, and what seemed an unlimited right of private data-collecting agencies, and especially of the government, to invade individual privacy. The main point of the study is that *all* automated data systems, not just federal systems, should come under a Code of Fair Information Practice. According to these recommendations, all data systems with individually identifiable information should have the following minimum safeguards: 1) one person should be directly responsible for the system; 2) each employee should be informed about the system and the legal consequences for leaking information to unauthorized persons, with specific consequences for such acts; 3) reasonable precautions must be taken to protect the system, in terms of both physical and electronic access; 4) no transfer of information may be made to other systems without verifying that security requirements will be maintained; 5) a complete and accurate record of all instances of access to the system must be kept; 6) the file must be as complete, up-to-date, and accurate as possible to minimize potential harm to individuals; 7) data must be eliminated from the files when it is no longer timely; 8) annual notices must be published describing each extant system and must cover: kind of information held, how many subjects are covered, policies concerning storage, the use to be made of data, and procedures whereby individuals can examine or correct files; and 9) specific procedures must be clearly delineated whereby the individual can challenge the data held, and a person must be able to obtain remuneration in court if all other avenues fail.

The regulations were necessary because few of these safeguards were being used by those responsible for data banks or computer systems.

The law, as finally enacted, states that only information necessary to the original purpose of the file can be collected, and that it must be removed from the file as soon as the original purpose is no longer served. It does not allow for the use of a Social Security number for any purpose except one connected with Social Security, and any information form asking for individual data to be fed to such a computer must show which questions are mandatory and which are optional.

Library data abuses

This new guideline brings up some very interesting questions about current practices in library borrower registration procedures. Librarians dimly perceive the surveillance nature of circulation records. They have asked for driver's license numbers, Social Security numbers, place of work, and other data not needed for the purpose of circulation. One library which has computerized its borrowers' records still asks some of these questions—then puts only the name and address into the computer and throws away the application. Libraries have never, to my knowledge, indicated whether or not omitting answers to questions would deprive prospective borrowers of library privileges.

The Privacy Act of 1974 applies only to federal computers and data banks, but also creates a commission "to prepare model privacy legislation for state and local governments." Such legislation, which would bring state and local governmental data bank jurisdictions under at least the same controls as the federal ones, is now pending.[20] Some local jurisdictions have already gone further. Berkeley, California, has enacted an ordinance which requires a social impact statement for any new or additional automated systems, and a study of alternate ways of doing the job, even of not doing the job at all.[21] It requires that new data programs have wide publicity within the city, and a public hearing before implementation of any new data bank plan.

The new federal bill will bring to a halt certain other abuses some librarians with new computer systems seem unable to resist. One of these is putting economic or occupational information into the computer in order to do a use study at some future date. The new bill will make the collection of such nonessential information by public libraries illegal.

People greatly fear the fact that computers create "unforgetting and unforgiving" record systems. They are especially apprehensive that the people who work with the computers treat "printouts" as gospel, and that clerks assume machines can't make mistakes. Westin and Baker point out, however, that machine records tend to contain more mistakes, not fewer, and that people who think record keepers, especially civil servants, have ever been noted for taking an individual's side in a debate with a written record have obviously never heard of Kafka.

Some libraries have already begun looking for ways to safeguard circulation and borrowers' records in computer situations. Some of these safeguards are: 1) the registration file can be kept separately from the computerized file and/or manually; 2) all circulation records can be erased from the file when the item is returned, and a record can still be kept showing how many times a book circulates; 3) books can be charged by an identification number instead of by borrower's name; 4) minimum data can be requested from the patron, extra questions, if asked, can be clearly indicated as "optional."

Librarians must weigh carefully whether the added ability to query a library user about books overdue or lost in another jurisdiction is worth the additional negative surveillance impact this will have with many borrowers. At issue here are the conflicting ideals of the law and order "wrong-doers should be punished" forces against those of forgiveness, the "people should be able to escape their past" group. The more data one has about patrons, the more it will be used. Challenging patrons from such data involves doing so face-to-face and in public. There are few people who would continue to use the library after such an affront to their dignity, and many bystanders are likely to be almost as greatly offended. These patrons are lost to the library. Can any of us afford such an image? What is the true cost of "efficiency" in such a situation?

Personal personnel records

The problems involved in the keeping of public records in libraries will still be relatively easy of solution compared to those of administrative files of employee's records, and the problem of reducing the prevalence of the "buddy system."

James Rule found that no subject aroused more defensiveness and antagonism among administrators than this one. Why do employers think they must, or ought to, have so much information on applications that is not job-related? Do questions such as past medical history, psychoanalysis, past hospitalization, treatment for drug abuse, sex life, sex orientation, union membership, political activism or beliefs, or religious beliefs, really become problems on the job to the extent that routine violation of personal privacy and due process are justified? It is still common for interviewers to ask questions of a personal nature, especially whether women are going to get married, or have a baby and leave, and whether unmarried men are homosexuals. Two years ago, a delegation from the University of California, Berkeley, School of Librarianship came to a meeting of the San Francisco Bay Area Social Responsibilities Round Table to ask that the group investigate what they considered improper questions regarding their sex lives asked during oral interviews. SRRT did not do so because the students were too apprehensive about being identified to give even the names of the interviewing institutions.

Police are notoriously helpful at supplying wanted information to all governmental jurisdictions, and both police and private employers have virtually unlimited access to credit bureau investigation if they care to use them, which they often do.[22] New laws will not necessarily be a corrective remedy for these practices, for many of them now go on in disregard of existing laws and institutional regulations. Nothing can stop these practices but an increased awareness that personal privacy is being invaded and a decreased tolerance for them. When administrators see such practices as dangerous, that is, potentially leading to law suits, or as threatening to the organization, they will cease according to Rule.

Surveillance in our society

Our concepts of privacy have changed during the last two decades or so, and it is difficult to discuss how that has happened without a further discussion of surveillance in American life. Most Americans are now aware that they have probably been the subject of a dossier of some kind, as an employee (especially of a federal employer, or as a scientist), as a recipient of state or federal aid of any kind, as a credit bureau subject, as the result of an encounter with the police, but most likely, as someone who has come to the attention of one of the local police intelligence units, the FBI, or one of the more than 20 federal agencies collecting intelligence on private citizens.[23]

Evidence of their scope is all around us: the FBI opens mail of anyone who has been to Russia, including Boy Scouts. At the time of the Peace Marches in San Francisco, the employees in at least one Bay Area library were told by someone in the Sheriff's Office that they had photographs of all employees who had participated. Dossiers are opened on school children, carefully noting "anti-social" behavior, such as preferring to work alone.[24] No status provides protection. Congressmen are monitored also. Only just recently, Congressman Dellums complained his office was bugged. J. Edgar Hoover used to amuse various presidents with stories of the private wrongdoings of Congressmen, and Congressmen have greatly feared the dossier consequences of voting against appropriation requests of the FBI.[25] Dr. Martin Luther King's private life was monitored for years, and the FBI tried to blackmail him with the resultant tapes.[26] No one seems too unimportant for investigation; it is well-known that both FBI and CIA and all of the Armed Forces have secret investigators and informers on campuses.[27]

One might well ask, what do all of these people investigate? Anyone who is, or who is potentially, a dissenter to the U.S. government. That would include anyone who actually speaks out against the government, anyone who might become a leader and might possibly dissent in the future, all groups with potential power, especially all minority groups and potential minority leaders, labor unions, groups such as the ACLU or NAACP and individuals interested in constitutional rights, those involved in "Earth Day," etc. In fact, they seem for the most part to be investigating people involved in fully legal activities. It has been argued that the surveillance of legal activities produces a "chill" and an inhibition about continuing, or beginning, such activities. It also causes the activity to be looked on as "tainted," or somehow illegal, and those who engage in it as socially stigmatized. Additionally, it has been noted that there is a significant difference between the tolerance of dissentors in Britain and America, and it is believed that the lesser tolerance of Americans has been produced by systematic and continued surveillance as official policy by our government over a period of several decades. Even if surveillance stopped tomorrow, political activity would remain repressed, perhaps through several generations. Awareness of such all-pervading stigma does not disappear overnight.[28]

My generation learned its lesson watching our elders suffer during McCarthy's time for their political beliefs in the thirties and forties, and this generation has seen those politically involved in the sixties reduced to silence during the Nixon administration. The infamous "Houston Plan" approved by Nixon, included six recommendations amounting to a virtual definition of all citizens as "enemies." The plan included: 1) intensifying electronic surveillance of all domestic security threats and foreign diplomats; 2) increased monitoring of American citizens using international communications facilities; 3) increased mail coverage; 4) more informants on college campuses; 5) listing restraints on "surreptitious entry"; and 6) the establishment of an interagency group to coordinate existing intelligence and internal security agencies, with representatives from the White

House, FBI, CIA, NSA, DIA, and the three militaries.[29] According to the recent revelations concerning the CIA, all of these things have already been done, except the last two, which were seemingly prevented by Watergate.

It would be comforting to think that it was the paranoia of our late intrepid FBI leader, reinforced by that of Nixon, which had brought us to our present acquiescence in the loss of our civil liberties, and that our institutions will automatically now revert to ones respecting due process and privacy, as befits a democratic country. The fact is, however, that Nixon's recommendations could not have been effected had not our civil liberties already been eroded.

John Raines, an Assistant Professor of Religion at Temple University, has written a most informative book reviewing the developments through which we lost our civil liberties. Raines says that it is through the conversion of the government into a guarantor of big business, necessitated by the New Industrial State (as described by Galbraith) which marked the change from a government of the people. This need for big business to control the market necessitated enormous amounts of social control, which only the government could provide. As Raines points out: "This is the result, not of bureaucratic necessity . . . but of the pursuit of human ambition and the bending of society for that purpose."[30] That this has been achieved is the real lesson of Watergate. Raines reminds us that it is the *right* of the people to watch the government, not vice versa, and that cosy regulation of business by the government for what is plainly their mutual benefit can be maintained only by the privatization of power and the pacification of public protest. In order for this to be effected, the affairs of the state must be secret, defined as "national security," and the affairs of the citizens must be public.

This has been accomplished by: 1) trivializing private needs; 2) stigmatizing activity which supports individual feelings of self-worth and self-reliance; and 3) humiliating people by forcing them to trade privacy for needed services. To quote Raines again: "Humiliation is the invasion of our inner silences and self-space to render us docile to the interests of others. It is an attack upon our dignity and reserve as persons."[31]

NCLIS and privacy

It has been necessary to wander into the society at large briefly in order to provide perspective on the issue of a national system of libraries as proposed by the National Commission of Libraries and Information Science.[32] The NCLIS plan is conceived of as a bibliographic, communication, and retrieval network of massive and inclusive proportions, involving public libraries, universities and colleges, information retrieval service companies, and other private companies involved in information services, including publishers.

Space does not allow a full discussion of the civil liberties issues which would be affected by this plan. Several of them can be touched upon here. Further discussion should be forthcoming.

First of all, the plan places an emphasis on machine retrieval and communication, including a heavy commitment of the federal government to support further research and development of all computer communications technology by private industry, and funding of all aspects of the program.[33] The plan envisions large public libraries forming the "backbone" of the network, although it would clearly be advanced researchers, scientists, and technicians who would benefit most by such a sophisticated information network, people who are not now served by the public libraries at all, but by special libraries and universities and colleges. The plan would do little for the public library user, or for school libraries, and most special libraries are of such a nature that they would receive little benefit. Such a network would necessitate a complete reordering of priorities away from public services in public libraries, because funds, personnel, materials, and time would of necessity have to be given to the network priority. There is little likelihood that sufficient funds would be available for both services and technology. For most of the public, this simply means less access to materials and services. The NCLIS package also includes the proposal to pass on the enormous costs of the technological package by charging the patron for information and services, which appears as a serious threat to the tradition of free public library access. The controversy over who will pay for what, and how much, is already raging.[34]

As now written the NCLIS plan is paradoxically capable of solving some of the acquisition and access problems of universities and special libraries while potentially lessening the services and materials available in public libraries. One acquisitions librarian commented to me that networking tends to limit the acquisition of unusual or "underground" material simply because there is no ready-made procedure for cataloging it. In Peter Simmons' paper previously cited it is noted that in general, network participation tends to diminish local autonomy.

The Commission Report states that they see the agency controlling a federal network as "neither all-encompassing, nor authoritarian, nor prescriptive, nor regulatory, but rather, that it should be supportive and coordinating." But participating agencies who accept grants for cooperation with the plan would be subject to the regulations of the granting agency. Therefore the granting agency could be described as a regulatory agency. Many other commentators see such an agency as both potentially powerful and possibly dangerous. One scientist takes the view that "regulation and control is the proper function of government."[35] Olson, Shank, and Olsen state flatly that a national system will not work without regulation, or even "monolithic control."[36] "One reason for doubt about effective action on the national level is the lack of centralized control over information services in the U.S.," they state, and go on to cite a study which lists eight centers of influence in U.S. librar-

ies. The study expresses further doubt that such a network involving all libraries can be established under any circumstances.

We would do well, therefore, to concern ourselves with the implications of federal control. One model we have to look at is the Federal Communications Commission. The FCC is known to have a black list of thousands of names to whom it will not issue licenses; and in November 1975 the Washington *Post* printed an article attacking the FCC for not being able to keep up with technology and being too close to the companies they are supposed to be regulating.[37] In short, most government regulating bodies we are familiar with behave as Raines describes. If such a body is needed to carry out this plan, it behooves us to wonder if the benefits could possibly outweigh the civil liberties threats involved.

Attention should also be paid to the problems that will arise as publishing via a computer becomes commonplace, especially if that computer is part of a national system. It is expected that growth of publishing by machine will greatly accelerate, and that growth of scientific publishing will virtually explode. Machines have in fact already begun to change the nature of publishing.[38] The demand for less scientific duplication,[39] and the expense of information retrieval will all contribute to the necessity of controlling information at the source of publication.

Finally, one can only question why information is suddenly of federal priority status. Does the federal government really care about the dangers of "information chaos"? They have not heretofore been known as generous supporters of either libraries in general, or even of federal libraries,[40] although they have put over $1 billion into computers.[41] Can it be that libraries, information sources, and the "private sector" are now recognized as essential adjuncts to the research necessary to increase the G.N.P., insure national defense, and aid "internal security"? If the growth of the products of technological communications, especially 2-way cable TV, leads to the necessity for making communication products more homogenous (as books are in Russia), in order for the "private sector" to make a profit, so much the better. Control need not be repressive in intent to be repressive in fact. It need only be total. Consider the highly mechanized "model" libraries in Russia, mentioned by Simmons.

We now are at a turning point and must make a choice. The "easy rider" approach is before us. We can ride on the backs of the federal priorities, where the big money is, and establish, or attempt to establish, a national system of disparate parts with uncertain outcome, and unknown costs. Or, we can continue to look for solutions for parts of the problem, establish homogenous networks, explore further ways of sharing, etc., while we carefully consider alternate structures. More answers are needed, by far. Would the public commit us to a national plan if they were asked? I for one do not see any more reason for thinking there exists only one solution than that there is only one problem for all libraries.

In the end, there is one important question, and that is whether 1984 will happen while we are admiring the efficiency of it all, or whether we will insist that machines must be used for social objectives that include human values as their basic component.

REFERENCES

1. American Library Association. Policy on Confidentiality of Library Circulation Records. Chicago, ALA, 1970.

2. "Library records are confidential in Texas," *Newsletter on Intellectual Freedom*, September 5, 1975, p. 133f.

3. Privacy Act of 1974. 5 USC 552a.

4. Westin, Alan F., & Michael A. Baker. *Databanks In a Free Society: Computers Recordkeeping and Privacy.* (Report of the project on computer databanks . . . National Academy of Sciences.) Quadrangle, 1972. p. 200f.

5. Miller, Arthur R., "Computers, data banks, and individual privacy: an overview," in *Surveillance, Dataveillance, and Personal Freedoms; Use and Misuse of Information Technology; a Symposium.* ed. by the Staff of the *Columbia Human Rights Law Review.* Fair Lawn, N.J., R. E. Burdick, 1973. p. 20.

6. Raines, John C. *Attack on Privacy.* Valley Forge, Pa., Judson Pr., 1974. p. 30f.

7. Neier, Aryeh. *Dossier: The Secret Files They Keep on You.* Stein & Day, 1974. Chapter 9, "The Scarlet Letter: Conviction Records."

8. U.S. Equal Employment Opportunity Commission. *Affirmative Action and Equal Employment: A Guide for Employers.* Washington, D.C., U.S. GPO, 1974. Vol. 1, p. 41f.

9. Askin, Frank. "Surveillance, the Social Science Perspective," in *Surveillance, Dataveillance, and Personal Freedoms: Use and Misuse of Information Technology; A Symposium.* Ed. by the staff of the *Columbia Human Rights Law Review.* Fair Lawn, N.J., R. E. Burdick, 1973. p. 90.

10. Neier, *op. cit.,* Chapters 5, 6, 11.

11. Askin, *op. cit.,* p. 92f.

12. Ervin, Sam J., Jr. "The First Amendment: a Living Thought on the Computer Age," in *Surveillance, Dataveillance, and Personal Freedoms; Use and Misuse of Information Technology; A Symposium.* Ed. by the staff of the *Columbia Human Rights Law Review.* Fair Lawn, N.J., R. E. Burdick, 1973. p. 50.

13. Solano County, California, "Disclosure of Personal History Files." October 1975.

14. Baker, Michael A., "Record Privacy as a Marginal Problem: The Limits of Consciousness and Concern," in *Surveillance, Dataveillance, and Personal Freedoms; Use and Misuse of Information Technology; A Symposium.* Ed. by the staff of the *Columbia Human Rights Law Review.* Fair Lawn, N.J., R. E. Burdick, 1973. p. 109.

15. Miller, Arthur R. *The Assault on Privacy: Computers, Data Banks, And Dossiers.* Ann Arbor, Univ. of Michigan Pr., 1971. p. 83f. Also: Thomas Whiteside, "Credit Bureaus," *New Yorker,* April 21, 1975, p. 45f.

16. Simmons, Peter. "Library Automation," In *Annual Review of Information Science*

and Technology. American Society for Information Science, Vol. 8, 1973. p. 180.

17. Rule, James B. *Private Lives and Public Surveillance; Social Control in the Computer Age.* Schocken, 1974. p. 29f, 333f.

18. Ervin, *op. cit.*, p. 33.

19. U.S. Department of Health, Education, and Welfare. *Report of the Secretary's Advisory Committee on Automated Personal Data Systems: Records, Computers, and the Rights of Citizens.* GPO, 1973.

20. H.R. 1984, 94th Congress, 1st Session. January 23, 1975. Also: Barry M. Goldwater, Jr., "Bipartisan Politics," *The Civil Liberties Review,* Summer 1974, p. 744.

21. Ordinance No. 4732 N.S., October, 1974.

22. Shields, Hannah & Mae Churchill. "Criminal Data Banks: The Fraudulent War on Crime," *Nation,* December 21, 1974, p. 648.

23. Miller, *op. cit.*, p. 21.

24. Neier, *op. cit.*, Chapters 1-3.

25. Askin, *op. cit.*, p. 95.

26. Donner, Frank, "Electronic Surveillance: The National Security Game," *Civil Liberties Review,* Summer 1974, p. 15f. Also: Raines, *op. cit.*, p. 32.

27. Donner, Frank J. "Political Intelligence: Cameras, Informers, and Files," *Civil Liberties Review,* Summer 1974, p. 8f. Also: Raines, *op. cit.*, p. 32.

28. Ervin, *op. cit.*, p. 30f., 74f.

29. Raines, *op. cit.*, p. 34.

30. Raines, *ibid.*, p. 44.

31. Raines, *ibid.*, p. 58.

32. National Commission on Libraries and Information Science. *Toward a National Program for Library and Information Service: Goals for Action,* GPO, 1975.

33. ———. *Annual Report to the President and Congress: 1973-74,* GPO, 1975.

34. Wright, Christopher. "Pricing knowledge: Annual Meeting of the American Society for Information Science," *American Libraries,* January 1975, p. 8f. Also: "New computerized services provide speedy (but not free) copies 'on demand,'" *Publishers Weekly,* 206:21. Also: Penner, Rudolf J., "The practice of charging users for information service," *Journal of the American Society for Information Science,* January-February 1970, p. 67f.

35. "The growth of scientific and technical information—A Challenge." *Information.* 3:3, 1974, p. 9.

36. Olson, Edwin E., Russell Shank, and Harold A. Olsen, "Library and Information Networks." In *Annual Review of Information Science and Technology.* American Society for Information Science, Vol. 7, 1972, p. 307.

37. Ervin, *op. cit.*, p. 29.

38. "Data base publishers vying for key roles as rapid growth looms in business use," *Publishers Weekly,* September 16, 1974, p. 36f.

39. Garfield, Eugene. "Is there a future for the scientific journal?" *Sci-Tech News,* April 1975, p. 42f.

40. Martin, Susan K., "Library Automation." In *Annual Review of Information Science and Technology,* American Society for Information Science, Vol. 7, 1972, p. 250.

41. Simmons, *op. cit.*, p. 179.

Let It All Hang Out: A Think Piece for Luddite Librarians

Sanford Berman

IF ANYBODY really loves libraries today, it must be the power companies and electronics industry, for we gleefully purchase, so it seems, almost anything that plugs in, flashes, bleeps, or hums. There are the giant computers, some of which occasionally spew out— at enormous cost—cumbersome, promptly outdated lists of serial holdings, or the siren-activating, turnstile-locking detection systems to encourage pilferers to reach new levels of sophistication.

Bright young circuitry-men and information-retrievers speak enchantedly about their programs and machines as if these were inestimable *ends* in themselves. Research, teaching, and development money appears increasingly directed to mechanical gimmickry. Despite all the lofty talk about "social responsibility," the electric socket seems to enjoy progressively more dollars-and-cents attention than the flesh-and-blood reader. Librarianship, of course, is not unique in this. In the nation itself (let alone the world), about a third of the populace, including 5,000,000 aged, the "old folks" who safely and devotedly squired many of us through wars and depression, is under-fed and under-housed. Yet national resources are overwhelmingly channeled into either an

expensive, circus-like, ego-tripping space-race or to pacify the uppity, ungrateful "natives" of Southeast Asia, Africa, and Latin America. Experts acknowledge that the delivery system for medical care verges on a breakdown, that only the fortunate fraction of our citizenry who can pay for it receive full medical attention. Yet "medical" funding for esoteric research and gadgetry, together with frenzied "empire building"—both unrelated to immediate human needs—escalate, while federal grants for cancer study have declined. Unemployment is chronic, presently exceeding six percent of the employable. (Sweden, as a comparative example, proclaims a national crisis when this figure approaches two percent.) Yet job-killing automation continues unabated, and necessary, job-generating social projects remain unbegun. Our environment nears catastrophe. Yet the very corporate interests who profit from junk production, blissfully pollute the atmosphere, and haphazardly alienate the land suffer only polite knuckle-rappings—for they bulwark the whole politico-economic structure.

A classical Luddite might indiscriminately damn *all* the multiplying soft- and hardware. But that would be foolishly naive, sentimental, Utopian. The

341

age of cottage industry and idyllic agriculture is past. And that many library-related machines perform essential, service-improving tasks cannot be challenged. (Indeed, the warmly welcome *Alternative Press Index* owes its existence to a computer. So does the annual *Periodicals in East African Libraries,* which vastly facilitates interlibrary borrowing among a number of otherwise isolated, "developing" institutions.) Still, the suspicion grows that an untouchable elite is developing within the profession: a coalition of technocrats and bureaucrats dedicated—even if somewhat unwittingly—to making themselves indispensable by virtue of their ability to manipulate and expand the "new technology" plus the more complicated administrative-budgetary apparatus associated with it. If many colleagues share this suspicion, it might be well to profoundly re-assess our fundamental attitudes and priorities before things get totally out of hand.

To what extent, for instance, may super-mechanization of libraries—and its all too likely depersonalization of services—actually "turn off" current and potential users, many of whom want little more than access to the books, magazines, and nonprint items that will satisfy their personal interests and curiosity, and who "dig" the opportunity to rap at leisure with another sensitive, literate, helpful person? (Should this sound preposterously old-fashioned, undertake a simple experiment: Try rapping with a teaching machine or microfilm reader. It's a frustrating experience, certainly less pleasurable than discourse with a live, albeit imperfect, human. One fellow's encounter with a talking cigarette-automat a few years ago in Germany proved completely lop-sided. The contraption never stopped its own guttural rumbling long enough to understand that, since no weed packet had been ejected, the would-be smoker only wanted his Deutsch-Mark back.)

To what extent might library automation contribute to worsening unemployment? Or has already done

so? Is it considered as a factor in deciding whether to install new machinery or systems that such "innovations" may permanently displace or eliminate some of the library labor force? Even acknowledging "efficiency" and cost reduction *per se* as cardinal elements in our Western, industrial mythology, may it not be socially *ir*responsible to heartily embrace labor-*saving* devices that will unconscionably dump people into an economy ill-prepared to ensure them a decent livelihood (not to mention soul satisfying work)? Or, on the positive side, have we sufficiently explored the possibility, for instance, of hiring capable, unemployed youths and senior citizens to perform exit-checks instead of relying upon magnetic fields that don't have to pay rent or buy bread?

To what extent may the mounting emphasis on technology impose inflexibility on many of our operations and, further, permit or dictate certain regressive policies? To illustrate: Reform of obsolete or offensive subject headings has been opposed in some places not because such reform is itself unwarranted, but rather due to a[1] fear that local alterations will not mesh or harmonize with, say, the computerized LC scheme upon which individual institutions may have become dependent. In other words, a library might reluctantly choose to retain the slaver-derived, black-denounced, ambiguously-assigned head, "Negroes," rather than replace it with the more accurate and patently acceptable terms, "Afro-Americans," "Afro-Brazilians," etc., solely out of an anxiety that to deviate from the computer standard would wreak havoc in its catalog or, correlatively, invite heavy expenditures in changing the centrally provided data on tapes and cards. LC's recently developed music headings have already alarmed several catalogers, who allege that they were constructed not with music and users as the primary foci, but rather to placate the computer. And an ostensibly admirable project like Bell & Howell's micro-package of UPS titles, while a thoughtful and requisite gift to future generations of scholars, could equally function as a ready-made alibi for subscribing libraries not to stock the inky, perishable—but immensely more enticing and readable—"underground" originals for the benefit of right-now patrons. The unhurried researcher may be content to scan a six-month-old run of *Kaleidoscope* in a quiet, secluded micro-cubicle. Others, however, for whom tabloids like *Kaleidoscope* express vital aspects of their daily life and furnish instantly usable information, want the latest edition as quickly as the library can get it—and are sure to "groove" on it all the more when they can relax with it, perhaps even share it with nearby brethren. The danger, in short, is that of sacrificing immediate reader needs and satisfactions to what is essentially an archival, elitist, long-term objective. (The solution, clearly, is to take *both* media forms, yet the temptation will undoubtedly be to buy the micro-package and then argue that this fulfills the two distinct obligations. The same argument, of course, could be applied to the *New York Times* and *London Times*. But won't be.)

Returning to priorities, to attitudes: Given that any library—and the profession as a whole—has resource limits in labor and funds, how are these resources to be distributed? What projects more urgently demand our money and creative energy than others? It may be —as much of the recent professional literature and agitation suggest—that we have reached a philosophical, if not also spiritual, watershed. Which way do we go? Which side are we on?

Now that gadgetry apostles, administrative autarchs, and those whom Phillip Berrigan has termed "passive robots in the technological waxworks" have probably dismissed most of the foregoing as retrograde nonsense or Leftist cant, let's get to the nitty-gritty:

The libraries we work in, where we get our kicks, where we think we're doing something worthwhile and socially productive, the libraries in which

we've invested our training, imagination, adrenalin, and lives, could soon become magnificently irrelevant to ourselves, our society, our world. This is not to predict a sudden apocalypse, only to note a discernible drift.

Much verbiage has been expended on how to become "relevant." Much doubt, however, surrounds the question of whether that verbiage has in fact transformed many attitudes or notably redirected our available resources. All of us suppose that libraries do something valuable, that they have some impact, some effect. (Otherwise, why willfully make a career of librarianship?) Okay. Is that effect in reality benign or malignant? Are we retreating to "safe," static conventionality or moving toward a dynamic involvement with our fast-changing human and physical milieu? Sure, the answers depend on your values, your *Weltanschauung*. A value judgment can't be escaped, except at the price of outright surrender to external pressures (like Government and its military-industrial puppeteers) or strong, self-propelled internal elements (call them, collectively, the Techno-Bureaucratic Library Establishment). While admittedly an over-simplification, the value problem seems to resolve itself into polar choices: people vs. things, participation vs. pyramidal authority, compassion vs. convenience, engagement vs. neutrality. Were our profession magically transmuted in time and space to Germany of the 1930s, would it be "neutral" about Yellow Stars, Blitzkriegs, KZs, book-burning, forced labor, organization-banning, Gypsy guinea pigs, etc.? Would these events and practices not be regarded as anathema to humane values, to uninhibited scholarship, learning, and dialogue, to the very well-being of our clientele and colleagues? If we rejected "neutrality" under those circumstances, how can we be "neutral" or dispassionate about the American onslaught in Asia (replete with torture, massacre, and charred infants), widespread repression of dissent at home (by means of gun, gavel, computer-bank, and publicly-paid spies), continued subjugation of racial and ethnic minorities (who require no brightly colored, sew-on symbols to identify them), and "criminalization" of our long-haired young (achieved through pot-busts, police-induced "riots," rigid appearance-codes etc.)? Are these events no less anathema to humane values, to a climate of trust and unfettered dialogue, to a rational distribution of resources? Will the "good Germans" claim that they are not our concern, that war and racism—as outstanding examples—don't affect libraries, or—more cogently—that libraries can exert no influence on them? If we opt for people, participation, compassion, and engagement, there are things to talk about and do. Some, already well-stated—like heightened recruitment and promotion of minority group members; swift, concrete support for the censor's victims; the professional imperative to declare for peace; sanctions against segregated libraries; urging publishers to midwife prejudice-free, interracial books for children; and opposition to governmental prying into patrons' reading habits—need no repeating here. Still others, though, have hardly—if ever—been raised (and fellow "Luddites" can undoubtedly refine these, as well as citing many more):

1. *Outreach.* On the Association level, the one serial publication devoted to servicing outside groups—in this case, labor—has been discontinued. The tragedy in this is not entirely that a useful, horizon stretching newsletter has folded, but that it was the only such publication to begin with. Not only should the labor vehicle be reinstated, but sister publications are manifestly needed to chronicle, analyze, and assist library services to many more specific groups whose needs are at once pressing and distinctive: Indians, Mexican-Americans, blacks, GIs and draft-age men, women, and the poor. Also, providing it doesn't restrict the mag's independence, money might be allocated to enlarge *Sipapu*'s format and circulation so that

it becomes an effective catalyst/clearinghouse in the slightly chaotic realm of radical and "underground" literature.

The ALA suspension is perhaps ominously symptomatic of the profession's attitude toward innovative "outreach" programs themselves. How many public libraries, for instance, have established (in easy-to-reach locations; e.g., storefronts) special collections of material on welfare rights, the draft, child care, community organizing, and the like—perhaps staffed by local people, with qualified counselors appearing at regularly-scheduled times? Some, to be sure. Indeed, some—like the Free Library of Philadelphia—appear to have wisely harnessed the computer to meet the unmistakable, wide-ranging information requirements of the urban "underprivileged." Some, then. But enough to make a difference, to redress the terrific imbalance between services hesitatingly supplied to low-income ghetto or migrant peoples and those unstintingly offered to Beverly Hills-variety affluents or some far from underprivileged multiversity students now pampered with phone-requested, direct-to-dorm book delivery? Are even the existing programs funded securely enough to guarantee their continuation, or likely to collapse—like so many other highly-touted, "pilot" enterprises—when the voracious military-space moguls decree more rockets and bombs? Has a lobby been mounted to press the Bureau of Indian Affairs to supply pertinent, identity-bolstering library collections, together with wanted bookmobile, oral-history, and other services to the wonderfully neglected "reservations"? Have hitherto submerged elements like street "gangs," junkie communities, and welfare mothers been asked what kind of library service they want? Have well-endowed universities which so painlessly maintain Colleges of Business Administration been pushed to create legal aid and other Goliath-dismembering literature that libraries might then promulgate throughout the inner city? Have library school students been encouraged, perhaps in lieu of theses, to develop reading and media programs for slum-dwellers, farmworker families, etc.? And has . . .?

2. *Subject and classification schemes.* Our fundamental "tools of the trade"— Dewey, LC, Sears—in many respects embody the conceits and wrongheadedness of another era. Far from being the disinterested, universally applicable, and fair-minded schema that an enlightened profession could employ—and disseminate abroad—with pride, they are appallingly marred by pro-Christian bias, Western chauvinism, misogyny, prudery, and WASPish racism; often denigrate the young; defame the sexually unorthodox; and largely underwrite a magisterial, laissez-faire view of economic and social life. In short, they subtly reinforce pernicious stereotypes and questionable, if not untenable, notions concerning humankind. If this judgment seems rash, only examine the Dewey "Religion" schedules; note the DDC equation of "premarital relations" and "homosexuality" with "perversion"; compare the disparate treatment of "Capitalism" and "Socialism" in both Dewey and LC; and then consider—merely as examples—these active LC subject heads, many of which Sears echoes:

LITERATURE, IMMORAL
ART, IMMORAL
CHILDREN—MANAGEMENT
DISCIPLINE OF CHILDREN
NATIVE RACES (as both a primary and subhead)
MAMMIES
JEWISH QUESTION
RACE QUESTION (as a subhead)
JEWS *AS* FARMERS [SCIENTISTS, etc.]
INDIANS OF NORTH AMERICA, CIVILIZATION OF (i.e., Anglo-Saxon efforts to "civilize" the Indians)
NEGROES *AS* BUSINESSMEN [COWBOYS, etc.]
JAPANESE [CHINESE, MEXICANS, etc.] IN THE U.S. (but never *Americans*)
WOMEN *AS* AUTOMOBILE DRIVERS [LIBRARIANS, etc.]

MANAGEMENT RIGHTS (but no "LABOR RIGHTS")
YELLOW PERIL
HOMOSEXUALITY
    XX Sexual Perversion
LESBIANISM
    XX Sexual Perversion
CATHOLIC [JEWISH, NEGRO] CRIMINALS (uniquely)
SABOTAGE
    XX Socialism
SOCIETY, PRIMITIVE
ANARCHISM AND ANARCHISTS
    XX Terrorism
NAPALM
    XX Metallic Soaps (!)
HEROES (but no "HEROINES")
PAGANISM
DISCOVERY AND EXPLORATION (subdivision under names of continents and countries "discovered" and "explored" by Europeans)
KAFIRS (i.e., in South African parlance, "niggers")

The situation seems sufficiently alarming to warrant thoroughgoing, critical studies of all the major cataloging tools and then their urgent revision to accord with modern knowledge, as well as elementary canons of human decency and dignity.

3. *Selection.* If a single keyword or rubric encompasses the multitude of overlapping movements and ideas that within the past decade have forcefully emerged among blacks, students, Jews, teachers, Chicanos, women, the young, Asian-Americans, servicemen, Indians, ecophiliacs, still-colonized peoples, workers, the impoverished, homosexuals, and even some psychiatrists, athletes, retirees, sociologists, and librarians, it is "liberation." The library press and SRRT have suitably reported aspects of this many-faceted "liberation" scene, as well as engendering extensive booklists, bibliographies, and other selection-aids (e.g., *Alternative Books in Print*). The hangup, evidently, lies not with the library press nor SRRT, but rather with libraries. The "liberation" materials have been identified. They can

easily be acquired. It is now incumbent upon collection developers to *get* them —in order, naturally, to document the whole phenomenon for posterity—but even more compellingly to satisfy the contemporary informational needs of "liberation" activists and spectators alike. The multi-pronged "movement" has obviously assumed such proportions that it can no longer be regarded as a temporary fad. (Its roots, in any event, reach deep into the past, and many of its organs have attained a "respectable" longevity.) A library that cannot furnish at least a few appropriate books and magazines, together with knowledgeable advice, to patrons who want material on Gay Liberation, Workers' Control, senior citizen's campaigns for lower transportation rates and higher Social Security benefits, or Third World revolutionary struggles risks becoming utterly useless and pointless to those patrons.

If it's not thought unbecoming nor unusual to lavishly provide directories, newsletters, magazines, and special information services like *Barron's, Moody's, The Wall Street Transcript, Advertising Age,* and *Fortune* for businessmen, investors, and stock market speculators, why flinch at providing even a modest amount of material to "liberationists" who, as equally bona fide members of the community, have no less right to library resources? Further, *LJ,* the *Booklist,* and *Choice* could much enhance the ongoing identification-selection process by more frequently reviewing the books and pamphlets generated by offbeat, "liberationist" presses such as the powerful graphic statements by *L.A. Free Press* cartoonists Ron Cobb and Ed Badajos published respectively by Sawyer and Olympia, *War Incorporated: The Complete Picture of the Congressional-Military-Industrial-University Complex,* and *Autopsy of the A.M.A., an Analysis of American Health Care Delivery Systems,* both confected by Berkeley Student Research Facility, or the Africa Research Group's explosive tract, *The*

Extended Family. Also, we need to abandon our condescending, curatorlike, rubber-gloves-and-forceps mentality with regard to "alternative" publications. They belong on open shelves, not in glass cases nor padlocked vaults. Students of social problems and current affairs may well find that articles in *Radical America, Women,* and *Tricontinental Magazine* are just as fitting and citable for term papers and dissertations as material culled from *Foreign Affairs, Time,* and *Business Week.* The oft-enunciated dictum that such matter should only be collected as fodder for the historian, much as intriguing cadavers are gathered and then pickled and frozen for later study by anatomists must be rejected as wholly repugnant species of in-group arrogance.

4. *Participation.* If the boards and committees upon which we increasingly sit have no decision-making power, why sit on them? Without authority to actually enact change or create policy, the activity qualifies as a dreary, spirit-killing charade, a successful management device for co-optation, spawning the illusion that our views and desires really figure in the decision-making calculus. It is altogether too much to expect that libraries will shortly undergo complete democratization, that all employee-strata will soon participate effectively in the decision-making process. But we can sure as hell begin discussing the subject, begin exposing the present shams that pass for "participation," begin devising participative models, and—when sufficient strength and solidarity develop—begin demands for real power-sharing.

5. *Publishing.* Judging from its recent output, ALA appears to regard itself as a scholarly publisher. Some colleagues could certainly produce manuscripts that, while not conforming to a stiff, conventional definition of "scholarship," nonetheless dealt in depth with clearly significant topics and honestly represented dissident, "heretical" opinions not yet accorded book-length treatment. Remarkably few such titles, though, have ever appeared under the

ALA imprint. This is not to gainsay the bibliographic and historical value of works, for instance, on Carnegie libraries or German exile publishing in the U.S. It is only to observe that such works seem to constitute the norm, while possible tomes of much greater immediacy—and intellect-stimulating controversiality—go unprinted. If ALA Publishing Services haven't so far done so, why not speedily commission:

—a Frommian-Goodmanesque critique of traditionally hierarchic, authoritarian library administration?

—a pro-and-con symposium on library unionism, perhaps including case studies of unions-in-operation and appending a few representative contracts?

—an anthology in which *Synergy*-type "Young Turks" forthrightly rap about the numerous skeletons in our professional closets?

—a collection of all major documents and reports relating to the abolition of "pornography" censorship in Denmark, indicating why and how it came about, together with its results?

—an exploratory study on how libraries —like schools—might become subject to genuine community control, with evidence (if any) from wherever it has actually occurred?

—a women-authored volume—perhaps comparable to E. J. Josey's recent opus dealing with black librarianship —on the historic and current status of women within the profession?

—a survey and discussion of current professional priorities which, among other things, assembles comprehensive budgetary and manpower statistics so we can determine less intuitively in what directions—electronic, "outreach," etc.—we're now travelling?

—a levity-laden tome composed of parodies, satires, graffitti, caricatures, and cartoons—however irreverent— that booby-traps professional pomposity and reveals the frolicsome, funny dimension of librarianship?

—a compendium of historical, evaluative, and bibliographic writings on the Underground Press, "counter-culture," and "liberation" publishing, plus a cross-section of views on what the library attitude should be toward such materials and some objective data on how libraries have actually responded to them thus far in terms of selection, display, publicity, access, and censorial encounters?

6. *Watchdogging.* If any group has the competence and wherewithal to first identify and then exercise pressure to correct malpractice or delinquencies in tax-supported, federally operated libraries, it's ALA. The same holds for state and municipal associations with respect to state, county, and city institutions.

Prison libraries are notoriously understocked and poorly staffed. Moreover, prison officials often deliberately and arbitrarily restrict the reading opportunities of inmates according to their own, private beliefs or whims about "what's good for the cons." At minimum, ALA could sponsor a survey of prison library facilities and practices (which should include interviews with convicts, penologists, and warders), prepare basic guidelines, and—where necessary—intercede with authorities to improve conditions.

USIS. Library and general periodicals have abundantly disclosed that the globe-spanning U.S. Information Service library system practices a "mainstream," Babbitt-like censorship which largely excludes material by radicals, pacifists, black militants, avant-garde literati, counter-culturists, and even extreme rightists. The agency, for example, will apparently not even consider buying a book issued by International Publishers in New York, whose list includes major works by W. E. B. DuBois, John Reed, Herbert Aptheker, Clarence Major, Phillip S. Foner, and "Big Bill" Haywood. In all likelihood, a similar ban obtains for the Pathfinder Press, formerly Merit Publishers, whose catalog features a half dozen titles by and about Malcolm X, a collection of Eugene Debs' speeches, the stenographic record of the IWW's founding convention, and a pamphlet on Chicano studies —all important pieces of Americana. The "image" these collections project to overseas readers is a distortion. It is not the everyday America we know, at once hopeful and floundering, imaginative and mediocre, violent and gentle, hate-ridden and loving. The thoroughly sanitized, plastic-packaged "America" marketed by USIS libraries insults us and affronts literate people abroad, many of whom surely recognize the put-on and can hardly think well of a nation that by perpetrating such deceit plainly thinks so little of *them*. Our national reputation would indisputably suffer less from candor than from bullshit. A possible ALA role might be to initially investigate USIS selection policy, not merely examining official statements and other documentary evidence, but also conducting first-hand checks at random facilities, and then—if the data so indicate—simultaneously make these findings public and demand change, perhaps with an explicit threat of sanctions.

Military libraries have long ignored the Library Bill of Rights' injunction to represent all possible political and other viewpoints. It is doubtful that any presently receive and openly display GI anti-war papers, scores of which have blossomed in the States, Europe, and Asia, although their relevance to servicemen is perfectly obvious. And one Special Services librarian in Europe not so long ago encountered truly incredible static when he attempted to add the "Wolfenden Report," several outspoken volumes on the Afro-American experience,

and some modern literary classics—by Henry Miller, William Burroughs, Allen Ginsberg, Lawrence Ferlinghetti, Jean Genet, and others—to a local collection. Of these works it was said either that "We have enough of that sort of thing already" or "No one will read them," both contentions being equally absurd. The system had, in fact, bought Sartre's treatise on Genet, but balked at stocking anything by the celebrated playwright-novelist. Additionally, the operative myth regarding homosexuals in uniform is that there are none. Later, when that same librarian protested against the official distribution and endorsement of palpably right-wing material produced by the Freedoms Foundation, he was advised by superiors that he might be happier working someplace else.

Moreover, the implicitly sanctioned role of military librarians—almost exclusively women—has been as much that of high-caste sex-ornament and morality-maid as book-jockey and mind-vibrator. And, at least a few years ago, off-duty social liaisons with enlisted men were definitely taboo, a sure-fire way to dis-ingratiate oneself with the higher ups. If military libraries remain oblivious to many soldiers', sailors', and airmen's authentic interests and needs (even when these conflict with brass-pronounced orthodoxy) and continue to thrust degrading, sexist roles upon our sisters who staff them, the situation merits attention by the whole profession. A first step might be for present and former military librarians to openly document the matter from their own experience. The *Wilson Library Bulletin,* for example, could profitably devote a full issue to the topic, possibly including contributions from GI library users, as well. Were such a symposium to demolish the above allegations: Beautiful! If not, the necessity would persist to "shape up."

Finally, given an honest commitment to "social responsibility," to tackling, library-wise, the manifold problems of poverty, imperialism, discrimination, and public waste, ALA cannot in the future hold its meetings in plush hotels and racist atmospheres, nor charge impecunious colleagues and even ordinary (but concerned) folk what may be a prohibitive fee to simply watch the Association at work.

UNLIMITED PUSHBUTTONS AND PARAPHERNALIA TO THE TECHNO-BUREAUCRATS!

DYNAMIC, RESPONSIVE, SANELY-EQUIPPED LIBRARIES TO THE PEOPLE!

Under which banner do we proceed?

Processing for the People

Maurice J. Freedman

BY THE YEAR 2000, unless something happens to deflect the current juggernaut, all processing will be solely Library of Congress (LC) based, or worse yet, will emanate from LC and the uncontrolled data base of the Ohio College Library Center (OCLC), consistent with policies determined by a research library biased American Library Association (ALA), and studies funded by the Council on Library Resources (CLR).

This possibility is not new, at least regarding LC and ALA, but its realization grows closer:

> The rules issued by the . . . catalog committee of the American Library Association (ALA) are expressly designed to be made for the use of a learned library. The old catalogs were not made for children, but the modern ones have to be, especially in a circulating library, for the children are the library's best clients. That the [ALA catalog] committee has always understood the public's views, estimated correctly its power of changing them, and drawn the.line in the right place between a conservative regard for custom and a wish to lead the public toward a desirable simplicity and consistency is too much to assume.[1]

Charles A. Cutter stated this at the turn of the 20th Century in the introduction to his final edition of cataloging rules, and more importantly on the occasion of the end of the "golden age of cataloging." The "golden age" was ended with the anticipated universal availability of LC cards; essentially each library would no longer need to do its own cataloging nor have its own staff of catalogers except for those few needed to handle the small percentage of titles not covered by LC.

In the late 1960s, Cutter's warning became even more urgent. Prior to 1968, libraries had many sources from which to meet their cataloging needs, plus some remnants of a local staff. In 1964[2] and 1969,[3] articles appeared in *Library Resources and Technical Services* (LRTS) and in other places listing processing center products and services, both nonprofit and commercial, available in the United States. An examination of those listed reveals that a full range and variety of cataloging services were available. Some nonprofit ones provided full LC cataloging and others used Sears subject headings, abridged Dewey numbers, and title page author entries. Some commercial firms furnished one or the other, or a choice of the two. (Although cataloging and processing are not synonymous, for this paper's purpose they will be used somewhat interchangeably. As it is the basic cataloging data which forms the nucleus for all processing services, such components as pockets, spine labels, etc. cannot be created without the prior production of the cataloging record.) In addition to LC as a main source, many cataloging services were available either on a regional basis, primarily used by public libraries, school systems and in some rare cases even academic libraries; or nationally, commercial services used mainly by college, public, and school libraries. Centralization and standardization before the advent of MARC and massive computerization allowed various kinds of libraries to select either jointly or separately a processing service which furnished cataloging data tailored or suited to their respective libraries. The diversity of distributors and their lack of absolute dependence on a single source for cataloging data permitted them the freedom to choose from among the many established authorities and to attempt to be more responsive to the diverse needs of their customers or users. In a 1964 article, for example, Elizabeth Adcock pointed out that in a response to a vote of one center's users and a change in policy by one of the center's commercial sources, the center changed from LC to title page author entry.[4]

The existence of a variety of commercial and centralized processors, many of whom independently selected and defined the content of the catalog records they created and distributed, had benefits and drawbacks. On the positive side, they could attempt to meet the needs of their narrowly defined constituencies. Already cited was an example of a given processor which switched to title page author entry because of its greater suitability for its member libraries. Some of LC's subject terms are particularly unsatisfactory for nonresearch libraries. For example, the *Sears List of Subject Headings* uses the explicit and direct term, "Busing (School integration)," while LC calls it "School children—Transportation." Card formats from central processors are frequently simpler and more intelligible than the LC card, eliminating such descriptive items as city of publication, spine size, and lengthy notes, while providing valuable annotations. In Westby's directory of processors, there are sample cards illustrating this point.[5] Note that LC currently provides annotations and alternate headings for children's books—a valuable service.

But the multiplicity of standards and the various exceptions to the standards contributed to conflicts in the individual catalogs. One can find a short history of processing services embedded in many public library catalogs. LC cards, LJ cards, Wilson cards, local processor cards, and handwritten nonprofessionally produced cards, intermixed in the same catalog with their concomitant inconsistency in entry and format, frequently added up to a dismal situation for their patrons.

Although there have been many social and political movements up to and through the 1960s, they seemed to have little effect on the racist, sexist, colonialist, and other slanted headings perpetuated by LC's canonization of prevailing bigotries (e.g. "Mammies," "Kafirs," "Women as librarians," "Yellow peril," "Jewish question," etc. *ad nauseum*);[6] LC's anachronisms such as "European war, 1914-1918," "Motor-trucks," "Moving pictures," etc.; and LC's failure to recognize new terms before a large segment of materials on that topic are cataloged under an improperly general term, such as "Rock music" being put under "Jazz" years after rock was created, all of these criticisms were basically ignored by the dominant cataloging authorities.

Because there were a large variety of processing services and still some local cataloging staff, at least some of these centrally disseminated horrors were properly dealt with and not enshrined in some neighborhood 3 x 5 card tray. As we approached the present era of au-

tomation, standardization and inflation, there did exist
some variation in local practice, and as pointed out, not
all of it for the good. Processing for the people, certainly
as coming from LC, was not a reality, but on the other
hand cataloging had not yet been totally divorced from
the reality of local needs.

Automation and standardization

Automation in libraries did not begin to have a major impact until the late 1960s and early 1970s. The automated cataloging systems in various stages of development around the country were built to accept or enter
into the computer, cataloging data, but not to provide
bibliographical control. With one exception, the New
York Public Library automated system,[7] these systems
did not automate any of the professional cataloging functions such as authority checking, establishment of entry,
cross-reference control, etc.[8] (This is an especially important point to keep in mind regarding the OCLC system
and data base.) By 1975 the impact of automation has become overwhelming. The three largest library jobbers all
have MARC (*MA*chine *R*eadable *C*ataloging) based
catalog card and processing services. (MARC is the service wherein LC currently sends out weekly in computer
readable form its current cataloging information for
English language and some other Roman language
titles.) LC's Catalog Distribution Service (formerly the
Card Division) is sending to its subscribers computerized
"letterpress quality" MARC based cards (as well as letterpress, offset, and photocopies of other cards), and the
Ohio College Library Center, the nation's most ubiqui-
tous alternative, is mailing out over half-a-million cards
per week (as of July 11, 1975).[9]

However, the OCLC system has some drawbacks.
Insofar as there is no rigorous bibliographical or authority control built into the system controlling the entry of
cataloging information into the OCLC data base, OCLC
is a threat to the traditional integrity of the catalogs of *all*
of its member libraries, not just the nonresearch libraries.
But it is important to note that "integrity," such as consistency in the form, spelling and fullness of entries, is no
longer a universal value. Many librarians feel that the re-
tention of traditional cataloging values is no longer economical. To them the sloppiness embodied in several en-

tries for the same work, a not uncommon occurrence in the OCLC data base, is not a drawback. To me it is bad service because it will lead, at least in some cases, to the user not finding a work that is in the collection. The traditional integrity of the catalog, be it on-line, card, book or microform, does not necessarily have to be sacrificed in the name of automation and cooperation.[10]

ISBD—the wrong kind of rule

Concomitantly the drive toward standardization, advanced in the names of international cooperation, economics, and efficiency (Motherhood was omitted), and substantially financed by the Council on Library Resources, has seen an almost lemming-like pursuit of "international standards," or most recently, "universal bibliographical control" (UBC). Originally billed as an optional format required for the purposes of computerizing catalog data, the International Standard Bibliographical Descriptive (ISBD) with its esoteric punctuation conventions and Latin abbreviations was adopted officially as a tool enabling the research libraries of the western world to communicate cataloging information.

Many public librarians feel that ISBD has little value, that it will further confuse their users. While no study has been attempted demonstrating this negative effect on the user, the original ISBD proponents did no formal user study either. Assuming that the lack of studies are a tradeoff, other considerations could be most informative. Seymour Lubetzky, one of the greatest theoreticians of descriptive cataloging, publicly decried the ISBD as being unnecessarily redundant because it requires the author's name after the title, even when it is identical to the main entry, and it introduced confusing punctuation.[11] Lubetzky's objections were numerous, but in brief he rejected ISBD.

ISBD *is* the wrong kind of cataloging rule to be taken up at the international level. In a discussion of what should be the concerns of an international cataloging code, as well as national, regional, local, and bibliophilic codes, S. R. Ranganathan was most helpful. For Ranganathan, when librarians of different nationalities sit down to create an international code, they should only accept past practices of permanent value, be free from lower emotions, such as decadent imperialism, inhibiting camp bearerism, prejudice of colour, east-west or realistic-practical, and every other kind slogan-phobia. As a meeting of intellectual peers . . . brought together to find what is best and true, the Round-Table should first determine the normative principles to guide their further work. . . . Unlike classification, *catalogue cannot use a purely artificial international symbolic language.*[12]

In specifically taking up international catalog codes, and in view of the groundwork he has already set forth, Ranganathan stated that such matters as normative principle, choice of heading for main entry, etc. ". . . can be bodily adapted by . . . [national] codes . . . [but] . . . an international code on rendering of names and style of writing can only be taken as directives by a [national] code."[13] The Japanese language illustrates why international legislation for detailed punctuation and rendering routines are necessarily bound to failure. Japanese sentences have no punctuation marks. As a result of the impossibility for the Japanese to use ISBD's codes for Japanese language cataloging records going into Japan's catalogs, a JSBD had to be developed.[14] Ranganathan's "Law of Parsimony" is violated when the occurrence of an author's name after the title duplicates the main entry. Ranganathan would have many reasons to find ISBD most objectionable. The IFLA cataloging experts who created ISBD and who have more goodies coming our way should give Ranganathan's *Heading and Canons* (from which all of these quotes were taken) a most careful reading.

ISBD is a most unfortunate development, probably a precursor of even greater calamities for the users of America's nonresearch libraries, and a perfect example of what Cutter was warning us about. It is ironic that over 70 years later his words could again be timely and even urgent.

The Library of Congress, in the words of William J. Welsh, director of the world's largest processing department, has publicly avowed that "LC's first constituency is in fact the research community."[15] This statement in the proceedings of an Association of Research Libraries (ARL) program, coupled with his *American Libraries* article (September 1975, p. 459) constitute a mandate for America's public libraries (and to some, *all* of the nonresearch academic libraries,)[16] to look for an alternative to the LC standard. It is most important to underscore the need for an *alternative* standard as opposed to an abandonment of standards.

Narrowed options

Options have continuously narrowed through the closings, bankruptcies, and consolidations of commercial and nonprofit processors. Several commercial card and/ or processing services have recently gone out of business, and the largest ones remaining are mainly computer based. In the commercial sphere, the H. W. Wilson Company, Richard Abel, Canadian Book Wholesale Company, and most recently Ingram have all gone out of the card business. (Abel and Canadian Book went out of business altogether.) Inflation, the inability to successfully utilize the computer and/or other considerations have resulted in the California State Library processing center (CLASS), the Iowa State Library processing center, and the Colorado Academic Library Book Processing Center (CALBPC) getting out of the processing business. Josten's Catalog Card Corporation, Bro-Dart, and Baker and Taylor, the biggest commercial services, and OCLC and LC's Catalog Distribution Service in the nonprofit sphere, are all providing MARC based cards with the aforementioned defective LC authorities and ISBD conventions. OCLC does give its users the option of changing any portion of the catalog record LC or any member library has entered in the system. Albeit a somewhat time-consuming manual process, it is the positive side of the nonbibliographical control of its data base. None of the commercial services provide this option.

At much greater cost to them, the commercial firms mentioned are also providing title-page entry, Sears headings, and abridged Dewey cataloging to their customers. All of this requires original cataloging for the limited titles they cover, plus input to the computer. It is less and less economical for them to continue to provide alternative cataloging services because they require both professional staff and keyboarders. These people costs are always the most expensive elements in an automated production system.

Further changes in the cataloging rules will of course be incorporated into the MARC record LC distributes to these and other major disseminators of cataloging products. Libraries producing their own cards using the LC unit record (be it a proof slip, NUC record, microform copy of same, etc.) as a master will put all of those "goodies" such as ISBD on every card they make. This means that all of the public, school, and other non-research libraries using LC-based cataloging products are getting cataloging data from a "national" library which regards their needs as—at best—its second concern. Consequently ISBD and other superfluous data is showing up in library catalogs all over the country.

Who makes the rules?
One of the chief reasons for ISBD and the previously cited name and topical headings has been the near absence of public library people on the standing ALA bodies which develop and administer cataloging policies and rules. Illustration A will graphically demonstrate the imbalances of representation. An examination of the membership of three key groups within the Resources and Technical Services Division (RTSD) for the 1974-1976 period, and one for the 1975-1976 year, should illustrate the problem. Out of 78 people, 57 are academic librarians, 14 are library school faculty, and four are public library technical services professionals.[17]

This almost total absence of the public library view on RTSD cataloging committees is at least in part the fault of public librarians. At least some, especially administrators, see the catalog as a necessary evil and have literally and figuratively relegated catalogers to the back room, given them the lowest status of their professional staff, and allotted meager funds for their attendance at meetings. Direct service to the public, building buildings, and nodding toward selection have been the foci of many public librarians and it shows in their representation in the ALA structure—they have not had their say in technical services matters because they in significant part have not recognized its importance. This is sad because they are spending money on processing but not really getting full value for it, while others have to pay more than they really should to get reasonable public library cataloging service. For example, the Hennepin County Library has a most vital program, at least as evidenced by its *Cataloging Bulletin*, of enhancing, correcting, and changing LC cataloging so as to adequately serve its clientele. Unfortunately, Hennepin must bear all of the costs of its improved service because the "national" library output has public libraries as its secondary concern, and the ALA rule-makers are not representative of the interests of public libraries. The academic and library school monopoly of interest, and the lack of participation by public librarians through, in part, their own neglect, leaves us ever more mindful of Cutter's admonition about leaving it to ALA.

Forcing change at LC, CLR

LC staffers, regardless of their personal views, have basically maintained stolid conservative policies in terms of their contributions. Changes in large part, have come as a result of outside criticism and attack: such terms as "Kafirs," "Aeroplanes," "Electronic calculating machines," "Negroes," etc. were eliminated only after external pressure was exerted. This LC intransigence or at best, resistance to change, in combination with CLR appointed and funded bodies, is leading to cataloging policies which will even further disregard public library service, and will probably create some real problems for the academic library user. In its efforts toward national and international standardization, and through the massive input of funds, CLR has been a driving force to establish the ISBD. In other areas CLR has not seemed to be reluctant to establish and fund ad-hoc committees to develop standards which it finds desirable at a given time. It is true that the recommendations of CLR appointed bodies must be approved by the appropriate ALA committee. However the CLR subsidized group meets as frequently as is necessary. The members of ALA groups have no such ready availability of funds, meet twice a year at the ALA annual and midwinter meetings, and in effect have to deal with the almost *fait accompli* of the CLR committee recommendations in the very short time available.

For example, the Committee on the Encoding of Machine-readable Bibliographic Information (CEMBI) set up by CLR did work which had to be reviewed by the ALA RTSD/ISAD/RASD committee on Representation in Machine-Readable Form of Bibliographic Information (MARBI) for it to become an ALA standard. The problem was that CEMBI was better funded by CLR and could meet as often as necessary, while its ALA

counterpart, MARBI, was limited to meeting twice a
year. Neither ALA nor the institutions they represented
could afford the expense of frequent meetings. If a MAR-
BI member wanted to study a matter in greater depth, the
delay would be six months, until the next ALA meeting.
That person would then be subject to criticism for delay,
obstructionism, holding up national projects, etc. If
MARBI rather than CLR's handpicked committee had
been funded to originally study the matter, or at least had
been kept closely abreast of the CLR group's activities,
then that duplicative, time-consuming process might
have been avoided, and the MARBI members would
have had much better conditions under which to deal with
CLR's proposals.

Of gravest concern is the current situation in which
the Advisory Group on National Bibliographic Control
was established. This group of six people selected by
CLR and the National Science Foundation (NSF) has at
best two people on it identified with the library community (as opposed to publishing or abstracting and indexing): William Welsh of the Library of Congress, and
Jerrold Orne, formerly director of the University of
North Carolina library and now head of the University's
library school. Orne is a key figure in the area of national
library standards with the American National Standards
Institute (ANSI). In major part this Group will be following up on a CLR-NSF sponsored meeting (April 17-
20, 1974) on "National Bibliographic Control." That
meeting had 40 participants, none of whom was identified
with a public library. There were six LC people, four were
from CLR, six ARL people, and three library school faculty among others. The following general recommendation was made at the meeting:

> The participants join in supporting an effort (by or through
> [CLR and NSF]) to identify or create an ongoing
> body ... that could ... take appropriate actions to advance
> social objectives and national needs in the fundamental as-
> pects of bibliographical control including (but not limited to)
> such activities as developing national strategies, identifying
> areas for standardization, protecting system integrity, pro-
> viding national direction for international participation, and
> assigning responsibility to accomplish specific tasks.[18]

Between the participants and the recently chosen Advisory Group on National Bibliographic Control, the bibliographic needs of the public library community are totally

unrepresented. It is of the utmost importance that those who want to see the library catalog be a catalog serving the public libraries, and not just the needs of the international research library cataloging community, actively concern themselves with the confidential work of the Advisory Group's surrogates or working parties before it is writ in stone because, "Working papers ... will be treated as confidential until such time as it is appropriate to publicize results and invite public comment."[19]

The Library of Congress

LC used to be the premier supplier of card sets in the country. It still is selling more catalog cards than any other supplier in the country, but the nature of its business—the methods of card production, its clientele, its position of unquestioned leadership—has changed.

In the early 1960s, for a variety of reasons, LC's ability to provide a prompt and complete card service declined. In the late 1960s LC tried to create an automated system which would supersede the manual methods of card production and order fulfillment. A primary design goal was to reproduce, in effect by automation, the traditional LC card which had been printed by hot-type and reprinted by photo-offset techniques.[20] The equipment available at that time was a high-speed electronic photo-composition device and the Videocomp, a particular model that was probably the best of its kind. Unlike the computer line printer with its single type font and type size which produces the catalog cards sold by Josten's, Baker & Taylor, OCLC, and a host of other services, the Videocomp, with the capacity for an unlimited number of type fonts and type sizes could be programmed to take a MARC record and produce offset masters for LC cards that are virtually identical to the hot-type cards traditionally printed by LC. In other words, the computer was used to produce the same LC product as before. In addition, another goal was to use automation to furnish the LC card set on demand. LC would stock no cards at all, but would only print the cards needed from its computerized data base when it received the order. This latter goal, according to current LC staff, was unrealistic. The equipment could not be economically utilized to print LC card sets on demand across the full range of card orders, although some individual orders are being fulfilled this

way for infrequently re(uested titles. All of the high
volume orders are filled from stocked, or, in effect, pre-
printed cards.

The Card Division automation project eventually
succeeded, although some of its goals changed. The
multi-million dollar effort involving the state-of-the-art
photocomposition equipment is successfully being used,
but LC's card service has subsequently earned less money
every year than it did in 1968.[21] (The Card Division, while
losing money, also lost its name: it became the Catalog
Distribution Service Division.) What accounts for the diminished business, the state-of-the-art equipment notwithstanding? The computer line-printer, *vis-à-vis*
OCLC, Josten's Catalog Card Corporation, Baker &
Taylor, Bro-Dart and others, has been able to produce
catalog card services in a manner more satisfactory to an
increasing number of the nation's libraries than LC. The
commercial firms offer kits with headings on appropriate
cards and full processing. OCLC mails its card orders out
in alphabetical arrangement. Using 20/20 hindsight, it is
easy to second-guess about what LC should have done.
Maybe a line-printer-based card and/or kit service would
have been or still could be a good approach. But it surely
would have been challenged by at least some of the library community which requires the highest quality
product from LC, but has no qualms about accepting less
from others. The automation project did essentially deliver what it was supposed to, but the Catalog Distribution
Service Division decreased sales attest to the fact that
something else is needed.

LC is still the mecca of card suppliers in the United
States, the 60 to 70 million cards sold per year is still un-
rivaled, but there are fewer libraries turning toward
Washington to have their card needs met. The competition, although still not too close, is growing. On the
other hand if all of the MARC based cards produced by
OCLC, the commercial jobbers, and all of the other
MARC subscribers who use MARC to print catalog
cards were added to LC's output, LC would probably
have an even larger percentage of the card sale market
than it did in the Card Division's best years. LC's current
position as MARC distributor and low profile card pur-
veyor seems to be the position it wants.

The reason for this extensive examination of the

quality of LC's cataloging, its research library commitment, and its comparatively less useful card service, is
to provide a background against which to judge the validity of LC's claim that: "The Library of Congress is the
logical agency to serve as the national bibliographic center."[22] The national bibliographic center cannot put service to the majority of the nation's population second to
the interests of the nation's research libraries and still be
considered *the* national center. LC can be the national
bibliographic center for research libraries, but not for the
rest of us. Obviously, the nonresearch libraries of the
country, certainly the nation's public libraries, need a national bibliographic service, but they must not accept one
which subordinates their needs to those libraries on the
membership list of the Association of Research Libraries.

Current alternatives

Coupling the developments of the availability of
MARC and the viability of the line-printer, commercial
processors, and others entered a whole new world of
processing. Instead of storing cards for distribution, they
can print the requisite card sets or kits as needed for actual orders. In addition through a little extra programming effort, machines could be made to pick out the trac-
ings and overprint them on the appropriate cards, a
service not available from LC. The acceptance by the
bulk of the nation's libraries of computer line-printer
cards was assured when they included fast turnaround,
additional services, and low prices.[23]

Automation has kept the purchase of cardsets and
processing services economical and timely. Inflation and
decreased funding (particularly the withdrawal of large
federal subsidies) have driven libraries toward standardization and centralized and/or commercial, but unfortunately flawed, services. In view of the problems with
OCLC's data base, including its lack of cross-references,
OCLC is not an ideal alternative to LC. OCLC has been
and will probably continue to be very successful, despite
all of this criticism. Consequently the decline in the ob-
servance of traditional cataloging standards as evidenced
by the OCLC data base will probably continue. For commercial processors the first priority is profit. It is not easy
to get these days. For example, Josten's does not give

service on the government documents included in the MARC data base, because it is not economical for them. Another jobber will not take the ISBD punctuation out of the catalog cards it creates from the MARC data base because there has not been a sufficient demand to justify the programming costs involved. None of the commercial services alters the LC catalog record to make it more usable. Josten's, something of an exception, deletes some data elements so it can avoid the cost of printing continuation cards (one of the problems created by the line-printer's single type size), but it does not change the name and topical headings provided in the MARC record. The commercial services do not generally adapt the LC created cataloging they distribute, to meet the needs of their nonresearch library clientele. They have neither the resources to do so, nor the crystal ball to help them divine what would be acceptable and/or desirable to these customers.

Membership by affiliation of members of three key Resources and Technical Services Division groups, 1974-1976, and one key committee, 1975-1976. Source: *ALA Handbook of Organization, 1974-1975* and telephone conversations with ALA official.

Body	Library School	Public/ School	Other	Academic	Total Members
1. RTSD Board	6	2/0	0	22	30
2. Cataloging & Classification Section Executive Board	5	0/0	0	17	22
3. Descriptive Cataloging Committee	1	0/1	1	11	14
4. Catalog Code Revision Committee (1975-76 only)	2	2/1	0	7	12
TOTALS:	14	4/2	1	57	78

The combination of rising local costs and MARC availability have driven many more public, and even school, libraries over to the LC cataloging entry and away from local processors, local practice, and a more local user oriented service. There is a new wave of converts to the unquestioned acceptance of LC cataloging. Only the truly committed and adequately funded libraries can do otherwise. The internal costs are mounting beyond the financial capacities of taxpayers. The net result is that ISBD-like, research library oriented cataloging is becoming more widespread in libraries. Such questionable service should not be imposed on their users. The non-LC based services, Sears, abridged Dewey, title page author, etc., are diminishing, but at least some of the computerized commercial ones seem to be strong.

Several references have already been made to Sears as an alternative to LC for some libraries. Unfortunately the *Sears list of subject headings* is not an adequate list for most public libraries. There is no central disseminator of cataloging data with Sears terms, only several services, none of which are comprehensive. Sears is neither extensive nor specific enough to serve the broad collection needs of most medium and large public libraries. Finally, there is no updating service for terms covering topics which are introduced between editions. The Sears list is most valuable for small public libraries and school libraries. Some of its choices of terms could be a model for some LC headings which tend to adumbrate rather than enlighten. Sears would not be a satisfactory alternative to LC, but it is clear why it is of value to processors serving school and small public libraries.

Processing for the people?

Things will get worse before they get better, if they get better at all. LC is still producing research library oriented bibliographical information. Sales of its card sets are on the wane. Computerized services outside of LC are having an increasingly dominant impact. Commercial processors whose clients are in both the academic and public sphere are now successfully selling MARC based cataloging services. OCLC has taken a preeminent position with its LC and local MARC records available in card or other forms to its hundreds of members. Many processing centers are still making it, but are subject to increasing economic pressures. Some have failed, others require increased subsidies, and still others are cutting back on services. Dallas Shawkey, chairperson, RTSD Commercial Processing Services (ad hoc) Committee, reports that one state processing center was forced to ask its legislature for a direct subsidy for the 1975-1977 biennium so as to avoid increased prices to its members. Another confided that his center would no longer be selling stand-alone cardsets—its members would have to buy processed books from the center, not just cardsets. The catalog rules will be changed more, consequently the LC catalog record created under them will be affected. These changes will have no useful results for the public library user's efforts to reach desired library materials and may even hinder them. With the increased help of automation and complementary technologies, that catalog record from LC will be placed into more and more catalogs in all formats.

National center for public libraries

There is an alternative: the establishment of a national bibliographic center for public libraries. This service would be concerned with cataloging rules as they relate primarily to the domestic public library user, and only incidentally to international and research library use. Catalog records in any form would then be designed to serve the overwhelming majority of America's library users.

The service would be sensitive to the needs and aspirations of ethnic, age, and sexual minorities. It would care whether a library patron could easily understand the information in the catalog, recognizing "new" terms like "Gospel music" (established by LC in 1975), "Rock music" (established by LC in 1972), and "Rhythm and blues" (still not established by LC) when they come into use rather than decades later. This service would provide full subject access to both adult and juvenile fiction, including "easy" books. The service would have to be computer based, have rigorous authority control, and first-rate professional catalogers who are aware of and in touch with public service concerns, as well as having the appropriate subject and specialty skills. It would have as its first priority the speedy availability of full and accurate cataloging records for current American imprints.

While Cataloging In Publication (CIP), an LC service, has been proposed as a solution to this latter need, it has been oversold. CIP is incomplete, often inaccurate—far more so than the final LC record—and leaves individual libraries with the task of producing a physical catalog record.[24] There are still some major publishers not participating in the program. Finding and funding such an outfit in this or any later year of our Ford might just be a soma trip, but it would be far better than forcing the majority of library users to struggle with the esoterica and unreality of research library cataloging data.

Because LC has been so remote from the needs of most of the nation's library users, and has usually responded with resistance or palliative, it would take a massive effort for LC to adjust to serve them. The only alternative is a consortium of public libraries, supported at the outset almost wholly by grant monies. If a national bibliographic center for public libraries could be established which would meet all of the requirements set forth and serve public libraries with the same intensity of effort LC serves research libraries, public libraries would be far better served than they are at present. Commercial processors, presently saddled with the costly options and original cataloging they must provide the non-LC based libraries, would welcome a standardized machine-readable cataloging record and/or a standardized format for products which they in turn could sell to all libraries. ALA cataloging committees concern themselves almost solely with international, nay universal, bibliographical control. Achieving a standard for U.S. library users will take either special perseverance or a different route altogether. Centralized processors, would better serve their customers by dealing with a bibliographic center established primarily to serve them rather than a different constituency.

People's MARC

The goal in effect is a PEOPLE'S/MARC. MARC, the computer communications format for cataloging data, is a remarkably flexible computer format—it is neutral. It solely concerns itself with how cataloging information is to be organized in machine terms, but does not dictate what the content of the catalog record is to be. Simply put, MARC can be used as the communications format for the cataloging produced from a national bibliographic center for public libraries, a People's MARC. Regardless of what agency, be it a rededicated LC, a consortium of public libraries, or some other alternative, a People's MARC from a national bibliographic center for public libraries is essential.

Those who care about the quality of the catalog as a public service tool essential to meeting and being responsive to the library needs of contemporary Americans *must* intensify their efforts to be heard, understood, and effective. The catalog must be a useable, responsive and vital tool. The alternative to such vigorous action is the complacent acceptance of the currently available and deficient options apparently accepted by the Cleveland Public Library, now in the process of converting from the Dewey to the LC classification scheme and joining OCLC. The Cleveland administration said that when all of this is accomplished, ". . . the library can get rid of its entire cataloging staff."[25]

REFERENCES

1. Cutter, Charles A., *Rules for a dictionary catalog*, 4th ed. rewritten, GPO, 1904, p. 6.
2. Hunt, James R., "The historical development of library centers in the United States," p. 60-62 gives essentially a list of nonprofit centers, in *Library Resources and Technical Services*, v.8, no. 1, Winter 1964.
3. Westby, Barbara M., "Commercial processing firms: a directory," p. 220-86 form the directory portion of the article, in *Library Resources and Technical Services*, v.13, no.2, Spring 1969.
4. Adcock, Elizabeth, "A comparison of the operation of various processing centers," *Library Resources and Technical Services*, v.8, no. 1, Winter 1964, p. 64-65.
5. Westby, *op. cit.*, p. 221-24 etc. show sample cards.
6. Berman, Sanford, *Prejudices and antipathies*, Scarecrow, 1971, is an exhaustive study of the defects of LC heading practices.
7. Malinconico, S. Michael, and James A. Rizzolo, "The NYPL automated book catalog subsystem," *Journal of Library Automation*, v.6, no.1, March 1973, p.3-36.
8. _____. "Role of a machine-based authority file in an automated bibliographic system," in: Canadian association of college and university libraries. *Automation in libraries: papers presented at the CACUL workshop on library automation*, Winnipeg, June 22-23, 1974, Ottawa, Canadian Library Association, 1975.
9. *OCLC Newsletter*, no. 84, July 15, 1975, p. 4.
10. Malinconico, S. Michael, "The library catalog in a computerized environment," a speech to be published in the pro-

ceedings of the ISAD/RASD/RTSD-CCS institute on: *The catalog: its nature and prospects*, New York City, October 9-10, 1975.

11. Lubetzky, Seymour, "The ideology of bibliographic cataloging progress and retrogression," a speech to be published in the proceedings of the ISAD/RASD/RTSD-CCS institute on: *The catalog: its nature and prospects*, New York City, October 9-10, 1975.

12. Ranganathan, S. R., *Heading and canons*, Madras, S. Viswanathan, 1955, p. 255-57.

13. *Ibid.*, p. 263-64.

14. *International cataloguing*, v.4, no.2, April/June 1975, p. 3.

15. Welsh, William J., response to a question in: *The future of card catalogs*, Association of Research Libraries, April 1975, p. 43.

16. Marshall, Joan, "The catalog in the world around it," a speech to be published in the proceedings of the ISAD/RASD/RTSD-CCS institute on: *The catalog: its nature and prospects*, New York City, October 9-10, 1975.

17. Source: *ALA handbook of organization, 1974-1975* and telephone conversation with ALA official.

18. *Library of Congress information bulletin*, v.33, no.25, June 21, 1974, p. A-110.

19. _____. v.34, no.37, September 12, 1975, p. A-221.

20. Welsh, William J., "The processing department of the Library of Congress in 1968," *Library Resources and Technical Services*, v.13, no.2, Spring, 1969, p.189-95.

21. Based on a review of several annual reports of the Librarian of Congress, appendices on card sales.

22. Welsh, William J., ". . . The Library of Congress as the national bibliographic center," *American Libraries*, v.6, no.8, September 1975, p. 459.

23. Freedman, Maurice, "Cataloging systems: 1973 applications status," *Library automation: state of the art II*, ALA, 1975, p. 58.

24. _____. "What do libraries really need?" *Library Journal*, October 15, 1974, p.2570-71, and Marvin Scilken, "Let's try COP," *Library Journal*, October 15, 1974, p. 2582-83.

25. "Cataloging switch eliminates job," *Library Journal*, August 1975, p.1373.

OTHER SOURCES

Bundy, Mary, "Behind central processing," *Library Journal*, October 1, 1963.

Fasana, Paul, "Impact of national developments on library technical services," *Journal of Library Automation*, v.7, no.4, December, 1974, p. 249-62.

Martin, Susan K., "Who will steer the ship?" an editorial in *Journal of Library Automation*, v.7, no.2, p. 71-72.

Social Responsibility: An Agenda for the Future

Patricia Glass Schuman

I LIVE IN NEW YORK CITY, a city on the verge of collapse the newspapers tell me. I listen to the polemics taking place on all levels of government with a conviction that "it can't happen here," but with a sneaking suspicion that it might, and elsewhere too. The bankruptcy of a city threatens not only jobs, but the support structures which make life possible in a complex urban environment. The depression of the 1930s was signalled by the stock market crash of 1929; will the depression of the 1970s be signalled by the economic bankruptcy of local governments? Why is it all such a numbing shock? Who can even guess at the outcome? Why didn't anyone even anticipate the problem? Doom has become boring.

The angry optimism many of us felt in the 1960s seems to have turned a bewildered skepticism in the 1970s. Librarians, along with most segments of society, have a feeling of powerlessness—as individuals and professionals. Events rush past us almost before we comprehend them. Our worst fears, and some we could never have imagined—institutionalized repression, economic chaos, immoral men in high office, illegal wars—have become the trite reality of the present. There is a curious sense of *déjà vu* as revelations of attempts to control through undemocratic means continue to emerge.

Those of us who spearheaded the movement for greater social responsibility of libraries in the late sixties viewed libraries as important and effective instruments of social change. A spirit of movement and action was pervasive and strong. Despite the labels hurled at us: "New Left," "Young Turks," "idealistic," "anti-intellectual," we envisioned libraries as places which would play a role in achieving a just, humane, and democratic society. Librarians were "change agents" who, through their information skills, might help the general populace to gain the information they needed to alter the quality of their lives. Libraries to the people. Power to the people. Naïve, perhaps, but certainly not very radical ideas in a democracy. Somehow these ideas never quite made it. Social responsibility as a philosophy of librarianship is still in a nascent stage. Although the movement generated over-reactive fears of apocalypse from those who misunderstood it, it has barely reached beyond formative action—resolutions which had very little effect, and a few innovative programs, many of which are now threatened due to a lack of funds. Although some people's consciousness may have been raised, many more heads were stuck in the sand. The latter regard this crusade against the status quo as a nihilistic and threatening concept.

Birth of SRRT

Up to now social responsibility has been defined organizationally, through the establishment of a Social Responsibilities Round Table (SRRT) of the American Library Association in 1969, which was to: "Provide a forum on the major issues; propose activities which will increase understanding of these issues; promote action towards resolution of attendant, critical problems." It was not until 1971 that social responsibility became a priority of the American Library Association, defined as: the contribution that librarianship can make in ameliorating or even solving the critical problems of society; support for all efforts to help inform and educate the people of the United States on these problems and to encourage them to examine the many views on, and the facts regarding, each problem; the willingness of ALA to take a position on current and critical issues with the relationship to libraries and library service clearly set forth in the position statement."

To date, SRRT has attempted to turn this definition into action. But, mild as these statements are, they were seen as the antithesis of library service. Some librarians felt that intellectual freedom and social responsibility were squarely at variance to each other, without realizing that intellectual freedom is part of social responsibility. Social responsibility proponents were not espousing the suppression of access, but rather the ideal that libraries must work for equality of access for all people, not just say that they do. Information on abortion is not a new phenomena; it is just *new to libraries*. Our operative mythologies blur our vision of reality.

Library mythology

Myth I is pervasive and insidious: *Institutions are neutral, and those within them must be neutral in order to be effective.* Professionals can and should strive for objectivity, but each of us is a product of our biological and intellectual environment. Objectivity demands that we attempt to recognize our own psychological and cultural biases, sift all the facts, and make judgments based on these facts. Neutrality allows us to believe that we have no effect. But, "to neutralize," is to make something lose its effect, to take a negative form of action. Recent revelations about activities of the CIA and FBI have made us all embarrassed witnesses to the horrifying results of what Warren Bennis terms "collective immorality": decisions and actions taken by moral men and women (including the decisions to remain silent) who, gathered together under an institutional umbrella, suppress their humanistic ideals in favor of institutional goals which basically negate the existence of humanity. Often these goals are no more than the preservation and perpetuation of the institution. Take the statement of the director of one of the nation's largest public libraries during the Vietnam moratorium: "It is not that the library is against peace, but neither is it against war." Substitute the words freedom and fascism, equality and racism, and the absurdity grows. Silence has been recorded throughout history as affirmation. It is surrender, as the "good" Germans learned to their dismay. (Speaking out does not mean, and never has meant, that one prevents others from doing likewise.)

Myth II is a basic tenet of our often misguided professional philosophy: *Intellectual freedom is an end in itself.* Intellectual freedom is certainly an essential means towards the creation and maintenance of a just, humane, democratic society. The end is a society in which intellectual freedom and all other freedoms guaranteed under the Bill of Rights will flourish. No one ideal can be guarded at all costs while others are allowed to languish, or they will all die. Too often, intellectual freedom has been used as a smokescreen to perpetuate existing ideas and prevent criticism of them. The virulence with which critics of sexist children's literature are attacked by those supposedly defending intellectual freedom is but one example. These critics are not suggesting the removal of materials: they are suggesting that alternatives to predominant materials be provided, that intellectual freedom become an active process which helps to achieve freedom from stereotyped socialization so that all children can have a shot at fulfilling their potentialities. True intellectual freedom is the free exchange of all ideas as a means towards achieving a truly open and legally free society.

Myth III is that *libraries provide free access to information on all sides of all issues.* This is a goal to strive for, but in reality libraries only provide some information on some sides of some issues to some people, and this information is certainly not free; it just depends on who is footing the bill—the taxpayer, the community, the city, the state, endowment funds, private industry, etc. Libraries are limited by their ability to handle that which is available, and their ability to pay not only for information products, but for services which will make information available to library users in a usable form. Rarely does our profession actively encourage such industries as publishing to make sure that materials are available, and even less often are we willing to collect "ephemeral" materials such as pamphlets and underground newspapers which might complicate our procedures. (The few libraries which have accepted this responsibility are, to a great extent, academic or research-oriented ones concerned with preservation—not dissemination.) Libraries specifically choose not just what information they provide, but when, where, and how. This heady goal of free access is slipping away from us daily during the current economic crunch.

Myth IV is that *libraries are not political institutions.* You could have fooled me. This is possibly another version of the neutrality myth. I was under the impression that libraries were competing in the political marketplace for funding and favorable legislation. Four Presidential vetoes of library funds, our opposition to the appointment of a historian as a librarian of Congress, and our position on copyright revision legislation should be enough to explode this myth once and for all.

Demystifying a profession

If we can finally face up to the demystification of our profession, then we can go one step further to the thesis that libraries are institutions whose service affects, and may even change, society. Francis Bacon said long ago, "Knowledge is power." Today, Daniel Bell and other social scientists tell us that information is very definitely power. They define our present society as "post-industrial," one in which the organization and codification of theoretical knowledge becomes paramount for societal innovation, and intellectual institutions become central to the social structure. This society has three dimensions: a change from a goods producing society to a service producing society; a rise of an intellectual technology as opposed to a machine technology; a centralization of theoretical knowledge. Information is the force which transforms in this post-industrial society, just as energy was the transforming force in industrial society, and natural forces were in agrarian society. Unfortunately, the majority of society is suffering from an information overload. Too much is hitting the senses at once. New ways of thinking of social structures which will help us to cope, sort out, and survive have not yet been developed.

Intellectual technology and the centrality and power of information contains the potential for great harm as well as good. Social scientists and communications theorists agree that some filtering is necessary in order to make the overload of information usable. Librarians have a vital role to play, a social responsibility, to work towards an invention of the future which is free and just for all. A participatory information structure may be the only antidote to the authoritarian potential of technology. Libraries are invisible; they may fast become obsolete. To become part of the information structure of the future the profession must overcome what Alvin Toffler so aptly terms "future shock." At present, the profession is an elitist one which views the flow of information in top-down terms. The flow of information from librarian to client is a static process. We can no longer attempt to fit the questions of our public into the mold of what exists in our collections, but must fit our active services to the questions—both those that lie on the surface, and those that are not quite so obvious.

The information loop

"Democracy is no longer a political luxury, but a primal necessity . . ." says Toffler. "The faster pace of change demands—and creates—a new kind of information system in society: a loop rather than a ladder. Information must pulse through this loop at accelerating speeds, with the output of one group becoming the input for many others, so that no group, however politically potent it may seem, can independently set goals for the other." The information loop points out two basics for the library profession. We have no right to set social goals by ourselves and hand them down, but neither can we accept goals blindly from a "higher" authority. We are obligated to participate in social goal setting and to aid in the creation of mechanisms for the participation of others. Libraries, as the only institutions which profess the goal of collecting and disseminating *all* information (unsuccessful as they may have been) have a responsibility, a social responsibility, to become curves on the information loop; to facilitate—and even to create—information power for all people. To provide such power, libraries and librarians must not only survive, but participate fully in the vital decisions to be made while shaping the future. It is foolish to believe that we are the only information agency vital to society, but it is realistic to realize that we are an information agency which allows for instant action and reaction. We are not merely traffic cops directing raw information to users. We are going to have to participate *with* (not sit back and wait—or force upon) people to sort out information priorities, to make information usable and understandable, and to provide the necessary information in time for it to be usable. In our capacity as librarians anticipating and filling information needs, users may have many needs they may not even be aware of, as any librarian who has ever answered a reference question knows.

Action on information needs necessitates dealing with problems—information problems. Is the information need of the user who requests information on his eligibility for welfare really going to have his need filled by having you hand him the welfare regulations? Will he be able to interpret them? If he does, do they include all the possibilities? Can he work through the bureaucratic application maze himself? And just suppose all of these problems are solved—by the library, by community referral, or by the user himself. Isn't the fulfillment of this particular information at best a tourniquet—and at worst a Band-Aid? The more complex questions are: Why is he on welfare? How can he get off? Why does the welfare system exist in the first place? What are the alternatives?

Creating tools for change

Libraries must begin to provide not only the information tools which will allow individuals to better manipulate the system, but those that will allow them to research and change the system. The provision of these tools implies not only the purchase of what exists through normal distribution channels, i.e., a book from a publisher, but the *creation* of information. Librarians do not seem to hesitate at the thought of computerized data bases for professional researchers, but they seem intimidated at the idea of selective dissemination of information to the public. We have MEDLARS; where is our "LEMEIS" data base? (Let Me Survive, or legal and medical information for survival.) Our elitist and passive role has so far recognized our obligation to organize information for some other professionals, but this role also allows us to abrogate our own obligation as information providers. This is not to say that librarians should become doctors or lawyers, but there is a good deal of medical and legal information the lay person must have access to in order to survive that need not be transmitted by other professionals at fees of $25 an hour or more. Some very basic examples of legal and medical information libraries might provide are materials on self-examination for breast cancer or handbooks on the right to privacy. We could work with legal and medical experts to set up a meaningful "LEMEIS" data base, one that is constantly made responsive through feedback and input by its users.

Toffler's information loop will be functional only if it is a flexible means to enable individuals, groups, and concerned organizations to continually posit questions and answers. There is an alternative contrary to those predicted in *1984* and *Brave New World*, and librarians have a role to play in achieving it. But first the old shibboleths must be laid to rest and we must accept the fact that we are responsible for whatever effect we have—or fail to have. The schizophrenic dichotomy librarians have tried for so long to preserve between their actions as private citizens and their actions as librarians who are employees of specific institutions just does not hold. "The loyalty of the professional is to his profession," John Gardner points out, "and not to the organization that houses him at any given moment." Breaking out of the hierarchy will not be easy. We will have to learn as we act and continuously define our role. The future of libraries may be in our very ability to define the social responsibilities of libraries and librarians. This cannot be done in a vacuum; it can only happen if we place ourselves in a constant input-output position with others. If we begin to identify issues, to take action, and begin to build a socially responsible information agenda. An agenda which will propel the world we know into a truly participatory society. It is one thing to provide information to people; it's quite another to help them to demand it as a right. Positing questions and trying out answers, of course involves informed judgment—an advocacy stance which forces us to continually ask: "Why not?" and a nondogmatic philosophy which allows us to move forward quickly enough to keep up with society in flux.

An agenda for libraries

How can we posit the questions and try out the answers? There is no easy prescription. Some of the steps librarians might initiate, in addition to making sure that NCLIS (the National Commission on Libraries and Information Science) deals with the information needs of all people, are to begin the information loop by seeking the realities of our services in order to discover the possibilities. This process could be started by:

Calling town meetings with our users, be they individuals, community groups, business people, students, or others.

Initiating a national, continuing communication with other professions and constituency groups (women, minority groups, political groups, etc.).

Making all future library conferences—regional and national—"think tank" sessions where we talk *with*, not at, each other.

Developing programs to bring representatives of *all* segments of the population and professions together to plan new information structures.

These are just beginnings. The process will be continuous, but flux will not prevent us from having to *choose* at many levels along the way. Eventually we *are* going to have to advocate a specific, flexible, course of action. As a profession, we will have to face head-on the question of our role in society. Events of the past few years clearly illustrate that libraries are often considered passive, expendable institutions in communities which have been forced to set priority goals in order to survive the present. Grimmer still is the possibility of a static profession—failing to take responsibility for molding its own future. As Daniel Bell recently warned the American Society for Information Science: "If you don't know where you're going, any road will take you there."

REFERENCES:
Alinsky, Saul D. *Rules for Radicals: A Pragmatic Primer for Realistic Radicals*. Random House, 1971.
Bennis, Warren. *Changing Organizations*. San Francisco: Chandler, 1966.
Dodson, Dan W. *Power, Conflict and Community Organizations*. New York: Council for American Unity, 1967.
Kahn, Herman & Anthony I. Weiner. *The Year 2000*. Macmillan, 1967.
McHale, John. *The Future of the Future*. Braziller, 1969.
Theobold, Robert. *Futures Conditional*. Bobbs-Merrill, 1972.
Toffler, Alan. *Future Shock*. Random House, 1970.

Professional Adaptation: Library Education Mandate

Paul Wasserman

CONTEMPORARY CONTEXT: Political, social, and institutional ferment. The issue before us: the adaptive capacity of libraries, librarianship, and the educational process for librarians. The cast of the analysis which I shall make is critical. Yet, it is partisan and it is hopeful. For as John W. Gardner has said, ". . . love without criticism brings stagnation, and criticism without love brings destruction. . . . The swifter the pace of change, the more lovingly men care for and criticize their institutions to keep them intact within turbulent pastures."

For in this culture, indeed in any culture, the university and the professional school within it exist not merely to reinforce the going value structure, but to question, to hold up for review and analysis the conventions, the traditions and the ideology of the society and its institutions.

Much is made of the power of our technology. Yet, technical provincialism leads to isolation and irrelevance, and ultimately to decay. The times we live in are ample testimony that technology without social responsiveness no longer suffices. Yet, many in librarianship see technology—computers and automation—as ultimate solace. It is

not, and it cannot be. To others, our professional and institutional problems all seem to be soluble in terms of simply increased sensitivity to the social, the human context—as if the very wanting to be useful and relevant without the demonstrated ability to do so were enough. It is not enough.

This is a time when fundamental questions of human import are addressed to those who have mastered the technology. And it is a time when social activism, without the capacity to exploit the technical and intellectual means which make the ends susceptible of attainment, is mere sloganeering. Because, as a teacher, I genuinely believe that it is as a consequence of education that progress is made, I propose that we look at education—at how and why and whether it can assist our discipline, librarianship, and those who practice it, to be viable and relevant to the needs of the times. And so I shall discuss some issues, or more nearly raise questions about them, and as I range over a number of concerns which are bound together by only the flimsiest thread—that they interest me—you will note that even though these remarks are addressed to matters of professional education in librarianship, they are at root questions for the wider university within which professional education is lodged.

Aims and Philosophy

There are many obvious ties between occupational structure and professional education, so it is not surprising that too often professional education is satisfied simply to deliver freshly-minted recruits equipped to march in the ranks and to keep them straight. Thus, the professional inductee is seen less as scholar and more as apprentice, and academia becomes a replacement training center, committed less to a questioning posture and rather more to imparting a thorough indoctrination into the conventional wisdom and folklore of the field, in which practice is seen as true and right and everlasting. The school, in the service of the field, serves as training ground: imparting skills, techniques, and discipline; operating the assembly line which is organized by three-credit processing units and which leads directly and unquestioningly to the reference desk or the circulation counter. In this kind of world, the presence of scholarship and intellect are almost embarrassing, for they do not jibe with the basic mission, and if they are present, they are seldom woven into the fabric of the educational experience or linked with occupational needs or expectations.

There are many low roads to professional practice. One wonders whether the university deserves a place on such a map of the territory. For in truth, the values and the methods developed and instilled in professional schools—not schools of librarianship—are coming to be increasingly accepted in the larger society. A most hopeful and striking phenomenon is the way in which the opinions, the concepts, and the advanced practices which are born in the professional schools ultimately are seen to have foreshadowed those of the professions which they serve, and in some

instances, by as much as a generation in advance of their acceptance.

There is and there will continue to be inevitable tension between theorist and practitioner. Many would argue that without theory or philosophy, practice is ultimately ritualistic and bankrupt. But in librarianship the lead/lag relationship, whether in conceptual or even practical ideology, still tends too often to be reversed, with practice in the vanguard and education puffing and panting to catch up. Here may be the key to the disillusion of librarians in their disdain for their own professional schools.

Because we are so pragmatic a craft, not only in the field but in the academy as well, our educational objectives tend to be shallow and perfunctory. Not only do we not know many of the essential things needed if we are to shape our own destiny, but seemingly do not care to know, and so we blissfully perpetuate ourselves in unquestioning innocence or stupidity. And as we strive for status, we revere the status quo, and do not even perceive the incongruity. Because we do not ask the hard questions, we complacently compartmentalize ourselves into the traditional containers and offer students the reassurance of our history. Only this no longer works in a culture and in a profession where our institutions and our ideology are the subject of excruciating re-examination and re-assessment. And if our intellectuals fail to seek in order to lead us, others with less insight may and indeed already do act upon us.

In every professional field, the future must rest upon balancing the organizational stability with the capacity to adapt and respond to a changing technological and political reality—business as usual plus innovation. This implies for library education and for library practice a whole new set of concepts about the profession and those who will come to practice it, if we are to maintain continuity with earlier experience and yet graft on new perspectives. Such a shift calls for a radical alteration in the view of authority, both in the professional school and in library organizations, if the forms of initiative that result from purposeful participation are to replace traditional rigidity. Such a shift calls for a new identification of requisite skills and definition of the professional role. And such a shift calls for engendering in the professional ranks the critical cast of mind which is founded upon individual capacity to intellectualize organizational and professional problems. Conducted in this way, the school would go beyond merely being lodged in academia, and would further the intellectual development of those who would no longer simply castigate themselves and their organizations in frustration, without the ability to modify and adapt the terms of their experience. They would have learned the habits of mind to solve problems in order to strike out purposefully toward solutions.

The problems faced by libraries (and other institutions in the culture) desperately call for more inquiring minds than can at present be mustered. Yet to adapt any ritualistic process, and educational ritual is perhaps the most recalcitrant of any, calls for answers to questions which library educators have only uncommonly asked. Let me recite some unanswered questions among many, answers to which, even partial answers, would more strongly undergird our educational structures.

How can accommodation be made to the need for new technical capacities in view of the continuing need for education for traditional processes? Who ultimately must judge competent professional performance—the lay clientele, professional peers, administrative superiors? What is the true state of development of library technology and at what level must the new entrant be prepared to perform in it?

How has the sex, age, and ethnic composition of the occupation been prescribed and determined? How do some individuals select themselves for career roles in the field and why do not others, who might function effectively to bring libraries to a higher level of attainment, make similar choices? What are seen as the special personal talents for this calling? What are the primary objectives and expectations of new entrants—service? personal gain? escape from boredom? self-expression?

What are the characteristics of the occupational role vis-à-vis the client—impersonality, value neutrality, identification with him, authority? To what degree does its practice involve independent choice by individual practitioner and to what extent institutional constraints? What are potential sources of strain and conflict between the profession, its clientele, its organizational hierarchy, and how are these negotiated?

What are the ethical commitments of the occupational role with regard to privacy and personal confidences, in relation to clients? How important is technical competence relative to other relationships between the professional and the client? How can the propensity of new entrants for innovative performance be identified, reinforced and extended?

The Context of Library Education

The setting for professional education is the university, on the supposition that specialized knowledge and theoretical understanding are more efficiently imparted here than through the trial and error process of apprenticeship in the workplace where such indoctrination was begun. Yet it is no easy task to prove decisively through empirical evidence what would appear to be such a self-evident assumption. It would seem reasonable to suppose that faculty members in professional schools, including library schools, would be expert in what they are trying to teach. It would also seem reasonable to assume that there is some relationship between the grades that students receive for their work and the success of faculty members in teaching whatever it is they try to teach. From this it would follow that there should be some reasonable expectation that there is a relationship between the grades a student receives in a professional school and his subsequent performance in a professional role. Yet the fact of the matter is that such correlations do not exist. And even that the reverse may be true.

Those who complete professional school and become practitioners are not necessarily good ones with demonstrated professional competence reflecting the level of their performance as students. Yet there is surely an expected difference in the probable level of competence between those who have completed professional school and those who do not enter. A professional school student certainly learns something in the course of his training, even if his professors are unable accurately to measure it. And the poor correlation between grades and later success may demonstrate only that professors cannot measure their own success in teaching whatever they seek to teach, rather than showing that what they teach is irrelevant to job performance. At least this is how we educators would like to view it.

But perhaps the important point is that the function of a professional school is not, or should not necessarily be, to impart a narrowly defined set of skills of the kind measured by examinations, but to define a set of criteria which individuals entering a profession ought to meet and to screen out those who do not measure up against such a yardstick. Obviously, the new entrant is supposed to demonstrate a certain amount of diligence and the right combination of assertiveness and receptivity, to accept the basic values and assumptions of the professional culture (if these can be divined and a consensual base achieved for them), to master the rudiments of professional

vocabulary and to learn something of the professional ethic. Normally, if he does this he gets through the course of study and if not, he does not. Whether he actually learns details of specific classification schemes, the titles of books on one or another subject, may be quite irrelevant, since probably if he gains entry to the profession he can fill the gaps in his technical knowledge later on. The schools, in any event, cannot do the whole job for him. The primary role of the professional school may thus be seen as socialization or acculturation rather than training.

If this is so, the library schools can legitimately breed dissatisfaction with the present condition and encourage higher levels of aspiration for the profession's future. They can identify where and why and how change is needed. And they can assume a mandate to serve as proving ground for the change agents necessary to make the type of dramatic metamorphosis in libraries and of the library profession which seems needed to transform a basically passive, uncommitted, outside-the-fray occupation to something fundamentally different. They can conceive their mission, not in the hortatory terms of do-gooders who believe that the fusion of person and book is a holy alliance, but as shapers of strategies for imparting sophistication and problem-solving skills to their students. Then their view of their graduates becomes one of an educated elite, of shock troops who are going out in waves to do battle with all the familiar institutional dragons of indifference, of ritual, of entrenched business-as-usual. Indoctrination is not enough however. More important is the intellectual orientation to skills and methods, both technical and behavioral, if one is to be effective in such roles of advocacy.

And even if faculties are complacent, students need not be so. For this is what the student movement everywhere in the world is saying to us. Students have the power to be an influence. It is they who sense and understand the now imperatives for change.

Libraries are in trouble. At the local level, the public library seems powerless. In periods of fiscal drought it is a target; its support, except perhaps in unusual circumstances, most often is a reflection of parental nostalgia for a dream of an institution of yesterday. Seldom viewed as information hub of its culture, the library rests on its laurels, appeals to shrinking numbers, calculates few alternate strategies, holds on for a little while longer awaiting salvation. Staff associations grudgingly give way to unions. Yet the zeal for seniority and security, at least in the short run, translates into terms which further harden bureaucratic arteries. The intelligence base needed in urban life for planning and for decision-making is never or seldom viewed as the province of the library—neither by those who have the responsibility for the decisions nor by those who have responsibility for the library.

For the man in the street, the public library is a symbol without meaning. For the disenfranchised in the culture, it is unknown, unused, coldly remote and forbidding, attuned to the requirements of others. When a library is built, it is not their library. When it burns, the loss is not theirs. For students, it is an alternative, but only during hours when access to school and college libraries is cut off. In its essence, the public library is seen as recourse for housewives and children, for casual, undisciplined use. Once it was almost the sole means of access to books, but books are no longer so expensive. And while there are stirrings and strivings to redirect the public library—ghetto and media efforts are two instances—it remains fundamentally unaltered, and business goes on as usual. But business has been slow lately in many institutions.

Let us look at some of the adaptations which have been made by library organizations to contemporary pressures. Specialization of task is one theme which has reached libraries. Automation efforts add system analysts to the staff; subject specialists are enlisted to handle collections; library technicians are shouldering clerical routines —these changes are tending to become commonplace. The growing scale of library bureaucracy is its predominant contemporary characteristic, for size is seen as intrinsically desirable. The notion of collection growth as measure of organizational utility, and the consequent scramble of acquisition, spawn the need for ever larger work forces with which to harness the growing inventory, to house it, to prepare it for use. Only uncommon leadership, or the limits of space and funds (as in the case of many special libraries) resists this trend and leads to a reliance on interrelationships, with their concomitant pooling of resources and development of efficient transfer mechanisms. Networks and regional groups come grudgingly into existence, for the route to professional esteem tends to remain in the separate institution, not in the union of many; beyond this, the political problems of cooperation are deeply rooted.

Response to clients is another casualty of scale; indifference and neglect are accentuated by scale, and the bureaucratic values of academic, public, and governmental libraries transcend the human values they were created to serve. With few exceptions, the organizational culture nurtures organizational values, and those—notably the value of size—are impediments to change. As one consequence of this, newer, smaller agencies tend more frequently to be the spawning ground for innovative advance.

Because change is widely perceived as an imperative, education for librarianship is in ferment. And while the ultimate direction is yet undiscernible, some characteristics of the shifting scene are clearly in evidence. Librarianship and information science sometimes polarize, often converge. Computer issues, mathematics, systems analysis, draw nearer in prototypal programs. Behavioral issues, politics, economics, while not yet fully in focus, are coming to be viewed as necessary elements of the information scene, with hospitality to outside disciplines seen as the route of choice. Social commitment is an issue reborn—what is the responsibility of librarianship to social forces and how express it? And so recruitment becomes germane. The passive, uncommitted student, indecisive in choice of career option, seems poor prospect for an activist role in a librarianship of social conscience or one founded upon a more measurable scientific rigor and expertise. The educational community in librarianship is diversified, and in it the more traditional concerns of libraries—children, general readers, schools—face off against more technologically and methodologically oriented commitment. Some of the more recent and formidable academic entrants veer toward information science. But what of their progeny —what role will they take, and in what organization? The question ultimately is how to harness the technical requisites of information processing in tandem with value perspectives essential to the determination of choice, or to put it another way, where, how, for whom, for what ends, is the information system to be?

A number of information developments in the present culture, still only dimly perceived, yet with presumably significant implications for library education, are scarcely susceptible of precise classification or even orderly sorting out. Much less is their relevance for librarianship of tomorrow understood. These include the emergent information industry; the melange of publishers, embryo information utilities, and other proprietary information organs, suggesting a forceful voice and role for private interests in competition with public monopoly; the State Technical Services Act program, correlate of, often substitute for, genuine library

programs (where effective, excellent; where not, another embarrassment of involvement of the information dissemination function with the regionalized political pork barrel); the Neighborhood Information Center movement, without library involvement or counsel, awkwardly illustrating how libraries are seen by social workers as irrelevant to human needs and aspirations; the experimental library prototypes such as MIT's Intrex and Robert Taylor's Hampshire College adventure in new library forms and uses, linking up computer and book store to the traditional paraphernalia of the college library; the multi-media approach and client orientation of Washington, D.C.'s Federal City College; the transformation of the traditional school library into learning resource center—embracing new forms, new methods and applications; the manufacture and distribution of MARC tapes by the Library of Congress, providing the ultimate prospect of freeing local effort while perhaps freezing information patterns into a homogenized mold; the attempts at systematizing bibliographic control by discipline (the ERIC system in education is one such illustration) and the consequence for library programs and services; the international cooperative schemes oriented to disciplines, as in the field of atomic energy.

These are some of the most dramatic illustrations of where it is at. But what is not happening? Stated baldly, what is not happening is responsible concern. Adequacy of performances is not happening. New alternatives, new client responses, adapted priorities, are overdue. In actuality, it is the inadequacy and irrelevance which are themselves disbelieved. Controversy and dissent are uncommon. Library school students and those new to librarianship raise the doubts—practitioners silence them. And meanwhile, clients who find libraries irrelevant and unworkable, all too frequently abandon them for alternate problem-solving strategies. The evidence of urgent preoccupation with reevaluation, reassessment and reconstruction of library perspectives is the rare, the isolated phenomenon.

Leadership for change is nowhere to be found. No single great institution stands at center stage, dramatically demonstrating variation in organizational form, clientele response, imaginative utilization of talent and expertise. There is no perceptible demonstration of organizational vitality in any one place to exert its powerful influence upon others who would observe and emulate, or even profit from errors made in testing dramatic alternatives. For while the voices of younger elements in the profession are raised in growing chorus, they are seemingly inaudible to those who hold power and assume responsibility for organizational leadership.

These sought-for changes are not tied to technological functions and procedures exclusively. For the latter are merely instruments enlisted in the provision of service to the client. Yet when technical advances are made, too often they are viewed as ends in themselves rather than as devices for dramatically enlarging the scope of client service. At issue is the intrinsic institutional purpose: knowledge for what, libraries for whom? Seldom in librarianship or in library organizations is the precision and clarity required to answer these questions in evidence. Yet these are the questions the culture asks. While libraries, whatever their type, remain value-neutral, they remain the arbitrary and bureaucratic servants of power which is nameless and uncommitted to the service of mankind.

You who come new to librarianship, don't be satisfied with complacency. Don't let the system grind you down— neither the educational indoctrination nor the facts of here and now library "truths." You come in a time of high adventure, in a time of desperate need, and if your faculty preach to you in tried and true Panglossian terms that all is well in the best of all possible worlds in the world of librarianship,

you will know that it is not so. Visit and use some libraries yourselves to test this proposition. As new recruits to this profession, our problems are your problems. And it will be your responsibility as it is my responsibility, to question the state of affairs and to work toward something better. This will come not by blinking it all away, but by honest perception of reality, and by calculating the strategy needed to set things right.

The Library School Culture

Some faculty members and even one or two administrators would like their students to act like apprentices, both socially and intellectually, and if students do not do so, the reaction of the faculty and administrators is that they don't belong in the university. But in some fields, and particularly in librarianship, faculty members are more eager to have their students adopt a particular style than to become imitative and not very capable carbon copies of themselves. In some instances the students are looked to as agents of the political mandate and ambitions of the faculty, either in alliance with them, or in compensation for the faculty's inability to play partisan roles in practice. For some have become professors in recent years in order to do precisely this—to use the university as the platform and to urge on each successive generation of students a commitment to go forth and do battle, to change the library world in ways which conform with the views of such partisan professors. Be wary of such faculty members. Do not be drawn to their banner unknowingly and naively. Yet be on notice that they reflect a wholesome alternative to those who gravitate to academic berths to escape the more exacting demands of the culture of practice.

Library school faculties are improving. And faculty members are tending to encounter more students who are well prepared and who seem genuinely interested in their course of studies. When this is the case, graduate instruction tends toward a relationship between senior and junior colleagues, with new entrants being indoctrinated in a common field of professional concern. In a time when there is much bewailing of the fact that it is only younger faculty members who spend time with students, while their seniors flee the classroom to engage in more status- and incentive-laden preoccupations, it may also be the case that it is the junior faculty who know more and have most to impart. It is likewise the younger faculty who tend to have more commitment, with more at stake in change. It is they who are likely to care more deeply about the future than senior colleagues who have reason to romanticize the past and dread the future.

I would encourage you to seek out the good teachers. The caring ones—those who care intellectually, those who care about you as an individual human being. How to identify them is something which your student culture knows far more about than I can tell you and I shall not attempt to probe such mysteries. For these are private matters among students.

The days of educational innovation are upon us in academia if only to shield ourselves from the assault of aroused students. Special courses, seminars, independent study, and the like are becoming more the pattern than the exception. The faculty task is to devise a program which can touch the lives and the life styles of those who are in many instances merely going through the motions in preparation for careers which they have not clearly perceived or correctly assessed. The faculty succeeds best when they delineate styles by their own lives which exemplify the potential for the life of the mind in the profession; students will seek to emulate them. Yet such teachers are a rare species. A handful have sometimes been known to inhabit library schools. I can only wish you good luck in your quest for them.

One difficulty in library education, and perhaps in all professional education, may be the rigidity of performance conditioned by the writing of papers and the consequent communicating with one another only in academic rather than in real terms. This is the sequence of scholarship, in which the individual is groomed, like his teacher, to prepare formal technical papers which others then read and criticize. Because academics place little value upon knowledge derived from individual subjective experience, when they speak of "research" for courses, it is frequently the sterile and irrelevant paper to which they refer. Thus they insist upon knowledge that is objective, in the sense that others can be told how it was acquired and can repeat the same operation and learn the same things. Is this not perhaps what a footnote is all about? But this kind of effort has a pattern and a logic which neglects to take account of the individual's personal experience. And such course work tends to have little effect on the rest of the student's life, while his earlier experiences are seen to have little effect upon his course work. One contemporary doctrine, deeply ingrained in the new young culture of relevance and activism, is that an important ingredient of education is understanding achieved by actually doing or observing or participating. In and through such a communication process, both instructor and students can more reasonably be moved to respond as human beings to questions at issue. The net effect of an over-reliance on more sterile forms of writing and research, may be a sterility of outlook which forces those on both sides of the process to be concerned more with the precision of the paper and less with the human enterprise—which is what professional practice is all about.

To put this another way would be to

suggest that in a field like librarianship we are social scientists and we must be conditioned by political and social passions as well as intellectual ones. We need to care whether something works or does not work and if we find by looking at it in the real world that something does or does not work or affects or does not affect the way in which the process took place, then this should influence our way of perceiving the reality of professional practice and of professional ideology. For the fact of the matter is that when we really care about something, the caring will influence what we bring to the task and we shall improve the professional practice as a direct consequence of this concern. Yet only uncommonly do professors conceive of themselves as being in the business of helping to extend a student's experience or perception through real observations into genuine areas. What they try to do instead is to substitute a new type of learning which then will permit the student to use the same skills in the same ways no matter where they come from and no matter what their personal lives are going to be. Perhaps one of the things which the times are saying to us is that individual experience must be related to professional knowledge and skill and that in the final analysis librarianship is the practice of one human being reacting upon another. And that unless the student is encouraged to translate his method of performance beyond the level of papers and examinations into such a philosophy of commitment, it is all useless.

You are students in a very large school. Perhaps I should say something about the fact that many of our professional schools are growing larger. The current folklore suggests that in the good old days academia was a place where faculty and students had close contact with each other each day. This was said to be a time when the faculty were not busy with their research or consulting and so they had time and energy for students. Perhaps this illustrates the American propensity or the universal human mistake of assuming that if things are not so good now, they used to be better—instead of realizing that things today are likely to be considered bad precisely because they are at last getting better. For the fact of the matter is that student/faculty relations have probably never been so good or so open.

Of course the precise character of the inter-generational conflict depends in large measure upon the ages of the participants and in library education there is oftentimes not such a great disparity between the ages of those who are on the receiving end from those who are dispensing wisdom. The university in its essence is a societal design to familiarize the young with what are deemed to be the best ideas which their elders have, to give them a sense of the relationship between their problems and those of the previous generation, and so to spare them from learning everything by trial and error. Of course this sometimes has just the opposite effect. Too frequently a faculty is over-committed to transmitting the conventional wisdom of practice rather than questioning or expanding it and it is the student body and the student culture which makes the university the instrument of social change. This is precisely what can happen whether the faculty in the professional school welcomes it or not; the new professional generation can shape its own values and acquire a sense of its own identity rather than one shaped by that which had gone before and acquired from the sense of their instructors as to the ideals of history and purpose for their institutions. For as never before, students have their destiny in their own hands and they are beginning to assert themselves. For they are free to form their own sub-culture and to bargain with their faculty in ways heretofore viewed to be inappropriate, in order to bring about change and adaptation and modification and variation in virtually any and every element of the academic program which requires it. This is the lesson of upheaval in the university and it is a prerogative open to any and to all. Library school students in more than one institution have obviously learned the lesson well.

In professional education all too often the school's culture has been benevolently derived by the faculty. And it is typically a culture firmly anchored in the values of the past. Yet it is the students who have a greater stake in the future. As there is a growing self-awareness among students and an identification of individual interest with responsibility for social purpose and aims, so there is the capacity to influence the academic culture which resides as much with the students as it does with their instructors. But in this the students also have the responsibility for taking the lead and not waiting for someone to coerce them into joining together and forming conventional alliances and associations. The faculties need not be told to organize. Neither should the students. For the students of a professional discipline have a stake in where the discipline is headed and this implies a responsible voice in shaping that future. Such expression is the consequence of a political constituency.

I can cite one experience in which students, in league with aroused faculty colleagues, recalled one library school to its social responsibility. And out of such an alliance of cause there has begun a special program of recruitment, selection and identification of financial support for black students in order to right an imbalance of long standing in only one school among many where the balance sheet of equity is a hundred years out of kilter.

Apropos of the selection process for new students, it is unquestionably true that the way in which the schools and the students who come to the schools choose each other is just as important, if not more important, than what the schools may be trying to teach. We in education find it exceedingly difficult to accept the very conclusive fact that it is far simpler to change the character of our program by changing our admission requirements than by changing our curriculum. A professional school has a student for only a short period of time and there is only a limit to what can be done with the intellectual raw material under these terms. To the extent that this raw material is chosen in some preconceived way, there can be significant influence upon the profession which is being served.

In librarianship, we have set standards based upon academic performance. We have never delineated precisely the qualifications needed by individuals for specific work roles. Yet it is very clear, particularly in a culture torn by dissent, one which is questioning fundamental values, that there may be honest differences about the appropriate methods of selecting human beings for life roles. The choice of individuals who have been successful in certain ways in academia, by conventional methods of measurement, does not mean that such human beings will be successful practitioners. For there is little or no correlation between performance in professional school and performance on the job. And since this is so, our traditional selection criteria, including Graduate Record Examinations and undergraduate performance, may be subject to some very fundamental questions.

Whether we are prepared to concede it or not, students who cannot successfully complete courses in professional schools cannot be proved to make incompetent practitioners. Similarly, those who do very well academically do not necessarily live up to the promise which their academic success would seem to imply for them. We do know that in certain occupations it is clear that some individuals, who have only an intuitive grasp of the field in which they perform, may achieve more than those who may be steeped in the technical competency which professional education so frequently imparts. Without going into the problems of an educational sequence which cannot distinguish problem-solving capacity from rote learning skills, suffice it to say that in many very demanding professions (and I would characterize modern day librarianship as one of them) the field of practice requires superb generalists who can do everything well or technical people who can accept a role in an organization divided by specialization. The professional schools tend to be structured by specialty and most frequently either ignore the need for the generalist or have not yet found the mechanism for generating him.

Library school faculties are rarely activist. While in a number of other disciplines students are beginning to receive formal credit or acknowledgment for doing work like organizing unions, or teaching in summer head-start programs, the same is not yet true of librarianship. A student can of course write a paper about an experience, but he is not acknowledged for doing anything, only for writing about it. Faculties have yet to acknowledge that their system must be restructured in such ways that students will try to learn new things and master new skills; the system must be sufficiently flexible so that students know they can achieve even if their skills are not those currently recognized. A student who has the capacity and the motivation to play one specific role—effectively—in a particular library culture should be encouraged to do so, for this contribution may be infinitely more relevant to the accomplishment of institutional goals than those deriving from more general professional qualifications. Perhaps there should be a system of weighing assets and liabilities so that a human being who is really good at anything which is professionally desirable, may be utilized, despite limitations which may become apparent during his professional education.

The Learning Perspective

There are essentially three ways that a student can regard a teacher. First a student may believe that the teacher is giving the correct answer and it must be correct because he is the teacher. The second is that the teacher has not given the right answer because that is not his job or his role. Instead, he has developed certain facts and has posed a problem. It is the student's job to find the right answer. The third view is that there is not any one right answer, but any number of right answers depending upon the context. Gradually, students in this society have been moving from the first perspective to the third.

In the first alternative, the position of instructor is a polar one between good and bad, right and wrong. The faculty member is placed on a pedestal and he is the one who imparts knowledge. When facts are the case in point, a student is correct when he answers the question with a specific fact to which the answer is known and he must therefore be right or wrong and the question of right or wrong is a very simple one. With increased sophistication, and of course students are growing more sophisticated all the time, students begin to perceive that there is diversity in the world and that life is not so simple. Yet some students may expect that a competent authority structure will sort out the world for them and everything will be black or white, open or shut. This is the plea of the library school student who wants answers to questions, formulae or conditioned responses to particular problems. With sophistication comes realization of uncertainty, and as sophistication advances to the next stage, students gradually perceive the world as so uncertain that there are no anchors of right and wrong and that individuals personally, must eventually sort out for themselves a philosophy, a commitment, and so in effect, do their own thing. The most sophisticated and intellectually mature student finds convincing and plausible the fact that he no longer must rely very much upon official figures of authority. And then, once the individual begins to think he is just as good as the authorities, to think in relativistic terms, to think he has the right to decide what an artist is expressing, what a poet means, what a library should do, he also has the right to put himself in the shoes of a political figure or anyone that he chooses, and he then can come to assume that he is just as good at making decisions for a library as its administrator is. The difference is that the authorities have to act and while they are often wrong, the student does not have to act and so is not often wrong.

We live in a time when authority is everywhere being challenged. Unfortunately, in higher education, by virtue of a recent history of some very confused decision-making, we have been making it appear more and more to the students that responsible officials are pretty naive and simple because they are enforcing upon the students the need to accept authority for its own sake simply because it is authority. Perhaps the lesson for education and for educational leadership is that if authority enforces bad judgments, in these times students can see such choices as patent nonsense. And once this becomes clear to them, they are going to be willing to second guess faculty members and administrators along a broad range of questions even though they might have been too timid to make the challenge before. So that if somebody makes students memorize obviously inane things in courses which seem to be irrelevant anyway, this will be seen to be kind of stupid by students and it will open the door to them to the possibility that the faculty member can make other mistakes and the student's respect for the teacher is weakened if not ultimately destroyed. In the past, students have been submissive, and library school students have been particularly sub-missive. Times are changing; library school students are not and need not be submissive any longer. Unless faculty members grow wise enough to share their concerns and enlist students as junior colleagues in the process of seeking better answers to questions which are not simply and readily resolved, then the entire academic enterprise may be in jeopardy.

Of course the interesting thing is that when there is concession of uncertainty, when academics will concede to their students that they do not know and are themselves striving for answers and indeed simply trying to identify the right questions, then all kinds of new questions are raised and people begin to try new things and some of the new ideas may even work. And then in essence we have an establishment which no longer needs to protect itself by virtue of relying upon its authority. For then no longer is it the facts of position and status and power which set the faculty member apart from the student. As we look at our institutions, with libraries as good an illustration as any, we see that in many ways they are failing, not meeting the needs of the times or the needs of those for whom they are intended. To enlist all the intelligence at our command in the cause of better decision processes, is the first and most important step to take.

When the head of a library makes bad mistakes, when a faculty member makes poor choices, the traditional authorities come into question. Of course at the other extreme, the student may dismiss all authority and make the erroneous judgment that in an uncertain world he is as prepared to make significant judgments about what is appropriate and inappropriate without the background or preliminary understanding of the issues. It is in such a context that the faculty wisely identifies the difference between choice determination built upon sufficient substantive understanding of issues and without it.

The Process of Change

If I would leave a single thought with you, it is that librarianship and library education stand in need of change. And change is a difficult process, for most of us fear it and are repulsed by it. New modes of action appear difficult, unnatural, anxiety producing, and even reprehensible. The behavior of organizations like the behavior of the individual acts to maintain and reinforce identity, and thus resists adaptation. As long as an individual lives or as long as an institution survives, change is possible; yet the longer the behavior is perpetuated, the more authority it assumes. But because we can do what we choose to do, as individuals and as institutions we have the capacity to change. Often we have become what we are not by choice, but by drifting. Personal freedom and educational freedom depend upon an awareness of alternatives and the ability to choose from among them. An individual life or an individual organization can be enlarged or it can be constrained. In the life which is most free and the organization which is most adroit at adaptation and modification, there is an awareness of choice so that change can still occur.

We are striving in librarianship, as human beings and as human institutions, to play important roles. We would be ill-advised to see our profession or our institutions as closed; indeed, doing the work which the culture requires of us must be our overriding concern. It is toward such a goal that our change must be oriented. Still, no matter how effective our resources and how satisfied we are with our professional educational processes, if in our educational preparation we do not equip human beings who are both competent and committed to expanding the potential of man, of our culture and our society, we are doomed to failure.

List of Contributors

BARBARA E. ANDERSON, former Education Librarian at San Francisco State University, is a part-time lecturer at the University of California (Berkeley) School of Librarianship, a research assistant for the UCB Institute of Library Research, and a doctoral student. "Ordeal at San Francisco State College" originally appeared in the April 1, 1970 issue of *Library Journal*.

SANFORD BERMAN is Head Cataloger at Hennepin County Library, Edina, Minnesota. "Let It All Hang Out: A Think Piece for Luddite Librarians" originally appeared in the June 15, 1971 issue of *Library Journal*.

JOHN N. BERRY III is Editor-in-Chief of *Library Journal*. "A Tip from Detroit" originally appeared in the July 1975 issue of *Library Journal*.

FAY M. BLAKE is Chief of Public Services at the California State Polytechnic College, Pomona, California. "Libraries in the Marketplace" originally appeared in the January 15, 1974 issue of *Library Journal*. "The Useful

Academic Librarian" originally appeared in the November 15, 1971 issue of *Library Journal*.

LARRY EARL BONE is former Assistant Director of Libraries for Public Services, Memphis-Shelby County Public Library and Information Center. "Study in Renewal: A Library in Search of Itself" originally appeared in the March 1, 1972 issue of *Library Journal*.

MARY LEE BUNDY is affiliated with Urban Information Interpreters, Inc., College Park, Maryland. "Urban Information and Public Libraries: A Design for Service" originally appeared in the January 15, 1972 issue of *Library Journal*.

ROBERT CABELLO-ARGANDOÑA is Coordinator, Bibliographic Research and Collection Development Unit, Chicano Studies Center, University of California, Los Angeles. "Recruiting Spanish-Speaking Library Students" originally appeared in the May 15, 1976 issue of *Library Journal*.

391

JOHN M. CARTER spent many years in libraries in the Southeast and is now Deputy State Librarian of Wyoming. "A Boll Weevil Six Feet Long" originally appeared in the October 15, 1969 issue of *Library Journal.*

KAY CASSELL is Director of the Bethlehem Public Library in Delmar, New York. "The Legal Status of Women" originally appeared in the September 1, 1971 issue of *Library Journal.*

GERALDINE CLARK is Assistant Director, Center for Library, Media, and Telecommunications, New York City Board of Education. "Bureaucracy or Commitment?" originally appeared in the January 15, 1970 issue of *Library Journal.*

REED COATS is Institutional Library Consultant (for people of all ages confined to state institutions) at the Virginia State Library in Richmond. "Two Years After . . . Reflections from YAP" originally appeared in the March 15, 1973 issue of *Library Journal.*

PAUL COWAN is affiliated with *The Village Voice,* New York City. "Bearing Witness: Some Thoughts on Zoia Horn" originally appeared in the June 15, 1972 issue of *Library Journal.*

ROBERT CRONEBERGER, JR. is Assistant Director of Libraries for the Memphis-Shelby County Public Library and Information Center, Memphis, Tennessee. "Defining Information and Referral Service" originally appeared in the November 1, 1975 issue of *Library Journal.* "I & R = Reference" originally appeared in the January 15, 1976 issue of *Library Journal.*

JOYCE M. CROOKS is Head of Reference at the J. F. Kennedy Library, Solano County, California. "Civil Liberties, Libraries, and Computers" originally appeared in the February 1, 1976 issue of *Library Journal.*

MILDRED DICKEMAN is Professor of Anthropology at California State College, Sonoma. "Racism in the Library: A Model from the Public Schools" originally appeared in the February 1973 issue of *School Library Journal.*

DR. JOSEPH C. DONOHUE is Library and Information Management Scientist, Bureau of Foods, Food and Drug Administration, Washington, D.C. "Some Experiments Fail," published first in the June 15, 1975 issue of *Library Journal,* was developed for earlier inclusion in *Information for the Community,* edited by Manfred Kochen and Joseph C. Donohue and published by the American Library Association in 1976.

C. EDWIN DOWLIN is the State Librarian of New Mexico. "Ohio's BOOKS/JOBS Program" originally appeared in the October 1, 1970 issue of *Library Journal.*

GEOFFREY DUNBAR was formerly affiliated with the Area Reference Library, Serra Regional Library System, El Centro, California. "Librarian and/or Citizen?" originally appeared in the January 1, 1972 issue of *Library Journal.*

RENEE FEINBERG is a reference librarian at Brooklyn College Library, Brooklyn, New York. "What Price Professionalism?" originally appeared in the February 1971 issue of *School Library Journal.*

FLORENCE N. FIELD is Staff Associate, Program Development, Consumers' Health Group/North Communities Health Foundation, Evanston, Illinois. "Branch Power" originally appeared in the October 1, 1969 issue of *Library Journal.*

CAROLYN FORSMAN is Head, Telephone Reference, Washington Public Library, Washington, D.C. "Crisis Information Services to Youth: A Lesson for Libraries?" originally appeared in the March 15, 1972 issue of *Library Journal*.

MAURICE J. FREEDMAN is Coordinator of Technical Services, The Branch System, New York Public Library. "Processing for the People" originally appeared in the January 1, 1976 issue of *Library Journal*.

LEONARD H. FREISER is Director of Libraries and the Graduate Program in Library Science at the National College of Education, Evanston, Illinois. "Community, Library, and Revolution" originally appeared in the January 1, 1970 issue of *Library Journal*.

AGNES M. GRIFFEN, former Deputy Library Director for Staff and Program Development at the King County Library System, Seattle, Washington, is currently Deputy Library Director at Tuscon Public Library, Tuscon, Arizona. "Libraries and Hunger" originally appeared in the October 15, 1971 issue of *Library Journal*.

ROBERT P. HARO is affiliated with the Department of Ethnic Studies at the University of California, Berkeley. "College Libraries for Students" originally appeared in the June 1, 1969 issue of *Library Journal*.

BILL HINCHLIFF describes himself as a community bibliographer and a "crusading library hobbit who dreams of children's paperback libraries on every block in every city, town, and village." "Ivory Tower Ghettos" originally appeared in the November 1, 1969 issue of *Library Journal*.

E. J. JOSEY is Chief, Bureau of Specialist Library Services, New York State Education Department. "Can Library Affirmative Action Succeed?" originally appeared in the January 1, 1975 issue of *Library Journal*.

ELEANOR F. KLEPEIS is Institutional Coordinator of the King County Library System, Seattle, Washington. "The King County Youth Service Center" originally appeared in the April 1973 issue of *School Library Journal*.

S. J. LEON is the Northeast Area Administrator for the Free Library of Philadelphia. "Book Selection in Philadelphia" originally appeared in the May 1, 1973 issue of *Library Journal*.

HELEN LOWENTHAL is Director of the Goodnow Library, Sudbury, Massachusetts. "A Healthy Anger" originally appeared in the September 1, 1971 issue of *Library Journal*.

CAROLYN LUCK is Head of Information and Referral Service for the Memphis-Shelby County Public Library and Information Center, Memphis, Tennessee. "Defining Information and Referral Service" originally appeared in the November 1, 1975 issue of *Library Journal*. "I & R = Reference" originally appeared in the January 15, 1976 issue of *Library Journal*.

CELESTE MACLEOD, writer and librarian, lives in Berkeley, California, where she is currently working on a book. "Prison Law Libraries and You" originally appeared in the November 1, 1972 issue of *Library Journal*. "Reconstitution for Peace and Relevancy" originally appeared in the May 1, 1971 issue of *Library Journal*.

GORDON MCSHEAN'S story of his struggle with the censors will be told in his new book *Running a Message Parlor, or The Library's Lascivious Legacy,* to be published by Multinational Media in late 1976. "From Roswell to

Richmond . . . to Your Town" originally appeared in the February 15, 1970 issue of *Library Journal*.

EDWARD MAPP is Chief Librarian at New York City Community College Library, Brooklyn, New York. "The Invisible Librarian" originally appeared in the November 1, 1970 issue of *Library Journal*.

LOWELL A. MARTIN is a Professor Emeritus of the School of Library Service, Columbia University, New York City. "The Changes Ahead" originally appeared in the February 15, 1968 issue of *Library Journal*.

REGINA MINUDRI, former Coordinator of YAP, is Assistant County Librarian, Alameda County Library, California. "Two Years After . . . Reflections from YAP" originally appeared in the March 15, 1973 issue of *Library Journal*.

RICHARD MOSES is Chief Librarian, Oakville Public Library, Oakville, Ontario, Canada. "Hindsight on High John" originally appeared in the May 1, 1972 issue of *Library Journal*.

SUE OPIPARE MURDOCK is Head Librarian, Library for the Blind and Physically Handicapped, Carnegie Library of Pittsburgh. "Breaking into Jail" originally appeared in the September 15, 1971 issue of *Library Journal*.

MAJOR OWENS is a New York State senator. "A Model Library for Community Action" originally appeared in the May 1, 1970 issue of *Library Journal*.

RICHARD PARSONS is Coordinator of Interorganizational Development for the Baltimore Public Library. "Help! A Crisis Services Project" originally appeared in the February 1973 issue of *School Library Journal*.

DR. EDITH L. PERLMUTTER is Assistant Professor of Economics, Loyola Marymount University. "Libraries in the Marketplace" originally appeared in the January 15, 1974 issue of *Library Journal*.

PEGGY PORTER is Coordinator of Information Services, Community College of Allegheny County, Allegheny Campus, Pittsburgh, Pennsylvania. "Breaking into Jail" originally appeared in the September 15, 1971 issue of *Library Journal*.

IDA REED is Head of the Music and Art Department at the Carnegie Library of Pittsburgh. "Breaking into Jail" originally appeared in the September 15, 1971 issue of *Library Journal*.

BERNARD E. RICHARDSON is Director of Library Services, Cornell College, Mt. Vernon, Iowa. "A Wind Is Rising" originally appeared in the February 1, 1975 issue of *Library Journal*.

LILLIAN L. SHAPIRO, formerly a supervisor of high school libraries in New York City and Director of Media Services in the United Nations International School, is now a school library consultant. "Bureaucracy and the School Library" originally appeared in the April 15, 1973 issue of *Library Journal*.

JOSEPH E. SHUBERT is State Librarian of Ohio. "Ohio's BOOKS/JOBS Program" originally appeared in the October 1, 1970 issue of *Library Journal*.

PATRICIA GLASS SCHUMAN, former Senior Acquisitions Editor at the R. R. Bowker Company, is President, Neal-Schuman Publishers, Inc., New York City. "Social Responsibility—A Progress Report" originally appeared in the May 15, 1969 issue of *Library Journal*. "Southern Integration: Writing off the Black Librarian" originally appeared in the May 15, 1971 issue of *Library Journal*. "Social Responsibility: An Agenda for the Future" originally appeared in the January 1, 1976 issue of *Library Journal*.

HELEN W. TUTTLE is Assistant University Librarian for Technical Services at the Princeton University Library. "Women in Academic Libraries" originally appeared in the September 1, 1971 issue of *Library Journal*.

DR. PAUL WASSERMAN is Professor, College of Library and Information Services, University of Maryland. "Professional Adaptation: Library Education Mandate" originally appeared in the April 1, 1970 issue of *Library Journal*.

KATHLEEN WEIBEL, a former public librarian in New York and Chicago, is a doctoral student at the University of Wisconsin Library School, Madison. "Toward a Feminist Profession" originally appeared in the January 1, 1976 issue of *Library Journal*.

BILLY R. WILKINSON is Staff Relations Officer, New York Public Library, New York City. "A Screaming Success As Study Halls" originally appeared in the May 1, 1971 issue of *Library Journal*.

Index